MATHEMATICAL LOGIC
AND THE
FOUNDATIONS OF MATHEMATICS

MATHEMATICAL LOGIC

AND THE

FOUNDATIONS OF MATHEMATICS

An Introductory Survey

G. T. KNEEBONE

Bedford College
University of London

D. VAN NOSTRAND COMPANY LIMITED
LONDON

TORONTO   NEW YORK
PRINCETON, NEW JERSEY

D. VAN NOSTRAND COMPANY LTD.
358, Kensington High Street, London, W.14

D. VAN NOSTRAND COMPANY INC.
120, Alexander Street, Princeton, New Jersey
24, West 40 Street, New York 18, New York

D. VAN NOSTRAND COMPANY (CANADA) LTD.
25, Hollinger Road, Toronto 16

Library of Congress Catalog Card No. 62–19535

Made and printed in Great Britain by
William Clowes and Sons, Limited, London and Beccles

PREFACE

This introduction to mathematical logic and the philosophy of mathematics is based on courses of lectures given in the University of London, and attended both by undergraduates in the final year of an honours course in mathematics and by graduates beginning research for higher degrees. Planned with a variety of needs in mind, it is addressed both to readers who require only a general survey of the topics with which it deals and to intending specialists in mathematical logic and foundations of mathematics.

The general reader may pass quickly over sections marked with an asterisk, and he will also be able to omit many of the formal proofs in other sections without losing the thread of the main argument. No very detailed knowledge of mathematics is demanded, although a general familiarity with the concepts, terminology, and methods of modern mathematics is desirable. Readers who are not mathematicians should be able to understand, without undue difficulty, most of Parts I and III, and even to follow the broad argument of Part II; but only those with a mathematical background will be in a position to appreciate all the details of the discussion.

For mathematicians who are proposing to turn to serious study of some aspect of mathematical philosophy, the book is intended as a general introduction to this entire field. It is indeed offered specifically as a preliminary survey, and not as an exhaustive account of the present state of knowledge; but anyone who has worked carefully through it, following up the suggestions for supplementary reading, should be ready to begin independent work in whatever branch of the subject he may choose. Specialized research in mathematical philosophy needs the support of a sound knowledge of the classical literature; and it is with the work of the classical phase—which in the study of the foundations of mathematics may be said to have lasted up to about 1939—that the book is for the most part concerned.

The student is thus meant to use this book very much as a perceptive traveller, journeying abroad, uses his Baedeker. The ideal guide-book enables the visitor to a strange country to travel round and explore by himself. With its aid, he can learn in a reasonably short time to find his way about for practical purposes; and in addition it helps him to gain some understanding of the topography of the country, the outward appearance of its towns and buildings and the historical development of its architecture, the language and traditions of its people, and some of the facets of its present-day life.

The survey of mathematical philosophy that is offered here is not intended to be, and indeed cannot be, a substitute for direct study of original writings. For this reason the details of long or difficult proofs are often omitted when they are already accessible elsewhere in a suitable form, though precise indication is always given of where they are to be found. This is not so much a matter of economy as of deliberate choice. The writings of great creative thinkers, whether mathematicians or philosophers, have a profundity that cannot be exhausted by the extraction from them of what bears on any specific problem or what is relevant to the concerns of any one age; and the works of such authors as Kant, Dedekind, Russell, and Hilbert need to be read afresh by every student who is forming his own conceptions in mathematical philosophy.

The present book is thus designed to serve in the first instance, when supplemented by reference to original sources, as a comprehensive introduction to the earlier phases of the historical development of the philosophy of mathematics. But since study of the classical literature of a subject serves mainly to prepare the way for active participation in current research, many signposts are provided, partly in notes at the ends of the chapters and partly in the appendix on developments since 1939, in order that paths may readily be found which lead through the more recently published work on mathematical philosophy to the frontiers of present knowledge. By setting out along such a path, and then relying for further guidance upon the reviews of new books and papers that have been published over the years in the *Journal of Symbolic Logic* (since 1936) and in *Mathematical Reviews* (since 1940), the reader should be able to make himself sufficiently familiar with recent advances in whatever branch of mathematical philosophy he wishes to concentrate upon.

When studying Part I, which is concerned exclusively with logic, the reader is recommended to work systematically through Hilbert & Ackermann: *Principles of Mathematical Logic* (editions earlier than the fourth if it is read in the original German). The presentation of symbolic logic in that book is so clear and so elegant that no attempt has been made here to cover the ground again in detail. In Part II, where the central place is taken by Hilbert's metamathematics, the argument follows closely the development of ideas in Hilbert & Bernays: *Grundlagen der Mathematik*, the most authoritative presentation of this fundamental contribution to the study of foundations of mathematics. The choice of logical symbolism in the present book has, in fact, been dictated by the importance of easy comparison with that standard treatise, although in certain historical sections alternative systems of

notation are also mentioned.   In Part II, frequent page references to
Grundlagen der Mathematik are given, so that particular arguments
can quickly be found.   Those readers who require an account of metamathematics in English should consult Kleene: *Introduction to Metamathematics.*

Another indispensable work on the logical foundation of mathematics is Bernays & Fraenkel: *Axiomatic Set Theory*; and the *Éléments
de Mathématique* of Bourbaki is equally important, though in a different way.   Bourbaki is neither a logician nor a philosopher of mathematics in the narrower sense, but rather a working mathematician who
makes the fullest possible use of modern logical technique in order to
construct a unified system of rigorous mathematics; and his *Éléments*
thus carries over the theoretical study of symbolic logic into the realm
of significant application.

The author is heavily indebted to various friends and colleagues for
substantial help in the preparation of this book.   Professor Alice Ambrose Lazerowitz (Smith College) read most of the original manuscript
and criticized it in detail from the point of view of a philosopher.
Mr D. Pager (then of Bedford College) read the entire manuscript and
checked its formal accuracy.   Mr B. Rotman (Sir John Cass College)
gave much help with Chapter 11.   Finally, the author's greatest debt,
which no formal acknowledgement could discharge, is to Dr L. Mirsky
(Sheffield).   Not only has Dr Mirsky read successive drafts with immense care and made innumerable suggestions for their improvement,
but many of the ideas in the book have themselves developed out of
conversations which the author has had with him over a considerable
number of years.

The transformation of a manuscript into a printed book can be an
onerous task, but in the present instance the process has been greatly
lightened for the author by the help and encouragement which he has
received from the publishers.   He is indeed most grateful to them for
their concern and understanding in interpreting his intentions; and he
would like to acknowledge also the excellent work of the printers in
their treatment of the logical symbolism.

ACKNOWLEDGEMENTS

The author and publishers gratefully acknowledge the kindness of the authorities listed below in granting permission for the quotation of extracts from the copyright works mentioned. Numbers in square brackets refer to the Bibliography, pp. 401–423, and an asterisk against an entry indicates that a quotation has been translated into English. Die Akademie der Wissenschaften in Göttingen: Hilbert [3*]. The American Mathematical Society: Post [3]. The Association for Symbolic Logic: Bourbaki [3]. Basil Blackwell & Mott Ltd, Oxford, and Dr Theodor Marcus, Graubünden: Frege [2], English version. Cambridge University Press: Eddington [1]; Euclid [1]; Whitehead [5]; Whitehead & Russell [1], second edition. Edizioni Cremonese, Rome: Peano [6*], edition of 1901. Dover Publications Inc., New York: G. Cantor [1], English version. Encyclopædia Britannica Ltd, London: Church [12]; Wolf [1]. Hermann & Cie, Paris: Bourbaki [1*]. M. F. Le Lionnais and M. J. Ballard, Paris: Bourbaki [2*]. The London Mathematical Society: Turing [1]. Macmillan & Co. Ltd, London: Burnet [1]. The Mathematical Association of America: Gödel [6]. Methuen & Co. Ltd, London: Ross [1]. Mrs Klara von Neumann-Eckart, La Jolla, Mrs Marina von Neumann Whitman, Pittsburgh, and Walter de Gruyter & Co., Berlin: von Neumann [1*]. The North-Holland Publishing Company, Amsterdam: Fraenkel & Bar-Hillel [1]. Verlag von Hermann Pohle, Jena: Frege [4*]. Princeton University Press: von Neumann & Morgenstern [1]; Weyl [3], English version. The Royal Society: Weyl [6]. Routledge & Kegan Paul Ltd, London: Wittgenstein [1], edition of 1922. The Earl Russell O.M., F.R.S.: Russell [2]. Professor Thoralf Skolem, Oslo: Skolem [1*, 2*]. Springer-Verlag, Berlin: Ackermann [3*]; Hilbert & Bernays [1*]; Peano [4*]; Zermelo [1*]. Springer-Verlag, Vienna: Brouwer [2*]; Gödel [2*]. B. G. Teubner Verlagsgesellschaft m.b.H., Stuttgart: Hilbert [2*]; Schönflies [1*]. F. Vieweg & Sohn Verlag, Brunswick: Dedekind [1*, 2*].

The publishers have not been able to trace the successors of Hermann Pohle, Jena, but trust that this acknowledgement will be accepted as a substitute for their permission.

CONTENTS

PART I
MATHEMATICAL LOGIC

Chapter 1 Traditional Logic

Supplementary notes on Chapter 1

Chapter 2 Symbolic Logic I—The Propositional Calculus

Supplementary notes on Chapter 2

PART II

FOUNDATIONS OF MATHEMATICS

PART III

PHILOSOPHY OF MATHEMATICS

PART I

Mathematical Logic

Chapter 1

TRADITIONAL LOGIC

1 Introduction: mathematics and logic

In the course of this book a variety of topics will be discussed, some of them closely connected and others apparently standing more or less by themselves. All the topics, however, have one feature in common, namely their relevance to our understanding of mathematics and its epistemological status. They are all, in a general sense, philosophical, although most of the argument will be conducted in more mathematical language than has in the past been customary in books of philosophy. This departure from an ancient tradition is forced upon us by the nature of the subject, and it is indeed typical of the modern philosophy of mathematics.

Philosophy, of whatever kind it may be, is critical analysis of rational activity; and every form of rational activity calls into existence a corresponding branch of philosophy, with the task of disengaging the general principles implicit in that activity, and so enabling the activity itself to be pursued more purposefully and perhaps more efficiently. The specific activity of mathematicians falls, by long-established tradition, within the province of logic, and indeed mathematical demonstration approximates more closely than any other type of reasoning to the logician's ideal. But in the course of the last three centuries mathematics has undergone a complete transformation, developing during that period from an 'elementary' deductive science to a discipline of extreme subtlety and complexity. It still has, even today, a logical articulation that can be analysed in terms of a small number of basic principles; but the technique of analysis that is used must match in delicacy the reasoning to which it is applied, and thus the development of mathematics has led to a comparable development of logic also.

The interplay between mathematics and logic is, in fact, the key to the understanding of the extensive literature on foundations of mathematics that now exists. In the present introduction to the subject we shall discuss the type of logic that has been evolved for the critical analysis of modern mathematics, and we shall also consider the new understanding of mathematics itself to which this analysis has led.

In order to make sufficiently definite the starting-point of the discussion, and the movement of thought that constitutes its initial phase, we now prefix to the main argument an informal characterization of the two disciplines to which the later discussion chiefly relates. This is the function of the next two sections, on mathematics and logic respectively.

2   The nature of mathematics

The subject of mathematics has a dual nature, for it may be studied purely for its intrinsic interest (and in this capacity it is one of the most highly developed of all theoretical studies) or alternatively it may be studied for the sake of its manifold applications to other realms of knowledge. Today we are in the fortunate position of being able to give a satisfactory account of why it should be that mathematics has these two complementary aspects; and our ability to do this is a direct result of the clarification of the nature of mathematics that has been progressively achieved, during the past half-century, by those mathematicians and logicians who have concerned themselves with the foundations of mathematics.

Mathematics, as the author of one of the most important of modern mathematical treatises uncompromisingly asserts,[1] is simply the study of abstract structures, or formal patterns of connectedness; and abstract structures can be of interest in a variety of ways. They often appeal powerfully to the aesthetic sense, for instance, by reason of what has been called, in a different context,[2] the quality of 'significant form' —a quality which, though elusive and hard to analyse, is familiar to people with a capacity for aesthetic enjoyment. Or again, a person who comes across some particular mathematical structure may be stimulated in a more strictly intellectual way by the problem of tracing back the immediately obvious features of the structure to others which are more fundamental; and response to such stimulus may vary in seriousness from idle preoccupation with puzzles and games of skill to devotion of one's whole life to academic research in some such subject as the theory of numbers.

Of such purely contemplative kinds, then, may be the inspiration of *pure* mathematics, or the study of structures for their own sake. In applied mathematics the motives are different, and other considerations come into play as well. Applied mathematics, no less than pure mathematics, may be interpreted as a study of structure, but it does not possess the complete freedom of pure mathematics. It is essentially a theoretical study of various realms of actual experience, undertaken with the object of bringing to light their structural articulation. Nevertheless, although it is firmly rooted in actuality, applied mathematics is not a strictly empirical study; for the applied mathematician

---

[1] Nicolas Bourbaki: *Éléments de Mathématique* (Paris, in progress since 1939).
[2] Clive Bell: *Art* (London, 1914).

has the delicate task of idealizing actual experience sufficiently to make it amenable to precise mathematical handling, while not running too great a risk of losing contact with the world to which his conclusions are intended to apply.

The 'experience' with which an applied mathematician begins may be experience of observed phenomena of the physical world, as is the case, for instance, in statics or dynamics or electromagnetic theory; but there is no necessity for 'experience' to be limited to this physical kind. The theory of statistics, for example, is a branch of applied mathematics that has a great diversity of applications in many different spheres—and right at the non-physical extreme of the spectrum of applied mathematics there is to be found the science of formal logic. It is with this last study that the present chapter and the other chapters of Part I are particularly concerned, and in these chapters logic will be exhibited as a highly developed branch of applied mathematics,[1] concerned with the mathematical analysis of the structure of deductive argument.

3 The nature of logic

The primary subject-matter of formal logic, then, is the structural pattern of demonstrative inference. Taken in the widest possible sense, however, logic is much more than this, being the theoretical study of the structure of reasoning in all its possible forms, and it was indeed so understood by the great logicians of the nineteenth century. These logicians directed their main attention towards *judgements*, that is to say acts of assertion which are backed by adequate grounds for maintaining whatever it is that is asserted. This was still very much the outlook adopted by Abraham Wolf in his article 'Logic' in the fourteenth edition of the *Encyclopaedia Britannica*, published in 1929. Wolf's article begins as follows:

'Logic is the systematic study of the general conditions of valid inference . . . . *Inference* is the act or process of deriving one judgment or proposition from another or from others . . . . By a "proposition" is here meant a judgment expressed in words, the judgment itself being the actual thought or belief in the mind, which may or may not be expressed in a proposition, though we cannot discuss it until it is so expressed.'

Logic, as understood by Wolf, is considerably wider than formal logic; but the general tendency in recent years has been to confine logic more and more to its purely formal side. In the latest edition of

---

[1] To be an applied science in this sense is the *initial* character of logic. But we shall see that, like many other branches of applied mathematics, logic has now developed also a 'pure' side, and logical systems based on arbitrarily postulated axioms are widely studied for the interest of the investigation itself.

the *Encyclopaedia Britannica* (1959) there is a new article 'Logic', written this time by one of the foremost authorities on symbolic logic, Alonzo Church. Church proceeds in a very different manner from Wolf, and his article opens with these words:

'Logic is the systematic study of the structure of propositions and of the general conditions of valid inference by a method which abstracts from the content or *matter* of the propositions and deals only with their logical *form*. This distinction between form and matter is made whenever we distinguish between the logical soundness or validity of a piece of reasoning and the truth of the premisses from which it proceeds, and in this sense is familiar in everyday usage. However, a precise statement of the distinction must be made with reference to a particular language or system of notation, a *formalized language*, which shall avoid the inexactnesses and systematically misleading irregularities of structure and expression that are found in ordinary (colloquial or literary) English and in other natural languages, and shall follow or reproduce the logical form—at the expense, where necessary, of brevity and facility of communication. To adopt a particular formalized language is thus to adopt a particular system or theory of logical analysis. And the formal method may then be characterized by saying that it deals with the objective form of *sentences* which express propositions, and provides in these concrete terms criteria of meaningfulness, of valid inference, and of other notions closely associated with these.'

We see here how the main object of discussion has ceased to be the *act* of judgement and has become the sentence or verbal statement, which can be considered purely in itself, without being taken in relation to a mind at all.

The logic with which Church is concerned is essentially the theory of the formal structure of deductive systems, and this is obviously of direct relevance to mathematics. But there is another branch of logic, usually known as 'inductive logic', which has been written about extensively in recent times, and which might also be expected to have some bearing on the philosophy of mathematics by reason of its relation to natural science and scientific method. By *induction* is meant argument from the particular to the more general, and the most important type of induction is the process whereby general scientific laws are inferred from the results of observation and experiment. The logic of induction, however, has even now hardly evolved beyond the initial tentative phase in which possible ideas are tried out, in ways usually suggested by analogy, in the hope that some among them will eventually develop into satisfactory theoretical concepts. We shall return to the subject of induction in Chapter 14, but in the other chapters of this book the term 'logic' will almost always be used in the restricted sense of 'deductive logic'.

Logic goes back, as a systematic study, to Aristotle; and its early history presumably extends even further into the past. The ground was doubtless prepared for Aristotle's definitive formulation of the theory by generations of earlier philosophers, for concepts as general and as mature as those which Aristotle was able to use are only formed very slowly, and are normally the ultimate outcome of a prolonged process of inquiry, the earlier phases of which may not even have reached the threshold of conscious and deliberate theorizing. However that may be, Aristotle was in a position to give final form to a theory of deductive inference, and he did so in a number of writings that have been handed down under the general title of *Organon*, or instrument of reasoning.[1] This *Organon* exerted an immense influence all through the Middle Ages and on into modern times, and was the basis of 'traditional' or 'aristotelian' logic, the logic of the mediaeval Scholastic philosophers or Schoolmen.

It is characteristic of Aristotle's logic that, in common with ancient Greek science generally, it was very sparing in its introduction of technical concepts and special symbols. The Greeks ordinarily used everyday concepts, denoted by words with immediate intuitive meaning, in situations where we now prefer mathematical symbols (which, incidentally, we can manipulate without faltering, even though we may be unable to interpret them intuitively), and this could sometimes be a serious bar to progress. Aristotelian physics and cosmology, for example, notable achievements though they were, eventually stagnated until Galileo and his fellow-scientists of the seventeenth century introduced a more mathematical way of conceiving physical phenomena; and even geometry was unable to advance much beyond Euclid until the advent of Cartesian ideas, which only became possible when mathematics was extended by the creation of an abstract concept of number (cf. p. 137). There is, indeed, a remarkable parallel between Euclid's geometry and Aristotle's logic. Both the *Elements* of Euclid and the *Organon* of Aristotle were compiled at roughly the same time, round about 300 B.C.; both works were treated with the utmost veneration for some two thousand years, with the result that they became integral parts of the European intellectual tradition; and the content of each of them has in the end been so generalized and transmuted, in the course of the development of modern mathematics, that we now have for the first time a just appreciation of both their greatness and their limitations. When these classics are compared with modern books on the same subjects it becomes apparent, in particular, that for all their unsurpassed excellence of construction they are fundamentally non-technical works, written in the language of ordinary educated

[1] For a brief indication of the contents of the *Organon* see Note 1 at the end of this chapter, p. 21.

discourse. We shall find that the mathematical logic to which we turn in the next chapter is no longer non-technical in this way, and that it compares with aristotelian logic rather as modern algebraic geometry compares with the 'elementary' geometry of Euclid.

Logic is a discipline that is not merely descriptive, but normative as well, being concerned more with how we *ought* to reason than with how we habitually do so. The activity of reasoning involves a succession of thoughts, and in studying this activity we can set to work in two different ways. If we adopt the point of view of the experimental psychologist, we may investigate the types of succession of thoughts that most frequently occur, tracing these back to association of ideas, mental habits acquired from schooling, and so forth. We are then asking what actually occurs when people think, that is to say how their minds work—and it may well turn out that, for the understanding of the phenomena of psychology, incorrect reasoning is no less interesting and informative than reasoning which is correctly performed. This is one possible approach; but there is also the alternative possibility that we may wish to concern ourselves with the philosophy or logic of reasoning rather than with its psychology, and in that case our method will be entirely different. Psychological facts will still be relevant to the inquiry, but they will no longer control it. We shall seek to construct an ideal theory of correct reasoning, based on a small number of general principles which we postulate as 'laws of thought'. Such a system of logic will be related to actual thinking as euclidean geometry is related to processes of drawing and measuring, or newtonian mechanics to the carrying out of physical experiments and observations. In all theoretical sciences, indeed, the conclusions reached must fit the empirical facts; but the ideal concepts and general laws that are introduced go beyond what is directly given in experience.

4　Terms and propositions

Since it is our purpose to treat logic as applied mathematics, never losing sight of its relation to the actual processes of reasoning which it serves to idealize and systematize, it would be inappropriate to present mathematical logic from the beginning as an axiomatic system—that is to say to treat it as if it were pure mathematics. A more fitting course is to go back first of all to traditional aristotelian logic in order to gain understanding of the simple concepts that have underlain all subsequent investigations. We shall then be in a position to see clearly what modern symbolic logic achieves as, with the aid of a more mathematical technique, it gives its own analysis of the structure of deductive arguments.

Every branch of applied mathematics has its appropriate subject-matter—statics dealing with forces, kinematics with velocities and accelerations, and so forth—and the subject-matter of formal logic consists of statements or assertions. This is so because the primary purpose of deductive argument is to lead ultimately to the making of statements which are true and whose truth is guaranteed; and logic has accordingly to concern itself with those formal relations between statements which ensure that conclusions follow from premisses. The statements originally envisaged by Aristotle were all of one very simple type, being statements in subject-predicate form; and although it has since been found necessary for mathematical logic to take more elaborate forms of statement into account, the simple aristotelian type was sufficient to meet the quite considerable needs of mediaeval Scholastic philosophy. In traditional logic, then, every statement is treated as being analysable into subject and predicate, and this means that it can only express either the agreement or the difference of two things or general notions. Typical statements in subject-predicate form are 'Socrates is a man', 'All men are mortal', 'Some men are liars', and 'No man is perfect'.

The two things which are compared in such a statement are known as its *terms*, and to make a statement involving a certain term is simply to use a certain name—either the name of a thing or class of things or that of a quality. The concept of name has been succinctly defined by Thomas Hobbes as follows:

'A *name* is a word taken at pleasure to serve for a mark, which may raise in our mind a thought like to some thought we had before, and which being pronounced to others, may be to them a sign of what thought the speaker had, or had not before in his mind.'[1]

Such a definition, however, makes the use of names seem a much simpler matter than it really is, and we need to bear in mind that idealization may be carried too far. In logic especially, over-simplification of situations can easily deprive theoretical inquiries of most of their practical utility.

Names need not, of course, be single words; and in mathematics we make continual use of such composite names as 'the sum of the first n terms of the infinite series whose rth term is $(-1)^r x^r$' and 'less than any assignable quantity'. This is something that can be taken into account merely by a slight modification of the definition just quoted; but there are other difficulties that are much more fundamental. Ideas and thoughts are not, in actual fact, discrete or self-contained entities, and we do not as a rule use words 'at pleasure' as signs of them. Ideas and the words that we use for them are historical products, and in thinking and speaking we draw, sometimes more and sometimes less

[1] Thomas Hobbes of Malmesbury: *Elements of Philosophy* (1655). The definition, which Hobbes set down as a convenient starting-point for his very careful discussion of names, must not be taken too literally in view of its essentially epigrammatic character.

consciously, upon their history, which supplies a penumbra of associations and may often induce, without our even being aware of it, a particular orientation of mind. Such is the more typical use of names; and those names called proper names, which may indeed be assigned at pleasure, function in a way that is wholly trivial by comparison. If we treat logic as if it dealt only with Hobbesian names, we must be prepared to find that its scope as applied mathematics is severely limited. Traditional logic is treated, in fact, in just this way; and the reason why it has any significant applications at all must be sought in the circumstance that, within the frame of any particular deductive theory, we freeze our concepts. In developing such a theory we take whatever concepts we need, as they are currently understood, and we treat them for the purposes of the theory as if they were sharply defined and unchanging. But when a new and revised theory comes subsequently to be constructed, the concepts may possibly be redefined; and in this way the continuous historical evolution of ideas is artificially replaced by a series of jumps from one definite conception to the next.

According to traditional logic, then, the basic constituents of statements are terms, i.e. names of entities or of classes of entities. It is customary to classify terms as *singular* and *general* (a distinction in logic which comes near to the grammatical distinction between proper and common nouns) and also as *positive* and *negative*. A statement in subject-predicate form is constructed by taking two terms, one as subject and the other as predicate, and connecting them by a *copula*, namely the verb 'is' or 'are' if the statement expresses agreement between the terms, and the verb 'is not' or 'are not' if it expresses difference. If the terms actually do agree or differ as is asserted, then the statement is *true*; if not, it is *false*.

As typical examples of statements in subject-predicate form we might take 'Socrates is mortal' and 'Athenians are not Greeks'. The first of these statements, which has a singular subject 'Socrates' and a general predicate 'mortal', expresses agreement between its terms, and it is in fact true. The second is false, since it incorrectly expresses difference between the subject 'Athenians' and the predicate 'Greeks'. The subject and predicate are both general in this case, since they apply to many individuals. A singular term can only apply (in a given context) to a unique individual, as was the case with the term 'Socrates'.

It may be remarked that not all meaningful sentences are statements, for sentences can be interrogative or imperative or exclamatory. A statement or assertion is an indicative sentence, and such sentences are referred to in the terminology of logic as *propositions*.[1] Propositions

---

[1] This was the usage in traditional logic. More recently, a distinction has come to be recognized between the 'sentence', or specific form of words, and the 'proposition', or meaning of the sentence. Thus 'Socrates is a man' and 'Sokrates ist ein Mensch' are

can be conditional, like 'If the winter is severe, sparrows are not timid', or unconditional, like 'Sparrows are not timid'; but it is only with unconditional propositions that we shall for the present be concerned. Such propositions are said to be *categorical*, and they make simple, direct statements of alleged fact.

Categorical propositions in subject-predicate form are traditionally subdivided with respect to quality and again with respect to quantity, and the resulting fourfold classification needs to be firmly grasped, as it underlies the entire traditional theory of inference.

As regards *quality*, a proposition is *affirmative* if the subject and predicate are declared to agree and *negative* if they are declared to differ. Quality thus depends on whether the copula that is involved is a positive or a negative one.

As regards *quantity*, a proposition is either universal or particular. It is *universal* if the predicate is affirmed or denied of the whole of the subject, as in 'All men are mortal' and 'No man is perfect'; and it is *particular* if the predicate is affirmed of some incompletely specified part of the subject, as in 'A few men are wise' and 'Some men are not self-seeking'. A *singular* proposition—that is to say one like 'Socrates is mortal', with a particular individual as its subject—is to be counted as universal since, the subject being indivisible, the predicate is affirmed of the whole of it.

The fourfold classification of propositions can be set out in tabular form as follows:

| | | QUALITY | |
		Affirmative	Negative
QUANTITY	Universal	**A**	**E**
	Particular	**I**	**O**

The letters **A**, **I**, **E**, **O** attached to the various cases are traditional symbols which should be committed to memory, and this may easily be done with the aid of the mnemonic *affirmo—nego*. In aristotelian logic, as in Latin grammar, there are many mnemonics, some of them highly ingenious.

two sentences which express the same proposition. A proposition is now conceived as the common meaning of an entire class of sentences which are mutually translatable one into another, and any sentence of the class can stand for the proposition. In much the same way, the different arithmetical expressions $2+4$, 2.3, and $3!$ all stand for one and the same number 6.

The four standard forms of proposition may be represented by schematic sentences as follows:

A	All X is Y,
I	Some X is Y,
E	No X is Y,
O	Some X is not Y.

The two affirmative forms express agreement between the subject, 'all X' in case **A** and 'some X' in case **I**, and the predicate 'Y', whereas the negative forms **E** and **O** express difference between these same pairs of terms. The universal negative form **E** is the assertion that all X differs from Y, and this is put most naturally as 'No X is Y'. As stock examples of the four types we shall take the following propositions:

A	All men are mortal,
I	Some men are mortal,
E	No man is mortal,
O	Some men are not mortal.

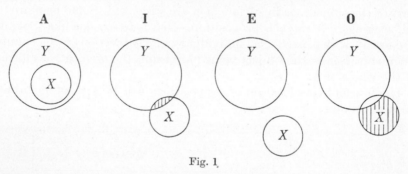

Fig. 1.

Any term that is affirmed or denied universally in a proposition is said to be *distributed* there, and distribution of a term thus means the making of some assertion about the whole of it. Of our four standard types of proposition, exactly two (**A** and **E**) distribute the subject, and exactly two (**E** and **O**) distribute the predicate. **A** asserts agreement and **E** asserts difference between the whole of X and Y. **E** and **O** assert difference between the whole of Y and all or some of X. It is plain that every negative proposition must distribute its predicate, since to say something about exclusion from Y is to refer implicitly to the whole of Y.

An expressive pictorial device for illustrating the relation between the terms in any proposition in subject-predicate form was introduced by Euler.[1] The extent of each term is represented as a region enclosed

---

[1] Euler used the device in his *Lettres à une Princesse d'Allemagne sur divers sujets de physique et de philosophie* (Mitau & Leipzig, St. Petersburg, 1770–1772), letters 102–105. Some earlier uses of circles for a similar purpose are also known. For the more elaborate diagrams used by Venn, see Note 3, p. 24.

by a circle, with the result that any agreement between two terms can be shown as an overlapping of the corresponding circular areas. In this way the four basic types of proposition give rise to 'Euler diagrams' as in Fig. 1.

When these diagrams are used to illustrate our four stock examples, the small circle X represents the totality of men and the large circle Y represents the totality of mortal beings.

The logical relations between the four propositions, one of each of the types **A**, **I**, **E**, **O**, that can be formed from two given terms X and Y are expressed in certain technical terms, traditionally displayed in the following 'square of opposition':

A, O and **E, I** are two pairs of *contradictory* propositions. One proposition of each pair is true, and the other is false.

A and **E** are *contraries*. They cannot both be true, but it is possible for both to be false. They are the extremes of affirmation and denial.

In each of the pairs of *subalterns* **A, I** and **E, O** the two propositions are related as stronger and weaker, the universal (upper) entailing the particular (lower) but not conversely.

Exercise. Follow out these various relations for the square of opposition obtained when the four stock propositions 'All men are mortal', etc. are inserted in place of the letters **A, I, E, O**.

An important part of traditional logic, which is quasi-mathematical in form, deals with what are known as operations of *conversion*. If from a proposition that has a term X as subject and a term Y as predicate we derive a consequence with Y as subject and X as predicate, then this new proposition is said to have been obtained from the original one by conversion.

Propositions of types **I** and **E** are convertible by *simple conversion*, i.e. by mere interchange of the terms X and Y; for 'Some X is Y' clearly entails 'Some Y is X', and 'No X is Y' entails 'No Y is X'.

Conversion of a proposition of type **A** only yields a proposition of the weaker type **I**, for from 'All X is Y' we cannot infer more than 'Some Y is X'. We could not even infer this much if it were not taken for granted in traditional logic that a statement 'All X is Y' is not true unless there is some X. The type of conversion that we have here is known as *conversion by limitation* (*conversio per accidens*).

Neither of the above methods of conversion can be applied to a proposition of type **O**, and for such propositions conversion in the full sense is not possible at all. The best that we can do in this case is to apply the indirect process known as *conversion by negation*. Suppose, for example, that the proposition which we wish to convert is

'Some X is not Y'.

This can be reformulated as

'Some X is not-Y',

and then simple conversion yields the proposition

'Some not-Y is X',

with X as predicate, but only the complementary term not-Y as subject, instead of Y itself as in true conversion.

Let us apply the above methods of conversion to the four standard propositions on p. 12. From 'All men are mortal', which is of type **A**, we obtain, on converting by limitation, the proposition 'Some mortal beings are men'; and we also obtain this same proposition when we convert 'Some men are mortal', which is of type **I**, by simple conversion. The negative proposition 'No man is mortal', of type **E**, converts simply into 'No mortal being is a man'. Finally, the proposition of type **O**, namely 'Some man is not mortal', has to be converted by negation, when it yields the proposition 'Some immortal being is a man'.

5 Syllogistic inference

In the previous section we considered *terms*, that is to say objects of thought, and also *propositions*, that is to say assertions of agreement or difference between terms; and we are now ready to pass to the third stage in the construction of the traditional system of logic, that which has to do with *inference*. Inference is a process in which we affirm a certain proposition, the *conclusion* of the inference, on the ground of other propositions, its *premisses*, which we accept as true, or at least treat as if they were true.

From a single premiss we cannot infer very much. We may simply restate the premiss as conclusion (a trivial or tautological inference);

or we may infer a subalternate particular from the corresponding universal, **I** from **A**, or **O** from **E**; or we may pass from a universal proposition to a particular proposition subsumed under it, as from

'All men are mortal'

to

'Socrates is mortal'.

This last type of inference is an application of the logical principle known as the *dictum de omni et nullo* of Aristotle: 'Whatever is predicated of a term distributed whether affirmatively or negatively may be predicated in like manner of everything contained in it.'

A pair of premisses allows much greater scope than a single premiss, but in order that a non-trivial conclusion may be inferable it is obviously necessary for the premisses to have something in common. The simplest case is that which arises when the inference proceeds by elimination of a common term—that is to say when, from a proposition which involves two terms M and P and another proposition which involves M and a further term S, we infer a proposition connecting S and P. This form of inference, known as the *syllogism*, was singled out by Aristotle as the fundamental constituent out of which chains of reasoning are constructed; and one of Aristotle's major achievements was to give an exhaustive classification of the valid forms of syllogism.

The term M, which occurs in both premisses, is called the *middle term* of the syllogism; the predicate P of the conclusion is called the *major term*; and the subject S of the conclusion is called the *minor term*. The premiss that contains the major term P is called the *major premiss*, and the premiss that contains the minor term S is called the *minor premiss*. The three constituent propositions of a syllogism are written, according to the usage of traditional logic, in the invariable order: major premiss, minor premiss, conclusion. When the major term, the minor term, and the middle term of a syllogism have respectively been specified, the subject and predicate of the conclusion are determined; but it still remains an open question which of the two terms M and P is the subject and which the predicate of the major premiss, and similarly with M and S in the minor premiss. Since the two pairs M, P and M, S can be ordered independently in four possible ways, we obtain four distinct *figures* of the syllogism. In representing these schematically, it is convenient to adopt the convention that the term which is the subject of a proposition shall be written before the term which is the predicate. Then '$X\ Y$', say, will stand for some proposition with X as subject and Y as predicate (a proposition that may be of any of the four types **A**, **I**, **E**, **O**), while '$Y\ X$' will stand for a proposition with Y as subject and X as predicate. We thus have the following table of the figures of the syllogism:

Figure I	Figure II	Figure III	Figure IV
$M\ P$	$P\ M$	$M\ P$	$P\ M$
$S\ M$	$S\ M$	$M\ S$	$M\ S$
$S\ P$	$S\ P$	$S\ P$	$S\ P$

The fourth figure was not recognized by Aristotle, but the mediaeval logicians included it in their enumeration of permissible types.

When a syllogism is assigned to a definite figure, this determines which of the two terms in each proposition is the subject and which is the predicate; but the quality and quantity of each of the three propositions still remain to be specified. For each individual proposition there are the four possibilities **A**, **I**, **E**, **O**, and the number of different determinations for the whole set is accordingly 4^3, i.e. 64. Thus each of the four figures has 64 *moods*, and there are in all 256 syllogistic schemes to be considered. Some of these are valid—that is to say, the premisses really do entail the conclusion—and some are invalid or fallacious. In Figure I, for instance, the mood **AAA** gives the scheme

$$\text{All } M \text{ is } P$$
$$\text{All } S \text{ is } M$$
$$\overline{\text{All } S \text{ is } P,}$$

which corresponds to a valid inference, e.g.

$$\text{All continuous functions are integrable}$$
$$\text{All polynomials are continuous functions}$$
$$\overline{\text{All polynomials are integrable.}}$$

The mood **IAA**, on the other hand, gives the scheme

$$\text{Some } M \text{ is } P$$
$$\text{All } S \text{ is } M$$
$$\overline{\text{All } S \text{ is } P,}$$

which is manifestly invalid.

In Figure II the mood **AAA** is invalid. It corresponds to the inference

$$\text{All } P \text{ is } M$$
$$\text{All } S \text{ is } M$$
$$\overline{\text{All } S \text{ is } P,}$$

which involves the fallacy of the *undistributed middle*. Although P and S are both connected in the premisses with the term M, they are only connected with unspecified parts of it. These parts may be non-overlapping, and so there is no effective middle term at all in the inference. Only when at least one of the premisses refers to the whole of M can we be sure that there is something to which both premisses refer simultaneously. As an illustration of the fallacious inference just considered, we might take the following argument:

All differentiable functions are continuous
All polynomials are continuous

All polynomials are differentiable functions.

The conclusion, as it happens, is a true assertion, but nevertheless it does not follow from the premisses.

Whether a syllogism of given figure and mood is valid or not can always be decided by inspection—most easily, perhaps, with the aid of Euler's diagrams—and indeed there is no appeal in this matter beyond the appeal to self-evidence. But when we wish to determine systematically which of the 256 possible syllogisms are valid, we can proceed more economically by first establishing certain general principles, known as the 'canons of valid reasoning', and then using them to cast out the invalid moods.[1] These rules, the correctness of which may easily be seen, run as follows:

1. Every syllogism has three and only three terms.
2. Every syllogism contains three and only three propositions.
3. The middle term must be distributed once at least.
4. No term may be distributed in the conclusion which is not distributed in at least one of the premisses.
5. From two negative premisses nothing can be inferred.
6. If one premiss is negative, the conclusion can only be negative; and if the conclusion is negative, one of the premisses must be negative.

It is usual to add to these six canons two further rules which follow from them:

7. From two particular premisses no conclusion can be drawn.
8. If one premiss is particular, the conclusion must be particular.

If we test the 256 possible syllogisms by means of these rules, we find that all except 24 are invalid. Of these 24, moreover, five are of little use, since they have what is known as a weakened conclusion. In the first figure, for instance, the moods **AAA** and **AAI** are both valid; but since **AAA** gives the conclusion 'All S is P', whereas **AAI** yields no more than the subalternate proposition 'Some S is P' from the same premisses, only the first of the two moods is worth retaining. When

[1] See, for example, W. S. Jevons: *Elementary Lessons in Logic* (London, 1870), Lessons XV and XVI.

the five weakened moods are discarded, we are left with the following set of nineteen valid syllogistic schemes:

Figure I	Figure II	Figure III	Figure IV
AAA	**EAE**	**AAI**	**AAI**
EAE	**AEE**	**IAI**	**AEE**
AII	**EIO**	**AII**	**IAI**
EIO	**AOO**	**EAO**	**EAO**
		OAO	**EIO**
		EIO	

The nineteen valid moods are traditionally referred to by gibberish Latin names, of mediaeval origin, in order that they may be remembered with the aid of a Latin hexameter mnemonic:

> *Barbara, Celarent, Darii, Ferio*que, prioris;
> *Cesare, Camestres, Festino, Baroko*, secundae;
> Tertia, *Darapti, Disamis, Datisi, Felapton,*
> *Bokardo, Ferison*, habet; Quarta insuper addit
> *Bramantip, Camenes, Dimaris, Fesapo, Fresison.*

Each name (written in italics) contains three vowels, and these indicate the mood of the corresponding syllogism.

As we have already said, the fourth figure was not included by Aristotle in his original theory of the syllogism. Aristotle distinguished, moreover, between the 'perfect' syllogisms of the first figure and the 'imperfect' ones of his other two figures, which he looked upon as somewhat less direct than the perfect ones; and he accordingly sought to reduce every syllogism in one or other of these two figures, by suitable logical transformation, to an equivalent syllogism in the first figure. This was the origin of the theory of *reduction of syllogisms*, which has a central place in traditional logic, and which we include here, in spite of the fact that it is now obsolete, because it gives a very good idea of the way in which the apparatus of aristotelian logic used to be handled. Knowing something of the mode of operation of the older logic, we shall be much better able to appreciate the greater power of modern symbolic logic, and to understand the difficulties that this new logic has been designed to overcome.

6   The reduction of syllogisms

By *reduction* of a syllogism in one of the last three figures is meant transformation of the syllogism into an equivalent one in the first figure, that is to say a syllogism in the first figure by means of which the same conclusion can be inferred from the same premises. The transformations that are used depend on the standard processes of conversion of propositions that we have already discussed (p. 13). Each mood has its own proper mode of reduction, and this can be read off at once from the name given to the mood in the mnemonic verse. In this name, in fact, the vowels give the mood of the syllogism itself, the initial consonant indicates the mood in the first figure to which it is reducible, and the remaining consonants specify the steps necessary to effect the reduction. The key to the code is as follows:

(i) The letter *s* indicates simple conversion of the proposition denoted by the preceding vowel.

(ii) The letter *p* indicates conversion by limitation (*per accidens*) of the proposition denoted by the preceding vowel.

(iii) The letter *m* indicates interchange (*mutare*) of the two premisses.

We may take as an illustration the reduction of the following syllogism in Camestres (the mood **AEE** in the second figure):

$$\begin{array}{ll} \text{All } P \text{ is } M & \textbf{(A)} \\ \underline{\text{No } S \text{ is } M} & \textbf{(E)} \\ \text{No } S \text{ is } P. & \textbf{(E)} \end{array}$$

The coded instructions are to convert simply both the minor premiss and the conclusion, and also to interchange the premisses. Doing all this, we obtain the result

$$\begin{array}{ll} \text{No } M \text{ is } S & \textbf{(E)} \\ \underline{\text{All } P \text{ is } M} & \textbf{(A)} \\ \text{No } P \text{ is } S, & \textbf{(E)} \end{array}$$

that is to say a syllogism in Celarent (as we expect from the initial *C*) with *S* as major and *P* as minor term.

The two moods Baroko and Bokardo both present a special difficulty, since each has a premiss of type **O**, which cannot be converted either simply or by limitation. These exceptional moods are reduced by a special process (indicated by the presence of the letter *k* in the name) which is known as *indirect reduction* or *reductio ad impossibile*. This procedure may be compared to Euclid's method of proof by *reductio ad absurdum*. As an illustration of indirect reduction, let us apply the method to the mood Baroko (Figure II):

$$\begin{array}{ll} \text{All } P \text{ is } M & \textbf{(A)} \\ \underline{\text{Some } S \text{ is not } M} & \textbf{(O)} \\ \text{Some } S \text{ is not } P. & \textbf{(O)} \end{array}$$

We begin by taking as a new premiss the negation of the original

3—M.L.

conclusion, namely 'All S is P'. Combining this with the original major premiss, we can form the following syllogism in Barbara:

$$\begin{array}{ll}
\text{All } P \text{ is } M & \textbf{(A)} \\
\underline{\text{All } S \text{ is } P} & \textbf{(A)} \\
\text{All } S \text{ is } M. & \textbf{(A)}
\end{array}$$

But the conclusion of this syllogism is incompatible with the original minor premiss; and since the assumption that the original conclusion is false leads in this way to an impossibility, we may regard that conclusion as having been established indirectly by means of a syllogism in Barbara. In this special sense, then, Baroko is reducible to Barbara; and the reader may verify that the same is true also of Bokardo.

7   Deductive arguments of more complex form

We have now carried our survey of traditional logic to a point where the basic ideas have all been discussed, and most of the features of the older logic that are now incorporated in modern symbolic logic have been introduced. One topic in traditional logic that we have not so far mentioned is the theory of forms of argument that are more complex than the syllogism. Much deductive reasoning can be carried out by combining syllogisms in suitable ways, but there are also certain patterns of inference that are accorded separate treatment in the standard manuals.

One such pattern is the type of extended syllogism known as the *sorites*. This takes the form

$$\begin{array}{l}
\text{All } A \text{ is } B \\
\text{All } B \text{ is } C \\
\quad \cdot \quad \cdot \quad \cdot \\
\underline{\text{All } H \text{ is } K} \\
\text{All } A \text{ is } K,
\end{array}$$

and it may evidently be considered as a telescoped system of syllogisms in Barbara.

As an example of a pattern of inference that is not trivially reducible to the syllogism in this way we may take the *dilemma*, which has three different forms:

(i) *The simple constructive dilemma:*

$$\begin{array}{l}
\text{If } A \text{ is } B,\ C \text{ is } D;\ \text{and if } E \text{ is } F,\ C \text{ is } D \\
\underline{\text{Either } A \text{ is } B,\ \text{or } E \text{ is } F} \\
C \text{ is } D.
\end{array}$$

(ii) *The complex constructive dilemma:*

If A is B, C is D; and if E is F, G is H
Either A is B, or E is F
_____
Either C is D, or G is H.

(iii) *The destructive dilemma:*

If A is B, C is D; and if E is F, G is H
Either C is not D, or G is not H
_____
Either A is not B, or E is not F.

The following illustration of the destructive dilemma has been given by Archbishop Whately in his *Elements of Logic* (1826): 'If this man were wise, he would not speak irreverently of Scripture in jest; and if he were good, he would not do so in earnest; but he does it, either in jest, or earnest; therefore he is either not wise, or not good.'

It becomes apparent, when we reach patterns of inference as complicated as the dilemmas, that we are dealing with subject-matter which is more appropriately handled by mathematical symbolism than by ordinary language. Traditional logic thus has a severely limited range; and in order to develop logical theories that go substantially beyond the theory of the syllogism we shall have to turn to the more modern logic that makes fuller use of mathematical methods.

SUPPLEMENTARY NOTES ON CHAPTER 1

1. *Aristotle's 'Organon'.* The *Organon* consists of the following six books, English translations of which make up the first volume of the standard Oxford edition of Aristotle's works: *Categories, De Interpretatione, Topics, Sophistic Elenchi, Prior Analytics, Posterior Analytics.* For an indication of the contents of these books, as well as of Aristotle's other writings, the reader may consult Ross [1].[1] Ross summarizes the arrangement of the *Organon* as follows:

'The logical treatises fall into three main parts: (1) the *Prior Analytics*, in which Aristotle aims at laying bare the structure which he regards as common to all reasoning—the syllogism—and at exhibiting its formal varieties, irrespective of the nature of the subject-matter dealt with. This may fairly be called a formal logic or logic of consistency. (2) The *Posterior Analytics*, in which he discusses the further characteristics which reasoning must have if it is to be not merely self-consistent but in the full sense scientific. This is emphatically a logic interested not in mere consistency but in truth. (3) The *Topics* and *Sophistic Elenchi*, in which he studies those modes

_____
[1] References of this form are to the Bibliography at the end of the book.

of reasoning which are syllogistically correct but fail to satisfy one or more of the conditions of scientific thought. The *Categories* and the *De Interpretatione*, which roughly speaking study the term and the proposition respectively, may be regarded as preliminary.'

A fundamental contribution to Aristotelian studies has been made by Łukasiewicz in his book *Aristotle's Syllogistic from the Standpoint of Modern Formal Logic* (1951), in which Aristotle's treatment of the syllogism is examined afresh in relation to the modern conception of logic. Łukasiewicz shows that the accounts of Aristotle's thought given by even such eminent scholars as Prantl and Maier are inadequate and often misleading; and he is able to improve substantially upon earlier interpretations because of the new insight that he gains from his knowledge of symbolic logic.

2. *Transitional logic.*   Before the middle of the nineteenth century, some logicians were already beginning to feel that aristotelian logic is too restricted to give a satisfactory account of the whole of deductive reasoning, and a number of attempts were made at that time to achieve greater generality.

(a) Sir William Hamilton, professor of logic and metaphysics at Edinburgh, already believed in 1833 that Aristotle, 'by an oversight, marvellous certainly in him', left his treatment of the syllogism in an incomplete state, since only the subject of a proposition could be quantified, and not the predicate also.   Hamilton maintained that the two terms involved in a proposition in subject-predicate form ought to be treated in the same way, and that the want of symmetry in the accepted treatment distorts and makes erroneous the traditional account of conversion of propositions.   He was not satisfied, for instance, with the existing distinction between the two types of affirmative proposition **A** and **I**, that is to say 'All X is Y' and 'Some X is Y', but demanded the further subdivision of **A** into the more specific types 'All X is all Y' and 'All X is some Y', and a similar subdivision of the types **I**, **E**, and **O**.   See W. Hamilton [1], vol. 4, pp. 249 ff.

(b) Augustus De Morgan, professor of mathematics at University College, London, adopted a more elaborate method than direct quantification of the predicate for improving upon the traditional fourfold classification of propositions.   His new classification is elaborated in his *Formal Logic* (1847), where it is used as the basis of a revised theory of the syllogism.

De Morgan begins by defining a proposition in the following way : 'A proposition is the assertion of agreement, more or less, or disagreement, more or less, between two names.   It expresses that of the objects of thought called Xs, there are some which are, or are not, found among the objects of thought called Ys ; that there are objects which have both names, or which have one but not the other, or which have neither.'   Together with each name X, De Morgan takes its contrary x, i.e. not-X ; and this introduction of coupled pairs of terms gives rise to a certain duplication of the traditional four types of proposition **A**, **I**, **E**, **O**.   Denoting the four schematic statements 'All X is Y', 'Some X is Y', 'No X is Y', and 'Some X is not Y' by the expressions

'X)Y', 'XY', 'X.Y', and 'X:Y' respectively, De Morgan introduces the following set of eight basic forms:

$A_,$:   X)Y = X.y = y)x, A':   x)y = x.Y = Y)X,

$I_,$:   XY = X:y = Y:x, I':   xy = x:Y = y:X,

$E_,$:   X.Y = X)y = Y)x, E':   x.y = x)Y = y)X,

$O_,$:   X:Y = Xy = y:x, O':   x:y = xY = Y:X.

Propositions of any of these eight forms are said to be *simple*. The information which a simple proposition gives about the relation between its two terms X and Y is in every case incomplete. Complete information can only be given by a *complex* proposition, that is to say a conjunction of a certain set of simple propositions, which together specify fully the way in which X and Y are related. The eight simple propositions derived from a given pair of terms X and Y are far from independent; and as a result the number of essentially different complex propositions that can be constructed from them is not $2^8 = 256$, as might at first appear, but only seven. These seven possibilities are the following:

$$P = O' + O_, + I' + I_,$$

$D = A_, + A',$ $C = E_, + E',$

$D_, = A_, + O',$ $C_, = E_, + I',$

$D' = A' + O_,$ $C' = E' + I_,.$

The form **P**, for instance, the *complex particular*, may be written out in full as 'Some not-X is Y and some X is not-Y and some not-X is not-Y and some X is Y', and it thus asserts that the four possibilities 'X and Y', 'not-X and Y', 'X and not-Y', and 'not-X and not-Y' are all realized, i.e. that the class of Xs and its complement both intersect the class of Ys and its complement.

D is the assertion of extensional *identity* of X and Y, **D**, the assertion of the relation of *subidentity*, and **D'** the assertion of that of *superidentity* (i.e. the assertions that the class of Xs is coextensive with the class of Ys, is a proper part of it, and contains it as a proper part respectively).

C is the assertion that X and Y are *contraries*, **C**, the assertion that X is a *subcontrary* of Y, and **C'** the assertion that X is a *supercontrary* of Y.

By using this classification of the possible types of complex proposition (which expresses in the terminology of logic the basic relations that are possible between two classes) De Morgan was able to construct his improved treatment of the syllogism.

(c) De Morgan's approach to logic was clearly that of a mathematician, although he chose to retain the ordinary language of logic. An even more thoroughgoing attempt to assimilate logic to mathematics was made by George Boole, who published an important logical treatise [2] in the same year as De Morgan. Boole's purpose was to reformulate logic in mathematical terms, and he adapted to this requirement the familiar symbolism

of algebra.   For a brief account of his work see Note 4, p. 51, at the end of
the next chapter.

An elementary survey of the developments that took place in logic during
the phase of transition from the traditional conception of this discipline to
the modern mathematical conception is to be found in Jevons [2], Lessons
XXII and XXIII.

3. *Venn's diagrams.*   In a paper [1] of 1880, John Venn proposed a new
form of diagrammatic representation for logical relationships between terms,
and he incorporated this method in his book *Symbolic Logic.*   The superiority
of Venn's form of representation over that of Euler resides in the fact that
Venn first of all represents all the terms involved, and also their contraries,
by certain regions of the plane, and then, by marking the basic diagram
appropriately, he inserts whatever specific information may be given.   His
mode of representation is thus related to Euler's very much as De Morgan's
classification of complex propositions, outlined in the previous note, is
related to the older use of the four types of proposition **A**, **I**, **E**, **0**.

Suppose that, in some context, there are n terms $X_1, \ldots, X_n$ to be
considered.   For each term X_i Venn takes a simple closed curve c_i, the
curves being chosen in such a way that each divides the interior of every
other into two portions, with the result that the plane is split up altogether
into 2^n regions.[1]   If the interior of c_i is used to represent the extension of X_i
and the exterior is used to represent the extension of its contrary not-X_i,
or x_i in De Morgan's notation, the 2^n regions are in one-one correspondence
with the 2^n conjunctive terms (intersections of classes) $X_1 X_2 \ldots X_n$,
$X_1 X_2 \ldots x_n$, $\ldots$, $x_1 x_2 \ldots x_n$.

For given terms $X_1, \ldots, X_n$, we may have information that certain of the
2^n *a priori* possibilities $X_1 X_2 \ldots X_n$, etc. are excluded (i.e. their extensions
are known to be null) or else are realized (i.e. their extensions are known to
be non-null); and all the logical relations between terms that are taken into
account in traditional logic—or even in the extended logic of De Morgan—
can be expressed in this way.   Venn's method of indicating that a particular
extension is null is by shading the corresponding region, and his method of
indicating that it is non-null is by placing a number in the region (or the same
number in each part of the region if this happens to be subdivided).   With
these conventions, the four standard propositional schemes **A**, **I**, **E**, **0**,
formed from a given subject-term X and a given predicate-term Y, are
represented by the diagrams:

A   I   E   0

---

[1] If n is 2 or 3, circles will do as the curves; but for larger values of n curves of more
complicated shape are needed in order that they may be able to intersect in the manner
required.

These diagrams, unlike those of Euler for the same four propositional schemes
(p. 12), are all derived from a single basic figure:

$X \quad Y$

For a discussion of Venn's diagrams see Suppes [1], pp. 195–201, or Ambrose & Lazerowitz [1], pp. 218–229.

4. *Additional reading.* For admirable surveys of both the content and
the history of logic, the articles 'Logic', by Church, and 'Logic, History of',
by Church and others, in editions of the *Encyclopaedia Britannica* from 1959
onwards may be consulted.

A very readable elementary book on traditional logic, which has con-
siderably influenced the writing of the present chapter, is Jevons: *Elementary
Lessons in Logic.* Two more detailed traditional manuals are Whately:
Elements of Logic and Bain: *Logic* (Part first, Deduction).

A classic in the literature of logic, which is devoted largely to induction
and scientific method, is John Stuart Mill: *A System of Logic* (1843).

5. '*The Development of Logic*'. A book that will be of much value to
any reader who wishes for a fuller account than is given here of the history
of logic—or indeed of almost any aspect of logic other than the detailed
construction of symbolic calculi—is *The Development of Logic* (1962) by
William and Martha Kneale. As this major historical work did not appear
until the present book was already in the press, no use could in fact be made
of it; but since over four hundred of its pages are devoted to logic since the
Renaissance, and full weight is given to the mathematical element in logical
investigations, this new account of the development of logic follows on very
naturally from the considerably more elementary discussion of the same
subject in the present book.

Chapter 2

SYMBOLIC LOGIC I:
THE PROPOSITIONAL CALCULUS

1 Propositional logic

Logic, in the present context, is to be thought of as the theory of the formal structure of deductive reasoning. Since the traditional logic that we have discussed in Chapter 1 originated in ancient Greece and was perfected by the mediaeval Scholastic philosophers, the forms of argument which it analysed were those practised by ancient and mediaeval thinkers. In modern times, however, with the unprecedented development of mathematics and the mathematical sciences, procedures of deduction have become immeasurably more subtle and more complex than ever before; and this elaboration of reasoning has made necessary a corresponding revision of deductive logic. The systematization of logic that is applicable to deductive argument as we now know it is no longer the traditional logic based on Aristotle's *Organon*, but modern symbolic logic.

A characteristic difference between ancient and modern reasoning is that, whereas in former times the complexity of a theory resided wholly in the logical sequence of the inferential steps, it now enters no less into the constitution of the actual propositions of which the theory is composed. We marvel, for instance, at the ingenuity shown by Euclid in his construction of the edifice of propositions in Book I of the *Elements*, which begins with very simple theorems such as the *Pons Asinorum* (I, 5) and yet culminates in the theorem of Pythagoras (I, 47); but we see at the same time that the propositions themselves are all elementary by current mathematical standards. It is very different when we open any textbook of modern mathematical analysis, for there we encounter propositions of elaborate logical form on almost every page. It is hardly to be wondered at, therefore, that modern logic is concerned much more with structural analysis of propositions than with formalization of possible procedures of demonstration (cf. p. 6).

The traditional analysis of propositions into subject, predicate, and copula is so elementary that it is scarcely even heard of in discussions of modern logic. Propositions are today analysed in a much more significant and complete way, with the aid of an essentially mathematical symbolism that was devised for this specific purpose; and in turning our attention in this chapter to the most elementary part of symbolic logic we must begin by making ourselves familiar with the symbolism and the intuitive ideas to which the various symbols and symbolic devices correspond.

The classical presentation of symbolic logic is that developed by Bertrand Russell and Alfred North Whitehead in the first volume of *Principia Mathematica* (1910)—see below, Chapter 6, §3.1.   A greatly simplified treatment of the elements of symbolic logic was subsequently given by David Hilbert and Wilhelm Ackermann in their *Grundzüge der theoretischen Logik* (1928), of which an English translation is now available.   Symbolic logic is also discussed very fully in the two volumes of *Grundlagen der Mathematik* (1934 & 1939) by David Hilbert and Paul Bernays, a work that exists in German only.   Our discussion will be based in the main on the treatment of Hilbert and Ackermann, to which the reader should turn for those details of the systematic development which we are obliged to omit.   We shall in addition refer from time to time to the *Grundlagen*, especially when considering the applications of symbolic logic to mathematics; and we shall also need to turn back to *Principia Mathematica* as a historical source.   It is important to note that, for the fourth edition of the *Grundzüge* (1959), Ackermann has radically overhauled the text, changing both the notation and the manner of development of the theory in order to bring the book up to date.   This latest edition of the *Grundzüge* is now better suited than the earlier ones to the needs of the advanced student; but in our present introduction to symbolic logic and the foundations of mathematics we prefer to adhere to the simpler treatment of the earlier editions.   All our references to the *Grundzüge* are to the second edition (1938), which is the one from which the English translation was made.

2   Propositional variables and the basic connectives

The primary entities with which we have to deal in logic are propositions, and we accordingly adopt a system of notation in which propositions are represented by literal symbols.   More precisely, we use capital Greek letters to stand for particular propositions, and capital Latin letters to stand for what are known as *propositional variables*.   Logic proper (as distinct from applied logic) cannot involve particular propositions, for it is concerned exclusively with the *form* of statements, and makes total abstraction of their material content.   The idea of a propositional variable may be explained by saying that a propositional variable X bears the same relation to a determinate proposition Φ as does a numerical variable x in mathematics to a determinate number or 'constant' a.

In elementary algebra we use 'variables' for the purpose of representing fixed patterns that are exhibited by arithmetical calculations, no matter what the particular numbers may be to which the calculations are applied. The identity $x^2 - y^2 \equiv (x + y)(x - y)$, for instance, tells us that two particular sequences of arithmetical operations, when applied to any pair of numbers whatever, necessarily yield the same result. The x and y in the identity are not themselves numbers, but merely abstract symbols. Numbers can be inserted in place of them, however, and then each side of the identity can be evaluated arithmetically. As mere symbols, x and y do not denote anything; but they occur in formal expressions in such a way that, whenever numbers are substituted for them, expressions are obtained which have arithmetical meaning. Symbols used in this way are referred to in mathematics as *indeterminates*, or more often (though less exactly) as *variables*. Strictly speaking, there is no question of variation, and all that can happen is that 'values are given to the variables', i.e. particular numbers are substituted for them.

When we speak of 'propositional variables', these also are to be understood as indeterminates. Formal expressions can be built up out of them, with the aid of standard symbols that we shall introduce for various simple logical operations, and these expressions become composite propositions whenever particular propositions are substituted for the propositional variables. In this way we obtain an 'algebra of propositions' that is in some respects analogous to the more familiar 'algebra of numbers'.

As well as using the Greek and Latin alphabets for propositions and propositional variables, we also make considerable use of the German alphabet. The precise mode of employment of German letters in our system of symbolic logic is explained in Note 1 on p. 86, and it will be sufficient for the present if we think of such letters simply as names for certain unspecified symbols or combinations of symbols. Using this convenient device we could, for instance, express the statement made in the second sentence of the previous paragraph as follows: If, in any expression $\mathfrak{A}$ that is formed out of the propositional variables $X_1, \ldots, X_n$ and suitable symbols for logical operators, we substitute particular propositions $\Phi_1, \ldots, \Phi_n$ for $X_1, \ldots, X_n$, then the resulting expression $\mathfrak{B}$ is a proposition. We could also express the same idea by saying that, if $\mathfrak{A}(X_1, \ldots, X_n)$ is an expression of the kind specified, and $\Phi_1, \ldots, \Phi_n$ are propositions, then $\mathfrak{A}(\Phi_1, \ldots, \Phi_n)$ is a proposition.

Coming now to the introduction of suitable symbols[1] for the basic logical operators that can be applied to propositions and propositional

---

[1] Unfortunately there is no generally accepted set of conventions for logical symbolism, and usage varies greatly from book to book and from paper to paper. The conventions adopted here are essentially those of Hilbert & Ackermann: *Grundzüge der theoretischen Logik* and Hilbert & Bernays: *Grundlagen der Mathematik* (see Note 1, p. 86). We have, however, followed the more recent practice of Bernays in using '↔' in place of the earlier ' ∼ '.

variables, we write the negation 'not-$\mathfrak{A}$' of $\mathfrak{A}$ as $\bar{\mathfrak{A}}$, and we also write
'$\mathfrak{A}$ or $\mathfrak{B}$', '$\mathfrak{A}$ and $\mathfrak{B}$', 'If $\mathfrak{A}$, then $\mathfrak{B}$', and '$\mathfrak{B}$ if and only if $\mathfrak{A}$' as $\mathfrak{A} \vee \mathfrak{B}$,
$\mathfrak{A} \& \mathfrak{B}$, $\mathfrak{A} \to \mathfrak{B}$, and $\mathfrak{A} \leftrightarrow \mathfrak{B}$ respectively.   We shall sometimes refer
to the operators $^{-}$, $\vee$, $\&$, $\to$, $\leftrightarrow$ as *logical constants*, and sometimes to
the last four of them, which always stand between two propositional
symbols, as *connectives*.   The intuitive concepts that are symbolized
in this way naturally require some clarification before they can take
their place in a systematic treatment of logic.   The explanations that
now follow should be sufficient at this initial stage, but later on, when
the theory is made more formal, reconsideration of the status of the
symbols $^{-}$, $\vee$, $\&$, $\to$, $\leftrightarrow$ will become necessary (cf. p. 41).

Negation may perhaps be thought to be sufficiently clear as an intuitive idea, but the same certainly cannot be said of all the elementary
logical operations on propositions that have just been enumerated.
Thus in common speech the word 'or', to take the stock example, is
used sometimes inclusively and sometimes exclusively—sometimes like
the Latin *vel* and sometimes like *aut*.   If, for instance, one of the rules
of a club provides that 'A member shall pay a reduced subscription if
he is under 25 or if he lives outside London' it is intended that a member
who is under 25 and who also lives in the country shall qualify for the
reduction; but if a rule runs 'A member may vote in person or register
a vote by post' the intention is then clearly that each member must
choose just one of the possible methods of voting.   The meanings
given to the logical constants 'not', 'or', etc., by common usage are
thus not always sufficiently definite for the more theoretical needs of
logic, and formal definition of these constants is accordingly required.
A fully satisfactory way of achieving this is to make use of 'truth-
tables', in a way now to be explained.

X	$\bar{X}$
T	F
F	T

From our present logical point of view, all that need be known concerning a proposition is whether it is true or false; for in assessing the
correctness of deductive chains, such as those which are constructed
when a mathematical theory is presented axiomatically, we ask only
that if the premisses are true propositions then the conclusions must
necessarily be true also.   In deductive logic, therefore, we abstract
from everything in a proposition except its *truth-value*, that is to say its
truth or falsity.   This being so, all that we need to know about the

operator $^-$, say, which converts any proposition into its negation, is that it reverses the truth-value of any proposition to which it is applied. Denoting the two possible truth-values by T and F, we can accordingly define $\bar{X}$ as a truth-function of X by the truth-table on p. 29.

More generally, to define a particular truth-function $\Phi(X_1, X_2, \ldots, X_n)$ of a set of n arguments we shall need to use a truth-table with 2^n entries, one for each of the possible sets of truth-values of the arguments $X_1, X_2, \ldots, X_n$:

X_1	X_2	$\ldots$	X_n	$\Phi(X_1, X_2, \ldots, X_n)$
T	T		T	*
T	T		F	*
$\cdot\ \cdot\ \cdot$	$\cdot\ \cdot$	$\cdot\ \cdot\ \cdot$	$\cdot\ \cdot$	$\cdot\ \cdot\ \cdot\ \cdot\ \cdot\ \cdot$
F	F		F	*

The asterisks mark the places of the 2^n values, T or F, of the truth-function in question. In particular, the truth-functions $X \vee Y$, $X \& Y$, $X \rightarrow Y$, and $X \leftrightarrow Y$, each a function of two arguments, have definitions which may be combined in the following composite table:[1]

X	Y	$X \vee Y$	$X \& Y$	$X \rightarrow Y$	$X \leftrightarrow Y$
T	T	T	T	T	T
T	F	T	F	F	F
F	T	T	F	T	F
F	F	F	F	T	T

If Φ and Ψ denote any particular propositions, this table makes possible the determination of the truth-values of the propositions $\Phi \vee \Psi$, $\Phi \& \Psi$, etc. as soon as the truth-values of Φ and Ψ are known. In this way the table makes precise the use of the basic connectives $\vee$, $\&$, $\rightarrow$, $\leftrightarrow$.

$X \vee Y$ is known as the *disjunction* of X and Y, and $X \& Y$ is known

[1] Cf. also Note 3, p. 50.

as their *conjunction*. It will be seen that in the formal definition of the disjunction we select the inclusive meaning of 'or', this being the one that is normally appropriate in mathematical contexts.

The relation symbolized by '$\rightarrow$' is most conveniently referred to as *implication*,[1] although it does not quite correspond to implication in the everyday sense. When we say that a proposition Φ 'implies' a proposition Ψ we ordinarily mean that, apart from any question of truth-values, there is some connexion between the contents of the propositions. When Izaak Walton wanted to establish the antiquity of angling, for instance, he argued thus: '... and in the Book of Job ... mention is also made of fish-hooks, which must imply Anglers in those times'. Thus the proposition 'Fish-hooks are mentioned' implies the proposition 'There are anglers'; and it does so because of the connexion between fish-hooks and their use. But in modern formal logic we abstract entirely from the *meaning* of statements and pay attention only to their *truth-values*; and when we do this, all that can be retained of the everyday notion of implication is the feature that 'Φ implies Ψ' rules out the possibility that Φ is true and Ψ is false. This, as we shall see, is as much as is needed in the formalization of deduction. For suppose we know that $\Phi \rightarrow \Psi$ is true. If we are now told that Φ is true, we can at once conclude that Ψ is true also. Thus when we are assured of the validity of the logical implication $\Phi \rightarrow \Psi$, we are in a position to 'deduce Ψ from Φ'. The truth-values that are to be ascribed to $\Phi \rightarrow \Psi$ in cases in which Φ is false are unimportant, since we do not draw conclusions from premisses unless these are known to be true, or at least assumed true for the sake of argument; but it greatly simplifies the formal logic of propositions if we define the truth-value of $\Phi \rightarrow \Psi$ in all cases, taking it as T whenever Φ has the truth-value F (cf. such conventional definitions in mathematics as $a^0 = 1$ and $0! = 1$). We thus arrive at the definition of the truth-function $X \rightarrow Y$ given in the table above.

Finally, the symbol '$\leftrightarrow$' for the relation that we call *bi-implication* (or alternatively *equivalence*) is defined in such a way that $X \leftrightarrow Y$ amounts to the two-sided implication $(X \rightarrow Y)$ & $(Y \rightarrow X)$.

By multiple use of the logical connectives, as in the expression last written down, we can build up formal combinations of propositional variables of unlimited complexity. Such combinations of symbols will be referred to as *propositional formulae*, or often more simply as *formulae*.

3   Equiveridicity of formulae

Now that the basic logical operators $^{-}$, $\vee$, &, $\rightarrow$, $\leftrightarrow$ have been defined by means of truth-tables, we can turn to the details of the 'algebra

---

[1] On this usage see Note 6, p. 54, at the end of the chapter.

of propositions' to which we alluded on p. 28.   This logical algebra is
an abstract theory, expressed in terms of propositional formulae; and
it is usually referred to as the *propositional calculus*.   As we shall see in
§4, it is similar in many respects to ordinary algebra, though not
identical with it.   It is known to mathematicians as *boolean algebra*,
a name that commemorates George Boole, the nineteenth-century
mathematician who first conceived the idea of handling logic by means
of algebraic symbolism (see Note 4, p. 51).   Boole's application of
mathematical methods to logic led him in actual fact to the algebra of
classes, which has essentially the same structure as the propositional
calculus.

  We say in elementary algebra that two expressions $f(x_1, \ldots, x_n)$ and
$g(x_1, \ldots, x_n)$, or more precisely two polynomials, containing the same
'variables' $x_1, \ldots, x_n$, are *identical* if they both take the same numerical value whenever numbers are substituted for the variables; and
when this is the case we write '$f(x_1, \ldots, x_n) \equiv g(x_1, \ldots, x_n)$'.   The
sign '$\equiv$' is not, strictly speaking, an algebraic symbol at all, but a sign
of abbreviation used in making certain statements about algebraic expressions.   In very much the same way we shall now say that two pro-
positional formulae $\mathfrak{A}(X_1, \ldots, X_n)$ and $\mathfrak{B}(X_1, \ldots, X_n)$ are *equiveridic*
if they both take the same truth-value whenever propositions are sub-
stituted for the variables in them; and for this relation we shall write
'$\mathfrak{A}$ eq $\mathfrak{B}$'.   Plainly a necessary and sufficient condition for equiveridicity of $\mathfrak{A}$ and $\mathfrak{B}$ is that the truth-tables for the two formulae shall be
the same.

X	Y	Z	$\mathfrak{Y}$	$\mathfrak{Z}$
T	T	T	T	T
T	T	F	T	T
T	F	T	T	T
T	F	F	T	T
F	T	T	F	F
F	T	F	F	F
F	F	T	F	F
F	F	F	F	F

The definition of equiveridicity just given is for a pair of formulae that contain the same variables, but this restriction on its generality is only apparent. Suppose, for example, that $\mathfrak{Y}$ and $\mathfrak{Z}$ are the formulae $X \mathbin{\&} (Y \vee \bar{Y})$ and $X \vee (Z \mathbin{\&} \bar{Z})$ respectively. Then, adopting the normal mathematical convention, we can treat them both as truth-functions of the same set of variables X, Y, Z, with Z not actually present in the first nor Y in the second. The truth-tables of the two formulae can then be combined as on the opposite page. Since the last two columns of the resulting table are identical, we may say that $\mathfrak{Y}$ and $\mathfrak{Z}$ are equiveridic.

The relation of equiveridicity between formulae is (i) reflexive ($\mathfrak{A}$ eq $\mathfrak{A}$), (ii) symmetrical (if $\mathfrak{A}$ eq $\mathfrak{B}$, then $\mathfrak{B}$ eq $\mathfrak{A}$), (iii) transitive (if $\mathfrak{A}$ eq $\mathfrak{B}$ and $\mathfrak{B}$ eq $\mathfrak{C}$, then $\mathfrak{A}$ eq $\mathfrak{C}$). It is thus an instance of what is known in mathematics as an *equivalence relation*; and by a standard theorem on such relations the totality of propositional formulae is partitioned by it into disjoint sets of mutually equiveridic formulae. Each such set is, in fact, the set of all formulae that determine some particular truth-function.

Among the possible truth-functions there are certain very special ones that take the truth-value T only, and we call these *identical truth-functions*. Thus the formula $X \vee \bar{X}$ determines an identical truth-function of the single propositional variable X; and, more generally, the formula $(X_1 \vee \bar{X}_1) \mathbin{\&} (X_2 \vee \bar{X}_2) \mathbin{\&} \ldots \mathbin{\&} (X_n \vee \bar{X}_n)$ determines an identical truth-function of $X_1, \ldots, X_n$. Any propositional formula that determines an identical truth-function is said to be an *identical formula* of the propositional calculus. Identical formulae are also referred to sometimes as *tautologies*.

If, in an identical formula $\mathfrak{A}(X_1, \ldots, X_n)$, we substitute any propositions $\Phi_1, \ldots, \Phi_n$ whatever for $X_1, \ldots, X_n$, we obtain a proposition $\mathfrak{A}(\Phi_1, \ldots, \Phi_n)$ that is true solely by reason of its logical form, no matter what may be the truth-values of the constituent propositions $\Phi_1, \ldots, \Phi_n$.

A clear distinction must be made between the symbol 'eq' that we have introduced for the relation of equiveridicity between formulae and the logical connectives '$\vee$', '$\&$', '$\rightarrow$', '$\leftrightarrow$'. These latter connectives form part of the 'language' of symbolic logic itself, whereas the symbol 'eq' is part of the language that we use in making statements about symbolic logic (cf. the sign '$\equiv$' in algebra, referred to on p. 32). We shall find it more and more important, as our discussion of mathematical logic proceeds, to keep separate the two spheres of *logic* and *metalogic*. Logic is the primary theory to which the whole discussion relates, while metalogic is the theory of this theory. Propositional formulae, for instance, are expressed in the language or symbolism of logic, and they are part of logic proper (although they can also be referred to in statements about logic). But when use is made of German letters, these do not themselves form part of the logical system, since they are employed for the purpose of making metalogical statements about the system. In the same way, the verb 'eq', standing between formulae, is a metalogical symbol.

There is a simple connexion between the metalogical symbol 'eq' and the logical connective '↔', which we formulate as follows:

THEOREM 1. *If* $\mathfrak{A}$ *and* $\mathfrak{B}$ *are propositional formulae* (*which need not involve the same set of variables*) *then* $\mathfrak{A}$ eq $\mathfrak{B}$ *if and only if the formula* $\mathfrak{A} \leftrightarrow \mathfrak{B}$ *is a tautology.*

Proof. From the definition of $X \leftrightarrow Y$ as a truth-function, a proposition $\Phi \leftrightarrow \Psi$ is true if and only if Φ and Ψ have the same truth-value; and therefore $\mathfrak{A} \leftrightarrow \mathfrak{B}$ is a tautology if and only if $\mathfrak{A}$ and $\mathfrak{B}$ have the same truth-value, whatever propositions may be substituted for the variables that occur in them, i.e. if and only if $\mathfrak{A}$ eq $\mathfrak{B}$.

4 Elementary transformations in the propositional calculus

Every propositional formula $\mathfrak{A}$ determines one and only one truth-function, but the truth-function does not determine the formula uniquely. In other words, to any formula $\mathfrak{A}$ there correspond many others that are equiveridic to it. In particular, there are certain canonical or normal forms to which all propositional formulae can be reduced. In order to make use of these normal forms we need some simple way of converting any given formula into any other equiveridic formula; and the required transformation can in fact always be carried out, as we shall show on p. 39, by a suitably chosen sequence of steps of a small number of standard types. We shall refer to these basic transformations as *elementary transformations*, and by an elementary transformation we shall understand the passage from a given formula to a formula that is equiveridic to it by virtue of one of the following rules (cf. Hilbert & Bernays: *Grundlagen*, I, p. 49):

I. Rules of substitution

(a) Let $\mathfrak{U}$ and $\mathfrak{B}$ be two equiveridic formulae, and let $X_1, \ldots, X_n$ be the variables involved in them. Let $\mathfrak{U}'$ and $\mathfrak{B}'$ be the formulae that are obtained from $\mathfrak{U}$ and $\mathfrak{B}$ when certain formulae $\mathfrak{A}_1, \ldots, \mathfrak{A}_n$ are substituted for $X_1, \ldots, X_n$. Then $\mathfrak{U}'$ and $\mathfrak{B}'$ are equiveridic.

(b) If $\mathfrak{U}$ and $\mathfrak{B}$ are equiveridic formulae, $\mathfrak{C}$ is a formula with $\mathfrak{U}$ as a component, and $\mathfrak{C}'$ is the formula obtained when this component of $\mathfrak{C}$ is replaced by $\mathfrak{B}$, then $\mathfrak{C}$ and $\mathfrak{C}'$ are equiveridic.

II. Rules for conjunction and disjunction

(a) $(\mathfrak{A} \,\&\, \mathfrak{A})$ eq $\mathfrak{A}$ and $(\mathfrak{A} \vee \mathfrak{A})$ eq $\mathfrak{A}$;

(b) $\mathfrak{A} \,\&\, (\mathfrak{B} \,\&\, \mathfrak{C})$ eq $(\mathfrak{A} \,\&\, \mathfrak{B}) \,\&\, \mathfrak{C}$,

$\mathfrak{A} \,\&\, \mathfrak{B}$ eq $\mathfrak{B} \,\&\, \mathfrak{A}$,

$$\mathfrak{A} \lor (\mathfrak{B} \lor \mathfrak{C}) \text{ eq } (\mathfrak{A} \lor \mathfrak{B}) \lor \mathfrak{C},$$
$$\mathfrak{A} \lor \mathfrak{B} \text{ eq } \mathfrak{B} \lor \mathfrak{A};$$

(c) $(\mathfrak{A} \And \mathfrak{B}) \lor \mathfrak{C}$ eq $(\mathfrak{A} \lor \mathfrak{C}) \And (\mathfrak{B} \lor \mathfrak{C}),$

$(\mathfrak{A} \lor \mathfrak{B}) \And \mathfrak{C}$ eq $(\mathfrak{A} \And \mathfrak{C}) \lor (\mathfrak{B} \And \mathfrak{C}).$

III. Rules for negation

(a) $\overline{\overline{\mathfrak{A}}}$ eq $\mathfrak{A}$;

(b) $\overline{\mathfrak{A} \And \mathfrak{B}}$ eq $\overline{\mathfrak{A}} \lor \overline{\mathfrak{B}}$ and $\overline{\mathfrak{A} \lor \mathfrak{B}}$ eq $\overline{\mathfrak{A}} \And \overline{\mathfrak{B}}.$

IV. Rules of cancellation

(a) $\mathfrak{A} \And (\mathfrak{B} \lor \overline{\mathfrak{B}})$ eq $\mathfrak{A}$ and $\mathfrak{A} \And (\mathfrak{B} \lor \overline{\mathfrak{B}} \lor \mathfrak{C})$ eq $\mathfrak{A}$;

(b) $\mathfrak{A} \lor (\mathfrak{B} \And \overline{\mathfrak{B}})$ eq $\mathfrak{A}$ and $\mathfrak{A} \lor (\mathfrak{B} \And \overline{\mathfrak{B}} \And \mathfrak{C})$ eq $\mathfrak{A}$.

V. Rules for implication and bi-implication

(a) $\mathfrak{A} \to \mathfrak{B}$ eq $\overline{\mathfrak{A}} \lor \mathfrak{B}$;

(b) $\mathfrak{A} \leftrightarrow \mathfrak{B}$ eq $(\mathfrak{A} \And \mathfrak{B}) \lor (\overline{\mathfrak{A}} \And \overline{\mathfrak{B}}).$

These rules can all be justified by reference to the definitions of $\overline{X}$, $X \lor Y$, $X \And Y$, $X \to Y$, $X \leftrightarrow Y$ as truth-functions.

If we compare the set of rules II with the familiar 'laws of algebra', that is to say the identities that express the associative, commutative, and distributive properties of arithmetical addition and multiplication, we see that there is a twofold analogy between the logic of propositions and the algebra of numbers. We can take '$\lor$' and '$\And$' either as corresponding respectively to '$+$' and '$.$' or as corresponding to '$.$' and '$+$'. In both cases we have an analogy that holds up to a certain point; but the boolean algebra of propositions differs essentially from ordinary algebra in the properties expressed by rules II(a) and II(c). In the language of mathematics, these rules can be expressed by the statements that each of the operations denoted by '$\lor$' and '$\And$' is idempotent, and the two operations are distributive both ways.

If we dispense with the connectives $\to$ and $\leftrightarrow$, as we can by the use of rules V(a) and V(b), we obtain a formal system that involves the remaining connectives $\And$ and $\lor$ symmetrically; and then to every relation of equiveridicity there corresponds a *dual* relation, which we get from it if we replace the sign '$\lor$' everywhere by '$\And$' and the sign '$\And$' by '$\lor$'. The two parts of rule II(c), for example, are dual to each other, and so also are the two parts of rule III(b).

5 Normal forms

Suppose, now, that some particular propositional formula $\mathfrak{A}$ is given. We can eliminate the connectives $\to$ and $\leftrightarrow$ by the use of rule V(a) and rule V(b), and we can then arrange matters, by the use of rule III(b), so that negation signs occur only above single propositional variables. By III(a) moreover, every variable, X say, with more than one negation bar can be replaced by X itself if the number of bars is even and by $\bar{X}$ if the number of bars is odd. Finally, using II(c), we can multiply the resulting formula out in either of two ways, so as to obtain either a conjunctive or a disjunctive normal form for the original formula $\mathfrak{A}$. The *conjunctive normal form* $\mathfrak{C}$ is a conjunction $\mathfrak{D}_1$ & $\mathfrak{D}_2$ & ... & $\mathfrak{D}_r$ of formulae $\mathfrak{D}_i$, each of which is a disjunction of propositional variables and negations of propositional variables. (It is understood that a variable or formula, standing by itself, is to be counted both as a conjunction and also as a disjunction with a single component.) The *disjunctive normal form* $\mathfrak{D}$ is of the dual type, that is to say it is a disjunction $\mathfrak{C}_1 \vee \mathfrak{C}_2 \vee \ldots \vee \mathfrak{C}_s$ of conjunctions $\mathfrak{C}_j$.

EXAMPLE. Let us take the formula $(X \to Y)$ & $\overline{\overline{X} \to (Y \ \& \ Z)}$. Carrying out the procedure indicated above, we have:

$$(X \to Y) \ \& \ \overline{\overline{X} \to (Y \ \& \ Z)}$$
$$\text{eq} \ (\bar{X} \vee Y) \ \& \ \overline{\overline{\overline{X}} \vee (Y \ \& \ Z)}$$

$$\text{eq} \ (\bar{X} \vee Y) \ \& \ (\overline{\overline{\overline{X}}} \ \& \ \overline{Y \ \& \ Z})$$
$$\text{eq} \ (\bar{X} \vee Y) \ \& \ \overline{\overline{\overline{X}}} \ \& \ (\bar{Y} \vee \bar{Z})$$
$$\text{eq} \ (\bar{X} \vee Y) \ \& \ \bar{X} \ \& \ (\bar{Y} \vee \bar{Z}) \tag{1}$$
$$\text{eq} \ (\bar{X} \ \& \ \bar{X} \ \& \ \bar{Y}) \vee (\bar{X} \ \& \ \bar{X} \ \& \ \bar{Z}) \vee (Y \ \& \ \bar{X} \ \& \ \bar{Y}) \vee (Y \ \& \ \bar{X} \ \& \ \bar{Z}). \tag{2}$$

Formula (1) is a conjunctive normal form for the formula with which we began. Formula (2) is a disjunctive normal form for the same formula. Formula (2) can be further reduced by elementary transformations to the formula

$$(\bar{X} \ \& \ \bar{Y}) \vee (\bar{X} \ \& \ \bar{Z}) \vee (\bar{X} \ \& \ Y \ \& \ \bar{Z}),$$

which is also in disjunctive normal form.

This example shows that we cannot properly refer to *the* conjunctive or *the* disjunctive normal form of a given formula, for the same formula can be equiveridic to more than one formula—indeed to infinitely many formulae—in each of the normal forms.

Exercises. (i) Obtain expressions for the formula

$$(X \to Y) \leftrightarrow [Y \vee (\bar{X} \ \& \ Z)]$$

in conjunctive and disjunctive normal form.

(ii) Prove that the process outlined above for reducing any given formula to conjunctive or disjunctive normal form must yield the required result in a finite number of steps.

We can use the process of reduction to conjunctive normal form in order to determine whether or not a given formula is a tautology without having to set up a truth-table for it. The appropriate criterion is supplied by the following theorem.

THEOREM 2. *If $\mathfrak{A}$ is a given formula, and $\mathfrak{D}_1 \,\&\, \mathfrak{D}_2 \,\&\ldots\&\, \mathfrak{D}_s$ is a formula in conjunctive normal form that is equiveridic to $\mathfrak{A}$, then a necessary and sufficient condition for $\mathfrak{A}$ to be a tautology is that each of the disjunctions $\mathfrak{D}_j$, $j = 1, \ldots, s$, shall contain some variable together with its negation.*

Proof. Any disjunction of the form $\ldots \vee X \vee \ldots \vee \overline{X} \vee \ldots$ is a tautology, and so therefore is any conjunction of such disjunctions. The condition is accordingly sufficient.

Suppose now that $\mathfrak{A}$ is a formula which can be written in conjunctive normal form as $\mathfrak{D}_1 \,\&\ldots\&\, \mathfrak{D}_s$, and that there is at least one component $\mathfrak{D}_i$ in which no variable occurs both barred and unbarred. If we assign the truth-value F to all the variables in $\mathfrak{A}$ that are unbarred in $\mathfrak{D}_i$ and the truth-value T to all those that are barred in $\mathfrak{D}_i$, and we complete the assignment of truth-values to the variables in $\mathfrak{A}$ by giving arbitrary truth-values to any variables in $\mathfrak{A}$ that do not occur in $\mathfrak{D}_i$, then, for this particular choice of truth-values, the component $\mathfrak{D}_i$ of the conjunctive expression for $\mathfrak{A}$, and therefore $\mathfrak{A}$ itself, will take the truth-value F. Thus $\mathfrak{A}$ is not a tautology in this case; and the necessity of the condition has accordingly been established.

Exercises. (i) State and prove a theorem which gives a corresponding criterion for a formula to be identically false, i.e. for it to determine a truth-function that takes only the truth-value F.

(ii) Use Theorem 2 to show that the formula

$$(X \to Y) \to [(Z \vee X) \to (Z \vee Y)]$$

is a tautology; and verify this conclusion by drawing up a truth-table for the formula.

The conjunctive and disjunctive normal forms for propositional formulae are often of considerable use in the practical handling of symbolic logic, but their value as metalogical instruments is severely limited by the fact that they are not unique. Fortunately, however, by a slight modification of these otherwise convenient normal forms we can define rather more specialized forms that have the desired property of uniqueness. It will be sufficient if we explain how this is to be done for the conjunctive normal form, since the treatment of the disjunctive normal form is similar.

Let $\mathfrak{A}$ be any given formula, and let $X_1, \ldots, X_n$ be the variables that are actually involved in it. We begin by resolving $\mathfrak{A}$ into conjunctive normal form in the usual way, and we thus arrive at a formula $\mathfrak{C}$ of the type $\mathfrak{D}_1 \,\&\ldots\&\, \mathfrak{D}_s$. Let us assume, first of all, that $\mathfrak{A}$ is not a tautology. Then there is at least one among the components $\mathfrak{D}_j$ of $\mathfrak{C}$ in which no variable occurs both barred and unbarred. By the rule of cancellation IV(a), we may drop from the conjunction $\mathfrak{C}$ all those components that do not have this property; and we may also suppress all repetitions of variables within the components. We are then left with a conjunction $\mathfrak{D}_1' \& \ldots \& \mathfrak{D}_t'$ in which every component $\mathfrak{D}_k'$ is a disjunction of distinct variables, each of which may be either barred or unbarred. Taking each component $\mathfrak{D}_k'$ in turn, we supply any of the variables $X_1, \ldots, X_n$ that may be missing from it by rewriting it as

$$\mathfrak{D}_k' \vee (X_h \& \bar{X}_h) \vee \ldots \vee (X_l \& \bar{X}_l);$$

and we finally restore the conjunction to conjunctive normal form by use of the distributive rule II(c). In this way we obtain for $\mathfrak{A}$ an expression $\mathfrak{C}^*$ in conjunctive form which is such that, in each of its components $\mathfrak{D}_i^*$, each of the variables $X_1, \ldots, X_n$ occurs once and once only, either barred or unbarred. In other words, $\mathfrak{C}^*$ is a subconjunction of the formula

$$(X_1 \vee X_2 \vee \ldots \vee X_n) \& \ldots \& (\bar{X}_1 \vee \bar{X}_2 \vee \ldots \bar{X}_n) \qquad (1)$$

which is obtained when the identically false formula

$$(X_1 \& \bar{X}_1) \vee (X_2 \& \bar{X}_2) \vee \ldots \vee (X_n \& \bar{X}_n)$$

is multiplied out in accordance with II(c). Such reduction of $\mathfrak{A}$ to $\mathfrak{C}^*$ is possible as long as $\mathfrak{A}$ is not a tautology; and in this one exceptional case we may take $\mathfrak{A}$ to be represented conventionally by the empty subconjunction of (1), i.e. the subconjunction which has no component at all.[1]

When a propositional formula $\mathfrak{A}$ is reduced in the above manner to a subconjunction $\mathfrak{C}^*$ of the conjunction (1), we say that $\mathfrak{A}$ is expressed in *special conjunctive normal form* for the set of variables $X_1, \ldots, X_n$.[2] The above argument shows that such reduction is always possible; and we now show further that the resulting expression is unique.

It is easy to see that no two distinct subconjunctions of the conjunction (1) are equiveridic. For suppose $\mathfrak{C}_1^*$ and $\mathfrak{C}_2^*$ are two subconjunctions of (1), and $\mathfrak{C}_1^*$ contains some component $\mathfrak{D}_i^*$, say $X_1 \vee \bar{X}_2 \vee \ldots \vee X_n$, which does not occur in $\mathfrak{C}_2^*$. We can then assign truth-values to X_1, $X_2, \ldots, X_n$ in such a way that $\mathfrak{D}_i^*$ has truth-value F, and every other component of the conjunction (1) consequently has truth-value T. In the example given, the chosen truth-values would be $F, T, \ldots, F$.

---

[1] The empty subconjunction is not, of course, a formula in the proper sense; and if we adopt the convenient device suggested here we shall have to make sure that suitable interpretations can be given to all statements in which reference is made to normal forms of the type that has just been introduced.

[2] The term used by Hilbert and Ackermann is *ausgezeichnete konjunktive Normalform*.

With such a determination of truth-values for the variables, the truth-values of $\mathfrak{C}_1^*$ and $\mathfrak{C}_2^*$ are F and T respectively; and this proves that $\mathfrak{C}_1^*$ and $\mathfrak{C}_2^*$ are not equiveridic.

Now since the conjunction (1) has 2^n components, the number of subconjunctions that it possesses (including the empty one) is $2^{(2^n)}$; and, as we have just seen, these all determine different truth-functions of $X_1, X_2, \ldots, X_n$. But the total number of truth-functions of n variables is also $2^{(2^n)}$—this being the number of distinct truth-tables—and hence there is a one-one correspondence between truth-functions of $X_1, \ldots, X_n$ and formulae in special conjunctive normal form for these variables.

It should be noted further that we can express a formula $\mathfrak{A}$, which contains only the variables $X_1, \ldots, X_n$, in special conjunctive normal form for any larger set of variables $X_1, \ldots, X_n, Y_1, \ldots, Y_p$, simply by applying the process of reduction already described to the formula $\mathfrak{A} \vee (Y_1 \mathbin{\&} \overline{Y}_1) \vee \ldots \vee (Y_p \mathbin{\&} \overline{Y}_p)$, which is equiveridic to $\mathfrak{A}$.

The main conclusion from the above discussion can now be stated as a theorem in the following terms:

THEOREM 3. *Every propositional formula that involves some or all of the variables $X_1, X_2, \ldots, X_n$, but no other variable, is equiveridic to one and only one formula in special conjunctive normal form for the set of variables $X_1, X_2, \ldots, X_n$.*

COROLLARY 1. *If two propositional formulae are equiveridic, then each can be transformed into the other by a finite sequence of elementary transformations.*

Proof. If two formulae $\mathfrak{A}$ and $\mathfrak{B}$ are equiveridic, they can both be transformed, by elementary transformations, into the same formula $\mathfrak{C}^*$ in special conjunctive normal form (for an appropriately chosen set of variables); and $\mathfrak{A}$ can then be transformed into $\mathfrak{B}$ by way of $\mathfrak{C}^*$. Corollary 1 is the result referred to on p. 34.

COROLLARY 2. *Every truth-function (defined by a truth-table) of a set of propositional variables $X_1, X_2, \ldots, X_n$ can be represented by a propositional formula that involves these variables and the two logical constants $^-$ and $\vee$ only.*

Proof. We have seen, in the argument leading up to Theorem 3, that there is a one-one correspondence between truth-functions and formulae in special conjunctive normal form. Since the connective '&' can be eliminated from any such formula by the use of rule III(b), any truth-function can be represented in the manner specified.

EXAMPLE. To reduce the following formulae to special conjunctive normal form:

(i) $[X \to ((X \to X) \to Y)] \ \& \ (\overline{X} \to Z)$,

(ii) $[X \ \& \ (X \to Y)] \to Y$.

(i) $[X \to ((X \to X) \to Y)] \ \& \ (\overline{X} \to Z)$

eq $[\overline{X} \vee (\overline{\overline{X} \vee X} \vee Y)] \ \& \ (\overline{\overline{X}} \vee Z)$

eq $[\overline{X} \vee ((X \ \& \ \overline{X}) \vee Y)] \ \& \ (X \vee Z)$

eq $(\overline{X} \vee Y) \ \& \ (X \vee Z)$

eq $[\overline{X} \vee Y \vee (Z \ \& \ \overline{Z})] \ \& \ [X \vee (Y \ \& \ \overline{Y}) \vee Z]$

eq $(\overline{X} \vee Y \vee Z) \ \& \ (\overline{X} \vee Y \vee \overline{Z}) \ \& \ (X \vee Y \vee Z) \ \& \ (X \vee \overline{Y} \vee Z)$.

(ii) $[X \ \& \ (X \to Y)] \to Y$

eq $\overline{X \ \& \ (\overline{X} \vee Y)} \vee Y$

eq $\overline{X} \vee (X \ \& \ \overline{Y}) \vee Y$

eq $(\overline{X} \vee X \vee Y) \ \& \ (\overline{X} \vee \overline{Y} \vee Y)$.

In this latter case the formula is a tautology, and its normal form is therefore the empty conjunction.

Exercise. Show that the truth-function $\Phi(X,Y)$ defined by the truth-table

X	Y	$\Phi(X,Y)$
T	T	F
T	F	T
F	T	T
F	F	F

is represented by the formula $(X \ \& \ \overline{Y}) \vee (\overline{X} \ \& \ Y)$ in special disjunctive normal form, the disjunction containing a component for each line of the truth-table in which the truth-value of $\Phi(X,Y)$ is T. By generalizing this result for an arbitrary truth-function of n variables, give an alternative proof of Corollary 2 to Theorem 3 on the previous page.

6   Axiomatic treatment of the propositional calculus

Our further treatment of the propositional calculus owes even more than the discussion in the earlier sections of this chapter to the example of mathematics. In that subject it has become the accepted practice to present theories axiomatically, especially when their structure is sufficiently simple for this to be done without excessive formal complication. The axiomatic method is applied with more or less strictness according to circumstances. In geometry, for instance, a comparatively free mode of argument can be the most illuminating when once the axiomatic foundation of the subject has been carefully laid. In algebra and analysis, on the other hand, strictly formal development is appropriate throughout. A very high degree of formal rigour is considered appropriate in the modern theory of groups, for example, while in Landau's well-known book *Grundlagen der Analysis* we have an equally austere treatment of the number-system of analysis.

Although the abstract axiomatic method is especially characteristic of pure mathematics, it can also be used in applied mathematics when a sufficient degree of idealization is attainable. When we use this method we abstract altogether from the nature of any intuitively conceived entities with which the theory that is being formalized may originally have dealt. Replacing these by wholly abstract entities— or alternatively, as we may also express the matter, operating with mere symbols—we simply *postulate* the existence of certain relations among the primitive entities, treating these relations as undefined except in that they are required to satisfy the postulated axioms of the theory.

The propositional calculus is a system that can be treated axiomatically in this purely formal way; and not only do we then have a new and elegant mathematical theory, but such a treatment of logic also enables us to establish a number of general metalogical theorems concerning the propositional calculus itself and other wider systems of formal logic.

Our first step must be to specify the symbols that are to be used in the propositional calculus, now that we are treating this as an axiomatic theory. First of all, there will be capital Latin letters; and although these do not now have any meaning or interpretation within the system, which is wholly abstract, we shall nevertheless continue to refer to them for convenience as 'propositional variables'. In addition, we also need formal counterparts of the special logical symbols. We shall see that it is sufficient to take two such symbols, namely ' $^{-}$ ' and ' $\lor$ ', to be read as 'not' and 'or'. From these two constant symbols and the propositional variables we can build up composite expressions, which will be referred to as 'formulae'. The symbols ' $^{-}$ ' and ' $\lor$ ' and the variables are thus taken as undefined or *primitive*; and we shall have to lay down suitable axioms which characterize them implicitly. We shall introduce further symbols, as the need arises, by *explicit definition*, defining them always in such a way that expressions in which they occur can be taken as abbreviations for expressions that involve primitive symbols only. This new use of explicitly defined symbols as abbreviations must be clearly distinguished from our earlier use of German letters as abbreviations in quite another sense (cf. p. 28). German letters are used sometimes as names of unspecified symbols or

expressions (as in the statement of rules I(a) and I(b) on p. 34) and
sometimes as 'syntactic variables' for which arbitrary formulae may be
substituted (as in rules II–V). In any case they are *metalogical* symbols, used only in making statements about the formal system, whereas
symbols introduced by explicit definition actually belong to the formal
system itself. We shall continue to use German letters for metamathematical purposes when discussing the axiomatic propositional calculus,
as we have already used them in our earlier and more intuitive treatment of propositional logic. With the aid of this notational device we
can now define three further connectives (further, that is, to the two
primitive symbols '$^{-}$' and '$\vee$') by adopting the following explicit definitions. It should be noted that these definitions are consistent with the
definitions of the same symbols in terms of truth-functions that we
gave on p. 30.

DEFINITIONS. $\mathfrak{A} \ \& \ \mathfrak{B} \ = \ \overline{\overline{\mathfrak{A}} \vee \overline{\mathfrak{B}}}$ Df

$\mathfrak{A} \to \mathfrak{B} \ = \ \overline{\mathfrak{A}} \vee \mathfrak{B}$ Df

$\mathfrak{A} \leftrightarrow \mathfrak{B} \ = \ (\mathfrak{A} \to \mathfrak{B}) \ \& \ (\mathfrak{B} \to \mathfrak{A})$ Df

where $\mathfrak{A}$ and $\mathfrak{B}$ denote arbitrary formulae built up from the primitive
symbols and possibly also the symbols '&', '$\to$', and '$\leftrightarrow$'.

The standard form in which we shall write explicit definitions is
'$\ldots = \ldots$ Df'. In the definitions just given, the letters '$\mathfrak{A}$' and '$\mathfrak{B}$'
are syntactic variables; and if any specific formulae are substituted for
them, the expressions '$\mathfrak{A} \ \& \ \mathfrak{B}$', '$\mathfrak{A} \to \mathfrak{B}$', and '$\mathfrak{A} \leftrightarrow \mathfrak{B}$' all become new
constituents of the formal system itself, defined as abbreviations for
$\overline{\overline{\mathfrak{A}} \vee \overline{\mathfrak{B}}}$, etc.

In what we have been saying, we have used the word 'formula' in a
technical sense. The meaning that is intended should be clear from
our earlier intuitive use of the same term—namely an expression that
becomes a proposition whenever propositions are substituted for the
variables, and the logical operators are given their interpretation by
truth-tables—but intuitive clarity of this kind is not sufficient in a
strictly formal development. The technical term 'formula' can easily
be defined syntactically, that is to say by reference solely to the manner
in which expressions are formed from their constituent symbols, and
this would have to be done in a fully systematic presentation of the propositional calculus as an axiomatic system. We do not go into such
details here, because in the next chapter we discuss the axiomatization
of the calculus of predicates, a more comprehensive system of logic
which includes the propositional calculus as its most elementary part.
The term 'formula' is defined syntactically for this wider system on
p. 65.

We come now to the axioms of the propositional calculus, of which four are required:

(a) $(X \vee X) \to X$,

(b) $X \to (X \vee Y)$,

(c) $(X \vee Y) \to (Y \vee X)$,

(d) $(X \to Y) \to [(Z \vee X) \to (Z \vee Y)]$.

By the 'theorems' of propositional logic we are to understand all the formal consequences of the axioms, but here some caution is required. In constructing axiomatic theories within mathematics we ordinarily establish theorems by arguing *informally*, though with very careful attention to logical rigour, from the axioms; but to do this in the present case would be to risk allowing the whole undertaking to be vitiated by circularity. The formal system that we are now dealing with is constructed with the aim of studying, in the most abstract manner possible, the structural pattern of deductive inference; and if the propositional calculus is to be used later on in order to criticize or justify deductive arguments, it must not presuppose deductive procedures in its own construction. In order to circumvent this difficulty, we now replace the notion of proof (as ordinarily understood in mathematics) by the more precise notion of *formal derivation*.

We lay down two entirely formal rules of manipulation of formulae, the rule of substitution (α) and the rule of inference (β); and we then say that a formula $\mathfrak{F}$ of the propositional calculus is *derivable* if and only if there exists a finite sequence of formulae $\mathfrak{F}_1, \ldots, \mathfrak{F}_n$ such that (i) $\mathfrak{F}_n$ is $\mathfrak{F}$, and (ii) each of the formulae $\mathfrak{F}_1, \ldots, \mathfrak{F}_n$ is either an axiom, or is derived in accordance with the rule (α) from an earlier formula of the sequence, or else is derived in accordance with the rule (β) from two earlier formulae. The two rules referred to run as follows:

(α) *For any particular variable that occurs in a given formula $\mathfrak{A}$ we may substitute, wherever it occurs, one and the same formula $\mathfrak{C}$.*

(β) *From two formulae $\mathfrak{A}$ and $\mathfrak{A} \to \mathfrak{B}$ we may pass to the further formula $\mathfrak{B}$.*

Rule (β), also known as *modus ponens* (a term borrowed from traditional logic), is often written as a *schema*

$$\mathfrak{A}$$
$$\mathfrak{A} \to \mathfrak{B}$$
$$\overline{}$$
$$\mathfrak{B}.$$

Such a schema is to be understood as indicating that from the pair of formulae above the line we may pass to the formula beneath it.

It may be noted that we could dispense altogether with the rule of substitution if we took, instead of the axioms (a)–(d), corresponding *axiom-schemata* (a')–(d') with syntactic variables $\mathfrak{A}$, $\mathfrak{B}$, $\mathfrak{C}$ in place of the propositional variables X, Y, Z.[1] In that case we would not derive the formula $X \to (X \vee X)$, for instance, by substituting X for Y in axiom (b) in accordance with the rule of substitution, but by substituting X for the syntactic variable $\mathfrak{A}$ and X for the syntactic variable $\mathfrak{B}$ in the axiom-schema (b'), namely $\mathfrak{A} \to (\mathfrak{A} \vee \mathfrak{B})$, i.e. by making $\mathfrak{A}$ and $\mathfrak{B}$ specific in this particular way. Axiom-schemata will not be used, however, in the treatment of symbolic logic that is to be given in this book.

Formal derivation is essentially a process of calculation in conformity with prescribed rules, and in itself it has nothing to do with inference in the ordinary sense. Its rules are chosen, however, with formalization of deductive inference in mind, and it will be applicable to deductive logic to the extent to which it faithfully mirrors the structure of deductive argument. In other words, our intention is that the derivable formulae of the present axiomatic system shall be formally the same as our earlier tautologies, or formulae that symbolize 'truths of logic'.

It is easy to see that every derivable formula is a tautology. The four axioms, in fact, all have this characteristic, and the characteristic is plainly left invariant by any application of the rules (α) and (β). What is not so obvious is that all tautologies are formally derivable. Such is in fact the case, however, and we shall shortly prove a metalogical theorem to this effect (p. 47).

We now have at our disposal two alternative treatments of the propositional calculus—either as a theory of identical truth-functions or as an abstract axiomatic system—and the two are precisely coextensive. The first way brings out best the logical significance of the calculus, but the second has the advantage of putting the calculus on a simple mathematical basis and freeing it from dependence on intuitive ideas. The two modes of treatment are often distinguished as *semantic* and *syntactic* respectively for the first makes use of the semantic notion of truth, while the second involves nothing beyond the formal structure or syntax of the system of symbolism that is used.[2]

An admirably clear and concise summary of the detailed building up of the axiomatic propositional calculus is given by Hilbert and Ackermann in §§10 and 11 of the first chapter of their book (editions earlier than the fourth), where full derivations of twenty carefully selected

---

[1] It will be observed that the word 'schema' is used in two quite different senses: (i) for a rule of procedure expressed with the aid of the horizontal line, (ii) for an 'axiom-pattern', expressed in terms of syntactic variables.

[2] For the meaning of the term 'semantic' see Note 1 on p. 49.

derivable formulae are to be found.   The twenty formulae are derived in succession from the axioms, and they are so chosen that the derivations themselves illustrate thoroughly the handling of the formalism, while among the results obtained there are formal versions of many important and interesting logical principles.   As it would scarcely be possible to improve upon Hilbert and Ackermann's treatment of the present axiomatic system, no attempt will be made here to cover the same ground.   The much more summary remarks which follow are intended merely to give a first idea of the development of the formal theory.   To facilitate reference, Hilbert and Ackermann's numbering of the derived formulae is adopted.

As far as formal handling of the calculus is concerned, the most powerful of the axioms (a)–(d) is the fourth, namely

$$(X \to Y) \to [(Z \lor X) \to (Z \lor Y)].$$

Making the substitution $\bar{Z}/Z$ in this axiom (i.e. putting $\bar{Z}$ everywhere in place of Z), and using the definition of $\to$ given on p. 42, we immediately derive Formula (1):

(1) $(X \to Y) \to [(Z \to X) \to (Z \to Y)].$

This formula is very useful as a lemma, since it embodies the transitivity of the connective $\to$.   We have, in fact, by the substitution $\mathfrak{B}/X, \mathfrak{C}/Y, \mathfrak{A}/Z,$

$$(\mathfrak{B} \to \mathfrak{C}) \to [(\mathfrak{A} \to \mathfrak{B}) \to (\mathfrak{A} \to \mathfrak{C})].$$

This schematic formula, by two applications of the rule (β), justifies the following schema[1] as a metalogical rule:

$$\frac{\begin{array}{c} \mathfrak{A} \to \mathfrak{B} \\ \mathfrak{B} \to \mathfrak{C} \end{array}}{\mathfrak{A} \to \mathfrak{C}.}$$

(V)

This derived schema, incidentally, may be compared with the syllogism in Barbara (see p. 18) which, by transposition of the premisses, can be written as

$$\frac{\begin{array}{c} \text{All } A \text{ is } B \\ \text{All } B \text{ is } C \end{array}}{\text{All } A \text{ is } C.}$$

In the one case we have transitivity of the connective $\to$, and in the other case transitivity of the relation of inclusion of one class in another.

Rule V may be used to derive Formula (2), namely $\bar{X} \lor X$; or

---

[1] More accurately, any *application* of the schema, with definite formulae in place of the syntactic variables, can be justified in this way.

alternatively, if we prefer to go back to first principles, the derivation may be given as follows:

Formula (2): $\bar{X} \vee X$

$$X \to (X \vee X) \qquad\qquad\qquad\qquad \text{[(b) } X/Y]$$
$$(X \vee X) \to X \qquad\qquad\qquad\qquad \text{[(a)]}$$
$$[(X \vee X) \to X] \to [(X \to (X \vee X)) \to (X \to X)]$$
$$\qquad\qquad\qquad\qquad\qquad \text{[(1) } (X \vee X)/X,\ X/Y,\ X/Z]$$
$$X \to X \qquad\qquad\qquad\qquad\qquad \text{[(}\beta\text{) twice]}$$
$$\bar{X} \vee X. \qquad\qquad\qquad\qquad\qquad \text{[Definition of } \to\text{]}$$

We now give derivations of the next four formulae of the sequence.

Formula (3): $X \vee \bar{X}$

$$(\bar{X} \vee X) \to (X \vee \bar{X}) \qquad\qquad \text{[(c) } \bar{X}/X,\ X/Y]$$
$$X \vee \bar{X}. \qquad\qquad\qquad\qquad \text{[(}\beta\text{), using (2)]}$$

Formula (4): $X \to \bar{\bar{X}}$

$$\bar{X} \vee \bar{\bar{X}} \qquad\qquad\qquad\qquad \text{[(3) } \bar{X}/X]$$
$$X \to \bar{\bar{X}}. \qquad\qquad\qquad\qquad \text{[Definition of } \to\text{]}$$

Formula (5): $\bar{\bar{X}} \to X$

$$\bar{X} \to \bar{\bar{\bar{X}}} \qquad\qquad\qquad\qquad \text{[(4) } \bar{X}/X]$$
$$(X \vee \bar{X}) \to (X \vee \bar{\bar{\bar{X}}}) \qquad\qquad \text{[By use of (d)]}$$
$$X \vee \bar{\bar{\bar{X}}} \qquad\qquad\qquad\qquad \text{[(}\beta\text{), using (3)]}$$
$$\bar{\bar{X}} \vee X \qquad\qquad\qquad\qquad \text{[By use of (c)]}$$
$$\bar{\bar{X}} \to X. \qquad\qquad\qquad\qquad \text{[Definition of } \to\text{]}$$

Formula (6): $(X \to Y) \to (\bar{Y} \to \bar{X})$

$$Y \to \bar{\bar{Y}} \qquad\qquad\qquad\qquad \text{[(4) } Y/X]$$
$$(\bar{X} \vee Y) \to (\bar{X} \vee \bar{\bar{Y}}) \qquad\qquad \text{[By use of (d)]}$$
$$(\bar{X} \vee \bar{\bar{Y}}) \to (\bar{\bar{Y}} \vee \bar{X}) \qquad\qquad \text{[(c) } \bar{X}/X,\ \bar{\bar{Y}}/Y]$$
$$(\bar{X} \vee Y) \to (\bar{\bar{Y}} \vee \bar{X}) \qquad\qquad \text{[Rule (V)]}$$
$$(X \to Y) \to (\bar{Y} \to \bar{X}). \qquad\qquad \text{[Definition of } \to\text{]}$$

Formulae (2) and (3) jointly provide a counterpart in the propositional calculus of the law of excluded middle (*tertium non datur*) in traditional logic, that is to say the principle 'Either A or not-A'.

Formula (6) is the principle of transposition. If in it we make the double substitution $\bar{Y}/X,\ \bar{X}/Y$, we obtain the formula

$$(\bar{Y} \to \bar{X}) \to (\bar{\bar{X}} \to \bar{\bar{Y}}).$$

Then using (4) and (5), which express the principle of double negation, we are able to pass to

$$(\bar{Y} \to \bar{X}) \to (X \to Y);$$

and from this and (6) we finally obtain, with the aid of Rule IX below, the bi-implication

$$(X \to Y) \leftrightarrow (\overline{Y} \to \overline{X}).$$

We have here a formal proof that two propositions which can be written as $\mathfrak{A} \to \mathfrak{B}$ and $\overline{\mathfrak{B}} \to \overline{\mathfrak{A}}$ make essentially the same assertion. The proposition $\mathfrak{B} \to \mathfrak{A}$, on the other hand, makes quite a different assertion from $\mathfrak{A} \to \mathfrak{B}$. It is said to be the *converse* of $\mathfrak{A} \to \mathfrak{B}$; and it can be written in the alternative form $\overline{\mathfrak{A}} \to \overline{\mathfrak{B}}$.

Many of the remaining fourteen formulae in the set of twenty derived by Hilbert and Ackermann are simple laws of propositional algebra, as for example

(11) $$(X \& Y) \to (Y \& X)$$

(16) $$[(X \lor Y) \lor Z] \to [X \lor (Y \lor Z)],$$

(19) $$[X \lor (Y \& Z)] \to [(X \lor Y) \& (X \lor Z)].$$

A result of some formal interest is Formula (18):

(18) $$X \to [Y \to (X \& Y)].$$

This can be written in terms of $^-$ and $\lor$ as

$$\overline{X} \lor (\overline{Y} \lor \overline{\overline{X} \lor \overline{Y}}),$$

and we can derive it from Formula (3), $X \lor \overline{X}$, by making the substitution $(\overline{X} \lor \overline{Y})/X$ and using the associativity of $\lor$ (Formula (16)). With Formula (18) at our disposal, we are able freely to pass from any pair of derived formulae $\mathfrak{A}$ and $\mathfrak{B}$ to their conjunction $\mathfrak{A} \& \mathfrak{B}$ by making two applications of the rule (β). In other words, we may use the schema[1]

(IX)
$$\frac{\begin{array}{c} \mathfrak{A} \\ \mathfrak{B} \end{array}}{\mathfrak{A} \& \mathfrak{B}.}$$

Exercises. (i) Give in full the derivation, outlined in the text, of the formula $(\overline{Y} \to \overline{X}) \to (X \to Y)$.

(ii) Justify the following schema:

$$\frac{\mathfrak{A} \to \mathfrak{B}}{(\mathfrak{B} \to \mathfrak{C}) \to (\mathfrak{A} \to \mathfrak{C}).}$$

Having followed the development of the axiomatic propositional calculus thus far, we are now in a position to prove the metalogical theorem alluded to on p. 44, which asserts that all identical formulae of the propositional calculus (i.e. all tautologies) are derivable from the

---

[1] This schema is not given a number by Hilbert and Ackermann, but we shall refer to it as Rule IX.

axioms. This theorem tells us that the axioms that we have adopted for the propositional calculus are in fact sufficient to yield a *complete* formalization of the calculus, as based on the concept of truth-function.

THEOREM 4. *The axiomatic propositional calculus is complete, in the sense that every formula which determines an identical truth-function is formally derivable from the axioms.*

Proof. Let $\mathfrak{A}$ be any identical formula of the propositional calculus. Then $\mathfrak{A}$ may be transformed, by a finite sequence of elementary transformations, into a formula $\mathfrak{C}$ in conjunctive normal form; and by Theorem 2 (p. 37), $\mathfrak{C}$ is a conjunction $\mathfrak{D}_1 \,\&\ldots\&\, \mathfrak{D}_s$ in which every component $\mathfrak{D}_i$ is a disjunction of the special type

$$\ldots \vee X \vee \ldots \vee \overline{X} \vee \ldots,$$

containing some variable X together with its negation. Now it is easily seen that:
(i) the formula $X \vee \overline{X}$ is derivable (Formula (3));
(ii) if a formula $\mathfrak{U}$ is derivable, then so also is every formula $\mathfrak{U} \vee \mathfrak{B}$ (by use of Axiom (b));
(iii) if a disjunction is derivable, then so also is any disjunction that is obtained from it when the order of its components is changed (by use of Axiom (c));
(iv) if the separate components of a conjunction are all derivable, then so is the conjunction itself (by use of Rule IX).

It follows that the above formula $\mathfrak{C}$, in conjunctive normal form, is derivable. But $\mathfrak{C}$ can be transformed back into $\mathfrak{A}$ by a sequence of elementary transformations; and this resultant transformation of $\mathfrak{C}$ into $\mathfrak{A}$ can readily be converted into a formal derivation of $\mathfrak{A}$ from $\mathfrak{C}$. Thus $\mathfrak{A}$ is itself a derivable formula, as was to be proved.

Now that Theorem 4 has been established, we have no further need actually to construct derivations in the propositional calculus, even when we wish to treat this calculus as a formal system. A formula is derivable if and only if it is identical, and we can therefore decide whether it is derivable or not simply by setting up a truth-table for it. Consider, for example, the following three formulae:

$$X \to (Y \to Z), \qquad Y \to (X \to Z), \qquad (X \,\&\, Y) \to Z.$$

It may be verified that they all determine the same truth-function; and from their mutual equiveridicity it then follows that any implication between two of them is an identical formula. Thus all the six possible implications are derivable, and any of the given formulae can therefore be derived from any other by an application of the rule (β).

We have here a simple justification of the following very useful schemata, given by Hilbert and Ackermann as their derived rule VII:

$$(\text{VII}) \quad \frac{\mathfrak{A} \to (\mathfrak{B} \to \mathfrak{C})}{\mathfrak{B} \to (\mathfrak{A} \to \mathfrak{C}),} \quad \frac{\mathfrak{A} \to (\mathfrak{B} \to \mathfrak{C})}{(\mathfrak{A} \ \& \ \mathfrak{B}) \to \mathfrak{C},} \quad \frac{(\mathfrak{A} \ \& \ \mathfrak{B}) \to \mathfrak{C}}{\mathfrak{A} \to (\mathfrak{B} \to \mathfrak{C}).}$$

Exercise. Show that, if $\mathfrak{A}$ and $\mathfrak{B}$ are formulae of the propositional calculus such that $\mathfrak{B}$ is obtainable from $\mathfrak{A}$ by a finite sequence of elementary transformations (see p. 34), then the bi-implication $\mathfrak{A} \leftrightarrow \mathfrak{B}$ is formally derivable.

SUPPLEMENTARY NOTES ON CHAPTER 2

1. *The term 'semantic'.* To say that a word or a concept is *semantic* is to say that it has to do with the relationship between words or other signs and what they mean or refer to. Thus the concepts of truth, of meaning, and of definition are all semantic, and so also is the concept of an empirically verifiable assertion, for in all these cases more is involved than the purely internal structure of whatever language is being used.

The semantic characteristics of natural languages are always more or less ill-defined; but when a formalized language (i.e. a logical calculus) is used instead of a natural one, semantics can be made into an exact study. This is a development to which we return in Note 2, p. 128.

2. *The logical notation of Łukasiewicz.*—Logical symbolism is much less standardized than mathematical symbolism (cf. p. 28), and not only does the literature of symbolic logic reveal innumerable variations of detail, but several quite distinct kinds of notation have been proposed by different authors.

(i) In the first place we have an extensive family of related systems, all descended through *Principia Mathematica* from Peano's *Formulaire*. To this family belongs the system of Hilbert, adopted with slight modification in the present book.

(ii) An entirely different system is that of Frege (see Chapter 6, §4.1), which was used systematically by him though not by any of his successors.

(iii) Yet another system, which has established itself as a recognized alternative to the systems of the family (i), is the one invented by the Polish logician Jan Łukasiewicz (1878–1956). This system has been adopted, in particular, by A. N. Prior, who uses it in his *Formal Logic* (1955).

Łukasiewicz prefers not to introduce quasi-mathematical symbols for logical constants, but rather to adapt ordinary letters to this purpose; and he invariably places letters which denote logical operators in front of any arguments on which they operate. For the molecular forms 'not-p', 'p or q', 'p and q', 'if p, then q', and 'q if and only if p', he writes Np, Apq, Kpq, Cpq, and Epq respectively. In his symbolism, for instance, the formula that we write in this book as $(X \ \& \ Y) \leftrightarrow \overline{X} \vee \overline{Y}$ is written as $EKpqNANpNq$. A considerable advantage when Łukasiewicz's notation is used is that the manner in which the atomic constituents are associated in a molecular expression is unambiguous, even when no brackets are inserted. A disadvantage is that the constitution of such an expression is not as immediately apparent as when the more usual logical notation is employed.

3. *The sixteen truth-functions of two propositional variables.* The number of distinct truth-functions of two variables is $2^{(2^2)}$, i.e. 16. Any particular function $\Phi(X,Y)$ in the set can be specified by a truth-table with four entries:

X	Y	$\Phi(X,Y)$
T	T	v_1
T	F	v_2
F	T	v_3
F	F	v_4

where each of the four values v_i is either T or F. The table can also be written more compactly as a truth-matrix:

Φ	T	F
T	v_1	v_2
F	v_3	v_4

We may use the symbol $(v_1,v_2,v_3,v_4 \rangle X,Y)$ to denote the truth-function $\Phi(X,Y)$ that is thus defined. Then $X \to Y$, for instance, is the truth-function $(T,F,T,T \rangle X,Y)$.

In the system of Łukasiewicz, described in the previous note, fixed symbols are assigned to all the sixteen truth-functions of a pair of propositional variables p,q. Arranged lexicographically, with 'T' always preceding 'F', the set of functions is

$$Vpq,\ Apq,\ Bpq,\ Ipq,\ Cpq,\ Hpq,\ Epq,\ Kpq,$$
$$Dpq,\ Jpq,\ Gpq,\ Lpq,\ Fpq,\ Mpq, Xpq, Opq.$$

The sixteen truth-functions of two variables are by no means independent. We know, for instance, that $X \leftrightarrow Y$ eq $(X \to Y)$ & $(Y \to X)$, i.e. Epq eq $KCpqCqp$. If we have negation at our disposal, that is to say Łukasiewicz's function Np of a single variable, we only need to take one function of two variables, e.g. the disjunction Apq, in order to be able to

form composite expressions for all the sixteen (cf. p. 39). And even negation can be dispensed with if we take as primitive either joint denial, Xpq,
or incompatibility, Dpq; for Np can then be expressed as Xpp or Dpp, and
Apq as $NXpq$ or $DNpNq$. The function Dpq, i.e. $(F,T,T,T \wr p,q)$, is in fact
Sheffer's stroke function $p \mid q$, adoption of which as a primitive connective
was advocated in the second edition of *Principia Mathematica*.

4. *Boole's application of algebraic symbolism to logic.* George Boole
(1815–1864) was both a mathematician and an early pioneer in symbolic
logic. He was the author of textbooks on differential equations and finite
differences that remained in use for many years, and also of a work on logic
that has lately been reissued as a classic: *An Investigation of the Laws of
Thought, on which are founded the Mathematical Theories of Logic and Probabilities* (London, 1854; reprinted New York, 1951). Boole described his
purpose in writing the *Laws of Thought* in these words:

'The design of the following treatise is to investigate the fundamental
laws of the mind by which reasoning is performed; to give expression to
them in the symbolical language of a Calculus, and upon this foundation to
establish the science of Logic and construct its method; to make that
method itself the basis of a general method for the application of the mathematical doctrine of Probabilities; and, finally, to collect from the various
elements of truth brought to view in the course of these inquiries some
probable intimations concerning the nature and constitution of the human
mind.'

Boole's first published account of his system was given in a work entitled
*The Mathematical Analysis of Logic, being an Essay towards a Calculus of
Deductive Reasoning* (Cambridge, 1847; reprinted Oxford, 1948). This work
is included, with other papers, in George Boole: *Studies in Logic and Probability* (London, 1952), a volume that also contains an informative obituary
notice by the Rev. Robert Harley, originally published in 1866 in the *British
Quarterly Review*.

Boole, as Harley's account of his life shows, had the remarkable distinction
of being a self-educated man who took his place as the equal of the leading
British mathematicians of his generation; and at the same time he was 'a
man of great goodness of heart'. His father, a Lincoln shoemaker, could
only afford a simple schooling for him; and after that he had to study from
books as best he could. He soon mastered Latin and Greek, and then he
turned to higher mathematics. From the age of 16 to the age of 34 he was
a schoolmaster, for much of this time conducting his own school, but all the
while he steadily pursued his mathematical studies and gradually built up a
considerable reputation by a succession of papers on mathematical topics.
In 1844 the Royal Society of London awarded him a Royal Medal for his
fundamental paper 'On a General Method in Analysis'. Eventually, in
1849, he was appointed to the chair of mathematics in the newly established
Queen's College at Cork, an appointment which he held until his early
death in 1864. His later work on logic was thus done during his years in
Ireland.

The unifying thread of Boole's work, in mathematics as well as in logic, is

5—M.L.

clearly revealed in the Royal Society paper just referred to, where he introduces his subject in the following way:

'Much attention has of late been paid to a method in analysis known as the calculus of operations, or as the method of the separation of symbols. ... Mr. GREGORY lays down the fundamental principle of the method in these words: "There are a number of theorems in ordinary algebra, which, though apparently proved to be true only for symbols representing numbers, admit of a much more extended application. Such theorems depend only on the laws of combination to which the symbols are subject, and are therefore true for all symbols, whatever their nature may be, which are subject to the same laws of combination." The laws of combination which have hitherto been recognized are the following, π and ϱ being symbols of operation, u and v subjects.

1. The commutative law, whose expression is

$$\pi\varrho u = \varrho\pi u.$$

2. The distributive law,

$$\pi(u + v) = \pi u + \pi v.$$

3. The index law,

$$\pi^m \pi^n u = \pi^{m+n} u.$$

Perhaps it might be worth while to consider whether the third law does not rather express a necessity of notation, arising from the use of general indices, than any property of the symbol π.

The above laws are obviously satisfied when π and ϱ are symbols of quantity. They are also satisfied when π and ϱ represent such symbols as $\frac{d}{dx}$, Δ, &c., in combination with each other, or with *constant* quantities . . . .

The object of this paper is to develope a method in analysis, which . . . operates with symbols apart from their subjects, and may thus be considered as a branch of the calculus of operations . . . .'

The method in question is a method of handling differential equations by manipulation of the operator D, and Boole goes on to give a comprehensive treatment of its applications.

Boole's work in analysis thus depended on the *formal* handling of symbols, in abstraction from their specific meaning; and it was this same idea that led him to try to fit a mathematical pattern to logical relationships.

The symbolism that Boole chose to employ was that of ordinary algebra, and he devised a way of expressing logical connexions by means of equations. Although he saw clearly the formal means that were needed for his purpose, he evidently had second thoughts about the interpretation of the symbols. This is revealed by a comparison of the two treatments of 1847 and 1854. In his earlier essay he associated with every class X an operator x, conceived as an *elective symbol*: 'The symbol x operating upon any subject comprehending individuals or classes, shall be supposed to select from that subject all the Xs which it contains.' The universe is represented by 1, and thus $x1$ (or x, as Boole usually writes it for short) denotes the result of applying the selection operator x to the universe, i.e. it denotes the class of all Xs. The advantage of treating x in the first instance as an operator is that operators can be compounded by successive application; and thus a product such as xy has a natural interpretation. In this way Boole arrives at the use of xy (i.e. $xy1$) to denote the intersection of the classes X and Y; and he can show that $xy = yx$. He goes on further to introduce the plus sign for formation of the union of two classes (though only of classes that are disjoint) and the notation $1 - x$ for the complement of x. Logical relationships are then expressible by means of equations, e.g. 'All X is Y' by $x(1 - y) = 0$, and 'Some X is Y' by $v = xy$, v being an elective symbol that is indeterminate except that it is required to be non-null.

In the *Laws of Thought*, Boole reinterprets his symbolism in the following way. The symbols $x, y, \ldots$ are now introduced as 'appellative or descriptive signs, expressing either the name of a thing, or some quality or circumstance belonging to it', and they are supposed to be interpreted extensionally : 'Let us then agree to represent the class of individuals to which a particular name or description is applicable, by a single letter, as x.' In this way Boole sets up an algebra of classes, which differs from the modern algebra (given, for instance, in Birkhoff & MacLane [1]) chiefly in the restriction of logical addition to disjoint components.

Boole shows how the formulae in his logical system often take a simpler form than corresponding formulae in ordinary algebra because of the law $x^2 = x$; and he also introduces a certain analogue of Taylor's theorem, namely :

$$f(x) = f(1)x + f(0)(1 - x),$$

by which logical expressions can be developed in a standard way—a principle of expansion that forms the basis of much of his manipulation of the symbolism.

Opinions vary on the significance of Boole's contribution to logic. Lewis and Langford discuss his logical method in the historical chapter with which they begin their *Symbolic Logic*, and they give a high place to his achievement. In their view, Boole was 'the second founder of symbolic logic'— the first being Leibniz—and they describe the method that he introduced as 'even in its original form . . . an entirely workable logical calculus'.

For more information about Boole's life and work, see Kneale's article [1], which was written to mark the centenary of the publication of the essay of 1847.

5. *Logical sum and logical product.* In older accounts of symbolic logic, the terms 'logical sum' and 'logical product' are often used where 'disjunction' and 'conjunction' would now be preferred. These terms were at one time used in mathematics also, to denote the union and intersection of sets, but they are now obsolete in both fields. There is indeed an analogy between the arithmetical operations of addition and multiplication on the one hand, and the two basic operations in propositional logic and in the theory of sets on the other; but whereas arithmetic involves its two operations in different ways, both logic and the theory of sets involve

their operations symmetrically (cf. p. 35).   For this reason there is much to
be said for the avoidance of the terms 'sum' and 'product' when the two
combinations in question behave in a symmetrical or dual manner, and for
the introduction of suitable pairs of related symbols, such as ' ∨ ' and ' ∧ '
for 'or' and 'and' in logic, and '∪' and '∩' for the connectives which yield
the union and the intersection of two sets.   Many authors, indeed, now
adopt ' ∧ ' in preference to the dot or the ampersand as the symbol for
logical conjunction.   It may be noted, furthermore, that the 'logical product' of two propositions has been taken both as their conjunction (by
Russell) and as their disjunction (by Hilbert and Ackermann), though
admittedly with a recommendation, in the latter case, against the use of
the term at all.

6. *C. I. Lewis's modal logic of strict implication.*   Although we have
chosen, for convenience, to read the formal expression '$X \to Y$' as 'X implies
Y', there are certain well-known objections to this course.   One is that the
word 'implies' is part of the vocabulary of metalogic, not of logic; and so,
since the expression '$X \to Y$' belongs to the logical calculus itself, it would
be more accurate to render it as 'If X, then Y'.

A second objection to our use of 'implies' is that the relation formalized
by the arrow does not altogether correspond to the intuitive notion of
implication, which involves the idea of some necessary connexion between
two propositions of which one can be said to imply the other.   An alternative system of symbolic logic, in which the intuitive notion of implication
is more adequately formalized, has in fact been constructed by C. I. Lewis.
This system is the 'system of strict implication', discussed in detail in Lewis
& Langford [1].

Lewis's notation is modelled on that of *Principia Mathematica*, small
Latin letters being used as propositional variables, and dots serving both as
brackets and as symbols for conjunction.   There are four primitive logical
constants:

negation: $\sim p$, 'not-p';
logical product: pq or $p.q$, 'p and q';
self-consistency or possibility: $\Diamond p$, 'p is possible';
logical equivalence: $p = q$, 'p is equivalent to q'.

Definitions in this system, which take the form '$\mathfrak{A} = \mathfrak{B}$', are expressed with
the aid of the relation of logical equivalence; and additional logical constants
are defined as follows:

disjunction: $p \vee q .=. \sim (\sim p \sim q)$;
strict implication: $p \prec q .=. \sim \Diamond (p \sim q)$;
material implication: $p \supset q .=. \sim (p \sim q)$;
material equivalence: $p \equiv q .=: p \supset q.q \supset p$;
consistency: $p \circ q .=. \sim (p \prec \sim q)$.

Logical equivalence also admits of definition, namely

$$p = q .=: p \prec q.q \prec p,$$

but this definition is of limited value since the relation '=' involved in the act of defining must itself still be taken as primitive.

The system is based on eight postulates or axioms:

$$pq \cdot \langle \cdot qp,$$
$$pq \cdot \langle \cdot p,$$
$$p \cdot \langle \cdot pp,$$
$$(pq)r \cdot \langle \cdot p(qr),$$
$$p \cdot \langle \cdot \sim(\sim p),$$
$$p \langle q \cdot q \langle r : \langle \cdot p \langle r,$$
$$p \cdot p \langle q : \langle \cdot q,$$
$$\Diamond(pq) \langle\!\langle \Diamond p.$$

The rules of derivation may be summarized as follows:

Rules of substitution. (a) If an expression of the form $\mathfrak{A} = \mathfrak{B}$ has been assumed or derived, then $\mathfrak{A}$ and $\mathfrak{B}$ may be substituted freely for each other. (b) Any well-formed formula may be substituted for a propositional variable in any assumption or derived formula, provided that this is done throughout the formula.

Rule of adjunction. If $\mathfrak{A}$ and $\mathfrak{B}$ can both be asserted, then so also can $\mathfrak{A}\mathfrak{B}$.

Rule of inference. If $\mathfrak{A}$ and $\mathfrak{A} \langle \mathfrak{B}$ can both be asserted, then so also can $\mathfrak{B}$.

It will be seen that this logical calculus of Lewis is more comprehensive than the ordinary propositional calculus, for it makes provision for both ordinary or material implication $(p \supset q)$ and implication in a new and strengthened sense $(p \langle q)$, and it also has the modal operator '$\Diamond$', which formalizes the intuitive notion of possibility.

In an appendix to Lewis & Langford [1], five possible sets of axioms S1–S5 are formulated, which yield systems of strict implication of various strengths (see p. 500 of the second edition). The system summarized in the present note is effectively S2.

7. *Many-valued logics.*   In most treatments of deductive logic it is taken for granted that every proposition is either true or false—a principle that finds formal expression in the axiomatic propositional calculus in the law of excluded middle $X \vee \overline{X}$, and that is also acknowledged in the semantic conception of the calculus when the logical connectives are defined by means of truth-tables which involve precisely two truth-values T and F. There are concrete situations, however, in which reasoning is used that does not fit at all readily into this simple scheme, and to which the dichotomy of true and false seems inappropriate. Reichenbach, for instance, has argued in [3] that quantum mechanics calls for a three-valued logic, in which propositions may be true, false, or indeterminate. Such a system of logic is formally possible, and indeed an n-valued logic can be set up for any given n.

Systems of logic with more than two truth-values were first studied by Łukasiewicz [1] in 1920, and independently by Post [1] in 1921; and the theory of such systems was worked out in detail by Łukasiewicz and Tarski in 1930—see Łukasiewicz [2] and Łukasiewicz & Tarski [1].

The simplest many-valued logic is one with three possible truth-values T, F, I; and Łukasiewicz has proposed a system based on the following truth-tables:

X	$\bar{X}$
T	F
I	I
F	T

X	Y	$X \vee Y$	$X \,\&\, Y$	$X \to Y$	$X \leftrightarrow Y$
T	T	T	T	T	T
T	I	T	I	I	I
T	F	T	F	F	F
I	T	T	I	T	I
I	I	I	I	T	T
I	F	I	F	I	I
F	T	T	F	T	F
F	I	I	F	T	I
F	F	F	F	T	T

This three-valued system is discussed in Lewis & Langford [1], Chapter VII; and a more general treatment of many-valued logics is given in Rosser & Turquette [1], where the calculus of predicates is considered as well as the propositional calculus.

8. *Books on symbolic logic.* In addition to Hilbert & Ackermann [1], which should be read in conjunction with the present chapter and the two succeeding chapters, which are all on symbolic logic, the earlier sections of Hilbert & Bernays [1] may also be consulted.

As elementary introductions to modern logic, Suppes [1] and Ambrose & Lazerowitz [1, 2] are recommended. These books are amply illustrated by concrete examples.

The reader who is already familiar with the rudiments of symbolic logic should certainly study Church [10], a book which, though not altogether easy for a beginner, is especially authoritative in view of the author's immense erudition, both as a historian of logic and as a logician. Church has been responsible for the editing of the *Journal of Symbolic Logic* since its inception in 1936, and the bibliography of symbolic logic that he published in volumes 1 and 3, together with the reviews in this *Journal* of all contributions to the subject that have appeared since 1936, are of the highest value. Church has also published a brief bibliography of formal logic [9], in which the selected items are classified according to subject.

A standard system of symbolic logic is presented in Quine [2]; and a more recent book in this general field that is not restricted to the purely formal treatment of logical calculi is Prior [1].

Whitehead and Russell's introduction to *Principia Mathematica*, as well as those chapters of the first volume in which the details of the logical calculus are developed, can still be read for other than purely historical reasons. The exposition is not difficult to follow, since each chapter begins with a short section in which the main results in the chapter are singled out and commented upon. A reprint has been issued (Cambridge, 1962) of the initial part of the *Principia*, up to *56.

Chapter 3

SYMBOLIC LOGIC II:
THE RESTRICTED CALCULUS OF PREDICATES

1 Propositional functions

The propositional calculus, which we have been discussing in Chapter 2, is only the most elementary part of symbolic logic, and its aim is a modest one. This calculus, in fact, deals only with the very simplest aspects of propositional structure, namely those which relate to what may be called the molecular structure of propositions. When a proposition is compounded of simpler propositions by means of the logical operators $^-$, $\vee$, &, $\rightarrow$, $\leftrightarrow$, we may think of it as molecular and of its irreducible components—or at any rate those components which we do not choose to resolve further in this way—as atomic.[1]

It is obvious that a system of logic which stops short at the analysis of molecular structure will be a very weak one, and that unless we go also into the atomic constitution of propositions we have little hope of exhibiting any but the most superficial features of deductive argument of the kind that is used in mathematics. Even traditional logic, elementary as it certainly is in relation to the needs of mathematics, offers an analysis of atomic propositions into subject, copula, and predicate ; and what we need to do is to carry this analysis further with the aid of modern mathematical symbolism. This will be our task in the present chapter. We shall proceed, as we did in Chapter 2, by first introducing the appropriate symbols in an informal way, and then showing afterwards how the enlarged system of symbolic logic to which we are thus led can be treated as a formal axiomatic theory.

In logic, as in mathematics, one of the most powerful general notions now available is that of *function*. A mathematical function, as understood informally, is an incompletely specified quantity (the dependent variable) whose identity depends on the identity of one or more unspecified quantities (the independent variables). Thus when we write $y = f(x)$ we mean that, if a definite number a is taken as the *value* of x, there is a well-defined number b which is the *value* $f(a)$ of the function $f(x)$ for $x = a$. We say then that y is a function of the single *argument*

---

[1] It is not part of our purpose to maintain that there are such things as absolutely atomic propositions or facts, as Wittgenstein asserted in the theory of the 'world' which he outlined in his *Tractatus Logico-Philosophicus* (cf. p. 317 below).

x. The x and y are not themselves numbers, but when appropriately specified they have numbers as their values; and we use equations involving 'variables'—for instance the equation $y = x^2$—to exhibit the precise manner of the dependence of corresponding values of these variables (cf. p. 27). Similar considerations apply to the more general type of functional relation $y = f(x_1, \ldots, x_n)$, in which the simultaneous dependence of a variable y on a number of variables $x_1, \ldots, x_n$ is expressed by means of a function of several arguments.

The situation in logic is closely analogous to that in mathematics. Consider the propositions 'Socrates is mortal', 'Plato is mortal', 'Aristotle is mortal', etc. These are propositions in subject-predicate form, and they differ only in their subjects. We may therefore think of them as all arising by specification of x in the schematic propositional expression 'x is mortal'; and it is then a natural further step to think of every proposition in subject-predicate form as derived by appropriate specification of the 'variable' subject x and the 'variable' predicate F in a schematic expression $F(x)$. Such an expression may be called a *propositional function*. Just as the mathematical expression $f(x)$ denotes a definite number when a particular function (e.g. sin) is taken for f and a numerical value is given to x, so the logical expression $F(x)$ denotes a definite proposition when a particular predicate (e.g. mortal) is taken for F and the name of a particular individual is put in place of x. The copula is now no longer required, since the connexion between subject and predicate which it asserts is already implicit in the notion of function of an argument.

In addition to propositional functions of a single argument we need also to consider propositional functions of two or more arguments, which we represent by such expressions as $F(x, y)$ and $F(x_1, \ldots, x_n)$. A distinction may also be drawn (although this proves to be of secondary significance) between a function $F(x)$ in which F is variable, like the f in the unspecified mathematical function $f(x)$, and a function $\Phi(x)$ in which 'Φ' stands for some definite predicate such as 'mortal'. However, both $F(x)$ and $\Phi(x)$ will be referred to as propositional functions.

In the propositional calculus we used only capital Latin letters, and these were understood, in the intuitive interpretation of the calculus, as propositional variables. But now, in the wider system of symbolic logic that we are about to construct, we shall need further symbols to correspond to propositional functions and their arguments. We shall use small Latin letters as *individual variables*, and capital Latin letters followed by brackets enclosing argument-spaces as *predicate variables*. For an individual variable we can substitute the name of any individual (for which a small Greek letter may be used), and for a predicate variable with n argument-spaces we can substitute the name of any property of an ordered set of n individuals.

It is convenient to use the term 'predicate' now in an extended sense, suggested by mathematical usage with functions, and we shall no longer confine it to cases in which a predicate has a single subject. Propositions in traditional subject-predicate form are of the type $\Phi(\alpha)$, but we shall now say that the 'Φ' in any proposition of the form $\Phi(\alpha_1, \ldots, \alpha_n)$ is a predicate. Predicates with two or more arguments are often referred to as *relations*, as is natural in the case of such propositional functions as 'x is the father of y', '$x < y$', and 'x is between y and z'. A very special relation, essentially logical in character, is the relation of *identity* $x = y$ (see Chapter 4, §1).

2 Quantification

The traditional logic of propositions in subject-predicate form, including the central theory of the syllogism, is built round the two notions of 'all' and 'some'. These give rise to the four basic types of proposition: universal affirmative **A** and universal negative **E**, and particular affirmative **I** and particular negative **O** (cf. p. 11). In symbolic logic, the notions 'all' and 'some' are expressed by the *quantifiers* (x) and (Ex).

If $\mathfrak{A}(x)$ is an expression that involves the variable x, then the expressions $(x)\mathfrak{A}(x)$ and $(Ex)\mathfrak{A}(x)$ stand respectively for the statements 'For every x, $\mathfrak{A}(x)$' and 'For some x, $\mathfrak{A}(x)$'. We call the symbol '(x)' a *universal quantifier* and the symbol '(Ex)' an *existential quantifier*.

It is clear from the intuitive significance of quantification that the universal and existential quantifiers are not independent, and that either can be expressed in terms of the other with the aid of negation. The negation of 'For every x, $\mathfrak{A}(x)$' is 'There is some x for which $\mathfrak{A}(x)$ does not hold', and $\overline{(x)\mathfrak{A}(x)}$ thus reduces to $(Ex)\overline{\mathfrak{A}(x)}$. In a similar way, $\overline{(Ex)\mathfrak{A}(x)}$ reduces to $(x)\overline{\mathfrak{A}(x)}$. We can therefore identify $(Ex)\mathfrak{A}(x)$ with $\overline{(x)\overline{\mathfrak{A}(x)}}$, and $(x)\mathfrak{A}(x)$ with $\overline{(Ex)\overline{\mathfrak{A}(x)}}$.

If $\Phi(x)$ is a propositional function with no variable in it except x, then $(x)\Phi(x)$ and $(Ex)\Phi(x)$ are propositions; if $\Psi(x, y)$ is a propositional function with x and y as its only variables, then $(x)\Psi(x,y)$ is a propositional function of y only; and so forth. Quantification thus eliminates variables from propositional functions; and the x in $(x)\mathfrak{A}(x)$ is an *apparent* or *dummy* variable, no more involved in the final result than is k in $\sum_{k=1}^{n} a_{ik}x_k$ or t in $\int_a^b f(t)dt$. It is plain too that, if $\mathfrak{z}$ is any variable that does not occur in $\mathfrak{A}(x)$, then $(x)\mathfrak{A}(x)$ and $(\mathfrak{z})\mathfrak{A}(\mathfrak{z})$ represent exactly the same proposition or propositional function. The dummy variables used in quantification are often referred to as *bound variables*, in contrast to the *free variables* on which propositional functions properly depend.

We now have two quite different procedures whereby propositional functions can be converted into propositions. If, to take the simplest case, $\Phi(x)$ is a propositional function with a single free variable x, we can on the one hand substitute some definite individual α for x, in which case we obtain the proposition $\Phi(\alpha)$. But instead of doing this we can quantify the propositional function in either of the two possible ways, and then we obtain one or other of the propositions $(x)\Phi(x)$ and $(Ex)\Phi(x)$. The three propositions $(x)\Phi(x)$, $\Phi(\alpha)$, and $(Ex)\Phi(x)$, taken in this order, make assertions of decreasing strength; and we have the two obvious implications

$$(x)\Phi(x) \to \Phi(\alpha)$$

and

$$\Phi(\alpha) \to (Ex)\Phi(x),$$

in which α is an arbitrary individual. The first of these implications is the symbolic counterpart of the *dictum de omni et nullo* of traditional logic (cf. p. 15).

Now let us consider the various quantified propositions that can be formed from a given propositional function $\Psi(x,y)$ of two variables. If we bind one of the variables by a quantifier we obtain a propositional function of the other variable only, and then this variable may be bound in turn, the final result being a proposition. Thus we might pass from $\Psi(x,y)$ to $(x)\Psi(x,y)$, and then from this function of y to $(Ey)[(x)\Psi(x,y)]$—which we write more simply as $(Ey)(x)\Psi(x,y)$. By such means we can form the following set of eight propositions:

$$(x)(y)\Psi(x,y), \qquad (y)(x)\Psi(x,y);$$
$$(x)(Ey)\Psi(x,y), \qquad (Ey)(x)\Psi(x,y);$$
$$(Ex)(y)\Psi(x,y), \qquad (y)(Ex)\Psi(x,y);$$
$$(Ex)(Ey)\Psi(x,y), \qquad (Ey)(Ex)\Psi(x,y).$$

The second expression of each pair is obtained from the first by inverting the quantifiers.

It is easily seen, by consideration of intuitive meanings, that the two propositions of the first pair are equivalent, and likewise the two propositions of the fourth pair. It may also be seen in the same way (though only after closer consideration) that the propositions of the other two pairs are related but not equivalent. In each of these pairs we have a relation of stronger to weaker, giving rise to the following implications:

$$(Ey)(x)\Psi(x,y) \to (x)(Ey)\Psi(x,y),$$
$$(Ex)(y)\Psi(x,y) \to (y)(Ex)\Psi(x,y).$$

This situation may be illustrated by a concrete example. Let the individuals under discussion be human beings, and let $\Psi(x,y)$ be the propositional function 'y is the father of x'. Then $(x)(Ey)\Psi(x,y)$ is 'For all x there is a y such that y is the father of x', i.e. 'Everyone has a father'; whereas $(Ey)(x)\Psi(x,y)$ is 'There is a y such that, for all x, y is the father of x', i.e. 'Everyone has the same father'. The first proposition is true, but the second, which asserts more, goes beyond the facts and is false.

The distinction between the two forms of expression $(x)(Ey)\mathfrak{A}(x,y)$ and $(Ey)(x)\mathfrak{A}(x,y)$, though comparatively subtle, is familiar to mathematicians. It arises in mathematical analysis, for example, when the distinction is made between simple convergence for all values of a parameter in a given set and uniform convergence in the set. Consider a sequence $\{s_n(x)\}$ of real-valued functions of a real variable x that converges, for all values of x, to a certain limit function $s(x)$ as n tends to infinity. The statement '$s_n(x)$ converges to $s(x)$ for all x' can be rendered in symbols as

$$(\varepsilon)[\varepsilon > 0 \to (x)(En_0)(n)(n \geqslant n_0 \to |s_n(x) - s(x)| < \varepsilon)],$$

while the statement '$s_n(x)$ converges to $s(x)$ uniformly for all x' yields the slightly different form

$$(\varepsilon)[\varepsilon > 0 \to (En_0)(x)(n)(n \geqslant n_0 \to |s_n(x) - s(x)| < \varepsilon)].$$

The two statements can be abbreviated as

$$(\varepsilon)[\mathfrak{A}(\varepsilon) \to (x)(En_0)\mathfrak{B}(x,n_0,\varepsilon)]$$

and

$$(\varepsilon)[\mathfrak{A}(\varepsilon) \to (En_0)(x)\mathfrak{B}(x,n_0,\varepsilon)]$$

respectively, where '$\mathfrak{A}(\varepsilon)$' stands for '$\varepsilon > 0$' and '$\mathfrak{B}(x,n_0,\varepsilon)$' for '$(n)(n \geqslant n_0 \to |s_n(x) - s(x)| < \varepsilon)$'. Now, as we have just seen, we have the implication

$$(En_0)(x)\mathfrak{B}(x,n_0,\varepsilon) \to (x)(En_0)\mathfrak{B}(x,n_0,\varepsilon) ;$$

and hence, by Formula (1) of the propositional calculus (p. 45), we have also the implication

$$[\mathfrak{A}(\varepsilon) \to (En_0)(x)\mathfrak{B}(x,n_0,\varepsilon)] \to [\mathfrak{A}(\varepsilon) \to (x)(En_0)\mathfrak{B}(x,n_0,\varepsilon)].$$

Since this last implication is valid for arbitrary ε, it is intuitively clear that the implication

$$(\varepsilon)[\mathfrak{A}(\varepsilon) \to (En_0)(x)\mathfrak{B}(x,n_0,\varepsilon)] \to (\varepsilon)[\mathfrak{A}(\varepsilon) \to (x)(En_0)\mathfrak{B}(x,n_0,\varepsilon)]$$

is also valid; and thus we see that uniform convergence for all real x is a stronger condition than simple convergence for every real value of x.

We may now sum up the facts concerning repeated quantification by saying simply that quantifiers of the same kind are always commutative (i.e. they may be freely inverted), but the combination $(Ex)(y)$ of unlike quantifiers yields a stronger assertion than the combination $(y)(Ex)$.

The universal and existential quantifiers provide a generalization, in the logic of predicates, of the conjunctive and disjunctive operators & and ∨ of the propositional calculus. A proposition $(x)\Phi(x)$ may be thought of as the 'conjunction' of all possible propositions of the form $\Phi(\alpha)$, obtained by allowing α to run through the entire totality of individuals; and $(Ex)\Phi(x)$ may be interpreted similarly as the corresponding 'disjunction'. Whether we have conjunctions and disjunctions in the strict sense already defined, or in an extended analogical sense, depends on whether the set of individuals is finite or infinite.

It is important to observe that, now that we are taking propositional functions into account as well as propositions—which gives us the system of symbolic logic known as the *calculus of predicates*—the expressions that we have occasion to consider may make implicit reference to a totality of individuals. This happens whenever we have an expression that contains a quantifier. Now deductive reasoning, as is evident, is always carried out within some fixed universe of discourse, the whole 'world' of entities and concepts that is recognized for the purposes of the argument in hand; and an essential constituent of this universe is the *domain of individuals*. The individuals postulated may vary from one deductive argument to another. In arithmetic, for instance, we have numbers; in geometry, we have points; and in the reasoning that is used to illustrate the older textbooks of logic, which abound in propositions of the type 'Socrates is mortal', we have human beings. What chiefly matters is that every application of deductive logic presupposes its appropriate universe of discourse, and therefore, in constructing an abstract calculus of predicates to systematize deductive logic, we must make this calculus relative to a postulated domain of individuals. What this involves will become clearer later in the chapter (cf. p. 71). And we shall see that the implicit reference that is made to such a domain makes the calculus of predicates very much more complicated as an object of metalogical investigation than the propositional calculus, already discussed in Chapter 2.

Suppose now that, in some particular application of the calculus of predicates, the domain of individuals has only a finite number of members $\alpha_1, \ldots, \alpha_k$. Then $(x)\Phi(x)$ means the same[1] as $\Phi(\alpha_1)$ & ... & $\Phi(\alpha_k)$, and $(Ex)\Phi(x)$ means the same as $\Phi(\alpha_1) \vee \ldots \vee \Phi(\alpha_k)$. In such a case, therefore, $(x)\Phi(x)$ and $(Ex)\Phi(x)$ are obtainable by finite iteration of the operations denoted by the connectives & and ∨, and they may

---

[1] This is only a first approximation to the truth, since '$(x)\Phi(x)$' says more than '$\Phi(\alpha_1)$ & ... & $\Phi(\alpha_k)$' unless we add '& $\alpha_1, \ldots, \alpha_k$ are the only individuals' to the conjunction, while the conjunction also says more than '$(x)\Phi(x)$' in that it actually names the individuals covered.

accordingly be interpreted as truth-functions. And any predicate $\Phi(x)$ can itself be defined explicitly as a 'truth-function of x' by assigning the truth-value T or F, as the case may be, to each of the k propositions $\Phi(\alpha_1), \ldots, \Phi(\alpha_k)$.

The calculus of predicates is thus trivially reducible to the propositional calculus when the domain of individuals happens to be finite. When this domain is infinite, however, no such reduction is possible; and if the finitude of the domain of individuals is to remain open when the calculus of predicates is presented in abstract form, we cannot avoid taking at least one of the types of quantification, universal or existential, as an essentially new logical notion, not definable in terms of the propositional connectives.

3   Axiomatic treatment of the calculus of predicates

When we wished, in Chapter 2, to give a mathematically rigorous treatment of propositional logic, there were two courses open to us, the one semantic and the other syntactic. The semantic possibility was to interpret the formulae of the propositional calculus as truth-functions of their constituent propositional variables, defining the various logical operators by means of truth-tables. There was an intuitive element in this (although it could evidently be eliminated by treating truth-tables formally, as the multiplication tables of abstract groups are treated) but the appeal made to intuition was in any case innocuous since everything could be defined and decided in a finite number of steps. The syntactic treatment, on the other hand, abjured all interpretation of the symbols from the very outset, presenting the propositional calculus as an abstract axiomatic theory. The two ways of handling the calculus proved to be entirely equivalent in scope, since the identical formulae of the first treatment could be shown by metalogical argument to coincide with the derivable formulae of the second.

Turning now from the propositional calculus to the calculus of predicates, we find that, if we require a rigorous treatment of the more general system, the semantic approach that we used before is now no longer available. We cannot define the new operators (x) and (Ex) in terms of truth-functions, because such a definition cannot be completed in a finite number of steps unless the domain of individuals is finite, and to postulate this would be to confine the logical calculus in advance to essentially trivial applications. We therefore have no option but to treat the calculus axiomatically as a formal system.

Although the axiomatic calculus that we are about to set up is much more comprehensive than the propositional calculus, it is still not the most general formalization of the logic of propositional functions, and for this reason it is often referred to as the *restricted calculus of predicates*. The precise nature of the restriction is explained in §6 of Chapter 4, where the wider system of symbolic logic known as the *extended calculus of predicates* is discussed.

The symbols used in the present system are small Latin letters ('individual variables'), capital Latin letters ('propositional variables'), capital Latin letters with places for arguments ('predicate variables'), the logical operators ‾, ∨, &, →, ↔ of the propositional calculus, and the quantifiers (ɹ) and (*E*ɹ). German letters are used, as in the propositional calculus, to serve as syntactic variables in metalogical discussions.

Not every expression that can be formed by juxtaposition of symbols and perhaps insertion of brackets has significance if the usual intuitive interpretation is given to the symbols, and we need to distinguish in the formal system between 'significant' expressions, or *well-formed formulae* as they are usually called, and symbolic gibberish such as ' & (*Ex*) → *A* '. This must be done syntactically, however, that is to say entirely by reference to structural properties and without any appeal to 'meaning'.

We have first of all to make precise the distinction between free and bound variables. An individual variable is said to occur *bound* in an expression 𝔄 if it occurs within the 'scope', indicated if necessary by brackets, of a quantifier in which it is the variable. Thus, for example, in the expression

$$(x)[(Ey)(A(x,y,z) \to B(y)) \to C(x)]$$

the scope of the quantifier (*x*) is the entire expression in square brackets, while the scope of (*Ey*) is the expression $A(x,y,z) \to B(y)$; and all occurrences of the individual variables are therefore bound except that of *z* in $A(x,y,z)$. An individual variable that occurs in an expression without being bound is said to occur *free*. For the present no variables other than individual variables can occur in quantifiers, and all occurrences of other kinds of variables are necessarily free.

We now define *well-formed formula* inductively as follows:

1. A propositional variable is a well-formed formula.
2. A predicate variable whose argument-places are occupied by individual variables is a well-formed formula.
3. If 𝔄 is a well-formed formula, then so also is 𝔄̄.
4. If 𝔄 and 𝔅 are both well-formed formulae, such that no variable occurs both bound in one and free in the other, then 𝔄 ∨ 𝔅, 𝔄 & 𝔅, 𝔄 → 𝔅, and 𝔄 ↔ 𝔅 are all well-formed formulae.
5. If 𝔄(ɹ) is any well-formed formula in which the individual variable ɹ occurs free, then (ɹ)𝔄(ɹ) and (*E*ɹ)𝔄(ɹ) are both well-formed formulae.

The calculus of predicates has six axioms, of which the first four are the axioms of the propositional calculus:

(a) $(X \vee X) \to X$,

(b) $X \to (X \vee Y)$,

(c) $(X \lor Y) \rightarrow (Y \lor X)$,

(d) $(X \rightarrow Y) \rightarrow [(Z \lor X) \rightarrow (Z \lor Y)]$,

(e) $(x)F(x) \rightarrow F(y)$,

(f) $F(y) \rightarrow (Ex)F(x)$.

There are more rules of derivation for the calculus of predicates than for the propositional calculus, where only two are required. The rules for the calculus of predicates may be stated in the following terms,[1] the word 'formula' being used throughout in the sense of 'well-formed formula'.

(α) *Rules of substitution:*

(α1) If $\mathfrak{A}$ is a formula which contains a certain propositional variable $\mathfrak{X}$, and $\mathfrak{B}$ is any formula, we may replace $\mathfrak{X}$ by $\mathfrak{B}$ in $\mathfrak{A}$, as long as we do so wherever $\mathfrak{X}$ occurs in $\mathfrak{A}$, and provided that there is no individual variable that occurs in both $\mathfrak{A}$ and $\mathfrak{B}$.

(α2) In any formula $\mathfrak{A}$, a free individual variable $\mathfrak{x}$ can be replaced by another individual variable $\mathfrak{y}$, as long as this is done wherever $\mathfrak{x}$ occurs in $\mathfrak{A}$, and provided that the variable $\mathfrak{y}$ does not occur bound in $\mathfrak{A}$.

(α3) If $\mathfrak{A}$ is any formula and $\mathfrak{F}$ is a predicate variable with n arguments that occurs in $\mathfrak{A}$, we may replace $\mathfrak{F}$ in $\mathfrak{A}$ by a formula $\mathfrak{B}$, with at least n free variables, in the following way: Let the free individual variables in $\mathfrak{B}$ be $\mathfrak{x}_1, \ldots, \mathfrak{x}_{n+r}$ $(r \geqslant 0)$, and let some particular n of these, say $\mathfrak{x}_1, \ldots, \mathfrak{x}_n$, be singled out. Then, if $\mathfrak{F}(\mathfrak{a}_1, \ldots, \mathfrak{a}_n)$ is any occurrence of $\mathfrak{F}$ in $\mathfrak{A}$, we replace $\mathfrak{F}(\mathfrak{a}_1, \ldots, \mathfrak{a}_n)$ by $\mathfrak{B}(\mathfrak{a}_1, \ldots, \mathfrak{a}_n, \mathfrak{x}_{n+1}, \ldots, \mathfrak{x}_{n+r})$. Such a substitution must be made wherever $\mathfrak{F}$ occurs in $\mathfrak{A}$; and replacement of $\mathfrak{F}$ by $\mathfrak{B}$ in this way in $\mathfrak{A}$ is permitted only when $\mathfrak{A}$ and $\mathfrak{B}$ have no individual variables in common.

(β) *Rule of inference:*

From two formulae $\mathfrak{A}$ and $\mathfrak{A} \rightarrow \mathfrak{B}$ we may pass to the further formula $\mathfrak{B}$.

(γ) *Rules for the quantifiers:*

(γ1) If $\mathfrak{A} \rightarrow \mathfrak{B}(\mathfrak{y})$ is any formula such that the variable $\mathfrak{y}$ occurs free in $\mathfrak{B}(\mathfrak{y})$ but does not occur at all in $\mathfrak{A}$, and if the variable $\mathfrak{x}$ is either $\mathfrak{y}$ itself or else some variable different from $\mathfrak{y}$ that does not occur free in $\mathfrak{A}$ or at all in $\mathfrak{B}(\mathfrak{y})$, then we may pass to the formula $\mathfrak{A} \rightarrow (\mathfrak{x})\mathfrak{B}(\mathfrak{x})$.

(γ2) With the same provisos as in (γ1), we may pass from $\mathfrak{B}(\mathfrak{y}) \rightarrow \mathfrak{A}$ to $(E\mathfrak{x})\mathfrak{B}(\mathfrak{x}) \rightarrow \mathfrak{A}$.

---

[1] The rules that we give here are those of Hilbert and Ackermann, with modifications proposed by D. Pager in a note due to appear in the *Journal of Symbolic Logic*. The original rules were incorrectly stated, and Pager's amendments are designed to put into effect the actual intention of Hilbert and Ackermann. Cf. the remarks of Church in his *Introduction to Mathematical Logic* (original version of 1944), p. 63.

(δ) Rule of relabelling of bound variables:

If, in a formula $\mathfrak{A}$, a letter $\mathfrak{x}$ is used as a bound variable, then, for any particular quantifier in which $\mathfrak{x}$ occurs, the letter $\mathfrak{x}$ may be replaced by any letter $\mathfrak{y}$, as long as this is done both in the quantifier and throughout its scope, and provided also that $\mathfrak{y}$ is either new to $\mathfrak{A}$ or else occurs in $\mathfrak{A}$ and is bound there by a quantifier with a scope that does not overlap the scope of the given quantifier.

It should be noted, in connexion with rule (δ), that if a common letter $\mathfrak{x}$ occurs in more than one quantifier, as in the formula $(z)F(z) \rightarrow (Ez)F(z)$, the different quantifiers and their respective scopes are entirely independent.

The rules (β) and (γ) can be expressed in the form of schemata as follows:

$$(\beta) \quad \frac{\mathfrak{A} \qquad \mathfrak{A} \rightarrow \mathfrak{B}}{\mathfrak{B},} \qquad\qquad (\gamma 1) \quad \frac{\mathfrak{A} \rightarrow \mathfrak{B}(\mathfrak{y})}{\mathfrak{A} \rightarrow (\mathfrak{x})\mathfrak{B}(\mathfrak{x}),} \qquad\qquad (\gamma 2) \quad \frac{\mathfrak{B}(\mathfrak{y}) \rightarrow \mathfrak{A}}{(E\mathfrak{x})\mathfrak{B}(\mathfrak{x}) \rightarrow \mathfrak{A}.}$$

Looked at purely in relation to the axiomatic calculus of predicates (this being conceived as a syntactically defined system) the rules (α)–(δ) are nothing more than postulated rules which form part of the specification of the calculus. But the axiomatic system is set up as a formalization of logic, and its formulae *can* therefore be given an intuitive meaning. When this is done, the rules are seen to correspond to principles of inference for which a measure of intuitive justification can be found. In the intuitive explanations that now follow we shall use the term 'propositional function' in a wider sense than hitherto, applying it to any form of expression that contains variables and that becomes a proposition whenever definite 'values' are assigned to these variables.

(α1): If a propositional function containing $\mathfrak{X}$ expresses a 'truth of logic', and if we replace $\mathfrak{X}$ in it by a propositional function or a proposition, then we shall obtain either a further truth of logic or a true proposition.

(α2): Replacement of one free variable by another makes no essential difference, provided that it does not cause a variable that was previously free to become bound by an existing quantifier, as would be the case, for instance, if we replaced 'y' by 'x' in $(x)(F(x) \lor G(y))$.

(α3): This is similar to (α1). Here we replace a predicate variable by some propositional function with a corresponding set of arguments, and possibly with further arguments which then behave as parameters. For example, in the axiom (f), namely $F(y) \rightarrow (Ex)F(x)$, we might substitute the predicate '$- = w$' for '$F(-)$'; and then we would obtain the expression $(y = w) \to (Ex)(x = w)$, with the additional free variable w as a parameter.

(β): The rule of inference has the same intuitive justification here as in the propositional calculus.

($\gamma 1$): '$\mathfrak{A} \to \mathfrak{B}(\mathfrak{y})$', where $\mathfrak{y}$ is free, may be interpreted roughly as '$\mathfrak{A}$ implies $\mathfrak{B}(\alpha)$, for any arbitrary individual α'; and from this we infer '$\mathfrak{A}$ implies that $\mathfrak{B}$ always holds', i.e. '$\mathfrak{A}$ implies $(\mathfrak{x})\mathfrak{B}(\mathfrak{x})$'.

($\gamma 2$): '$\mathfrak{B}(\mathfrak{y}) \to \mathfrak{A}$' may be interpreted roughly as '$\mathfrak{A}$ follows from $\mathfrak{B}(\alpha)$, where α is arbitrary'; and from this we infer '$\mathfrak{A}$ follows if there is some α with the property $\mathfrak{B}$', i.e. '$(E\mathfrak{x})\mathfrak{B}(\mathfrak{x})$ implies $\mathfrak{A}$'.

(δ): The rule of relabelling simply expresses the fact that bound variables are dummy variables.

Reverting to the formal development of the axiomatic calculus of predicates, we now consider derivations. By a *derivation* of a formula $\mathfrak{F}$ we are to understand a finite sequence of formulae $\mathfrak{F}_1, \ldots, \mathfrak{F}_n$ such that $\mathfrak{F}_n$ is $\mathfrak{F}$ and each of the formulae $\mathfrak{F}_1, \ldots, \mathfrak{F}_n$ is either an axiom or else a formula that is obtained from a formula or a pair of formulae standing earlier in the sequence by an application of one of the rules (α)–(δ). Every derivation in the propositional calculus is *a fortiori* a derivation in the calculus of predicates; and since we already know, by Theorem 4, p. 48, that the derivable formulae of the propositional calculus are the same as the identical formulae (tautologies), we are at liberty to simplify the handling of the calculus of predicates by permitting unrestricted use of such identical propositional formulae as *initial formulae* in derivations, that is to say formulae which are used, like the axioms, without being themselves derived from earlier formulae.

When we come to apply the calculus of predicates to mathematical theories, we shall need to work with 'derivations' in an extended sense. In order to give a formal treatment of arithmetic, for example, we shall have to have special symbols by means of which we can designate the individual numbers $0, 1, 2, \ldots$, as well as symbols for constant arithmetical predicates such as $x < y$; and the axioms of the logical calculus will have to be supplemented by further axioms which formalize some of the basic properties of numbers. By a 'well-formed formula' we shall then understand an expression, constructed syntactically in the same way as the formulae of the logical calculus, but which may involve arithmetical symbols as well as the symbols of symbolic logic; and a 'derivation' will be a finite sequence of formulae $\mathfrak{F}_1, \ldots, \mathfrak{F}_n$ with the same structural connectedness as previously, except that arithmetical as well as logical axioms are permitted as initial formulae. (Cf. Chapter 4, §3.)

Examples of standard derivations in the calculus of predicates are given by Hilbert and Ackermann in §6 of Chapter 3 of their book. Among the formulae there derived are the following:

(26) $(x)(A \vee F(x)) \leftrightarrow (A \vee (x)F(x))$,

(28) $(x)(A \,\&\, F(x)) \leftrightarrow (A \,\&\, (x)F(x))$,

(33a) $(Ex)F(x) \leftrightarrow \overline{(x)\overline{F(x)}}$,

(31) $(x)[F(x) \rightarrow G(x)] \rightarrow [(x)F(x) \rightarrow (x)G(x)]$,

(34) $(x)[F(x) \rightarrow G(x)] \rightarrow [(Ex)F(x) \rightarrow (Ex)G(x)]$,

(29) $(x)(y)F(x,y) \leftrightarrow (y)(x)F(x,y)$,

(36) $(Ex)(y)F(x,y) \rightarrow (y)(Ex)F(x,y)$.

It will be observed that some of these formulae are bi-implications, while others are only simple implications.   An intuitive reason for this difference may be found in the interpretation of the formulae as logical principles.

As a specimen of a typical derivation in the calculus of predicates, the derivation of Formula (26) may be summarized as follows, some of the details that belong essentially to the propositional calculus being omitted.

$(x)(A \vee F(x)) \rightarrow (A \vee F(y))$ [(e) $(A \vee F(\mathfrak{x}))/F(\mathfrak{x})$]

$(x)(A \vee F(x)) \rightarrow (\overline{\overline{A}} \vee F(y))$ [Using $X \rightarrow \overline{\overline{X}}$]

$(x)(A \vee F(x)) \rightarrow (\overline{A} \rightarrow F(y))$

$[(x)(A \vee F(x)) \,\&\, \overline{A}] \rightarrow F(y)$ [Rule VII, p. 49]

$[(x)(A \vee F(x)) \,\&\, \overline{A}] \rightarrow (x)F(x)$ [($\gamma 1$)]

$(x)(A \vee F(x)) \rightarrow (\overline{A} \rightarrow (x)F(x))$ [Rule VII]

$(x)(A \vee F(x)) \rightarrow (A \vee (x)F(x))$.

As a further specimen, let us take the derivation of Formula (29).

$(x)(y)F(x,y) \rightarrow (y)F(u,y)$ [(e) $u/y, \ (y)F(\mathfrak{x},y)/F(\mathfrak{x})$]

$(y)F(u,y) \rightarrow F(u,v)$ [(e) $y/x, \ v/y, \ F(u,\mathfrak{z})/F(\mathfrak{z})$]

$(x)(y)F(x,y) \rightarrow F(u,v)$ [Rule V, p. 45]

$(x)(y)F(x,y) \rightarrow (x)F(x,v)$ [($\gamma 1$)]

$(x)(y)F(x,y) \rightarrow (y)(x)F(x,y)$.   [($\gamma 1$)]

The converse implication $(y)(x)F(x,y) \rightarrow (x)(y)F(x,y)$ can now be derived similarly—or alternatively by making the substitution $F(\mathfrak{y},\mathfrak{x})/F(\mathfrak{x},\mathfrak{y})$ in the formula just obtained, and then changing x into y and y into x by (δ)—and finally the two separate implications can be combined in a single bi-implication in accordance with Rule IX, p. 47.

There are many derived schemata that are useful in the present calculus.   One simple one

(γ') $$\frac{\mathfrak{A}(\mathfrak{y})}{(\mathfrak{x})\mathfrak{A}(\mathfrak{x})}$$

(with the obvious proviso that $\mathfrak{x}$ must be either $\mathfrak{y}$ or else some variable that does not occur in $\mathfrak{A}(\mathfrak{y})$) completes the formalization, partially attained in the axiom (e), of the intuitive equivalence of the two assertions 'For all x, $\Phi(x)$' and 'Whatever choice may be made of an individual α, then $\Phi(\alpha)$'. The rule (γ') may be justified by the following schematic derivation, based on $(\gamma 1)$:

$\mathfrak{A}(\mathfrak{y})$

$\overline{(X \vee \overline{X})} \to \mathfrak{A}(\mathfrak{y})$ [Using (b) and (c)]

$(X \vee \overline{X}) \to (\mathfrak{x})\mathfrak{A}(\mathfrak{x})$ [$(\gamma 1)$]

$(\mathfrak{x})\mathfrak{A}(\mathfrak{x})$.   [Using Formula (3), p. 46]

By means of the axiomatic calculus of predicates, we are now able to eliminate the remaining element of intuition from the mathematical proof, already partially formalized on p. 62, that uniform convergence of a sequence is a stronger property than simple convergence. The only intuitive steps left in that proof were the inversion of the quantifiers (En_0) and (x), and the final introduction of the quantifier (ε); and the whole argument can now be made strictly formal as follows:

$(En_0)(x)\mathfrak{B}(x,n_0,\varepsilon) \to (x)(En_0)\mathfrak{B}(x,n_0,\varepsilon)$

$[\mathfrak{A}(\varepsilon) \to (En_0)(x)\mathfrak{B}(x,n_0,\varepsilon)] \to [\mathfrak{A}(\varepsilon) \to (x)(En_0)\mathfrak{B}(x,n_0,\varepsilon)]$

$(\varepsilon)[[\mathfrak{A}(\varepsilon) \to (En_0)(x)\mathfrak{B}(x,n_0,\varepsilon)] \to [\mathfrak{A}(\varepsilon) \to (x)(En_0)\mathfrak{B}(x,n_0,\varepsilon)]]$

$(\varepsilon)[\mathfrak{A}(\varepsilon) \to (En_0)(x)\mathfrak{B}(x,n_0,\varepsilon)] \to (\varepsilon)[\mathfrak{A}(\varepsilon) \to (x)(En_0)\mathfrak{B}(x,n_0,\varepsilon)]$.

The justifications of the four lines are [(36)], [(1)], [(γ')], and [(31)] respectively.

Exercise. Use Formula (26) in order to derive the formula

$$(Ex)(F(x) \& A) \leftrightarrow ((Ex)F(x) \& A).$$

[*Hint.* Make the substitution $\overline{F(x)}/F(x)$, $\overline{A}/A$ in (26), negate both sides of the bi-implication, etc.]

4   Completeness of the restricted calculus of predicates

We have now seen how the restricted calculus of predicates can be formulated as an axiomatic theory, but we still have to assess the sufficiency of the resulting system as a formalization of intuitive logic. It will be remembered that when we were considering only the molecular structure of propositions we were able to show that the abstract propositional calculus is fully adequate to the limited purpose for which it is designed. The propositional calculus is in fact *complete*, in the sense that a formula built up from its symbols is identically true when interpreted as a truth-function if and only if it is formally derivable from the axioms. We now have to ask whether it can be said also of the calculus of predicates that any formula of this wider calculus which expresses a 'truth of logic' is derivable from the axioms.

In the propositional calculus, the notion of a truth of logic has an intuitive meaning that is precise enough to serve as a basis for meta-logical argument, for every formula determines unambiguously a truth-function which is finitely definable.   When we come to the calculus of predicates, however, we find that the situation is more complicated, because the use of quantifiers involves implicit reference to an unspeci-fied domain D of individuals, the abstract counterpart of the universe of discourse in any application of the calculus of predicates.   When we interpret the logical symbolism intuitively, propositions of the forms $(x)\Phi(x)$ and $(Ex)\Phi(x)$ are understood as asserting that the property Φ holds for all individuals or for some individual *of the relevant domain D*.

In order to give precise meaning to the notion of identical truth of a formula, we shall suppose that some definite domain D has been chosen. Then, by a *truth-specification* for a predicate variable $F(x_1, \ldots, x_n)$ rela-tive to D we shall understand some particular correlation of a well-defined truth-value T or F with every ordered n-tuple $(\alpha_1, \ldots, \alpha_n)$ of individuals in D—i.e. a truth-function of n individual arguments, defined in D.

We may then say that a formula of the calculus of predicates is *identical for the domain D* if it assumes the truth-value T whenever definite individuals in D are substituted for any free individual variables which occur in it, truth-values are assigned to any propositional vari-ables, truth-specifications in D are prescribed for any predicate variables, and all quantifiers are interpreted intuitively as generalized conjunctions or disjunctions.

We may also say that a formula is *satisfiable in D* if there is some choice of elements of D for its free individual variables, truth-values for its propositional variables, and truth-specifications for its predicate variables which makes it assume the truth-value T.

Plainly, a formula $\mathfrak{F}$ is identical in D if and only if its negation $\bar{\mathfrak{F}}$ is not satisfiable in D.

Plainly also, if $\mathfrak{F}$ is identical or satisfiable for a particular domain D, then $\mathfrak{F}$ is likewise identical or satisfiable for any other domain D' that can be put in one-one correspondence with D.   In other words, the characteristics of being identical and being satisfiable are relative simply to the cardinal number of the domain D in question.

EXAMPLES.   (i) Consider the formula

$$F(y) \rightarrow (x)F(x).$$

This formula is identical for all domains with a single element, but not for any domain with more than one element.   Suppose, for instance, that $D = \{\alpha, \beta\}$.   If we take the truth-specification for $F(x)$ in which $F(\alpha)$ has the truth-value T and $F(\beta)$ has the truth-value F, and if we substitute α for y, the given formula takes the truth-value F.

(ii) Let $\mathfrak{A}_1$, $\mathfrak{A}_2$, $\mathfrak{A}_3$ be respectively the formulae

$$(x)\overline{F(x,x)},$$

$$(x)(y)(z)[(F(x,y) \ \& \ F(y,z)) \rightarrow F(x,z)],$$

$$(x)(Ey)F(x,y),$$

and let $\mathfrak{B}$ be their conjunction $\mathfrak{A}_1 \ \& \ \mathfrak{A}_2 \ \& \ \mathfrak{A}_3$. Then, if the domain of individuals is finite, $\mathfrak{B}$ is unsatisfiable (and $\overline{\mathfrak{B}}$ is therefore identically true). For if $\mathfrak{B}$ were satisfied by a predicate $\Phi(x,y)$, and if we were then to take any particular individual α_1, there would exist a second individual α_2, distinct from α_1, such that $\Phi(\alpha_1,\alpha_2)$; then a third individual α_3, distinct from α_1 and α_2, such that $\Phi(\alpha_2,\alpha_3)$; and so on. The formula $\mathfrak{B}$ can be satisfied, however, for a domain of individuals with cardinal number $\aleph_0$—for we need only take the natural numbers as individuals and put the truth-function corresponding to the relation $x < y$ in place of $F(x,y)$.

Reverting now to the formal calculus of predicates, we can readily show that every derivable formula of this calculus is identical for any domain of individuals whatever; for the axioms have this property, and the property is left invariant by all transformations permitted by the rules of derivation (α)–(δ). A much more difficult task is to establish the converse of this result, or in other words to show that every formula that is identical for all domains of individuals is derivable. This can in fact be shown, and the calculus of predicates is accordingly complete; but the proof is long, and an outline of the idea of it is as much as can appropriately be given here.[1]

The proof of completeness depends on the use of a certain normal form for the formulae of the calculus of predicates, and we therefore begin with a brief survey of the normal forms that are available in this calculus. When we say that an expression $\mathfrak{A}$ in a formal system can be reduced to a normal form $\mathfrak{N}$, we mean that $\mathfrak{N}$ is an expression of some specified standard kind which is equivalent to $\mathfrak{A}$ in an appropriate sense (cf. Chapter 2, §5). In the calculus of predicates there is more than one kind of normal form that is important, and we also have more than one relation of equivalence to consider. Taking first the question of equivalence, we need to distinguish between two different metalogical relations, which we call 'deductive equivalence' and 'convertibility'.[2]

---

[1] Full details are given by Hilbert and Ackermann, *Grundzüge*, Chapter 3. See §8 for the Skolem normal form and §10 for Gödel's proof of the completeness theorem itself. The outline of the proof that we give here is based directly on Hilbert and Ackermann's account.

[2] For a discussion of deductive equivalence and convertibility see Hilbert & Bernays: *Grundlagen*, I, pp. 132, 149. The terms there used for 'deductively equivalent' and 'convertible' are respectively *deduktionsgleich* and *überführbar*. The relations denoted by these terms are not discussed by Hilbert and Ackermann.

Two formulae $\mathfrak{A}$ and $\mathfrak{B}$ are said to be *deductively equivalent* if and only if each is derivable from the other. It is plain that, when this is the case, $\mathfrak{A}$ and $\mathfrak{B}$ have exactly the same derivable consequences.

A formula $\mathfrak{A}$ is said to be *convertible* into a formula $\mathfrak{B}$ if and only if the bi-implication $\mathfrak{A} \leftrightarrow \mathfrak{B}$ is a derivable formula; and since convertibility, as so defined, is a symmetrical relation, we may say in such circumstances that $\mathfrak{A}$ and $\mathfrak{B}$ are mutually convertible.

Both deductive equivalence and convertibility are readily seen to be equivalence relations. We can also see without much difficulty that convertibility is the stronger relation of the two. Deductive equivalence follows from convertibility since, when $\mathfrak{A} \leftrightarrow \mathfrak{B}$ is a derivable formula, $\mathfrak{A}$ and $\mathfrak{B}$ are derivable from each other by the rule of inference (β). Convertibility, on the other hand, does not follow from deductive equivalence; for the two formulae $F(y)$, with y as a free variable, and $(x)F(x)$ are deductively equivalent but not convertible. They are deductively equivalent since $F(y)$ can be derived from $(x)F(x)$ by the use of axiom (e), and $(x)F(x)$ can be derived from $F(y)$ by the rule (γ') obtained on p. 69. They are not convertible since the implication $F(y) \rightarrow (x)F(x)$, which is not an identical formula for all domains of individuals (see p. 71), is underivable, and *a fortiori* the bi-implication $F(y) \leftrightarrow (x)F(x)$ is underivable.

THEOREM 1. *If* $\mathfrak{U}$ *is a formula of the restricted calculus of predicates that is built up by means of the logical operators* $^-$, $\vee$, &, $\rightarrow$, $\leftrightarrow$ *out of certain component formulae, of which* $\mathfrak{A}$ *is one, and* $\mathfrak{A}$ *is convertible with* $\mathfrak{B}$, *then* $\mathfrak{U}$ *is convertible with any formula that is obtained when* $\mathfrak{A}$ *is replaced by* $\mathfrak{B}$ *at some or all of the places where it occurs in* $\mathfrak{U}$.

Proof. We need only verify that, if $\mathfrak{A}$ and $\mathfrak{B}$ are convertible, then so are $\overline{\mathfrak{A}}$ and $\overline{\mathfrak{B}}$, and so also are $\mathfrak{A} \vee \mathfrak{C}$ and $\mathfrak{B} \vee \mathfrak{C}$ for any $\mathfrak{C}$.[1]

It should be noted particularly that, in transforming formulae into other formulae whose convertibility with them is guaranteed by this theorem, we are able to make *partial* substitutions, whereas the rules of substitution (α) of the calculus of predicates—though not the rule of relabelling (δ)—permit only *total* substitution throughout a formula.

We shall show now that every formula of the calculus of predicates is convertible with a formula in which all the quantifiers stand at the beginning and have a scope that extends right to the end of the formula. A formula of this special kind is said to be in *prenex normal form*. The formula $(x)(Ey)(F(x,y) \rightarrow G(x,y))$, for example, is in prenex normal form, but the formula $(Ex)(F(x,y)$ & $(z)H(z))$ is not.

Suppose we wish to put a given formula $\mathfrak{U}$ into this special form. We first eliminate the connectives $\rightarrow$ and $\leftrightarrow$, replacing them by the

---

[1] Strictly speaking 'for any $\mathfrak{C}$ such that $\mathfrak{A} \vee \mathfrak{C}$ and $\mathfrak{B} \vee \mathfrak{C}$ are both well-formed'; but for the sake of clarity we shall ordinarily leave such qualifications to be understood.

appropriate combinations of $^{-}$, $\lor$, and &. Next we transfer all negation signs to single propositional variables or predicate variables by
replacing $\overline{\mathfrak{A} \lor \mathfrak{B}}$ by $\overline{\mathfrak{A}}$ & $\overline{\mathfrak{B}}$, $\overline{\mathfrak{A} \text{ & } \mathfrak{B}}$ by $\overline{\mathfrak{A}} \lor \overline{\mathfrak{B}}$, $\overline{(\mathfrak{x})\mathfrak{A}(\mathfrak{x})}$ by $(E\mathfrak{x})\overline{\mathfrak{A}(\mathfrak{x})}$, and
$\overline{(E\mathfrak{x})\mathfrak{A}(\mathfrak{x})}$ by $(\mathfrak{x})\overline{\mathfrak{A}(\mathfrak{x})}$ repeatedly until this part of the reduction is accom-
plished. In this way we arrive at a formula $\mathfrak{B}$. To complete the
reduction of $\mathfrak{U}$ to prenex normal form we now relabel bound variables
in $\mathfrak{B}$, where necessary, so as to ensure that the letters used in the
various quantifiers are all different; and then, with the aid of such
standard derivable formulae as

$$[A \lor (x)F(x)] \leftrightarrow (x)[A \lor F(x)]$$
and
$$[(Ex)F(x) \text{ & } A] \leftrightarrow (Ex)[F(x) \text{ & } A],$$

(cf. pp. 69 and 70) we bring all the quantifiers to the beginning of the
whole formula, keeping their relative order unchanged. We thus
arrive ultimately at a formula $\mathfrak{W}$ in prenex normal form; and a formal
derivation of the bi-implication $\mathfrak{U} \leftrightarrow \mathfrak{W}$ can then be constructed without
difficulty.

   Exercise. Supply the details of the proof that has just been outlined,
   giving, in particular, a complete catalogue of the 'standard derivable
   formulae' that are required.

Although the reduction of formulae to prenex normal form substantially simplifies the calculus of predicates as an object of metalogical investigation, this simplification is still not quite sufficient to
enable us to establish the completeness of the calculus. For although
the quantifiers in a formula in prenex normal form all stand at the
beginning, some of them may be universal and some existential, and
essentially different combinations of quantifiers in great variety still
have to be taken into account. There is, however, a refinement of the
prenex normal form, due to Thoralf Skolem, in which all the existential
quantifiers come first, with all the universal quantifiers following; and
we can show that every formula is deductively equivalent to a formula
in this *Skolem normal form*. It should be noted that when we restrict
the general prenex normal form to Skolem's more specific type we have
to relax the associated type of equivalence from convertibility to deductive equivalence.

In proving that every formula is reducible to Skolem normal form,
we may obviously confine the argument to formulae that are already in
prenex normal form. We may also assume that the formula to be
reduced contains no free individual variables; for any formula
$\mathfrak{F}(\mathfrak{x}_1, \ldots, \mathfrak{x}_n)$, in which $\mathfrak{x}_1, \ldots, \mathfrak{x}_n$ are free, is deductively equivalent to
a formula $(\mathfrak{x}_1) \ldots (\mathfrak{x}_n)\mathfrak{F}(\mathfrak{x}_1, \ldots, \mathfrak{x}_n)$ without free variables. The proof
will be by induction with respect to the number of universal quantifiers

that have existential quantifiers anywhere to the right of them, a number that we shall refer to as the *degree* of the formula concerned. Formulae of degree 0 are already in Skolem normal form, and so we have only to show that, if all formulae of degree $n - 1$ are deductively equivalent to formulae in Skolem normal form, then so also are all formulae of degree n.

Suppose, then, that $\mathfrak{A}$ is some formula, in prenex normal form, which is of degree n $(n \geqslant 1)$. Then $\mathfrak{A}$ may be written more fully as $(E\mathfrak{x}_1)\ldots(E\mathfrak{x}_m)(\mathfrak{y})\mathfrak{B}(\mathfrak{x}_1, \ldots, \mathfrak{x}_m, \mathfrak{y})$, where $\mathfrak{B}(\mathfrak{x}_1, \ldots, \mathfrak{x}_m, \mathfrak{y})$ contains no free variables other than those shown. The number m may be zero, in which case $\mathfrak{A}$ will be of the form $(\mathfrak{y})\mathfrak{B}(\mathfrak{y})$. $\mathfrak{B}(\mathfrak{x}_1, \ldots, \mathfrak{x}_m, \mathfrak{y})$ may be written more fully as $\mathfrak{Q}_1 \ldots \mathfrak{Q}_s \mathfrak{C}(\mathfrak{x}_1, \ldots, \mathfrak{x}_m, \mathfrak{y}, \mathfrak{z}_1, \ldots, \mathfrak{z}_s)$, where $\mathfrak{Q}_1$, $\ldots$, $\mathfrak{Q}_s$ are the quantifiers, universal or existential, which bind $\mathfrak{z}_1, \ldots, \mathfrak{z}_s$, and where the complete prefix of quantifiers in $\mathfrak{A}$ is $(E\mathfrak{x}_1)\ldots(E\mathfrak{x}_m)$ $(\mathfrak{y})\mathfrak{Q}_1 \ldots \mathfrak{Q}_s$.

Our method of reduction is to introduce a predicate variable with $m + 1$ arguments, $H(-, \ldots, -)$ say, which does not already occur in $\mathfrak{B}(\mathfrak{x}_1, \ldots, \mathfrak{x}_m, \mathfrak{y})$, and with it to construct the formula

$$(E\mathfrak{x}_1)\ldots(E\mathfrak{x}_m)[(E\mathfrak{y})(\mathfrak{B}(\mathfrak{x}_1, \ldots, \mathfrak{x}_m, \mathfrak{y}) \,\&\, \overline{H(\mathfrak{x}_1, \ldots, \mathfrak{x}_m, \mathfrak{y})}) \vee$$
$$\vee (\mathfrak{z})H(\mathfrak{x}_1, \ldots, \mathfrak{x}_m, \mathfrak{z})],$$

which we will call $\mathfrak{D}$. Then $\mathfrak{A}$ and $\mathfrak{D}$ are deductively equivalent, as we can show in the following way:

(i) Making the substitution $\mathfrak{B}(-, \ldots, -)/H(-, \ldots, -)$ in $\mathfrak{D}$, we are able to derive $\mathfrak{A}$.

(ii) The formula

$$(y)F(y) \to [(Ey)(F(y) \,\&\, \overline{G(y)}) \vee (y)G(y)]$$

is derivable from Formula (31), p. 69, by means of the identical formula $[X \to (Y \to Z)] \to [Y \to (\overline{X} \vee Z)]$ of the propositional calculus; and by making the double substitution $\mathfrak{B}(\mathfrak{x}_1, \ldots, \mathfrak{x}_m, -)/F(-)$, $H(\mathfrak{x}_1, \ldots, \mathfrak{x}_m, -)/G(-)$ in it, and relabelling the last bound variable, we derive the formula

$$(\mathfrak{y})\mathfrak{B}(\mathfrak{x}_1, \ldots, \mathfrak{x}_m, \mathfrak{y}) \to [(E\mathfrak{y})(\mathfrak{B}(\mathfrak{x}_1, \ldots, \mathfrak{x}_m, \mathfrak{y}) \,\&\, \overline{H(\mathfrak{x}_1, \ldots, \mathfrak{x}_m, \mathfrak{y})}) \vee$$
$$\vee (\mathfrak{z})H(\mathfrak{x}_1, \ldots, \mathfrak{x}_m, \mathfrak{z})].$$

We can then derive $\mathfrak{D}$ from $\mathfrak{A}$ by using Formula (34) m times in conjunction with this last formula and applying the rule of inference (β).

The formula $\mathfrak{A}$ with which we began is thus deductively equivalent to the formula $\mathfrak{D}$, which, when written in full, takes the form

$$(E\mathfrak{x}_1)\ldots(E\mathfrak{x}_m)[(E\mathfrak{y})(\mathfrak{Q}_1 \ldots \mathfrak{Q}_s \mathfrak{C}(\mathfrak{x}_1, \ldots, \mathfrak{x}_m, \mathfrak{y}, \mathfrak{z}_1, \ldots, \mathfrak{z}_s) \,\&$$
$$\&\, \overline{H(\mathfrak{x}_1, \ldots, \mathfrak{x}_m, \mathfrak{y})}) \vee (\mathfrak{z})H(\mathfrak{x}_1, \ldots, \mathfrak{x}_m, \mathfrak{z})].$$

This formula, in turn, is deductively equivalent to the formula

$$(E\mathfrak{x}_1)\ldots(E\mathfrak{x}_m)(E\mathfrak{y})\mathfrak{O}_1\ldots\mathfrak{O}_s(\mathfrak{z})[(\mathfrak{C}(\mathfrak{x}_1,\ldots,\mathfrak{x}_m,\mathfrak{y},\mathfrak{z}_1,\ldots,\mathfrak{z}_s)\;\&$$
$$\&\;\overline{H(\mathfrak{x}_1,\ldots,\mathfrak{x}_m,\mathfrak{y})})\vee H(\mathfrak{x}_1,\ldots\mathfrak{x}_m,\mathfrak{z})],$$

which is in prenex normal form and is of degree $n-1$ only. This completes the proof by induction of the required result, which we may now state formally as follows:

THEOREM 2 (*Skolem's Theorem*). *Any well-formed formula of the restricted calculus of predicates is deductively equivalent to a formula in which all the quantifiers stand at the beginning, and all the existential quantifiers are to the left of all the universal quantifiers.*

It will be seen from the above discussion that we are able to simplify the prefix of quantifiers in a formula in prenex normal form at the cost of introducing additional predicate variables. The process described is a constructive one, which we can use in order to obtain a Skolem normal form for any given formula. Consider, for example, the formula $(x)(Ey)F(x,y)$, which is certainly not deductively equivalent to the formula $(Ey)(x)F(x,y)$ that is obtained when the quantifiers are merely interchanged (cf. p. 61). The Skolem normal form for this formula that is yielded by our standard procedure is $(Ex)(Ey)(z)[(F(x,y)\;\&\;\overline{H(x)})\vee H(z)]$.

We are now ready to consider the proof of the completeness of the calculus of predicates. The completeness of this calculus was first established in 1930, by Kurt Gödel,[1] and the outline of the argument that now follows is based on the version of Gödel's proof that is given by Hilbert and Ackermann.

Let $\mathfrak{U}$ be any formula of the calculus of predicates, and let $\mathfrak{B}$ be a formula in Skolem normal form to which $\mathfrak{U}$ is deductively equivalent. Then $\mathfrak{U}$ and $\mathfrak{B}$ are derivable from each other, and hence if one of them is absolutely derivable—i.e. derivable from the axioms of the calculus alone—then so also is the other. Since, furthermore, any formula that is derivable from identical initial formulae is itself identical, it follows that if either of $\mathfrak{U}$ and $\mathfrak{B}$ is identical then so also is the other. It will be sufficient, therefore, in proving that every identical formula of the calculus of predicates is derivable from the axioms, to consider only formulae in Skolem normal form.

Suppose, then, that we are given the following formula $\mathfrak{B}$ in Skolem normal form:

$$(Ex_1)\ldots(Ex_k)(y_1)\ldots(y_l)\mathfrak{A}(x_1,\ldots,x_k;y_1,\ldots,y_l).$$

[1] K. Gödel: 'Die Vollständigkeit der Axiome des logischen Funktionenkalküls', *Monatsh. Math. Phys.*, **37** (1930), 349–360. For an alternative proof of the same result see L. Henkin: 'The completeness of the first-order functional calculus', *J. Symb. Logic*, **14** (1949), 159–166,

Taking a denumerable set of individual variables $\{x_0, x_1, \ldots\}$, we first of all arrange in a sequence all the k-tuples that can be formed from these variables, repetition being allowed. The ordering is in the first instance by the sum of the k suffixes, and then lexicographically for those k-tuples which yield any fixed value for this sum. Writing the nth k-tuple as $(x_{n_1}, x_{n_2}, \ldots, x_{n_k})$, we denote the formula

$$\mathfrak{A}(x_{n_1}, \ldots, x_{n_k}; x_{(n-1)l+1}, x_{(n-1)l+2}, \ldots, x_{nl})$$

by $\mathfrak{B}_n$, so that

$$\mathfrak{B}_1 \equiv \mathfrak{A}(x_0, \ldots, x_0, x_0; x_1, x_2, \ldots, x_l),$$
$$\mathfrak{B}_2 \equiv \mathfrak{A}(x_0, \ldots, x_0, x_1; x_{l+1}, x_{l+2}, \ldots, x_{2l}),$$
$$\mathfrak{B}_3 \equiv \mathfrak{A}(x_0, \ldots, x_1, x_0; x_{2l+1}, x_{2l+2}, \ldots, x_{3l}),$$

and so forth. For each n, we denote the disjunction

$$\mathfrak{B}_1 \vee \mathfrak{B}_2 \vee \ldots \vee \mathfrak{B}_n$$

by $\mathfrak{C}_n$.

The formulae $\mathfrak{C}_n$ are molecular combinations of atomic constituents which are either propositional variables or predicate variables with individual variables as arguments, and the atomic constituents of any particular formula $\mathfrak{C}_n$ are constituents also of $\mathfrak{C}_{n+1}, \mathfrak{C}_{n+2}, \ldots$. We now replace by propositional variables all atomic constituents, other than propositional variables, which occur in the formulae $\mathfrak{C}_n$, doing this in such a way that the variables introduced are different from any that already occur in the formulae $\mathfrak{C}_n$, and that distinct atomic components are always replaced by distinct propositional variables. When this has been done, we have, in place of the sequence $\{\mathfrak{C}_1, \mathfrak{C}_2, \ldots\}$ of formulae of the calculus of predicates, a sequence $\{\mathfrak{E}_1, \mathfrak{E}_2, \ldots\}$ of formulae of the propositional calculus; and there are now two mutually exclusive alternatives:

(i) for some n, $\mathfrak{E}_n$ is an identical formula;

(ii) the formula $\mathfrak{E}_n$ is not identical for any n.

Hilbert and Ackermann prove that in case (i) $\mathfrak{B}$ is a derivable formula of the calculus of predicates, while in case (ii) $\overline{\mathfrak{B}}$ is satisfiable when the totality of natural numbers is taken as the domain of individuals. It follows from this that if the original formula $\mathfrak{U}$, of which $\mathfrak{B}$ is supposed to be a Skolem normal form, is identically true for all domains of individuals, then $\mathfrak{U}$ is derivable in the calculus of predicates. This proves the required completeness theorem, which we may state formally as follows:

THEOREM 3 (*Gödel's Completeness Theorem*). *Any well-formed formula of the restricted calculus of predicates that is identical for all domains of individuals is derivable from the axioms of the calculus.*

The proof that we have outlined yields more than the bare completeness theorem, and we have in addition the following important corollary:

THEOREM 4 (*Löwenheim's Theorem*[1]).   *If a well-formed formula of the restricted calculus of predicates is identical for some denumerably infinite domain of individuals, then it is identical for any domain of individuals whatever.*

Proof.   Let the formula $\mathfrak{U}$ in the previous argument be identical for some particular denumerably infinite domain of individuals D.   Then $\mathfrak{U}$ is also identical for every domain equipotent to D, and in particular for the domain of natural numbers.   Thus $\bar{\mathfrak{u}}$, and therefore also $\mathfrak{V}$, is not satisfiable for the domain of natural numbers, and the alternative (ii) is accordingly excluded.   The only possibility is then alternative (i), which means that $\mathfrak{U}$ is a derivable formula of the calculus of predicates, and is consequently identical for all possible domains.

5   The deduction theorem

Before leaving the calculus of predicates, we need to look once again at the two metalogical relations of convertibility and deductive equivalence in order to see how they are related.   It will be recalled that two formulae $\mathfrak{A}$ and $\mathfrak{B}$ are said to be convertible if $\mathfrak{A} \leftrightarrow \mathfrak{B}$ is an absolutely derivable formula (i.e. a formula that is derivable from the axioms of the calculus of predicates alone) and deductively equivalent if each is derivable from the other (cf. p. 72).   As we have already seen, convertibility is a stronger relation than deductive equivalence.   If, in fact, the implication $\mathfrak{A} \to \mathfrak{B}$ is absolutely derivable, then $\mathfrak{B}$ is at once derivable from $\mathfrak{A}$; but from the derivability of $\mathfrak{B}$ from $\mathfrak{A}$ we cannot, in general, infer the absolute derivability of $\mathfrak{A} \to \mathfrak{B}$.   Nevertheless, there is a wide class of situations in which the existence of a relative derivation of $\mathfrak{B}$ from $\mathfrak{A}$ is sufficient to guarantee the existence of an absolute derivation of $\mathfrak{A} \to \mathfrak{B}$; and this is the import of the powerful metalogical theorem known as the deduction theorem, which we may state in the following terms:

THEOREM 5 (*Deduction Theorem*).   *If $\mathfrak{A}$ and $\mathfrak{B}$ are well-formed formulae of the restricted calculus of predicates, such that no variable occurs both free in one and bound in the other, and if $\mathfrak{B}$ is derivable from $\mathfrak{A}$ in such a way that all free variables that occur in $\mathfrak{A}$ are kept unchanged (as parameters) throughout the derivation, then the formula $\mathfrak{A} \to \mathfrak{B}$ can be derived without use of $\mathfrak{A}$ as an initial formula.*

The general idea of the argument by which Theorem 5 is to be proved

---

[1] L. Löwenheim: 'Über Möglichkeiten im Relativkalkül', *Math. Ann.*, **76** (1915), 447–470.

is essentially simple, in spite of the somewhat complicated details of the full proof; and in order to convey its simplicity we give first of all a rough indication of the procedure to be employed. The idea is, in fact, to build up an absolute derivation of $\mathfrak{A} \to \mathfrak{B}$ by suitably modifying the postulated derivation of $\mathfrak{B}$ from $\mathfrak{A}$.

The derivation of $\mathfrak{B}$ from $\mathfrak{A}$ is a finite sequence of well-formed formulae, which we shall denote by $(\mathfrak{F}_i)$, or more specifically by $(\mathfrak{F}_1, \ldots, \mathfrak{F}_n)$. The end-formula $\mathfrak{F}_n$ is $\mathfrak{B}$, and every formula of the sequence is either an initial formula (which can only be one of the axioms (a)–(f) or the formula $\mathfrak{A}$) or else the product of an application of one of the rules (α)–(δ) to a formula or pair of formulae taken from the preceding part of the sequence. Our first step is now to prefix to every line $\mathfrak{F}_i$ of the given derivation the complex of symbols '$\mathfrak{A} \to$', so as to form the sequence of expressions $(\mathfrak{A} \to \mathfrak{F}_i)$ or $(\mathfrak{A} \to \mathfrak{F}_1, \ldots, \mathfrak{A} \to \mathfrak{F}_n)$, i.e. $(\mathfrak{A} \to \mathfrak{F}_1, \ldots, \mathfrak{A} \to \mathfrak{B})$. This sequence ends with $\mathfrak{A} \to \mathfrak{B}$, and if it were a derivation in the calculus of predicates we would of course have reached our goal; but this is altogether too much to expect, and the sequence will normally need considerable modification before the required derivation is arrived at.

The first point to be noted is that although, as a result of the restrictions imposed on $\mathfrak{A}$ and $\mathfrak{B}$ in the statement of Theorem 5, the expression $\mathfrak{A} \to \mathfrak{B}$ is necessarily a well-formed formula, it does not follow that $\mathfrak{A} \to \mathfrak{F}_1, \ldots, \mathfrak{A} \to \mathfrak{F}_{n-1}$ are all well-formed also. This difficulty is not very serious, however, and we can arrange matters, by carrying out a suitable preliminary relabelling of bound variables, so as to ensure that $(\mathfrak{A} \to \mathfrak{F}_i)$ is in fact a sequence of well-formed formulae. Having done this, we then have to face the more serious question of whether the sequence $(\mathfrak{A} \to \mathfrak{F}_i)$ has the structure of a derivation. Even though a formula $\mathfrak{F}_k$ may be derived in $(\mathfrak{F}_i)$ from an earlier formula $\mathfrak{F}_h$ in accordance with one of the rules (α), (γ), (δ), or from two earlier formulae $\mathfrak{F}_i$ and $\mathfrak{F}_j$ in accordance with the rule (β), the transition from $\mathfrak{A} \to \mathfrak{F}_h$ to $\mathfrak{A} \to \mathfrak{F}_k$ or from $\mathfrak{A} \to \mathfrak{F}_i$ and $\mathfrak{A} \to \mathfrak{F}_j$ to $\mathfrak{A} \to \mathfrak{F}_k$ need not be of the same elementary kind. Fortunately, however, every such transition can be justified by a finite number of applications of the rules (α)–(δ)—that is to say by an auxiliary derivation—and we can thus make the sequence of formulae $(\mathfrak{A} \to \mathfrak{F}_i)$ into a derivation by interpolating suitable additional formulae wherever there is a gap in the demonstrative chain. By such means we are able to build up a derivation of $\mathfrak{A} \to \mathfrak{B}$ from initial formulae of the types $\mathfrak{A} \to$ (a), $\ldots$, $\mathfrak{A} \to$ (f), $\mathfrak{A} \to \mathfrak{A}$, where (a)–(f) are the axioms. But $\mathfrak{A} \to$ (a), $\ldots$, $\mathfrak{A} \to$ (f), $\mathfrak{A} \to \mathfrak{A}$ are themselves easily derivable from the axioms, and so we arrive finally at the required absolute derivation of $\mathfrak{A} \to \mathfrak{B}$.

We come now to the detailed implementation of this plan, and we begin by discussing the means needed for making the sequence $(\mathfrak{A} \to \mathfrak{F}_i)$ into a coherent derivation. Since the procedure to be adopted is in no way dependent on the fact that the '$\mathfrak{A}$' in '$\mathfrak{A} \to \mathfrak{F}_i$' is itself one of the initial formulae of the derivation ($\mathfrak{F}_i$), we shall change to a neutral notation for the purpose of this particular discussion.

LEMMA 1.   *Let* $(\mathfrak{F}_i) \equiv (\mathfrak{F}_1, \ldots, \mathfrak{F}_n)$ *be a given derivation of a formula* $\mathfrak{F}_n$ *from initial formulae* $\mathfrak{I}_1, \ldots, \mathfrak{I}_r$ *(among which are included any of the axioms* (a)–(f) *that are used) and let* $\mathfrak{G}$ *be a formula which does not contain as a free variable either any letter for which a substitution is made in the course of the derivation* $(\mathfrak{F}_i)$ *or any letter that is the operative variable*[1] *in an application of* $(\gamma 1)$ *or* $(\gamma 2)$. *Then, provided that all the expressions* $\mathfrak{G} \to \mathfrak{F}_i$ *are well-formed formulae, the sequence* $(\mathfrak{G} \to \mathfrak{F}_1, \ldots, \mathfrak{G} \to \mathfrak{F}_n)$ *can be amplified in such a way that it becomes a derivation of the formula* $\mathfrak{G} \to \mathfrak{F}_n$, *in which the only initial formulae that are used are* $\mathfrak{G} \to \mathfrak{I}_1$, $\ldots, \mathfrak{G} \to \mathfrak{I}_r$.

Proof.   We consider in turn the various ways in which the separate lines $\mathfrak{F}_k$ of the original derivation ($\mathfrak{F}_i$) may have been obtained.

(i) If $\mathfrak{F}_k$ arises from an earlier formula $\mathfrak{F}_h$, either by repetition or by application of one of the rules of substitution (α), then, since no variable for which a substitution is made is present in $\mathfrak{G}$, the formula $\mathfrak{G} \to \mathfrak{F}_k$ arises in exactly the same way from $\mathfrak{G} \to \mathfrak{F}_h$.

(ii) If $\mathfrak{F}_h$ results from an application of the rule (β), say

$$\frac{\mathfrak{C} \qquad \mathfrak{C} \to \mathfrak{F}_k}{\mathfrak{F}_k,}$$

we shall have in $(\mathfrak{G} \to \mathfrak{F}_i)$ the corresponding transition

$$\frac{\mathfrak{G} \to \mathfrak{C} \qquad \mathfrak{G} \to (\mathfrak{C} \to \mathfrak{F}_k)}{\mathfrak{G} \to \mathfrak{F}_k.}$$

This transition can be effected by two applications of (β), with the aid of the identical formula

$$(X \to Y) \to [(X \to (Y \to Z)) \to (X \to Z)].$$

(iii) If $\mathfrak{F}_i$ is a formula $\mathfrak{C} \to (\mathfrak{x})\mathfrak{D}(\mathfrak{x})$, derived by an application

$$\frac{\mathfrak{C} \to \mathfrak{D}(\mathfrak{y})}{\mathfrak{C} \to (\mathfrak{x})\mathfrak{D}(\mathfrak{x})}$$

of the rule $(\gamma 1)$, we shall have in $(\mathfrak{G} \to \mathfrak{F}_i)$ the step

$$\frac{\mathfrak{G} \to (\mathfrak{C} \to \mathfrak{D}(\mathfrak{y}))}{\mathfrak{G} \to (\mathfrak{C} \to (\mathfrak{x})\mathfrak{D}(\mathfrak{x})).}$$

---

[1] By the *operative variable* in an application of $(\gamma 1)$ or $(\gamma 2)$ we mean the free variable that is denoted by '$\mathfrak{y}$' in the original formulation of these rules on p. 66.

Since, in view of the original validity of $(\gamma 1)$, the operative variable $\mathfrak{y}$ cannot occur in $\mathfrak{C}$, and by the hypothesis of Lemma 1 it does not occur in $\mathfrak{G}$, the following application of $(\gamma 1)$ is valid:

$$\frac{(\mathfrak{G} \ \& \ \mathfrak{C}) \to \mathfrak{D}(\mathfrak{y})}{(\mathfrak{G} \ \& \ \mathfrak{C}) \to (\mathfrak{x})\mathfrak{D}(\mathfrak{x})};$$

and Rule VII, p. 49, then enables us to complete the derivation of $\mathfrak{G} \to (\mathfrak{C} \to (\mathfrak{x})\mathfrak{D}(\mathfrak{x}))$ from $\mathfrak{G} \to (\mathfrak{C} \to \mathfrak{D}(\mathfrak{y}))$.

(iv) Applications of $(\gamma 2)$ can be dealt with in a similar way, this time with the help of the first of the three schemata that make up Rule VII.

(v) If, finally, $\mathfrak{F}_k$ is derived from $\mathfrak{F}_h$ by an application of the rule of relabelling (δ), $\mathfrak{G} \to \mathfrak{F}_k$ can be derived in the same way from $\mathfrak{G} \to \mathfrak{F}_h$.

We are thus able to enlarge the sequence of formulae $(\mathfrak{G} \to \mathfrak{F}_i)$ to a correct derivation; and this derivation plainly has end-formula $\mathfrak{G} \to \mathfrak{F}_n$ and initial formulae $\mathfrak{G} \to \mathfrak{F}_1, \ldots, \mathfrak{G} \to \mathfrak{F}_r$, as required by the lemma.

We now prove as a further lemma a special case of the deduction theorem, from which we shall afterwards be able to deduce the much more general case, Theorem 5, that we are primarily interested in.

LEMMA 2. *Let $\mathfrak{A}$ and $\mathfrak{B}$ be two well-formed formulae of the restricted calculus of predicates, such that no variable occurs both free in one of them and bound in the other, and let $(\mathfrak{F}_i)$ be a derivation of $\mathfrak{B}$ which uses no initial formulae except the axioms* (a)–(f) *and the formula $\mathfrak{A}$. Let this derivation be such that no letter[1] occurs in $\mathfrak{A}$ as a free variable if it is used anywhere in $(\mathfrak{F}_i)$ either* (i) *as a free variable for which a substitution is made in accordance with* $(\alpha 1)$, $(\alpha 2)$, *or* $(\alpha 3)$ *in the course of the derivation, or* (ii) *as the operative variable in an application of* $(\gamma 1)$ *or* $(\gamma 2)$. *Then a derivation can be formed which has $\mathfrak{A} \to \mathfrak{B}$ for its end-formula and which uses no initial formulae other than the axioms* (a)–(f).

Proof. We first of all relabel bound variables in $\mathfrak{A}$, wherever necessary, so as to ensure that no letter that is used as a free variable anywhere in $(\mathfrak{F}_i)$ is used also as a bound variable in $\mathfrak{A}$. Let the formula which results from $\mathfrak{A}$ by this operation be denoted by $\mathfrak{A}^*$. Next relabel bound variables in $(\mathfrak{F}_i)$, wherever necessary, in such a way that no letter that occurs in $\mathfrak{A}$ as a free variable is also used in $(\mathfrak{F}_i)$ as a bound variable. We can carry out this process in such a way that every formula $\mathfrak{F}_i$ is changed into a well-formed formula, and the modified sequence of formulae is still a derivation, the only essential change being that where there were occurrences of the axioms (e) or (f) as initial formulae in

---

[1] For this purpose a propositional variable A and predicate variables $A(-)$, $A(-, -), \ldots$ with different numbers of argument-places are all to be counted as different letters.

($\mathfrak{F}_i$) there may now be formulae obtained from these axioms by relabelling the bound variable. Let the modified derivation be denoted by ($\mathfrak{F}_i^{**}$).

We now prefix to each formula of the sequence ($\mathfrak{F}_i^{**}$) the complex of symbols '$\mathfrak{A}^* \to$', obtaining in this way a sequence ($\mathfrak{A}^* \to \mathfrak{F}_i^{**}$) of well-formed formulae $\mathfrak{A}^* \to \mathfrak{F}_i^{**}$. Then, by Lemma 1, this sequence can be amplified to yield a derivation of the formula $\mathfrak{A}^* \to \mathfrak{F}_n^{**}$ from initial formulae of the form $\mathfrak{A}^* \to \mathfrak{J}^{**}$, where $\mathfrak{J}^{**}$ is either one of the axioms (a)–(d) or a formula derived from (e), (f), or $\mathfrak{A}$ by a possible relabelling of bound variables. But every such formula $\mathfrak{A}^* \to \mathfrak{J}^{**}$ is derivable from the axioms (a)–(f) alone, by use of the identical formulae $X \to (Y \to X)$ and $X \to X$ and the rules of the logical calculus; and the derivation of $\mathfrak{A}^* \to \mathfrak{F}_n^{**}$ from formulae $\mathfrak{A}^* \to \mathfrak{J}^{**}$ can therefore be prolonged backwards to a derivation of $\mathfrak{A}^* \to \mathfrak{F}_n^{**}$ from (a)–(f). Since, moreover, $\mathfrak{A}$ is obtainable from $\mathfrak{A}^*$ and $\mathfrak{F}_n$ from $\mathfrak{F}_n^{**}$ by suitable relabelling of bound variables, the derivation of $\mathfrak{A}^* \to \mathfrak{F}_n^{**}$ from (a)–(f) can be prolonged forwards to a derivation of $\mathfrak{A} \to \mathfrak{F}_n$ from the axioms. We are thus able in these circumstances to construct an absolute derivation of the formula $\mathfrak{A} \to \mathfrak{B}$.

The deduction theorem, as we originally stated it in the enunciation of Theorem 5, is much wider than the special case embodied in the lemma that we have just proved, and our final task must be to remove the unnecessary restrictions on its generality. We were able to express the general theorem in a particularly compact form, free from elaborately formulated conditions, by requiring simply that the free variables in $\mathfrak{A}$ should function as 'parameters' in the derivation of $\mathfrak{B}$; and the concept of a parameter in a derivation must be made more precise before we can turn to the proof of the theorem. The term 'parameter' is borrowed, of course, from the language of mathematics, and analogy with mathematical usage gives a reasonably clear indication of its meaning; but we certainly cannot leave the interpretation of the precise conditions involved in so fundamental a metalogical theorem as the deduction theorem to the guidance of analogy, which is often treacherous. We now explain what is intended by the reference to parameters, and, when this explanation has once been given, the brief formulation of the deduction theorem on p. 78 will be seen to characterize adequately the situation that it is intended to cover.

In a derivation in the calculus of predicates, every non-initial formula is obtained either from a single earlier formula by repetition or by application of one of the rules (α), (γ), (δ), or else from a pair of earlier formulae by application of the rule (β); and we can distinguish those free variables which are properly involved in any such transition from those which are left unaffected by it. All unaffected variables will be said to be *parameters* for the transition in question. In the case of repetition, all free variables in the repeated formula are parameters. In an application of one of the rules (α), all free variables in the original formula are parameters, with the single exception of the one that is replaced. In an application of (β), in which a formula $\mathfrak{B}$ is derived from two formulae $\mathfrak{U}$ and $\mathfrak{U} \rightarrow \mathfrak{B}$, all the free variables in $\mathfrak{U}$ and in $\mathfrak{B}$ are parameters. Those in $\mathfrak{B}$ are strictly unaffected, while those in $\mathfrak{U}$ but not in $\mathfrak{B}$ simply disappear in the transition, without being otherwise involved. In an application of ($\gamma 1$) or ($\gamma 2$) the operative variable is not a parameter, but all other free variables in the original formula are parameters. And lastly, in any application of (δ), as in repetition, all free variables are parameters.

Unless it disappears in an application of (β), every parameter retains its identity through the transition from the earlier formula or formulae to the later formula, and it does so, moreover, not merely as a certain letter of the alphabet but as a specific occurrence of that letter. If, therefore, we fix our attention on an occurrence of a particular free variable at a definite place in the derivation, we can keep track of this variable, as we proceed downwards through the derivation, for as long as it continues to be a parameter. If the variable remains a parameter until it either reaches the end-formula or else is eliminated in an application of (β), we shall say that it is a parameter for the derivation.

Proof of Theorem 5. By hypothesis, every free variable in every occurrence of $\mathfrak{A}$ in the given derivation ($\mathfrak{F}_i$) of $\mathfrak{B}$ from $\mathfrak{A}$ is a parameter for the whole derivation, and it therefore retains its identity right to the end, or until it is eliminated. At no stage, therefore, can such a variable become the operative variable for an application of ($\gamma 1$) or ($\gamma 2$) or can a substitution be made for it in accordance with ($\alpha 1$), ($\alpha 2$), or ($\alpha 3$). This does not, however, preclude a letter of the alphabet which occurs as such a variable from also occurring independently (i.e. not consequentially upon an occurrence of $\mathfrak{A}$) elsewhere in the derivation, and being involved there in an operation (γ) or (α). We shall separate off the parameters introduced through $\mathfrak{A}$ from alphabetically identical letters that are not parameters by a device of relettering that we now describe. We take in turn each letter that occurs free in $\mathfrak{A}$ and is properly involved elsewhere in ($\mathfrak{F}_i$) in an application of (γ) or (α), and we replace it in $\mathfrak{A}$ by another letter of the appropriate kind (small Latin letter or capital Latin letter with or without argument-places) that has not hitherto been used; and we denote the resulting formula by $\mathfrak{A}^*$. Next we replace $\mathfrak{A}$, wherever it occurs in ($\mathfrak{F}_i$) by $\mathfrak{A}^*$, and we then take every substitution that has been made for any free variable in any occurrence of $\mathfrak{A}$ and apply it also to all the consequential occurrences of that free variable as a parameter in the derivation. The resulting sequence of formulae $(\mathfrak{F}_i^*)$ can only fail to be a derivation in one way. If there is in $(\mathfrak{F}_i)$ a step

$$\frac{\begin{array}{c} \mathfrak{U} \\ \mathfrak{U} \to \mathfrak{B} \end{array}}{\mathfrak{B}}$$

there will be in $(\mathfrak{F}_i^*)$ a corresponding step

$$\frac{\begin{array}{c} \mathfrak{U}^* \\ (\mathfrak{U} \to \mathfrak{B})^* \end{array}}{\mathfrak{B}^*,}$$

but $(\mathfrak{U} \to \mathfrak{B})^*$ is not necessarily the same as $\mathfrak{U}^* \to \mathfrak{B}^*$. It may be that one of the two premisses $\mathfrak{U}$ and $\mathfrak{U} \to \mathfrak{B}$ in $(\mathfrak{F}_i)$ was derived by means of $\mathfrak{A}$ and the other one independently of $\mathfrak{A}$, and that a free variable in $\mathfrak{U}^*$ is not now the same as the corresponding free variable in $(\mathfrak{U} \to \mathfrak{B})^*$. In such a case, however, we can always alter the derivation of the premiss that is independent of $\mathfrak{A}$ so as to make that premiss match the one that has been modified, and the validity of the application of (β) in $(\mathfrak{F}_i)$ then extends to $(\mathfrak{F}_i^*)$ at the place in question.

How this is to be done is best made clear by using the procedure for unravelling the strands of a derivation that is introduced for another purpose on p. 215. If the derivation $(\mathfrak{F}_i)$ is unravelled and then displayed schematically, we can convert it in the following way into a sequence of formulae $(\mathfrak{F}_i^*)$ that is again a derivation. We first make the necessary substitutions, as previously specified, in every occurrence of $\mathfrak{A}$, and then we continue them down every strand to the end-formula (or to where the variable that is being substituted for is eliminated). After this, we work upwards from each place where a substitution has been made, proceeding along every strand until we come either to an initial formula or to a place where the variable that is being substituted for was itself introduced into $(\mathfrak{F}_i)$ by a substitution, and there we stop.

When all this has been done, we have a derivation of a formula $\mathfrak{B}^*$, the formula obtained when certain substitutions are made for free variables in $\mathfrak{B}$, from the formula $\mathfrak{A}^*$, the axioms (a)–(f), and possibly certain formulae derived from these axioms by substitution for the free variables in them. This derivation can at once be made into a derivation of $\mathfrak{B}^*$ from $\mathfrak{A}^*$ and the six axioms, a derivation, moreover, which satisfies the conditions of Lemma 2. It now follows that an absolute derivation of the formula $\mathfrak{A}^* \to \mathfrak{B}^*$ can be constructed; and this derivation can be prolonged to a derivation of $\mathfrak{A} \to \mathfrak{B}$ by a finite number of applications of the rules (α). Theorem 5 is accordingly proved.

As an illustration of the process of substitution involved in the above proof, let us take the following abbreviated derivation of $\mathfrak{B} \equiv F(y)$ from $\mathfrak{A} \equiv (x)(F(x) \mathbin{\&} G(x))$, which is adapted from Hilbert & Bernays: *Grundlagen*, I, p. 153.

(1) $(x)F(x) \to F(y)$ [(e)]

(2) $(x)(F(x) \mathbin{\&} G(x)) \to (F(y) \mathbin{\&} G(y))$ [(1): (α3)]

(3) $(x)(F(x) \mathbin{\&} G(x))$ [i.e. $\mathfrak{A}$]

(4) $F(y) \mathbin{\&} G(y)$ [(3), (2): (β)]

(5) $(X \mathbin{\&} Y) \to X$ [Identical formula]

(6) $(F(y) \mathbin{\&} G(y)) \to F(y)$ [(5): (α1)]

(7) $F(y)$.   [(4), (6): (β)]

Unravelling the strands, we obtain the schematic derivation

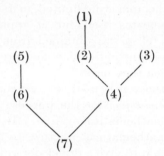

Here the occurrence of a substitution for $F(-)$ in the passage from (1) to (2) means that $F(-)$ must be replaced by a new predicate variable, $H(-)$ say, in $\mathfrak{A}$, and consequentially in the derivation. We first make this change in (3), where $\mathfrak{A}$ is directly involved. Then we carry it downwards into (4) and (7). From (7) we must ascend again to (6), and from (4) to (2); but we do not ascend from (6) to (5), nor from (2) to (1).

Remarks on the deduction theorem. (i) The force of the proviso, in the statement of Theorem 5, that all free variables in $\mathfrak{A}$ must be parameters throughout the given derivation of $\mathfrak{B}$ from $\mathfrak{A}$, is illustrated by the following simple example of a situation in which the theorem fails to apply. Let $\mathfrak{A}$ and $\mathfrak{B}$ be the formulae $F(y)$ and $(x)F(x)$ respectively. Then $\mathfrak{B}$ may be derived from $\mathfrak{A}$ as follows:

$$F(y)$$
$$\overline{X \vee \bar{X} \vee F(y)} \quad \text{[By (b) and (c)]}$$
$$(X \vee \bar{X}) \to F(y)$$
$$(X \vee \bar{X}) \to (x)F(x) \quad \text{[(γ1)]}$$
$$(x)F(x). \quad \text{[(β), using the identical formula } X \vee \bar{X}]$$

Since the free variable y in $\mathfrak{A}$ is not a parameter—being the operative variable for the application of $(\gamma 1)$—we are not able to invoke the deduction theorem in order to infer the derivability of $\mathfrak{A} \to \mathfrak{B}$, i.e. $F(y) \to (x)F(x)$. We already know, of course, that this latter formula is not a derivable formula of the calculus of predicates (cf. p. 71).

(ii) The proof of the deduction theorem that we have given is constructive. The theorem, in other words, is not merely an existence theorem, which does no more than guarantee the derivability of $\mathfrak{A} \to \mathfrak{B}$ when a derivation of $\mathfrak{B}$ from $\mathfrak{A}$ is already available. It actually enables us to produce a derivation of $\mathfrak{A} \to \mathfrak{B}$ by transforming the given derivation of $\mathfrak{B}$ from $\mathfrak{A}$ in a systematic way. In this respect the deduction theorem is unlike the theorem on the completeness of the calculus of predicates (Theorem 3, p. 77), which is only an existence theorem.

(iii) The deduction theorem is not limited, in its range of applicability, to the calculus of predicates itself, but it applies also to formalized mathematical theories (cf. p. 98), obtained from this calculus when it is supplemented by constant individuals and predicates, together with suitable axioms in which they occur.

(iv) The deduction theorem is used very extensively by Bourbaki, in his *Éléments de Mathématique*, for the purpose of simplifying formal derivation within the mathematical system. It is often easier, as well as nearer to normal mathematical practice, to derive a conclusion $\mathfrak{B}$ from a hypothesis $\mathfrak{A}$ than to give a direct derivation of the implication $\mathfrak{A} \to \mathfrak{B}$. In Bourbaki's system, moreover, the deduction theorem takes a particularly simple form (cf. p. 120).

SUPPLEMENTARY NOTES ON CHAPTER 3

1. *Some points concerning symbolism.* (i) We have already alluded, on p. 28, to the multiplicity of systems of logical notation that are used in the literature. Some of the more commonly occurring symbols are indicated in the table opposite.

(ii) An important constituent of the syntax of any formalized language is the means used to eliminate ambiguity in the structure of composite expressions. Some form of bracketing is usually adopted, although in the exceptional instance of Łukasiewicz's system of notation, in which operators are always placed before the symbols on which they operate, this is theoretically unnecessary (cf. p. 50). Even here, however, brackets are often useful in practice, as an aid to clarity.

In Peano's *Formulaire*, and also in *Principia Mathematica*, dots are used in preference to brackets (see below, p. 164), and this useful convention has been adopted sporadically by later writers on logic.

The number of brackets or dots that have to be employed is substantially reduced if a fixed order of precedence is laid down for the logical connectives.

Concept	Symbol		
	Whitehead & Russell	Hilbert's school	Other authors
not	$\sim$	$\overline{}$, $\overrightarrow{}$	N, $\neg$
or	$\vee$	$\vee$	A
and	$\cdot$	$\&$	K, $\wedge$
if ... then ...	$\supset$	$\rightarrow$	C
if and only if	$\equiv$	$\sim$, $\leftrightarrow$	E
for some x	$(\exists x)$	(Ex)	Σx, $\exists x$
for all x	(x)	(x)	Πx, $\forall x$

Hilbert and Ackermann, for instance, take '$\rightarrow$' and '$\sim$' (i.e. '$\rightarrow$' and '$\leftrightarrow$' in our notation) as binding less closely than '$\vee$' and '$\&$', in the manner in which the algebraic connective '$+$' binds less closely than the connective '$\times$' or '$\cdot$'. Thus, just as '$a + b \cdot c$' is read without ambiguity as '$a + (b \cdot c)$' and not as '$(a + b) \cdot c$', so '$X \rightarrow X \vee Y$' is to be read as '$X \rightarrow (X \vee Y)$' and not as '$(X \rightarrow X) \vee Y$'.

(iii) In the present book, in conformity with the practice of Hilbert and Bernays, we make use of German letters for two important purposes, both of them metalogical:

(a) German letters are frequently employed as *syntactic variables*, as in the schemata (β) and ($\gamma 1$) on p. 67, namely

$$\frac{\begin{array}{c}\mathfrak{A}\\ \mathfrak{A} \rightarrow \mathfrak{B}\end{array}}{\mathfrak{B}} \quad \text{and} \quad \frac{\mathfrak{A} \rightarrow \mathfrak{B}(\mathfrak{y})}{\mathfrak{A} \rightarrow (\mathfrak{x})\mathfrak{B}(\mathfrak{x}).}$$

Here '$\mathfrak{A}$' and '$\mathfrak{B}$' are syntactic variables for which well-formed formulae may be substituted, while '$\mathfrak{x}$' and '$\mathfrak{y}$' are syntactic variables for which individual variables (i.e. small Latin letters) may be substituted. With the aid of syntactic variables we are able, in effect, to make statements about *arbitrary* formulae or variables of the logical calculus, as in elementary algebra we can make statements about arbitrary numbers. In later chapters of this book, moreover, we shall extend the use of syntactic variables to further kinds of entities, e.g. arithmetical functions $\mathfrak{f}(x)$, $\mathfrak{g}(x,y)$.

(b) Our second use of the German alphabet is to provide names for specific entities, as when we say 'Let $\mathfrak{A}$ be the given formula', or 'Let a natural number $\mathfrak{n}$ be chosen'.

(iv) An alternative to the naming of entities by German letters, as in (iii b), is the construction of names with the aid of inverted commas. We might have occasion to say, for example, 'Let $\mathfrak{A}$ be a well-formed formula in which the letter "x" occurs as a free variable', and we would then be using the double inverted commas with a letter between them as a name for the last letter but two of the Latin alphabet. By introducing inverted commas in this way, we make explicit the distinction between *use* and *mention* of a symbol. When a symbol is actually used—say in the course of a derivation—it is written in the ordinary way, without inverted commas; but when it is merely mentioned, in a metalogical context, it is placed between inverted commas. Since, however, inverted commas are needed for a variety of other purposes in addition to this particular one, we prefer on the whole not to distinguish explicitly between use and mention unless confusion would otherwise be possible. Our choice would be different if the nature of the argument were such that the distinction between use and mention needed always to be kept before the reader. Then stricter attention to this use of inverted commas would be appropriate. Inverted commas are used meticulously, for instance, in the fourth edition of Hilbert & Ackermann [1].

2. *A strong sense of 'complete'.* A formal axiomatic theory may be said to be *complete* if every formula which is intuitively valid when the symbols are given some agreed interpretation is derivable from the axioms. The notion of 'semantic completeness' of a logical calculus that we have considered in Chapter 2, §6 and Chapter 3, §4 is of just this kind. There is, however, an alternative syntactic notion of completeness that makes no reference to any extraneous interpretation of the axioms or their possible consequences; and a theory is said to be complete in this sense if the addition to its axioms of any formula that is not derivable from them renders the system inconsistent. We have here completeness of a very strong kind; and although the propositional calculus is complete in the syntactic as well as the semantic sense, the restricted calculus of predicates is only complete in the weaker semantic sense (cf. Hilbert and Ackermann's discussions of completeness for these two logical calculi).

Chapter 4

FURTHER DEVELOPMENT OF SYMBOLIC LOGIC

1 The relation of identity

We have now devoted two chapters to the subject of symbolic logic —one to the propositional calculus, and another to the calculus of predicates. We began, in Chapter 2, by introducing in a fairly intuitive way the basic ideas of the propositional calculus, and after that we proceeded to put this calculus into axiomatic form and to discuss its metalogical characteristics. Then, in Chapter 3, we began anew with the calculus of predicates, a wider system of symbolic logic that includes the propositional calculus as its most elementary part; and once again we constructed a formal axiomatic theory and made it an object of metalogical discussion.

The propositional calculus, as we now see, is very limited in scope, since it merely permits exhibition of the molecular structure of composite propositions, while leaving the inner constitution of the atomic constituents of such propositions wholly unanalysed. The calculus of predicates, on the contrary, provides an analysis of atomic structure that goes far beyond the relatively crude separation into subject and predicate that is all that is envisaged by traditional logic. This new analysis has been made possible by two innovations: (i) the application to predicates of the mathematical symbolism for dependence of functions on arguments, and (ii) the introduction of a special notation for the key ideas of 'all' and 'some'. The calculus of predicates provides in this way appropriate means for treating properties of individuals and relations between individuals. There still remain, however, several important logical notions, familiar enough in mathematical and other discourse, that are as yet unprovided for in the formal system, and we need to see to what extent we can find ways of incorporating these also.

A very common logical notion that the calculus of predicates makes no provision for is the relation of *identity*. To say that a and b are identical amounts to saying that 'a' and 'b' are symbols, names, descriptive phrases, or other representative marks, which stand for the same individual. We say, for example, that Corno di Bassetto is identical with George Bernard Shaw, that $7 + 5$ is identical with 12, and that the propounder of the general theory of relativity is identical with Albert Einstein.   Identity is thus a constant predicate with two arguments (as opposed to the predicate *variables* which alone have a place in the formal calculus of predicates) and we could adopt for it some such notation as $\mathfrak{Jd}(x,y)$, using '$\mathfrak{Jd}$' as a constant symbol.   It is much more convenient, however, to take over from mathematics the sign of equality, which indeed is ordinarily used in the sense of logical identity, and to write the propositional function 'x is identical with y' in symbols as '$x = y$'.   We shall also use $x \neq y$ as an abbreviation for the negation $\overline{x = y}$ of $x = y$, that is to say for the relation of *diversity*.

The most familiar formal characteristics of the relation of identity are that it is reflexive, symmetrical, and transitive; but these three properties are not by themselves sufficient to determine the relation uniquely.   They apply equally to all 'equivalence relations', of which there are many examples in mathematics alone, as for instance congruence and similarity of geometrical figures.   A *definition* of identity was proposed in 1903 by Bertrand Russell, in his book *The Principles of Mathematics*, §24, where he said, in effect, that $\mathfrak{a}$ is identical with $\mathfrak{b}$ if every property of $\mathfrak{a}$ is also a property of $\mathfrak{b}$.   This definition is closely related to Leibniz's famous principle of the Identity of Indiscernibles, according to which [1] 'there are not in nature two indiscernible real absolute beings' or 'no two substances are completely similar, or differ *solo numero*'.   We might try to put the definition into symbols by writing

$$(x = y) \;=\; (F)(F(x) \leftrightarrow F(y)) \quad \text{Df,}$$

but to do this would take us beyond the limits of our present calculus, as we would have a quantifier (F) binding a *predicate* variable.   So radical an innovation does not prove to be necessary, however, since a characterization of identity that is adequate for mathematical purposes is provided by the following pair of formal axioms, adopted by Hilbert, in which '$=$' is a primitive symbol:

$$(\mathrm{J}_1) \qquad\qquad\qquad a = a,$$

$$(\mathrm{J}_2) \qquad\qquad a = b \to (F(a) \to F(b)).$$

When identity is introduced with the aid of these axioms, we are able to show in the following way, by formal derivation in the calculus of predicates, that the new relation is indeed reflexive, symmetrical, and transitive.

---

[1] See Bertrand Russell: *A Critical Exposition of the Philosophy of Leibniz* (London, 1900), §23.

(i) The axiom (J_1) is itself the assertion of reflexivity.

(ii) $a = b \to (a = c \to b = c)$ (1) $[(J_2)\ x = c/F(x)]$
      $a = b \to (a = a \to b = a)$ $[(1)\ a/c]$
      $a = a \to (a = b \to b = a)$ [Rule VII, p. 49]
      $a = b \to b = a.$ (2) $[(\beta)$, using $(J_1)]$

(2) is the assertion of symmetry.

(iii) $b = a \to (b = c \to a = c)$ (3) $[(1)\ b/a\ a/b]$
      $a = b \to (b = c \to a = c)$ $[(2), (3)]$
      $(a = b\ \&\ b = c) \to a = c.$ (4)   [Rule VII]

(4) is the assertion of transitivity.

Exercise. Derive in a similar way the formula

$$(a = c\ \&\ b = c) \to a = b,$$

which formalizes the assertion that two things which are identical with the same thing are identical with each other. (Cf. Euclid's first 'common notion', quoted on p. 136.)

2 Descriptions and the ι-symbol

Every application of the calculus of predicates relates to some definite domain of individuals, and we usually think of the members of this domain as identifiable by appropriate names. In arithmetic, for example, when we wish to discuss the natural numbers we can refer to them individually by their names $0, 1, 2, \ldots$. But instead of mentioning the number 6, say, we might have occasion to talk about 'the highest common factor of 36 and 42', and this would be equally specific. The use of descriptive phrases can be just as efficacious as actual naming for the purpose of singling out individuals, and it has the very important advantage of enabling us to speak of a particular individual, which we are interested in because it has a certain property, even when we do not know what the name of this individual happens to be—that is to say, when the identity of the individual is not known to us. What we have here is therefore much more than a mere device of nomenclature; and in it we must recognize a fundamental logical procedure that has not yet been taken into account in our formalization of deductive logic.

Descriptive phrases of the type 'the such and such', i.e. 'the individual with the property P', are known to logicians as 'descriptions', this being the name given to them by Bertrand Russell in his account of the subject in *Principia Mathematica*, a treatment that has formed the basis of all subsequent work on the use of descriptive phrases. Russell returned to the same topic in his *Introduction to Mathematical Philosophy* (1919), where he drew a distinction between *indefinite* descriptions (of the form '*a* such and such') and *definite* descriptions (of the form '*the* such and such'). In the present context we are concerned only with definite descriptions, and for these we shall adopt Hilbert's modified version of Russell's original treatment. If a property P is symbolized by a predicate $\mathfrak{A}(x)$, with a single argument-place, we shall write the definite description 'the individual with the property P' in symbols as $\iota_x \mathfrak{A}(x)$. The letter x is, we observe, a bound variable in this expression, not properly involved in it, and hence replaceable by any other suitable letter.

Now although descriptions certainly serve to denote particular individuals, they are essentially different from names. A name is an arbitrarily assigned label, and it denotes that individual to which the name has been given. A description, on the contrary, is a specification; and it applies to whatever individual may satisfy the requirements that it comprises. In formulating such a specification, we do not necessarily guarantee that there is anything at all to which it applies. Thus the descriptions 'the present king of France' and 'the round square' are both void, since there is no entity that is denoted by either of them. Again, it may well be that a descriptive phrase applies to more than one individual, in which case English usage would normally prefer the indefinite form 'a such and such' to the definite form 'the such and such'. In symbolic logic, rigorous limitation of the form of expression $\iota_x \mathfrak{A}(x)$ to those instances in which the propositional function $\mathfrak{A}(x)$ is satisfied by one and only one object proves to be highly desirable.

In *Principia Mathematica*, Russell made existence and uniqueness of the object referred to a part of the meaning to be attributed to any sentence that involves a description. The definition of descriptions that he gave was indeed not an explicit definition at all—that is to say a declaration whereby the thing to be defined is identified with something already known—but a 'definition in use' or contextual definition. He did not attempt to analyse or define the description $\iota_x \mathfrak{A}(x)$ taken in isolation, but contented himself with giving precise meaning to any statement $\mathfrak{B}(\iota_x \mathfrak{A}(x))$ in which it may occur as argument of a predicate. The form of statement $\mathfrak{B}(\iota_x \mathfrak{A}(x))$ was analysed by him as the composite assertion 'There is one and only one individual $\mathfrak{a}$ such that $\mathfrak{A}(\mathfrak{a})$; and, for this same individual, $\mathfrak{B}(\mathfrak{a})$'. In other words, $\mathfrak{B}(\iota_x \mathfrak{A}(x))$ is to be taken as an abbreviation for

$$(Ex)[\mathfrak{A}(x) \ \& \ (y)(\mathfrak{A}(y) \to y = x) \ \& \ \mathfrak{B}(x)].$$

On this view, the proposition $\mathfrak{B}(\iota_x \mathfrak{A}(x))$ is to be counted as false if there is nothing that has the property symbolized by the predicate $\mathfrak{A}(x)$, and also if there is more than one thing with this property. Thus, for example, the propositions 'The present king of France is bald' and 'The real number whose square is 2 is irrational' are both false on Russell's reckoning.

Although Russell's way of interpreting statements of the form $\mathfrak{B}(\iota_x\mathfrak{A}(x))$ yields a logically satisfactory theory of descriptions, the meaning that has to be given to ostensibly simple assertions can often be very complicated; and we may well feel that a somewhat less artificial treatment of definite descriptions would be preferable—a treatment more immediately related to the way in which phrases of the type 'the such and such' are commonly used. A modified form of Russell's theory, designed to satisfy this demand, has in fact been developed by Hilbert, and to this we now turn.

In common speech we are not troubled by sentences containing descriptions which refer either to no object at all or else to a multiplicity of objects, for we never use a phrase of the form '*the* individual with the property P'—except when speaking loosely or idiomatically— unless we believe that it refers to a unique individual; and this suggests that in the formal system we might make the introduction of a description symbol $\iota_x\mathfrak{A}(x)$ conditional on the prior derivation of the associated *uniqueness formulae* $(Ex)\mathfrak{A}(x)$ and $(x)(y)[(\mathfrak{A}(x)\ \&\ \mathfrak{A}(y)) \to x = y]$. We accordingly widen the rules of substitution (α) of the calculus of predicates, stated on p. 66, so as to permit substitution of an ι-expression $\iota_x\mathfrak{A}(x)$ for a free individual variable, *provided that the two uniqueness formulae for* $\mathfrak{A}(x)$ *have previously been derived.* We also adopt, as an additional rule for the derivation of new formulae, the ι-*schema*

$$\frac{(E\mathfrak{x})\mathfrak{A}(\mathfrak{x}) \quad (\mathfrak{x})(\mathfrak{y})[(\mathfrak{A}(\mathfrak{x})\ \&\ \mathfrak{A}(\mathfrak{y})) \to \mathfrak{x} = \mathfrak{y}]}{\mathfrak{A}(\iota_{\mathfrak{x}}\mathfrak{A}(\mathfrak{x})).}$$

Semantically, ι-expressions stand for individuals, and there is therefore an essential difference between them and all the other composite expressions that have occurred hitherto in our logical calculus. The earlier expressions were without exception *formulae*, and they stood for propositions or propositional functions. Syntactically, a formula can only be substituted for a propositional or predicate variable, whereas an ι-expression can only be substituted for an individual variable. Any expression with the syntactic status of an individual (that is, an expression which can be an argument of a predicate symbol) will henceforth be referred to as a *term.* In the system of symbolic logic that we have so far built up there are just two kinds of terms, namely individual variables and ι-expressions. From now on we shall usually refer to ι-expressions as ι-terms.

We have already pointed out that the 'x' in the ι-term $\iota_x\mathfrak{A}(x)$ is a bound variable, which may be changed into a different letter without essential modification of the term. As in the case of the quantifiers, however, we must take good care that no clash of bound variables is allowed to occur; and if we were giving a detailed and rigorous account of the incorporation of the formal theory of descriptions in the calculus of predicates we would have to include suitable provisos in the definitions of well-formed formula and well-formed term, and also in the modified rules of derivation. To illustrate what is meant by avoidance of clashes, let us suppose that we are able to derive the uniqueness formulae for some formula $\mathfrak{A}(y)$ of the form $(Ex)[\mathfrak{B}(x) \rightarrow \mathfrak{C}(x,y)]$, containing y as a free variable. We are then at liberty to introduce the ι-term $\iota_y \mathfrak{A}(y)$, that is to say $\iota_y(Ex)[\mathfrak{B}(x) \rightarrow \mathfrak{C}(x,y)]$; but we could not change the bound variable 'y' into 'x', writing the ι-term as $\iota_x(Ex)[\mathfrak{B}(x) \rightarrow \mathfrak{C}(x,x)]$.

The ι-symbol may be applied to formulae which contain more than one free individual variable. A particular variable must be selected as the variable to be bound by the ι-symbol, and it is necessary that the corresponding uniqueness formulae should be derivable. We have, for example, the following schema:

$$(E\mathfrak{y})\mathfrak{A}(\mathfrak{x},\mathfrak{y})$$
$$\frac{(\mathfrak{y})(\mathfrak{z})[(\mathfrak{A}(\mathfrak{x},\mathfrak{y}) \ \& \ \mathfrak{A}(\mathfrak{x},\mathfrak{z})) \rightarrow \mathfrak{y} = \mathfrak{z}]}{\mathfrak{A}(\mathfrak{x},\iota_{\mathfrak{y}}\mathfrak{A}(\mathfrak{x},\mathfrak{y})).}$$

Here $\iota_{\mathfrak{y}}\mathfrak{A}(\mathfrak{x},\mathfrak{y})$ is a term that involves $\mathfrak{x}$ as a free variable or 'parameter'. Such a term may be referred to as a 'function of $\mathfrak{x}$'—not a propositional function, however, but an individual function. A propositional function is an expression, containing one or more free variables, which yields a *proposition* whenever suitable individuals, propositions, or predicates are substituted as 'values' for all the free variables in it; while an individual function is an expression, containing free variables that may again be of any of the three kinds, which yields an *individual* whenever 'values' are given to all the variables. If we wish to introduce an abbreviation for an ι-term in which free variables are present, we adopt some such explicit definition as

$$\mathfrak{f}(x) = \iota_y \mathfrak{A}(x,y) \quad \text{Df.}$$

When this is done, the expression $\mathfrak{A}(x,\mathfrak{f}(x))$ is a derivable formula.

We have now indicated how it is possible to incorporate the theory of descriptions in our earlier system of logic (that is to say in the restricted calculus of predicates, extended by the addition of the sign of identity and the axioms (J_1) and (J_2)) by adjoining to this system the ι-symbol and the ι-schema and amending suitably the definitions and rules; and it might be expected that this further extension of the resources of symbolic logic would allow additional formulae of the original system to be derived. Such is not the case, however, for it can be shown that use of the ι-schema merely facilitates the process of derivation, without rendering derivable any formulae that were previously underivable. That this is so is asserted by a fundamental metalogical theorem, which may be formulated in the following terms.

THEOREM 1 (*Theorem on the Eliminability of the ι-Symbol*). *If a formula* $\mathfrak{A}$ *of the restricted calculus of predicates, extended by incorporation of the theory of identity, is derivable with the help of the ι-symbol and the ι-schema, and if no ι-symbol occurs in* $\mathfrak{A}$ *itself, then* $\mathfrak{A}$ *is derivable without use of the ι-symbol.*

Since the proof of this theorem is long and very closely reasoned, it would not be appropriate to include it here. Full details are given by Hilbert and Bernays (*Grundlagen*, I, pp. 422–457).

It should be mentioned that Theorem 1 admits of considerable generalization. This theorem is not restricted to the calculus of predicates with identity, but applies equally to formal systems which include symbols for particular individuals, predicates, and individual functions, and also additional axioms, as long as any such axioms (except the arithmetical axiom of induction if it is one of them) are free from propositional and predicate variables. The notion of a formal system of this wider kind will be discussed later in this chapter (see §3, p. 98).

2.1 Characteristic functions of formulae

As an illustration of the utility of the ι-symbol in applied logic, we shall show in this section how the symbol can be used for the purpose of formalizing the often convenient mathematical device of *characteristic function*. We are now in a position, in fact, to define characteristic functions of propositional variables and of formulae of more general kinds. Since such functions are used chiefly when the logical calculus is applied to the properties of numbers, within the frame of a formalized system of arithmetic, it will be sufficient if we define such functions in terms of two constant individuals 0 and 1. There is nothing essentially arithmetical in what we do, however, since all that we require is that there shall be available two constant individual symbols 0 and 1 such that $0 \neq 1$ can be asserted.

Looking at the matter intuitively in the first instance, we shall understand by the characteristic function of a propositional variable X a term $\omega(X)$—i.e. an individual function with the propositional variable X as argument—whose only possible 'values' are 0 and 1. If any proposition with truth-value T is substituted for X, the value assumed by $\omega(X)$ is to be 0; and if any proposition with truth-value F is substituted for X, the value of the function is to be 1. We thus require to introduce, in a purely formal way, a term $\omega(X)$ such that the formula

$$(X \to \omega(X) = 0) \,\&\, (\overline{X} \to \omega(X) = 1)$$

is derivable.

We begin by forming the expression

$$(X \to a = 0) \ \& \ (\bar{X} \to a = 1),$$

which we denote by $\mathfrak{A}(X,a)$; and then we derive the two uniqueness formulae

$$(Ex)\mathfrak{A}(X,x)$$

and

$$(x)(y)[(\mathfrak{A}(X,x) \ \& \ \mathfrak{A}(X,y)) \to x = y].$$

Having done this, we are at liberty to introduce the ι-term $\iota_x\mathfrak{A}(X,x)$; and by the ι-schema we then have

$$(X \to \iota_x\mathfrak{A}(X,x) = 0) \ \& \ (\bar{X} \to \iota_x\mathfrak{A}(X,x) = 1).$$

If, therefore, we denote the term $\iota_x\mathfrak{A}(X,x)$, in which X occurs as a free variable, by $\omega(X)$, we have the required formal assertion

$$(X \to \omega(X) = 0) \ \& \ (\bar{X} \to \omega(X) = 1).$$

We now complete the argument with an outline of the derivations of the uniqueness formulae for $\mathfrak{A}(X,x)$. The following identical formulae of the propositional calculus are available for use:

(i) $Y \to (X \to Y)$,

(ii) $X \to (\bar{X} \to Y)$,

(iii) $\bar{X} \to (X \to Y)$,

(iv) $[(X \to Y) \ \& \ (X \to Z)] \leftrightarrow [X \to (Y \ \& \ Z)]$,

(v) $[(X \to Z) \ \& \ (Y \to Z)] \leftrightarrow [(X \vee Y) \to Z]$,

(vi) $X \vee \bar{X}$,

(vii) $[(Y \vee Z) \to W] \to [((X \to Y) \ \& \ (\bar{X} \to Z)) \to W]$.

(a) *Derivation of* $(Ex)\mathfrak{A}(X,x)$.

$X \to (X \to 0 = 0)$ [(J_1), using (i) twice]

$X \to (\bar{X} \to 0 = 1)$ [(ii)]

$X \to [(X \to 0 = 0) \ \& \ (\bar{X} \to 0 = 1)]$ [(iv)]

$[(X \to 0 = 0) \ \& \ (\bar{X} \to 0 = 1)] \to (Ex)[(X \to x = 0) \ \& \ (\bar{X} \to x = 1)]$

$X \to (Ex)[(X \to x = 0) \ \& \ (\bar{X} \to x = 1)]$

$\bar{X} \to (X \to 1 = 0)$ [(iii)]

$\bar{X} \to (\bar{X} \to 1 = 1)$ [(J_1), using (i) twice]

$\bar{X} \to (Ex)[(X \to x = 0) \ \& \ (\bar{X} \to x = 1)]$ [as before]

$(X \vee \bar{X}) \to (Ex)[(X \to x = 0) \ \& \ (\bar{X} \to x = 1)]$ [(v)]

$(Ex)[(X \to x = 0) \ \& \ (\bar{X} \to x = 1)]$ [(vi)]

i.e. $(Ex)\mathfrak{A}(X,x)$.

(b) *Derivation of* $(x)(y)[(\mathfrak{A}(X,x)$ & $\mathfrak{A}(X,y)) \to x = y]$.

$(a = 0 \ \& \ b = 0) \to a = b$ [cf. p. 91, exercise]

$(a = 1 \ \& \ b = 1) \to a = b$ [ditto]

$[(a = 0 \ \& \ b = 0) \vee (a = 1 \ \& \ b = 1)] \to a = b$ [(v)]

$[(X \to (a = 0 \ \& \ b = 0)) \ \& \ (\overline{X} \to (a = 1 \ \& \ b = 1))] \to a = b$ [(vii)]

$[(\overline{X} \vee (a = 0 \ \& \ b = 0)) \ \& \ (X \vee (a = 1 \ \& \ b = 1))] \to a = b$

$[(\overline{X} \vee a = 0) \ \& \ (\overline{X} \vee b = 0) \ \& \ (X \vee a = 1) \ \& \ (X \vee b = 1)] \to a = b$

$[((X \to a = 0) \ \& \ (\overline{X} \to a = 1)) \ \& \ ((X \to b = 0) \ \& \ (\overline{X} \to b = 1))] \to a = b$

$(\mathfrak{A}(X,a) \ \& \ \mathfrak{A}(X,b)) \to a = b$

$(x)(y)[(\mathfrak{A}(X,x) \ \& \ \mathfrak{A}(X,y)) \to x = y]$.   [(γ′)]

The characteristic function $\omega(X)$ of a propositional variable is not in itself of much interest; but we are able to substitute any formula for the variable X, and in this way we can obtain characteristic functions of a much more general kind. Suppose, for instance, that we are given some particular predicate $\Phi(x)$, represented formally by a formula $\mathfrak{F}(x)$ which contains x as a free variable. Then $\omega(\mathfrak{F}(x))$ is a term $\mathfrak{f}(x)$ in which x again occurs free; and the formula

$$(\mathfrak{F}(x) \to \mathfrak{f}(x) = 0) \ \& \ (\overline{\mathfrak{F}(x)} \to \mathfrak{f}(x) = 1)$$

is derivable.

Once again by the exercise on p. 91, we have

$$(\mathfrak{f}(x) = 0 \ \& \ \mathfrak{f}(x) = 1) \to 0 = 1.$$

But, by hypothesis, $0 \neq 1$; and hence

$$\mathfrak{f}(x) \neq 0 \vee \mathfrak{f}(x) \neq 1,$$

i.e.

$$\mathfrak{f}(x) = 0 \to \mathfrak{f}(x) \neq 1.$$

But transposition of the implication

$$\overline{\mathfrak{F}(x)} \to \mathfrak{f}(x) = 1$$

yields the implication

$$\mathfrak{f}(x) \neq 1 \to \mathfrak{F}(x),$$

and hence we have

$$\mathfrak{f}(x) = 0 \to \mathfrak{F}(x).$$

Similarly we can derive the formula

$$\mathfrak{f}(x) = 1 \to \overline{\mathfrak{F}(x)};$$

and combining into a single formula the various implications that have been derived, we have finally the complete relation

$$(\mathfrak{F}(x) \leftrightarrow \mathfrak{f}(x) = 0) \ \& \ (\overline{\mathfrak{F}(x)} \leftrightarrow \mathfrak{f}(x) = 1),$$

now with the sign for bi-implication in each component. Thus the individual function $\mathfrak{f}(x)$ formalizes the characteristic function of the predicate $\Phi(x)$ with which we began, that is to say the function which takes the value 0 for every individual to which the predicate applies and the value 1 for every individual to which it does not apply.

Now the language of predicates or propositional functions may be looked upon as the typical language of logic, and that of equations as the typical language of mathematics; and what we have shown means, therefore, that each of these languages may be freely translated into the other.

3   Formalized mathematical theories

Already on a number of occasions we have envisaged the possibility that a formal system may include more than the bare logical calculus, and we have noted, in particular, that both the deduction theorem (p. 78) and the theorem on the eliminability of the ι-symbol (p. 95) are valid for formal systems of wider scope. Such formalized theories have indeed come to play a large part both in the study of foundations of mathematics and in mathematics itself, and we need to make more precise than we have done hitherto the notion of an axiomatic theory that is based on a mixed set of logical and mathematical axioms.[1]

By a *formal theory* (which will as a rule be set up as a formalization of some more intuitively conceived theory of the ordinary mathematical kind) we shall understand an axiomatic system F which consists of a suitable logical calculus, amplified by the adjunction of special symbols that serve as proper names for certain particular individuals, predicates, or individual functions, together with axioms in which these various constants appear. The logical calculus will usually be the restricted calculus of predicates, supplemented by the theory of identity and perhaps also by the ι-symbol. The definition of well-formed formula in this calculus must be appropriately extended, and a definition of well-formed term must also be supplied; and the rules of derivation must be properly reformulated for the extended system. When this has all been done, any formula that can be derived from the axioms in accordance with the rules of derivation will count as a theorem of the system F.

As an illustration of this idea of a formal system we may take the very simple system (A_0) of formalized arithmetic that is discussed below in Chapter 7 (see p. 210). In this system the domain of individuals is an abstract counterpart of the totality of natural numbers, and we have the constant symbol 0 for one particular individual, the

---

[1] The distinction that we have drawn here between a logical calculus in itself and a formal theory obtained by making additions to such a calculus should be compared with Church's distinction between a pure functional calculus and an applied functional calculus. See his *Introduction to Mathematical Logic*, I, §30.

formula $x < y$ for a certain constant predicate with two arguments, and the term x' for an individual function that serves to formalize the notion of the successor of x. The underlying logic is the restricted calculus of predicates with identity; and the system is based on the logical axioms (a)–(f) and the axioms (J_1) and (J_2), together with five formalized arithmetical axioms $(<_1)$, $(<_2)$, $(<_3)$, (P_1), (P_2).

In the elaboration of formalized mathematical theories, extensive use is made of explicit definitions, since only by introducing standard abbreviations for the more interesting composite predicates and functions are we able to focus attention on the mathematically significant features of the system. Up to now we have expressed such definitions in the form

$$\mathfrak{A} = \mathfrak{B} \quad \mathrm{Df},$$

$\mathfrak{A}$ being the new symbol or expression that is introduced, and $\mathfrak{B}$ an equivalent expression formed from symbols that are already available in the system. The form of statement '$\ldots = \ldots$ Df' is to be understood as permitting either of the two expressions that are connected by the sign ' $=$ ' to be replaced at any time by the other. Hilbert and Bernays, however, adopt a different convention, writing an explicit definition of a formula $\mathfrak{A}$ always in the form

$$\mathfrak{A} \leftrightarrow \mathfrak{B}$$

and an explicit definition of a term $\mathfrak{a}$ in the form

$$\mathfrak{a} = \mathfrak{b}.$$

A definition that is formulated in one of these ways has precisely the same force as one of the type '$\ldots = \ldots$ Df', since substitution of $\mathfrak{B}$ for $\mathfrak{A}$ or of $\mathfrak{b}$ for $\mathfrak{a}$, as the case may be, is readily justifiable by the logical calculus. We shall conform from now on to the usage of Hilbert and Bernays.

Suppose, to take a simple illustration, that the formal system F with which we are dealing is a formalization of part of the arithmetic of the real numbers, and that by $\mathfrak{A}(x,y)$ we mean the particular formula $y > 0 \,\&\, x^2 = y \,\&\, x > 0$. If we are able to derive the uniqueness formulae for $\mathfrak{A}(x,y)$, treated as a function of x, we can then introduce the ι-term $\iota_x\mathfrak{A}(x,y)$; and it will be a natural further step to adopt the customary notation for the square root of a number by taking as an explicit definition the equation

$$+\sqrt{y} = \iota_x(y > 0 \,\&\, x^2 = y \,\&\, x > 0).$$

The notion of a formalized mathematical theory will be more amply illustrated in Chapter 7, where various systems of formalized arithmetic will be considered in addition to the system (A_0) already mentioned on p. 98. We shall see in Chapter 11, moreover, that certain formal theories of a very comprehensive kind, in which axioms for abstract sets are adjoined to the logical axioms, now offer to mathematicians a reasonable hope of a nearer approach than has previously proved possible to their ideal objectives of perfect rigour and perfect lucidity in the presentation of mathematics in general.

4   Hilbert's ε-symbol

The ι-term $\iota_x \mathfrak{A}(x)$ gives formal expression in the logical calculus to the intuitive idea of 'the individual x such that $\mathfrak{A}(x)$'; and in the formal handling of the ι-symbol this interpretation is reflected in the condition that the term $\iota_x \mathfrak{A}(x)$ may only be introduced into a derivation when the corresponding uniqueness formulae

$$(Ex)\mathfrak{A}(x)$$

and

$$(x)(y)[(\mathfrak{A}(x) \ \& \ \mathfrak{A}(y)) \rightarrow x = y]$$

have already been derived.[1] Hilbert has shown in his later work, however, that for many purposes the uniqueness formulae can be dispensed with; and in the *ε-symbol* that then replaces the ι-symbol he has produced a new logical instrument of great power. A lucid account of this further development of the calculus of predicates is given by Hilbert and Bernays in §1 of their second volume, and the brief remarks which now follow are based on what is said there.[2]

The *formal* introduction of the ε-symbol (like that of the earlier ι-symbol) must be carried out by strictly syntactic means, and nothing is in fact required beyond a suitable specification of those expressions containing 'ε' that are to count as well-formed terms, one new axiom, and a number of obvious amendments to the rules of procedure of the existing calculus. As long as we treat the logical calculus syntactically, this is as much as we need, and any intuitive interpretation that we may at other times give to the ε-symbol is wholly irrelevant. This is a very important consideration, for it means that the *formal* correctness of theories or derivations into which the new symbol enters does not depend on intuitive considerations, which in this instance are rather less compelling than elsewhere in symbolic logic; but we shall want nevertheless to have in reserve some intuitive meaning for the symbol, for use as a clue to the formal steps that are called for in particular arguments.

Suppose, then, that $\mathfrak{A}(x)$ is some formula in which x occurs as a free variable. From it we can form an *ε-term* $\varepsilon_x \mathfrak{A}(x)$, in which x is now a

---

[1] We take this opportunity of observing that there are certain objections to making the introduction of a new syntactically defined expression dependent on what has already been derived, and that a modified treatment of the ι-symbol that is not open to any such objection has recently been given by Bernays. See below, p. 297.

[2] See also Note 3, p. 130, at the end of this chapter.

bound variable; and this term is to be interpreted intuitively as follows.[1] If there is at least one entity $\mathfrak{a}$ such that $\mathfrak{A}(\mathfrak{a})$, then $\varepsilon_x \mathfrak{A}(x)$ designates some entity, not further specified, with this property; but if there is no $\mathfrak{a}$ such that $\mathfrak{A}(\mathfrak{a})$, then $\varepsilon_x \mathfrak{A}(x)$ does not designate anything at all. Such an interpretation obviously makes $(Ex)\mathfrak{A}(x) \to \mathfrak{A}(\varepsilon_x\mathfrak{A}(x))$ a true proposition, and this suggests that a suitable axiom for the ε-symbol in the formal system might be

$$(Ex)F(x) \to F(\varepsilon_x F(x)),$$

which is a weakened version of the ι-schema (p. 94), with the second uniqueness formula left out of account. The axiom actually chosen by Hilbert and Bernays, and called by them the *ε-formula*, is the deductively equivalent formula

$$F(y) \to F(\varepsilon_x F(x)),$$

with a free variable y instead of the variable x bound by the existential quantifier.

Since the letter 'x' that occurs in the ε-term $\varepsilon_x \mathfrak{A}(x)$ is a bound variable, we shall want to be able to replace it by any other suitable letter, and the rule of relabelling (δ) must be amended to permit this to be done. Furthermore, the formula $\mathfrak{A}(x)$ to which the operator 'ε_x' is applied may itself contain free variables other than 'x', and also variables that are already bound by quantifiers, ι-symbols, or ε-symbols; and the formal definition of ε-term will have to be framed in such a way that no clash of bound variables is permitted to occur (cf. p. 94).

The power of the ε-symbol as an instrument of deduction may be gauged from the fact that it provides, in our system of formalized logic, a counterpart to the mathematical axiom of choice (cf. p. 289). This axiom asserts (in one of its possible forms) that, if $\{\mathfrak{C}_i\}$ is a set of non-empty sets $\mathfrak{C}_i$, the suffix ranging over some set $\mathfrak{J}$, then there exists an operator which selects from each set $\mathfrak{C}_i$ one of its elements as 'representative' of the set. Plainly the ε-symbol is just such an operator, since $\varepsilon_x(x \varepsilon \mathfrak{C}_i)$ stands, with the intuitive interpretation that we have already given, for a 'selected' but otherwise unspecified element e_i of $\mathfrak{C}_i$. More generally, if $\mathfrak{A}(a, \ldots, k, x)$ is a formula, in which $a, \ldots, k, x$ are the only free variables, and for every set of individuals $\mathfrak{a}, \ldots, \mathfrak{k}$ there is at least one individual $\mathfrak{x}$ such that $\mathfrak{A}(\mathfrak{a}, \ldots, \mathfrak{k}, \mathfrak{x})$, then $\varepsilon_x \mathfrak{A}(a, \ldots, k, x)$ is a function—in the mathematical sense—which associates with every set of 'values' of the arguments $a, \ldots, k$ a unique 'value' of x. To infer the existence of such a function in mathematics we would be obliged, except in very special cases, to have recourse to the axiom of choice.

---

[1] An ε-term may be thought of as formalizing an indefinite description, somewhat as an ι-term formalizes a definite description (cf. p. 91).

Since the ε-symbol is so powerful as a logical operator, we might expect it to absorb the weaker ι-symbol whenever that symbol can be used; and such is indeed the case. If, for some formula $\mathfrak{A}(x)$, the uniqueness formulae

$$(Ex)\mathfrak{A}(x) \tag{1}$$

and

$$(x)(y)[(\mathfrak{A}(x) \ \& \ \mathfrak{A}(y)) \to x = y] \tag{2}$$

are both derivable, we are able by the ι-schema to derive the formula

$$\mathfrak{A}(\iota_x\mathfrak{A}(x)). \tag{3}$$

But since, by substitution in the ε-formula (p. 101), we have

$$\mathfrak{A}(\iota_x\mathfrak{A}(x)) \to \mathfrak{A}(\varepsilon_x\mathfrak{A}(x)),$$

the derived formula (3) at once yields the formula

$$\mathfrak{A}(\varepsilon_x\mathfrak{A}(x)). \tag{4}$$

From (2), (3), and (4) we now easily derive the formula

$$\varepsilon_x\mathfrak{A}(x) = \iota_x\mathfrak{A}(x);$$

and thus the ε-term is demonstrably identical with the ι-term whenever the latter may be introduced.

What is perhaps rather more surprising than the absorption of the ι-symbol in the ε-symbol is the fact that the ε-symbol is capable also of taking over the work of the quantifiers; but we can show without difficulty that this, too, is the case.

Taking first of all the ε-formula, i.e.

$$F(y) \to F(\varepsilon_x F(x)),$$

we can at once derive, by the schema ($\gamma 2$), the formula

$$(Ex)F(x) \to F(\varepsilon_x F(x));$$

and then, taking the axiom (f), i.e.

$$F(y) \to (Ex)F(x),$$

and substituting the term $\varepsilon_x F(x)$ for the free variable y, we derive also the formula

$$F(\varepsilon_x F(x)) \to (Ex)F(x).$$

Combining the two implications into a single formula by Rule IX, p. 47, we have finally the bi-implication

$$(Ex)F(x) \leftrightarrow F(\varepsilon_x F(x)).$$

If we now substitute $\overline{F(x)}$ for $F(x)$ and use the identical formula $(X \leftrightarrow Y) \rightarrow (\overline{X} \leftrightarrow \overline{Y})$, we readily obtain the further bi-implication

$$(x)F(x) \leftrightarrow F(\varepsilon_x \overline{F(x)}).$$

This argument shows that, if we have already taken the ε-symbol as primitive and adopted the ε-formula

(g) $$F(y) \rightarrow F(\varepsilon_x F(x))$$

as an axiom, we can introduce the quantifiers by explicit definition as follows:

$$(Ex)F(x) \leftrightarrow F(\varepsilon_x F(x)),$$
$$(x)F(x) \leftrightarrow F(\varepsilon_x \overline{F(x)}).$$

When this course is adopted, the formulae (e) and (f) can be omitted from the list of axioms, since (f) is then the ε-formula (g) itself, and (e) may be derived from (g) by the following sequence of steps:

$$\overline{F(y)} \rightarrow \overline{F(\varepsilon_x \overline{F(x)})} \qquad \qquad [\text{(g)} \ \overline{F}/F]$$
$$F(\varepsilon_x \overline{F(x)}) \rightarrow F(y)$$
$$(x)F(x) \rightarrow F(y).$$

Like the ι-symbol, the ε-symbol is eliminable whenever it occurs in the course of a derivation but does not occur either in the initial formulae or in the end-formula. To give precise expression to this obviously important metalogical principle we must revert to the calculus of predicates as we originally conceived it, with the quantifiers taken as primitive and the formulae (e) and (f) adopted as axioms. The ε-symbol is to be adjoined to this calculus, and the ε-formula (g) taken as a further axiom, but the quantifiers are to be retained as primitive constituents of the calculus. We can then formulate the following theorem on the possibility of eliminating the ε-symbol, which embodies both the *second ε-theorem* of Hilbert and Bernays (*Grundlagen*, II, p. 18) and a refinement of the same theorem (*ibid.*, p. 141).

THEOREM 2. (i) *Let a formula* $\mathfrak{A}$ *be derivable in the formal system* F *which we obtain from the restricted calculus of predicates when we take as additional symbols the ε-symbol and certain symbols for constant individuals, predicates, and individual functions (i.e. terms which involve free individual variables), and as additional axioms the ε-formula and certain axioms* $\mathfrak{P}_1, \ldots, \mathfrak{P}_k$ *which do not contain either the symbol ε or any propositional or predicate variable. Then, provided that* $\mathfrak{A}$ *does not itself contain any ε-symbol, it can be derived from the axioms* $\mathfrak{P}_1, \ldots, \mathfrak{P}_k$ *by means of the calculus of predicates alone, without use of the ε-symbol.*

(ii) *Let a formula* $\mathfrak{B}$ *be derivable in the formal system* F' *which we obtain*

*from the restricted calculus of predicates when we take as additional symbols
the ε-symbol and the symbol for identity, and as additional axioms the
ε-formula and the axioms* (J_1) *and* (J_2). *Then, provided that* $\mathfrak{B}$ *does not
itself contain any ε-symbol, it can be derived without use of the ε-symbol.*

It might be imagined at first glance that (ii) was no more than a
special case of (i), with (J_1) and (J_2) as $\mathfrak{P}_1$ and $\mathfrak{P}_2$. This is not the case,
however, since the second axiom for identity (J_2), namely

$$a = b \rightarrow (F(a) \rightarrow F(b)),$$

contains the predicate variable $F(-)$; and the presence of this variable
in fact adds very considerably to the difficulty of proving the theorem.
For a full discussion of the proof of both parts of the theorem the reader
should consult the second volume of Hilbert and Bernays.

4.1 Symbolic resolution of existential axioms

When Hilbert introduced his ε-symbol to take the place of the older
ι-symbol, he did not do so lightly, merely for the sake of achieving
greater generality. The ε-symbol was in fact devised for a quite
specific purpose, and in the present section we shall try to indicate what
it was that Hilbert was trying to do and to what extent the ε-symbol
met his requirements.

Hilbert's main achievement in the realm of foundations of mathematics was, as we shall see in Chapter 7, his creation of the new discipline known as metamathematics, in which entire mathematical
theories and their structural properties are taken as objects of study.
The typical metamathematical procedure is first of all to convert some
mathematical theory, by formalization of its intuitive content, into a
formal system of the kind that we have described in §3, and then to
prove general theorems about the properties of this formal system.
The central problem is always that of proving the consistency of the
theory under consideration; and the standard way of solving this
problem is by showing that some particular formula of the corresponding formal system is underivable in that system. In the case of arithmetic, the formula $0 \neq 0$ is the one usually considered.

Now the procedure for setting up a formal system is, as we have seen,
to take a suitable logical calculus and then to adjoin to it the necessary
additional symbols and axioms. The logical calculus that is chosen
must obviously be powerful enough to allow formalization of the essential inferences that are used in the mathematical theory to which the
formal system is meant to correspond; but, in view of the fact that it
is the structure to which this calculus gives rise that has to be studied
metamathematically, we certainly do not want the logic to be more
elaborate than is absolutely necessary. Much the same can be said
also of the formalized mathematical axioms. These should be taken

in the simplest form that is consonant with their being strong enough
to serve as the ultimate mathematical premisses of the system.

The strategy at which Hilbert ultimately arrived is expounded in
detail in the two volumes of *Grundlagen der Mathematik*, and particularly in the first three sections of Volume II.   The first move is to
begin with what might be called a 'straight' formalization of the
mathematical theory, which we obtain by taking the calculus of predicates and adjoining to it ordinary mathematical axioms, expressed
formally in the symbolism of this calculus.   Such a formal system will
correspond in the most direct manner possible to the intuitive theory
on which it is modelled, but we may expect it to be more complicated
than is necessary as an object of metamathematical investigation.   It
must therefore be modified, with the object of reducing as far as
possible its formal complexity without sacrificing any of its mathematical content. Hilbert has shown that two important kinds of modification can be effected: (i) total elimination of bound variables from the
axioms, and (ii) replacement of the full calculus of predicates by what
is known as the *elementary calculus with free variables*.   This elementary
calculus is a weakened system of symbolic logic, which we obtain from
the calculus of predicates when we exclude bound variables from well-
formed formulae, at the same time dropping the axioms (e) and (f) and
the rules (γ) and (δ).

Let us consider first the elimination of bound variables from the
axioms.   Any axiom may be put in prenex normal form $\mathfrak{A}$, with all the
quantifiers at the beginning (see p. 73); and then, if it contains quantifiers at all, it either begins with a universal quantifier and is of the
form [1] $(x)\mathfrak{A}_1(x)$, or else it begins with an existential quantifier and is of
the form $(Ex)\mathfrak{A}_1(x)$.   In the first case we simply replace $(x)\mathfrak{A}_1(x)$ by
$\mathfrak{A}_1(a)$, with a free variable a instead of the bound variable x; and we
then know (cf. p. 73) that $(x)\mathfrak{A}_1(x)$ and $\mathfrak{A}_1(a)$ are deductively equivalent.   In the second case we replace $(Ex)\mathfrak{A}_1(x)$ by $\mathfrak{A}_1(\varepsilon_x\mathfrak{A}_1(x))$, at the
same time extending the calculus of predicates by incorporating in it
the ε-symbol and the ε-formula.   Then $(Ex)\mathfrak{A}_1(x)$ and $\mathfrak{A}_1(\varepsilon_x\mathfrak{A}_1(x))$ are
convertible, and *a fortiori* deductively equivalent.   If the expression
$\mathfrak{A}_1(x)$ in either of the two cases is free from quantifiers, we have achieved
our initial purpose; but if not, we repeat the same procedure, with $\mathfrak{A}_1$
in place of $\mathfrak{A}$, in order to eliminate a second quantifier.   Continuing
in this way, we are able to eliminate all quantifiers from $\mathfrak{A}$ in a finite
number of steps.

If, when the quantifier (Ex) is eliminated from $(Ex)\mathfrak{A}_1(x)$ in the manner described, the formula $\mathfrak{A}_1(x)$ contains no free variable except x, the

---

[1] Since the 'x' and 'a' in the argument that follows could equally well be any other
letters, we ought strictly to use syntactic variables '$\mathfrak{x}$' and '$\mathfrak{a}$'; but to do this would
be to blur an even more important distinction on p. 106.

term $\varepsilon_x \mathfrak{A}_1(x)$ will involve no free variable at all; but if $\mathfrak{A}_1(x)$ contains the free variables $x, a, \ldots, k$, this ε-term will itself contain $a, \ldots, k$ as free variables. In the first case we accordingly introduce a new (constant) individual symbol, $\mathfrak{s}$ say, for $\varepsilon_x \mathfrak{A}_1(x)$, while in the second case we introduce a function symbol $\mathfrak{f}(a, \ldots, k)$. If we now lay down an explicit definition

$$\mathfrak{s} = \varepsilon_x \mathfrak{A}_1(x)$$

or

$$\mathfrak{f}(a, \ldots, k) = \varepsilon_x \mathfrak{A}_1(x, a, \ldots, k),$$

as the case may be, we can write the axiom by which $(Ex)\mathfrak{A}_1(x)$ is to be replaced as $\mathfrak{A}_1(\mathfrak{s})$ or $\mathfrak{A}_1(\mathfrak{f}(a, \ldots, k), a, \ldots, k)$. If explicit definitions are used in this way whenever existential quantifiers are eliminated from the original axiom $\mathfrak{A}$, we shall obtain finally an axiom $\mathfrak{A}^*$ which contains only free variables and symbols for constant individuals and functions. Thus—taking the examples adduced by Hilbert and Bernays (*Grundlagen*, II, p. 7)—we can rewrite an axiom of the form

$$(Ex)(y)(Ez)\mathfrak{A}(x,y,z)$$

as

$$\mathfrak{A}(\mathfrak{s}, a, \mathfrak{f}(a)),$$

and one of the form

$$(x)(Ey)(Ez)(u)(Ev)\mathfrak{A}(x,y,z,u,v,a,b)$$

as

$$\mathfrak{A}(c, \mathfrak{f}(a,b,c), \mathfrak{g}(a,b,c), d, \mathfrak{h}(a,b,c,d), a, b).$$

The process of eliminating existential quantifiers from axioms by introducing new symbols, such as $\mathfrak{s}$ and $\mathfrak{f}(a, \ldots, k)$, for the individuals and functions that are declared to exist, is referred to by Hilbert and Bernays as 'symbolic resolution' (*symbolische Auflösung*) of existential axioms. Plainly, the formal procedure that we have described can always be used to remove the existential quantifiers from an axiom when this has been put in prenex normal form—but we still have to ask whether the totality of derivable formulae remains the same as it was initially. Indeed this totality is obviously enlarged, since there are now derivable formulae in which the newly-introduced symbols occur; but, by Theorem 2 on p. 103, we can assert that any formula which is derivable from the new axioms is also derivable from the original axioms, *provided only that it does not itself contain any of the symbols introduced by the process of symbolic resolution*. Since the old axioms are readily derivable from the new ones by the rules of the calculus of predicates, we see that a formula in which none of the new constant symbols appears is derivable in the old system if and only if it is derivable in the new one. We are thus able, in particular, to prove the consistency of the original system by showing that there is a formula in that system which cannot be derived from the modified axioms.

The argument just developed presupposes that the axioms of the formal system considered are all what are called *proper* axioms (*eigentliche Axiome*), that is to say axioms that contain no propositional or predicate variables, for it is only in such circumstances that Theorem 2 is applicable.

We turn now to the second way in which formal systems can sometimes be simplified for metamathematical purposes, namely by replacement of the calculus of predicates by the elementary calculus with free variables. That such simplification is possible follows from another very general theorem established by Hilbert and Bernays, and called by them the *first ε-theorem*. This theorem can be stated in the following terms (*Grundlagen*, II, p. 79):

THEOREM 3. *Let* F *be a formal system which is obtained from the restricted calculus of predicates by adjunction of* (1) *the ε-symbol and the ε-formula,* (2) *the symbol for identity and the axioms* (J_1) *and* (J_2), *and* (3) *certain constant symbols for individuals, functions, and predicates, together with proper axioms* $\mathfrak{P}_1, \ldots, \mathfrak{P}_k$, *without bound variables, that contain these symbols. Then if* $\mathfrak{A}$ *is a formula, free from bound variables, that is derivable in* F, *a derivation of* $\mathfrak{A}$ *can be constructed which uses only the elementary calculus with free variables.*

Our task in proving the consistency of a given formal system F is to show that some one formula $\mathfrak{E}$ is underivable in F; and we have already seen (p. 106) that to this end we may replace the given system F by one with all bound variables removed from the axioms, though perhaps at the cost of introducing the ε-symbol into the logical calculus on which the system is based. Theorem 3 now assures us that, as long as we have chosen for $\mathfrak{E}$ a formula that contains no bound variables, the only derivations that need to be taken into account are those which can be carried out by means of the severely restricted elementary calculus with free variables.

5 Classes and relations

The system of symbolic logic that we now have at our disposal is well suited to the analysis of deductive arguments, and it finds its most characteristic applications, of course, in the field of mathematics. Not only can the logical structure of mathematical theories be clarified with the aid of the logical calculus, but many mathematical concepts can themselves be analysed in purely logical terms. We have already seen how to handle formally the mathematically important relation of identity, and we have also seen how the ι-symbol and the ε-symbol can be used in order to formalize definite and indefinite descriptions;

but there is still one very widely used logical concept that we have not yet dealt with—namely the concept of *class* or *set*—and we must now consider how this, too, can be incorporated in our formal system.

Much has been written by philosophers on the subject of classes, and the arguments are often difficult and subtle; but we can confine ourselves for the present to the purely formal part of the theory, and this is relatively simple. By a *class* we ordinarily mean some aggregate or totality of entities, distinguished from all other entities by their possession of a particular common characteristic. Expressing this rather vague idea in the language that we have been using, we might say that a class is a part of the domain of individuals which is obtained by separating off all those of its members which have a certain property. We begin, therefore, with a propositional function $\Phi(x)$ of one argument, represented in the formal system by a formula $\mathfrak{A}(x)$ in which the variable x occurs free, and we separate those individuals $\mathfrak{a}$ for which the proposition $\Phi(\mathfrak{a})$ has the truth-value T from those for which it has the truth-value F. The individuals of the first kind make up a class, and we denote this class by $\{x \,|\, \mathfrak{A}(x)\}$,[1] using the letter '$x$' as a bound variable. We shall also want to be able to use single letters as names of classes, and for clarity we shall reserve small Greek letters for this purpose. If α is any class, we express the statement 'the individual $\mathfrak{a}$ belongs to the class α' in symbols by writing $\mathfrak{a} \in \alpha$.

The language of classes is intuitively very suggestive, which may explain why it appeals so strongly to mathematicians; but in principle, nevertheless, it is superfluous. We shall treat it as derivative from the primary language of propositions and propositional functions. The only type of reference to classes that we ultimately need is that made in atomic propositions of the form $\mathfrak{a} \in \alpha$, which assert that such and such an individual belongs to such and such a class; and if $\alpha = \{x \,|\, \mathfrak{A}(x)\}$, then the statement $\mathfrak{a} \in \alpha$ amounts to exactly the same thing as the statement $\mathfrak{A}(\mathfrak{a})$. We are able in this way to introduce the language and symbolism of classes, and then to make formal statements that are closely modelled on familiar statements of mathematics, without any essential strengthening of our existing system of logic.

If $\alpha = \{x \,|\, \mathfrak{A}(x)\}$ and $\beta = \{x \,|\, \mathfrak{B}(x)\}$, we can define the *union* $\alpha \cup \beta$ and the *intersection* $\alpha \cap \beta$ of α and β in terms of the logical connectives $\vee$ and $\&$ by putting

$$\alpha \cup \beta = \{x \,|\, \mathfrak{A}(x) \vee \mathfrak{B}(x)\}$$

and

$$\alpha \cap \beta = \{x \,|\, \mathfrak{A}(x) \,\&\, \mathfrak{B}(x)\},$$

---

[1] In the older literature the notation $\hat{x}\mathfrak{A}(x)$, introduced by Russell, is used instead of $\{x|\mathfrak{A}(x)\}$, and we shall occasionally have reason to designate classes in this alternative way.

and we can also define the *complement* $\complement\alpha$ of α (with respect to the entire domain of individuals) by putting

$$\complement\alpha = \{x \mid \overline{\mathfrak{A}(x)}\}.$$

Every formula that is built up out of certain formulae $\mathfrak{A}_1(x), \ldots, \mathfrak{A}_n(x)$ by means of the operators of the propositional calculus now defines a class that is expressible in terms of the n classes $\{x \mid \mathfrak{A}_i(x)\}$ by means of the operators $\cup, \cap, \complement$ which have just been defined; and every identical formula of the propositional calculus that has the form $\mathfrak{B} \leftrightarrow \mathfrak{C}$ gives rise, when arbitrary predicates with a single argument x are substituted for the propositional variables in it, to an identity between classes. It is thus a direct consequence of the connexion between the logical constants $\vee, \&, {}^{-}$ of the propositional calculus and the operators $\cup, \cap, \complement$ of the theory of classes that boolean algebra, which we originally met (p. 32) as an algebra of propositions, has an alternative interpretation as an algebra of classes.

A further basic relation in the theory of classes is the relation of *inclusion*, $\alpha \subset \beta$, which we are now able to define explicitly by writing

$$\alpha \subset \beta \leftrightarrow (x)(x \in \alpha \rightarrow x \in \beta).$$

If $\alpha = \{x \mid \mathfrak{A}(x)\}$ and $\beta = \{x \mid \mathfrak{B}(x)\}$, the condition for α to be included in β reduces to $(x)(\mathfrak{A}(x) \rightarrow \mathfrak{B}(x))$. And if we can make the stronger assertion $(x)(\mathfrak{A}(x) \leftrightarrow \mathfrak{B}(x))$, then α and β are each included in the other, and thus in this case $\alpha = \beta$.

The *empty class*[1] (or *null class*) Λ and the *universal class* V (i.e. the entire domain of individuals) can be defined respectively by means of any identically false and any identically true propositional function. We can, in particular, adopt the definitions

$$\Lambda = \{x \mid x \neq x\}$$

and

$$V = \{x \mid x = x\}.$$

Just as a formula $\mathfrak{A}(x)$ with a single free variable determines a class of individuals $\{x \mid \mathfrak{A}(x)\}$, so a formula $\mathfrak{A}(x,y)$ with two free variables determines a class of ordered pairs of individuals, the elements of this class being all those ordered pairs $(\mathfrak{a},\mathfrak{b})$ for which the proposition expressed by $\mathfrak{A}(\mathfrak{a},\mathfrak{b})$ is true. We denote the class of ordered pairs by $\{xy \mid \mathfrak{A}(x,y)\}$. Now a class of ordered pairs is just a *relation* taken 'in

---

[1] The empty class is important in mathematics, and mathematicians often denote it by $\emptyset$, in preference to the symbol Λ that is more usual in symbolic logic. Mathematicians are also in the habit of distinguishing between a wider and a narrower relation of inclusion between classes. Thus (i) they say that α *is included in* β, or α *is a subclass of* β, if $(x)(x \in \alpha \rightarrow x \in \beta)$, and for this relation they often write $\alpha \subseteq \beta$; and (ii) they say that α is *strictly included* in β, or is a *proper subclass* of β, if $\alpha \subseteq \beta \ \& \ \alpha \neq \beta$, and for this narrower relation they then write $\alpha \subset \beta$.

extension', that is to say as the actual totality of related pairs, and not as some 'intensional' functional connexion by virtue of which these pairs are all associated. The class $\{xy \mid \mathfrak{A}(x,y)\}$ is thus that relation $\mathfrak{R}$ which holds between $\mathfrak{a}$ and $\mathfrak{b}$ if and only if $\mathfrak{A}(\mathfrak{a},\mathfrak{b})$. When $\mathfrak{a}$ and $\mathfrak{b}$ stand in the relation $\mathfrak{R}$ we can express this fact symbolically by writing $\mathfrak{a}\mathfrak{R}\mathfrak{b}$, with the symbol '$\mathfrak{R}$' for the relation placed between the name '$\mathfrak{a}$' of the *referent* and the name '$\mathfrak{b}$' of the *relatum*, as is customary in the case of such common relations as $=$, $\rightarrow$, and $\in$.

Every relation $\mathfrak{R}$ has a *converse* $\breve{\mathfrak{R}}$; and if $\mathfrak{R} = \{xy \mid \mathfrak{A}(x,y)\}$, then $\breve{\mathfrak{R}} = \{xy \mid \mathfrak{A}(y,x)\}$. If $\breve{\mathfrak{R}} = \mathfrak{R}$, the relation $\mathfrak{R}$ is said to be *symmetrical*, and this is the case if and only if $(x)(y)(\mathfrak{A}(x,y) \leftrightarrow \mathfrak{A}(y,x))$. It should be clear from these simple examples how formal properties of relations can be handled by means of the calculus of predicates.

Relations of the type $\{xy \mid \mathfrak{A}(x,y)\}$ will sometimes be referred to more specifically as *two-term relations*. Any propositional function $\mathfrak{A}(x_1, \ldots, x_n)$ of n arguments gives rise in a similar way to an *n-term relation* $\{x_1 \ldots x_n \mid \mathfrak{A}(x_1, \ldots, x_n)\}$, i.e. a class of ordered *n*-tuples.

Such, then, is the symbolism needed for classes and relations, as commonly conceived by mathematicians. We shall give further details of the handling of relations in Chapter 6, when discussing *Principia Mathematica*; and we shall take up the subject of classes again in Chapter 11, where we give an account of the axiomatic theory of sets that has now largely supplanted the older 'logical' treatment of classes.

6   The extended calculus of predicates

The basis of symbolic logic, as we now understand it, is the calculus of predicates, presented axiomatically as in Chapter 3, §3; and the various extensions and refinements that we have been discussing in the present chapter can all be accommodated in this basic calculus by adjunction of additional symbols together with suitable axioms. There is one particular extension, however, which cannot be effected without changing fundamentally the elementary character of the calculus, but which must nevertheless be undertaken if symbolic logic is to be made comparable in generality with the logic implicit in ordinary mathematical reasoning. The calculus of predicates, as it at present stands, certainly does not have the greatest degree of generality that we could look for in a system of symbolic logic, for the only variables that can occur bound, or that can be arguments of predicates, are individual variables. For this reason, this particular calculus is often referred to as the *restricted* calculus of predicates (*engerer Prädikatenkalkül*), in contrast to the *extended* calculus of predicates (*erweiterter Prädikaten-kalkül*), in which predicate variables can be handled with the same freedom as individual variables.

It frequently happens in mathematics that we encounter forms of statement, as well as inferences, that cannot be formalized at all, or at best can only be formalized in an indirect and awkward way, when predicate variables are not allowed to occur as arguments or as bound variables. We often have occasion, for example, to consider classes of classes; and, in view of what we have said in §5 on the subject of classes, this amounts to considering predicates of predicates.

Again, we pointed out earlier in this chapter, when discussing the relation of identity, that in order to define identity in purely logical terms we would need to write

$$x = y \leftrightarrow (F)(F(x) \leftrightarrow F(y)),$$

with F occurring as a bound predicate variable. We were only able to avoid introducing a bound predicate variable in this way by taking ' = ' as an additional primitive symbol and adopting as axioms for it the two formulae

(J$_1$) $a = a$,

(J$_2$) $a = b \rightarrow (F(a) \rightarrow F(b))$,

in which the variables are all free. These axioms are in fact sufficient for purely formal purposes, although they do not comprise a full logical analysis of identity.

In Cantor's theory of cardinal numbers, to give yet a further example, bound predicate variables appear to be unavoidable. We say in this theory that two classes α and β are *equipotent* if and only if they can be put in one-one correspondence. If $\alpha = \{x \mid \mathfrak{A}(x)\}$ and $\beta = \{x \mid \mathfrak{B}(x)\}$, the condition for equipotency is accordingly

$$(EF)\{(x)[\mathfrak{A}(x) \rightarrow (Ey)[F(x,y) \And \mathfrak{B}(y) \And (z)((F(x,z) \And \mathfrak{B}(z)) \rightarrow y = z)]] \And$$
$$\And (y)[\mathfrak{B}(y) \rightarrow (Ex)[F(x,y) \And \mathfrak{A}(x) \And (z)((F(z,y) \And \mathfrak{A}(z)) \rightarrow x = z)]]\},$$

with the predicate variable F bound by an existential quantifier.

There is, of course, no difficulty whatever in extending the *symbolism* of the calculus of predicates in such a way that expressions like this can be written down. What gives us trouble is the problem of fashioning the resulting totality of formal expressions into a coherent system, whether this be a semantically conceived system of symbolic logic, based on some suitable intuitive interpretation of the formulae, or an abstract system that is defined syntactically.

The first obstacle to be overcome is a latent circularity in the logic of predicates, to which Russell drew attention in *The Principles of Mathematics* (1903). When provision is made in the logical symbolism for predicates of predicates, a fundamental distinction that we made when we first introduced predicates into the logical calculus is at once lost, namely the distinction between predicates as such, denoted by capital letters, and arguments of predicates (i.e. individuals) denoted by small letters. There is now nothing to prevent one and the same symbol from occurring in a formula in both capacities, and we can even go so far as to construct the formula $F(F)$, which expresses in symbols the circular utterance 'F is a predicate of itself'. Provision within the logical system of such unrestricted means of formal expression, however, renders the system inconsistent. Consider, for example, the formula $F(F)$ already mentioned, in which F is a predicate with a single argument. This formula expresses a property (i.e. a predicate) of F, namely self-reference, and we may introduce a symbol for this property by explicit definition:

$$\Re\mathfrak{f}(F) \leftrightarrow F(F).$$

Now let us substitute the constant predicate $\overline{\Re\mathfrak{f}}$ for the predicate variable F in this bi-implication. We then have

$$\Re\mathfrak{f}\,(\overline{\Re\mathfrak{f}}) \leftrightarrow \overline{\Re\mathfrak{f}\,(\overline{\Re\mathfrak{f}})},$$

a formula which expresses a contradiction.

The antinomy or paradox that we have here can be developed equally well for predicates and for classes, and it is indeed in terms of classes that it is best known. It was propounded in this form by Bertrand Russell, who saw clearly its paramount importance for logic, and took steps to safeguard his logical system in *Principia Mathematica* against such a possibility of contradiction.

6.1   Russell's antinomy

A class is to be counted as well-defined when, no matter what entity may be chosen, either this entity is a member of the class or it is not a member of the class. But classes are themselves entities, and we can therefore significantly ask, in relation to any class α, whether or not α itself is among the members of α. The class of all natural numbers, for instance, is not a natural number, whereas the class of all classes is a class. Now let us denote by ω the class of those classes that are not members of themselves, i.e. the class $\{x \mid x \notin x\}$; and let us then consider the proposition $\omega \in \omega$. By the law of excluded middle, expressed in the propositional calculus by the formula $X \vee \bar{X}$, either $\omega \in \omega$ or $\omega \notin \omega$ is a true assertion; but it is easily seen that each of the two propositions leads to a contradiction and is thus disproved. For suppose first of all that $\omega \in \omega$. Then, as a member of ω, the entity ω must have the defining property of this class, and thus $\omega \notin \omega$. If, on the other hand, we suppose that $\omega \notin \omega$, then this means that ω has the defining property of the class ω, and therefore $\omega \in \omega$.

Since the argument that we have developed issues in this way in a flat contradiction, it must somehow be fallacious; and Russell himself traced the fallacy to a breach of what he called the 'vicious-circle principle'. In the chapter of *Principia Mathematica* in which this topic is dealt with he assembled a collection of seven different paradoxes,[1] all of which were based on the same circular type of reasoning, and then he resolved them by making their circularity explicit. We cannot do better than quote his own words on the subject of vicious circles.

'An analysis of the paradoxes to be avoided shows that they all result from a certain kind of vicious circle. The vicious circles in question arise from supposing that a collection of objects may contain members which can only be defined by means of the collection as a whole. Thus, for example, the collection of *propositions* will be supposed to contain a proposition stating that "all propositions are either true or false". It would seem, however, that such a statement could not be legitimate unless "all propositions" referred to some already definite collection, which it cannot do if new propositions are created by statements about "all propositions". We shall, therefore, have to say that statements about "all propositions" are meaningless. More generally, given any set of objects such that, if we suppose the set to have a total, it will contain members which presuppose this total, then such a set cannot have a total. By saying that a set has "no total", we mean, primarily, that no significant statement can be made about "all its members". . . .

The principle which enables us to avoid illegitimate totalities may be stated as follows: "Whatever involves *all* of a collection must not be one of the collection"; or, conversely: "If, provided a certain collection had a total, it would have members only definable in terms of that total, then the said collection has no total." We shall call this the "vicious circle principle", because it enables us to avoid the vicious circles involved in the assumption of illegitimate totalities. Arguments which are condemned by the vicious-circle principle will be called "vicious-circle fallacies". Such arguments, in certain circumstances, may lead to contradictions, but it often happens that the conclusions to which they lead are in fact true, though the arguments are fallacious. Take, for example, the law of excluded middle, in the form "all propositions are true or false". If from this law we argue that, because the law of excluded middle is a proposition, therefore the law of excluded middle is true or false, we incur a vicious-circle fallacy. "All propositions" must be in some way limited before it becomes a legitimate totality, and any limitation which makes it legitimate must make any statement about the totality fall outside the totality. Similarly, the imaginary sceptic, who asserts that he knows nothing, and is refuted by being asked if he knows that he knows nothing, has asserted nonsense, and has been fallaciously refuted by an argument which involves a vicious-circle fallacy. . . .

[1] See Note 1 on p. 127, below.

The paradoxes of symbolic logic concern various sorts of objects: propositions, classes, cardinal and ordinal numbers, etc. All these sorts of objects, as we shall show, represent illegitimate totalities, and are therefore capable of giving rise to vicious-circle fallacies.'[1]

Russell's antinomy has thus revealed a circularity that infects the outlook of what may be called "naive logic', a circularity which must be eradicated if this logic is to be transformed into a satisfactory formal theory. To see how this can be done, we need first of all to look more closely at the genesis of vicious circularity.

There are two distinct ways in which illegitimate totalities can give rise to vicious circles. The first way is the one that we have already illustrated by means of Russell's class $\{x \mid x \notin x\}$; and here the circularity is explicit, as we expressly define a totality by means of a predicate which is not itself completely defined unless this same totality is already taken into account. The second way, on the contrary, involves an implicit kind of circularity, produced by a quantifier which is tacitly assumed to range over a totality that is in fact illegitimate. Consider, for example, the paradox of omnipotence: Can an omnipotent being create an indestructible object?

If $\mathfrak{A}$ is omnipotent, then

$$(x)(\mathfrak{A} \text{ can do } x), \tag{1}$$

and it follows from this that $\mathfrak{A}$ can create an object $\mathfrak{a}$ to any given specification. Now let the specification be

$$(y)(y \text{ cannot destroy } \mathfrak{a}). \tag{2}$$

Then, with this choice of $\mathfrak{a}$, we can make the assertion

$$\mathfrak{A} \text{ cannot destroy } \mathfrak{a}; \tag{3}$$

and (1) is plainly contradicted by (3).

In this reasoning we certainly have a vicious-circle fallacy, but one in which the circularity is generated by the universal quantifiers embodied in the definitions of omnipotence and indestructibility, which range over illegitimate totalities.

It will be plain by now that, in trying to construct an extended calculus of predicates, we shall have to control the use of the undiscriminating notion of 'everything'; and to this end we must adopt safeguards sufficient to ensure that all our arguments are anchored securely to the basic domain of individuals, which is supposed given once and for all in the context of each particular discussion, and which can never be enlarged by circular definitions of further entities. Vicious circles can, in fact, be prevented from occurring by a certain device of strati-

---

[1] *Principia Mathematica*, I, second edition, p. 37.

fication, due originally to Russell, the basic idea of which can be expressed quite simply in the following terms. The individuals by themselves constitute a fixed and well-defined totality. So also do the classes of individuals, so do the classes of classes of individuals, and so on. Although we cannot speak significantly of 'all entities', we are justified in speaking of 'all individuals', 'all classes of individuals', etc., for as long as we are careful to keep the various levels entirely separate we do have a genuine totality at each level. The relation of membership $x \in y$, moreover, is only significant when y belongs to the level next above that of x; and we cannot have a meaningful utterance that involves $x \in x$, $x \in y$ & $y \in x$, or any other closed cycle of relations of membership. If we restrict the relation $\in$ in this way, and if we confine quantifiers always to a single level, we can construct a logic of classes from which vicious circles are totally excluded.

When we turn from classes to predicates, however, we find that the situation is more complicated. Individuals still account for the lowest level, but at the next level we now have predicates with a single individual argument, predicates with two individual arguments, and so forth; while higher still in the system of levels we shall meet predicates with arguments that are at several lower levels, as for example $F(x,y) \leftrightarrow F(y,x)$, which is a predicate $\mathfrak{G}(x,y,F)$ with two individuals and one predicate of two individuals as its arguments. The conception of a simple sequence of levels thus breaks down, and what is needed to bring order into this state of affairs is an inductively defined separation of predicates into homogeneous, legitimate totalities—or *types*, as these totalities have come to be called. The original theory of types was proposed by Russell in *Principia Mathematica* (see Chapter 6, §3.2, below) but the treatment that is best suited to our present purpose is the following simplified version of Russell's theory, given by Hilbert and Ackermann.

Every individual or individual variable is said to be of type i; and if a predicate or predicate variable $\mathfrak{A}(x_1, \ldots, x_n)$ has arguments $x_1, \ldots, x_n$, of types $\mathfrak{a}_1, \ldots, \mathfrak{a}_n$ respectively, then $\mathfrak{A}(x_1, \ldots, x_n)$ is said to be of type $(\mathfrak{a}_1, \ldots, \mathfrak{a}_n)$. Thus, for example, any predicate with two individual arguments is of type (i,i), while a predicate with a single argument that is itself a predicate with two individual arguments is of type $((i,i))$. The predicate $\mathfrak{G}(x,y,F)$ of our earlier example is of type $(i,i,(i,i))$.

Having introduced the hierarchy of types in this way, we shall now require bound variables always to be of some definite type. Every quantifier will then range over the totality of all entities of the same type as the bound variable. When this is done, we have a very comprehensive logical calculus (the *Stufenkalkül* of Hilbert and Ackermann) which is secure against vicious circularity and yet is no longer subject to the limitations that we referred to at the beginning of §6.

6.2   Axiomatization of the extended calculus of predicates

The theory of types, then, enables us to eliminate vicious-circle fallacies in a satisfactory way from the extended calculus of predicates; but there still remains a second formidable obstacle in the way of formalization of this calculus. In a famous paper of 1931, Kurt Gödel established certain very general theorems concerning the inherent limitations of formal systems, which we shall discuss in Chapter 8; and one consequence of Gödel's results is that no complete system of axioms for the extended calculus of predicates can exist. In other words, whatever finite set of axioms we may adopt, there will always be formulae, identical for all domains of individuals, that cannot be formally derived. The situation thus brought about is discussed by Hilbert and Ackermann, who stress the fact that the incompleteness of the extended calculus of predicates that was revealed by Gödel, interesting though it is from a theoretical point of view, is of little moment in practice. Whatever system of axioms we choose, there will indeed be formulae that are identically true and yet underivable; but it is not at all difficult to find axioms capable of yielding all the logical principles that are ever likely to be required in mathematical or any other demonstrative reasoning. In Chapter 4, §5 of their book, Hilbert and Ackermann give a system of axioms, a natural extension of the system given earlier for the restricted calculus of predicates, which they believe to be adequate in this sense.

The axioms in this system are of two rather different kinds. On the one hand we have ordinary logical axioms: first the axioms of the propositional calculus, and then the axioms[1]

$$(G)F(G) \to F(H)$$

and

$$F(H) \to (EG)F(G),$$

in which G and H can be of any type $\mathfrak{a}$ and F must then be of type $(\mathfrak{a})$. These new axioms are obvious generalizations of the axioms (e) and (f) of the restricted calculus of predicates.

But then, in addition to the logical axioms, we need two further axioms that fit rather more naturally into the mathematical theory of sets than into symbolic logic. These are the axiom of choice and the axiom of extensionality (cf. Chapter 11, below).

When the extended logic of predicates is made axiomatic in some such way as this, a powerful calculus is obtained, which appears to be sufficient for the formalization of the whole of existing mathematics.

---

[1] Strictly speaking, these new axioms are *axiom-schemata* rather than axioms in the proper sense, and they should be written with syntactic variables $\mathfrak{F}$, $\mathfrak{G}$, $\mathfrak{H}$. Any substitution of proper variables F, G, H (i.e. symbols of the calculus itself) of appropriately related types for the syntactic variables would then yield a formula which would count as a proper axiom.

Hilbert and Ackermann illustrate the use of their extended calculus for this purpose by giving a rapid outline of a formal treatment of the theory of real numbers, and they include in their brief account a derivation of one of the fundamental theorems of analysis, namely the theorem that every bounded set of real numbers possesses a least upper bound.

The extended calculus of predicates thus compares favourably, as regards deductive power, with the intuitive logic that it is meant to formalize, and so we have at last reached a point where it is possible to maintain that the problem of constructing a completely rigorous system of deductive logic has been solved.   This being so, one might imagine that the extended calculus of predicates would have been generally accepted as the standard logic of the present day, and that mathematicians, in particular, would rely heavily upon it.   Such is very far from being the case, however, for the extended calculus of predicates is rarely mentioned in the literature of mathematics, and most mathematicians are hardly even aware of its existence.   One reason for this surprising state of affairs may possibly be that mathematicians tend to be suspicious of the technicalities of logic ; and in any case they have discovered that many of the duties of a logical calculus can in fact be taken over by an essentially mathematical instrument, the axiomatic theory of sets.

Mathematics, as it exists today, is extensional rather than intensional. By this we mean that, when a propositional function enters into a mathematical theory, it is usually the extension of the function (i.e. the totality of entities or sets of entities that satisfy it) rather than its intension (i.e. its 'content' or meaning) that really matters.   This leaning towards extensionality is reflected in a preference for the language of classes or sets over the formally equivalent language of predicates with a single argument ; and in modern mathematics relations, functions, mappings, and the like are all conceived in a similar spirit as classes of ordered pairs.   Thus, even when predicates could equally well be used, classes tend on the whole to be preferred ; and this preference of mathematicians is reinforced by the fact that, as we have already mentioned, some of the axioms needed for the extended calculus of predicates are more naturally formulated for classes than for predicates.   There are thus compelling reasons why a logic of classes (or sets, as they are now more commonly called in mathematics) should be preferred to the logic of predicates.

We shall see in Chapter 11 that the axiomatic theory of sets, in the form given to it by Bernays, is the product of a complete fusion of the more narrowly mathematical treatment of sets, which goes back to Cantor, with the restricted calculus of predicates.   It is this system of Bernays, rather than the extended calculus of predicates, that now has

the strongest claim to recognition as the true heir to the restricted calculus of predicates itself, as a practical system of symbolic logic.   We
shall discuss Bernays's system in Chapter 11, §5.

7   The logical calculus of Bourbaki's 'Éléments de Mathématique'

As we shall see when we come to Chapter 11, Bernays is not alone in
wishing to reinforce elementary symbolic logic by combining with it
the mathematical theory of sets.   Today there are in existence two
major systems of mathematical logic, differing somewhat in the manner
of their presentation though closely allied in ultimate purpose, in which
the restricted calculus of predicates is supplemented by the abstract
theory of sets in the construction of what is believed to be an adequate
logical foundation for a comprehensive system of the whole of pure
mathematics.   One of these logical instruments is the system of
Bernays, to which we have already referred in the previous section,
and the other is that of Bourbaki.

Nicolas Bourbaki, the eminent French mathematician whose profound and invigorating influence upon the mathematical outlook of the
present generation is entirely commensurate with the brilliance of the
varied talents that are united in his person, has now been at work for a
quarter of a century on his great treatise, the *Éléments de Mathématique*,
of which nearly thirty instalments have so far been published (1962).
This work is addressed primarily to working mathematicians, and the
role assigned in it to symbolic logic is accordingly a subordinate one.
Bourbaki has himself acknowledged, in an address[1] delivered before
the Association for Symbolic Logic, that 'in matters pertaining to pure
logic he is self-taught, and labours under all the handicaps that this
implies'; and he has also affirmed his conviction, on the same occasion,
that logic 'must allow the mathematician to say what he really wants
to say, and not try to make him conform to some elaborate and useless
ritual'.   But true though this may be, it is still logic that has to support
the entire edifice of the *Éléments*, which is in fact raised on a foundation
of axioms very similar in scope to those adopted by Bernays in his
rather more theoretical treatment of the unified logic of predicates and
sets.

We must postpone to a later stage consideration of the more specifically mathematical aspects of Bourbaki's system—his axiomatic
treatment of the theory of sets to Chapter 11, and his conception of pure
mathematics as a study of structure to Chapter 12.   In the present
chapter we confine our remarks to the logical calculus on which the
axioms for sets are subsequently to be grafted.   Bourbaki's treatment
of this calculus is to be found at the beginning of the *Éléments*, in

---

[1] This address is printed in the *Journal of Symbolic Logic*, **14** (1949), 1–8, under the
title 'Foundations of mathematics for the working mathematician'.

Book I ('Théorie des Ensembles'), Chapter I ('Description de la mathématique formelle'). When we compare the way in which Bourbaki sets up his system of symbolic logic with the corresponding treatment given by Hilbert and Bernays in their *Grundlagen der Mathematik*, we find that Bourbaki has substantially simplified the handling of the logical calculus by making extensive use of the more recent innovations of Hilbert and his collaborators. Thus, for example, Bourbaki's calculus is based from the outset on the ε-symbol.

Bourbaki's system of logic is in essence the restricted calculus of predicates, extended by inclusion of the relation of identity and the ε-symbol, but his presentation of this calculus diverges in a number of ways from the one that we have so far been considering. We may note, first of all, a number of superficial differences of notation and terminology. The logical operators that are taken as primitive for the propositional calculus are 'not' and 'or' as usual, but 'not' is represented by the symbol '⌐' in preference to '‾'. Connectives, moreover, are written in front of the symbols which they connect instead of between them, so that the use of brackets is unnecessary (cf. Note 1, p. 86, above). The quantifiers 'for all x' and 'for some x' are written as $(\forall x)$ and $(\exists x)$ respectively; and Hilbert's ε-symbol now appears as a τ-symbol, with the Greek letter changed. This latter symbol is taken as primitive, and the quantifiers are defined by means of it.

Bourbaki makes the usual distinction between formulae and terms, but for 'formula' he uses the (French) word *relation*. Any well-formed expression in which only primitive symbols occur is said to be an *assemblage*, though almost from the beginning of his exposition Bourbaki freely uses explicitly defined abbreviated forms of expression in order to avoid much of the cumbrousness of the *assemblages* proper. As the development of the system proceeds, moreover, *abus de langage* is countenanced whenever formal accuracy can with advantage be subordinated to intuitive perspicuity. In general it is Bourbaki's considered policy to simplify the handling of his system both by assimilating his formal procedure to common mathematical practice and also by taking advantage, wherever possible, of metalogical considerations in order to by-pass tedious formal manipulations. He makes extensive use of syntactic variables, for example, (using bold-face Latin type for this purpose) and he works with axiom-schemata in preference to axioms in the narrower sense.

The axiomatic basis of the propositional calculus is provided by four axiom-schemata S1–S4, which are simply our earlier axioms (a)–(d), p. 43, with the propositional variables replaced by syntactic variables. For the calculus of predicates a further axiom-schema S5 is added. This is almost identical with Hilbert's ε-formula (p. 101, above), but the free individual-variable in that formula is replaced by a syntactic term-

variable. The axiom-schema S5 and the ε-formula are easily seen to be
of equal deductive power.

Bourbaki relies heavily upon the deduction theorem as a means of
shortening demonstrations.   This theorem (the *critère de la déduction*
C14; I, §3, No. 3) is directly established only for the propositional calculus, but it extends automatically to the calculus of predicates because
Bourbaki is able to dispense with the rules (α) and (γ) which made our
proof of the theorem so complicated (see Chapter 3, §5, above).

A further simplification that Bourbaki has introduced into the
calculus of predicates is the complete avoidance, in principle though
not in practice, of bound variables, with all the complications that
these give rise to through the possibility of clashes.   His method is
a very simple one.   He introduces a new constant symbol '□', which
is to take over all the functions of bound variables (that is to say
variables bound by τ-symbols, since the quantifiers are here defined in
terms of τ).

If a τ-term contains only one τ-symbol (which may bind more than
one occurrence of the associated variable) Bourbaki replaces the bound
variable, everywhere within the scope of τ, by the symbol '□', and he
joins 'τ' by a bond to each symbol thus introduced.   If a τ-term contains several τ-symbols, binding different variables, all occurrences of
all these variables are to be replaced by a '□', but each '□' must be
connected by a bond to the 'τ' to which it belongs.   Consider, for
example, the formula

$$x \in y \lor x = x,$$

which takes the form

$$\lor \in x \, y = x \, x$$

when it is written strictly according to the rules as an *assemblage*.
From it we may form the τ-term

$$\tau_x \tau_y \, (x \in y \lor x = x),$$

that is to say the *assemblage*

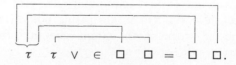

$$\tau \quad \tau \quad \lor \quad \in \quad \square \quad \square \quad = \quad \square \quad \square.$$

Needless to say, the entire apparatus of squares and bonds is wholly
theoretical, and in practice Bourbaki normally writes τ-terms as
$\tau_x R$, $\tau_x \tau_y S$, etc.

The system of logic that Bourbaki builds up by the means that we
have now outlined is already a powerful one, and its power is further

increased when axioms of the abstract theory of sets are added to the more narrowly logical axioms that we have so far considered. It is this aspect of Bourbaki's system that we shall return to in Chapter 11.

8*   Gentzen's calculus of natural deduction

The logical calculus that we have been chiefly concerned with up to now—that is to say the restricted calculus of predicates, treated axiomatically—represents an outstandingly successful application of the methods of mathematics to logic. Its formal simplicity is wholly admirable, and from a purely mathematical point of view it is worthy to be ranked with such perfect embodiments of the mathematical ideal as axiomatic projective geometry and the abstract theory of groups. Its immense value, moreover, as an instrument for use in the study of the structure of deductive systems is placed beyond doubt by the fact that both *Principia Mathematica* and the whole corpus of Hilbert's metamathematics are based directly on it. Strictly as a presentation of logic, however, the axiomatic calculus of predicates is open to criticism on certain counts, and a somewhat different formalization of deductive logic has therefore been proposed by Gerhard Gentzen.[1] Gentzen has called his system a 'calculus of natural deduction', and he claims that it corresponds more closely than does the older form of the calculus of predicates to the kind of argument that is normally used in mathematical proofs.

When working with the calculus of predicates, we are not permitted to use any formula as an initial formula in a derivation unless it is an axiom (either of the logical calculus itself or of the particular mathematical theory to which this calculus is being applied) or else a formula that has already been derived. No provision is made, in other words, for the introduction of hypotheses or temporary assumptions; and yet such assumptions play a very considerable part in ordinary mathematical reasoning. Let us now see, in a few specific cases, how Gentzen formalizes modes of argument that are based on the use of temporary assumptions.

(i) Suppose that, in a mathematical treatise, a proof has to be given of a theorem of the form 'If $\mathfrak{A}$, then $\mathfrak{B}$'. Instead of deriving the implication $\mathfrak{A} \to \mathfrak{B}$ directly, by methods similar to those used in the propositional calculus, the author will most probably suppose that $\mathfrak{A}$ is true, deduce $\mathfrak{B}$ from this hypothesis, and finally assert the required conclusion 'If $\mathfrak{A}$, then $\mathfrak{B}$'. Gentzen accordingly takes as part of

---

[1] Gerhard Karl Erich Gentzen was born in 1909 at Greifswald, on the Baltic coast of Germany, and died in 1945 at Prague. He studied under Weyl and also worked with Hilbert, and although his life was short he made fundamental contributions to both logic and metamathematics. The calculus of natural deduction formed the subject of his inaugural dissertation at Göttingen, which was published under the title 'Untersuchungen über das logische Schließen', *Math. Z.*, **39** (1935), 176–210 and 405–431.

the axiomatic foundation of his calculus of natural deduction the schema

$$\text{(FE)} \quad \frac{\overset{[\mathfrak{A}]}{\mathfrak{B}}}{\mathfrak{A} \to \mathfrak{B},}$$

which is to be interpreted as meaning that if, from the temporary assumption $\mathfrak{A}$, we are able to derive $\mathfrak{B}$ by a finite number of permitted steps, then $\mathfrak{A} \to \mathfrak{B}$ is to count as a derivable formula. Thus, when a formula $\mathfrak{A}$ in square brackets stands above another formula $\mathfrak{B}$, this indicates the availability of a 'derivation' of $\mathfrak{B}$, in accordance with Gentzen's rules, in which $\mathfrak{A}$ may be used as an initial formula. The schema FE is a powerful one, which may be looked upon as asserting from the outset, by way of an 'axiom', the conclusion of the deduction theorem (p. 78 above), without any restriction being imposed on the behaviour of free variables in $\mathfrak{A}$ in the course of the postulated derivation of $\mathfrak{B}$ from $\mathfrak{A}$. It is not in reality quite as sweeping, however, as it may appear at first sight, for Gentzen's rules of derivation only permit $\mathfrak{B}$ to be obtained from $\mathfrak{A}$ in ways that correspond more or less to derivations in the calculus of predicates that satisfy the conditions of the deduction theorem. No provision is made in the calculus for substitution for free variables, and Gentzen also imposes the general restrictive condition that we quote below on p. 124.

(ii) Reverting once more to the logic of ordinary mathematics, we next observe the very extensive use that is made by mathematicians of argument by cases—again a procedure that has no direct representation in the propositional calculus. Suppose we have an exhaustive (though not necessarily exclusive) set of cases, specified by a disjunction $\mathfrak{A}_1 \vee \mathfrak{A}_2 \vee \ldots \vee \mathfrak{A}_r$, and we wish to show that a certain conclusion $\mathfrak{B}$ always holds. We first assume $\mathfrak{A}_1$, and on this assumption we deduce $\mathfrak{B}$. We then begin afresh, assuming $\mathfrak{A}_2$ in place of $\mathfrak{A}_1$, and again we deduce $\mathfrak{B}$, possibly in some quite different way. Continuing in this way, we show that $\mathfrak{B}$ follows from each of the separate assumptions $\mathfrak{A}_1, \ldots, \mathfrak{A}_r$; and then we conclude that $\mathfrak{B}$ holds without qualification. While such a chain of reasoning can readily be justified by the propositional calculus, in which we have the identical formula

$$[(X \to Z) \mathbin{\&} (Y \to Z)] \to [(X \vee Y) \to Z],$$

the justification is rather unwieldy, and so Gentzen once again postulates a schema, namely

$$\text{(OB)} \quad \frac{\mathfrak{A} \vee \mathfrak{B} \quad \overset{[\mathfrak{A}]}{\mathfrak{C}} \quad \overset{[\mathfrak{B}]}{\mathfrak{C}}}{\mathfrak{C}.}$$

(iii) Thirdly, we may mention the following form of argument: 'There exists some individual with the property $\mathfrak{F}$. Let $\mathfrak{a}$ be such an individual. Then, from the fact that $\mathfrak{a}$ has the property $\mathfrak{F}$, we may conclude that $\mathfrak{C}$. Hence $\mathfrak{C}$.' This is an argument that can be formalized with the aid of the ε-symbol, which allows us to identify the '$\mathfrak{a}$' of the argument with the ε-term $\varepsilon_x\mathfrak{F}(x)$; and the theorem on the eliminability of the ε-symbol (p. 103) tells us that using the argument does not really take us beyond the limits of the restricted calculus of predicates. All the same, we are then using elaborate means to deal with what is ostensibly a basic and elementary type of inference; and here also Gentzen prefers to represent the inference directly in his calculus by a schema:

$$
(EB) \qquad \cfrac{(E\mathfrak{x})\mathfrak{F}(\mathfrak{x}) \qquad \begin{array}{c}[\mathfrak{F}(\mathfrak{a})]\\ \mathfrak{C}\end{array}}{\mathfrak{C}.}
$$

It will be seen from what we have been saying that Gentzen's method is to work with *schemata* that represent typical inferential steps instead of with *axioms* that represent basic truths of logic.[1] He has fourteen such schemata, introduced systematically in the following manner. For each of the six logical constants[2] &, $\lor$, $(-)$, $(E-)$, $\to$, $^-$, (*Und-, Oder-, All-, Es-gibt-, Folgt-,* and *Nicht-Zeichen*), there are two schemata, one for introduction (*Einführung*) and one for elimination (*Beseitigung*); and there are two further schemata which do not directly introduce or eliminate constants in quite this way. The complete catalogue of schemata is given as follows.

$$
\text{UE} \qquad\qquad \text{UB} \qquad\qquad\qquad \text{OE}
$$

$$
\cfrac{\mathfrak{A} \quad \mathfrak{B}}{\mathfrak{A} \,\&\, \mathfrak{B}} \qquad \cfrac{\mathfrak{A} \,\&\, \mathfrak{B}}{\mathfrak{A}} \quad \cfrac{\mathfrak{A} \,\&\, \mathfrak{B}}{\mathfrak{B}} \qquad \cfrac{\mathfrak{A}}{\mathfrak{A} \lor \mathfrak{B}} \quad \cfrac{\mathfrak{B}}{\mathfrak{A} \lor \mathfrak{B}}
$$

$$
\text{OB} \qquad\qquad \text{AE} \qquad\qquad \text{AB}
$$

$$
\cfrac{\mathfrak{A} \lor \mathfrak{B} \quad \begin{array}{c}[\mathfrak{A}]\\ \mathfrak{C}\end{array} \quad \begin{array}{c}[\mathfrak{B}]\\ \mathfrak{C}\end{array}}{\mathfrak{C}} \qquad \cfrac{\mathfrak{F}(\mathfrak{a})}{(\mathfrak{x})\mathfrak{F}(\mathfrak{x})} \qquad \cfrac{(\mathfrak{x})\mathfrak{F}(\mathfrak{x})}{\mathfrak{F}(\mathfrak{a})}
$$

---

[1] Schemata have been used in a similar way by Ackermann in his completely revised fourth edition (1959) of *Grundzüge der theoretischen Logik,* in which 'a more modern system of axioms of the Gentzen type is now adopted for the identically true formulae'.

[2] In describing the calculus of natural deduction we continue here to use the same logical symbolism as for the earlier calculus of predicates, although Gentzen's own usage differs in several respects from ours.

$$\text{EE} \qquad\qquad \text{EB} \qquad\qquad \text{FE}$$

$$\frac{\mathfrak{F}(\mathfrak{a})}{(E\mathfrak{x})\mathfrak{F}(\mathfrak{x})} \qquad\qquad \frac{(E\mathfrak{x})\mathfrak{F}(\mathfrak{x}) \quad \overset{[\mathfrak{F}(\mathfrak{a})]}{\mathfrak{C}}}{\mathfrak{C}} \qquad\qquad \frac{\overset{[\mathfrak{A}]}{\mathfrak{B}}}{\mathfrak{A} \to \mathfrak{B}}$$

$$\text{FB} \qquad\qquad \text{NE} \qquad\qquad \text{NB}$$

$$\frac{\mathfrak{A} \quad \mathfrak{A} \to \mathfrak{B}}{\mathfrak{B}} \qquad\qquad \frac{\overset{[\mathfrak{A}]}{\curlywedge}}{\overline{\mathfrak{A}}} \qquad\qquad \frac{\mathfrak{A} \quad \overline{\mathfrak{A}}}{\curlywedge} \qquad \frac{\curlywedge}{\mathfrak{D}} \qquad \frac{\overline{\overline{\mathfrak{A}}}}{\mathfrak{A}}$$

In these schemata, the letter $\mathfrak{a}$ always represents a variable; and the symbol $\curlywedge$ is a logical constant which stands, when intuitively interpreted, for a certain definite proposition, namely 'the false proposition' (*das falsche Aussage*).   Gentzen also uses the symbol $\curlyvee$ to denote 'the true proposition' (*das richtige Aussage*).

Applications of the schemata are all subject to a certain proviso, which Gentzen formulates in the following terms: 'We call the variable that is denoted by the letter $\mathfrak{a}$ in a schema AE or EB the *proper variable* (*Eigenvariable*) of the schema (assuming that it exists, i.e. that the bound individual variable that is denoted by $\mathfrak{x}$ actually occurs in the formula denoted by $\mathfrak{F}(\mathfrak{x})$).   A derivation must then satisfy the following condition: The proper variable of an AE may not occur in the formula denoted by $(\mathfrak{x})\mathfrak{F}(\mathfrak{x})$ in the schema, or in any assumption-formula on which this formula depends; and the proper variable of an EB may not occur in the formula denoted by $(E\mathfrak{x})\mathfrak{F}(\mathfrak{x})$ in the schema, nor in the formula denoted by $\mathfrak{C}$, nor in any assumption-formula on which this is dependent, except the assumption-formula, belonging to the schema, that is denoted by $\mathfrak{F}(\mathfrak{a})$.'

A *derivation* in the calculus of natural deduction is a concatenation of a finite number of applications of the postulated schemata, arranged

$$\frac{\dfrac{\overset{2}{F(a)}}{(Ex)F(x)} \text{ EE} \quad \dfrac{1}{(Ex)F(x)}}{\dfrac{\dfrac{\dfrac{\dfrac{\curlywedge}{F(a)} \text{ NE2}}{\overline{F(a)}}}{(y)\overline{F(y)}} \text{ AE}}{(Ex)F(x) \to (y)\overline{F(y)}} \text{ FE1}} \text{ NB}$$

in the form of a 'tree', so that the formalized argument ultimately converges upon a single end-formula. Gentzen illustrates the process of derivation by the example shown at the foot of p. 124. The tree-structure of this derivation can be represented thus:

If we try to trace a way in reverse through a given derivation, starting from the end-formula and working all the time upwards, we may come to nodes where there is a choice of routes. At any application of UE, EB, FB, or NB, in fact, there are two branches, and at any application of OB there are three. Taking all possible ways through the derivation from the end-formula, we obtain a finite number of finite sequences of formulae ('threads' or *Beweisfäden* in the terminology of Hilbert, cf. p. 215 below), each of which begins at the end-formula of the derivation and ends at an assumption-formula.

If, now, we look at the derivation again in the ordinary way (i.e. reading downwards to the end-formula), we may say that, in any particular thread, all the successive formulae are *dependent* on the assumption-formula at the top of the thread, up to the point at which the assumption is 'discharged'. Discharge occurs when one of the following schemata is used: OB, EB, FE, NE. The conclusion of the schema (i.e. the formula below the line) is then no longer dependent on the assumption in force up to that point. When a derivation is set down, every application of one of the four 'discharging schemata' is given a number, and the same number is written over each assumption-formula discharged by it. In the example given, the assumption $\overline{(Ex)F(x)}$ is discharged by FE1, and the assumption $F(a)$ by NE2. Every well-formed derivation is such that all assumptions are discharged by the time the end-formula is reached. An assumption-formula may occur more than once, provided that all the occurrences are in threads which converge on the discharging schema (cf. the derivation of the formula (a) given below).

By means of the calculus of natural deduction we can readily derive the four axioms (a)–(d) of the propositional calculus without using anything except the schemata already given. The derivations, which now follow, may serve also to provide illustrations of the way in which the new calculus is handled.

(a) $(X \vee X) \to X$:

$$\cfrac{\cfrac{\overset{2}{X \vee X} \quad \overset{1}{X} \quad \overset{1}{X}}{X} \text{ OB1}}{(X \vee X) \to X.} \text{ FE2}$$

(b) $X \to (X \vee Y)$:

$$\cfrac{\cfrac{\overset{1}{X}}{X \vee Y} \text{ OE}}{X \to (X \vee Y).} \text{ FE1}$$

(c) $(X \vee Y) \to (Y \vee X)$:

$$\cfrac{\overset{2}{X \vee Y} \quad \cfrac{\overset{1}{X}}{Y \vee X} \text{ OE} \quad \cfrac{\overset{1}{Y}}{Y \vee X} \text{ OE}}{\cfrac{Y \vee X}{(X \vee Y) \to (Y \vee X).} \text{ FE2}} \text{ OB1}$$

(d) $(X \to Y) \to [(Z \vee X) \to (Z \vee Y)]$:

$$\cfrac{\overset{3}{Z \vee X} \quad \cfrac{\overset{1}{Z}}{Z \vee Y} \text{ OE} \quad \cfrac{\cfrac{\overset{1}{X} \quad \overset{2}{X \to Y}}{Y} \text{ FB}}{Z \vee Y} \text{ OE}}{\cfrac{\cfrac{Z \vee Y}{(Z \vee X) \to (Z \vee Y)} \text{ FE3}}{(X \to Y) \to [(Z \vee X) \to (Z \vee Y)].} \text{ FE2}} \text{ OB1}$$

The four axioms of the propositional calculus have now all been derived, and it is a simple matter to derive also the further axioms (e) and (f) of the restricted calculus of predicates. For axiom (e), i.e. $(x)F(x) \to F(y)$, we use AB with FE; and for axiom (f), i.e. $F(y) \to (Ex)F(x)$, we use EE with FE.

Since the axioms of the calculus of predicates are thus contained implicitly in the schemata of the calculus of natural deduction, it now seems likely that, in making symbolic logic conform more closely to the pattern of deduction as actually practised, Gentzen has not weakened it. In his original paper he went, in fact, fully into the metalogic of his system, and he was able there to establish the complete equivalence of his calculus with the restricted calculus of predicates.   Thus, *a for-mula in the restricted calculus of predicates is derivable in the calculus of natural deduction if and only if it is derivable in the calculus of predicates itself, and therefore if and only if it is an identical formula of that calculus.*

Exercise.   Since the formula $F(y) \to (x)F(x)$ is not identical (cf. p. 71) it is not derivable.   Why can we not derive it by AE and FE, just as we can derive the formula $(x)F(x) \to F(y)$ by AB and FE?

SUPPLEMENTARY NOTES ON CHAPTER 4

1. *The vicious-circle paradoxes.*   In this note we collect together those vicious-circle paradoxes which are most frequently referred to in the litera-ture of mathematical logic (cf. *Principia Mathematica*, I, second edition, p. 60).   For historical information concerning these paradoxes see Fraenkel & Bar-Hillel [1], Chapter 1.

(1) Russell's antinomy (1903): This is the paradox of the class $\{x \,|\, x \notin x\}$, which we have already discussed on p. 112.

(2) Burali-Forti's antinomy (1897): The ordinal numbers, taken in their natural order, form a well-ordered series, and this series accordingly itself has an ordinal number Ω.   But the ordinal number of any segment of the series of ordinal numbers exceeds every number of that segment, and there-fore Ω exceeds any ordinal number whatever.

(3) Cantor's antinomy: The cardinal number of any set S is less than the cardinal number of the set of subsets of S.   In particular, therefore, the cardinal number of the set U of *all* sets is less than the cardinal number of the set of subsets of U, although this latter set is itself a subset of U.

(4) The antinomy of the liar: If a man says 'I am lying', his utterance is self-contradictory, and it cannot be either true or false.   The oldest form of this particular paradox, in the words of *Principia Mathematica*, is that of Epimenides the Cretan, 'who said that all Cretans were liars, and all other statements made by Cretans were certainly lies'.

(5) Richard's antinomy (1905): Let E be the class of all non-terminating decimals that can be defined in a finite number of words.   Since the defini-tions can be arranged lexicographically in a sequence, E can also be formed into a sequence.   Now let the nth digit of the nth member of this sequence be altered systematically according to some definite rule—say by being increased by 1 unless it happens to be 8 or 9, and by being replaced by 1 in these exceptional cases; and let the digit so obtained be taken as the nth digit in a new decimal N $(n = 1, 2, \ldots)$.   Then N differs in at least one decimal place from every member of E, and it therefore does not belong to E; but it is nevertheless a non-terminating decimal, defined in a finite number of words.   See Richard [1].

(6) The possible definitions of specific ordinal numbers can be arranged in a sequence, and there are therefore at most $\aleph_0$ of them.   But the totality of ordinal numbers is not denumerable, and so there exist ordinal numbers which cannot be individually defined.   Among such indefinable ordinals

there is a least, and thus it appears that the description 'the least indefinable ordinal' yields a definition of an entity that cannot be defined.

(7) A paradox similar to (6) can be derived from the description 'the least integer not nameable in fewer than nineteen syllables', which is itself a name that contains only eighteen syllables.

(8) The Grelling-Nelson antinomy (1908): There are adjectives, such as 'English' and 'short', which apply to themselves, and also adjectives, such as 'Latin' and 'long', which do not apply to themselves. Let adjectives of the second kind be described as *heterological*. Then the question 'Is the adjective "heterological" itself heterological?' leads to a contradiction whether it is answered affirmatively or negatively. See Grelling & Nelson [1].

The eight paradoxes that we have here are by no means all of the same kind, and there is more than one natural way of grouping them. One significant distinction is that between those which are strictly logical and those which involve a semantic element as well. The first three may be treated as purely logical, since they can be formulated in the symbolism of a system such as *Principia Mathematica* (though not, of course, derived within the system if this has proper safeguards against inconsistency). The remaining five paradoxes are all of the semantic kind, since they make use of ideas of truth, definability, nameability, and self-reference, which are concerned in one way or another with relations between symbols and what they mean or stand for.

The logical paradoxes have been instrumental in bringing about fundamental advances in logic. It was Russell's antinomy that first revealed the circularity of the extended calculus of predicates, as naively formulated, and thus demonstrated the need for a theory of types or some equivalent restrictive device. And many years later, Rosser's derivation of the Burali-Forti antinomy within the framework of Quine's *Mathematical Logic*, as this was originally set up, forced Quine to reconsider the basic concept of elementhood. See Rosser [3] and Quine [3].

In a somewhat similar way, the semantic paradoxes have also stimulated fundamental inquiry, namely Tarski's formal analysis of truth and other semantic concepts. The results of this investigation are presented in detail in Tarski [2], and we give a brief indication of their nature in the next note.

2. *Tarski's formalization of semantics*. Tarski has insisted that the semantic paradoxes are not to be brushed aside as mere curiosities. In the antinomy of the liar, in particular, entirely normal use of English issues in a flat contradiction; and this shows that the English language breaks down when it is used to express semantic ideas. Tarski comes to the conclusion that a consistent language can never be semantically closed, that is to say it cannot provide for the complete expression of its own semantics. Just as the logical paradoxes point to the need for a hierarchy of types, so the semantic paradoxes show that a hierarchy of languages is equally necessary. For if some given language L is consistent, its semantics cannot all be expressed in L itself, but only in a richer language L'; and then, if L' is consistent, a still richer language L" will be required for its semantics, and so on indefinitely. We thus arrive at a sequence L, L', L", ... of languages

of increasing richness of expression; and when any particular one of these languages is taken as object-language, its successor in the sequence is needed as a metalanguage.

Since natural languages such as English are comparatively ill-defined, and in such languages many things that would be made part of the syntax of a formalized logical language are taken care of tacitly by idiomatic usage, or may even be left to the judgement of whoever employs the language, no rigorous treatment of the semantics of a natural language is possible. Tarski accordingly limits his analysis of semantic concepts to artificial, completely formalized languages.

Tarski concerns himself primarily with one particular semantic concept, namely truth. He does not attempt to give a complete philosophical analysis of this concept, but undertakes only the more limited task of constructing a definition of the term 'true sentence' which shall be both materially adequate and formally correct. His definition is in fact intended to isolate the formal element in the classical notion of truth, the conception expressed by Aristotle in the words: 'To say of what is that it is not, or of what is not that it is, is false, while to say of what is that it is, and of what is not that it is not, is true' (*Metaphysics*, 1011^b).

In order to formulate the criterion of material adequacy that he wishes to apply to proposed definitions of truth, Tarski introduces the sentential function 'X is true if and only if p'. A definition of truth is to be deemed materially adequate if its consequences include every sentence that we are able to obtain from this sentential function by inserting some particular sentence in place of 'p' and a name of this sentence in place of 'X'.

The definition of truth that Tarski puts forward is of a recursive kind. We are supposed to be dealing with some particular object-language L and a suitable metalanguage L', capable of providing names for all the sentences in L. The idea is then to define truth explicitly for some suitable totality of 'elementary' sentences in L, i.e. some totality of sentences out of which all further sentences in L can be formed by logical operations, and to relate the truth-values of composite sentences systematically to the truth-values of their constituents. This idea cannot be implemented directly, however, since the primary use of the logical connectives and the quantifiers is not to generate sentences from sentences but to generate sentential functions from sentential functions. Tarski accordingly develops first of all a theory of the satisfaction of sentential functions, and he then obtains his required theory of the truth of sentences as a special case of this wider theory. In his basic paper [2], he explains the procedure by carrying it out in a particular instance, with a certain fragment of the formalized theory of sets as object-language. More recently, in [4], he has recapitulated his train of thought, this time without giving details of the formal development.

Semantic ideas have also been studied systematically by Carnap, who has attempted to construct a new abstract science of semantics. See his two books *Introduction to Semantics* (1942) and *Meaning and Necessity* (1947), as well as the reviews of these books in Church [6] and Bernays [2] respectively. For a compact introduction to this whole field of study, see Kemeny's article [5] in the *Encyclopædia Britannica*.

3. *The ε-symbol as a selection operator.* Some brief but lucid and informative remarks on Hilbert's ε-operator are made by Fraenkel and Bar-Hillel, [1], pp. 183–185. On the one hand these authors regard the ε-symbol as a logical instrument of such importance that 'the early introduction of ε-terms in the teaching of elementary logic should be seriously considered, in spite of the obvious objections'. But at the same time they are chary of over-estimating the power of the symbol : 'There clearly exists a close connection between the ε-formula and the axiom of choice. This connection should however not be overstated, as it is occasionally done, in the form that the ε-formula is a kind of logical (or generalized) axiom of choice. Indeed, the ε-formula allows for a single selection only, while the axiom of choice allows for a simultaneous selection from each member of an (infinite) set of sets, and guarantees the existence of the set comprising the selected entities. There is, then, no reason to suppose that in a set theory constructed on the basis of an ε-calculus the principle of choice would become generally derivable, unless the specific axioms of that set theory contain ε-terms themselves.' Since an ε-term may involve free variables as parameters, it is certainly capable of taking care of a totality of simultaneous choices ; but whether it provides a formal counterpart of the *set* of selected entities depends on the particular axioms for sets by which the purely logical axioms are supplemented (cf. Chapter 11, below).

Hilbert had only a limited objective in view when he originally introduced the ε-symbol, namely that of facilitating certain metamathematical processes, in particular the symbolic resolution of existential axioms. The more ambitious project of constructing an *ε-calculus*, or system of symbolic logic which embodies a selection operator, has been undertaken more recently by Günter Asser, who has given a thorough and rigorous treatment of the subject in his Berlin *Habilitationsschrift* 'Theorie der logischen Auswahl-funktionen', printed in the *Zeitschrift für mathematische Logik und Grundlagen der Mathematik*, **3** (1957), 30–68. Asser discusses both the axiomatic treatment of possible ε-calculi and the intuitive interpretations that can be given to these calculi as systems of logic ; and he also examines the relation which the treatment of the ε-symbol that is given by Hilbert and Bernays bears to them.

4. *Additional reading.* Any of the books recommended in Note 8 on p. 56 as sources for the propositional calculus may be consulted for further information concerning symbolic logic in general. Among older works, both *Principia Mathematica* and Lewis & Langford [1] are of considerable value in this respect. For a modern survey of symbolic logic see Hermes & Scholz [1], the opening article of the most recent edition of the *Enzyklopädie der mathematischen Wissenschaften* (1952), in which a masterly account of mathematical logic is compressed into eighty pages.

A treatment in English of Gentzen's calculus of natural deduction is to be found in Quine's paper [5].

PART II

Foundations of Mathematics

'Was beweisbar ist, soll in der Wissenschaft nicht ohne Beweis geglaubt werden.'
R. Dedekind: *Was sind und was sollen die Zahlen?*

Chapter 5

THE CRITICAL MOVEMENT IN MATHEMATICS
IN THE NINETEENTH CENTURY

1 Symbolic logic in relation to the foundations of mathematics

Although symbolic logic, as it exists today, has a secure place as a system of logic in its own right, which has indeed supplanted and rendered wholly obsolete the traditional logic that persisted from the time of Aristotle until less than a century ago, this modern logic nevertheless owes much more to mathematicians than it does to pure logicians, for it originated largely as a by-product of investigations into the logic of mathematics. Close study of the foundations of mathematics, pursued with much vigour and with striking success since the middle of the nineteenth century, and more especially during the past seventy years, has led to a thorough reconsideration of the nature of mathematics and mathematical argument, which has had philosophical repercussions far beyond the boundaries of mathematics itself. In Parts II and III of this book we shall survey, from a historical point of view, the main lines of inquiry that have been traced out by those mathematicians and philosophers who have sought to lay bare the foundations of mathematics; we shall discuss the relationship of mathematics to logic; and we shall attempt to evaluate the epistemological status of mathematical knowledge in the light of what has been discovered.

The connexion between mathematics and logic proves to be far less simple than we might expect; and although symbolic logic provides us with a satisfactory theory of the structure of deductive systems, this is by no means enough to resolve the fundamental problems of the philosophy of mathematics. Mathematical knowledge, we might initially be inclined to say, is set apart from the rest of human knowledge by certain characteristics which spring from its abstract nature. Thus although it may, and frequently does, have applications to the actual world, it is valid primarily—that is to say as 'pure' mathematics—in the realm of ideas; and therefore nothing which may be discovered in the future by scientific observation or experiment can ever shake its established conclusions. Mathematical theorems are accordingly absolute truths, exempt from all further dispute when once they have been proved, and mathematics is the one domain of thought where certainty is attainable.   But plausible as such a view of mathematics may be, we now know that it needs much qualification; and indeed we are today in a position to go far in qualifying it, even though we eventually come up against difficulties that are at present insurmountable.   One conclusion that does seem certain in the light of what has been discovered is that mathematics must be looked upon as an *activity* of thinking, not as a totality of facts of some special kind.   This being so, it is essential that we should see mathematics always in relation to its historical development; for thought is an autonomous process, controlled by principles and criteria which it has itself evolved in the course of its own earlier phases.   We shall therefore examine, first of all, the way in which mathematics has come to possess its characteristic features of apparent absoluteness and certainty, and then in due course we shall pass on to a closer investigation of these features themselves.

2   Greek mathematics

The ideal method of mathematical argument, which does not merely yield knowledge that is demonstrably true but which also exhibits clearly the logical relations that hold between the individual items of knowledge, is traditionally regarded as having found its classical embodiment in the *Elements*, the immortal treatise on geometry and algebra that was written by Euclid in about 300 B.C., probably at Alexandria; and it was indeed in the ancient Greek world that mathematics first assumed its now familiar character of a deductive body of knowledge.   Much factual mathematical information had doubtless existed in considerably earlier times—associated, for example, with Egyptian surveying and building and with Babylonian astronomy— but the Greeks transformed mathematics by making it into a rational system.   We can gather some idea of the nature of the Greek achievement from the mode of construction of the geometrical books of the *Elements*.   A very full discussion of the structure of the *Elements* has been given by Sir Thomas Heath in the introductory chapters of his definitive English translation of the work.[1]   Heath quotes (vol. I, p. 117) a long passage from Aristotle's *Posterior Analytics*, containing a very careful analysis of the idea of a demonstrative science, and he then summarizes Aristotle's view in the following words:

'Every demonstrative science, says Aristotle, must start from indemonstrable principles: otherwise, the steps of demonstration would be endless.   Of these indemonstrable principles some are (*a*) common to all sciences, others are (*b*) particular, or peculiar to the particular science; (*a*) the common principles are the *axioms*, most commonly

---

[1] T. L. Heath: *The Thirteen Books of Euclid's Elements*, translated from the text of Heiberg, with introduction and commentary (3 volumes: Cambridge, 1926, second edition).

illustrated by the axiom that, if equals be subtracted from equals, the remainders are equal. Coming now to (*b*) the principles peculiar to the particular science which must be assumed, we have first the *genus* or subject-matter, the *existence* of which must be assumed, viz. magnitude in the case of geometry, the unit in the case of arithmetic. Under this we must assume *definitions* of manifestations or attributes of the genus, e.g. straight lines, triangles, deflection etc. The definition in itself says nothing as to the existence of the thing defined: it only requires to be understood. But in geometry, in addition to the *genus* and the *definitions*, we have to assume the *existence* of a few *primary* things which are defined, viz. points and lines only: the existence of everything else, e.g. the various figures made up of these, as triangles, squares, tangents, and their properties, e.g. incommensurability etc., has to be proved (as it is proved by construction and demonstration). In arithmetic we assume the *existence* of the *unit*: but, as regards the rest, only the *definitions*, e.g. those of odd, even, square, cube, are assumed, and *existence* has to be *proved*. We have then clearly distinguished, among the indemonstrable principles, *axioms* and *definitions*. A *postulate* is also distinguished from a *hypothesis*, the latter being made with the assent of the learner, the former without such assent or even in opposition to his opinion.'

Such, then, was the conception of a demonstrative science, as it had been developed by Greek mathematicians and philosophers; and it was a science of just this kind that Euclid expounded in his *Elements*—for Euclid and Aristotle lived at almost the same time. The *Elements* opens with an enumeration of the first principles that are to be adopted, classified under the three heads of definitions, postulates, and common notions.

There are twenty-three *definitions*, of which the following are typical:

1. A *point* is that which has no part.

2. A *line* is breadthless length.

3. A *straight line* is a line which lies evenly with the points on itself.

8. A *plane angle* is the inclination to one another of two lines in a plane which meet one another and do not lie in a straight line.

10. When a straight line set up on a straight line makes adjacent angles equal to one another, each of the equal angles is *right*, and the straight line standing on the other is called *perpendicular* to that on which it stands.

15. A *circle* is a plane figure contained by one line such that all the straight lines falling upon it from one point among those lying within the figure are equal to one another.

23. *Parallel* straight lines are straight lines which, being in the same plane and being produced indefinitely in both directions, do not meet one another in either direction.

There are five *postulates*, expressed as follows:

Let the following be postulated:

1. To draw a straight line from any point to any point.
2. To produce a finite straight line continuously in a straight line.
3. To describe a circle with any centre and distance.
4. That all right angles are equal to one another.
5. That, if a straight line falling on two straight lines make the interior angles on the same side less than two right angles, the two straight lines, if produced indefinitely, meet on that side on which are the angles less than two right angles.

Finally, there are five *common notions*:

1. Things which are equal to the same thing are also equal to one another.
2. If equals be added to equals, the wholes are equal.
3. If equals be subtracted from equals, the remainders are equal.
4. Things which coincide with one another are equal to one another.
5. The whole is greater than the part.

Using only the first principles that he had enumerated, Euclid was able to establish, by a systematic process of construction and demonstration, the properties of rectilinear plane figures and circles that make up the most elementary part of what is now known as euclidean geometry; and a generation later similar methods were used by Apollonius in his treatment of the euclidean properties of the conic sections.[1] Euclid began his treatise by considering problems and theorems which concern only the simplest figures, and then, as his store of demonstrated theorems increased, he was able to extend his deductive treatment to figures and situations of a more complicated character. In this way the truths of geometry were lifted out of the sphere of contingent fact and exhibited as truths of reason.

Now when the civilization of the ancient world broke up, mathematics, in common with most of the other forms of rational activity perfected by the Greeks, became stagnant. Fortunately some of the most important mathematical works were preserved, chief among them being Euclid's *Elements* and Ptolemy's *Almagest*.[2] For many centuries, however, mathematics made little progress; and the next major advance, when it eventually came, took place in a new part of the world. This was during the Middle Ages, when the work of Arabian and Indian

---

[1] See Apollonius of Perga: *Treatise on Conic Sections*, edited in modern notation, with introductions including an essay on the earlier history of the subject, by T. L. Heath (Cambridge, 1896).

[2] *Almagest* was the name given by the Arabs to the *Megale Syntaxis* of Claudius Ptolemaeus (Μαθηματικῆς Συντάξεως βιβλία ιγ), the great work in which the famous Alexandrian astronomer of the second century A.D. analysed the motions of the planets by means of a system of epicycles.

mathematicians brought about the emancipation of number from the thraldom of geometry by the creation of an abstract science of arithmetic and algebra. The development of Greek mathematics beyond a certain point had been hampered by the absence of any abstract conception of number, since magnitudes were always thought of as lengths, areas, or volumes; and the highly developed science of demonstration had not been paralleled by any corresponding technique of calculation. This the new Arabic mathematics now made possible.

3   The beginnings of modern mathematics

When the modern era began, the already existing mathematical tradition embraced both the ancient ideal of mathematics as a demonstrative science and the new conception of number as an abstract magnitude. The rise of mathematics as we know it today dates back to the seventeenth century, when two decisive innovations made it possible for mathematics to grow vastly in power and to develop with steadily increasing momentum. The first of these innovations was made by Descartes (1596–1650), who brought into close relation the two then quite separate realms of geometry and algebra. The use of coordinates made it possible to specify curves by equations, and so to determine their geometrical properties by algebraic calculation; and by allowing equations to be represented by graphs, it also prepared the way for the metamorphosis of algebra into analysis, as ideas of functional dependence took shape, and variables and functions came to be thought of in terms of geometrical representations. The second great innovation, out of which evolved the study that came later to be known as analysis, was of course the invention of the infinitesimal calculus by Newton (1642–1727) and Leibniz (1646–1716).

After its modern reawakening, mathematics developed with great rapidity, but at the cost of relinquishing the very high standard of demonstrative rigour that had characterized its earlier phase. Gottlob Frege, the great logician and philosopher of mathematics, looking back in 1884 over the centuries, described what had happened in the following terms:

'After deserting for a time the old Euclidean standards of rigour, mathematics is now returning to them, and even making efforts to go beyond them. In arithmetic, if only because many of its methods and concepts originated in India, it has been the tradition to reason less strictly than in geometry, which was in the main developed by the Greeks. The discovery of higher analysis only served to confirm this tendency; for considerable, almost insuperable, difficulties stood in the way of any rigorous treatment of these subjects, while at the same time small reward seemed likely for the efforts expended in overcoming them. Later developments, however, have shown more and more clearly that in mathematics a mere moral conviction, supported by a mass of successful applications, is not good enough. Proof is now demanded of many things that formerly passed as self-evident. Again and again the limits to the validity of a proposition have been in this way established for the first time. The concepts of function, of continuity, of limit and of infinity have been shown to stand in need of sharper definition. Negative and irrational numbers, which had long since been admitted into science, have had to submit to a closer scrutiny of their credentials. In all directions these same ideals can be seen at work—rigour of proof, precise delimitation of extent of validity, and as a means to this, sharp definition of concepts.'[1]

Demonstrative rigour had been lost, and then, slowly and laboriously, it was recovered again; and Frege, one of the most penetrating of logical critics of mathematics, devoted his life's work to the task of making arithmetic so rigorous that it would surpass even Euclid's geometry in this respect. The gradual recovery, mainly in the course of the nineteenth century, of rigour of mathematical demonstration was the prologue to a much more deliberate study of the foundations of mathematics. This study is, in fact, the topic of Part II of the present book, and the remainder of this chapter will accordingly be devoted to an account of the process that led up to it.

In the seventeenth century, and even well on into the eighteenth, mathematicians of the eminence of Leibniz, Bernoulli, and Euler were ready to put forward for serious consideration arguments involving infinitely small quantities, 'sums' of divergent series, and the like, which are not merely seen today to be erroneous in the light of subsequently acquired knowledge, but which made use of concepts that were not clearly defined even at that time. It is hardly to be wondered at, however, that when the calculus was still a new discovery mathematicians were carried away by the spirit of adventure and were more interested in exploiting the new techniques than in building systematic theories. The magnitude of the discovery that had been made was indeed tremendous. Greek mathematics, it has been said, attained its zenith in the work of Archimedes (287–212 B.C.), who even anticipated the modern identification of the area of a curvilinear figure with a definite integral; but Archimedes could make only limited use of this idea, for want of knowledge of the process of differentiation and its inverse relation to that of integration. As soon as that key had been found, mathematical problems in immense variety were there to be solved. The phase of bold and often hazardous application of the new methods lasted until almost the end of the eighteenth century, when eventually a more critical mood began to prevail. The first half of the nineteenth century was a period in which consolidation of ground

[1] G. Frege: *The Foundations of Arithmetic*, translated by J. L. Austin (Oxford, 1950), §1.

already won went on steadily, while further big advances continued to be made. The great mathematicians of this age, led by Gauss (1777–1855) and Cauchy (1789–1857), were in fact equally active as innovators and as critics.

4   The first phase of the critical movement

The history of the development of mathematics in the nineteenth century has been narrated in masterly fashion by Felix Klein,[1] who tells how the need for more rigour in mathematical demonstration had already begun to be appreciated at the end of the preceding century. The new attitude found its first expression, says Klein, in Legendre's *Éléments de Géométrie* (1794) and Lagrange's *Théorie des Fonctions*[2] (1797), although neither of these works would satisfy us today. Then there came Gauss's *Disquisitiones Arithmeticae* (1801), the argument of which leaves nothing to be desired, even though Gauss was content to accept the elementary operations of arithmetic and algebra as too familiar to need discussion. Gauss concerned himself throughout his life with the important work of strengthening the foundations of mathematics, as we can see from his repeated attempts to devise a satisfactory proof of the 'fundamental theorem of algebra', the theorem which asserts that in the domain of complex numbers every algebraic equation has a root. The notion of complex number itself, which had hitherto remained obscure and controversial, was finally clarified by Gauss. In Klein's words, 'by his geometrical interpretation [of complex numbers] he lifted calculation in a doubly extended manifold once and for all out of the sphere of mystical fantasies into that of clear ideas' (*Entwicklung*, I, p. 54). The extension of analysis from the real to the complex domain was largely the work of Cauchy, who created the theory of functions of a complex variable. Cauchy was perhaps even more influential through his comprehensive reform of the entire realm of analysis, a reform which involved the final banishment from mathematics of the unsatisfactory notions of infinitely small quantities and sums of infinite numbers of terms. Cauchy's method was first of all to give precise meaning to the concept of limit, by means of the ε-definition, and then to define such further concepts as convergence and continuity in terms of this basic concept.

The work of tightening up concepts and proofs went on all through the nineteenth century, until in the end it was the discipline of analysis that came to be accepted as the standard of comparison in questions of

---

[1] F. Klein: *Vorlesungen über die Entwicklung der Mathematik im* 19. *Jahrhundert* (Berlin, 1926).

[2] J.-L. Lagrange: *Théorie des fonctions analytiques, contenant les principes du calcul différentiel, dégagés de toute considération d'infiniment petits et d'évanouissans de limites ou de fluxions, et réduits à l'analyse algébrique des quantités finies* (Paris, Imprimerie de la République, an v.).

rigour, and geometry lost its former pre-eminence in this respect. Analysis owed its eventual perfection very largely to the work of Karl Weierstrass (1815–1897) who, over a period of more than thirty years as professor at Berlin, gave many courses of lectures in which the main branches of analysis were presented with extreme care in severely deductive form. These lectures had an immense influence on the younger mathematicians of the time, who accepted them without question as completely authoritative; and Weierstrass was universally acknowledged by the end of his life as the supreme authority in mathematics—'notre maître à tous', in Hermite's phrase.

There, then, we have one aspect of the critical movement in mathematics, which can be seen as a movement of reform, carried through by mathematicians for the well-being of their subject. But the critical movement also had a second and more specifically logical side, which is even more relevant to our present inquiry. This particular trend is seen most clearly in the work of Dedekind, who was possibly the most logically-minded of all the great creative mathematicians. Richard Dedekind (1831–1916) was born at Brunswick,[1] and he eventually became professor at the *Technische Hochschule* of that city, having in the meantime studied under Gauss at Göttingen. Although he is perhaps best known for his theory of real numbers and his introduction into algebra of the fundamental concept of ideal, he is equally important for the essential part that he played in moulding the new tradition of abstract reasoning that issued directly in the development of 'modern algebra', as presented, for example, by van der Waerden in his well-known book on the subject.[2]

When, in 1872, Dedekind published his famous essay *Stetigkeit und irrationale Zahlen* [Continuity and irrational numbers], he explained in his preface what it was that had prompted him to write it.

'The reflections which are the subject of this little essay date from the autumn of the year 1858. I then found myself, as professor at the Federal Polytechnic at Zürich, for the first time in the position of having to lecture on the elements of the differential calculus, and I felt more keenly than ever before the lack of a rigorous foundation of arithmetic. In dealing with the idea of the approach of a variable quantity to a fixed limiting value, and particularly in proving the theorem that any quantity which increases steadily but not beyond all bounds must tend to a limiting value, I had recourse to geometrical evidence. Indeed I still maintain today that such invoking of geometrical intuition is ex-

---

[1] An account of Dedekind's life and mathematical achievements was given by Landau in the memorial address which he delivered at Göttingen on 12 May 1917. The address is to be found, together with a catalogue of Dedekind's published works, in the *Göttinger Nachrichten* for 1917. It is in the series *Geschäftliche Mitteilungen*, not the series *Mathematisch-physikalische Klasse*.

[2] B. L. van der Waerden: *Moderne Algebra* (Berlin, 2 volumes, 1930 and 1931).

tremely useful and even indispensable from the didactic point of view in the early teaching of the calculus if too much time is not to be lost. But no one will deny that this way of introducing the calculus can make no claim to being systematic.   My feeling of dissatisfaction at that time was so overwhelming that I firmly resolved to go on reflecting until I had found a purely arithmetical and absolutely rigorous basis for the principles of the calculus.   It is so often said that the calculus deals with continuous quantities, and yet no explanation of this continuity is ever given, and even the strictest presentations of the calculus do not base their proofs on continuity, but either appeal more or less consciously to geometrical or geometrically inspired ideas or else make the proofs rest on theorems which are never themselves proved arithmetically.   One such theorem is the one that I have mentioned, and closer investigation convinced me that this or any equivalent theorem can be taken as a sufficient foundation for infinitesimal analysis.   It only remained to discover its origin in the elements of arithmetic, and so at the same time to obtain a real definition of the essence of continuity.   This I succeeded in doing on 24 November 1858. . . .'

Dedekind found the solution of the problem that had been troubling him in his new definition of real numbers as sections of the ordered set of rational numbers, and in his theorem that to every section of the ordered set of real numbers there corresponds a real number.   This is only one example of the fundamental work that he did in giving strictly conceptual definitions of mathematical ideas that had hitherto been vague or intuitive.   Another example is his replacement of Kummer's fictitious ideal factors, in the theory of algebraic number fields, by ideals, in the now familiar sense, defined as certain sets of actual numbers (see Note 2, p. 153).

We shall have occasion to say more about Dedekind in the next chapter (p. 158), when we discuss the logical analysis of mathematical concepts, but here we must turn to another great pioneer in the field of foundations of mathematics, Giuseppe Peano.

5   Peano's 'Formulaire de Mathématique'

Even though Dedekind had a more lively interest in questions of logical analysis than men such as Cauchy and Weierstrass, who were only concerned with logic in so far as it was involved in their purely mathematical work, he was still essentially a mathematician, and not a logician or a philosopher.   But a turning point in the whole critical movement was reached with Peano, who, after having begun his career as a critical mathematician of a somewhat similar type to Dedekind, devoted himself specifically to the study of foundations of mathematics for its own sake.   For this reason alone, Peano must be looked upon as a pivotal figure in the history of this particular branch of study.   His was, moreover, an unusual and engaging personality; and since some knowledge of the man is necessary for the proper understanding of his thought, we give here a few biographical details.

Giuseppe Peano was born in 1858 (the very year of Dedekind's great discovery) and died in 1932, having spent almost the whole of his life at Turin, where for many years he was professor of infinitesimal analysis. He had wide mathematical interests, as well as major interests outside mathematics, and the number of his published papers exceeds two hundred. Although he was a meticulous scholar, who always liked, for example, to trace statements and discoveries to their original sources, he was no pedant; and he is also said to have been a remarkably enthusiastic and inspiring teacher. He never tired of trying to persuade other teachers that they fail in their task unless they are able to make every fact which they have to communicate come to life in the student's mind, so that he sees it as something directly relevant to his own thinking.

Peano's career falls naturally into three phases, since his chief interest was successively in the infinitesimal calculus, in foundations of mathematics, and in linguistic studies; but all three preoccupations were in some measure with him throughout his life.

Like Dedekind, Peano was made aware of the need for a higher standard of rigour in mathematics by his experience of teaching the infinitesimal calculus. His first book[1]—which he published under the name of Angelo Genocchi, his revered former teacher at Turin—was a treatise on the calculus, of the customary form but very much improved in the details of the exposition. In all his mathematical work Peano strove towards a twofold ideal of simplicity and rigour, and his book on the calculus is exemplary in both these respects. Beginning with a strict definition of real number, essentially that of Dedekind, he develops the calculus systematically, formulating every theorem with the greatest possible accuracy and precision, and strictly avoiding in the proofs any illegitimate appeal to intuitive properties of curves. When the customary enunciations of theorems are too loose, or conditions that need to be satisfied are not as a rule clearly stated, Peano often constructs counter-examples to show that assertions made in standard textbooks are incomplete or erroneous.

Both Peano and Dedekind traced much of the still prevalent lack of rigour in analysis to unwarranted reliance upon intuition. The languages of analysis and geometry are to some extent translatable into each other, by reason of the connexion between functions and their graphs, but their equivalence is by no means as complete as has often been supposed. At a comparatively naive level of mathematical thinking (corresponding historically to the state of mathematics before

---

[1] A. Genocchi: *Calcolo differenziale e principii di calcolo integrale, pubblicato con aggiunte dal D.ʳ Giuseppe Peano* (Turin, 1884).

the beginning of the critical movement), where the concepts of function and curve are interpreted in a common-sense way, it is reasonable to regard these concepts as interchangeable. As a result of the critical movement, however, the concepts of number and function are now no longer intuitive, and they have been found to require elaborate logical definition. If, therefore, we reason intuitively about curves—arguing, for example, that if a continuous curve has points on both sides of a straight line then it must 'obviously' have at least one point of intersection with the line—we are not justified in translating our conclusions into statements about functions in the sense in which they are now understood in analysis. Since the concepts of analysis are abstract concepts, having strictly logical definitions, we can only prove the theorems of analysis by arguing exclusively from these definitions. The intuitive properties of graphs may suggest to us new analytical theorems, and they may also make existing theorems more readily intelligible, but they can never be grounds of proof.

Peano gave a striking illustration of the way in which intuitively evident conclusions may cease to be valid if the concepts involved in them are idealized theoretically when he devised his famous space-filling curve. He published this discovery in a short paper entitled 'Sur une courbe, qui remplit toute une aire plaine' (*Math. Ann.*, **36** (1890), 157–160), introduced as follows :

'In this note we determine two one-valued and continuous functions x and y of a single (real) variable t, which, as t varies in the interval (0,1), take all pairs of values such that $0 \leqslant x \leqslant 1$, $0 \leqslant y \leqslant 1$. If, in accordance with custom, we use the term *continuous curve* for the locus of those points whose coordinates are given continuous functions of one variable, we obtain in this way a curvilinear arc which passes through all the points of a square. Hence, if an arc of a continuous curve is given, about which nothing further is assumed known, it is not always possible to enclose the arc in an arbitrarily small area.'

It is thus clearly demonstrated that idealization of the notion of function makes impossible the retention of the simple intuitive notion of the dimensionality of a set of points. Details of the functions which Peano used in the definition of his curve are to be found in Note 1, p. 152, at the end of the present chapter.

As a result of his work on the properties of functions, Peano arrived at the conclusion that, in the refounding of mathematics, half-measures are useless. It is of no avail to tinker with common sense and intuition ; for we are now committed to defining such notions as number and function in a more formal way, and this means that intuitive mathematics and abstract mathematics have entirely different presuppositions. As mathematicians, therefore, we must renounce intuition altogether, and develop mathematics strictly by its own proper means. With the clear recognition of this principle, Peano entered upon the second phase of his career, devoted to the transformation of mathematics into a self-contained formal system.

Peano followed the ancient Greek precedent in presenting his system of mathematics in demonstrative form; but his abandonment of intuition as a sufficient foundation made it necessary for him to modify the Greek method in several essential respects. In the first place, the entities to be considered—numbers, functions, points, etc.—are neither entities given in intuition nor entities whose properties are dependent on their being idealizations of something given in intuition (although they may in fact have originated in that way); and it follows from this that they must all be either postulated or defined. Again, since mathematics is to be logically independent of intuition the axioms of the demonstrative system cannot be justified by appeal to self-evidence. They too must be simply postulated, and they neither require nor admit of any further justification within the formal theory. When once the entities in the system and their initial properties have been postulated, the theorems must all be derived by purely logical processes; and here it is particularly necessary to guard against involuntary appeal to intuition. To this end Peano introduced two safeguards, each of which inaugurated an enduring tradition in the study of mathematics and its foundations. In the first place, he renounced ordinary language and determined to rewrite mathematics entirely in terms of a new symbolism. He had a number of reasons for doing this—the fact that ordinary language is often imprecise, and that its structure does not always match the structure of mathematical demonstration; the desirability of using entirely neutral symbols, so that there is no danger of appealing tacitly to the intuitive associations of common words (as the older analysts were led to do when they inferred properties of functions from those of curves); and the universality of mathematical symbolism, as compared with the diversity of national languages. And secondly, he formalized the logic of mathematical argument as well as the language in which mathematics is expressed, undertaking for this purpose the task of replacing intuitive inference by application of a limited number of stated logical rules. In other words, he constructed and used a symbolic logic, by the aid of which the inferring of a conclusion from premises was replaced by the derivation of one symbolic expression from other such expressions by quasi-algebraic calculation.

The new form that the theories of pure mathematics were to assume, then, was of the following nature. Each theory would involve a small number of primitive ideas, to be represented by suitably chosen symbols; and these ideas would be left undefined, simply being enumerated at the beginning of the exposition. There would also be a small number of primitive propositions, containing the primitive ideas, which would likewise be enumerated.   Development of the theory would be wholly by derivation of symbolically formulated propositions, either from the primitive propositions themselves or from propositions already derived, in accordance with the stated principles of symbolic logic.   New entities might be introduced in the course of the development, either by explicit definition as some particular combination of given entities or, in the case of arithmetic, by the special process of 'recursive definition' (see p. 147).

The work of formalization of mathematics involved the rewriting of existing theories in symbolic form, and it also involved a great deal of amplification and reorganization of the deductive sequence in order to make the system conform to the new logical canons, which were much more exacting than any that had been recognized previously.   This vast work was carried out by Peano, in collaboration with a number of colleagues and assistants, and the results were published in the *Rivista di Matematica* and the *Formulaire de Mathématique*.   The first of these two publications was a journal, founded by Peano in 1891 for the dissemination of the results obtained in his circle, and published until 1906, while the second was a cumulative exposition of the whole system as worked out to date.

The *Formulaire* appeared in five successive editions or volumes.   The series began in 1894, with an introductory pamphlet entitled 'Notations de logique mathématique.   Introduction au Formulaire de Mathématique', and in 1895 there followed the first full volume of the *Formulaire* itself, in nine sections written by Peano and his collaborators: I. Mathematical logic; II. Algebraic operations; III. Arithmetic; IV. Theory of magnitudes (*grandeurs*) [Burali-Forti]; V. Classes of numbers; VI. Theory of sets (*ensembles*) [Vivanti]; VII. Limits [Bettazzi]; VIII. Series [Giudice]; IX. Contributions to the theory of algebraic numbers [Fano].   The second volume of the *Formulaire* was published in three parts in 1897, 1898, and 1899; and the third, fourth, and fifth volumes appeared respectively in 1901, 1902–1903, and 1908.

The relation between the different volumes is confused, since these are neither complementary volumes of a single work, like the three volumes of *Principia Mathematica*, nor successive editions of one and the same work.   Central topics, such as mathematical logic and arithmetic, are treated again and again, now briefly and now at much greater length, but peripheral theories may appear only once, when first formalized.   Thus the earlier volumes are not altogether superseded by the later ones, although the different volumes overlap to a considerable extent.

The version of the *Formulaire* that we shall discuss here is that of 1901, which is arranged in the following five parts: I. Mathematical logic; II. Arithmetic; III. Analytic functions; IV. Complex numbers; V. Vectors.

The section on mathematical logic is now of no more than historical interest; for Peano did not develop symbolic logic beyond a comparatively rudimentary stage, and the propositional calculus and the calculus of predicates, as formalized by him, were first worked out in full detail, as we shall describe in Chapter 6, by Russell and Whitehead in *Principia Mathematica* (1910). Nevertheless, the credit for introducing the essential notions and symbols belongs to Peano, as Russell himself has freely acknowledged. Peano used letters to denote propositions and propositional functions, devised notations[1]—of which some are still in use, while others have now been supplanted—for the logical constants 'not', 'implies', 'implies for all x', etc., and pointed out the fundamental significance of the relation of class-membership, reserving for it the initial letter of the Greek word ἐστί (*is*).

Apart from the section devoted to logic, the most important of the five divisions of the *Formulaire* of 1901 is undoubtedly the second one, on arithmetic. To this formulation of the basic properties of numbers (which owes much to Dedekind's essay *Was sind und was sollen die Zahlen?*, to be discussed in §2 of the next chapter) almost all subsequent work on the foundations of arithmetic can ultimately be traced back. Peano bases his treatment on three primitive ideas:

(i) N_0, the class of natural numbers;
(ii) 0, the particular number zero;
(iii) $a+$, the successor of the number a.

There are six primitive propositions, which we may write in a slightly modernized form as follows:

(i) $N_0 \in \mathrm{Cls}$;
(ii) $0 \in N_0$;
(iii) $a \in N_0 \to a+ \in N_0$;
(iv) $[s \in \mathrm{Cls}\ \&\ 0 \in s\ \&\ (x)(x \in s \to x+ \in s)] \to N_0 \subset s$;
(v) $(a,b \in N_0\ \&\ a+ = b+) \to a = b$;
(vi) $a \in N_0 \to a+ \neq 0$.

With the exception of (i), which belongs more to Peano's way of presenting arithmetic than to arithmetic itself, these primitive propositions

Peano, and Russell likewise, wrote 'p implies q' as '$p \supset q$'. Peano also wrote '$p .\supset_x. q$' to mean 'for all x, p implies q', where p and q were propositional functions involving the variable x; and Russell continued to use this notation, in the more explicit form '$\phi x \supset_x \psi x$', as an alternative to '$(x) .\phi x \supset \psi x$'. Hilbert subsequently replaced '$\supset$' by '$\to$', at the same time discontinuing the use of subscripts to indicate universal quantification. For 'x is a member of a' Peano wrote '$x \varepsilon a$', and for 'the class of entities x which satisfy the propositional function p' he wrote '$x \vartheta p$'. Russell changed this last usage to '$\hat{x}(\phi x)$'.

are simply the well-known 'Peano axioms' for the natural numbers.[1] They may be expressed in familiar language as follows: (i) N_0 is a class; (ii) 0 is a number; (iii) The successor of any number is a number; (iv) If a class s is such that (a) it contains 0, and (b) if it contains any number a then it also contains the successor $a+$ of that number, then s includes the whole of N_0; (v) No two numbers have the same successor; (vi) 0 is not the successor of any number.

The fourth of the primitive propositions is the axiom of induction, whose function in the system is to formalize the demonstrative procedure known as *mathematical induction*. This is the mode of argument that we commonly use in demonstrating a theorem $\mathfrak{A}(n)$, the statement of which involves an undetermined integer n as a parameter. We prove (a) that $\mathfrak{A}(0)$ holds, and (b) that if $\mathfrak{A}(n)$ holds then so also does $\mathfrak{A}(n+)$; and we then conclude that $\mathfrak{A}(n)$ is valid for every value of n. Proof by mathematical induction is fundamental to Peano's whole system, and indeed it is the only specifically arithmetical form of argument that is provided by the primitive propositions. In the working out of the system, Peano also makes essential use of the constructive counterpart of this demonstrative procedure, namely *recursive definition*. An arithmetical function $\mathfrak{f}(n)$ is said to be defined recursively if (a) an explicit definition of $\mathfrak{f}(0)$ is given, and (b) $\mathfrak{f}(n+)$ is defined in terms of $\mathfrak{f}(n)$ by means of functions that are already available. Interpreted intuitively, a recursive definition of $\mathfrak{f}(n)$ plainly provides a means of determining in succession the values $\mathfrak{f}(0)$, $\mathfrak{f}(1)$, $\mathfrak{f}(2)$, ... of the function. Peano uses the method in order to define the arithmetical sum and product, $a + b$ and $a \times b$, doing this in each case by recursion with respect to b:

$$a + 0 = a, \qquad a + (b+) = (a + b)+,$$
and
$$a \times 0 = 0, \qquad a \times (b+) = (a \times b) + a.$$

The familiar associative, commutative, and distributive laws can now be established in the formal system, and much of the elementary theory of numbers is then readily derivable by formal means.

Having proceeded thus far with the systematic construction of his system of arithmetic, Peano goes on to indicate much more briefly how rational numbers and real numbers can be obtained formally from the natural numbers; and he then turns, in the next two sections of the *Formulaire*, to a consideration of various topics in elementary analysis.

---

[1] In the literature, the 'natural numbers' are taken sometimes as 0, 1, 2, ... and sometimes as 1, 2, 3, ... Peano began the series with 0, and Hilbert adopted the same convention. Dedekind, on the contrary, took 1 as the first natural number, and this is now the normal practice in mathematics. The choice between the two possible conventions is of no theoretical importance, and we shall ordinarily conform to the usage of the author whose work we are discussing.

The concluding section of the work, which has the heading 'Vectors', is devoted to geometry.

Geometry was indeed yet another subject to which Peano gave a considerable amount of attention, and on which he even wrote a separate book[1]; but although his work on geometry is by no means without interest, it is of much less significance in the history of foundations of mathematics than his contribution to arithmetic. It arose out of the dissatisfaction which he, in common with certain other nineteenth-century mathematicians, felt with the way in which modern geometry had developed. The use of cartesian coordinates had made geometry less elementary than it was in classical times, and also, by rendering it dependent on processes of calculation, had reduced to a minimum its intuitive content. But the cartesian method relies on the introduction of a set of arbitrarily chosen axes, having no connexion with the figure under investigation; and during the nineteenth century several attempts were made to perfect a symbolic calculus which would apply more directly to geometrical entities, without intervention of an extraneous frame of reference. Möbius with his barycentric calculus (1827), Hamilton with his quaternions (1843), and Grassmann with his *Ausdehnungslehre* or calculus of extension (1844 and 1862) had all made contributions to this movement; and prompted by their example, Peano gave a new formal treatment of certain parts of geometry by means of a calculus of vectors, similar to the system now widely used in theoretical physics.

The adoption of vectorial ideas in physics and applied mathematics is not, however, due directly to Peano's influence, since the use of vectors was developed independently of him by Josiah Willard Gibbs (1839–1903) and Oliver Heaviside (1850–1925); and already in 1881 Willard Gibbs had some notes on vectors printed for circulation among his students. And even in the field of geometry, Peano's vectorial treatment has perhaps become something of a historical curiosity,[2] for geometry has in the meantime developed along quite other lines, becoming less and less dependent on geometrical intuition of any kind. Differential geometry is now handled, in fact, by the calculus of tensors, and algebraic geometry by means of a coordinate representation over a postulated ground-field, which makes possible the application to it of the no less powerful methods of modern algebra and topology.

In his later years Peano turned away from mathematics and its foundations, and devoted almost all of his time and energy to the task

---

[1] G. Peano: *Calcolo Geometrico, secondo l'Ausdehnungslehre di H. Grassmann, preceduto dalle operazioni della logica deduttiva* (Turin, 1888).

[2] This is not to say that it must always remain so. New ideas in mathematics are not always significant in the way that their originators intend, and history shows that an apparently barren innovation may become abundantly fruitful when a later age provides it with fresh soil.

of winning support for a new international auxiliary language, Interlingua, that he had invented. His interest in linguistic studies had
already been awakened much earlier in his career, and this part of his
activity, seemingly remote from mathematics, made a far from neglig-
ible contribution to the success of his mathematical and logical
researches.

Peano had expert knowledge of classical languages, as well as a lively
interest in comparative philology. At one time he made a number of
attempts to reduce the grammatical structure of various languages to
essentially mathematical form, in order to see if he could find any common structure belonging to all languages, and so, perhaps, inherent in
language as such. He became convinced in the end that no such structure exists, and that both grammar and idiom are wholly dependent on
the fortuitous circumstances of history. As time went on, he became
more and more concerned with communication in its various aspects.
The problems presented by communication of abstract or mathematical
knowledge were manageable, and Peano solved them so successfully
that his symbolic methods led directly to the creation of modern mathematical logic. Communication of more concrete experience—thoughts,
impressions, emotions, etc.—is very much more difficult, since the substance of what is to be communicated can exhibit infinite variety, and
so linguistic representation of elements in experience can only be
approximate. In many of its functions, language is evocative rather
than representational; but even in so far as it is representational its
effective use is much impeded by the existence of a multiplicity of different national forms. In his mathematical writing, addressed to
mathematicians at large, Peano changed over early on from his own
language of Italian to French, which is more widely known; but even
French is not fully international, and he looked back with regret to the
time, not so very distant, when Latin had been the universal language
of scholars.[1] In his day, unfortunately, comparatively few people
could write Latin, and the difficulty of the language was a bar to its
revival; but the idea came to him that most of the difficulty could be
avoided by the simple expedient of dispensing with the complexity of
Latin grammar (which is in any case historically fortuitous, and in no
way essential to the language as a medium of communication). Peano
thus arrived at his auxiliary international language of *latino sine
flexione*, afterwards named *Interlingua*. The vocabulary is that which
is to be found in any Latin dictionary, and there is virtually no grammar. Nouns are undeclined and verbs unconjugated, every noun
taking the invariable form of the Latin ablative singular and every verb
that of the singular imperative. Case is indicated, as in many modern

---

[1] In 1889 there had in fact appeared an essay of twenty-nine pages, written in Latin,
with the title *Arithmetices Principia nova methodo exposita, a Ioseph Peano*.

languages, by means of prepositions, and tense by means of adverbs. In his later mathematical publications, Peano consistently used Interlingua. The *Rivista di Matematica* was then called *Revista de Mathematica*, and when the final version of the *Formulaire* appeared in 1908 it was as *Formulario Mathematico*.

It emerges clearly, even from the present superficial account of his work, that Peano was a man of quite remarkable originality—original not merely in his ability to carry out mathematical research of the customary kind, but even more in his capacity for detaching himself from prevailing traditions and looking at them critically and dispassionately. He was able to confront in this way some of the most widely accepted presuppositions of his age, and to ask himself whether they really corresponded to the needs of the actual situation. He considered afresh, as we have already described, the whole question of communication between one mind and another, and he was led by his inquiries to advocate radical reforms in the two very different spheres of mathematics and linguistics. His mathematical innovations were to exercise a profound influence on the thought of mathematicians and philosophers of mathematics; but his long championship of Interlingua as an auxiliary language met with no lasting response. In mathematics, he recognized that there is an unbridgeable gulf between the intuitive outlook of common sense and the logical rigour that, by his day, had come to be looked upon as essential in the construction of mathematical theories. He came to the conclusion that mathematics must be constructed, independently of intuition, in a way that guarantees absolutely the validity of its theorems; and in order to satisfy this requirement he set to work to rewrite mathematics in symbolic form as an axiomatic system, based exclusively on postulated primitive notions and primitive propositions. This was an epoch-making step to take; and we shall see how heavily later writers on the foundations of mathematics have been indebted to Peano for his initiative.

6   The symbolic language of Leibniz

Although Peano was a man of outstanding ability he also had, to a most unusual degree, the quality of humility. This was so strong an element in his personality that he could never bring himself to accept the credit for his own achievements.[1]   He would certainly never have admitted to being an original thinker, and it was his nature to see his

---

[1] It is wholly characteristic of Peano that he expressed the wish that when he died, honoured though he was as a man of acknowledged eminence in the world of learning, he should be buried in the part of the cemetery that was reserved for the paupers of the city of Turin.   And in the brief report of Peano's funeral that is printed in *Schola et Vita*, 7 (1932), 103, we read that indeed, after a ceremony in the great hall of the university, 'funere move ad cæmeterio, ubi nostro caro et venerato prof. Peano es sepulto in campo commune, 3° sud, in fossa n. 674, inter pauperes'.

own work always as nothing but a continuation or fulfilment of someone else's—as for instance of Genocchi's when he wrote his book on the
infinitesimal calculus. In the case of symbolic logic, it was Leibniz
who received the credit. Peano had especial reverence for Leibniz,
which is partly accounted for by the fact that he was probably the first
man ever fully to appreciate some of the things that Leibniz did or conceived the idea of doing. In the preface to the *Formulaire* of 1901 we
find these words:

'Mathematical logic studies the properties of logical operations and
relations, which it denotes by symbols. A few of the principles of this
science are to be found in general logic (see Aristotle). Its true founder
is Leibniz, who enunciated the principal properties of the ideas now
represented by $\cap$, $\cup$, $-$ [not], $=$, $\supset$, Λ.'

Leibniz, as is generally acknowledged, may be compared to Aristotle
in the range of his abilities. He had prodigiously wide interests and
made highly original contributions to many different branches of
learning; and among his numerous projects was the construction of a
symbolic logical language. But the men of his time did not take him
seriously, and he himself never found the leisure needed to carry
through the immense task of working out a suitable symbolism in
detail, starting from the very beginning. Although, however, his project remained largely a dream, he worked at it intermittently and
obtained a number of fragmentary results. These were preserved
among his manuscripts in the royal library at Hanover, and some of
them were at length published in selections from his works; but once
again their significance was not appreciated. Eventually, when Peano
had been led by his own researches into the foundations of mathematics
to reflect independently on the same matters, he realized for the first
time the meaning of the results noted down by his great predecessor.
And so at last, just before the close of the nineteenth century, Peano's
colleague Giovanni Vacca went to Hanover to make an examination of
the manuscripts there. The extracts which Vacca published in the
Formulaire of 1899 inspired Louis Couturat to go more fully into the
matter; and in 1901 Couturat published *La Logique de Leibniz*, which
was followed in 1903 by a large volume containing the logical fragments
themselves.

Now that Peano had actually produced a logical calculus, and had
thus demonstrated that the project was not illusory, the true significance and importance of Leibniz's work could at last be appreciated.
That Leibniz himself had seen clearly, all the time, what he was about,
is proved by some words that he wrote in an often-quoted letter of 1714:

'If I had been less distracted, or if I had been younger or assisted by
young men in a position to help me, I would have hoped to give a kind

of *spécieuse générale*,[1] in which all truths of reason would be reduced to a calculus. This would be at the same time a sort of universal speech or writing, but infinitely different from all those proposed hitherto; for the characters, and the words themselves, would be governed by Reason; and errors, with the exception of those of fact, could only be mistakes in calculation. It would be very difficult to create or invent this language or characteristic, but very easy to learn it without the aid of a dictionary.'

The symbolic logic of Peano, though limited to a narrow range of discourse (namely the exposition of demonstrative theories) is just such an instrument as Leibniz had in mind.

SUPPLEMENTARY NOTES ON CHAPTER 5

1. *Peano's space-filling curve.* Peano's procedure for defining a curve which passes through every point of the square $0 \leqslant x \leqslant 1$, $0 \leqslant y \leqslant 1$ (cf. p. 143) may be summarized as follows. Let t be any real number in the range $0 \leqslant t \leqslant 1$, expressed in the scale of 3 in the form

$$a_1/3 + a_2/3^2 + \ldots + a_n/3^n + \ldots.$$

Denoting by **k** an operator which converts 0, 1, or 2 into its complement with respect to 2, so that $\mathbf{k}0 = 2$, $\mathbf{k}1 = 1$, $\mathbf{k}2 = 0$, we define two sequences $\{b_n\}$ and $\{c_n\}$ in the following way:

$$b_1 = a_1,$$
$$b_2 = \mathbf{k}^{a_2}a_3,$$
$$\cdot \quad \cdot \quad \cdot \quad \cdot$$
$$b_n = \mathbf{k}^{a_2 + a_4 + \ldots + a_{2n-2}}a_{2n-1};$$
$$\cdot \quad \cdot \quad \cdot \quad \cdot$$

and

$$c_1 = \mathbf{k}^{a_1}a_2,$$
$$c_2 = \mathbf{k}^{a_1 + a_3}a_4,$$
$$\cdot \quad \cdot \quad \cdot \quad \cdot$$
$$c_n = \mathbf{k}^{a_1 + a_3 + \ldots + a_{2n-1}}a_{2n},$$
$$\cdot \quad \cdot \quad \cdot \quad \cdot$$

If, now, we put

$$X = b_1/3 + b_2/3^2 + \ldots, \qquad Y = c_1/3 + c_2/3^2 + \ldots,$$

X and Y are continuous functions of t; and the parametric representation $x = X$, $y = Y$ then defines a curve with the required property. A number of details still have to be taken care of, but even when this is done Peano's entire paper occupies only four pages.

[1] Literally, 'generalized algebra'. The name *arithmétique spécieuse* was formerly used for algebra; cf. the article *Spécieuse* in the *Encyclopédie* of Diderot and d'Alembert (Paris, 1751–1765).

2. *Ideal numbers and ideals.* Kummer introduced ideal numbers into arithmetic with the aim of simplifying the discussion of algebraic number fields.

By an *algebraic number* is meant a (complex) number which satisfies an algebraic equation

$$x^n + a_1 x^{n-1} + \ldots + a_n = 0,$$

in which the coefficients $a_1, \ldots, a_n$ are rational numbers, i.e. elements of the rational field Q. If, more specifically, these coefficients happen to be rational integers, the algebraic number is said to be an *algebraic integer*. Now the set of all algebraic integers is a ring, and the set of all algebraic numbers is the field of quotients of this ring; but the arithmetical analogy with the rational integers and the rational numbers does not go very far, since there are no algebraic integers that are irreducible, i.e. prime.

The situation becomes much more like that in ordinary arithmetic if, instead of the field of *all* algebraic numbers, some restricted field $Q(\theta)$ is taken, that is to say the smallest field, containing Q, which has some specified algebraic number θ as one of its elements. The algebraic integers which belong to $Q(\theta)$ then form a ring, and $Q(\theta)$ is the field of quotients of this ring.

For some choices of θ, the arithmetic of $Q(\theta)$ is very similar to that of Q. In the case $\theta = \sqrt{3}$, for instance, we have a direct analogue of the theorem that every rational integer is expressible in one and essentially only one way as a product of prime factors; but in other cases there is no such analogy. Thus the number 21 has two distinct resolutions into factors which are irreducible in the field $Q(\sqrt{-5})$, namely 3.7 and $(1 + 2\sqrt{-5})(1 - 2\sqrt{-5})$. This is possible because, although the algebraic integers $3, 7, 1 + 2\sqrt{-5}$, $1 - 2\sqrt{-5}$ are all irreducible in the field $Q(\sqrt{-5})$, they have as common factors certain algebraic integers which do not belong to this field. We have, in fact,

$$1 + 2\sqrt{-5} = \sqrt{\lambda}\sqrt{-\varkappa'}, \quad 1 - 2\sqrt{-5} = \sqrt{\lambda'}\sqrt{-\varkappa},$$
$$3 = \sqrt{\lambda}\sqrt{\lambda'}, \quad 7 = \sqrt{\varkappa}\sqrt{\varkappa'},$$

where

$$\varkappa = 2 + 3\sqrt{-5}, \quad \varkappa' = 2 - 3\sqrt{-5}; \quad \lambda = 2 + \sqrt{-5}, \quad \lambda' = 2 - \sqrt{-5}.$$

The arithmetic of $Q(\sqrt{-5})$ is thus anomalous in that common factors, which have an effect on the multiplicative properties of the integers of the field, are sometimes missing from the field; and Kummer's idea was to postulate 'ideal' numbers of the field in order to fill any gaps that may exist. The field that he originally considered was not in fact $Q(\sqrt{-5})$ but a cyclotomic field, generated from Q by adjunction to it of a complex pth root of unity. In his own words:

'Es ist mir gelungen, die Theorie derjenigen complexen Zahlen, welche aus höheren Wurzeln der Einheit gebildet sind und welche bekanntlich in der Kreistheilung, in der Lehre von den Potenzresten und den Formen höherer Grade eine wichtige Rolle spielen, zu vervollständigen und zu vereinfachen; und zwar durch Einführung einer eigenthümlichen Art imaginärer Divisoren, welche ich *ideale complexe Zahlen* nenne; worüber eine kurze Mittheilung zu machen ich mir erlaube.

Wenn α eine imaginäre Wurzel der Gleichung $\alpha^\lambda = 1$, λ eine Primzahl ist und a, a_1, a_2, etc. ganze Zahlen sind, so ist $f(\alpha) = a + a_1\alpha + a_2\alpha^2 + \ldots a_{\lambda-1}\alpha^{\lambda-1}$ eine complexe ganze Zahl. Eine solche complexe Zahl kann entweder in Factoren derselben Art zerlegt werden; oder auch nicht. Im ersten Fall ist sie eine zusammengesetzte Zahl: im andern Fall ist sie bisher eine complexe Primzahl genannt worden. Ich habe nun aber bemerkt, daß, wenn auch $f(\alpha)$ auf keine Weise in complexe Factoren zerlegt werden kann, sie deshalb noch nicht die wahre Natur einer complexen Primzahl hat, weil sie schon gewöhnlich der ersten und wichtigsten Eigenschaft der Primzahlen ermangelt: nämlich, daß das Product zweier Primzahlen durch keine von ihnen verschiedene Primzahl theilbar ist. Es haben vielmehr solche Zahlen $f(\alpha)$, wenn gleich sie nicht in complexe Factoren zerlegbar sind, dennoch die Natur der zusammengesetzten Zahlen; die Factoren aber sind alsdann nicht wirkliche, sondern *ideale complexe Zahlen*.' ('Zur Theorie der complexen Zahlen', *J. reine angew. Math.*, **35** (1847), 319–326.)

The further step taken by Dedekind was the recognition that, in order to handle the arithmetic of a given algebraic field $Q(\theta)$, we do not need to be able actually to produce irreducible factors, since we can do all that is required by arguing in terms of those totalities of integers of the field that behave as if they were divisible by some common irreducible factor. These totalities are what are now known as *ideals*. The procedure here adopted by Dedekind may be compared with his own identification of real numbers with totalities of rational numbers which behave as if separated off by boundary numbers, and also with Frege's identification of the cardinal number of a class with the totality of all classes which behave as if possessing just as many members as that class.

For the use of ideals in the study of algebraic number fields see E. Hecke: *Vorlesungen über die Theorie der algebraischen Zahlen*, Chapter 5.

3. *Sources of historical information*. (a) *General*. The standard history of Greek mathematics is Heath [3].

A very comprehensive survey of the history of mathematics up to 1799, in four volumes, is M. Cantor [1]. For the subsequent development of modern mathematics, in the course of the nineteenth century, see Klein [2].

A collection of essays on the greatest mathematicians from the fifth century B.C. onwards, which is perceptive and informative beneath a somewhat racy style, is E. T. Bell: *Men of Mathematics*. The same author has also written a less popular work [2], in which the emphasis is more on mathematical discoveries than on biographical anecdotes.

Biographical details of modern mathematicians, as well as information concerning their work, are often most readily obtained from the obituary notices published by learned societies. See, in particular, the series *Obituary Notices of Fellows of the Royal Society* (1932–1955) and its continuation since 1956 as *Biographical Memoirs of Fellows of the Royal Society*, and also the obituary notices in the *Journal of the London Mathematical Society*.

(b) *For Peano*. There are a number of articles which give details of Peano's life and work. His contributions to mathematics are outlined in Levi [1] and his contributions to logic in Cassina [3]. Cassina's more elaborate notice [2] covers the whole of Peano's mathematical and logical work, and includes a full list of his publications. Yet another account of Peano's life and work, Cassina [1], is essentially the same as an article which Cassina wrote in 1928, with Peano's assistance, to mark Peano's seventieth birthday. For Peano's own writings, see the three volumes of *Opere scelte*, published 1957–1959.

Chapter 6

THE LOGISTIC IDENTIFICATION OF
MATHEMATICS WITH LOGIC

1 Russell's conception of mathematics

The topic of the previous chapter was the growth of the critical movement, or movement towards new and more exacting standards of rigour, which revolutionized mathematics in the course of the nineteenth century; and we have now brought the story of that movement to the point at which the study of the foundations of mathematics clearly emerged, in the work of Peano, as a discipline in its own right. This new study inherited from the critical movement that had prepared the ground for it two well-defined attitudes, each of which was to influence profoundly the investigations of the coming decades. One of these was the attitude of Peano himself, who had consistently maintained that mathematics must be emancipated by formalization from its traditional dependence upon intuition; while the other, which sprang from a more philosophical belief that the ultimate ground of mathematical truth can only be pure logic, had found its most eloquent advocate in Dedekind. The two points of view were complementary rather than opposed, since both Dedekind and Peano were of like mind in rejecting common sense as an adequate basis for mathematics; and the foundation of Peano's formal system, moreover, was his symbolic logic. There was, nevertheless, a considerable difference of emphasis, and subsequent developments were to produce widely divergent philosophies of mathematics in which this difference was greatly magnified. The logical conception of mathematics found full expression in the 'logistic' system elaborated by Russell, while the formal conception was developed more particularly by Hilbert in his philosophy of 'formalism'. We shall now discuss these two systems in turn, beginning in this chapter with Russell's, as the one that came first.

Russell arrived very early in his career at a clear conception of what he held to be the true nature of mathematics; and he epitomized this conception in the definition which stands at the beginning of *The Principles of Mathematics*, published in 1903. This definition runs as follows:

'Pure Mathematics is the class of all propositions of the form "p implies q", where p and q are propositions containing one or more variables, the same in the two propositions, and neither p nor q contains any constants except logical constants. And logical constants are all notions definable in terms of the following : Implication, the relation of a term to a class of which it is a member, the notion of *such that*, the notion of relation, and such further notions as may be involved in the general notion of propositions of the above form. In addition to these, mathematics *uses* a notion which is not a constituent of the propositions which it considers, namely the notion of truth.'

In *The Principles of Mathematics* Russell attempted to justify this definition by discussing in detail the main branches of pure mathematics, and analysing the concepts involved in them into concepts of pure logic. He did so discursively, strictly avoiding the use of logical symbolism, and for this reason important arguments were often merely mentioned or hinted at instead of being presented in a complete form. The theory could only be made fully cogent by a more systematic treatment, and to this end Russell subsequently adopted an elaborate and very precise symbolic language, based on that of Peano. In the three volumes of *Principia Mathematica* (1910–1913), the definitive version of the logistic theory, the entire formal system is presented in the new symbolism. The *Principia* is a work in which profound insight is matched by immense technical mastery, and it must be accounted one of the great classics of mathematical literature. In the writing of it Russell had the collaboration of A. N. Whitehead, who was then already the author of two important Cambridge Tracts on the axioms of geometry (cf. p. 342), as well as being an expert on the use of symbolic techniques, which he had studied in detail in his book *Universal Algebra* (1898).

Russell's theory of the nature of mathematics is based, as we have said, on an uncompromising identification of mathematics with logic, and it thus goes far beyond anything envisaged by Peano. Both Peano and Russell were committed to rewriting mathematics, entirely in symbols, as an axiomatic system ; but whereas Peano was content to base his mathematical system on undefined primitive concepts and undemonstrated primitive propositions, Russell held that the only primitive concepts that were necessary belonged already to logic, and that all mathematical concepts were definable and all mathematical theorems provable within the logical system.

But although it was from Russell's work that the logistic movement drew its main inspiration, and *Principia Mathematica* greatly influenced even those philosophers of mathematics who did not grant its basic assumptions, Russell was not in fact the first person to construct a systematic philosophy of mathematics on logistic principles. He had been anticipated in this, as we shall explain in §4, by Frege. And, earlier even than Frege's work, there had been an attempt by Dedekind to devise a purely logical treatment of arithmetic. We shall now give a brief account of Dedekind's theory, which will be followed by a considerably more detailed description of the content and mode of construction of *Principia Mathematica*. Finally, at the end of this chapter, we shall describe Frege's work and assess his contribution to the logistic movement.

2   Dedekind's analysis of number

It was in 1872 that Dedekind published *Stetigkeit und irrationale Zahlen* (see p. 140), and sixteen years later he followed this up with a longer essay on numbers, with the title *Was sind und was sollen die Zahlen?* [What are numbers and what is their purpose?]   In the earlier essay he had taken the rational numbers as already given, for his problem at that time was to clarify the concept of continuity, and this concept first becomes applicable when the irrational numbers are adjoined to the rational numbers so that the full totality of real numbers becomes available. But having once solved the problem of continuity, he could turn to even more fundamental issues, and in particular to the riddle of the genesis of the rational numbers themselves— or rather the genesis of the natural numbers, out of which the rational numbers are easily constructed.   In *Was sind und was sollen die Zahlen?* Dedekind expounded his theory of the natural numbers ; and in the preface to the essay he explained his point of view in the following terms :

'Whatever is provable ought not to be believed in science without proof.   Obvious as this requirement appears to be, I do not think it can by any means be regarded as satisfied even in the setting up of the simplest science of all, namely that part of logic which deals with the theory of numbers, as given in the most recent treatments.   In calling arithmetic (algebra, analysis) only a part of logic, I am already asserting that I hold the concept of number to be wholly independent of representations or intuitions of space and time, and that I hold it rather to be an immediate product of the pure laws of thought.   My principal answer to the question asked in the title of this essay runs as follows : numbers are free creations of the human mind, and they serve as a means for enabling the variety of things to be grasped more easily and with greater precision.   It is by the purely logical construction of the science of numbers, and by the continuous domain of numbers that this yields, that we are first put in a position to make a close examination of our representations of space and time, by relating these to the system of numbers that our mind has created.   If we look attentively at what occurs when we count sets of numbers or things, we are led to observe the ability of the mind to relate things to one another, to make one thing correspond to another, or to map one thing on another, without which ability no thinking is possible.   In my view, the entire science of numbers must be erected on this unique, and in any case indispensable, foundation.'

Dedekind first of all gives a careful treatment of such purely logical notions as class (*System*), union and intersection of classes, mapping of one class into another, and 'similar mapping' (a mapping such that distinct elements are always mapped on distinct elements); and in terms of these he then defines the further notion of a 'chain' with respect to a mapping. If φ is a mapping of a class S into itself, a subclass K of S is said to be a *chain* (with respect to φ) if $\varphi(K) \subset K$, i.e., in modern mathematical terminology, if K is closed under the mapping φ. If, furthermore, A is any subclass whatever of S, the *chain of* A (denoted by A_0) is the intersection of all chains that contain A.

A class S is said to be *infinite* if there exists a similar mapping which maps it on a proper subclass of itself; otherwise it is finite.

A *simply infinite* class can now be defined as a class N which has a similar mapping φ into itself, such that N is the chain of an element of N which does not belong to $\varphi(N)$.[1] For a class N to be simply infinite, therefore, there must exist a mapping φ and an element 1 of N such that (α) $\varphi(N) \subset N$, (β) $N = 1_0$, (γ) $1 \notin \varphi(N)$, and (δ) the mapping φ is similar (§71).

Dedekind now introduces the concept of natural number as follows (§73):

'If in considering a simply infinite class N, ordered[2] by a mapping φ, we abstract altogether from the particular nature of the elements, retaining only their distinguishability and the relations between them which arise from the mapping φ by which they are ordered, then these elements are called *natural numbers* or *ordinal numbers* or simply *numbers*, and the initial element 1 is called the *basic number (Grundzahl) of the number series* N. In view of this freeing of the elements from all other content (abstraction) we can justifiably call the numbers a free creation of the human mind.'

The properties of numbers are now all to be derived logically from the characteristic properties (α)–(δ) of a simply infinite class; and Dedekind is able, in particular, to prove the principle of mathematical induction as a theorem. This system of Dedekind obviously corresponds closely in its formal structure to Peano's later axiomatic theory, and the requirements (α), (γ), and (δ) are actually the same as three of Peano's axioms.

Although Dedekind certainly freed the concept of number from its

---

[1] What is meant is, of course, the chain of the class that has this element as its sole member; but Dedekind does not distinguish between single elements and unit classes (cf. p. 170 below).

[2] The mapping φ, in the definition of a simply infinite class N, associates with every element x of N a 'successor' $\varphi(x)$; and in this way φ gives rise to an ordering of N.

long-standing dependence on intuition, which was his main purpose, he was not fully successful in defining numbers in purely logical terms. His reference to 'abstracting altogether from the nature of the elements' cannot be regarded as satisfactory, as it is not a formal idea that can be expressed in the symbolism of a logical calculus. Dedekind's aim was thus some way short of Russell's, and his initial logical analysis of arithmetical notions still needed considerable refinement. The definition of number that was eventually adopted by both Frege and Russell was not in fact based directly on Dedekind's analysis, but rather on the alternative treatment of number that was proposed by Cantor.

2.1   Cantor's definition of cardinal and ordinal number

Georg Cantor (1845–1918) is known chiefly for his bold extension of the idea of number from finite to infinite classes, embodied in his theory of transfinite cardinal and ordinal numbers; but from our present point of view his work is of fundamental significance not so much because he showed that mathematics can deal with actual infinities no less than with the limiting infinity of analysis, as because he gave a strictly logical analysis of the concept of the number of elements in a class. His method was first of all to define equipotency of classes by saying that two classes M and N are *equipotent* ($M \sim N$) if and only if there exists a one-one correspondence between them. Equipotency is easily seen to be an equivalence relation (i.e. a relation that is reflexive, symmetrical, and transitive) and it therefore arranges the totality of classes into disjoint sets of mutually equipotent classes. All classes equipotent to a fixed class M have a common property (namely the property of belonging to the set of mutually equipotent classes that is determined by M) and Cantor in effect identified this common property with the *cardinal number* $\bar{\bar{M}}$ of M. Cantor himself, with an outlook similar to Dedekind's, preferred to think of cardinal number rather less formally as the product of a process of abstraction, and to prove from his definition that the relations $M \sim N$ and $\bar{\bar{M}} = \bar{\bar{N}}$ are equivalent. In his words:

'We will call by the name "power" or "cardinal number" of M the general concept which, by means of our active faculty of thought, arises from the aggregate M when we make abstraction of the nature of its various elements m and of the order in which they are given. We denote the result of this double act of abstraction, the cardinal number or power of M, by $\bar{\bar{M}}$.'

By abstracting only from the nature of the elements of a class, but retaining the order in which the elements are given, Cantor was also able to define a second kind of number, which he called 'ordinal number'. We can summarize this part of his theory as follows.

A class is said to be *simply ordered* if there is a non-reflexive, transitive relation $\prec$, such that, for any two distinct elements a and b of the class, either $a \prec b$ or $b \prec a$.   Two simply ordered classes M and N are said to be *similar* ($M \simeq N$) if there is a one-one correspondence between them which preserves all relations of order.   All simply ordered classes similar to a given simply ordered class M then have a common property, the *order-type* $\bar{M}$ of M.   A simply ordered class is said to be *well-ordered* if each of its non-empty subclasses has a first member (i.e. a member which precedes all the other members in the given ordering); and the order-type of any well-ordered class is said to be an *ordinal number*.

Every finite class has a finite cardinal number, which may be identified with the number of elements in the class in the ordinary sense; and the finite cardinal numbers may accordingly be denoted by the symbols $1, 2, \ldots$.   If a finite class is simply ordered, it is necessarily well-ordered, and it therefore has an ordinal number.   If the elements of the class are taken in a different order, the new ordered class is similar to the original one, and thus has the same ordinal number.   There is therefore a unique ordinal number that corresponds to each *finite* cardinal number, and it makes little difference whether we think of $1, 2, \ldots$ as cardinal or as ordinal numbers.

The cardinal number of a class M is said to be smaller than the cardinal number of a class N (i.e. $\bar{\bar{M}} < \bar{\bar{N}}$) if M is equipotent to a subclass of N but N is not equipotent to any subclass of M.   The smallest infinite cardinal number is $\aleph_0$, the cardinal number of any *denumerably infinite* class, or class that is equipotent to the class of finite cardinal numbers.   The smallest infinite ordinal number is ω, the ordinal number of the sequence $\{1, 2, \ldots\}$ of the finite cardinal numbers, taken in their 'natural' order.   For infinite classes, ordinal numbers behave quite differently from cardinal numbers.   If M is a given well-ordered infinite class, equipotent ordered classes can be found with ordinal numbers different from $\bar{M}$—and even without ordinal numbers at all, because they are not well-ordered.

These are the main ideas on which Cantor based his theory of cardinal and ordinal numbers.   Although he, no less than Dedekind, thought in terms of a process of abstraction, his definition of cardinal number was one from which reference to the activity of minds could readily be eliminated.   The simple but decisive further step of actually identifying the cardinal number of a class M with the class of all classes that are equipotent to M was in fact taken by Frege.

3   'Principia Mathematica'

Reverting now to Russell, and his attempted reduction of mathematics to logic, we need first of all to explain the distinction that he has drawn between pure and applied mathematics. Every mathematical theory, in Russell's view, is a totality of assertions; and the constituents of these assertions can be sorted into variables and constants. The assertion 'If x and y are any natural numbers, and $x < y$, then $x^2 < y^2$', for instance, contains two (apparent) variables x and y as well as several constants, which include the specific concept 'natural number', the relation '$<$', and the logical constants 'any', 'and', and 'if . . . then . . .'. Some mathematical assertions involve logical constants only, as for example De Morgan's theorem $\mathsf{C}(X \cup Y) = \mathsf{C}X \cap \mathsf{C}Y$ in the algebra of classes, while other mathematical assertions make essential reference also to non-logical constants, as for example the assertion that (perceptual) space is three-dimensional. Assertions of the latter kind are statements of contingent fact, whereas those of the former kind are statements of logical necessity; and Russell classifies these two types of statement as belonging respectively to applied mathematics and to pure mathematics.

With pure and applied mathematics delimited in this manner, some deviations are necessary from the customary classification of mathematical theories. Thus the subject of 'rational dynamics', to take an instance to which Russell himself has drawn attention, belongs to pure and not to applied mathematics, for it is based entirely on definitions and not at all on inductively established empirical laws. A particularly illuminating instance (and one that was largely instrumental in bringing about a reconsideration of what constitutes pure and applied mathematics) is that of geometry. After the discovery, in the nineteenth century, that a non-euclidean system of geometry is a possible object of mathematical thought, the systems of euclidean and non-euclidean geometry had to be accepted as equally valid branches of pure mathematics (cf. Note 1, p. 182); and the question of whether actual space (whatever this may mean) is euclidean or non-euclidean was then seen to be a question of empirical fact. There was thus geometry studied as pure mathematics, which could be euclidean or non-euclidean at the option of the geometer; and there was also geometry conceived as the study of the spatial structure of the physical world, this being part of applied mathematics. In Russell's view the theorems of pure geometry are, properly speaking, not *factual* statements but rather statements of implications. The theorem of Pythagoras, for example, should ideally be enunciated, not in the bare words of Euclid, I, 47: 'In right-angled triangles the square on the side subtending the right angle is equal to the sum of the squares on the sides containing the right angle', but in the amended form: 'The axioms of euclidean geometry imply that in right-angled triangles etc.'[1]

It was, and has remained, Russell's firm belief that his definition of

[1] Cf. Russell [2], §412, and also Whitehead [2], p. 2.

pure mathematics—the definition laid down in the opening paragraph of *The Principles of Mathematics*, and already quoted on p. 156 above— is sufficiently wide to encompass all that is traditionally included in this division of mathematics, and more besides. Pure mathematics, in other words, requires no primitive notions or primitive propositions other than those of logic. This is what *Principia Mathematica* set out to demonstrate, by presenting a complete system of pure mathematics, based on logic alone.

3.1   The logical calculus of 'Principia Mathematica'

Principia Mathematica opens, as it must, with a very detailed treatment of symbolic logic, based on a small set of axioms. The logical calculus, formulated in the first instance in terms of propositions and propositional functions, is soon expanded into a formal theory of classes and relations, the topics dealt with becoming gradually more specific until eventually the discussion issues in a purely logical theory of cardinal and ordinal numbers. All this takes up the first volume and the greater part of the second. Then follow several chapters on 'series', i.e. simply ordered classes, in which is to be found a generalized treatment of much of the logical content of mathematical analysis. Finally, Volume III concludes with a discussion of 'the kinds of applications of numbers which may be called measurement'. This closing discussion was meant to prepare the ground (in a way that may be inferred from the corresponding discussion in *The Principles of Mathematics*) for an eventual fourth and concluding volume on geometry, but this volume was never written. *Principia Mathematica* thus remains a truncated system of pure mathematics, devoted essentially to the logical analysis and construction of arithmetic.

The logic of the *Principia* differs somewhat, especially in notation, from the logical calculus that we have presented in the last three chapters of Part I. That calculus is essentially Russell's system of logic as modified by Hilbert. Modification of the original system of the *Principia* has been proposed by many authors (including Russell and Whitehead themselves, in the introduction to the second edition of their work, published in 1925) and some of the suggested changes undoubtedly constitute substantial improvements. As our present interest in *Principia Mathematica* is primarily historical, however, and as we already have a logical instrument that is sufficient for our practical needs in the system of symbolic logic which we developed in Part I, it will be best if we base the remarks which follow on the *Principia* as it was originally formulated.

In *Principia Mathematica*, then, small Latin letters are used to denote propositions and propositional variables; and the molecular forms 'not-p', 'p or q', 'p and q', 'if p, then q', 'q if and only if p' are

12—M.L.

symbolized by $\sim p$, $p \vee q$, $p.q$, $p \supset q$, $p \equiv q$ respectively.   Propositional functions with individual arguments are written as ϕx, $\phi(x,y)$, etc., and the quantified expressions 'for all x, ϕx' and 'there exists an x such that ϕx' (or 'ϕx always' and 'ϕx sometimes') as $(x)\phi x$ and $(\exists x)\phi x$.

As a rule the use of brackets as a means of rendering unambiguous the molecular constitution of a symbolic expression is avoided, the function of brackets being taken over by dots or groups of dots.   It had already been pointed out by Peano that instead of using brackets round part of an expression we can draw a line beneath that part, and then we can simplify the typography by using dots instead of the lines. A simple way of doing this is by omitting the lines and simply marking the positions of their extremities by dots (except at the beginning and end of the whole expression, where no indication is needed).   For example, we can write

$$(q \supset r) \supset ((p \vee q) \supset (p \vee r))$$

either as

$$q \supset r \supset \underline{p \vee q \supset p \vee r}$$

or as

$$q \supset r . \supset : p \vee q . \supset . p \vee r,$$

leaving one dot at the beginning and two at the end to be understood. The effect of the dots is to emphasize the connectives rather than the expressions which they connect, and this is an advantage since it helps to make the logical symbolism easier to read.   The use of dots in *Principia Mathematica* is based directly on Peano's practice.

Among the logical notions for which special provision was made in the *Principia* is that of *assertion*.   If a symbolic expression is set down as a theorem, with the understanding that if the statement which it denotes is in fact false then the authors stand convicted of error, the expression is preceded by the sign of assertion '$\vdash$', followed by as many dots as may be needed to bracket off the whole of the expression that is asserted.   An expression that is written down without an assertion sign is to be understood as merely under consideration.   The distinction between asserting and considering, which thus appeared in a comparatively rudimentary form in *Principia Mathematica*, has subsequently proved to be of fundamental importance in the study of formal systems, and it has been elaborated by Hilbert in a way that renders use of a special assertion sign obsolete.   Following the practice of Hilbert, logicians now draw a clear distinction (as we did in Part I) between (a) the primary formal system of logic or mathematics that is under construction, and (b) the metalogic or metamathematics of this system, which comprises an examination of the properties of the primary system and the expressions that occur in it.   In place of Russell's 'assertions' $\vdash . \mathfrak{A}$ we now have the derived formulae of the system, which alone can be items in its formal development.   Everything else is metalogical; and when an expression $\mathfrak{E}$ is being 'considered' it can only occur in a metalogical setting.   Thus the idea of metalogical discussion as an essential element in the treatment of symbolic logic is certainly present in *Principia Mathematica*, if somewhat confusedly, but the achievement of appreciating and making clear its exact status was Hilbert's.

The entire system of *Principia Mathematica* was initially based on the notion (abandoned in the introduction to the second edition) of 'assertion of a propositional function'.   Suppose that, taking some specific predicate ϕ, we set down the propositional function ϕx, that is to say a form of words which contains a 'variable' or unspecified name x.   Such an expression has the grammatical form of a statement, but it only becomes properly a statement when a definite name is substituted for the variable.   Strictly speaking, therefore, we cannot assert the propositional function ϕx, but only the proposition ϕa for some specific a.   Nevertheless we often have occasion to do something that is almost indistinguishable from asserting ϕx, and Russell characterizes this as 'asserting an ambiguous value of ϕx'.   When we say 'The square of a real number is positive', for instance, we are making an assertion about an individual real number, but not about any particular one rather than another.   We are thus asserting a propositional function, as standing for any of the propositions covered by it.   In the same way, when Russell lays down the axiom

$$\vdash: p \vee p . \supset . p,$$

he is also asserting a propositional function, since p is here a variable; and it follows at once that, if any expression that denotes a proposition or propositional function is substituted for p throughout the axiom, the assertion sign may be prefixed equally to the resulting expression.   In Hilbert's symbolic logic, of course, where we are concerned only with *formal* derivation from the stated initial formulae, the principle that arbitrary expressions of the appropriate kind can be substituted for variables finds strictly formal expression in the rules of substitution (α).

The variables that occur bound in assertions made in *Principia Mathematica* do not necessarily denote individuals, and letters standing for propositional functions, classes, relations, etc. are allowed as apparent variables.   In other words, the logic of the system is not the *restricted* calculus of predicates but a much extended calculus; and a theory of types is accordingly needed in order to exclude vicious-circle fallacies such as the fallacy in Russell's own argument that leads to the antinomy of the class of all classes that are not members of themselves (cf. p. 112 above).

3.2   Russell's theory of types

It follows from the vicious-circle principle (cf. *P.M.*, I, p. 40) that no predicate can figure among its own arguments.   An ostensible proposition like $\phi(\phi)$, where ϕ is some specific predicate, must therefore be a form of expression that is neither true nor false, but devoid of significance; and the most obvious requirement to be satisfied by the theory of types is that it must exclude meaningless symbolic expressions of such a kind.   We accordingly set up a stratification of formal expressions into individuals, first-order functions (whose arguments are individuals), second-order functions (whose arguments are first-order functions, and possibly individuals as well), and so on.   This is not enough, however, for a function with an individual as its only argument may well *presuppose* a totality of functions, even though it does not have any function as argument (cf. p. 114).   Suppose we take a function ϕx, in which both ϕ and x are variables.   Then ϕx has two arguments— the variable predicate or function ϕ, or $\phi \hat{x}$ as it is written in *Principia Mathematica*, and the variable individual x.   If we now make ϕx the argument of some specific function $f\hat{z}$, we get a function $f(\phi x)$ of $\phi \hat{x}$ and x; and if we prefix to this function the universal quantifier (ϕ) we obtain finally a function $(\phi)f(\phi x)$ of x alone.   This new function is not an 'elementary' function ψx of the kind obtained when a specific predicate ψ is applied to a variable individual x, however, but a function which presupposes the entire totality of such elementary functions; and $(\phi)f(\phi x)$ and ϕx need therefore to be counted as being of different type.   The rough stratification of functions that we introduced above must accordingly be made more elaborate.

The classification of propositional functions that we ultimately arrive at is based on the concept of a *matrix*,[1] or propositional function in which no quantifiers are involved.   Matrices, or *predicative functions* as they are also called, are distinguished in the symbolism by an exclamation mark placed immediately after the symbol for the function. We begin the classification, as before, with the totality of individuals, which the vicious-circle principle allows us to count as a legitimate totality.   Next we have the first-order matrices (i.e. elementary propositional functions $\phi!x$, $\phi!(x,y)$, etc.); and any function or proposition that is obtained from a first-order matrix by quantification of some or all of the (individual) variables involved in it is said to be a first-order function or proposition.   A second-order matrix is a matrix that has for its arguments at least one first-order matrix, and possibly individual variables as well.   Examples of second-order matrices are $\sim \phi!a$, where $\phi!\hat{x}$ is a variable first-order matrix and a is a fixed individual, and $\phi!x \mathbin{.} \supset \mathbin{.} \psi!x$, where the arguments are the two first-order matrices $\phi!\hat{x}$

---

[1] This use of the term 'matrix' has, of course, no connexion with the use of the same term in algebra.

and $\psi!\hat{x}$ and the individual variable x. A propositional function or proposition that is derived from a second-order matrix by quantification is called a second-order function or proposition. Matrices, functions, and propositions of higher order than the second are defined in a similar way.

The order of a matrix, as here defined, is necessarily higher than the order of any of the arguments of the matrix, and matrices of fixed order accordingly form legitimate totalities. In other words, we may convert into an apparent variable any individual variable or any variable that carries an exclamation mark.

By a *type*, in the present theory, is meant the range of significance of some propositional function, i.e. the totality of arguments that render the function significant. Thus a function $f(\hat{x}_1, \ldots, \hat{x}_n)$ of n arguments, which may be individual variables or function variables, defines a type which is the totality of n-tuples $(a_1, \ldots, a_n)$ for which $f(a_1, \ldots, a_n)$ is significant. If there is only one argument, so that we have simply a function $f\hat{x}$, the type determined by this function is the totality over which the apparent variable ranges in the quantified expressions $(x)fx$ and $(\exists x)fx$.

Since the limitations imposed on the logical calculus by this theory of types proved to be so stringent that important parts of ordinary mathematics (among them Dedekind's theory of the real continuum) could not be incorporated in the system of *Principia Mathematica*, Russell and Whitehead were obliged to have recourse to a special axiom that would reinstate those excluded deductive procedures that were not themselves logically suspect. They chose for this purpose the axiom

$$\vdash: (\exists f): \phi x . \equiv_x . f!x,$$

which they called the *axiom of reducibility*. It asserts that to every propositional function $\phi\hat{x}$ of a single variable there corresponds a formally equivalent *predicative* function $f!\hat{x}$, i.e. a predicative function $f!\hat{x}$ such that ϕx and $f!x$ are equivalent *for all* x. This axiom was admittedly nothing but an *ad hoc* expedient; but Russell and Whitehead regarded it as a reasonable assumption since it is weaker than the assertion that every propositional function $\phi\hat{x}$ determines a class $\hat{z}(\phi z)$ of arguments that satisfy it. For, if such a class can be treated as a proper entity, we have

$$\vdash: \phi x . \equiv_x . x \in \hat{z}(\phi z);$$

and since the expression $\hat{x} \in \hat{z}(\phi z)$ contains no quantifier, it is a predicative function $f!\hat{x}$. We certainly cannot go as far as to make this unrestricted assumption about classes, since that is one way in which known vicious circles can be produced, but perhaps we can safely postulate the weaker axiom of reducibility.

The treatment of types given in *Principia Mathematica* is known as the *ramified theory of types*, and it is very much more complicated than the *simple theory of types*, which we discussed in Part I (cf. p. 115).   In the simple theory, the type to which any function $f(x_1, \ldots, x_n)$ belongs may be represented directly by the symbol $((x_1), \ldots, (x_n))$, where (x_i) denotes the type of x_i; but in the theory as given in *Principia Mathematica* (to express the matter somewhat roughly) every such simple type must be subdivided into infinitely many subordinate types, corresponding to the possible orders of $f(x_1, \ldots, x_n)$ for the prescribed types of the arguments.   The function $f(x_1, \ldots, x_n)$ may, in fact, be of any order superior to all the orders of the x_i, its order actually being one higher than the highest of all the orders of the variables, apparent as well as real, involved in $f(x_1, \ldots, x_n)$.   This fine structure of the types was introduced with the aim of ensuring strict observance of the vicious-circle principle.   But the only known paradoxes that are not ruled out by even the simple theory of types are the semantic ones, typified by the paradox of the liar, who utters the self-contradictory statement 'The assertion that I am now making is untrue'.   These paradoxes, of which several famous examples are given in *Principia Mathematica* (pp. 60 ff. ; see also Note 1 on p. 127 above), involve various notions, such as truth and definability, which are not purely syntactic.   In view of this fact—and even more because the extended calculus of predicates with the simple theory of types can be proved free from contradiction by metalogical argument[1]—the ramified theory of types, and with it the axiom of reducibility, has now been largely abandoned.

There are two further points relating to the treatment of types in *Principia Mathematica* that should perhaps be mentioned.   One is that only *relative* types matter in any given context, so that it is not essential to identify the zero level of the individuals ; and the other is that many of the propositional functions and other symbols used in *Principia Mathematica* possess *typical ambiguity*.   The relation of identity $x = y$, for example, is a different propositional function for each of the possible types to which x and y may belong.   But all these separate identities have the same formal characteristics, and it is quite harmless to gloss over the distinction of type, leaving it to be understood that the symbol '$=$' always denotes the particular species of identity that is called for by the context.   If it were not for the possibility of such systematic 'abuse of language', the logical calculus of the *Principia* would be altogether unmanageable.

3.3   The formal development of 'Principia Mathematica'

Principia Mathematica is chiefly valuable today, apart from its paramount interest as a historical source, as an exceptionally rich repository

[1] G. Gentzen: 'Die Widerspruchsfreiheit der Stufenlogik', *Math. Zeitschrift*, **41** (1936), 357–366.

of logical ideas and symbolic devices.   In the present section we shall attempt to summarize its more immediately interesting symbolic features.

We take first the relation of *identity*.   This was conceived by Russell in Leibnizian terms (cf. p. 90 above); and since his system of logic allowed quantifiers to be applied to functions (i.e. predicates) as well as to individuals, there was no obstacle in the way of his giving a purely logical definition of identity, namely

$$x = y . = : (\phi):\phi!x . \supset . \phi!y \quad \text{Df.}$$

Using the axiom of reducibility, we get from this the assertion

$$\vdash:. \ x = y . \supset : fx . \supset . fy,$$

whether $f\hat{x}$ is predicative or not.   The variables x and y can be of any order (the same for both, since both are possible arguments of the same function $f\hat{x}$) and then '$=$' is of the next higher order.

Classes are not admitted as actual entities at all, but a notation for them is nevertheless introduced in order that the very useful mathematical language of classes (cf. Chapter 4, §5 above) may be translated into the logical symbolism.   The class determined by a propositional function $\psi\hat{z}$ is denoted by $\hat{z}(\psi z)$.   This symbol is not defined explicitly but only contextually, since the chosen definition serves merely to give meaning to its use, by analysing certain composite expressions of which it can form part.   This definition runs as follows:

$$f[\hat{z}(\psi z)] . = : (\exists\phi):\phi!x . \equiv_x. \psi x : f[\phi!\hat{z}] \quad \text{Df.}$$

The relation of class-membership, denoted by ϵ, has a definition which leads at once to the basic equivalence

$$\vdash: x \ \epsilon \ \hat{z}(\psi z) . \equiv . \psi x.$$

Classes are commonly denoted, by way of convenient abbreviation, by small Greek letters.

A class is said to *exist* if it has at least one member.   This is a different sense of existence from that which is embodied in the existential quantifier, and a modified symbol is introduced for it by the following definition:

$$\exists!\alpha . = . (\exists x).x \ \epsilon \ \alpha \quad \text{Df.}$$

The empty class Λ and the universal class V are introduced by the definitions $\Lambda = \hat{x}(x \neq x)$ Df and $V = \hat{x}(x = x)$ Df, typical ambiguity here being involved; the union and intersection of two classes are defined in terms of the disjunction and conjunction of the propositional functions that give rise to the classes; and the detailed working out of the theory of classes now proceeds very much as it does in standard mathematical presentations of the subject.

Just as a propositional function $\phi\hat{x}$ with one argument can be looked upon as defining a class $\hat{x}(\phi x)$, so a propositional function $\psi(\hat{x},\hat{y})$ with two arguments can be looked upon as defining a *relation* $\hat{x}\hat{y}[\psi(x,y)]$, understood as the class of ordered couples (x,y) for which the function becomes a true proposition (cf. p. 109). Relations are very important later in the *Principia*, when symbolic logic is applied to the development of arithmetic.

Coming now to *descriptions*, we have the symbol $(\imath x)(\phi x)$, which has the interpretation '*the* entity x which satisfies $\phi\hat{x}$', and which only denotes something when there is precisely one entity with the stated property (cf. p. 92 above). The definition of a description, like the definition of a class, is once again a definition in use, which gives a meaning only to certain expressions in which $(\imath x)(\phi x)$ occurs. It runs as follows:

$$\psi(\imath x)(\phi x) . = : (\exists b): \phi x . \equiv_x . x = b: \psi b \quad \text{Df.}$$

Since the expression $(\imath x)(\phi x)$ does not denote anything unless $\phi\hat{x}$ is satisfied by a unique argument, we need a notation for yet another sense of existence, and so we put

$$\text{E!}(\imath x)(\phi x) . = : (\exists b): \phi x . \equiv_x . x = b \quad \text{Df.}$$

A particularly important kind of description is the *descriptive function*, which is derived in the following way from a relation. Suppose we have a relation xRy, such that whenever a definite value is given to the variable y there is one and only one value of x for which the relation holds. We are then able to make use of the expression $(\imath x)(xRy)$, which denotes a function of y since y is involved in it as a parameter. Such a function is not a propositional function, however, but an individual function (supposing that x is here an individual variable), i.e. a function that takes individuals as its values. It is, in fact, an *ι-term* in the sense of Chapter 4, §2. In *Principia Mathematica* $(\imath x)(xRy)$ is denoted by $R'y$, read as 'the R of y'. If, to take a simple example, xRy is 'x and y are father and son', then $R'y$ denotes 'the father of y', and we have $\text{E!}R'b$ for every man b; but if we consider the converse relation $\breve{R}$, we do not have $\text{E!}\breve{R}'a$ unless a has a unique son. The familiar one-valued functions of mathematics are descriptive functions in the sense just explained; and in the present notation we would have to write $\sin'x$, for example, instead of $\sin x$.

There is an important logical distinction, appreciated for the first time by Peano and Frege, between a single entity x and the class whose sole member is x. This *unit class* is denoted, in the symbolism of the *Principia*, by $\iota'x$. Recognition of the difference between x and $\iota'x$ incidentally clears up a certain obscurity in traditional logic. It will be recalled that this older logic has some features that are repugnant to a mind trained in modern mathematics, one of these being the counting of any singular proposition, such as 'Socrates is mortal', as universal on the ground that it distributes its (indivisible) subject (cf. p. 11).   In traditional logic, in fact, we have to regard the two syllogisms

All men are mortal	and	All men are mortal
All Greeks are men		Socrates is a man
All Greeks are mortal		Socrates is mortal

as both being of the same form Barbara; but the symbolism of *Principia Mathematica* reveals an essential structural difference between them, for when they are expressed more exactly they take the respective forms

Men $\subset$ mortal beings	and	Men $\subset$ mortal beings
Greeks $\subset$ men		Socrates ϵ men
Greeks $\subset$ mortal beings		Socrates ϵ mortal beings.

The second syllogism could only be properly assimilated to the first, with class-inclusion used throughout, if it were expressed in the modified form

Men $\subset$ mortal beings

ι' Socrates $\subset$ men

ι' Socrates $\subset$ mortal beings.

In this way, by using precise logical symbolism in place of the comparatively blunt instrument of everyday language, we are now able to distinguish clearly between the relations ϵ and $\subset$ and between the entities x and ι'x, thus bringing into sharp relief significant details of logical form that previously remained indistinct.

With the aid of the notation ι'x, an unordered pair (or *cardinal couple*) can be defined as the union ι'$x \cup \iota$'y of two distinct unit classes. The ordered pair (or *ordinal couple*) that consists of x and y in that order can be defined as the relation $\hat{z}\hat{w}(z \epsilon \iota$'$x . w \epsilon \iota$'$y)$, written for short as $x \downarrow y$, which holds between the two particular entities x and y, and between no others.[1]

Among the many special symbols that are introduced for the treatment of relations, the following are especially worthy of note.   We refer all the time to some particular relation R.

If xRy, we say that x is a *referent* of y, and y is a *relatum* of x.   The

---

[1] In mathematics, it is not now usual to define an ordered pair in this way as a relation.   Instead, a definition is preferred in which the ordered pair (x,y) is identified with the class $\{\{x\},\{x,y\}\}$, i.e. the class which has two members, namely the unit class $\{x\}$ or ι'x and the unordered pair $\{x,y\}$.   This definition was proposed by Kuratowski (see his paper 'Sur la notion d'ordre dans la théorie des ensembles', *Fund. Math.*, **2** (1921), 161–171).

relation of the class of referents of y to y is denoted by $\vec{R}$, so that we have

$$\vec{R} \,.=.\, \hat{\alpha}\hat{y}[\alpha = \hat{x}(xRy)] \quad \text{Df.}$$

It follows that $\vec{R}`y = \hat{x}(xRy)$. $\overleftarrow{R}$ and $\overleftarrow{R}`x$ are obtained in a similar way, but by use of relata instead of referents.

The *domain* $D`R$ of $R$ is the class of entities $x$ that have the relation $R$ to something, and the *converse domain* $\mathrm{Œ}`R$ is the class of entities y to which something has the relation.   Thus

$$D`R = \hat{x}[(\exists y)xRy] = \hat{x}[\exists! \overleftarrow{R}`x].$$

The *field* of R, denoted by $C`R$, is the union of the domain and the converse domain: $C`R = D`R \cup \mathrm{Œ}`R$.

If R and S are two relations, their *relative product* $R\,|\,S$ is the relation which holds between x and z when there is an intermediate entity y such that xRy and ySz.   Thus maternal grandfather = father | mother, while paternal grandmother = mother | father.   The relative product $R\,|\,R$ of a relation R with itself is conveniently written as R^2.

If β is a given class, $R``\beta$ is used to denote the class of referents of the elements of β :

$$R``\beta = \hat{x}[(\exists y){:}y \,\epsilon\, \beta \,.\, xRy] \quad \text{Df.}$$

Many-one, one-many, and one-one relations can all be characterized logically; and then two classes α and β are defined to be equipotent or *similar*[1] (α sm β) if there exists a one-one relation with α as its domain and β as its converse domain.   From here it is only a short step to the concept of the cardinal number $\mathrm{Nc}`\alpha$ of a class α.   We put

$$\mathrm{Nc} = \overrightarrow{\mathrm{sm}} \quad \text{Df}$$

and

$$\mathrm{NC} = D`\mathrm{Nc} \quad \text{Df},$$

so that NC denotes the class of cardinal numbers.   Then

$$\vdash. \mathrm{Nc}`\alpha = \hat{\beta}(\beta \text{ sm } \alpha),$$

that is to say, the cardinal number of α is the classes of all classes similar to α.   The particular cardinal numbers 0, 1, 2 are respectively

$$\iota`\Lambda,$$

$$\hat{\alpha}[(\exists x).\alpha = \iota`x],$$

$$\hat{\alpha}[(\exists x)(\exists y){:}x \neq y \,.\, \alpha = \iota`x \cup \iota`y].$$

---

[1] This use of 'similar' must not be confused with Cantor's use (cf. p. 161).   The term used in *Principia Mathematica* for 'similar' in the sense of Cantor is 'ordinally similar'.

With this we conclude our summary of the contents of *Principia Mathematica*, which is intended mainly as an introduction to the reading of the work itself. We have tried to give an indication of how Russell, with the collaboration of Whitehead, succeeded in fashioning a system of logic which, by virtue of the penetrating analysis of logical ideas on which it was based and the powerful symbolic apparatus used in its construction, far surpassed traditional logic in both delicacy and scope, and also how this system of symbolic logic was used for the analysis of pure mathematics. On the formal side Russell owed much to the initiative of Peano, while his logical analysis of mathematical concepts was partly his own and partly Frege's, as we shall now see.

4 Frege's logical analysis of arithmetic

It is a remarkable fact that, although Russell conceived his project of reducing mathematics to logic quite independently, a very similar task had been embarked upon some years earlier by Gottlob Frege, whose remarks on the history of mathematical rigour we have already had occasion to quote (p. 137). In the preface to *The Principles of Mathematics* (1903) Russell made the following acknowledgement:

'In Mathematics, my chief obligations, as is indeed evident, are to Georg Cantor and Professor Peano. If I had become acquainted sooner with the work of Professor Frege, I should have owed a great deal to him, but as it is I arrived independently at many results which he had already established.'

Gottlob Frege (1848–1925), who was born at Wismar, spent his whole life as a teacher of mathematics in the university of Jena, where he eventually became professor. Although it is now clear that he was the greatest mathematical logician of the age in which he lived, his work was not much regarded in his lifetime, and it is only since his death that his ideas have become at all widely known. He invented a logical symbolism, to which he gave the name *Begriffsschrift* (concept-script), and this enabled him to exhibit the logical structure of propositions and demonstrations with much greater clarity than had previously been possible. Indeed, Frege's concept-script is in no way inferior, from a theoretical point of view, to the more familiar symbolism that goes back to Peano; and the main reason why it was Peano's system of notation that prevailed may well be that Peano had more of an eye than Frege for ease of reading and ease of printing,[1] and this allowed him to achieve a more satisfactory balance between accuracy and simplicity in the representation of logical ideas.

[1] Always a practical man, Peano bought his own press so that he could personally supervise the printing of his *Rivista* and *Formulaire*.

Frege's work on the foundations of mathematics is nearly all contained in the three books that he published:

(1) *Begriffsschrift, eine der arithmetischen nachgebildete Formelsprache des reinen Denkens* [Concept-script, a symbolic language of pure thought modelled on the language of arithmetic] (Halle, 1879);

(2) *Die Grundlagen der Arithmetik, eine logisch-mathematische Untersuchung über den Begriff der Zahl* [The foundations of arithmetic, a logico-mathematical investigation into the concept of number] (Breslau, 1884);

(3) *Grundgesetze der Arithmetik, begriffsschriftlich abgeleitet* [Fundamental laws of arithmetic, derived by means of concept-script] (Jena; 2 volumes, 1893 and 1903).

The *Begriffsschrift* is a short essay of 88 pages, in which the new symbolism is introduced and explained. It is, in fact, the earliest systematic presentation of the propositional calculus and the calculus of predicates. The *Grundlagen der Arithmetik*, which has been translated into English (see above, p. 138), is a comparatively non-technical account of Frege's logical analysis of the concept of cardinal number. *Grundgesetze der Arithmetik* is Frege's main work, in which the concept-script is applied to the construction of a system of arithmetic comparable with that contained in *Principia Mathematica*.

4.1*   The 'Begriffsschrift'

In his *Begriffsschrift* (1879) Frege presented a system of symbolic logic that amounts essentially to the calculus of predicates with identity. It was the extended calculus of predicates that he had in mind, although most of the discussion is in fact confined to the restricted calculus.

Frege conceives his system in terms of assertions or judgements (*Urteile*), and his notation for an assertion is $\vdash\!\!\!-\!\!-$ A. Here 'A' stands for some sentence that expresses a proposition; the horizontal line '$-\!\!-$' is the *content-stroke*, which serves to bracket off all that is placed to the right of it; and the vertical line 'I' is the *assertion-stroke*, which converts the mere expression $-\!\!-$ A, simply entertained as an object of intellectual contemplation, into the assertion $\vdash\!\!\!-\!\!-$ A, by which it is declared to be a fact (cf. the assertion sign '$\vdash$' in *Principia Mathematica*, which was suggested by Frege's notation).

The logical constants that Frege adopts as primitive for the propositional calculus are not the more usual 'or' and 'not', as in systems of symbolic logic derived from *Principia Mathematica*, but 'implies' and 'not'. For the asserted implication $B \to A$, Frege writes

which, as he says, signifies the assertion that the possibility 'A is denied and B is affirmed' is excluded and one of the other three possibilities 'A is affirmed and B is affirmed', 'A is affirmed and B is denied', and 'A is denied and B is denied' must be a fact. The 'A' and 'B' that occur here are capital Greek letters, which Frege employs as syntactic variables. If we separate out the constituent parts of the above formal expression by writing it as

$$\vdash\!\!\!-\!\!-\!\!\begin{array}{l} -\ A \\[4pt] \underline{}\ B, \end{array}$$

we see that it is made up of the following elements: (i) the assertion-stroke '$\vdash$', (ii) adjacent to this, the content-stroke of the whole assertion, (iii) the vertical *condition-stroke*, (iv) the content-strokes of the two sentences 'A' and 'B', and (v) these two sentences themselves. All formulae written in concept-script can be analysed into components in this way.

To represent the negation of a formula (or of a constituent of a formula) Frege appends a small vertical mark to the corresponding content-stroke. Thus he writes the assertions of the propositions 'B implies not-A' and 'not-(B implies A)' as

$$\vdash\!\!\!\!\begin{array}{l} \dashv\ A \\ \underline{}\ B \end{array} \qquad\text{and}\qquad \vdash\!\dashv\!\!\!\begin{array}{l} \ A \\ \underline{}\ B \end{array}$$

respectively.

The sign '$\equiv$' is used for a certain relation of equivalence (*Inhalts-gleichheit*). When Frege writes '$A \equiv B$', he understands this statement as meaning that 'the symbol A and the symbol B have the same conceptual content, so that either may be put in place of the other'.

Predicates are symbolized with the aid of the usual notation for functions. If $\Phi(A)$ is a predicate with a single argument, the quantified assertion 'The predicate Φ applies for all values of its argument' is written symbolically as

$$\vdash\!\!-\!\!\overset{\mathfrak{a}}{\smile}\!\!-\ \Phi(\mathfrak{a}),$$

with a German letter used for the bound variable.

These, then, are the primitive elements in Frege's system, and they are sufficient to permit analysis of the structure of all assertions that Frege wishes to consider. Thus assertions of the forms 'A and B' and 'There is some value of the argument A for which $\Phi(A)$ holds', for example, can be expressed by writing

$$\vdash\!\dashv\!\dashv\!\begin{array}{l} \ A \\ \underline{}\ B \end{array} \qquad\text{and}\qquad \vdash\!\dashv\!\overset{\mathfrak{a}}{\smile}\!\dashv\ \Phi(\mathfrak{a})$$

respectively.

Frege bases his treatment of the propositional calculus on the following six axioms:

1.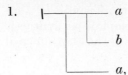

2.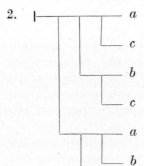

8.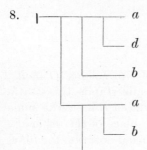

28.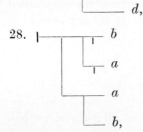

31.

41.

The letters $a, b, \ldots$ are here used as propositional variables. The numbers of the axioms are not consecutive, since Frege prefers to introduce the successive axioms gradually, deriving the more important standard formulae of the propositional calculus as soon as he is in a position to do so. The axioms themselves can be expressed in our earlier logical symbolism by the following formulae:

$$X \to (Y \to X),$$
$$[X \to (Y \to Z)] \to [(X \to Y) \to (X \to Z)],$$
$$[X \to (Y \to Z)] \to [Y \to (X \to Z)],$$
$$(X \to Y) \to (\bar{Y} \to \bar{X}),$$
$$\bar{\bar{X}} \to X,$$
$$X \to \bar{\bar{X}}.$$

Derivations in the propositional calculus are carried out by means of the two procedures of substitution and passage from a pair of formulae

$$\vdash A \quad \text{and} \quad \vdash \begin{array}{c} B \\ \hline A \end{array}$$

to the further formula

$$\vdash B,$$

i.e. *modus ponens*, the rule (β) of Chapter 2. These procedures are not embodied in stated rules, since they are so plainly justified by the interpretation that is given in the *Begriffsschrift* to the symbols used. The system, in fact, is not so much a *formal* axiomatic theory as a systematic presentation of logic with the aid of a suitable symbolic language; and, unlike Peano in the *Formulaire*, Frege treats the symbols as inseparable from their meaning.

The extension from the propositional calculus to the full calculus of predicates with identity necessitates the adoption of three further axioms:

52. $\vdash \begin{array}{c} f(d) \\ \hline f(c) \\ \hline (c \equiv d), \end{array}$

54. $\vdash (c \equiv c),$

58. $\vdash \begin{array}{c} f(c) \\ \hline \underset{\mathfrak{a}}{} \; f(\mathfrak{a}), \end{array}$

These axioms correspond respectively to our axioms (J_2), (J_1), and (e), namely $a = b \to (F(a) \to F(b))$, $a = a$, and $(x)F(x) \to F(y)$.

4.2*   The 'Grundgesetze der Arithmetik'

In his most ambitious work, the *Grundgesetze der Arithmetik* (1893 and 1903), Frege first of all gave a new and revised account of his logical calculus. By the time of writing of the *Grundgesetze* he had evolved his now well-known theory of sense and denotation (*Sinn* and *Bedeutung*) (see Note 2, p. 183), and he based his new treatment of logic on this theory. By the *sense* of a statement or proposition Frege understood its content, i.e. the 'meaning of the words' as we would ordinarily say, while by its *denotation* he understood its truth-value. He took propositions, in fact, as names, every true proposition being a name of the truth-value truth (*das Wahre*) and every false proposition a name of the truth-value falsity (*das Falsche*). He now needed an appropriate way of representing symbolically the truth-value of any given proposition, and for this purpose he modified his earlier use of the content-stroke. In the *Grundgesetze*, any combination of symbols of the form — $\varDelta$ denotes the truth-value truth when $\varDelta$ itself denotes truth and the truth-value falsity otherwise. Thus — $\varDelta$ denotes truth whenever $\varDelta$ is a true proposition, and it denotes falsity whenever $\varDelta$ is either a false proposition or not a proposition at all. The expression $\top \varDelta$ denotes the truth-value opposite to — $\varDelta$. If, in particular, A is a proposition, then — A is the truth-value of A; and if we prefix to this expression an assertion-stroke, writing $\vdash A$ in place of — A, we 'assert A' by declaring that the truth-value — A is in fact truth.

The incorporation in the concept-script of a symbol — A for the truth-value of any proposition A greatly increases the flexibility of the logical calculus. We can now write the bi-implication $A \leftrightarrow B$, for instance, simply as — $A = - B$, instead of having to use the complicated formula

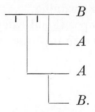

The earlier axioms are now replaced in part by rules for the transformation of formulae—for example, the axiom

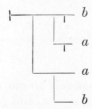

by a rule which states that a lower and an upper member in a proposition may be interchanged, provided that their truth-values are both reversed. The list of rules of procedure now also includes the rule of *modus ponens*, formulated explicitly.

In the *Grundgesetze*, the symbolism of the *Begriffsschrift* is extended by the adoption of a considerable number of special symbols for particular logical and arithmetical ideas. Especially important is the new notation for what Frege refers to as the 'course of values' (*Wertverlauf*) of a propositional function. This new concept is arrived at in the following way. Any propositional function $\Phi(\xi)$ associates with each value of its argument ξ a definite truth-value, truth or falsity; and if two functions $\Phi(\xi)$ and $\Psi(\xi)$ assign the same truth-values to all possible values of ξ, we would naturally say that they have the same course of values. Frege gives precision to this manner of speaking by introducing a new kind of expression $\acute{\varepsilon}\Phi(\varepsilon)$ to symbolize the course of values of $\Phi(\xi)$, and postulating as a new basic principle the formula

$$\vdash (\acute{\varepsilon}f(\varepsilon) = \acute{\alpha}g(\alpha)) = (\overset{\mathfrak{a}}{\smile} f(\mathfrak{a}) = g(\mathfrak{a})),$$

which thus functions as a contextual definition of $\acute{\varepsilon}\Phi(\varepsilon)$. The letter '$\varepsilon$' that occurs in $\acute{\varepsilon}\Phi(\varepsilon)$ is, of course, a bound variable, and it may be replaced by any other suitable letter.

Looking at the matter intuitively, we see that the course of values of $\Phi(\xi)$ is effectively the particular division into two classes that the function induces in the totality of possible arguments, namely the separation of the class of those arguments for which $\Phi(\xi)$ takes the truth-value truth from the complementary class of those arguments for which it takes the truth-value falsity. Thus $\acute{\varepsilon}\Phi(\varepsilon)$ provides a formal expression for the extension of the propositional function $\Phi(\xi)$, and Frege's $\acute{\varepsilon}\Phi(\varepsilon)$ therefore has a close affinity with Russell's $\hat{z}(\psi z)$. Frege himself leaves no doubt as to the importance of the new notation $\acute{\varepsilon}\Phi(\varepsilon)$, for he says (§9): 'The introduction of the way of symbolizing courses of values seems to me to be one of the most fruitful extensions of my concept-script that I have made since my first publication on this subject'.

A further valuable addition to the symbolic resources of the system is the symbol $\backslash\xi$, in which we may see a foreshadowing of Russell's definite description $(\imath x)(\phi x)$. The oblique stroke may be put in front of any symbol ξ that stands for a course of values or (as we shall permit ourselves to say slightly inaccurately, in order to convey more readily the underlying intention) any symbol ξ that stands for a class. If this class ξ has a unique member, then $\backslash\xi$ is this member; but if not, then $\backslash\xi$ is the class ξ itself. Frege's actual definition of $\backslash\xi$ runs as follows: 'If there is an object Δ such that $\acute{\varepsilon}(\Delta = \varepsilon)$ is the same as ξ, then the value of $\backslash\xi$ is Δ; but if there is no such object Δ, then ξ is itself the value of $\backslash\xi$.'

We can now state the axioms or 'laws' on which the revised logical calculus is based:

I. $\quad \vdash \quad a \quad$ and $\quad \vdash \quad a$
$$\qquad b \qquad\qquad a,$$
$$\qquad a$$

IIa. $\quad \vdash \quad f(a)$
$$\qquad \underset{\mathfrak{a}}{\quad} f(\mathfrak{a}),$$

IIb. $\quad \vdash \quad M_\beta(f(\beta))$
$$\qquad \underset{\mathfrak{f}}{\quad} M_\beta(\mathfrak{f}(\beta)),$$

III. $\quad \vdash \quad g\left(\underset{\mathfrak{f}}{\quad} \begin{array}{l} \mathfrak{f}(a) \\ \mathfrak{f}(b) \end{array}\right)$
$$\qquad g(a = b),$$

IV. $\quad \vdash \quad (\text{—} \; a) = (\text{—} \; b)$
$$\qquad {}_{\shortmid}(\text{—} \; a) = ({}_{\shortmid} \; b),$$

V. $\quad \vdash \quad (\grave{\varepsilon}f(\varepsilon) = \grave{\alpha}g(\alpha)) = (\underset{\mathfrak{a}}{\quad} f(\mathfrak{a}) = g(\mathfrak{a})),$

VI. $\quad \vdash \quad a = \backslash\grave{\varepsilon}(a = \varepsilon).$

It will be observed that the more usual sign ' = ' is now used in place of the earlier ' $\equiv$ '. Law (IIb) is an extension of law (IIa) to predicates of predicates, and law (V) is the contextual definition of course of values to which we have already referred. In postulating law (III), Frege is now adopting a Leibnizian treatment of identity in preference to the more formal Hilbertian treatment in the *Begriffsschrift*.

The purely logical part of the *Grundgesetze* is devoted to the calculus of propositions and predicates, the theory of classes (treated as courses of values of propositional functions with a single argument), and the theory of relations (*Doppelwertverläufe*, or courses of values of propositional functions with two arguments). But all this is preliminary to the main part of the work, the subject of which is arithmetic. The definition of cardinal number (*Anzahl*) on which the entire arithmetical discussion is based is one that Frege had already examined at length, from a more philosophical point of view, in *Die Grundlagen der Arithmetik* (1884). He argued there that number ought to be defined with reference to a concept or predicate, being, so to speak, a measure of the extension of the concept. He introduced the term 'equinumeric' (*gleichzahlig*) for the relation between two concepts which are such that the classes determined by them can be put in one-one correspondence, and he then defined cardinal number as follows: 'The cardinal number which belongs to the concept F is the extension of the concept "equinumeric to the concept F"'. In other words, the cardinal number that belongs to the concept F is the class of all concepts that are equinumeric to F. In the *Grundgesetze* this definition is applied directly to extensions of concepts instead of to concepts themselves, and a formal definition is given (Vol. I, §40) for the cardinal number $\mathfrak{y}u$ of any class u. The particular cardinal numbers zero and unity, which Frege writes as $\mathbb{0}$ and $\mathbb{1}$, are then defined as

$$\mathfrak{y}\,\grave{\varepsilon}\,(\top\,\varepsilon = \varepsilon) \quad \text{and} \quad \mathfrak{y}\,\grave{e}(\varepsilon = \mathbb{0})$$

respectively.

Cardinal number has now been defined in a way that yields infinite as well as finite numbers; and Frege next turns to a detailed discussion of cardinal arithmetic. This is followed, in the second volume of the *Grundgesetze*, by an account of the real continuum; and the volume concludes with a long section on the theory of quantity (*Grössenlehre*). The scope of the *Grundgesetze* is thus very similar to that of *Principia Mathematica*, and the development of the two works proceeds in very much the same way. This is of course largely because, although Russell worked out most of *The Principles of Mathematics* (1903) in ignorance of Frege's work, he and Whitehead had both volumes of the *Grundgesetze* before them when they were writing *Principia Mathematica* (1910–1913). In their preface, indeed, they acknowledge very specifically the extent of their indebtedness to Frege in the following words:

'Our chief obligations will be obvious to every reader who is familiar with the literature of the subject. . . . In all questions of logical analysis, our chief debt is to Frege. Where we differ from him, it is largely because the contradictions showed that he, in common with all other logicians ancient and modern, had allowed some error to creep into his premisses; but apart from the contradictions, it would have been almost impossible to detect this error.'

We see, then, how Frege and Russell arrived separately at the same logistic conception of mathematics, according to which the whole of mathematics can be expressed in purely logical terms. Frege was the first to carry out the detailed logical analysis of mathematical concepts that this view demanded; and the only major weakness of his system was the absence from it of any safeguard against vicious-circle fallacies. When Russell began his work he did so in ignorance of what Frege had already achieved, but soon afterwards he became acquainted with Frege's results; and eventually Russell and Whitehead produced their improved and extended version of the logico-mathematical system of the *Grundgesetze der Arithmetik*, in which a theory of types was now incorporated. It was this system that was to tower over the entire field of research into the logic of mathematics for many years; and Frege's influence on subsequent developments in the study of logic and the foundations of mathematics has been largely an indirect one, by way of *Principia Mathematica*.

SUPPLEMENTARY NOTES ON CHAPTER 6

1. *Non-euclidean geometry.* Until the nineteenth century, euclidean geometry was accepted without question as a body of necessary truth, and the critical work of mathematicians was directed solely to the removal of blemishes in Euclid's presentation of his system. One of the supposed blemishes was the mere postulation, without proof, of the fundamental fact concerning parallel lines (the fifth postulate of the *Elements*, quoted above on p. 136). Many attempts were made to prove this assertion, which is far from self-evident, by means of Euclid's other axioms and postulates; and an especially notable attempt was that of Gerolamo Saccheri (1667–1733). Saccheri adopted the method of *reductio ad absurdum*. Omitting the parallel postulate from Euclid's system, he considered the figure that is obtained when equal perpendiculars AC and BD are erected at the ends of a straight line AB, on the same side of the line. The angles ACD and BDC are readily shown to be equal, and Saccheri accordingly set up the three exhaustive hypotheses: (1) both angles are right angles, (2) both angles are obtuse angles, (3) both angles are acute angles. He then attempted to establish (1)—from which Euclid's postulate can be deduced—by refuting (2) and (3). His refutations were in fact both fallacious, but in constructing them he correctly deduced many lemmas which embody significant consequences of the assumptions (2) and (3) respectively.

Similar investigations were afterwards made by other mathematicians; and eventually János Bolyai (1802–1860) and Nikolai Ivanovich Lobachevsky (1793–1856), working independently of each other, reached the conclusion that a mathematically correct deductive system of geometrical theorems can be derived no less from Saccheri's hypothesis of the acute angle than from the hypothesis of the right angle. The same conclusion seems also to have been arrived at by Gauss, at the same time or even earlier. Saccheri's third hypothesis, that of the obtuse angle, was still felt to lead to consequences too bizarre for it to be taken seriously; but when Riemann eventually laid the foundation, in his inaugural dissertation of 1854 (cf. p. 334 below), for a more general conception of geometry, he revealed the hitherto unsuspected possibility of geometry on a pseudosphere (i.e. a surface of constant negative curvature), similar in many respects to the already familiar geometry on a sphere. This new geometry was closely related to the geometry that follows from Saccheri's hypothesis of the obtuse angle, and so Riemann was in effect the discoverer of a second type of non-euclidean geometry. His discovery was afterwards elaborated by Klein, who classified the three possible systems of geometry as *parabolic* (Euclid), *hyperbolic* (Bolyai and Lobachevsky), and *elliptic* (Riemann). All three systems are, of course, *abstract* mathematical theories, and whether any one of them applies to ordinary space is an empirical question, to be settled by the ordinary methods of scientific inquiry (cf. Chapter 13, below). It has often been asserted that Gauss attempted to decide the question of whether space is euclidean or non-euclidean by measuring the sum of the angles of a large triangle, with its vertices located at three of the peaks in the Harz mountains (Brocken, Inselberg, and Hoher Hagen), but it now seems that there is not sufficient evidence to show conclusively what purpose he had in mind when he made the measurements. See W. Klingenberg: 'Grundlagen der Geometrie', p. 123, in the *Gedenkband*, Gauss [2].

For an excellent introduction to the history and systematic development of non-euclidean geometry, see D. M. Y. Sommerville: *The Elements of Non-Euclidean Geometry* (1914). A basic work of more advanced character is F. Klein: *Vorlesungen über Nicht-Euklidische Geometrie* (1928). The history of non-euclidean geometry was the subject of an article 'Sulla teoria delle parallele e sulle geometrie non-euclidee', contributed by Roberto Bonola to the collection of essays which Enriques published in 1900 with the title *Questioni riguardanti la geometria elementare*. Bonola afterwards expanded his article into a book [2], which was translated into English by Carslaw in 1912. A reprint of Carslaw's translation, issued in 1955 by Dover Publications, New York, also contains English versions of the original memoirs of Bolyai and Lobachevsky.

2. *Sense and denotation*. Frege developed his theory of the sense and denotation of verbal expressions (cf. p. 178) in a paper entitled 'Über Sinn und Bedeutung', published in the *Zeitschrift für Philosophie und philosophische Kritik*, **100** (1892), 25–50.

Frege began by considering proper names, i.e. single words or descriptive phrases which refer to definite objects of thought. The 'sense' (*Sinn*) of such a name is that which is conveyed by the word or phrase, while the 'denotation' (*Bedeutung*) is the object, if any, to which the name in fact refers. Thus, for instance, the two names 'morning star' and 'evening star' have different senses, but their denotations are the same, namely the planet Venus. To appreciate the sense of a name we only need to understand the language to which it belongs, but to attach to it the correct denotation we must also be in possession of appropriate factual knowledge. The sense of a name must be carefully distinguished moreover, as Frege pointed out, from the private idea or image (*Vorstellung*) which the name conjures up in the mind of any particular individual. Sense is public, since to know a language is precisely to be familiar with the senses of the words and expressions which occur in it.

Having distinguished between sense and denotation in the case of names, Frege went on further to ask what we are to understand by the sense and the denotation of a statement or assertion. His conclusion here was the less immediately persuasive one that, whereas the sense of a statement is the 'thought' (taken in a public sense) which the words express, the denotation of the statement must be identified with its truth-value. For the considerations on which Frege based this identification, we refer the reader to the original paper.

3. *The algebra of logic.* Before symbolic logic took its modern shape, first in Peano's *Formulaire* and then more completely in *Principia Mathematica*, various attempts were made to bring traditional logic up to date (cf. the note on transitional logic on p. 22). The attempts consisted partly in extension or generalization of existing logical conceptions (as in the work of De Morgan, already discussed in the earlier note just referred to) and partly in the application to logic of algebraic symbolism, first carried out by Boole. Out of these investigations there developed an 'algebra of logic', seen in its most mature form in Schröder's *Algebra der Logik* (1890–1905). Although this logical algebra was eventually rendered obsolete by the calculi of propositions and predicates which make use of specifically logical connectives, and consequently it no longer exists as a separate discipline, much of its content was absorbed in *Principia Mathematica*, and there fused with the newer notions of symbolic logic. In this note we indicate briefly some of the main contributions to the early algebra of logic.

Boole's construction of a calculus of classes, whereby logical problems of a combinatorial character can be solved by a process of formal calculation, has already been described in Note 4, p. 51.

De Morgan approached logic in a less algebraic spirit than Boole, for in spite of being a mathematician he was evidently much in sympathy with the outlook of the Scholastic logicians; and he thought of the task facing the logicians of his own time as one of amending traditional logic rather than creating an entirely new logical system to take the place of the existing one. Nevertheless, he advanced far beyond the furthest point reached by logicians working within the aristotelian frame, and in particular he laid the foundation for a formal theory of relations.

De Morgan's logical work is mostly contained in a series of five papers, on the syllogism and various related matters, which he contributed to the *Transactions of the Cambridge Philosophical Society* over the years 1846 to 1862. In Paper No. I (1846) he gave an account of the ideas on the syllogism and the theory of probabilities which he also published in the following year in his *Formal Logic* (cf. p. 22 above); and in Paper No. II (1850) he developed these same ideas further. The third and fourth papers, which belong to a rather later phase of his work on logic, are more important than the first two from the present point of view. Paper No. III (1858) is arranged in two sections, the first of which comprises a general discussion of logic and prevailing attitudes towards it, while the second is a more formal essay entitled 'First Elements of a System of Logic'. It was in this essay that De Morgan gave his first systematic treatment of relations; and in Paper No. IV (1859) he went into the formal algebra of relations in greater detail. Paper No. V (1862) is relatively unimportant, since its chief purpose was to bring to a close the long controversy between De Morgan and Sir William Hamilton, who had died some years previously.

De Morgan accepts, in these papers, the traditional view of a proposition as consisting of two terms linked by a copula; but he rejects, as altogether too narrow, the customary conception of the copula itself. A proposition, in his view, is 'the presentation of two names under a relation' (III, p. 208). The relation *may* be one of the two 'onymatic' relations of identity and inclusion that are expressed by the word 'is', but it need not be of this restricted kind at all. The typical form of proposition is thus 'X is in the relation L to Y', with the relation L acting as copula between the subject X and the predicate Y; and De Morgan writes this form in symbols as 'XL..Y'. Plainly a logic of propositions, as thus understood, will have to be based on a theory of relations as well as on a theory of terms; and De Morgan is led in this way to undertake the construction of such a theory. Commenting on the need for a theory of relations, he points out that there is an evident weakness in traditional logic, since certain properties of the relation 'is' are constantly used, without ever being justified:

'The canons of ordinary syllogism cannot be established without help from our knowledge of the *convertible* and *transitive* character of identification: that is, we must know and use the properties "A is B gives B is A" and "A is B and B is C, compounded, give A is C". Can these principles be established by concession of "A is A, nothing is both A and not-A, and every thing is one or the other"? All my attempts at such establishment end in begging the question, when closely scrutinised.' (IV, p. 336.)

In Section 2 of his third paper, De Morgan introduces various ideas that are fundamental in the theory of classes and relations, e.g. intension and extension, aggregation and composition (i.e. union and intersection), and the converse of a relation.

'When X has a relation (A) to that which has a relation (B) to Y, X has to Y a *combined* relation: the *combinants* are A and B. Relations have both extension and intension. Thus, to take one of those relations which have appropriated the word in common life, the relation of *first-cousin* is the *aggregate* of son of uncle, daughter of uncle, son of aunt, daughter of aunt. The relation of minister to the crown is the *compound* of *subordinate* and *adviser*.' (III, p. 208.)

The following formal properties of relations are typical of those which De Morgan discusses in his fourth paper:

Contraries of converses are converses: thus not-L and not-L^{-1} are converses.

Converses of contraries are contraries: thus L^{-1} and $(\text{not-L})^{-1}$ are contraries.

The contrary of a converse is the converse of the contrary: not-L^{-1} is $(\text{not-L})^{-1}$.

If a first relation be contained in a second, then the converse of the first is contained in the converse of the second: but the contrary of the *second* is contained in the contrary of the *first*.

The conversion of a compound relation converts both components, and inverts their order: $(LM)^{-1}$ is $M^{-1}L^{-1}$. (IV, pp. 342–343.)

Although De Morgan undertook the study of relations with the analysis of syllogistic reasoning specifically in view, the theory that he constructed proved eventually to be of much wider application. De Morgan's insistence that relations other than those which can be expressed by the word 'is' ought to be treated in their own right was fully vindicated at the close of the nineteenth century, when the logical analysis of geometry was found to require a very general theory of relations, covering not only two-term relations of the kind originally considered but also such three-term and four-term relations as 'Q is between P and R' and 'P and R separate Q and S' (cf. Russell [2] and Whitehead [2,3]).

The symbolic methods of Boole and De Morgan, in which letters are used to designate qualities or classes, and (in Boole's system) equations are formed between expressions built up from such letters, were further developed by Jevons in his *Pure Logic* (1864) and his later textbooks. One of the improvements made by Jevons was the dropping of Boole's restriction of addition of classes to the case of disjoint summands. Jevons interpreted '$A + B$', which he wrote in his later work as '$A \cdot | \cdot B$', as 'A or B or both', i.e. 'A and/or B'.

The innovation which, in the work of Frege and Peano, ultimately made possible the transition from an elementary algebra of classes and relations to a logical calculus in the full sense, was the use of letters to stand for entire statements instead of for constituents of statements; and the earliest published use of symbols in this way is to be found in the papers of Hugh McColl. McColl's first systematic paper on the subject is 'The Calculus of Equivalent Statements and Integration Limits' (*Proc. London Math. Soc.*, **9** (1877–1878), 9–20), and in it he introduces a new type of logical algebra for the purpose of reducing to a process of systematic calculation the determination of the new limits of integration when the order of operations is changed in a repeated definite integral. Then, in a second paper in the same volume of the *Proceedings* and a third paper in the following volume, he develops the logical calculus for its own sake. In a fourth paper he applies it (as Boole and De Morgan also applied their formal methods) to the theory of probability.

McColl remarks in his second paper that he knows of Boole's 'celebrated works' from quotations in Bain's *Deductive Logic* but has not seen the books themselves. And then in his third paper he says that he has now been sent a copy of the *Laws of Thought* by the Rev. Robert Harley, and also a copy of *Pure Logic* by Jevons. He had previously criticized Jevons's symbolic method on the basis of the scanty indication of its nature that is given in the *Elementary Lessons on Logic*, but the fuller treatment contained in *Pure Logic* reveals that his objection arose from a misunderstanding. Now that he has read the work of Boole and Jevons, he sees that much of his own work has been anticipated; but he claims the credit for three innovations:

'(1) With me every single letter, as well as every combination of letters, denotes a statement.

(2) I use a symbol (the symbol :) to denote that the symbol following it is true provided the symbol preceding it is true.

(3) I use a special symbol—namely, an accent—to express denial; and this accent, like the minus sign in ordinary algebra, may be made to affect a multinomial statement of any complexity.'

McColl was thus working with a propositional calculus with special symbols for implication and negation. The two statements 'A implies B' and 'not-A' were written as A:B and A'; and the compound statement 'A and B' and the indeterminate statement 'A and/or B' were written as AB and A + B respectively. For 'A is true' and 'A is false', McColl wrote A = 1 and A = 0 respectively. Implication was not an unanalysed notion, for A:B was defined as A = AB. In his second paper, McColl gave various laws of propositional logic, e.g. if A:B then B':A', and if A:B then AC:BC.

McColl was in advance of his time with ideas such as these, and the older type of algebra of logic was still to undergo considerable development before being finally superseded. The use of algebraic symbolism in logic was carried much further than it had been hitherto by the American logician C. S. Peirce—a man of penetrating insight who was not nearly as influential as his abilities warranted, for the reason that he never worked up his ideas into a system. Peirce is now known to have anticipated many discoveries that were afterwards made independently by other logicians. He took up the theory of relations (or relatives, as he preferred to say) and developed it much further than De Morgan had done in his initial treatment of the subject. One of Peirce's more comprehensive works is his paper 'On the Algebra of Logic' (*Amer. J. Math.*, **3** (1880), 15–57), which consists of the following three chapters: I. Syllogistic; II. The Logic of Non-Relative Terms (i.e. the algebra of classes); III. The Logic of Relatives.

By the end of the century, a considerable body of writings on various aspects of the algebra of logic had accumulated. In addition to the primary works of Boole, De Morgan, and McColl, there was now a secondary literature of manuals and textbooks, the work of logicians such as Jevons and Venn, in which symbolic methods were adopted. Some of the writings of mathematicians also abutted on this field, particularly those of Dedekind. The largest single contribution to the formal development of logical algebra was undoubtedly that of Peirce, in his many papers on the subject.

All this material was finally assimilated and organized by Ernst Schröde (1841–1902) in his *Vorlesungen über die Algebra der Logik (Exakte Logik)*, the publication of which began in 1890 and ended posthumously in 1905. Schröder unified the various systems of notation that had been introduced by previous authors, and with the aid of his improved symbolism he gave a systematic treatment of the formal algebra of logic in its many different aspects. His book is in three volumes, the first of which is devoted to what he calls the *identischer Kalkul*. This is an abstract system which admits of interpretation either as a *Gebietekalkul* or calculus of domains (i.e. a formal theory of extension) or as a calculus of classes. The calculus is based on a certain constant relation $a \nsubseteq b$, which may be read as 'a is contained, though not necessarily as a *proper* part, in b'. This relation is governed by the principles '$a \subseteqq a$' and 'If $a \subseteqq b$ and $b \subseteqq c$, then $a \subseteqq c$'. Schröder defines further constants of the identical calculus contextually in terms of inclusion as follows:

$\qquad$ '$c \subseteqq ab$' means '$c \subseteqq a$ and $c \subseteqq b$';
$\qquad$ '$a + b \subseteqq c$' means '$a \subseteqq c$ and $b \subseteqq c$';
$\qquad$ 0 and 1 are entities of the system such that, for every a, $0 \subseteqq a$ and $a \subseteqq 1$.

For the case in which the calculus is taken as a calculus of domains, the negation a_1 of a is defined as that domain a_1 which is such that $a a_1 \subseteqq 0$ and $1 \subseteqq a + a_1$; and it is a postulate of the calculus that every domain has a negation.

Schröder gives, in his first volume, a very full and carefully worked out account of the identical calculus and its two most immediate applications; and then in his second volume he derives from it a calculus of propositions. Any proposition has a duration of validity (*Gültigkeitsdauer*), the union of all the stretches of time during which it is true; and $a \subseteqq b$ may be interpreted as meaning that the duration of validity of a is contained in that of b (the same symbol being used for the proposition and for its duration of validity). The constants 0 and 1 are now to be interpreted, of course, as the null duration and eternity respectively. Schröder follows Peirce (and his pupil Mitchell) in using $\sum_x$ and $\prod_x$ as quantifiers; but he makes no serious attempt to develop a full calculus of predicates on this basis. In his third volume, which is in many ways the most important of the three, he gives a very detailed treatment of the algebra of relations. A relation is here defined as a class of ordered pairs, which may be specified by a characteristic function a_{ij}, equal to 1 when the ordered pair $(i:j)$ belongs to the relation and equal to 0 when it does not belong to it.

Schröder's work may be seen as the ultimate fulfilment of the endeavour of logicians over half a century to evolve an adequate treatment of the formal side of logic. Within its terms of reference it is admirably executed (even though its axiomatic basis was shown by Huntington in [1] to need amendment) and it was the means of transmitting to the twentieth century most of what had been achieved in its domain in the nineteenth. Since, however, Schröder had little sympathy with the attitude towards logic of Peano and Frege, and as theirs was the attitude that was in fact to produce the next major advance, his book must be judged to close the preceding era rather than to open the following one. In this sense the whole 'algebra of logic' has become, together with Aristotelian and Scholastic logic, an object of mainly historical interest. Almost alone among twentieth-century logicians, Löwenheim has pressed the claims of the Schröder calculus as an alternative to symbolic logic of Peano's kind; and in a paper [2] of 1940 he deplored the general neglect of Schröder's methods.

4. '$\vdash$' *as a symbol for derivability.* In *Principia Mathematica* the assertion sign '$\vdash$' is prefixed to any formula that is either taken as an axiom or else derived from the axioms (see p. 164 above), but this usage is now obsolete. The symbol '$\vdash$' has been converted more recently into a sign for the meta-

logical relation of derivability; and a statement to the effect that, in some formal system F that is under consideration, certain formulae $\mathfrak{P}, \ldots, \mathfrak{W}$ are derivable from certain other formulae $\mathfrak{A}, \ldots, \mathfrak{H}$ (i.e. derivable in the system when $\mathfrak{A}, \ldots, \mathfrak{H}$ are adjoined to the axioms) is expressed concisely in symbols as '$\mathfrak{A}, \ldots, \mathfrak{H} \vdash \mathfrak{P}, \ldots, \mathfrak{W}$'.

5. *Introductory books on the foundations of mathematics.* Many good surveys of the foundations of mathematics have been published (see the reviews in the *Journal of Symbolic Logic*), and those mentioned in this note are simply a representative selection which may be useful to readers of various kinds. Other books, such as those of Kleene and Rosenbloom, are mentioned below, in the notes at the ends of the chapters to which they more specifically relate.
1. Max Black: *The Nature of Mathematics* (London, 1933). A brief but wide-ranging survey that is still stimulating to read.
2. R. L. Goodstein: *Mathematical Logic* (Leicester, 1957). A clear and readable introduction, of 100 pages, designed 'to introduce teachers of mathematics to some of the remarkable results which have been obtained in mathematical logic during the past twenty-five years'.
3. E. R. Stabler: *An Introduction to Mathematical Thought* (Reading, Mass., 1953). A modest, elementary book, in which the author tries to make students who are not specialists in mathematics aware of the logical structure of this subject.
4. R. L. Wilder: *Introduction to the Foundations of Mathematics* (New York, 1952). An admirably clear introduction, in which the author succeeds in incorporating much of the substance of the subject without making his account difficult for the reader who comes to it for the first time.
5. A. A. Fraenkel & Y. Bar-Hillel: *Foundations of Set Theory* (Amsterdam, 1958). In this companion volume to Fraenkel's *Abstract Set Theory* (Amsterdam, 1953), the authors concentrate on problems of foundations. They interpret their title in a very wide sense, taking most of mathematical philosophy to be relevant to the theory of sets. Their book, which is easy to read, contains a wealth of valuable information; and in addition it is provided with an extremely comprehensive bibliography.
6. S. Körner: *The Philosophy of Mathematics* (London, 1960). This is a book on foundations of mathematics, written by a professional philosopher who appreciates the nature of modern mathematics. It contains an excellent account of the subject, and it is in many ways complementary to similar books written by mathematicians.

6. *Books on the logistic conception of mathematics.* It is sufficient to mention a small number of works, since these are comprehensive enough to cover the more important ground. First of all must come the three major works of Russell: *The Principles of Mathematics* (1903), *Principia Mathematica* (1910–1913), and *Introduction to Mathematical Philosophy* (1919). To the same phase of development of the philosophy of mathematics also belongs F. P. Ramsey: *The Foundations of Mathematics and Other Essays* (1931), a posthumous volume of the work of Russell's brilliant follower and critic,

who was born in 1903 and died in 1930. The contribution made by Russell to logic and the foundations of mathematics has been examined very fully in *The Philosophy of Bertrand Russell* (1944), edited by P. A. Schilpp. This book contains an important article by Gödel: 'Russell's mathematical logic'.

As a more recent work in the logistic tradition, Quine's *Mathematical Logic* (1940) should also be mentioned.

7. *Sources.* (a) *Dedekind.* Dedekind's two essays on number, *Stetigkeit und irrationale Zahlen* and *Was sind und was sollen die Zahlen?*, are reprinted in the third volume of Dedekind's *Gesammelte mathematische Werke* (1932). They have also been published in English in Dedekind [3].

(b) *Frege.* For an introductory article on Frege's work and its general significance for logic, see Kneale [3]. Selected extracts from Frege's writings have been published, in English translation, in Frege [5].

(c) *The Peano axioms.* For some interesting remarks on the history of the Peano axioms, see Wang [2].

Chapter 7

FORMALIZED MATHEMATICS AND METAMATHEMATICS

Hilbert's new approach to the foundations of mathematics

For all the inspiration that *Principia Mathematica* has communicated to the mathematicians and philosophers of mathematics of the twentieth century, and for all its rich fecundity as a source of concepts and symbolic devices, this great work remains, in the literature of the foundations of mathematics, a lone classic without progeny.[1] That such should be the case may well seem puzzling; and indeed there does not appear to be any simple reason why the impetus of the logistic movement should have failed with the publication of the third volume of the *Principia*. It is an undoubted fact, however, that the leadership of research into the foundations of mathematics passed at that time from Russell to Hilbert, and that it is from Hilbert that most of the subsequent developments directly derive. Before turning to the details of his work, we must try to see, as best we can, how this sudden change came about.

Russell of the *Principia* was both a mathematician and a logician, though inclining, as we may infer from the outlook revealed in *The Principles of Mathematics*, more to the side of logic and philosophy than to that of mathematics, whereas Hilbert was one of the most professional of mathematicians. This difference may go a long way towards accounting for the greater readiness of mathematicians interested in the foundations of mathematics to align themselves with Hilbert than to follow Russell into the unfamiliar territory of philosophy.

There were also certain specific deficiencies in *Principia Mathematica* which must have made it appear that the solution there offered to the problems raised by the foundations of mathematics was not a complete or final one. The controversial nature of the theory of types, and in particular the intrusion of the admittedly arbitrary axiom of reducibility, constituted an obvious imperfection; and there was an even more fundamental weakness in the logistic view itself that had been shown

---

[1] On the logical side, the *Principia* has a direct descendant in Quine's *Mathematical Logic* (1940, revised 1951).

up by the discovery of the vicious-circle paradoxes.   The known para-doxes could indeed all be eliminated from the logistic system by the theory of types, but this still did not ensure that no other paradoxes would arise in the future, and the most that could be claimed was that the logic of the *Principia* was as rigorous as anyone then knew how to make it.   But if Russell had not happened to stumble upon his contra-diction, the *Principia* would presumably have been written (as indeed was Frege's *Grundgesetze der Arithmetik*) without any separation of types, and it is unlikely that logicians would have suspected that there might be something wrong with it.   Elimination of known fallacies is therefore not by itself a sufficient safeguard, and the ultimate logical justification of mathematics must include some more positive guarantee of its consistency.   The main concern of Hilbert, in the decades fol-lowing the publication of *Principia Mathematica*, was with the search for such a guarantee.

The approach of Hilbert to the problems of the foundations of mathe-matics was so closely bound up with his personal experience of the activity of mathematical creation that we can scarcely hope to under-stand it unless we see his work as a whole.   By good fortune we are in a position to trace the mathematical origin of his preoccupation with questions of foundations, for we possess an early though fully mature work of his in which we can see this interest in process of development. This work is the famous *Grundlagen der Geometrie* [Foundations of Geometry] of 1899, which we shall have to consider in some detail. But before turning to Hilbert's writings we must first summarize the main facts of his career.

David Hilbert was born in 1862 at Königsberg in East Prussia—the native city of Immanuel Kant, the great philosopher—and he became in turn a student, a lecturer, and a professor at the university of Königsberg.   In 1895 he went as professor to Göttingen, where he remained until his death in 1943; and he thus spent more than half his life at the university whose fame as a centre of mathematical research had begun with the presence there of the illustrious figure of Gauss and had been maintained by a succession of mathematicians of the highest eminence, from Dirichlet and Riemann to Klein.   Indeed, Hilbert himself must be numbered among the greatest creative mathematicians since Gauss, for besides making discoveries of fundamental importance in many different branches of mathematics, he influenced decisively the mathematical outlook of his whole generation.

In some fields of study Hilbert introduced concepts and methods that enabled research to go forward in entirely new directions, as with his theorem, described by Hermann Weyl[1] as 'one of the simplest and most important theorems in the whole of algebra', which asserts that

[1] See H. Weyl: *The Classical Groups* (Princeton, 1939), p. 251.

every ideal in a polynomial ring has a finite basis, and also with the concept that is now known by the name of 'Hilbert space'.   In the case of the classical theory of invariants he was able, by solving a fundamental problem that had been the ultimate objective of a vast amount of earlier work, to bring research virtually to an end.   Among the most important and influential of his publications (excluding those devoted specifically to the foundations of mathematics) are the book on geometry that we are about to discuss; the famous *Zahlbericht* of 1897, a report on the state of knowledge in the theory of algebraic numbers, drawn up for the *Deutsche Mathematiker-Vereinigung*; a book, *Grundzüge einer allgemeinen Theorie der linearen Integralgleichungen* (Leipzig and Berlin, 1912), in which are reprinted six fundamental papers on integral equations, originally published in the *Göttinger Nachrichten* between 1904 and 1910; and the two volumes of *Methoden der mathematischen Physik* (Berlin, 1924 & 1937), written in collaboration with Richard Courant, in which essentially algebraic methods are made the basis of a unified treatment of partial differential equations, integral equations, and the calculus of variations.

2   Hilbert's 'Grundlagen der Geometrie'

Hilbert's epoch-making book of 1899 was offered as a new presentation of euclidean geometry, written with the intention of taking fully into account the enhanced understanding of the axiomatic method that mathematicians had achieved in the centuries that had elapsed since the time of Euclid, and more particularly in the closing decades of the nineteenth century.   Not only did Hilbert profit by this recently acquired insight, but he himself raised the axiomatic method to a new level of efficiency; and of his book Hermann Weyl subsequently wrote as follows:

'The soil was well prepared, especially by the Italian school of geometers.   Yet it was as if over a landscape, wherein but a few men with a superb sense of orientation had found their way in murky twilight, the sun had risen all at once.   Clear and clean-cut we find stated the axiomatic concept according to which all geometry is a hypothetical deductive system; it depends on the implicit definitions of the concepts of spatial objects and relations which the axioms contain, and not on a description of their intuitive content.   A complete and natural system of geometric axioms is set up.   They are required to satisfy the logical demands of consistency, independence, and completeness, and by means of quite a few peculiar geometries, constructed *ad hoc*, the proof of independence is furnished in detail.'[1]

[1] H. Weyl: 'David Hilbert, 1862–1943', *Obituary Notices of Fellows of the Royal Society*, **4** (1942–1944), 547–553.   In this notice, Weyl gave an account of Hilbert's mathematical achievements and showed clearly why it was that his influence on the development of mathematics was so great.   A more detailed survey of Hilbert's work is contained in the longer obituary notice [5] that Weyl wrote for the American Mathematical Society.

In the opening chapter of the *Grundlagen der Geometrie* Hilbert laid his foundation for a new axiomatic treatment of euclidean geometry that was intended to be absolutely rigorous, although expressed without the aid of any special symbolism and in language no more technical than that of Euclid.   The later chapters of the book were then devoted to investigations, with the system of geometry itself as their object, of the kind described nowadays as *metamathematical*.   Chief among these investigations was one that established the consistency of geometry; and the others were mainly concerned with general questions of logical dependence of propositions on other propositions—whether certain important theorems are deducible from such and such axioms, and whether the axioms themselves are independent.

The formal system was constructed in accordance with the principles of Peano, although this feature was somewhat masked by Hilbert's use of ordinary language in preference to logical symbolism.   Hilbert had his reasons for this choice of language, the main consideration presumably being that he wished his work to be seen as a continuation of the age-old striving of geometers to evolve a purely rational theory of the spatial structure of the world.   That this was his motive is confirmed by the following words from the introduction to the book:

'Geometry, like arithmetic, requires for its systematic development only a small number of simple basic principles.   These principles are known as axioms of geometry.   Setting up axioms for geometry and investigating the way in which they are connected is a problem that has been discussed ever since the time of Euclid in numerous admirable contributions to the literature of mathematics.   The problem in question amounts to logical analysis of our intuition of space.'

The concluding sentence of this paragraph was no merely conventional remark, but a deliberate affirmation of ultimate intention.   Hilbert made this quite clear by placing at the head of the introduction, as a motto for the whole book, these famous words from Kant's *Critique of Pure Reason*: 'Thus all human knowledge begins with intuitions, goes from there to concepts, and ends with ideas.'   It had been Kant's firm conviction that theoretical knowledge and immediate intuition are inseparable, and that even the most abstruse scientific reasoning derives its significance and its objectivity from its continuity with the basic intuitions of the active mind.   In a rather similar way Hilbert believed that, although geometry is entirely self-sufficient as a deductive system, it is nevertheless dependent on the immediacy of intuition for the interest that makes it a recurrent challenge to the human mind instead of merely one among a whole infinity of arbitrary intellectual exercises.

Thus the language of the *Grundlagen* was the traditional language of elementary geometry; and where this language offered convenient synonyms, such as 'lies on' or 'belongs to' for 'is a point of', Hilbert used them freely to denote one and the same abstract concept.   From the point of view of the strict logician, however—and this was one of the points of view that Hilbert so skilfully kept distinct and yet at the same time never entirely separated—the concepts denoted by the geometrical terms were primitive concepts in the sense of Peano.   Among such concepts were 'point', 'line' (*Gerade*), and 'plane', conceived as three separate kinds of entity, and a number of basic relations such as 'belongs to' (i.e. 'is incident with'), 'is between', 'is congruent to', and 'is parallel to'.   The axioms or primitive propositions which comprised the implicit definitions of the primitive concepts were twenty in number, and they were classified in five sets as follows: I, 1–8, axioms of connexion; II, 1–4, axioms of order; III, 1–5, axioms of congruence; IV, the axiom of parallels; V, 1–2, axioms of continuity.   These axioms are a sufficient foundation for a strictly deductive treatment of Euclid's system of geometry, in which stated axioms take over the ill-defined function of such semi-intuitive procedures as establishment of congruence by the method of superposition.   We shall now give them in full.

I. *The axioms of connexion:*

1. If A and B are two points, there is always a line a that is incident with both of them.

2. If A and B are two points, there is not more than one line that is incident with both of them.

3. On a line there are always at least two points.   There are at least three points which do not lie on a line.

4. If A, B, C are any three points which do not lie on one and the same line, there is always a plane α which is incident with them all.   For every plane, there is a point that is incident with it.

5. If A, B, C are any three points which do not lie on one and the same line, there is not more than one plane that is incident with them all.

6. If two points A, B of a line a lie in a plane α, then every point of a lies in the plane α.

7. If two planes α, β have a point A in common, then they have at least one other point B in common.

8. There are at least four points which do not all lie in a plane.

II. *The axioms of order:*

1. If a point B lies between a point A and a point C, then A, B, C are three distinct points of a line, and B then also lies between C and A.

2. If A and C are two points, there is always at least one point B on the line AC which is such that C lies between A and B.

3. For any three points of a line, there is not more than one that lies between the other two.

4. Let A, B, C be three points which do not lie on a line, and let a be a

line in the plane ABC which does not pass through any of the points A, B, C. Then if the line a goes through a point of the segment AB [i.e. a point between A and B] it must go also through a point of the segment AC or through a point of the segment BC.

III. *The axioms of congruence:*

1. If A and B are two points on a line a, and if, further, A' is a point on the same or another line a', then a point B' can be found on the line a', on a given side of A', which is such that the segment AB is congruent or equal to the segment $A'B'$; in symbols:

$$AB \equiv A'B'.$$

2. If a segment $A'B'$ and a segment $A''B''$ are congruent to the same segment AB, then the segment $A'B'$ is congruent to the segment $A''B''$; in short, if two segments are congruent to a third, then they are congruent to each other.

3. Let AB and BC be two segments, without any points in common, on a line a, and also let $A'B'$ and $B'C'$ be two segments on the same or another line a', again without common points. If $AB \equiv A'B'$ and $BC \equiv B'C'$, then $AC \equiv A'C'$ also.

4. Let $\not\subset (h,k)$ be an angle in a plane α, and let a line a' in a plane α' and also a particular side of a' in α' be given. If h' denotes one ray of the line a' which issues from a point O', then in the plane α' there is one and only one ray k' such that the angle $\not\subset (h,k)$ is congruent or equal to the angle $\not\subset (h',k')$, and at the same time all the internal points of the angle $\not\subset (h',k')$ lie on the given side of a'; in symbols:

$$\not\subset (h,k) \equiv \not\subset (h'k').$$

Every angle is congruent to itself, i.e. always

$$\not\subset (h,k) \equiv \not\subset (h,k).$$

5. If, for two triangles ABC and $A'B'C'$, the congruences

$$AB \equiv A'B', \quad AC \equiv A'C', \quad \not\subset BAC \equiv \not\subset B'A'C'$$

all hold, then the congruence

$$\not\subset ABC \equiv \not\subset A'B'C'$$

is always satisfied also.

IV. *The axiom of parallels (Euclidean axiom):*

Let a be an arbitrary line and let A be a point that is not on a. Then, in the plane that is determined by a and A, there is at most one line that passes through A and does not meet a.

V. *The axioms of continuity:*

1. (*Axiom of measurement* or *Archimedean axiom.*)   Let AB and CD be any segments whatever.   Then there is a natural number n such that, if the segment CD is stepped off n times in succession along the ray from A which passes through B, a point beyond B will be reached.

2. (*Axiom of linear completeness.*)   The system of points on a line, with its relations of order and congruence, does not admit of any extension that preserves all relations between existing elements, and also all the fundamental properties of linear order and congruence which follow from the axioms I–III, and that preserves V, 1.

The twenty axioms have been stated here in the original sequence, but the later ones will be seen to involve concepts that have not been formally introduced.   This is because Hilbert himself interspersed between the separate sets of axioms various deductions of theorems and discussions of derivative notions.   For details of these, and of the way in which Euclid's basic theorems were deduced from the new set of axioms, the original memoir must be consulted.   It will be found that, despite its appearance of comparative informality, Hilbert's system of euclidean geometry is developed with great formal rigour.   In any case, important as was Hilbert's achievement of rewriting Euclid in the spirit of Peano, the *Grundlagen der Geometrie* was to prove even more significant as a metamathematical essay than as a treatise on geometry; and it is this aspect of the book that we need chiefly to discuss at present.

The first metamathematical topic that Hilbert considered was the consistency of his axioms, that is to say the freedom from contradiction of the deductive theory that is built upon them.   The method that he adopted for proving consistency was one of constructing an arithmetical model of the abstract system; and the use of models has since come to be very important in metamathematical investigations.   By a *model* of a formal axiomatic theory we understand a realization of that theory, constructed in some mathematical domain which is already available. The formal theory will be based, as always, on one or more postulated totalities of entities, certain constant predicates and functions, and suitable axioms which define these predicates and functions implicitly; and to construct a model of it we replace the postulated totalities of entities by certain specific mathematical totalities, and the constant predicates and functions by specific predicates and functions defined for these totalities.   If we are then able to show that, with this particular identification of the primitive elements of the formal theory, all the axioms become true propositions, we have succeeded in producing a model of the original theory.   A model of a formal theory is thus a well-defined mathematical system with the particular structure that is characterized by the theory.

What Hilbert did in the case of axiomatic euclidean geometry was to construct a model of the geometrical system within the domain of arithmetic. He could then argue that, if a contradiction were deducible from the geometrical axioms, a contradiction could also be reached by purely arithmetical reasoning. It follows that, when once the consistency of arithmetic is granted, the consistency of the system of euclidean geometry is assured. Thus, although the method of models does not establish the consistency of geometry in an absolute sense, it does nevertheless furnish a proof of the consistency of geometry relative to that of arithmetic—and even this is a substantial achievement.

Hilbert obtained two main results concerning freedom from contradiction. He began by taking a certain number field Ω, consisting of all the algebraic numbers that can be obtained by 'beginning with the number 1 and applying a finite number of times the four rational operations: addition, subtraction, multiplication, division, and the fifth operation $|\sqrt{(1 + \omega^2)}|$, where ω denotes any number already obtained by means of the five operations'. By defining a point as an ordered pair (x,y) of numbers in Ω, a line as a set of ratios $u:v:w$ with not both of u and v zero, the relation of incidence by the equation $ux + vy + w = 0$, the order of points on a line in terms of the order of magnitude of their coordinates, and so forth—prompted always by the familiar usages of coordinate geometry—he was able to construct a model that satisfied all those of his axioms that apply to plane geometry, with the single exception of V, 2 (the axiom of linear completeness); and the same method could readily be extended to the axioms for three-dimensional space. And if the restricted field Ω was replaced simply by the field of all real numbers, so that the model became identical with ordinary cartesian geometry, all the axioms were then satisfied, V, 2 included. The reason why Hilbert thought it worth while to give a separate proof of the less comprehensive consistency theorem was that the 'arithmetic' to which the consistency of geometry was made relative was logically much simpler in that case, and therefore even less open to philosophical doubt than the full arithmetic of the real continuum.

Having demonstrated the consistency of his axioms, Hilbert went on to show also that these were, in all essential respects, independent. This he did, in Weyl's phrase, 'by means of quite a few peculiar geometries, constructed *ad hoc*'; for a possible way of showing that some given axiom in a set is independent of the other axioms is by constructing a model for which all the axioms are satisfied, with the single exception of this particular one. Hilbert first of all inferred the independence of the axiom of parallels by appealing to the known model of non-euclidean geometry that can be set up by taking as the 'space' of the model the interior of a sphere in cartesian space, and defining 'congruence' in it by means of the collineations of the cartesian space that transform the sphere into itself.[1]

Besides the axiom of parallels, there are two more of the twenty axioms whose independence is of especial interest, namely the last of the axioms of congruence, III, 5, and the axiom of Archimedes, V, 1; and Hilbert dealt with these in the following way. He first of all modified three-dimensional cartesian geometry by defining 'distance' by means of the formula

$$\sqrt{[(x_1 - x_2 + y_1 - y_2)^2 + (y_1 - y_2)^2 + (z_1 - z_2)^2]},$$

instead of by the usual formula derived from the theorem of Pythagoras. This gave him a 'geometry' which satisfies all of the axioms except III, 5. And finally, in order to demonstrate the independence of axiom V, 1, he constructed a field $\Omega(t)$ of algebraic functions of t by proceeding exactly as in the construction of the earlier field Ω of algebraic numbers, but beginning now with the real variable t instead of with the number 1. Since every element of $\Omega(t)$ has a constant sign for all sufficiently large t, an ordering relation for this field may be defined by taking '$a(t) < b(t)$' to mean '$a(t) - b(t) < 0$, in the ordinary sense, for all sufficiently large t'. But, with this definition of order, no finite multiple $n.1$ of 1 can exceed t, and the field $\Omega(t)$ is therefore non-archimedean. The 'cartesian' geometry based on this field then satisfies all the twenty axioms except V, 1.

Two further metamathematical results, established in the *Grundlagen*, that have become part of common geometrical knowledge are concerned with the theorems of Pappus (or Pascal) and Desargues. The first of these theorems asserts that, if A, B, C and A', B', C' are triads of points on two intersecting lines, then the three points $BC'.B'C$, $CA'.C'A$, $AB'.A'B$ are collinear; and the second asserts that, if ABC and $A'B'C'$ are coplanar triangles such that the lines AA', BB', CC' are concurrent, then the three points $BC.B'C'$, $CA.C'A'$, $AB.A'B'$ are collinear. These theorems, which involve no relations but those of incidence, belong more properly to projective geometry than to euclidean geometry; and the well-known facts about them are that Desargues's theorem can be proved from axioms of incidence for space but not from axioms of incidence for the plane only, while Pappus's theorem cannot be proved at all from axioms of incidence alone, since it demands a commutative ground-field.[2]

---

[1] This model is due to Klein. Its existence establishes the consistency of non-euclidean geometry in much the same way as the existence of the cartesian model establishes the consistency of euclidean geometry. An alternative model for the same type of non-euclidean geometry was devised by Poincaré. On the subject of these models see Note 2, p. 227.

[2] H. F. Baker discusses the theorems of Pappus and Desargues in relation to the axioms of geometry in his *Principles of Geometry*, I, Foundations (1922).

Hilbert confined his discussion of the two theorems to the special cases in which the lines of collinearity that are asserted to exist are at infinity. For Desargues's theorem he proved the following result:

'There exists a plane geometry in which all the axioms I, 1–3, II, III, 1–4, IV*, V hold, i.e. all the linear and plane axioms except for the axiom of congruence III, 5, and for which Desargues's theorem is not true. Desargues's theorem is therefore not a consequence of the specified axioms; it requires for its proof either the space axioms or axiom III, 5 on the congruence of triangles.' The axiom IV* referred to is a strengthened form of the axiom of parallels IV, with the words 'at most one line' replaced by 'one and only one line'.

The treatment of Pappus's theorem depended on a purely algebraic result, to the effect that an ordered skew-field (i.e. an algebraic system for which all the axioms for an ordered field are postulated, with the single exception of the commutative law of multiplication $ab = ba$) is necessarily commutative if it is archimedean. The main conclusion that Hilbert was able to draw from this result was that Pappus's theorem can be proved without the axioms of congruence provided that a form of the Archimedean axiom V, 1 is taken, but not otherwise.

3   Axiomatic theories and their significance

With the publication in 1899 of his *Grundlagen der Geometrie*, Hilbert improved substantially upon the best that had previously been done by way of logical justification of euclidean geometry; and having achieved this initial success, he devoted the major part of his working life from that time on to the much greater task of applying his new metamathematical method to pure mathematics as a whole (though continuing at the same time to pursue more orthodox mathematical research as well). His conception of metamathematics became more precise as the work progressed, and his standard of rigour became correspondingly more stringent—so much so, indeed, that in the end even so modest an objective as the attainment of perfect rigour in the arithmetic of the natural numbers proved to be for ever out of reach. But in spite of the ultimate breakdown of the undertaking, the work done and the results obtained have greatly enhanced our knowledge and understanding of the formal articulation of both mathematics and logic; and through this work, no less than by his more strictly mathematical innovations, Hilbert has done much to shape the mathematical tradition inherited by the mid-twentieth century.

Hilbert evolved a distinctive personal philosophy of mathematics, which had very different presuppositions from the philosophy of Russell that we considered in Chapter 6; and his system is often referred to by the name of *formalism* in order to distinguish it from Russell's logistic system. The results of the researches that have centred round formalism are set forth with admirable lucidity in the two volumes of *Grundlagen der Mathematik*, which Hilbert published in 1934 and 1939 in collaboration with Paul Bernays, whose own further contribution to the foundations of mathematics we shall consider in Chapter 11 below. The account of formalism that now follows is directly based on this standard work, and the details that we are often obliged to omit are all to be found in its pages.

Whereas Russell has consistently maintained that the whole of pure mathematics is reducible to logic, Hilbert firmly believed mathematics to be an autonomous activity of the mathematician; and so formalism is more mathematical than philosophical in spirit, and it reflects very clearly the tendency towards total abstraction that was becoming dominant in mathematics at the time when the formalist outlook was being developed.   The general tendency in mathematics in the latter part of the nineteenth century had been in the direction of more and more extensive use of the axiomatic method, and Hilbert characteristically thought of mathematics in axiomatic terms.   The entire formalist programme was in fact based on a further development of the axiomatic principle; and in order to appreciate its aims we accordingly need to begin by clarifying the notion of an axiomatic theory.

At the beginning of the *Grundlagen der Mathematik* an important distinction is drawn between two accepted senses of the word 'axiomatic', there distinguished as 'concrete' (*inhaltlich*) and 'formal'.   In applying the *concrete* axiomatic method we take some body of empirical knowledge with which we are already tolerably familiar, and we try to make this knowledge systematic by idealizing the concepts which it involves and picking out from among the known facts a small number of basic principles from which all else can be derived by deduction. This is the method that was applied by Euclid to geometry and by Newton to mechanics; and it has been used more recently, though not yet with complete success, in the theory of probability.   The *formal* axiomatic method on the other hand, which is the method of pure mathematics *par excellence*, is not tied to any existing factual knowledge, since it is a method of constructing an abstract theory by beginning with arbitrary primitive ideas and primitive propositions, and then developing formal consequences without reference to any sort of meaning.

The concrete axiomatic method is a most powerful intellectual instrument, which can be used whenever a new science is taking shape—that is to say when familiarity with and understanding of some range of phenomena have reached a point at which general laws that govern it begin to be discernible.   Use of this method raises mere factual knowledge to the level of scientific theory; and in natural science the method is fully adequate to what is required of it.   But in mathematics, where empirical fact provides only the initial prompting for a mathematical investigation (and perhaps the material for subsequent application of the resulting theory), and where both logistic and formalist philosophers are agreed in recognizing only logic as final arbiter in questions of mathematical correctness, it is the *formal* axiomatic method that is needed.   Nevertheless, most mathematicians would admit that this formal method is not sufficient by itself.   We cannot be content with a mathematics that is imprisoned within a world of total abstraction,[1] a mathematics in which any axiomatic theory that may be arbitrarily set up is as good as any other.   Mathematics may indeed recognize no criteria of *correctness* but those of logic, but the *significance* of mathematical theories can hardly be altogether separated from the possibility of their application in wider realms of knowledge.   Mathematics is, in fact, indissolubly linked with scientific as well as with everyday thinking, and this connexion forms part of its significance as knowledge.   It is for this reason that the literature of foundations of mathematics contains important discussions relating to the *Anwendungsproblem* or problem of application; and this problem obviously calls for use of the concrete axiomatic method.   Pure mathematics provides logical analyses of various abstract structural patterns, and a particular mathematical theory can find an application in a particular range of experience if the pattern with which it deals is in fact present in that experience.   To reveal the possibility of the application, therefore, and to assess its precision, we need to isolate the pattern of the experience itself, by treating this axiomatically in the concrete manner.   That is a topic to which we shall return in Part III (cf. Chapter 13).

Quite apart from the question of whether a given abstract theory applies to a particular body of experience, we may also want to ask whether such a theory is significant *in itself*, that is to say as an abstract theory.   A formal axiomatic theory—which is nothing but an edifice of propositions that exists as an organic whole for no other reason than that the propositions are all deducible from certain propositions which have been adopted, by arbitrary fiat, as the axioms of the theory—is not 'significant' in the same sense as a concrete theory, rooted in already familiar knowledge; and for it some special sort of vindication is plainly needed.   The most obvious suggestion as to how a formal theory should be exhibited as non-trivial is that we ought to show that the structure which it analyses actually exists in some concrete domain —in other words, that we ought to point to some realization of the theory.   But although to do this would be quite sufficient to satisfy mathematicians and scientists that a particular branch of abstract

---

[1] It is of some interest to recall that Hilbert himself was an author of a book on intuitive geometry—D. Hilbert and S. Cohn-Vossen: *Anschauliche Geometrie* (Berlin, 1932); English translation *Geometry and the Imagination* (New York, 1956).

mathematics is significant, no philosophically acceptable demonstration of significance is in fact possible by such means; for almost every body of knowledge bristles with philosophical difficulties, and to try to justify abstract euclidean geometry, say, by pointing to empirically known facts concerning drawing and measuring would be to make the stronger partner lean upon the weaker. It is only in a few cases, moreover, that the theories which make up abstract mathematics have grown directly out of more intuitive knowledge at all, and there are now many branches of pure mathematics that have no immediate intuitive counterpart. Looking at the question of significance from the point of view of philosophy of mathematics, therefore, we must ask with reference to any given abstract mathematical theory not 'Has this theory a realization in some more concrete domain of knowledge?' but rather 'Does this theory in principle admit of realization?'. In other words, we shall ask if it is theoretically possible to replace the primitive concepts of the theory by well-defined specific concepts in such a way that the primitive propositions all become true assertions. Any such interpretation of the undetermined concepts will be said to yield a *realization* of the abstract theory (i.e. a model, in the sense of p. 197 above).

The idea of realizability that we have here is obviously related to the idea of satisfiability introduced in Chapter 3, but it applies to entire formal theories instead of to isolated formulae. We said earlier (p. 71) that a formula of the calculus of predicates is *satisfiable* for a given domain of individuals if predicates defined for this domain can be substituted for the predicate variables in it, and particular individuals and propositions for any individual and propositional variables that may be present, in such a way that the formula yields a true proposition. We now say that a formal theory is *realizable* if a domain of individuals can be chosen, and constant individuals and predicates taken, in such a way that, with this particular specification of the primitive elements of the theory, all the axioms are true propositions.

The most direct way of showing that an abstract theory is realizable, and ultimately the only one, is by actually producing a realization, though not necessarily in any concrete domain; but here we already find ourselves confronted with a fundamental difficulty. Only in a very few cases, in fact, can we claim actually to *produce* a realization, namely in those cases in which we can do this with a finite domain of individuals. For, unless the domain of individuals is finite, its very existence raises philosophical problems of the same order as those relating to the abstract system which our construction of the realization is designed to justify. If we are seeking a realization of the abstract theory of groups, say, we need only take some finite group, specified by a multiplication table which we can write out in full, and there, beyond all possibility of doubt, is a demonstration that the theory of groups is realizable. Or again, we have a completely satisfactory realization of abstract projective geometry of two dimensions in the well-known 7-point geometry (see Note 1, p. 224), and this model of the abstract theory can be defined combinatorially by a finite table of incidence relations. To produce in such a way a finite model is to give a perfect proof of realizability, but unfortunately there are quite simple systems of axioms for which no finite model can exist (cf. the example given on p. 72). This means that we are forced to deal with infinite domains of individuals; and so we must consider how these are to be handled.

4   The domain of numerals, treated by finitary means

The simplest infinite totality is that of the natural numbers, a progression which is usually defined implicitly by means of the Peano axioms. But if we adopt such a definition we make the domain of numbers itself dependent on an abstract axiomatic theory, which in turn gives rise to its own question of realizability; and so our whole method is vitiated by circularity. If we are to use the set of natural numbers, or some equivalent totality, as a domain of individuals for the construction of realizations, we must find a way of actually exhibiting this set directly, as an object of immediate perception or intuition, instead of characterizing it implicitly by means of axioms. Admittedly we cannot have the whole infinite collection before us, but we must at least be able to survey as much of it as is needed at any particular moment.

We can make a start by taking as the individuals of our progression the symbols I, II, III, ..., which we obtain one after another by starting with a single vertical stroke and then appending a further stroke at each stage of the construction. For the sake of clarity in the following discussion we shall call these stroke-symbols *numerals*, and we shall use small German letters (in metastatements, or statements about the primary theory) to stand for unspecified numerals. Given any two numerals, we can compare them with regard to length. By crossing off one stroke from each of them again and again we can decide in a finite number of steps whether or not they are of the same length; and if they are not, we find out in this way which is the shorter. We are thus able to define an order among the distinct numerals, by putting $\mathfrak{a} < \mathfrak{b}$ whenever the symbol $\mathfrak{a}$ is shorter than the symbol $\mathfrak{b}$. If $\mathfrak{a}$ and $\mathfrak{b}$ are any two numerals, we define their sum $\mathfrak{a} + \mathfrak{b}$ as the numeral obtained when $\mathfrak{b}$ is written immediately to the right of $\mathfrak{a}$, and we define their product $\mathfrak{a} \cdot \mathfrak{b}$ as the numeral that is obtained when $\mathfrak{a}$ is substituted for each of the strokes in the symbol denoted by $\mathfrak{b}$.

In order that the numerals may provide a non-hypothetical domain of individuals for realizations of axiomatic theories, we must be able to prove, by reasoning that never goes beyond the immediately given, all the arithmetical properties that we shall need in the construction of such realizations. Such non-hypothetical reasoning is referred to by Hilbert and Bernays as 'finitary inference' (*das finite Schließen*). To quote their words:

'We shall always use the word "finitary" to indicate that the discussion, assertion, or definition in question is kept within the bounds of thorough-going producibility of objects and thorough-going practicability of processes, and may accordingly be carried out within the domain of concrete inspection.'[1]

What is essential to finitary reasoning is thus that (a) the entities talked about are produced and not merely postulated, and (b) no process of definition or calculation is admitted unless it can be guaranteed to terminate in a finite number of steps, and a definite bound can be set to this number in advance.

All the definitions that we have so far laid down in relation to numerals are finitary; and we can also give finitary interpretations to the two fundamental arithmetical procedures of proof by mathematical induction and definition by recursion. A proof by induction of a theorem $\mathfrak{A}(n)$ gives us a means of verifying $\mathfrak{A}(\mathfrak{n})$, for any assigned numeral $\mathfrak{n}$, in a number of steps to which a bound can be assigned in advance; and a recursive definition of a function $\mathfrak{f}(n)$ similarly enables us actually to evaluate $\mathfrak{f}(\mathfrak{n})$, for any particular $\mathfrak{n}$, also in a previously bounded number of steps. With these basic procedures at our disposal, we can now reformulate in finitary terms the usual arguments by which it is customary to establish the associative, commutative, and distributive laws for addition and multiplication, we can introduce the concept of prime number, and we can prove the 'fundamental theorem of arithmetic', the theorem which asserts that every integer is representable, in one and essentially only one way, as a product of prime factors.

Adoption of the finitary point of view first reveals itself as an irksome limitation on arithmetical thinking when we have occasion to work with propositions that involve quantifiers. An assertion $(x)\mathfrak{A}(x)$ can only be understood as meaning that, for any choice of a numeral $\mathfrak{n}$, the proposition $\mathfrak{A}(\mathfrak{n})$ can be shown finitarily to be true; and an assertion $(Ex)\mathfrak{A}(x)$ has to be interpreted in such a way that it can only be made when we actually know some particular numeral $\mathfrak{n}$ for which $\mathfrak{A}(\mathfrak{n})$ is true, or at the very least when we have a process of calculation that can be guaranteed to lead to the determination of such a numeral in a previously bounded number of steps.

---

[1] 'Wir [wollen] allemal mit dem Worte ,,finit" zum Ausdruck bringen, daß die betreffende Überlegung, Behauptung oder Definition sich an die Grenzen der grundsätzlichen Ausführbarkeit von Prozessen hält und sich somit im Rahmen konkreter Betrachtung vollzieht.' (*Grundlagen der Mathematik*, I, p. 32.)

Finitary interpretation of non-elementary assertions presents even greater difficulty when the propositions that we wish to assert involve negation. The negation of an elementary proposition, that is to say one without quantifiers, is entirely unproblematic, but the situation is altogether changed when quantifiers are admitted. Let us consider first a proposition of the form $\overline{(Ex)\mathfrak{A}(x)}$. The most natural finitary interpretation of the assertion of this proposition is that, for any $\mathfrak{n}$ whatever, $\mathfrak{A}(\mathfrak{n})$ is false. With this interpretation, however, the alternatives $(Ex)\mathfrak{A}(x)$ and $\overline{(Ex)\mathfrak{A}(x)}$ are not exhaustive, for it may well happen that we have no means of determining an $\mathfrak{n}$ for which $\mathfrak{A}(\mathfrak{n})$ is true, and yet are unable to prove the falsity of $\mathfrak{A}(\mathfrak{n})$ for arbitrary choice of $\mathfrak{n}$. The two decisions, in fact, do not involve the same situation. Thus we find that, in the finitary logic of non-elementary propositions, the law of excluded middle 'A or not-A' (*tertium non datur*) fails to hold. Much the same considerations apply also to propositions of the form $\overline{(x)\mathfrak{A}(x)}$. There is more than one possible finitary interpretation of such an assertion—for instance availability of a counter-example, or derivability of a contradiction from the assumption that $\mathfrak{A}(\mathfrak{n})$ holds for arbitrary choice of $\mathfrak{n}$—but in any case the law of excluded middle is invalid.

It will be clear from what we have just seen that the virtual infallibility of finitary reasoning is only achieved at the cost of a heavy sacrifice of deductive power; and it turns out that this type of argument is too weak to enable us to develop a theory of numerals comparable, either in range or in logical simplicity, with ordinary arithmetic.

We see, then, that the arithmetic of the numerals I, II, III, . . . can never be a complete substitute for arithmetic as ordinarily understood by mathematicians, and it cannot even provide a realization of any formal theory that adequately represents ordinary arithmetic. In spite of this, however, the numerals themselves are of great value in metamathematics, for they do at least provide a potentially infinite system of entities, many properties of which can be treated by purely finitary means. The sequence of numerals I, II, III, . . ., in fact, is now available as a finitary counterpart of the sequence of natural numbers 1, 2, 3, ... If, moreover, as is often the case, we wish the progression of numbers to begin with 0 instead of 1, we can easily modify the numerals so that they behave in the corresponding way. All that we need to do is to replace the sequence of expressions I, II, III, . . . by the sequence 0, 0I, 0II, . . ., and to adapt the definitions of addition and multiplication suitably. The sum $\mathfrak{a} + \mathfrak{b}$ of two numerals in the extended sense is obtained by removing the initial '0' from $\mathfrak{b}$ and appending what remains to the right of $\mathfrak{a}$; and the product $\mathfrak{a}.\mathfrak{b}$ is obtained by removing the '0' from $\mathfrak{a}$ and substituting what is left (which may be nothing at all) for each stroke in the constitution of $\mathfrak{b}$.

5   The metamathematics of formalized theories

We now return to the fundamental question of mathematical significance. Pure mathematics, as it is understood nowadays, belongs to what Kant called the realm of ideas—a domain of pure thought, where the mind is no longer bound in any way by the conditions of sensory intuition or the exigencies of contingent fact—and mathematical theories can therefore only be conceived as abstract axiomatic theories. Such a theory must certainly be accepted as significant if a realization of it can be exhibited. When a finite realization is available, significance is guaranteed in the strongest possible way; but we shall also be satisfied if an infinite realization, based on the system of numerals discussed in §4, can be constructed by finitary means. In view of the fact, however, that only so limited a part of the arithmetic of the numerals is finitary, we can scarcely hope to produce even this kind of realization in any but a few favourable cases. The direct method of establishing significance thus soon fails, and we are obliged to have recourse to some weaker form of guarantee. The weakest criterion that can be held to meet the need at all is the one on which Hilbert based his philosophy of formalism, namely demonstrable consistency. Hilbert was prepared to accept any axiomatic theory as significant—that is to say as characterizing a possible structural pattern—if a proof could be given that no contradiction is deducible from its axioms.

Here, then, we have the essential problem of foundations of mathematics as Hilbert understood it in his later work. *A proof must be given, for each branch of mathematics, that the permitted procedures of demonstration can never yield two theorems* $\mathfrak{A}$ *and not-*$\mathfrak{A}$. This proof of consistency, furthermore, must be logically unassailable; and the metamathematical argument is accordingly required to be strictly finitary.

Now here there is a difficulty; for an ordinary axiomatic mathematical theory is a relatively ill-defined object of thought, whereas it is of the essence of finitary reasoning that it can only be applied to definite and constructively given entities. It was this consideration that produced a clear break in Hilbert's work on foundations of mathematics, which separates the earlier metamathematical discussion of euclidean geometry in the *Grundlagen der Geometrie* from the mature development of the philosophy of formalism, as presented in Hilbert's later papers and in the *Grundlagen der Mathematik*. In his earlier book, Hilbert first of all expounded an axiomatic treatment of geometry which was to be taken as presenting euclidean geometry in its most modern form—the abstract science that had grown out of pre-Euclidean empirical study of space—and the metamathematics that followed was intended simply to demonstrate by ordinary mathematical argument that this theory had certain important characteristics, especially that of consistency. In the *Grundlagen der Mathematik*, on the contrary, the essential task was to *justify* mathematics in its final abstract form, by exclusively finitary means. Here Hilbert was obliged to apply his metamathematical argument not to the mathematical theory itself, which would be built up merely in conformity with the ordinary canons of mathematical rigour, but to a much stricter formalized theory or *formalism*, of the type that we have described in Chapter 4, §3, chosen in such a way that it would faithfully represent the mathematical theory as far as its totality of theorems was concerned.

Formal theories, as set up by Hilbert, are required to be strictly syntactic in their construction. This means that any such theory must be based on a postulated domain of individuals, a finite set of initial formulae, and certain explicitly formulated rules of derivation (say those belonging to the syntactic treatment of the restricted calculus of predicates, as given on p. 66). Its derivable formulae will then be all those formulae that can be obtained from the initial formulae by a finite number of applications of the rules of derivation. The formal theory is to be set up in such a way that every provable theorem of the original mathematical theory has its counterpart in a derivable formula of the formal theory; and if this can be done, then we shall only need to demonstrate the consistency of the formal theory in order to justify (in the sense explained) the mathematical theory that it represents.

Throughout mathematics, frequent and essential use is made of non-finitary arguments, and the formal systems which are constructed to represent mathematical theories will consequently have to provide rules of derivation which correspond to non-finitary inferences. Hilbert considered, when he devised his metamathematical method, that this did not matter, because even if the intuitive interpretation of a formal system is not finitary, the system itself, treated as a totality of derivations (i.e. finite sequences of formulae, put together in accordance with stated rules) is constructively defined, and is therefore a possible object of finitary discussion. The formalist programme thus offered a reasonable hope that a finitary metamathematics would be able to justify a non-finitary mathematics. We must now examine in detail how the programme was put into effect.

6 Consistency of the restricted calculus of predicates

As a preliminary to Hilbert's main undertaking, it was necessary first of all to apply the new method to symbolic logic, by making the logical calculus that was to be used into a strictly formal system, and then establishing its freedom from contradiction by finitary means. The system of logic that was chosen was, in fact, the restricted calculus of predicates, treated syntactically in the manner that we have already specified in Chapter 3. In order to complete our account of this initial phase in the working out of the formalist philosophy of mathematics, therefore, we have only to show how the consistency of the restricted calculus of predicates can be demonstrated.   This is a simple matter.

THEOREM 1.   *The restricted calculus of predicates is free from contradiction, in the sense that two formulae $\mathfrak{A}$ and $\bar{\mathfrak{A}}$ cannot both be derived in the system.*

Proof.   (i) We consider first of all the propositional calculus, as presented syntactically in Chapter 2, §6, which forms the most elementary part of the restricted calculus of predicates.   The only undefined symbols that occur in it are propositional variables (capital Latin letters) and the logical symbols '$^{-}$' and '$\vee$'.   Taking two metalogical symbols 'T' and 'F', we can draw up a truth-table for any formula of the calculus, and in this way we can determine finitarily whether or not the formula is an identical one, i.e. one that has 'T' for every entry in its truth-table.   It can now readily be shown (again by finitary argument) that (1) the axioms (a)–(d) are identical formulae, and (2) the property of being identical is left invariant by all applications of the rules of procedure (α) and (β).   It follows from this that every derivable formula is identical, and hence that two formulae $\mathfrak{A}$ and $\bar{\mathfrak{A}}$ are never both derivable.

(ii) Turning now from the propositional calculus to the full calculus to which the theorem refers, we find that the same proof continues to apply if we simply strike out from every formula of the calculus of predicates any arguments and quantifiers that may be present in it, retaining only the bare capital letters and treating these as if they were propositional variables.   The axiom (e) for example, which reads $(x)F(x) \rightarrow F(y)$, is then changed into the identical formula $F \rightarrow F$, i.e. $\bar{F} \vee F$; and the rules of procedure become trivial in a similar way.

Remark.   The proof just given is plainly finitary.   The idea behind it may be expressed in general terms in the following way.   In order to show that two formulae $\mathfrak{A}$ and $\bar{\mathfrak{A}}$ are not both derivable, we introduce constructively a property of symbolic expressions which (i) belongs to all the axioms, (ii) is invariant with respect to the rules of procedure, and is therefore inherited by every derived formula, and (iii) cannot belong to both $\mathfrak{A}$ and $\bar{\mathfrak{A}}$.   It is an extension of this same idea that makes possible the proofs of consistency, shortly to be discussed, that Hilbert devised for various arithmetical formalisms.

7   Consistency of arithmetic

After carrying out his programme in the simple case of logic, Hilbert turned his attention to arithmetic, first of all taking a very small part of arithmetic and justifying it, and then by degrees strengthening the axioms so that more and more of ordinary arithmetic was represented in the formal system. The successive phases of this inquiry are discussed in the first volume of *Grundlagen der Mathematik*.

The systems that are considered are all based on Peano's formalization of arithmetic in terms of the three primitive concepts of number, zero, and successor. A domain of individuals is postulated, corresponding to Peano's class N_0 of numbers; a particular individual of this domain is designated by the (constant) symbol '0'; and a mathematical function a', which associates with every term a a uniquely defined term a', serves to represent the successor function in the formalism.

In the first and weakest of the successive arithmetical formalisms— which we shall call the system (A_0), although it is unnamed in the *Grundlagen*—there are two constant predicates, each with two arguments, namely the logical predicate of identity, $a = b$, and the arithmetical predicate of inequality, $a < b$. Seven axioms are taken in addition to the axioms (a)–(f) of the restricted calculus of predicates. These are the two axioms (J_1) and (J_2) for identity, three axioms $(<_1)$, $(<_2)$, $(<_3)$ for order of magnitude, and two of the Peano axioms, (P_1) and (P_2), for the successor function. We thus have the following set of axioms:

$$
\begin{array}{lll}
(J_1) & a = a, \\
(J_2) & a = b \to (A(a) \to A(b)), \\
(<_1) & \overline{a < a,} \\
(<_2) & (a < b \;\&\; b < c) \to a < c, & \quad (A_0) \\
(<_3) & a < a', \\
(P_1) & a' \neq 0, \\
(P_2) & a' = b' \to a = b.
\end{array}
$$

As we can easily see (cf. p. 72), the three axioms for order of magnitude are not satisfiable with a finite number of individuals, and the domain of individuals now postulated must accordingly be infinite.

The rules of derivation for the arithmetical formalism are those of the restricted calculus of predicates, trivially modified where necessary to take account of the fact that we now have certain constant symbols '0', ''', '=', '<' in addition to the symbols of the logical calculus itself. As usual, we allow all identical formulae of the propositional calculus to be used as initial formulae in derivations (cf. p. 68).

In order to prove that a formal system is consistent, we have to show that no two contradictory formulae $\mathfrak{A}$ and $\overline{\mathfrak{A}}$ can both be derived. This is something that is often best done indirectly, by showing that some particular formula is underivable in the system. In view of the usefulness of the principle that allows us to transform the problem in this manner, we shall begin our discussion of consistency by expressing this principle formally in a metamathematical theorem:

THEOREM 2. *A formal system* F *is consistent if and only if there is some formula of the system that is not derivable.*

Proof. (i) If F is consistent then, for any arbitrary choice of a formula $\mathfrak{A}$, it is impossible that both $\mathfrak{A}$ and $\bar{\mathfrak{A}}$ should be derivable, and it follows from this that $\mathfrak{A}$ & $\bar{\mathfrak{A}}$ is an underivable formula of the system.

(ii) If F is inconsistent, there are some two formulae $\mathfrak{A}$ and $\bar{\mathfrak{A}}$ that are both derivable. But then, if $\mathfrak{B}$ is any formula whatever, $\mathfrak{B}$ can be derived with the aid of the identical formula $X \to (\bar{X} \to Y)$ of the propositional calculus.

To establish the consistency of the arithmetical system (A_0), then, we require to show that there is some formula that cannot be derived. The formula chosen for this role by Hilbert was $0 \neq 0$, and we shall now give an outline of Hilbert's metamathematical proof that no derivation in the system (A_0) can have $0 \neq 0$ for its end-formula.

The proof hinges on the discovery of a property of formulae of the system that can be shown to belong to every derivable formula but not to $0 \neq 0$. When proving the consistency of the propositional calculus, we were able to obtain a property of the required kind by turning to the semantic interpretation of propositional formulae as truth-functions of their arguments; and we could do this because the use of truth-tables is an essentially finitary procedure. In the present situation we again find ready to hand an intuitive interpretation of the symbolic expressions—namely their interpretation as statements in elementary arithmetic—and this suggests that we might try to use the elementary interpretation in order to define a suitable formal property. But this interpretation, as we have already seen in §4, is not wholly finitary. Indeed, if it were finitary we would hardly need to apply the indirect procedures of formalist metamathematics to this part of mathematics. Some means has therefore to be found of extracting an appropriate finitary property of formal expressions from their intuitive arithmetical meaning. This has in fact been done by Hilbert, with the aid of an ingenious process of *reduction*, which plays a most important part in the whole metamathematical treatment of arithmetic.

What reduction achieves is the transformation of formulae that contain bound variables, without essential change of their intuitive truth-content, into formulae that are free from such variables. This is just what is needed, as it is precisely the presence of bound variables that makes arithmetic non-finitary. We shall see, moreover, that a process of reduction is only needed for formulae that do not contain propositional or predicate variables.

To illustrate the nature of the process of reduction, let us take the simple formula

$$(Ex)(\mathfrak{a} < x'' \text{ \& } x'' < \mathfrak{b}),$$

in which $\mathfrak{a}$ and $\mathfrak{b}$ are supposed to be given terms. To say that there is an x such that $\mathfrak{a} < x'' < \mathfrak{b}$ is to say that there is a $y \geqslant 0''$ such that $\mathfrak{a} < y < \mathfrak{b}$; and this is the case if and only if $\mathfrak{b}$ exceeds $0''$ and there is at least one number between $\mathfrak{a}$ and $\mathfrak{b}$. We can accordingly replace the original existential statement by the simpler statement

$$0'' < \mathfrak{b} \text{ \& } \mathfrak{a}' < \mathfrak{b}.$$

This is, in fact, the formula that would be obtained if the process of reduction, now to be defined, were applied to the original formula. It will be found that the fact that the natural numbers form a progression makes it always possible for us to eliminate existential quantifiers from formulae of the system (A_0) without altering their import as arithmetical statements.

Suppose, then, that $\mathfrak{F}$ is some formula of (A_0) which does not contain any propositional or predicate variable. If $\mathfrak{F}$ has no bound variables it requires no reduction, but if bound variables are present in it we proceed in the following manner: We first of all replace every universal quantifier by an existential quantifier, by the device of substituting $\overline{(E\mathfrak{x})\overline{B(\mathfrak{x})}}$ for $(\mathfrak{x})B(\mathfrak{x})$. Then we select an 'innermost' component of $\mathfrak{F}$ of the form $(E\mathfrak{x})\mathfrak{A}(\mathfrak{x})$, that is to say a component of this form which is such that $\mathfrak{A}(\mathfrak{x})$ does not involve any further existential quantifier. $\mathfrak{A}(\mathfrak{x})$ is therefore a combination, by means of the logical operators of the propositional calculus, of equalities $\mathfrak{a} = \mathfrak{b}$ and inequalities $\mathfrak{a} < \mathfrak{b}$, where $\mathfrak{a}$ and $\mathfrak{b}$ denote numbers (i.e. symbols of the form 0, $0'$, $0''$, etc.) or individual variables, free or bound, possibly with appended dashes. In the metamathematical discussion which follows, we shall find it convenient to write a term $\mathfrak{a}''\cdots'$, in which t dashes are appended to $\mathfrak{a}$, as $\mathfrak{a}^{(t)}$.

Having selected a suitable component $(E\mathfrak{x})\mathfrak{A}(\mathfrak{x})$ of $\mathfrak{F}$, we apply certain transformations to $\mathfrak{A}(\mathfrak{x})$, as follows:

(i) We first put $\mathfrak{A}(\mathfrak{x})$ into disjunctive normal form, so that it becomes a disjunction $\mathfrak{E}_1 \lor \ldots \lor \mathfrak{E}_r$, in which each component $\mathfrak{E}_i$ is a conjunction of equalities and inequalities and negations of equalities and inequalities.

(ii) We next eliminate all the negations, by replacing $\mathfrak{a} \neq \mathfrak{b}$ by $\mathfrak{a} < \mathfrak{b} \lor \mathfrak{b} < \mathfrak{a}$ and $\overline{\mathfrak{a} < \mathfrak{b}}$ by $\mathfrak{a} = \mathfrak{b} \lor \mathfrak{b} < \mathfrak{a}$; and then we put the expression once again into disjunctive normal form $\mathfrak{F}_1 \lor \ldots \lor \mathfrak{F}_n$.

(iii) In every equality or inequality of the form $\mathfrak{x}^{(t)} = \mathfrak{x}^{(l)}$ or $\mathfrak{x}^{(t)} < \mathfrak{x}^{(l)}$, with $\mathfrak{x}$ occurring on both sides, we substitute 0 for $\mathfrak{x}$, thus obtaining $0^{(t)} = 0^{(l)}$ or $0^{(t)} < 0^{(l)}$.

(iv) We now determine the maximum number of dashes, t say, appended to $\mathfrak{x}$ anywhere in the formula $\mathfrak{F}_1 \lor \ldots \lor \mathfrak{F}_n$, as modified in (iii), and we then make up the number of dashes on every $\mathfrak{x}$ in the formula to t by adding dashes to both sides of an equality or inequality wherever necessary. For example, the formula

$$(0 < \mathfrak{x}' \;\&\; \mathfrak{x} < a) \vee (\mathfrak{x}''' = a'')$$

would have to be changed into

$$(0'' < \mathfrak{x}''' \;\&\; \mathfrak{x}''' < a'') \vee (\mathfrak{x}''' = a'').$$

The formula $\mathfrak{A}(\mathfrak{x})$ will now have been transformed into a formula which we may write as

$$\mathfrak{C}_1(\mathfrak{x}^{(t)}) \vee \ldots \vee \mathfrak{C}_m(\mathfrak{x}^{(t)}) \vee \mathfrak{C}_{m+1} \vee \ldots \vee \mathfrak{C}_n,$$

each disjunctive component $\mathfrak{C}_i(\mathfrak{x}^{(t)})$, $i = 1, \ldots, m$, being a conjunction of expressions of the possible forms $\mathfrak{x}^{(t)} = a$, $\mathfrak{x}^{(t)} < a$, $a < \mathfrak{x}^{(t)}$, $a = b$, $a < b$; and we accordingly replace $(E\mathfrak{x})\mathfrak{A}(\mathfrak{x})$ by the disjunction

$$(E\mathfrak{x})\mathfrak{C}_1(\mathfrak{x}^{(t)}) \vee \ldots \vee (E\mathfrak{x})\mathfrak{C}_m(\mathfrak{x}^{(t)}) \vee \mathfrak{C}_{m+1} \vee \ldots \vee \mathfrak{C}_n.$$

Then, for each of the m formulae $(E\mathfrak{x})\mathfrak{C}_i(\mathfrak{x}^{(t)})$, there are two possibilities to be considered.

(1) At least one equality $\mathfrak{x}^{(t)} = a$ occurs in the conjunction $\mathfrak{C}_i(\mathfrak{x}^{(t)})$, so that $(E\mathfrak{x})\mathfrak{C}_i(\mathfrak{x}^{(t)})$ has the form

$$(E\mathfrak{x})(\mathfrak{x}^{(t)} = a \;\&\; \mathfrak{C}_i^*(\mathfrak{x}^{(t)})).$$

It is understood, of course, that the residual part $\mathfrak{C}_i^*(\mathfrak{x}^{(t)})$ of the quantified expression need not be present at all, and if it is present it need not actually involve $\mathfrak{x}$. When $(E\mathfrak{x})\mathfrak{C}_i(\mathfrak{x}^{(t)})$ is of the form just given, we replace it by the formula

$$(0^{(t)} = a \vee 0^{(t)} < a) \;\&\; \mathfrak{C}_i^*(a),$$

in which there no longer appears either the variable $\mathfrak{x}$ or the quantifier $(E\mathfrak{x})$.

(2) The conjunction $\mathfrak{C}_i(\mathfrak{x}^{(t)})$ involves $\mathfrak{x}^{(t)}$ in inequalities only. In this case we may write $(E\mathfrak{x})\mathfrak{C}_i(\mathfrak{x}^{(t)})$ in the form

$$\mathfrak{H} \;\&\; (E\mathfrak{x})(a_1 < \mathfrak{x}^{(t)} \;\&\; \ldots \;\&\; a_k < \mathfrak{x}^{(t)} \;\&\; \mathfrak{x}^{(t)} < b_1 \;\&\; \ldots \;\&\; \mathfrak{x}^{(t)} < b_p),$$

where $\mathfrak{H}$ is the conjunction of all the components of $\mathfrak{C}_i(\mathfrak{x}^{(t)})$ that do not involve $\mathfrak{x}^{(t)}$. We then replace $(E\mathfrak{x})\mathfrak{C}_i(\mathfrak{x}^{(t)})$ by the conjunction

$$\begin{aligned}
\mathfrak{H} \;\&\; 0^{(t)} < b_1 \;\&\; &\ldots \;\&\; 0^{(t)} < b_p \;\&\; \\
\;\&\; a_1' < b_1 \;\&\; &\ldots \;\&\; a_1' < b_p \;\&\; \\
\;\&\; a_2' < b_1 \;\&\; &\ldots \;\&\; a_2' < b_p \;\&\; \\
& \cdot \cdot \cdot \\
\;\&\; a_k' < b_1 \;\&\; &\ldots \;\&\; a_k' < b_p.
\end{aligned}$$

If there is no component of the form $a < \mathfrak{x}^{(t)}$, then only the first line is required; and if there is no component of the form $\mathfrak{x}^{(t)} < \mathfrak{b}$, then $(E\mathfrak{x})\mathfrak{E}_i(\mathfrak{x}^{(t)})$ may be replaced simply by $\mathfrak{H}$ if this expression is non-null and by $0 = 0$ otherwise.

When the process just described has been completed, one quantifier will have been eliminated from the original formula $\mathfrak{F}$ without change of the *intuitive* truth or falsity of the arithmetical statement to which $\mathfrak{F}$ corresponds if it contains no free variables, and without alteration in $\mathfrak{F}$ as a 'truth-function' otherwise; and a finite number of applications of the process therefore suffices to remove all the quantifiers from $\mathfrak{F}$. The formula which finally results is then free from bound variables; it contains exactly the same free variables as the original formula $\mathfrak{F}$; and its 'truth content' is the same as that of $\mathfrak{F}$.

Exercise. Apply the process of reduction to the formula

$$(x)(x < a \rightarrow b < x) \rightarrow a = 0,$$

in which a and b are free variables.

We can now use the procedure of reduction in order to define the metamathematical concept of verifiability for formulae of the arithmetical system (A_0) which do not contain propositional or predicate variables.

DEFINITION.   (a) A numerical formula (i.e. one without variables) is *verifiable* if it is true when interpreted in terms of the finitary arithmetic of numerals.

(b) A formula with free individual variables only is *verifiable* if a finitary proof can be given that it becomes a true statement whenever definite numerals are substituted for the variables in it.

(c) A formula with bound variables is *verifiable* if it can be transformed by the process of reduction into a formula that is verifiable in the sense of (a) or (b).

It should be observed that part (c) of the definition requires justification. The process of reduction is not unique (because of the ambiguity of the disjunctive normal form) and we need to show that all possible reductions of a formula lead to the same decision as to its verifiability. The proof of this is long and rather tedious but full details are given by Hilbert and Bernays.

The property of verifiability, as just defined, does not take us outside the sphere of finitary argument, and we are therefore at liberty to use it for metamathematical purposes. By its aid we are able, in fact, to adapt to the formal system (A_0) the general method for proving consistency that we have already described (p. 211). We require to show that the formula $0 \neq 0$ is not derivable; and this will be accomplished if we can demonstrate by finitary means that, if a formula is derivable, then it is also verifiable.

THEOREM 3.   *The formalized system of arithmetic* (A_0) *is free from contradiction*.

Proof.   Let $(\mathfrak{F}_i)$ be any derivation in the system (A_0).   We prove that the end-formula of this derivation cannot be $0 \neq 0$; and to do so we divide the proof into two parts.

(i) In the first part of the proof we assume that no bound variables occur in the given derivation $(\mathfrak{F}_i)$.   Thus the available initial formulae are the identical formulae of the propositional calculus and the seven special axioms (J_1), (J_2), $(<_1)$, $(<_2)$, $(<_3)$, (P_1), (P_2); and the only schema that can be used is the rule of inference (β), as given on p. 67. The derivation $(\mathfrak{F}_i)$ is therefore a finite sequence of formulae, each of which is either (i) an identical formula of the propositional calculus or one of the seven special axioms, (ii) a repetition of an earlier formula of the sequence $(\mathfrak{F}_i)$ or else a formula obtained by making a substitution in an earlier formula, or (iii) a formula obtained by use of the schema (β).

Our first step is one of unravelling the given derivation $(\mathfrak{F}_i)$ into its separate strands (*Auflösung in Beweisfäden*), and this is achieved by starting with the end-formula and working back systematically to the initial formulae of the derivation.   We set out the result of the process schematically in the following manner.   First of all we put down the end-formula in the middle of the page.   Then above it we place the formula or pair of formulae from which it is immediately derived; above each such formula we place in the same way the formula or formulae from which it is immediately derived; and so on, until we have worked back in every instance to an initial formula.   If a formula $\mathfrak{W}$ in the resolved derivation is derived from two formulae $\mathfrak{U}$ and $\mathfrak{V}$ by use of the schema (β) we put

while if a formula $\mathfrak{W}$ is derived from a formula $\mathfrak{V}$ by repetition or substitution we put

In order to avoid confusion in the diagram it is desirable to begin by numbering off the successive formulae of the sequence $(\mathfrak{F}_i)$, so that these can be represented by their numbers in the resolved derivation $(\mathfrak{F}_i')$ when this is displayed schematically.

As an illustration of the process of resolution into strands, we give here an example which Hilbert and Bernays discuss on p. 226 of their first volume. The formula $0'''' \neq 0''$ may be derived as follows:

$$\quad\;\;(1) \qquad\qquad (A \to B) \to (\bar{B} \to \bar{A})$$
$$\to(2) \qquad (a' = b' \to a = b) \to (a \neq b \to a' \neq b')$$
$$\quad\;\;(3) \qquad\qquad\quad a' = b' \to a = b$$
$$\overline{\qquad\qquad\qquad\qquad\qquad\qquad\qquad\qquad\qquad}$$
$$\quad\;\;(4) \qquad\qquad\quad a \neq b \to a' \neq b'$$
$$\to(5) \qquad\qquad\quad a' \neq 0 \to a'' \neq 0'$$
$$\quad\;\;(6) \qquad\qquad\qquad\quad a' \neq 0$$
$$\overline{\qquad\qquad\qquad\qquad\qquad\qquad\qquad\qquad\qquad}$$
$$\quad\;\;(7) \qquad\qquad\qquad\quad a'' \neq 0'$$
$$\to(8) \qquad\qquad a'' \neq 0' \to a''' \neq 0''$$
$$\overline{\qquad\qquad\qquad\qquad\qquad\qquad\qquad\qquad\qquad}$$
$$\quad\;\;(9) \qquad\qquad\qquad\quad a''' \neq 0''$$
$$\to(10) \qquad\qquad\qquad\quad 0'''' \neq 0''.$$

Key:

(1): [identical formula]   (2): [(1) $a' = b'/A$, $a = b/B$]
(3): [(P$_2$)]   (4): [(3), (2): (β)]
(5): [(4) a'/a, $0/b$]   (6): [(P$_1$)]
(7): [(6), (5): (β)]   (8): [(4) a''/a, $0'/b$]
(9): [(7), (8): (β)]   (10): [(9) $0'/a$].

The derivation $(\mathfrak{F}_i)$ that we have here, when written schematically as a resolved derivation $(\mathfrak{F}_i')$, takes the form:

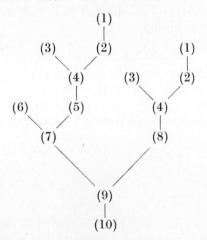

The formula (10) is the end-formula, and (1), (3), (6) are the initial formulae that are used.

Having unravelled the strands of $(\mathfrak{F}_i)$, we now work backwards through ($\mathfrak{F}_i'$), taking each strand in turn and going always from the end-formula of the derivation right back to the initial formula in which the strand originates.   In the example given, we would have to follow five different strands: (i) $(10) \to (9) \to (7) \to (6)$;   (ii) $(10) \to (9) \to (7) \to$ $\to (5) \to (4) \to (3)$;   (iii) $(10) \to (9) \to (7) \to (5) \to (4) \to (2) \to (1)$; (iv) $(10) \to (9) \to (8) \to (4) \to (3)$;   (v) $(10) \to (9) \to (8) \to (4) \to (2) \to$ $\to (1)$.   As we work along the strands, we carry all substitutions back to the initial formulae.   In other words, whenever we come to a link

which is such that $\mathfrak{W}$ is obtained from $\mathfrak{B}$ by one or more substitutions, we make the inverse substitutions in $\mathfrak{B}$ and in all the formulae that stand higher than $\mathfrak{B}$ in the strands which pass through $\mathfrak{B}$.   Let the derivation ($\mathfrak{F}_i'$), as thus modified, be denoted by ($\mathfrak{F}_i''$).   Then, whenever we have a pair of formulae

in ($\mathfrak{F}_i''$), $\mathfrak{W}$ is simply a repetition of $\mathfrak{B}$; and whenever we have a triad of formulae

in ($\mathfrak{F}_i''$), the passage from $\mathfrak{U}$ and $\mathfrak{B}$ to $\mathfrak{W}$ is a valid application of the rule (β).   Thus ($\mathfrak{F}_i''$) only differs from a proper derivation in that its initial formulae are not restricted to the identical formulae of the propositional calculus and the seven special axioms, but may be any formulae derived from these by substitution.

It is possible that some free variables may still be left in ($\mathfrak{F}_i''$).   This would be the case, for example, if ($\mathfrak{F}_i'$) contained some such sub-derivation as

$$A \vee \overline{A}$$
$$A(a) \vee \overline{A(a)} \qquad (A(a) \vee \overline{A(a)}) \to B$$
$$B$$
$$|\ .$$

We accordingly eliminate all remaining free variables from ($\mathfrak{F}_i''$) by making the following substitutions: $0 = 0$ for every propositional variable; $\mathfrak{a} = \mathfrak{a}$ for every predicate variable with a single argument $\mathfrak{a}$; $(\mathfrak{a} = \mathfrak{a} \ \& \ldots \& \ \mathfrak{k} = \mathfrak{k})$ for every predicate variable with the arguments

$\mathfrak{a}, \ldots, \mathfrak{k}$; and 0 for every individual variable. Then the array of formulae that we are left with is still a derivation in the same extended sense as $(\mathfrak{F}_i'')$; and every formula in the array is a numerical formula, that is to say a combination by means of the operators of the propositional calculus of equalities $\mathfrak{s} = \mathfrak{t}$ and inequalities $\mathfrak{s} < \mathfrak{t}$ between definite 'numbers' 0, 0', 0", etc. If, moreover, the original derivation $(\mathfrak{F}_i)$ had $0 \neq 0$ as its end-formula, the derivation yielded by the process that we have just described would also end with $0 \neq 0$.

Now it can be verified, by finitary argument, that (1) the initial formulae of the modified derivation are all true statements when they are given an interpretation based on the finitary arithmetic of the numerals 0, 0I, 0II, ...; (2) both the operation of repeating a formula and the operation of applying the rule (β) leave truth in this sense invariant; and (3) the formula $0 \neq 0$ is false in the corresponding sense. We thus have the required finitary proof of the underivability of the formula $0 \neq 0$, when 'derivable' is understood as meaning 'derivable without use of bound variables'. Our further task, in part (ii) of the proof, is to remove this limitation.

(ii) We now suppose that the derivation $(\mathfrak{F}_i)$ with which we begin uses the full resources of the restricted calculus of predicates. This means that the axioms (e) and (f), p. 66, which involve quantification, can now occur as initial formulae, and the two schemata $(\gamma 1)$ and $(\gamma 2)$ can now be used in addition to the schema (β).

We begin, as in part (i) of the proof, by unravelling the strands of the derivation, and by carrying back all substitutions to the initial formulae. Having done this, we eliminate all propositional and predicate variables as in case (i). But this time, because of the free variables that are essential to the schemata $(\gamma 1)$ and $(\gamma 2)$, we cannot eliminate all free *individual* variables without invalidating the derivation. Neither can we eliminate the bound (individual) variables that may occur. Consequently we are unable to transform the given sequence of formulae $(\mathfrak{F}_i)$ into an array of numerical formulae that retains the structure of a derivation, and so to prove as in (i) that the end-formula cannot be the false formula $0 \neq 0$. We can, however, use verifiability in place of numerical truth; and then a similar method of proof applies. We show that the initial formulae are all verifiable and that the property of verifiability is inherited by every formula in the modified derivation, and it then follows that $0 \neq 0$ cannot be the end-formula. The details of the argument, which we omit from this summary, are given in full by Hilbert and Bernays.

Here, then, we have in outline the proof of the first consistency theorem for formalized arithmetic, and we must now assess the value of what has been established. According to the formalist programme, in order to justify ordinary mathematics we are to formalize it and then to show that the formal system is free from contradiction. The proof just given has shown that the initial formalization of part of arithmetic by the system (A_0) is indeed consistent; and we must now ask how adequate this formalization is as a representation of intuitive arithmetic. In other words, we must raise the question of the completeness of the system. A formal theory may be said to be (semantically) complete if every intuitively valid statement that can be made in the symbolism of the theory is derivable; and in the present situation we shall make the notion of 'intuitively valid' precise by interpreting it to mean verifiable in the sense already laid down. The question, therefore, is whether every verifiable formula of the system (A_0) is derivable; and the answer is that this is not the case. Hilbert and Bernays prove (*Grundlagen*, p. 252) that the verifiable formula

$$a < b \rightarrow (a' = b \lor a' < b)$$

is not derivable from the axioms. To do this, they use the standard method for proving independence (cf. p. 198 above), devising a suitably distorted property of 'verifiability', which holds for the axioms and is invariant with respect to the rules of procedure, but does not hold for the formula in question. They then go on to prove (pp. 253–260) that all formulae that are verifiable in the original proper sense become derivable if the following five formulae are added to the axioms:

$$a \neq b \rightarrow (a < b \lor b < a),$$
$$a < b \rightarrow a' < b',$$
$$0 = a \lor 0 < a,$$
$$0 < a \rightarrow (Ex)(x' = a),$$
$$(a < c \ \& \ c < b) \rightarrow a' < b.$$

When these new axioms are added, some of the original ones become derivable, and hence superfluous. The extended list of axioms can eventually be condensed into the following set of seven only:

$$
\left.
\begin{aligned}
&a = b \rightarrow (A(a) \rightarrow A(b)),\\
&(a < b \ \& \ b < c) \rightarrow a < c,\\
&a \neq b \rightarrow (a < b \lor b < a),\\
&a < a',\\
&a < b \rightarrow \overline{b < a'},\\
&\overline{a < 0},\\
&a \neq 0 \rightarrow (Ex)(x' = a).
\end{aligned}
\right\} \quad (A)
$$

It is proved in the *Grundlagen* that these seven axioms are independent, and further that *a formula without propositional or predicate variables is derivable from them if and only if it is verifiable.* This last result shows that the system (A) is both consistent and complete.

All of Peano's five axioms except the axiom of induction are derivable in the system (A), but the axiom of induction is not derivable. This last statement is certainly plausible, for the axiom of induction

$$[A(0) \ \& \ (x)(A(x) \to A(x'))] \to A(a)$$

involves a predicate variable, and the only one of the axioms (A) in which any variable other than an individual variable occurs is the second axiom for identity (J_2). A formal proof of the independence of the axiom of induction is given by Hilbert and Bernays (p. 273).

We may note, incidentally, that instead of representing the principle of mathematical induction by the axiom just given, we could equally well formalize it by a schema:

$$\mathfrak{A}(0)$$
$$\frac{\mathfrak{A}(a) \to \mathfrak{A}(a')}{\mathfrak{A}(a).}$$

The two alternative ways of incorporating the principle in the formal system can be shown to have identical deductive power (*Grundlagen*, p. 266).

If we add the axiom of induction to the set of axioms (A), some of these axioms can be weakened or omitted altogether; and we thus arrive at the following revised set of axioms:

$$\left.\begin{array}{l} a = b \to (A(a) \to A(b)), \\ a < a, \\ (a < b \ \& \ b < c) \to a < c, \\ a < a', \\ a < b \to (a' = b \lor a' < b), \\ 0 = 0, \\ [A(0) \ \& \ (x)(A(x) \to A(x'))] \to A(a). \end{array}\right\} \quad \text{(B)}$$

The two systems (A) and (B) can be shown to be equivalent *for the derivation of formulae without propositional or predicate variables*—that is to say, any such formula that is derivable in one of the systems is also derivable in the other—but the systems are not equivalent for the derivation of formulae in which propositional and predicate variables may occur. The last assertion follows from the non-derivability of the axiom of induction from the set of axioms (A).

In the system (B) we are able to derive the very important arithmetical *principle of the least number* (*Grundlagen*, p. 284), expressed by the formula

$$A(a) \to (Ex)[A(x) \ \& \ (y)(A(y) \to (x = y \lor x < y))].$$

This principle is best utilized in conjunction with the ι-symbol, which provides an explicit expression for the least number in question. Let us denote by $\mathfrak{M}(c)$ the formula

$$A(c) \,\&\, (y)(A(y) \to (c = y \lor c < y)).$$

Then the formula just quoted may be written

$$A(a) \to (Ex)\mathfrak{M}(x).$$

By means of this formula we can derive (*Grundlagen*, p. 395) the two uniqueness formulae for the formula

$$((z)\overline{A(z)} \to a = 0) \,\&\, ((Ez)A(z) \to \mathfrak{M}(a)),$$

in which a is a free variable; and we are therefore at liberty to introduce the corresponding ι-term by means of the explicit definition

$$\mu_x A(x) \equiv \iota_x[((z)\overline{A(z)} \to x = 0) \,\&\, ((Ez)A(z) \to \mathfrak{M}(x))].$$

The term $\mu_x A(x)$ is the formal counterpart of the intuitive concept 'the least number with the property A if there is any such number, and 0 otherwise'.

The theorem on the eliminability of the ι-symbol (see above, p. 95) now permits us to assert, without further discussion, that *any formula, not itself involving the μ-symbol, that can be derived from the set of axioms* (B) *with the aid of the μ-symbol is also derivable from these axioms without use of the μ-symbol.*

Looking now at the way in which the axioms (B) have been obtained, we see that all of Peano's axioms are incorporated in the formal system, either implicitly through the symbolism or directly by derivable formulae; and this may seem to imply that the system is no less comprehensive than Peano's arithmetic. Such a conclusion is unwarranted, however, since Peano's treatment of arithmetic is actually based on more than the bare axioms. In the *Formulaire* extensive use is made of definitions, and we have already noted (p. 147) that as well as explicit definitions, which serve merely to introduce abbreviations, there are also *recursive definitions*, which are definitions in quite another sense and which make substantial additions to the system.

A recursive definition of a function $\mathfrak{f}(n)$ of one variable takes the form of a pair of equations

$$\mathfrak{f}(0) = \mathfrak{a},$$
$$\mathfrak{f}(n') = \mathfrak{b}(n,\mathfrak{f}(n)),$$

where $\mathfrak{a}$ is a term that does not involve any variable, $\mathfrak{b}(x,y)$ is a term that involves the variables x and y only, and neither $\mathfrak{a}$ nor $\mathfrak{b}(x,y)$ involves the function $\mathfrak{f}(-)$. For a function $\mathfrak{f}(a, \ldots, k, n)$, with parameters $a, \ldots, k$, the definition takes the more general form

$$\mathfrak{f}(a, \ldots, k, 0) = \mathfrak{a}(a, \ldots, k),$$
$$\mathfrak{f}(a, \ldots, k, n') = \mathfrak{b}(a, \ldots, k, n, \mathfrak{f}(a, \ldots, k, n)).$$

The adoption, within a given formal system, of a particular recursive definition always adds to the formal resources which the system provides, that is to say to the available means of symbolic expression, since we thereby acquire a new function-symbol; but it does not necessarily render the system any more comprehensive. We need, therefore, to distinguish between essential and non-essential extension of a formal system, the extension occasioned by a particular recursive definition being regarded as non-essential if the new function is one already representable in some alternative way in the original system. It is clearly important to give precise metamathematical meaning to the notion of formal representability of a function, and Hilbert and Bernays adopt the following definition (p. 352):

DEFINITION. Let a new function of one or more variables be adjoined to a given formal system by the introduction of a function-symbol $\mathfrak{f}(a, \ldots, k)$, together with associated formulae which permit calculation of the value of the function for any assigned numerical values of its arguments. The function is said to be *representable* in the original system if there is a formula $\mathfrak{A}(a, \ldots, k, l)$ of the system such that, for every substitution of numerical values $\mathfrak{a}, \ldots, \mathfrak{k}, \mathfrak{l}$ for the variables $a, \ldots, k, l$, the formula $\mathfrak{A}(\mathfrak{a}, \ldots, \mathfrak{k}, \mathfrak{l})$ is derivable if $\mathfrak{l}$ coincides with the value of $\mathfrak{f}(\mathfrak{a}, \ldots, \mathfrak{k})$ and the formula $\overline{\mathfrak{A}(\mathfrak{a}, \ldots, \mathfrak{k}, \mathfrak{l})}$ is derivable otherwise.

It can be shown (*Grundlagen*, p. 356) that the sum function $a + b$, which is definable by the equations of recursion

$$a + 0 = a,$$
$$a + n' = (a + n)',$$

is not representable in the system (B). We accordingly take ' $+$ ' as a new primitive symbol and incorporate this recursive definition in the system of axioms; and the usual sort of reorganization then leads to the following strengthened system:

$$
\left.
\begin{aligned}
&a = a, \\
&a = b \rightarrow (A(a) \rightarrow A(b)), \\
&a' \neq 0, \\
&a' = b' \rightarrow a = b, \\
&a + 0 = a, \\
&a + b' = (a + b)', \\
&[A(0) \,\&\, (x)(A(x) \rightarrow A(x'))] \rightarrow A(a).
\end{aligned}
\right\} \quad \text{(D)}
$$

The system (D) does not contain ' $<$ ' among its primitive symbols, but the predicate $a < b$ can be introduced by explicit definition, thus:

$$a < b \leftrightarrow (Ex)(x \neq 0 \; \& \; a + x = b).$$

The new system, as we have said, is stronger than the old; but once again we are able to assert that the system that we have before us is both consistent and complete. The process of reduction that we used before can be modified in such a way that it applies to formulae in (D), and we can then show that the totality of verifiable formulae of this system coincides with the totality of derivable formulae.

The assertion that the systems (B) and (D) are both complete, although the second is demonstrably wider than the first, has an air of paradox. There is not really any conflict, however, since completeness, as we have been interpreting this term, is always relative to the symbolic resources of the system concerned. And, even though the system (D) is complete in this internal sense, it is still far from complete as a formalization of intuitive arithmetic. We can show, in fact, that the product function $a.b$ is not representable in (D) (*Grundlagen*, p. 369). We accordingly add the symbol '.' and the relevant equations of recursion to the primitive elements of the system (D), passing thus to the following extended system of axioms:

$$
\left.
\begin{aligned}
&a = a, \\
&a = b \rightarrow (A(a) \rightarrow A(b)), \\
&a' \neq 0, \\
&a' = b' \rightarrow a = b, \\
&a + 0 = a, \\
&a + b' = (a + b)', \\
&a.0 = 0, \\
&a.b' = a.b + a, \\
&[A(0) \; \& \; (x)(A(x) \rightarrow A(x'))] \rightarrow A(a).
\end{aligned}
\right\} \quad \text{(Z)}
$$

Although the passage from (D) to (Z) appears to be of exactly the same kind as that from (B) to (D), involving nothing but the addition to the existing axioms of the recursive definition of one new function, this latest extension of the formalism in reality produces an entirely new situation. With addition and multiplication both at our disposal, we are now able to formalize the whole of the elementary theory of numbers, and we can in consequence represent in the system (Z) various propositions concerning the natural numbers that are as yet undecided, and that may even be undecidable by elementary means.

A famous undecided conjecture is Goldbach's hypothesis, according to which every even integer greater than 2 is expressible as a sum of two prime integers. In order to translate this assertion into the symbolism of the system (Z), we first of all formalize the propositional function 'n is prime' by defining a predicate $\mathfrak{Pr}(n)$ explicitly as follows:

$$\mathfrak{Pr}(n) \leftrightarrow n \neq 0 \;\&\; n \neq 0' \;\&\; (u)(v)((u \neq 0' \;\&\; v \neq 0') \to u.v \neq n).$$

Then we can express Goldbach's hypothesis in the form

$$(x)[0' < x \to (Ey)(Ez)(\mathfrak{Pr}(y) \;\&\; \mathfrak{Pr}(z) \;\&\; 0''.x = y + z)].$$

A second well-known conjecture concerning prime numbers is that there are infinitely many prime-pairs, or pairs of prime numbers which differ by only 2. It comes to the same thing to assert that there are arbitrarily large prime-pairs, and so we arrive at the formula

$$(x)(Ey)(x < y \;\&\; \mathfrak{Pr}(y) \;\&\; \mathfrak{Pr}(y'')).$$

The very fact that the formal system (Z) is wide enough to allow such translations into its symbolism to be made, which indicates that we are at last within sight of completeness of a mathematically interesting kind, signalizes also the breakdown of the method for proving consistency that has been applicable up to this point. That method depended on the existence of a process of reduction which could be used to define verifiability; and the effect of reduction was to convert any formula, without essential change of its intuitive truth-content, into a formula that could be handled by finitary means. Now since there are, among the formulae of the system (Z), some which correspond to problems in arithmetic that have for centuries defied all efforts to solve them, it seems very unlikely that any process of reduction for this system can be found.

The failure for the system (Z) of one particular method for proving consistency does not of itself imply that no finitary proof of consistency can be given for this system; but such is in fact now known to be the case on other grounds. One of the most famous theorems in metamathematics, proved in 1931 by Kurt Gödel, placed this virtually beyond doubt, and so brought to an abrupt end the phase of the development of formalism that we have been discussing in this chapter. The work of Gödel on the limitations of formalism is the topic of the chapter that now follows.

SUPPLEMENTARY NOTES ON CHAPTER 7

1. *Foundations of projective geometry.* The study of foundations of mathematics can be interpreted in a restricted sense, as an examination of the logical structure of deductive systems, or more widely, as a partly historical and partly critical consideration of the development of mathematical concepts and methods. From the latter point of view the history of projective

geometry is especially instructive, because of the progressive change of out-look that has taken place as this subject has become more thoroughly under-stood.

The story of projective geometry begins with Gérard Desargues (1593–1662), who in 1639 published his essay *Brouillon proiect d'une atteinte aux éuénemens des rencontres d'un cone auec un plan* [sketch of an inquiry into the results of the intersection of a cone with a plane]. In this work Desargues introduced a number of ideas characteristic of projective geometry, as for instance point at infinity, pole and polar, and involution of pairs of points on a line. His argument, however, was too abstruse for all but one or two mathematicians of the time, and the essay was soon entirely forgotten.

After a lapse of nearly two centuries, projective geometry was studied again, independently of Desargues, by Jean-Victor Poncelet (1788–1867). A military engineer by profession, Poncelet served with Napoleon's army; and when he eventually published his geometrical discoveries, in his *Traité des propriétés projectives des figures* (1822), he remarked of the book that it was 'the outcome of the investigations which I have carried on, since the spring of 1813, in the prisons of Russia'. In this book Poncelet developed the conception of duality, making use of the transformation by reciprocal polars determined by a fixed conic; and he also introduced (in an intuitive manner) such completely new ideas as that of the circular points at infinity.

A more systematic, though no less original contribution to projective geo-metry was made by August Ferdinand Möbius in *Der barycentrische Calcul* (1827). Möbius devised a way of representing the points of the plane (or of space) by homogeneous coordinates referred to an arbitrarily selected triangle (or tetrahedron) of reference—a way, moreover, that is essentially projective and that permits projective relationships to be expressed simply in algebraic terms. He defined cross ratio (as a quotient of position ratios) and he established the main properties of this important invariant. He also studied the 'net' of points—now known as a *Möbius net*—which is obtained from the vertices of a quadrangle when the two operations of joining two points of the plane by a line and taking the point of intersection of two given lines are repeated indefinitely often; and he was able to show that (i) in any coordinate system based on three of the vertices of the quadrangle as fundamental points and the remaining vertex as unit point, the points of the net are precisely those points which have rational coor-dinates, and (ii) every neighbourhood of any given point of the plane con-tains points of the net.

Up to this stage in its history, projective geometry had been conceived as just one particular division of the study of figures in ordinary space, namely that part which deals exclusively with relationships that are pro-jectively invariant; but now a more radical way of treating the subject emerged in the work of Georg Karl Christian von Staudt (1798–1868), who was professor of mathematics at Erlangen. Realizing that projective geometry is essentially non-metrical, von Staudt determined to treat it from the outset as a 'geometry of position'; and he carried this project through in his *Geometrie der Lage* (1847) and *Beiträge zur Geometrie der Lage* (1856–1860). He began with an intuitively conceived space, in which the concepts of straight line and plane had meaning, but no concept of distance was introduced; and he then attempted to build up the whole of projective geometry in terms of relations of incidence.   He had no means of introducing the metrical notion of cross ratio, but he was nevertheless able to define the harmonic relation by the quadrangle construction and then to make use of the properties of the Möbius net.   He defined two ranges of points (and similarly two two-dimensional or three-dimensional systems) to be projectively related when there is a correspondence between them which is such that harmonic tetrads correspond always to harmonic tetrads.   Appealing to considerations of continuity, he then attempted to justify the fundamental theorem that a projectivity between ranges is uniquely determined by three corresponding pairs; but in this one particular he went slightly wrong, since the argument that he used is invalid unless the line can be asserted to be a continuum in the sense of Dedekind.   The need for a special postulate to ensure this was pointed out in 1873 by Felix Klein, then in his turn professor at Erlangen.

Von Staudt's methodological principle that since projective geometry is logically independent of notions of spatial magnitude it ought to be developed non-metrically gained general acceptance; and towards the end of the nineteenth century many attempts were made to improve still further on the rigour of von Staudt's treatment by making the presentation strictly axiomatic.   An early contribution to this movement was made by Moritz Pasch, in his *Vorlesungen über neuere Geometrie* (1882).   Although Pasch believed that geometry ought to be grounded in intuition—and in consequence of this belief he chose to begin his treatment with finite linear segments rather than with straight lines of infinite extent—he considered at the same time that the logical basis of the deductive system must be made absolutely precise.   He accordingly based the development on a number of *Kernsätze*, in which were expressed the fundamental facts concerning incidence.   Other mathematicians (in particular Peano and Hilbert) soon went further still, recognizing that the logical structure of geometry is in fact independent of intuition.   They saw, in other words, that only *abstract* primitive notions and primitive propositions are needed, and that geometrical theorems are valid for all systems of entities that satisfy the appropriate axioms.

The formal properties of the relation of incidence constitute the most elementary part of projective geometry; and when incidence geometry is presented axiomatically it is seen to be a common substructure of many different systems of geometry, for instance of euclidean geometry and of the non-euclidean geometries as well as of projective geometry.   In particular, metrical geometries can be obtained when a suitable theory of congruence is set up.   For this aspect of the foundations of geometry see Hilbert [2] and Whitehead [2, 3].

A very careful investigation of the minimal assumptions that will suffice for the construction of a system of projective geometry of n-dimensional space was made by Gino Fano in a paper 'Sui postulati fondamentali della geometria proiettiva', published in 1891.   Fano showed that an explicit existential postulate is necessary in order to ensure that a line always contains more than two points, and that a further postulate is then necessary in order to ensure that points are not always their own harmonic conjugates. He did this by setting up models for which the postulates in question fail to hold, showing, for instance, that a two-dimensional projective geometry is possible in which there are only seven points, lying in threes on seven lines.

A complete axiomatic presentation of projective geometry, worked out with the aid of Peano's logical symbolism, but retaining few of the symbols in the published version, is contained in a paper of Mario Pieri, 'I principii della geometria di posizione composti in sistema logico deduttivo' (1899). Pieri's system is based on two primitive notions (point and the join of two points) and nineteen primitive propositions or postulates. The earlier postulates are concerned with properties of incidence, while the later ones deal with the relations which give rise to an order of the points of a line; and among these later postulates there is one which ensures that the line is a continuous series in the sense of Dedekind. Pieri considers that his set of postulates is complete, since he is able to derive all the principles used by von Staudt, and von Staudt has already derived the further theorems of projective geometry in detail, and has shown moreover that his points can be represented by real coordinates.

The attempts to make projective geometry rigorous that we have mentioned so far have all set out from a totality of 'geometrical' points, either supposed given intuitively or else postulated as primitive; but an analytical approach is also a possibility, and this has on the whole been preferred in recent times. The relation between the two possible approaches may be expressed in the following way. In a synthetic treatment such as that of Pieri, coordinates may be introduced by von Staudt's method. Rational coordinates are first of all determined for all the points of a Möbius net, and then real coordinates are determined by continuity for all other points. When this is done, points become in effect pairs of ratios $x:y:z$ of real numbers. But the same result would have been obtained more directly if a point had initially been *defined* as such a pair of ratios, a straight line as the totality of points which satisfy a given homogeneous equation, and so forth; and this is precisely the analytical approach.

When all geometrical entities are defined algebraically, it appears that there is no theoretical necessity for the coordinates to be *real* numbers, since the algebraic development requires only that they should be drawn from a field. Every field F thus yields corresponding spaces of 2, 3, or n dimensions; and if F happens to be a Galois field $GF(p^s)$, with only a finite number of elements, the corresponding projective spaces have each only a finite number of points. Since there are infinitely many Galois fields, one for each prime-power p^s, there are infinitely many finite projective geometries of given dimensionality. In the simplest case of all, when the ground-field is $GF(2)$, the projective plane has seven points, and projective space of three dimensions has fifteen. The finite geometries were first discussed in relation to Galois fields by Veblen and Bussey [1] in 1906.

2. *Models of non-euclidean geometry.* A brief account of the models of Klein and Poincaré for two-dimensional hyperbolic geometry is given by

Courant and Robbins, [1], pp. 219–224. Poincaré's model is mentioned also by Pedoe, [1], p. 58.

Klein developed the ideas involved in his model in his fundamental paper 'Über die sogenannte Nicht-Euklidische Geometrie' (1871), and they are treated very fully in his book *Vorlesungen über Nicht-Euklidische Geometrie* (1928). Hyperbolic geometry results when, in the real projective plane, a non-virtual conic is taken as absolute conic and only the points of its interior (i.e. those points from which no real tangent can be drawn) are treated as actual points. Angular measure can be introduced by the natural generalization of Laguerre's formula for euclidean geometry, with the proper absolute conic taking the place of the absolute point-pair (I,J); and distance can be defined in terms of cross ratio by the dual procedure. Collineations which leave the absolute conic invariant can then be interpreted as non-euclidean rotations. If a virtual conic is taken instead of a non-virtual one as the absolute conic, an elliptic metric is obtained instead of a hyperbolic metric.

3. *The literature of Hilbert's metamathematics.* Whereas Hilbert's *Grundlagen der Geometrie* has been translated into English (see the Bibliography), the *Grundlagen der Mathematik* of Hilbert and Bernays, which supplies the definitive account of Hilbert's later metamathematical work, at present exists in German only. Much of the substance of this book is contained, however, together with material from other sources, in Kleene's *Introduction to Metamathematics*. Kleene's book is also provided with a full and very useful bibliography.

Hilbert's many-sided contribution to mathematics, and his enormous influence on the creative work of other mathematicians, form the subject of a long commemorative article 'David Hilbert and his mathematical work', contributed by Hermann Weyl to the *Bulletin of the American Mathematical Society*, **50** (1944), 612–654. Weyl gives a clear and concise summary of Hilbert's achievement in each of the many fields in which he worked. There is a shorter notice by Weyl in the *Obituary Notices of Fellows of the Royal Society*, **4** (1942–1944), 547–553, and this also conveys clearly the unique position of Hilbert in the mathematical world of his time.

Chapter 8

GÖDEL'S THEOREMS ON THE INHERENT
LIMITATIONS OF FORMAL SYSTEMS

1 Gödel's new metamathematical method

We come now, in this chapter, to the celebrated metamathematical theorems of Gödel, which first revealed a fundamental disparity between formal axiomatic theories, of the type considered by Hilbert, and the intuitive mathematics that they are constructed to represent. The phase of formalism that lasted until 1930, and that was dominated by Hilbert's constructive work on metamathematics or theory of proof (*Beweistheorie*), can now be seen as a comparatively naive phase—intensely creative, and productive of the basic conceptions and techniques on which most later work has been based, but at the same time relatively uncritical of its own foundations and ignorant of its inherent limitations. By 1930, however, enough progress had been made on the constructive side for the process of formalization itself to be a possible object of critical study; and in a terse but incisive paper,[1] distinguished alike by astonishing originality, profundity of conception, and mastery of intricate detail, Gödel carried metamathematics over at a single stride into its second and more reflective phase.

Hilbert himself, in originally conceiving the idea of the formalist programme, had already taken a decisive step in the study of the formal aspect of mathematics. Even before this, the desirability of formalizing mathematical theories had been recognized by Peano, who had evolved a suitable technique for the purpose, but for Peano formalization was no more than an essential aid to rigour within mathematics. Hilbert, on the contrary, formalized mathematical theories in order to turn them into well-defined objects of discussion, thus making possible the new kind of investigation to which he gave the name 'metamathematics'. In his *Beweistheorie*, which we have outlined in the previous chapter, the mathematics is treated formally while the metamathematical discussion, though kept strictly within the bounds of finitary argument, proceeds in a more intuitive way. The further step which Gödel took was to devise a treatment of metamathematics that is itself

---

[1] K. Gödel: 'Über formal unentscheidbare Sätze der Principia Mathematica und verwandter Systeme I', *Monatsh. Math. Phys.*, **38** (1931), 173–198.

essentially formal in character; and this new advance was made possible
by a simple but ingenious device that he introduced for the 'arithmetization' of metamathematical reasoning.

A formalized mathematical theory, as understood by Hilbert, is an
edifice of symbolic expressions, made up of standard symbols that are
used again and again, and such that the constitution of its component
expressions (the well-formed formulae) and the manner in which these
expressions may be assembled into derivations are regulated by precisely formulated syntactic rules.   What Gödel realized was that, from
a theoretical point of view, the particular nature of the signs that are
chosen is totally irrelevant, so that we may as well adopt a standard
system of 'coding', in which each symbol that is used is represented by
a fixed natural number.   Any formula, which is simply a finite string
of symbols, will then be represented by a corresponding string of numbers; and by using the key to the code we shall be able to get back from
the string of numbers to the formula.   The coding can be arranged,
moreover, in such a way that the rules which govern both the formation
of well-formed formulae and the arrangement of such formulae in derivations can be expressed in terms of simple arithmetical operations on
the representative numbers.   When this is done, the metamathematical
assertions that we are mostly interested in no longer require formulation
in terms that refer specifically to the particular formal theory to which
they relate, but they are all of a single uniform type, being without
exception arithmetical propositions.   Thus metamathematics, no less
than the mathematics which forms its object, can be formalized, and it
then becomes much more sharply defined than it was previously, when
no limitation was imposed on it beyond that of being finitary.

When the new metamathematical technique is applied with formalized arithmetic itself as the primary theory, the way is made open for a
most significant development.   Since the metamathematics is now of
the same nature as the mathematics, both of them consisting of arithmetical propositions, every metamathematical assertion can be expressed within the primary theory (provided that this is sufficiently
comprehensive); and in this way the metamathematics of the formal
system becomes formalizable within that system itself.   A situation is
thus created which allows of the sort of exploitation of self-reference
that formed the basis of Cantor's proof that no class is equipotent with
the class of all its subclasses, and also of Richard's paradoxical argument
(see p. 127) and of the even simpler paradox of the man who declares
'The statement that I am now making is untrue'.   Seizing upon this
circumstance, Gödel was able to show that, if a system of formalized
arithmetic is wide enough, then (i) the system is necessarily incomplete,
in the sense that there exists a formula $\mathfrak{A}$ of the system such that
neither $\mathfrak{A}$ nor its negation is derivable, and (ii) if the system is con-

sistent, then no proof of its consistency is possible which can be formalized within it.

2 Gödel's heuristic argument

In the introduction to his paper of 1931, Gödel explained the general idea of his method by means of the following heuristic argument, formulated in relation to the logico-mathematical system of *Principia Mathematica*.

Consider all the formulae $R(x)$ which involve a single free variable x of the same type as the natural numbers. These formulae can be arranged, lexicographically for example, as a sequence $\{R_n(x)\}$.[1] Now the statement 'The formula $R_n(n)$, obtained when "n" is substituted for "x" in the nth formula of the sequence, is not derivable within the system' can itself be formalized within the system, and it is accordingly represented there by some formula $S(n)$. But the formula $S(x)$ then involves a single free variable x of the same type as the natural numbers, and therefore $S(x)$ coincides with $R_q(x)$ for some q. Thus $R_q(n)$ is a formal equivalent of 'The formula $R_n(n)$ is not derivable'; and consequently the formula $R_q(q)$ means 'The formula $R_q(q)$ is not derivable'. We therefore have, in $R_q(q)$, a formula that asserts its own underivability.

It now readily follows that this formula $R_q(q)$ is undecidable in the formal system. For suppose, first of all, that $R_q(q)$ were derivable. Then the proposition '$R_q(q)$ is underivable', expressed by this derivable formula, would be true. The assumption that $R_q(q)$ is derivable is therefore untenable. But now let us suppose that the negation $\sim R_q(q)$ of $R_q(q)$ were derivable. In that case the corresponding proposition 'not-[$R_q(q)$ is underivable]' would be true, and $R_q(q)$ would thus be derivable. If we assume that the formal system is consistent, we once again have an impossibility. Thus neither $R_q(q)$ nor $\sim R_q(q)$ can be derivable, and $R_q(q)$ is accordingly an undecidable formula of the system.

As Gödel says, this heuristic argument is plainly lacking in rigour, not only because we take for granted in it that the metamathematics of *Principia Mathematica* can be formalized within the *Principia* itself, but also because essential use is made of the non-formal semantic concept of truth of a proposition. In order to eliminate these deficiencies, Gödel proceeded in the body of his paper to develop the same line of argument fully and in a strictly formal manner, basing it not on *Principia Mathematica* itself but on a slightly different formal system,

---

[1] The convention on the use of symbols that we have adopted in earlier chapters would require $\{R_n(x)\}$ to be written as $\{\Re_n(x)\}$; but in this chapter we prefer to adhere closely to the usage of Gödel in order to facilitate comparison of our summary with his original paper.

namely an arithmetical system P that he constructed by combining together the extended calculus of predicates (with the simple theory of types) and Peano's axioms for the natural numbers.

3 The formal system P and its arithmetized metamathematics

In summarizing Gödel's main argument, we must begin with the specification of the formal system P on which it is based. The primitive symbols of this system include both constants and variables, as follows:
I. Constants: '$\sim$' (not), '$\vee$' (or), 'Π' (for all), '0' (zero), 'f' (the successor of), and the two brackets '(' and ')'.
II. Variables: variables of the first type 'x_1', 'y_1', 'z_1', ... (for individuals, i.e. natural numbers); variables of the second type 'x_2', 'y_2', 'z_2', ... (for classes of individuals); variables of the third type 'x_3', 'y_3', 'z_3', ... (for classes of classes of individuals); and so forth.[1]

In place of the symbolic expressions ϕx and $(x)\phi x$ that are used in *Principia Mathematica* for the propositional function 'x has the property ϕ' and the proposition 'Every individual has the property ϕ', we have in the system P the expressions $x_2(x_1)$ and $x_1\Pi(x_2(x_1))$.

The primitive symbols are to be supplemented by further constant symbols used as abbreviations. In particular, the symbols '.', '$\supset$', '$\equiv$', '(Ex)', '$=$' are used as '.', '$\supset$', '$\equiv$', '$(\exists x)$', '$=$' are used in *Principia Mathematica*.

By an *expression* (*Zeichen*) *of the first type* is meant an expression of one of the forms $a, fa, ffa, fffa, \ldots$, where a is either 0 or else a variable of the first type. An *expression of the nth type* ($n > 1$) can only be a variable of that type.

An *elementary formula* is an expression $a(b)$, where b is an expression of some type n and a is an expression of the next higher type $n + 1$.

The class of *formulae* is the smallest class that contains all the elementary formulae and is closed with respect to negation, disjunction, and universal quantification. By this we mean that, if a and b are formulae and x is any variable, then $\sim(a)$, $(a) \vee (b)$, and $x\Pi(a)$ are also formulae.

A formula with no free variables is said to be a *propositional formula*. A formula with exactly n free individual variables and no other free variable is said to be a *relation-formula with n arguments*. A relation-formula with one argument is also called a *class-formula*.

If a is any formula, v is a variable, and b is an expression of the same type as v, we are to understand by

$$\text{Subst } a \begin{pmatrix} v \\ b \end{pmatrix}$$

[1] No primitive symbols are needed for predicates. A predicate with one argument can be interpreted as a class of individuals, a predicate with two arguments as a class of ordered pairs of individuals, and so on; and an ordered pair $a \downarrow b$ can in turn be identified with a class of classes, namely $\{\{a\},\{a, b\}\}$ (cf. p. 171).

the formula which results when b is substituted for all the free occurrences (if there are any) of v in a.

A formula a is said to be obtained from a formula b by *elevation of type* if it is obtained when the type of every variable that occurs in b is raised by the same amount.

The axioms of the system P are arranged in five groups as follows:

I.   1. $\sim (fx_1 = 0)$,
      2. $fx_1 = fy_1 \supset x_1 = y_1$,
      3. $x_2(0) . x_1 \Pi(x_2(x_1) \supset x_2(fx_1)) \supset x_1 \Pi(x_2(x_1))$.

II. Every formula that can be obtained from the following schematic forms by substituting arbitrary formulae for p, q, r:

   1. $p \vee p \supset p$,
   2. $p \supset p \vee q$,
   3. $p \vee q \supset q \vee p$,
   4. $(p \supset q) \supset (r \vee p \supset r \vee q)$.

III. Every formula that can be obtained from the following schematic forms by making substitutions of the kind specified below for a, b, c, v, and, in the case of 1, carrying out the substitution indicated:

   1. $v\Pi(a) \supset \text{Subst } a \begin{pmatrix} v \\ c \end{pmatrix}$,
   2. $v\Pi(b \vee a) \supset b \vee v\Pi(a)$.

For a we may substitute an arbitrary formula, for v an arbitrary variable, for b a formula in which v does not occur free, and for c an expression of the same type as v, provided that c contains no variable that is bound in a where v is free.

IV. Every formula that can be obtained from the schematic form

   1. $(Eu)(v\Pi(u(v) \equiv a))$

by substituting for v and u variables of types n and $n + 1$ respectively, and for a a formula in which u does not occur free. (This axiom, which is related to the 'principle of comprehension' for classes, as formulated below on p. 285, takes the place in the system P of the axiom of reducibility in *Principia Mathematica*.)

V. The following formula, and every formula that is obtainable from it by elevation of type:

   1. $x_1 \Pi(x_2(x_1) \equiv y_2(x_1)) \supset x_2 = y_2$.

This axiom asserts that a class is completely determined by its members; cf. the axiom of determination in the theory of sets, as stated on p. 288 below.

No rule of substitution is required, since substitutions are already taken care of by the adoption of axiom-schemata in preference to specific axioms (cf. p. 44). The other rules of procedure are incorporated in the system P in the following manner: A formula c is said to be an *immediate consequence* of a and b (or of a) if a is the formula $(\sim(b)) \vee (c)$ (or if c is the formula $v\Pi(a)$, where v is any variable). The class of *derivable formulae* is defined as the smallest class of formulae which contains the axioms and is closed with respect to the relation of immediate consequence.

> *Exercise.* Rewrite the specification of Gödel's system P in the notation of the present book, using German letters as syntactic variables. Compare Gödel's axioms with those of (a) *Principia Mathematica*, (b) Peano's treatment of arithmetic, (c) Hilbert's formalization of logic and arithmetic, as given above in Chapters 3 and 7.

In order to arithmetize the metamathematics of the system P, Gödel had first of all to rewrite the entire formal system, using numbers everywhere in place of the special symbols $\sim$, $\vee$, Π, 0, f, $(\,,)$, x_1, y_1, $\ldots$; and this he did in principle by defining what has since come to be known as a *Gödel numbering* of the formal expressions. He first attached numbers to the constant primitive symbols in accordance with the following table:

Symbol	0	f	$\sim$	$\vee$	Π	$($	$)$
Number	1	3	5	7	9	11	13

Then, making use of the natural sequence of prime numbers p_1, p_2, p_3, $\ldots$ (i.e. the sequence $2, 3, 5, \ldots$), he assigned to the variables x_n, y_n, z_n, $\ldots$ of the nth type the numbers p_7^n, p_8^n, p_9^n, $\ldots$, i.e. the numbers 17^n, 19^n, 23^n, $\ldots$.

The coding of the symbols that is defined in this way is such that every primitive symbol of the system has a well-defined Gödel number, and distinct symbols always have distinct numbers. To any finite sequence $a_1, a_2, \ldots, a_k$ of primitive symbols there then corresponds a finite sequence $n_1, n_2, \ldots, n_k$ of natural numbers; and with this latter sequence we may associate in turn the single natural number $p_1^{n_1} p_2^{n_2} \ldots p_k^{n_k}$. By this process a one-one mapping is set up between the totality of finite sequences a of primitive symbols on the one hand, and a certain subset of the set of natural numbers on the other. We may denote this mapping by $a \longleftrightarrow \Phi(a)$. Then, since every formula a of the system P may be treated as a mere string of symbols, it has a well-defined Gödel number $\Phi(a)$.

EXAMPLE.   Consider axiom I 2, which runs

$$fx_1 = fy_1 \supset x_1 = y_1.$$

Written in terms of primitive symbols only, without use of abbreviations, this becomes

$$\sim (x_2 \Pi (\sim x_2(fx_1) \lor x_2(fy_1))) \lor x_2 \Pi (\sim x_2(x_1) \lor x_2(y_1)),$$

which is a string of 34 symbols.   From this string we obtain a sequence of 34 numbers 5, 11, 17^2, 9, 11, 5, 17^2, ..., 13; and the Gödel number of the formula is therefore

$$p_1^5 p_2^{11} p_3^{17^2} \cdots p_{34}^{13}.$$

Not every integer corresponds to a well-formed formula, of which it is the Gödel number, or even to a string of primitive symbols; but if a number is the Gödel number of a formula, this formula can actually be found by resolution of the number into its prime factors.

The Gödel coding can readily be extended from single formulae to finite sequences of formulae—among which, of course, are included derivations.   Let $a_1, \ldots, a_l$ be given formulae, and let the Gödel number $\Phi(a_i)$ of a_i be m_i, $i = 1, \ldots, l$.   Then we assign to the sequence $\{a_1, \ldots, a_l\}$ the single number $p_1^{m_1} \ldots p_l^{m_l}$.   When this has been done, every symbol, every formula, and every finite sequence of formulae in the system P is represented without ambiguity by a Gödel number.

Suppose now that we have some metamathematical predicate or relation $R(a_1, \ldots, a_n)$ that is defined for sets of n symbols, formulae, or sequences of formulae $a_1, \ldots, a_n$.   In the special case $n - 1$ the 'relation' is to be understood, as usual, as a class of symbols, etc.   Then the relation $R(a_1, \ldots, a_n)$ determines an 'induced' relation $R'(x_1, \ldots, x_n)$, defined for sets of natural numbers.   This induced relation holds for a particular set of numbers $x_1, \ldots, x_n$ if and only if there exist $a_1, \ldots, a_n$ in the formal system such that, for $i = 1, \ldots, n$, a_i has Gödel number x_i—in the appropriate sense—and $R(a_1, \ldots, a_n)$ is true.   Gödel represents the arithmetical relation R' that is derived in this way from any particular metamathematical relation R by putting the name of R into italics.   Thus, for example, *formula* is the class (i.e. predicate) whose members are the Gödel numbers of formulae; and 'm is a *derivation* of n' is the relation between two numbers m and n which holds whenever m is the Gödel number of a sequence of formulae that is a derivation, the end-formula of which has Gödel number n.

When Gödel had set up his numbering in the manner described, he had to go on to show that the arithmetized metamathematics of P was all contained in P; that is to say, he had to show that the various italic relations between numbers that are obtained from such metamathematical relations as 'formula', 'immediate consequence', and 'derivable' admit of formalization within P. He was able to do this with the aid of recursive arithmetic. Only the elements of recursive arithmetic were needed for this purpose, and Gödel gave the following explanation of what he understood by recursive functions and recursive relations. The explanation is expressed intuitively, of course, not formalized within the system P.

An arithmetical function $\varphi(x_1, x_2, \ldots, x_n)$ is said to be *recursively defined* in terms of a pair of given functions $\psi(x_1, x_2, \ldots, x_{n-1})$ and $\mu(x_1, x_2, \ldots, x_{n+1})$ if, for all $x_2, \ldots, x_n, k$,

$$\varphi(0, x_2, \ldots, x_n) = \psi(x_2, \ldots, x_n),$$
$$\varphi(k+1, x_2, \ldots, x_n) = \mu(k, \varphi(k, x_2, \ldots, x_n), x_2, \ldots, x_n).$$

A *function* φ is said to be *recursive*[1] if there exists a finite sequence of functions $\varphi_1, \varphi_2, \ldots, \varphi_n$ such that $\varphi_n = \varphi$, and every function φ_k of the sequence is either recursively defined in terms of two of its predecessors, or is obtained by substitution in one of its predecessors, or else is either a constant or the successor function $x + 1$.

A *relation* $R(x_1, \ldots, x_n)$ between natural numbers is said to be *recursive* if there exists a recursive function $\varphi(x_1, \ldots, x_n)$ such that, for any numbers $x_1, \ldots, x_n$, the relation $R(x_1, \ldots, x_n)$ holds if and only if $\varphi(x_1, \ldots, x_n) = 0$.

Recursiveness having thus been defined, the demonstration that the metamathematics of the system P can be formalized in P proceeds in two stages. First it is shown that all the relevant metamathematical relations are recursively expressible in terms of the Gödel numbering; and then recourse is had to a general theorem which asserts that every recursive relation is representable in P (cf. the definition of formal representability on p. 222 above).

Gödel states and proves from first principles for his formal system P the following theorem, which may be compared with the corresponding theorem for Hilbert's system (Z), which we give in Chapter 10 (p. 269):

THEOREM 1. *If $R(x_1, \ldots, x_n)$ is any relation in recursive arithmetic, there exists in* P *a relation-formula $\varrho(x_1^{(1)}, \ldots, x_1^{(n)})$, with n free variables, such that, for any set of n numbers $m_1, \ldots, m_n$, (i) if $R(m_1, \ldots, m_n)$ holds then $\varrho(m_1', \ldots, m_n')$ is derivable in* P, *and (ii) if $R(m_1, \ldots, m_n)$ does not hold then $\sim \varrho(m_1', \ldots, m_n')$ is derivable in* P, m_i' *denoting the symbol $ff \ldots f0$ that corresponds in* P *to the number m_i.*

This theorem appears in Gödel's paper as *Satz* V (p. 186).

That all the relevant metamathematical relations are recursive was shown by Gödel in a series of 46 lemmas. Typical of the relations that he considers are those which we can express (using the device of italic

---

[1] I.e. primitive recursive in current terminology (cf. Chapter 10, §6).

names to which we referred on p. 235) by the words 'x is a *variable of the nth type*', 'x is an *axiom*', and 'x is a *derivation* of the *formula y*'.

4*   The central argument of Gödel's paper

In attempting to summarize Gödel's argument in such a way that we can give some indication of the essential steps without going into too many formal details, we shall adopt a device of denoting the sequence of symbols (i.e the expression) that has a given Gödel number x by $\tilde{x}$, and the sequence of expressions that has a given Gödel number x by $\tilde{\tilde{x}}$. Then the statement 'x is a *derivation* of the *formula y*', for instance, can be expressed in the alternative form '$\tilde{\tilde{x}}$ is a sequence of formulae that is a derivation of the formula $\tilde{y}$'. We shall also use the notation 'x''', as in the theorem stated at the end of §3, for the expression $ff\ldots f0$ which represents the number x in the formal system P.

Gödel found it necessary to postulate that the system P is *ω-consistent*, or consistent in a stronger sense than that which is ordinarily envisaged, and the concept of *ω*-consistency must be explained before we can state his main theorem.   An arithmetical formalism is consistent in the ordinary sense—or *simply consistent*—if no two formulae 𝔄 and 𝔄̄ are both derivable in it; but consistency in this sense does not exclude the more subtle kind of contradiction that occurs when, for some formula 𝔄(n) that contains a free variable n, 𝔄(n) is derivable for each particular number n, and $\overline{(x)\mathfrak{A}(x)}$ is also derivable.   This possibility was first pointed out by Alfred Tarski.   It is easily seen that a system that is *ω*-consistent is also simply consistent, for if it were not simply consistent then every formula would be derivable in it (cf. p. 211); but Tarski has shown by an example that a system can be simply consistent without being *ω*-consistent.[1]

Gödel formulated his main argument in terms of any formal system that can be obtained by supplementation of the axioms of the basic system P by an arbitrary recursive class ϰ of additional formulae.   He first defined the *consequential set* (*Folgerungsmenge*) of ϰ as the smallest set of formulae that contains the axioms of P and the formulae belonging to ϰ, and is at the same time closed with respect to the relation of immediate consequence.   If ϰ is empty, its consequential set plainly reduces to the set of derivable formulae of P.

The two senses of consistency can now be redefined, with reference to such a class ϰ, as follows: A class of formulae ϰ is said to be *simply consistent* if its consequential set does not contain any formula together with its negation; and ϰ is said to be *ω-consistent* if there does not exist

---

[1] A. Tarski: 'Einige Betrachtungen über die Begriffe der ω-Widerspruchsfreiheit und der ω-Vollständigkeit', *Monatsh. Math. Phys.*, **40** (1933), 97–112.   In this paper Tarski claims priority in the introduction of the concept of ω-consistency though not in the use of this name for it.

any class-formula $a(v_1)$ such that (i) $a(n')$ belongs to the consequential set of $\varkappa$ for every natural number n, and (ii) $\sim (v_1 \Pi(a(v_1)))$ also belongs to this consequential set.

We can now state Gödel's key theorem (his *Satz* VI) in the following terms:

THEOREM 2. *If $\varkappa$ is any ω-consistent recursive class of formulae of the system* P, *there exists a formula* $\varrho(x_1)$, *which determines a recursive class of numbers, and which is such that neither* $v_1 \Pi(\varrho(v_1))$ *nor* $\sim (v_1 \Pi(\varrho(v_1)))$ *belongs to the consequential set of* $\varkappa$.

Proof. In outlining Gödel's proof, we shall use the term '$\varkappa$-derivation' to mean a derivation in which any formulae belonging to $\varkappa$ may be used as initial formulae.

We consider first of all the metamathematical propositional function '$\tilde{x}$ is not a $\varkappa$-derivation of the formula which results when y' is substituted for y_1 in the formula $\tilde{y}$'. The 'y_1' that is here referred to is the particular symbol of the system P that has Gödel number 19, and the letter 'y' in it has no connexion with the 'y' that is one of the variables involved in the propositional function. This propositional function is a relation, $Q(x,y)$ say, built up out of constituent notions such as 'immediate consequence' and 'substitution', whose italic counterparts are proved in the lemmas of Gödel's paper to be recursive; and it is therefore represented in P by a relation-formula $\tilde{q}(x_1,y_1)$, in such a way that (i) if $\tilde{x}$ is not a $\varkappa$-derivation of $\tilde{y}(y')$, then $\tilde{q}(x',y')$ is derivable, and (ii) if $\tilde{x}$ is a $\varkappa$-derivation of $\tilde{y}(y')$, then $\sim (\tilde{q}(x',y'))$ is derivable.

We now put

$$\tilde{p}(y_1) \equiv x_1 \Pi(\tilde{q}(x_1,y_1))$$

and

$$\tilde{r}(x_1) \equiv \tilde{q}(x_1,p').$$

Then

$$\tilde{p}(p') \equiv x_1 \Pi(\tilde{q}(x_1,p'))$$
$$\equiv x_1 \Pi(\tilde{r}(x_1)),$$

and

$$\tilde{q}(x',p') \equiv \tilde{r}(x').$$

Substituting p for y in (i) and (ii) above, we have: (i)′ if $\tilde{x}$ is not a $\varkappa$-derivation of $\tilde{p}(p')$, then $\tilde{q}(x',p')$ is derivable; and (ii)′ if $\tilde{x}$ is a $\varkappa$-derivation of $\tilde{p}(p')$, then $\sim (\tilde{q}(x',p'))$ is derivable. In other words, (i)″ if $\tilde{x}$ is not a $\varkappa$-derivation of $x_1 \Pi(\tilde{r}(x_1))$, then $\tilde{r}(x')$ is derivable; and (ii)″ if $\tilde{x}$ is a $\varkappa$-derivation of $x_1 \Pi(\tilde{r}(x_1))$, then $\sim (\tilde{r}(x'))$ is derivable.

At this point the argument divides into two parts:

1. We suppose that $x_1 \Pi(\tilde{r}(x_1))$ is $\varkappa$-derivable. Then it follows that $\tilde{r}(n')$ is $\varkappa$-derivable for any number n whatever. But, in view of (ii)″,

there is an n such that $\sim (\tilde{r}(n'))$ is $\varkappa$-derivable.   We thus have a $\varkappa$-derivable contradiction; and this proves, even if $\varkappa$ is assumed merely to be *simply* consistent, that the formula $x_1 \Pi(\tilde{r}(x_1))$ is not $\varkappa$-derivable.

2. We have shown in 1. that $x_1 \Pi(\tilde{r}(x_1))$ is not $\varkappa$-derivable, and thus, for any n whatever, $\tilde{n}$ is not a $\varkappa$-derivation of $x_1 \Pi(\tilde{r}(x_1))$.   Hence, by (i)", $\tilde{r}(n')$ is derivable for every choice of n.   If, therefore, $\varkappa$ is assumed to be ω-consistent, the formula $\sim (x_1 \Pi(\tilde{r}(x_1)))$ is not $\varkappa$-derivable.

1. and 2. together show that neither the formula $x_1 \Pi(\tilde{r}(x_1))$ nor its negation is $\varkappa$-derivable, and this proves the theorem.

Remarks (i) In the above version of the proof we have used the expression $\tilde{q}(x_1, y_1)$ to stand for the formula with Gödel number q, and to indicate at the same time that this formula contains x_1 and y_1 as free variables.   We have then used $\tilde{q}(x_1, p')$ to stand for the formula

$$\text{Subst } \tilde{q}(x_1, y_1) \begin{pmatrix} y_1 \\ p' \end{pmatrix}.$$

(ii) It has been shown by Barkley Rosser (*J. Symb. Logic*, **1** (1936), 87–91) that Gödel's original proof can be modified in such a way that the existence of an undecidable formula is shown to follow merely from simple consistency of $\varkappa$, the heavier requirement of ω-consistency being in fact superfluous.

(iii) After proving his main theorem on the existence of undecidable formulae, Gödel made the following comment on its range of application:

'In the proof of Theorem VI, no properties of the system P were used except the following:

1. The class of axioms and the rules of inference (i.e. the relation of "immediate consequence") are recursively definable (as soon as the primitive symbols have been replaced in some way by natural numbers).

2. Every recursive relation is definable within the system P (in the sense of Theorem V).

It follows that, in every formal system that satisfies the hypotheses 1 and 2 and is ω-consistent, there are undecidable propositions of the form $(x)F(x)$, where F is a recursively defined property of natural numbers, and the same is true of every extension of such a system by means of a recursively definable ω-consistent class of axioms.   The systems that satisfy the hypotheses 1 and 2 include, as may easily be verified, the Zermelo-Fraenkel and von Neumann systems of axioms for the theory of sets, and also the system of axioms for the theory of numbers that consists of the Peano axioms, recursive definitions, and the logical rules.   Hypothesis 1 is satisfied by any system whatever that has the usual rules of inference and whose axioms arise (as in the case of P) by substitution in a finite number of schemata.'

5   The impossibility of an 'internal' proof of consistency

In §4 of his paper, Gödel turned his attention to the second of his famous theorems, the one that establishes the impossibility of proving certain formal systems consistent from within.   The general idea of the argument (of which only the outline is sketched in the original paper) may be explained in the following terms.

The argument depends on the fact that in the system P we are able to formalize intuitive arithmetical reasoning.   That is to say, given an intuitive arithmetical proof, we can construct in P a corresponding formal derivation.   Suppose then, once again, that $\varkappa$ is an arbitrary recursive class of formulae of the system P.   We already know, by 1. on p. 238, that from the hypothesis that $\varkappa$ is simply consistent it follows that the formula $x_1 \Pi(\tilde{r}(x_1))$ is not $\varkappa$-derivable.   More precisely, we are able to give an intuitive proof (which is effectively arithmetical in view of our arithmetization of the metamathematics of the system P) that this conclusion follows.   Hence we can establish, by intuitive reasoning, the implication

($\varkappa$ is consistent) $\rightarrow$ (the formula $x_1 \Pi(\tilde{r}(x_1))$ is not $\varkappa$-derivable),

i.e. ($\varkappa$ is consistent) $\rightarrow$ $(x)(\tilde{\tilde{x}}$ is not a $\varkappa$-derivation of $x_1 \Pi(\tilde{r}(x_1)))$,

i.e. ($\varkappa$ is consistent) $\rightarrow$ $(x)(\tilde{\tilde{x}}$ is not a $\varkappa$-derivation of $\tilde{p}(p'))$,

i.e. ($\varkappa$ is consistent) $\rightarrow$ $(x)Q(x,p)$.

The intuitive proof of this implication can now be formalized by an equivalent derivation in P.   The metamathematical proposition '$\varkappa$ is consistent' will be formalizable in P by a certain propositional formula $\tilde{w}$; and since $Q(x,p)$ is formalizable, as we already know, by $\tilde{r}(x')$, it follows that $(x)Q(x,p)$ is formalizable by $x_1 \Pi(\tilde{r}(x_1))$.   The derivation in P will accordingly be a derivation of the formal implication

$$\tilde{w} \supset x_1 \Pi(\tilde{r}(x_1)).$$

If, now, $\tilde{w}$ were to be derivable in P, we would at once have a derivation of $x_1 \Pi(\tilde{r}(x_1))$—and this we know to be impossible if $\varkappa$ is consistent. Thus $\tilde{w}$ is not derivable in P, and so we have the following theorem:

THEOREM 3.   *If $\varkappa$ is any simply consistent recursive class of formulae in* P, *there does not exist any proof, formalizable in* P, *of the consistency of the system which results when the formulae in $\varkappa$ are adjoined to* P *as additional initial formulae.*

If, in particular, we take for $\varkappa$ the empty class, we see that Theorem 3 applies to the system P itself.

It was the publication of this theorem that effectively brought to a close the initial phase of the formalist movement, as we have indicated in §1 of this chapter.   Although, as Gödel was careful to point out, the theorem only rules out *formalizable* proofs of consistency, and does not say anything directly about *finitary* proofs, it does not seem likely that a finitary procedure could ever be devised that was not also formalizable.

Hilbert and Bernays have discussed Gödel's theory and its implications at length in the second volume of their *Grundlagen der Mathe-*

matik (1939). They modify the details of Gödel's paper, using an alternative way of arithmetizing metamathematics which brings the theory into more immediate relation with Hilbert's treatment of formalized arithmetic, but the basis of the theory remains substantially unchanged. The proofs are, of course, given in full; and for each of Gödel's theorems precise conditions are formulated which are sufficient to ensure that a formal system is one to which the theorem applies. It is eventually shown (*Grundlagen*, II, §5, 2, e) that the theorem on the impossibility of an internally formalizable proof of consistency holds, in particular, for the system (Z) of formalized arithmetic, as specified on p. 223 above.

We see, then, that the consistency of formalized arithmetic can only be proved by methods which are more general than any that are provided for in the arithmetical system itself. When Gödel had established this fact, it was natural that attempts should be made to prove the consistency of arithmetic by means which did not go too far beyond the previously recognized limits of strict finitariness, and in 1936 Gentzen succeeded in constructing a proof of consistency which depended on the application of transfinite induction. For this further development of metamathematics see Note 1, immediately following, and also Section 2 of the Appendix, p. 385.

SUPPLEMENTARY NOTES ON CHAPTER 8

1. *Gentzen's proof of the consistency of arithmetic.* It follows from Gödel's theorem on proofs of consistency (Theorem 3, p. 240) that, for any reasonably adequate formalization of arithmetic to be proved consistent, more powerful types of metamathematical argument must be allowed than those originally envisaged by Hilbert. The proof of consistency will then no longer provide the clear justification of arithmetic as a 'significant' formal theory that was at one time hoped for, and its value in this respect will vary inversely with the power of the methods of demonstration which it employs. But, whatever weight may now be given to proofs of consistency as an ultimate guarantee of the validity of mathematical theories, any precise indication of means that are sufficient to establish the consistency of formalized arithmetic is of major interest in its own right. In the proof of consistency which Gentzen constructed, finitary reasoning of the earlier kind was supplemented by a limited use of transfinite induction.

Gentzen's argument depended on the introduction of a process of reduction (cf. p. 211) which can be applied to any derivation in the arithmetical system that he considered. This process was defined in a recursive manner, and to complete the specification Gentzen had to show that the reduction of any given derivation can be accomplished in a finite number of steps. To show that the process of reduction always terminates, he introduced ordinal numbers as measures of the complexity of formulae and then applied transfinite induction to these ordinal numbers. For this purpose he needed transfinite induction for a certain segment of Cantor's second number class, namely the series of all ordinals below the first ε-number, i.e. the smallest ordinal number α such that $\omega^\alpha = \alpha$. A different proof of the consistency of arithmetic, also dependent on transfinite induction up to the first ε-number, has been given by Ackermann [2]. This proof makes essential use of the selection operator ε_x, which Hilbert originally introduced with the aim of extending to the arithmetical system (Z) the proofs of consistency that he had already constructed for weaker systems.

2. *Alternative accounts of Gödel's investigation.* A detailed presentation in English of the substance of Gödel's fundamental paper is contained in the mimeographed notes [3] of lectures which Gödel gave at Princeton in 1934. These notes were compiled by Kleene and Rosser. Rosser has published also, in the *Journal of Symbolic Logic* in 1939, an informal paper [2] which gives the gist of Gödel's work.

Gödel's theory is presented afresh by Mostowski in his book [1], again in considerable detail. A more elementary summary is that of N. R. Hanson [1]; and there is also a popular account by Nagel and Newman [1].

Chapter 9

INTUITIONISM

1 The intuitionist outlook

We have now traced the history of both the logistic and formalist attempts to provide mathematics once and for all with a secure foundation, and in the last three chapters we have given a general account of the two schools of research which these enterprises inspired.

The logistic movement began with Dedekind's endeavour to achieve a new and higher standard of rigour in the presentation of the infinitesimal calculus by rejecting arguments based on the alleged self-evidence of geometrical facts. Dedekind came at length to see that the degree of rigour which he regarded as necessary in mathematics could only be attained if this discipline were made wholly conceptual; and out of this realization there developed the logistic thesis that mathematics must be analysed in terms of logic alone. The traditional conception of logic was in due course sufficiently refined and elaborated, at the hands of Frege, Peano, and Russell, for such a reinterpretation of mathematics to be undertaken in detail; and ultimately, in *Principia Mathematica*, a system of logic and mathematics was produced which fulfilled the logistic intention. On the whole, however, mathematicians have not been inclined to accept the logistic analysis of mathematics as one that adequately reflects the real nature of their subject; and so *Principia Mathematica* has never gained general acceptance as a final solution to the central problem of foundations of mathematics. Furthermore, as we shall see in Chapter 12, there are various fundamental questions concerning the nature of logic which this system leaves unanswered.

Of rather more recent origin than the logistic movement is the other movement that has produced the philosophy of formalism—in its essentials the personal creation of Hilbert, although other mathematicians and logicians have subsequently contributed far-reaching discoveries in the field of metamathematics. The formalist philosophy has added much to our understanding of the formal basis of mathematical theories, and in its later developments has revealed unsuspected limitations of the formal axiomatic method itself. As we are now in a position to see, the solution to the main problem of the foundations of mathematics that Hilbert originally envisaged is illusory; and so, in the event, the work of formalism has not so much been to supply the details of such a solution as to reveal the deeper problems that arise in the second stage of the investigation, when the original problem has been left behind.

It appears, then, that the logistic and formalist movements have both made substantial constructive contributions to the study of foundations of mathematics, but without in fact doing anything to close the subject. Their achievement in each case has been to work out in detail the implications of a certain deep-rooted attitude to mathematics : on the one hand the belief that mathematics is wholly logical in character, and on the other hand the acceptance of mathematics as a process of intellectual construction which merely needs to be guaranteed against self-contradiction. These two conceptions of what constitutes the essence of pure mathematics are not, however, the only ones that have been advanced, and we must now turn to yet another critical approach that has appealed strongly to at least a very significant minority of mathematicians and philosophers of mathematics, and that has produced the philosophy of mathematics known as 'intuitionism'. As an explicit philosophy, intuitionism has been developed chiefly by L. E. J. Brouwer (b. 1881) and his Amsterdam school; but its general tenets have been shared by many working mathematicians, among whom should certainly be reckoned Kronecker, Poincaré, Borel, and Weyl. The fundamental beliefs which provide the chief inspiration of intuitionism are that mathematical theories are not significant unless they are about entities constructed out of something given immediately in intuition, and that definitions in mathematics must always be constructive.

One of the earliest manifestations of the spirit of intuitionism in the history of modern mathematics may be discerned in the work of Leopold Kronecker (1823–1891), who actually rewrote considerable portions of mathematics—especially the theory of algebraic number fields—in a form designed to satisfy the requirement that mathematics must be constructive. Kronecker fought bitterly against some of his fellow-mathematicians in support of the cause of restriction of mathematics to the constructive sphere, and his notorious feud with Cantor was precisely over this issue. The general trend in nineteenth-century mathematics, dominated as this was by the critical movement that we have described in Chapter 5, had been towards elimination of the infinite ; and, since the time of Cauchy, the use of the word 'infinity' in analysis, as in the proposition 'The function $\log n$ tends to infinity as n tends to infinity' had come to be recognized as nothing more than a convenient mode of abbreviation for more complicated forms of words that involve only finite numbers. And then, suddenly, Cantor broke into this world of security and caution, proclaiming that the actual infinite is a proper object of mathematical thought, and that numbers can be assigned to infinite as well as to finite aggregates. It was felt by some mathematicians, and above all by Kronecker, that to countenance such an innovation would be to allow the entire edifice of mathematical truth to be undermined. Cantor believed that, as long as logic was respected, statements about the infinite were significant; but Kronecker denied this and objected violently to the introduction into mathematics of entities that cannot be produced, even in principle, by any kind of finite construction.

The dispute between Kronecker and Cantor was fundamentally a conflict between two essentially different types of mathematical mind (both to be found also in other ages besides the mid-nineteenth century) which in the last resort are perhaps complementary rather than contradictory. Cantor had what we might call a 'metaphysical' outlook, using this term in the narrow sense given to it by the logical positivists. He believed that concepts can be significantly used in a purely conceptual setting, without any necessity for their being related to more intuitive data; and he was fully prepared to use familiar words in altogether new contexts or with reference to situations of a kind not previously envisaged, as in his attribution of a cardinal number to any aggregate whatever, finite or infinite, and his elaboration of an arithmetic of the new transfinite numbers (cf. p. 160). In Cantor's view, therefore, no bounds need be set to the conceptual sphere in which the mind can take its flight, provided only that the formal laws of logic continue to be observed. To Kronecker, on the contrary, such unrestricted speculation seemed mere word-spinning. Sentences might indeed be constructed in conformity with the accepted rules of grammar and deductions carried out according to the rules of logic, but in spite of this, unless the alleged entities to which reference was made could actually be produced, the conclusions drawn would be devoid of all significance.

Cantor's outlook has been shared by many mathematicians who have been influential in shaping modern mathematics. Ernst Zermelo, for instance, the creator of the axiomatic theory of sets, found it necessary to adopt in his work the essentially non-constructive postulate known as the axiom of choice—the postulate that, if K is any set of non-empty sets, there exists a function that makes correspond to each set X belonging to K a unique element of X. The axiom of choice has had to withstand much opposition, and even now it is still viewed with misgiving by some mathematicans, but it has nevertheless played a decisive part in the evolution of modern mathematics. As an explicit philosophy of mathematics, the 'metaphysical' conception of Cantor and Zermelo found its fullest development, of course, in the logistic system of *Principia Mathematica*, being united there with the further belief that mathematical concepts can actually be resolved into exclusively logical constituents.

The opposite view, that words are not being used significantly in mathematics unless the entities to which they purport to refer can in some sense be produced, has also found influential advocates in the recent history of mathematics. One of these was Émile Borel (1871–1956), who was resolutely opposed to the use of non-constructive arguments in the theory of sets of points and the theory of functions of a real variable, and who refused to recognize transfinite ordinal numbers beyond those in Cantor's second number class (the ordinal numbers of well-ordered series with cardinal number $\aleph_0$). Another such mathematican was Hermann Weyl (1885–1955), who in his early book *Das Kontinuum* (1918) attacked the use of non-constructive methods in analysis and attempted to lay the foundations for an unobjectionable treatment of the theory of functions of a real variable (see p. 256).

Kronecker's austere ideal of complete avoidance of non-constructive arguments received little whole-hearted support when it was first put forward, but by the time of Borel and Weyl the climate of opinion had become more favourable to such a way of thinking; and it was at this time that, through the initiative of Brouwer, intuitionism took shape as a definite philosophy of mathematics. Indeed, Brouwer did not merely refuse to accept non-constructive arguments; he even went so far as to reject traditional logic as a valid representation of the pattern of mathematical reasoning. We have already seen how the venerable logic of Aristotle was shown by such modern logicians as Frege and Peano to be only a very elementary part of logic, requiring extensive generalization and supplementation to make it adequate to the new needs of mathematics; but Brouwer's rejection of aristotelian logic was something altogether more radical than this. Brouwer maintained, in fact, that the common belief in the applicability of traditional logic to mathematics 'was caused historically by the fact that, firstly, classical logic was abstracted from the mathematics of the subsets of a definite finite set, that, secondly, an *a priori* existence independent of mathematics was ascribed to this logic, and that, finally, on the basis of this supposititious apriority it was unjustifiably applied to the mathematics of infinite sets'. There, in Brouwer's own words, we have his reading of the history of logic. He holds that (a) at some early stage, presumably in ancient Greece, elementary mathematics evolved into a deductive science; (b) by abstraction from such mathematical deduction, the laws of traditional logic were isolated; (c) these same laws were then taken to apply to *all* mathematical reasoning, however far its subject-matter might be generalized; and (d) much of modern mathematics is consequently based, not upon sound reasoning, but upon an unwarranted imitation of procedures that are only valid in a more restricted

domain.   We must accordingly go back to the original source of truth
—namely primitive intuition—since only by such means is genuine
mathematical knowledge to be obtained.   Brouwer believes that when
we return in this way to intuition we can in fact justify a considerable
part of modern mathematics, and that what we cannot so justify we
must relinquish.

The heroic course on which Brouwer embarked, then, was to set the
whole of existing mathematics aside and to start again from the beginning, using only concepts and modes of inference that could be seen to
have clear intuitive justification.[1]   His hope was that, when enough of
this programme had been carried out, he would be able to discern the
logical laws which intuitive mathematical inference actually obeys, and
would thus be in a position to compare intuitionist logic with traditional
logic.   This comparison, when it eventually came to be made, showed
that there were indeed big differences between the two types of logical
structure (see §4 of the present chapter, p. 254).   According to traditional logic, for instance, any linguistically correct statement Φ says
something that is true or false (*tertium non datur*), and the formula
$X \vee \bar{X}$ accordingly embodies a valid logical principle; but in intuitionist
logic this particular principle does not hold.   When truth and falsity
are understood in a constructive sense, purely hypothetical truth-
values have no significance.   We showed in an earlier chapter (p. 206)
how the law of excluded middle fails to hold in the case of finitary
reasoning; and what we said there applies equally to Brouwer's
intuitionism—for Hilbert's finitary reasoning is in effect intuitionist
reasoning that is applied to metamathematical subject-matter.

Brouwer's assertion that, since traditional logic has been arrived at
by abstraction from a circumscribed body of deductive argument, we
have no warrant for ascribing universal validity to it, is eminently
reasonable; and when we reflect on this view we may indeed find it
more persuasive than Russell's claim that abstract logic is the source
of all mathematical truth.   Philosophically there is much to be said
for it, as we shall see more clearly in Part III, and it also accords with
the natural outlook of many mathematicians.   Unfortunately, however, the new system of intuitionist mathematics, when worked out in
detail, has proved to be far from 'natural'.   This reformed mathematics is, in fact, intolerably complicated by comparison with the
'classical' mathematics that is based on naive acceptance of the traditional laws of logic.   It would seem that Brouwer's contention that
classical logic has no obvious claim to absolute validity is well-founded,
but the conception of 'intuition' as the ultimate source of mathematical
truth is not yet adequately understood, nor has the relation of this

[1] Cf. the even more radical attitude to tradition which Descartes described in his
Discours de la Méthode (1637).

intuition to logic been sufficiently worked out. The two aspects of intuitionism, positive and negative, are very well summed up in the following words of Weyl, whose mathematical career was profoundly influenced by the inspiration of the intuitionist ideal:

'Mathematics with Brouwer gains its highest intuitive clarity. He succeeds in developing the beginnings of analysis in a natural manner, all the time preserving the contact with intuition much more closely than had been done before. It cannot be denied, however, that in advancing to higher and more general theories the inapplicability of the simple laws of classical logic eventually results in an almost unbearable awkwardness. And the mathematician watches with pain the larger part of his towering edifice which he believes to be built of concrete blocks dissolve into mist before his eyes.'[1]

Although even Weyl has had to admit that intuitionism fails in the end to satisfy the aspirations of the mathematical mind, yet so great is the importance of intuitionism as a philosophical outlook that is not fettered by the presuppositions of the 'classical' tradition, and that in consequence may well point the way to fundamental advances in philosophy, that we must give at least some general idea of the basis of intuitionist mathematics and of the way in which mathematical theories have been treated intuitionistically.

2 Primary intuition

As a philosophy, intuitionism has some affinity—in mood if in nothing else—with the critical philosophy of Immanuel Kant (1724–1804). In the *Critique of Pure Reason* (1781) Kant developed his theory of what things it is possible for the human mind to have theoretical knowledge of, and why these things can be known at all. His view was that our theoretical knowledge can never be of anything but the world of phenomena, that is to say the world as accessible to sense perception and inference from sense perception in accordance with the 'categories' (unity, multiplicity, reality, causality, etc.). Any supposed 'metaphysical' knowledge of things in themselves, conceived as the reality lying behind phenomena, can only be illusion. Thus all theoretical knowledge is grounded ultimately in sensory intuition (*Anschauung*)— either that of outer sense (intuition of things in space) or that of inner sense (intuition of inner states, succeeding one another in time). Space and time are the pure forms of outer and inner sense respectively; and the categories might be described very crudely as supplying the form of conceptual thinking. Since all the content of our knowledge unavoidably has impressed upon it the forms of intuition and thought, it automatically possesses a structure that is objective *for us*, that is to

[1] H. Weyl: *Philosophy of Mathematics and Natural Science* (1949), p. 54.

say for all rational beings constituted as we are (cf. Chapter 13, §4, below).

In the section of the *Critique* that is devoted to the Axioms of Intuition (first edition, pp. 162–166), Kant argues that all perceived things (*Erscheinungen*) are extended magnitudes. He says: 'I give the name extended magnitude to that in which the presentation (*Vorstellung*) of the parts makes possible the presentation of the whole (and therefore of necessity precedes it). I cannot represent to myself any line, however small, without drawing it mentally, i.e. generating all its parts in succession, starting from one point. It is the same also with even the smallest time.' Kant goes on to explain that, since everything that is apprehended must be apprehended in space or time (that is to say by outer or inner sense) it must be grasped by 'successive synthesis', and is therefore an extended magnitude. Then he makes the following observation: 'On this successive synthesis of the productive imagination in the generation of shapes is founded the mathematics of extension (geometry), with its axioms that express the *a priori* conditions of sensory intuition, under which alone the schema of a pure concept of external appearance can come into being, e.g. between two points only one straight line is possible; two straight lines do not enclose a space; etc.'.

Kant's conception of mathematics has long been obsolete, and it would be quite misleading to suggest that there is any close connexion between it and the intuitionist outlook. Nevertheless it is a significant fact that the intuitionists, like Kant, find the source of mathematical truth in intuition rather than in the intellectual manipulation of abstract concepts.

Intuitionists naturally set out from the natural numbers, as being the simplest and most fundamental of all mathematical entities. Kronecker summed up his attitude in the well-known epigram 'God made the integers; all else is the work of man';[1] and Poincaré argued in *La Science et l'Hypothèse* (1902) that the creativeness of mathematical thinking springs from its freedom to use mathematical induction, a mode of argument, based on the successive generation of the natural numbers, which makes it possible for the mathematician to transcend the limitations of finitude.

The most rudimentary intuition of all is that which corresponds to Kant's inner sense, or the awareness of mental states which succeed one another in time, and consequently have the structure of a linear series. If it is possible for us to experience distinct acts of awareness, then the natural numbers are already implicit in the stream of our consciousness; and thus arithmetic may be conceived as growing directly out of

---

[1] Not to be found in any of his published works, since it comes from an after-dinner speech.

primary awareness. When once the natural numbers and their arith-metical properties have been isolated by more intellectual mental processes, able to reflect upon the products of intuitive awareness, mathe-matics can assume the form of a more conceptual construction; but intuitionists insist that conceptual thinking is not competent to put anything into mathematics that cannot already be found in intuition.

3* Intuitionist analysis

The natural numbers, as we have just seen, are accepted in intuition-ist mathematics as a datum, and further entities then have to be con-structed out of these numbers as required. The rational numbers do not occasion any serious difficulty, but when the real numbers are intro-duced the wide divergence between the classical and intuitionist out-looks at once becomes apparent. Methods by which the real numbers can be handled in an intuitionistically acceptable way have been de-vised by Brouwer; and a summary of the resulting theory has been given by Heyting in his book *Intuitionism* (Amsterdam, 1956).

In classical mathematics the real numbers are defined in terms of the rational numbers, and there are various standard ways in which this may be done. One of these is Dedekind's method of sections, and another, that of Cantor, depends on the use of 'Cauchy sequences', i.e. sequences $\{a_n\}$ of rational numbers which satisfy Cauchy's criterion of convergence: for any positive rational number ε, there exists a natural number $n_0 = n_0(\varepsilon)$ such that, for every $n \geqslant n_0$ and every $p > 0$, $|a_{n+p} - a_n| < \varepsilon$. Heyting takes this second method as the basis of his treatment of the continuum, but he has to modify it in order to meet the requirement that all Cauchy sequences that are used must be given constructively. For this reason, a sequence $\{a_n\}$ of rational numbers is only admitted as a *real number-generator* if it satisfies the requirement that, for every natural number k, a natural number $n = n(k)$ can be effectively determined which is such that, for every natural number p, $|a_{n+p} - a_n| < 1/k$. On the basis of this definition, an arithmetic of real number-generators is first of all worked out; and only at a considerably later stage (see below, p. 253) is the final transi-tion made from real number-generators to real numbers (i.e. to what would appear in an ordinary mathematical treatment as classes of Cauchy sequences that converge to a common limit).

In 'classical' analysis, two real numbers, defined by Cauchy sequences $\{a_n\}$ and $\{b_n\}$, are either equal or unequal; and which of the two cases obtains depends simply on whether or not the sequence $\{a_n - b_n\}$ con-verges to zero. In intuitionist analysis, on the contrary, where the law of excluded middle does not hold, more than two possibilities have to be distinguished.

Taking relations of 'equality' first of all, we have to distinguish between identity and coincidence of real number-generators. Two such generators $\{a_n\}$ and $\{b_n\}$ are said to be *identical* if $a_n = b_n$ for every n; and they are said to be *coincident* if, for every k, an $n = n(k)$ can be effectively found which is such that $|a_{n+p} - b_{n+p}| < 1/k$ for every p. For '$\{a_n\}$ is identical with $\{b_n\}$' we write '$\{a_n\} \equiv \{b_n\}$', and for '$\{a_n\}$ coincides with $\{b_n\}$' we write '$\{a_n\} = \{b_n\}$'.

We take as the negation of $\{a_n\} = \{b_n\}$ the relation $\{a_n\} \neq \{b_n\}$ which is defined as meaning that a contradiction can be deduced from the hypothesis $\{a_n\} = \{b_n\}$. But much more important than this negative relation is the positively conceived relation of *apartness*, $\{a_n\} \# \{b_n\}$, which holds if and only if an n and a k can be found, such that $|a_{n+p} - b_{n+p}| > 1/k$ for every p.

The four rational operations of addition, subtraction, multiplication, and division are defined for real number-generators in a way that closely follows the classical treatment; but whereas in classical analysis a product cannot be zero unless at least one of its factors is zero, the same is not necessarily the case in intuitionist analysis.[1] Heyting gives an example[2] of a product $\{a_n\}\{b_n\}$ which coincides with $\{0\}$ although neither $\{a_n\}$ nor $\{b_n\}$ does so. He is able to do this by defining $\{a_n\}$ and $\{b_n\}$ in such a way that we are unable to decide whether they coincide with $\{0\}$ or not, this being enough to make the propositions $\{a_n\} = \{0\}$ and $\{b_n\} = \{0\}$ both false.

Now, although individual real numbers can be defined satisfactorily when Cauchy sequences are introduced as number-generators, the same method cannot be used to generate the real continuum, which is needed as a foundation for analysis. The difficulty is that in order to produce an *arbitrary* real number we would have to operate with a Cauchy sequence given by an arbitrary law—and this is plainly an unacceptable conception. To meet the difficulty, Brouwer devised an essentially new way of introducing the continuum into mathematics, by treating it not as a set of existent entities but as the *potential* generation of a real number, with sufficient freedom incorporated in it for the range of possible outcomes of the process of construction to correspond to what a classical mathematician would refer to as the totality of all real numbers.

For this purpose an entirely new mathematical concept was needed, the concept of an *infinitely proceeding sequence*, i.e. a sequence of

---

[1] This peculiarity of intuitionist mathematics has nothing to do with divisors of zero, as known in non-intuitionist algebra. It is mathematically trivial, though perhaps not without some philosophical interest.

[2] See §2.2.5 of his book: 'If in the first n decimals of π no sequence 0123456789 occurs, $a_n = b_n = 2^{-n}$; if a sequence does occur in the first n decimals, let the 9 in the first sequence be the kth digit; now if k is odd, $a_n = 2^{-k}$, $b_n = 2^{-n}$ but if k is even, $a_n = 2^{-n}$, $b_n = 2^{-k}$. Neither for a nor for b are we able to decide whether it is 0 or not. But $ab = 0$!'

mathematical entities about which nothing need be known beyond the fact that it can be prolonged indefinitely. There need be no law governing the formation of such a sequence, and even the succession of numbers obtained in repeated throws of a die would fall under the mathematical concept. Although such a concept may seem at first sight too general for any mathematical assertions to be possible about it, this is not in fact the case. If, for instance, $\{a_n\}$ and $\{b_n\}$ are two infinitely proceeding sequences of natural numbers, then $\{a_n + b_n\}$ is also an infinitely proceeding sequence of natural numbers—and this is true whether the original sequences are given by mathematical laws or not.

Between the two extremes of an infinitely proceeding sequence that is determined by a definite law and one that is left completely free, there are infinitely many intermediate possibilities, with some limited restriction imposed on the development of the sequence. Consider, for example, an infinitely proceeding sequence $\{a_n\}$ of rational numbers which is required to be such that $|a_n - a_{n+p}| < 1/n$ for every n and p. For such a sequence, when any particular element a_n has been reached, there is only a restricted range of possibilities for the next element a_{n+1}; and the restriction in this case is plainly such that, however the elements may be determined within the permitted limits, the resulting sequence is bound to be a real number-generator.

Brouwer has expressed his conception of a range of possibilities of construction in very general terms in his definition of a *spread* (see §3.1.2 of Heyting's book). A spread is, in the first instance, a range of possibilities for the determination of a sequence $\{a_n\}$ of natural numbers. It is given by a 'spread-law', which Heyting defines as follows:

'A *spread-law* is a rule Λ which divides the finite sequences of natural numbers into admissible and inadmissible sequences, according to the following prescriptions: (1) It can be decided by Λ for every natural number k whether it is a one-member admissible sequence or not; (2) Every admissible sequence $a_1, a_2, \ldots, a_n, a_{n+1}$ is an immediate descendant of an admissible sequence $a_1, a_2, \ldots, a_n$ [i.e. it is obtained from such a sequence by the addition to it of one further number]; (3) If an admissible sequence $a_1, \ldots, a_n$ is given, Λ allows us to decide for every natural number k whether $a_1, \ldots, a_n, k$ is an admissible sequence or not; (4) To any admissible sequence $a_1, \ldots, a_n$ at least one natural number k can be found such that $a_1, \ldots, a_n, k$ is an admissible sequence.'

There are thus first of all certain permitted determinations (perhaps infinitely many) for a_1; for each of these there are then certain possible consequential determinations for a_2; and so on indefinitely. The determination of the successive numbers a_i may accordingly be pictured as a process of progressive ramification, each element a_i of the sequence being thought of as a node. At every node at least one branch must originate, and there may be any finite number of branches, or even infinitely many.

Each spread-law Λ defines in this way a mode of generation of an infinitely proceeding sequence of natural numbers. But now suppose that we are also given some previously formulated rule Γ, which associates with any finite sequence of natural numbers a well-defined mathematical entity of some particular kind. Then every infinitely proceeding sequence of natural numbers determines a second infinitely proceeding sequence of mathematical entities, one entity for each of the successive segments (a_1), (a_1, a_2), (a_1, a_2, a_3), . . . of the original sequence. In this way, when a spread-law Λ is taken in conjunction with a *complementary law* Γ, the basic process of generation is able to yield mathematical entities of any kind whatever. Such, in fact, is the device which Brouwer has adopted for the replacement of the classical (existential) notion of set by a notion that is more consonant with his constructivist outlook.

Suppose, now, that some 'totality' of mathematical entities has been defined, perhaps with the aid of one or more spreads, and that some constructively-defined property P is considered, which can apply to entities of the kind in question. The property P will select a well-defined subclass from the given totality; and such a subclass is (very roughly) what Brouwer calls a *species*. Heyting defines this concept as follows:

'A *species* is a property which mathematical entities can be supposed to possess. After a species S has been defined, any mathematical entity which has been or might have been defined before S and which satisfies the condition S, is a *member* of the species S.'

In particular the property, for real number-generators, of coinciding with a given real number-generator is a species in the sense of the above definition. This species is identified in Brouwer's system with the *real number* defined by the given number-generator.

The proviso, in the definition of species, that any member of a species S must be definable in advance of S itself has the effect of rendering vicious circles impossible, and it thus functions in a similar way to the classical theory of types. Indeed many features of the familiar theory of classes can be incorporated in the theory of species (cf. Heyting, §3.2). We may observe, in conclusion, that, since a species is effectively a subclass of some totality that is already given, the theory of species should be compared to a theory of classes based on Zermelo's *Aussonderungsaxiom* (p. 288) rather than to one based on the principle that every propositional function determines a class (the principle of comprehension).

4*   Heyting's formalization of intuitionist logic

We now conclude this chapter on intuitionism with a brief account of the intuitionist logical calculus of Heyting; but before going into formal details we must explain the intention behind this treatment of logic.   For intuitionists, logic has no independent existence, and in a sense it is superfluous.   There are simply mathematical constructions and mathematical arguments, and if these are valid this can be seen immediately, by direct intuition, without appeal to any general principles.   No logician is competent to say in advance what valid inferences there can be; for it is always possible that a mathematician will devise a new type of argument, never thought of before, which is then found to compel assent equally with the types that are already recognized.   All that logicians can do, therefore, is to examine the existing mathematics that is acceptable to intuitionists, with a view to isolating its structure.   If there are patterns of inference that can be seen to produce only intuitively valid arguments, these may be expressed in the form of logical principles; but, even if a coherent system of logic can be formulated, this must be taken as an open system, always liable to extension, and never to be appealed to for criteria of cogency.

With reservations such as these, Heyting put forward his intuitionist symbolic logic in a paper published in the *Sitzungsberichte der Preußischen Akademie der Wissenschaften* (1930), 42–71.   This paper is in two parts, the first of which is devoted to the propositional calculus, and the second to the restricted calculus of predicates and Peano's treatment of arithmetic.   We shall deal here with the first part only.

Heyting uses small Latin letters as propositional variables, and he requires four primitive constants $\supset$, $\wedge$, $\vee$, $\neg$.   The expressions $a \supset b$, $a \wedge b$, $a \vee b$, $\neg a$ are to be read as 'b follows from a', 'a and b', 'a or b' and 'not a' respectively.   Unlike the constants $\rightarrow$, $\&$, $\vee$, $^{-}$, in classical logic, Heyting's four constants $\supset$, $\wedge$, $\vee$, $\neg$ are independent, none of them being definable in his system in terms of the other three; and this circumstance leads to many formal complications.

The list of axioms is comparatively long, there being eleven formulae in all, which Heyting shows to be independent.   The axioms may be stated as follows:

$$a \supset (a \wedge a),$$
$$(a \wedge b) \supset (b \wedge a),$$
$$(a \supset b) \supset [(a \wedge c) \supset (b \wedge c)],$$
$$[(a \supset b) \wedge (b \supset c)] \supset (a \supset c),$$
$$b \supset (a \supset b),$$
$$[a \wedge (a \supset b)] \supset b,$$
$$a \supset (a \vee b),$$

$$(a \vee b) \supset (b \vee a),$$

$$[(a \supset c) \wedge (b \supset c)] \supset [(a \vee b) \supset c],$$

$$\neg a \supset (a \supset b),$$

$$[(a \supset b) \wedge (a \supset \neg b)] \supset \neg a.$$

As rules of derivation we have the rule of substitution, the rule that if a and b are correct formulae then so also is $a \wedge b$, and the rule of *modus ponens* (if a and $a \supset b$ are correct formulae then so also is b).

Many of the formulae of the classical propositional calculus are derivable in Heyting's system; but there are some which are only obtainable in a weakened or restricted form, and others which cannot be derived at all. Among the underivable formulae is $\neg\neg a \supset a$, which expresses part of the principle of double negation; but the formula $a \supset \neg\neg a$ that expresses the other part of this principle is derivable. Both of the implications $\neg\neg\neg a \supset \neg a$ and $\neg a \supset \neg\neg\neg a$ are derivable, however, and this means that, in spite of the failure of the principle of double negation, there is an intuitionist principle of triple negation, so that no more than two conjoined negation signs are ever necessary. The formula $a \vee \neg a$, which expresses the law of excluded middle, is naturally underivable in Heyting's system, but the rather more complicated formula $\neg\neg(a \vee \neg a)$ is derivable. This formula corresponds to Brouwer's principle of the 'absurdity of the absurdity of the law of excluded middle'.

Systems of intuitionist logic have been studied by many logicians since Heyting published his original paper. Gentzen, for instance, in the paper on natural deduction that we considered in Chapter 4, §8, set up his calculus in the first instance for a system NJ of intuitionist logic, only extending it later in the paper to the system NK of classical logic that we have described. The extension was brought about simply by adding one further schema

$$\frac{\overline{\mathfrak{A}}}{\mathfrak{A}}$$

to the schemata of NJ.

There is an interesting observation on Heyting's calculus in a paper of Kolmogorov ('Zur Deutung der intuitionistischen Logik', *Math. Z.*, **35** (1932), 58–65), where a 'calculus of problems' is set up. Kolmogorov shows that if problems are denoted by letters, and $a \wedge b$, $a \vee b$, $a \supset b$, and $\neg a$ are interpreted as the problems 'to solve both of a and b', 'to solve at least one of a and b', 'to solve b, given a solution of a', and 'to deduce a contradiction from the hypothesis that a is solved', then a formal calculus can be set up which coincides with the logical calculus given by Heyting.

SUPPLEMENTARY NOTES ON CHAPTER 9

1. *Accounts of Brouwer's intuitionism.* The most complete survey of intuitionism is that contained in Heyting [3], although even this book does not present a fully worked out system. A concise summary of the main tenets of intuitionism was included by Heyting in his much earlier article [2] in *Ergebnisse der Mathematik* (1934). Brouwer himself has outlined his conception of an intuitionistic approach to mathematics in three papers [1], published from 1925 to 1927 in *Mathematische Annalen.*

2. *Weyl's intuitionism.* Weyl has indicated in *Das Kontinuum* (1918) how he came early to the conclusion that, in spite of the work of Cauchy, Weierstrass, and Dedekind, analysis at the beginning of the twentieth century would still not bear logical scrutiny, for its essential conceptions and procedures involved vicious circles to such an extent that 'every cell of the mighty organism is permeated by the poison of contradiction'. Having at length found what he considered to be a reasonable way of freeing analysis from circularity, Weyl developed his ideas (by then to some extent influenced by his eventual reading of the works of Frege and Russell) in *Das Kontinuum.*

The guiding principle of the reform proposed by Weyl was that every branch of mathematics must be grounded in one or more totalities of given entities, and certain given properties and relations (i.e. predicates) that are significant for these entities. The original entities and predicates are not to be arbitrarily postulated as primitive, without further discussion, as in Peano's *Formulaire*, but must on the contrary be 'given' in an intuitive sense (*'unmittelbar gegeben', in der Anschauung aufgewiesen*). In particular, the natural sequence of numbers $1, 2, \ldots$ will usually be one of the given categories of entities, and the relation of identity $x = y$ will be among the initial predicates.

Further predicates (which can equally well be interpreted, by a mere change of language, as classes) can be built up logically by the following permitted operations:

1. Formation of the negation of a predicate that is already available.

2. Replacement of different variables in a propositional function by the same variable, as in the formation of the property $x = x$ from the relation $x = y$.

3. Formation of the conjunction of two predicates.

4. Formation of the disjunction of two predicates.

5. Replacement of a variable in a propositional function by a specific entity, e.g. y by a in the relation $x < y$ to form the property $x < a$.

6. Existential quantification of a variable in a given propositional function.

Weyl points out that if classes defined by predicates are themselves treated as entities, and adjoined to the original entities to provide an extended domain of operation, steps must be taken to exclude vicious circles. One possibility is the introduction of a hierarchy of types, but this makes analysis extremely complicated and is unacceptable. A different possibility, which Weyl adopts, is the confining of existential quantification (operation 6) to the initially given entities (i.e. limitation of the logic that is used to little more than the restricted calculus of predicates). With this restriction, many central results of classical analysis are not provable—in particular Dirichlet's principle that any bounded set of real numbers has a least upper bound—

but Weyl is prepared to accept this as part of the price that must be paid for the security of mathematics. He thus insists on restricting analysis to what can be done in terms of natural numbers with the aid of his six logical operations and the process of 'iteration', i.e. primitive recursion; and he does not allow any statement of the form 'there is a class of natural numbers such that . . .' or 'there is a relation between natural numbers such that . . .'.

Returning to the subject of the circularity of analysis in 'Über die neue Grundlagenkrise der Mathematik' (1921), Weyl declared that it was now apparent that, in the course of inquiries with a similar inspiration to his own, Brouwer had succeeded in coming nearer to the true essence of the real continuum than he had; and he therefore felt obliged to give up his own attempted reconstruction of analysis and simply to accept Brouwer's main conclusions. He considered above all that Brouwer's new understanding of a real number as something in process of determination, rather than an entity already existent in some mysterious sense, was a very substantial addition to the conceptual resources of mathematics.

Weyl's mathematical career has been described by M. H. A. Newman in two obituary notices [1,2], and these notices give also a brief indication of Weyl's attitude towards the foundations of mathematics.

Chapter 10

RECURSIVE ARITHMETIC

1 The class of natural numbers as a progression

Critical examination of the foundations of mathematics has been carried further in some branches of the subject than it has in others, and by far the greater part of the work that has been done in this field has been directed towards arithmetic—that is to say the mathematical treatment of the natural numbers. Among the more obvious reasons for this bias are the logical simplicity of arithmetic in comparison with most other branches of mathematics, and also the peculiarly fundamental role of numbers throughout mathematics and in many other realms of knowledge. In earlier chapters we have dealt with three standard presentations of arithmetic, in each of which the attainment of complete rigour is an avowed aim: (a) Peano's axiomatic treatment, as given in the *Formulaire de Mathématique*, (b) the logistic theory of *Principia Mathematica*, and (c) Hilbert's formalization of arithmetic in his system (Z). Hilbert's treatment may be looked upon as a refinement of Peano's, in which the basing of the system on a logical calculus is made fully explicit. The calculus used is the restricted calculus of predicates, which, although more limited than the extended calculus of *Principia Mathematica*, nevertheless goes far beyond the bounds recognized as permissible by intuitionists. An alternative way in which Peano's basic ideas can be developed, in a manner more acceptable to intuitionist critics, was proposed in 1923 by Thoralf Skolem in his fundamental paper 'Begründung der elementaren Arithmetik durch die rekurrierende Denkweise ohne Anwendung scheinbarer Veränderlichen mit unendlichem Ausdehnungsbereich'.[1] Skolem showed that, by exploiting more thoroughly Peano's reliance on the two complementary procedures of proof by mathematical induction and definition by recursion, it is possible to develop a substantial part of the theory of the natural numbers in a strictly constructive way. The notion of recursive definition is one that we have already touched upon several times (cf. pp. 147, 221, 236), but now in the present chapter we shall deal systematically with this important element in formal arithmetic.

---

[1] 'Foundation of elementary arithmetic by means of the recursive mode of thought, without application of apparent variables with an infinite range of extension.' See Bibliography.

The idea of recursion was familiar already to Dedekind (cf. *Was sind und was sollen die Zahlen?*, §9), and we have seen how Peano used it in building up his abstract theory of arithmetic.   The system of Peano was essentially a translation into symbolic language of the most natural common-sense way of handling the properties of the whole numbers. Unlike Cantor, Frege, and Russell, who sought to *analyse* number in terms of general logical concepts, Peano based his treatment on the immediate structural features of everyday experience of numbers as these are actually used in counting and reckoning.   From such a point of view, the most fundamental characteristic of the whole numbers is the fact that they form a natural sequence or progression, being obtainable in regular succession by unlimited repetition of a single generating act (cf. the intuitionist conception of the natural numbers).   Various accounts might be given by different people of the nature of the intuitive step by which they pass from one element of the number sequence to the next, but such psychological details are irrelevant in formal mathematics, where all that need be taken into account is the pure pattern of the process of successive generation.   It was this pattern that Peano isolated in his axiomatic theory.

In order, then, to generate the sequence of natural numbers, we need to have an initial number and also an operation which converts any number into its successor.   The notation that is used for the representation of numbers is, of course, arbitrary, but there are obvious advantages in conforming to the established usage of mathematics.   Peano accordingly began with an artificial notation $0, 0+, 0++, \ldots$ which reflected the structure of his number system, and then he passed quickly to the more familiar notation $0, 1, 2, \ldots$ by laying down appropriate explicit definitions of the customary symbols.   It makes little difference in principle whether the initial number is taken to be 0 or 1, but there are formal advantages that make the choice of 0 preferable (cf. p. 147).   The totality N_0 of natural numbers is thus conceived as a progression that can be generated by taking the initial number 0, and then passing again and again from the number x that has last been reached to its successor $x+$, or x' as this is now usually written.   Something has to be postulated, of course, concerning the function x'.   Two properties are in fact essential: (i) that the operation of passing from x to x' shall generate an infinite sequence of numbers, without ever returning cyclically upon itself, and (ii) that any number whatsoever can be obtained by carrying the process of successive generation far enough.   In order to secure (i), Peano adopted the two axioms which assert that no two numbers have the same successor and that 0 is not the successor of any number; and in order to secure (ii) he adopted the axiom of induction, which we have expressed in symbols in the form

$$[A(0) \ \& \ (x)(A(x) \to A(x'))] \to A(a).$$

The system of entities N_0, as thus understood, has no properties beyond those which arise from its characteristic mode of generation; and the entire arithmetic of the natural numbers must therefore be deduced from the serial structure of the number system.   But now every mathematical theory has two aspects, the one constructive and the other demonstrative; for we have first of all to introduce such mathematical concepts as may be required, and then we must establish theorems which express the properties of the concepts.   Demonstration of theorems presented no problem in Peano's arithmetic, since the axiom of induction provides a sufficient basis for proof by mathematical induction, a mode of argument that meets all arithmetical needs.   On the constructive side, however, some innovation was necessary.   The traditional form of mathematical definition—referred to nowadays as 'explicit definition'—which is typified by Euclid's definition of a circle (Definition 15 of the *Elements*, quoted on p. 135 above) is of little immediate use here, because there are no non-trivial arithmetical concepts that can be defined explicitly in terms of the constant 0 and the successor function n' only.   To be of value, an arithmetical definition must be in some way constructive or creative; and so the procedure of definition in the strict sense has to give place to a procedure of systematic generation.   An arithmetical function $\mathfrak{f}(n)$ of a single variable n, for example, has an infinity of values $\mathfrak{f}(\mathfrak{n})$, which form a progression since the values $\mathfrak{n}$ of the variable n form a progression; and the function may be regarded as properly defined when a rule is given which permits the unambiguous production of the progression $\mathfrak{f}(0), \mathfrak{f}(0'), \ldots.$ We thus arrive at the notion of recursive definition of a function, or definition of its entire course of values by an iterative process.   In recursive definition, in fact, as in proof by mathematical induction, we are able to span an infinite succession of cases finitely by treating only the initial case and the manner of the transition from the general case to its immediate successor.

2   Recursive definitions

The simplest type of recursive definition may be represented by a schema of the following form:

$$\left.\begin{array}{l} \mathfrak{f}(0) = \mathfrak{a}, \\ \mathfrak{f}(n') = \mathfrak{b}(n, \mathfrak{f}(n)). \end{array}\right\} \quad (1)$$

Here $\mathfrak{f}(n)$ is the function that is being defined, while $\mathfrak{a}$ is a given number and $\mathfrak{b}(x,y)$ is a function of two variables that has already been introduced.   It will be seen that, since recursive definitions involve 'given' functions as well as the primitive constituents 0 and n' of the arithmetical system, the introduction of new functions is itself progressive. Functions can only be introduced, in fact, in a suitable order, though the introduction of functions is a ramifying process, and not a serial one like the formation of the basic sequence of numbers $0, 0', \ldots$. The actual order of introduction of the functions, moreover, can be varied within wide limits.

A schema of the form (1) may legitimately be regarded as a *definition* of the function $\mathfrak{f}(n)$ because it makes possible the unambiguous evaluation of $\mathfrak{f}(\mathfrak{n})$ for any assigned value $\mathfrak{n}$ of the variable. We have only, in fact, to use the schema repeatedly to evaluate the progression $\mathfrak{f}(0), \mathfrak{f}(0'), \ldots$ up to the required point $\mathfrak{f}(\mathfrak{n})$.

Functions of more than one variable can be defined recursively if one of the variables is singled out as the main variable and the others are all treated as parameters. We then speak of recursion with respect to the selected variable. The more general form taken by the schema of recursion when parameters are involved is as follows:

$$\left.\begin{array}{l} \mathfrak{f}(a, \ldots, k, 0) = \mathfrak{a}(a, \ldots, k), \\ \mathfrak{f}(a, \ldots, k, n') = \mathfrak{b}(a, \ldots, k, n, \mathfrak{f}(a, \ldots, k, n)). \end{array}\right\}$$

The terms on the right-hand side involve, at most, the parameters that are explicitly indicated.

3 Systematic development of recursive arithmetic

Many detailed accounts of recursive arithmetic are to be found in the literature, in particular in the books of Hilbert and Bernays, Rózsa Péter, Goodstein, and Kleene (see Note 1, p. 283). Rózsa Péter's account is especially authoritative, since the modern theory of recursive functions is to a large extent her creation. The outline of the elementary part of the theory that we give here is modelled closely on the version of Hilbert and Bernays (*Grundlagen der Mathematik*, T, §7).

The basic functions $a + b$ and $a.b$ are each introduced, as in Peano's treatment, by a recursion with one parameter:

$$\left.\begin{array}{l} a + 0 = a, \\ a + b' = (a + b)'; \end{array}\right\} \quad \begin{array}{l}(1)\\(2)\end{array}$$

$$\left.\begin{array}{l} a.0 = 0, \\ a.b' = a.b + a. \end{array}\right\} \quad \begin{array}{l}(3)\\(4)\end{array}$$

Plainly, the definition of $a + b$ must precede that of $a.b$.

From these definitions the well-known 'laws of algebra' are readily deducible. The following results can be established in succession:

(i) $0 + a = a$,

(ii) $a' + b = a + b'$,

(iii) $a + b = b + a$,

(iv) $a + (b + c) = (a + b) + c$,

(v) $0 . a = 0,$
(vi) $a' . b = a . b + b,$
(vii) $a . b = b . a,$
(viii) $a . (b + c) = a . b + a . c,$
(ix) $(b + c) . a = b . a + c . a,$
(x) $a . (b . c) = (a . b) . c.$

The proofs are all by induction, except in the case of the equality (ix), which can be inferred immediately from (vii) and (viii). The variables involved in the induction arguments are (i) a, (ii) b, (iii) a, (iv) c, (v) a, (vi) b, (vii) a, (viii) c, (x) c. To illustrate the mode of reasoning, we give the proof of (vi).

Let the result to be proved, $a' . b = a . b + b$, be denoted by $\mathfrak{A}(b)$. Then $\mathfrak{A}(0)$ is $a' . 0 = a . 0 + 0$; and this is true since, by (1) and (3), $a . 0 + 0 = 0 + 0 = 0 = a' . 0$. Now let us assume the validity of $\mathfrak{A}(b)$. Then

$$
\begin{aligned}
a' . b' &= a'b + a'   &&[(4)] \\
        &= (a . b + b) + a' &&[\mathfrak{A}(b)] \\
        &= a . b + (a + b') &&[(iv), (ii), (iii)] \\
        &= a . b' + b'.   &&[(iv), (4)]
\end{aligned}
$$

Thus $\mathfrak{A}(b')$ follows from $\mathfrak{A}(b)$; and this completes the proof of (vi) by induction with respect to b.

The basic principles of elementary arithmetic can thus all be justified from the recursive point of view (at the logical level of rigorous mathematics) and we can then go on without undue difficulty to establish the fundamental divisibility properties of the natural numbers. With this aim in view we introduce several auxiliary arithmetical functions, most of which are characteristic functions of simple predicates.

We first introduce three functions $\alpha(n)$, $\beta(n)$, $\delta(n)$ of a single variable by putting

$$
\left.\begin{aligned} \alpha(0) &= 0, \\ \alpha(n') &= 1; \end{aligned}\right\} \qquad
\left.\begin{aligned} \beta(0) &= 1, \\ \beta(n') &= 0; \end{aligned}\right\} \qquad
\left.\begin{aligned} \delta(0) &= 0, \\ \delta(n') &= n. \end{aligned}\right\}
$$

It will be seen that $\alpha(n)$ is the characteristic function of the predicate $n = 0$, $\beta(n)$ is that of the predicate $n \neq 0$, and $\delta(n)$ is the predecessor function (with the 'predecessor' of 0 defined conventionally as 0). Rózsa Péter writes the functions $\alpha(n)$ and $\beta(n)$ as $\mathrm{sg}(n)$ and $\overline{\mathrm{sg}}(n)$ respectively.

Next we introduce three functions $\delta(a,b)$, $\alpha(a,b)$, $\beta(a,b)$ of two variables, the first by recursion and the second and third explicitly:

$$
\left.\begin{aligned} \delta(a,0) &= a, \\ \delta(a,b') &= \delta(\delta(a,b)); \end{aligned}\right\}
$$
$$
\alpha(a,b) = \alpha(\delta(a,b) + \delta(b,a));
$$
$$
\beta(a,b) = \beta(\delta(a,b) + \delta(b,a)).
$$

It should be noted that, although the same letter 'α' is used in both the function $\alpha(n)$ of one variable and the function $\alpha(a,b)$ of two variables, these are quite separate functions; and the same is true of the other two pairs $\beta(n)$, $\beta(a,b)$ and $\delta(n)$, $\delta(a,b)$. Interpreted intuitively, $\delta(a,b)$ is the 'excess' of a over b, which is equal to the arithmetical difference $a - b$ if this is positive and is zero otherwise. The notation $a \div b$ is often used for this function instead of $\delta(a,b)$. The functions $\alpha(a,b)$ and $\beta(a,b)$ are respectively the characteristic functions of the relations $a = b$ and $a \neq b$.

If $t(n)$ is any given function of n, we can define the sum and product of a variable number of terms of the sequence $\{t(0), t(1), \ldots\}$ recursively by putting

$$\left. \begin{array}{l} \displaystyle\sum_{x \leqslant 0} t(x) = t(0), \\[2ex] \displaystyle\sum_{x \leqslant n'} t(x) = \left(\sum_{x \leqslant n} t(x) \right) + t(n'), \end{array} \right\}$$

and

$$\left. \begin{array}{l} \displaystyle\prod_{x \leqslant 0} t(x) = t(0), \\[2ex] \displaystyle\prod_{x \leqslant n'} t(x) = \left(\prod_{x \leqslant n} t(x) \right) . t(n'). \end{array} \right\}$$

Furthermore, the very useful description 'the least number x, not exceeding n, for which $t(x) = 0$, or 0 itself if there is no such number' can be handled recursively as follows (see Hilbert & Bernays: *Grundlagen*, p. 315). We begin with the recursive definition

$$\left. \begin{array}{l} \underset{0 < x \leqslant 0}{\text{Min}} \ [t(x) = 0] = 0, \\[2ex] \underset{0 < x \leqslant n'}{\text{Min}} \ [t(x) = 0] = \underset{0 < x \leqslant n}{\text{Min}} \ [t(x) = 0] + \\[3ex] \qquad\qquad + n' . \beta(\underset{0 < x \leqslant n}{\text{Min}} \ [t(x) = 0] + t(n')), \end{array} \right\}$$

and then we define $\underset{x \leqslant n}{\text{Min}} \, [t(x) = 0]$ explicitly by putting

$$\underset{x \leqslant n}{\text{Min}} \ [t(x) = 0] = (\underset{0 < x \leqslant n}{\text{Min}} \ [t(x) = 0]) . \alpha(t(0)).$$

There is obviously a close connexion between the recursively defined function $\underset{x \leqslant n}{\text{Min}} \, [t(x) = 0]$ and the ι-term $\mu_x[t(x) = 0]$ which we obtain when we substitute $t(x) = 0$ for $A(x)$ in the term $\mu_x A(x)$ defined on p. 221. But whereas the bound variable x in $\mu_x[t(x) = 0]$ ranges over the full totality of natural numbers, the x in $\underset{x \leqslant n}{\text{Min}} \, [t(x) = 0]$ is restricted to a finite set of values. This difference reflects the constructive character of recursive arithmetic (cf. p. 265 below).

The use of bound variables with a finite range can be developed further, as Skolem already showed in the paper refered to on p. 258. If we apply the operators $\sum_{x \leqslant n}$, $\prod_{x \leqslant n}$, and $\operatorname*{Min}_{x \leqslant n}$ to characteristic functions of arithmetical predicates, we can express in our symbolism the forms of statement 'There exists an x in the range $0 \leqslant x \leqslant n$ such that $\mathfrak{A}(x)$' and 'For all x in the range $0 \leqslant x \leqslant n$, $\mathfrak{A}(x)$', thus giving a recursive treatment of quantifiers with a restricted range (cf. *Grundlagen*, pp. 310–316).

In order to incorporate the properties of divisibility in recursive arithmetic, we need to define recursively the remainder and quotient for the division of b into a.   We do this by putting

$$\left.\begin{aligned} \varrho(0,b) &= 0, \\ \varrho(a',b) &= \varrho(a,b)' \cdot \alpha(b,\varrho(a,b)'), \end{aligned}\right\}$$

and

$$\left.\begin{aligned} \pi(0,b) &= 0, \\ \pi(a',b) &= \pi(a,b) + \beta(b,\varrho(a,b)'). \end{aligned}\right\}$$

It may readily be verified that these two recursive definitions are equivalent to the familiar division algorithm

$$a = b \cdot \pi(a,b) + \varrho(a,b) \quad (0 \leqslant \varrho(a,b) < b).$$

Exercise.   Show how to express the condition $0 \leqslant \varrho(a,b) < b$ without the symbols $\leqslant$ or $<$, by means of the function $\delta(x,y)$.

The fundamental relation of divisibility $b \mid a$, i.e. the relation 'b is a divisor of a', is now expressible in the form $\varrho(a,b) = 0$.

The assertion 'n is prime' can be paraphrased as 'n is neither 0 nor 1, and for all x up to n, either $x = 0$ or $x = 1$ or $x = n$ or x is not a divisor of n', and it therefore has for its characteristic function $\mathfrak{p}(n)$ the function

$$\alpha[\beta(n,0) + \beta(n,1) + \sum_{x \leqslant n} \alpha(x) \cdot \alpha(x,1) \cdot \alpha(x,n) \cdot \beta(\varrho(n,x))].$$

Our next step (the details of which we leave to the reader) is to introduce formally, by explicit definition, a function $\mathfrak{q}(n)$ whose intuitive meaning is 'the least number x such that (i) $0 \leqslant x \leqslant n$, (ii) $x \mid n$, and (iii) $x \neq 1$ unless $n = 1$'.   If $n!$ is the factorial function, given by the recursive definition

$$\left.\begin{aligned} 0! &= 1, \\ (n')! &= (n!) \cdot n', \end{aligned}\right\}$$

we can prove that $\mathfrak{q}(n! + 1)$ is a prime number that lies in the range from $n + 1$ to $n! + 1$ inclusive.   If yet another function $\mathfrak{u}(n)$ is now introduced, with the intuitive interpretation 'the least number x in the range from 1 to $n! + 1$ which is prime and also greater than n', then the equations of recursion

$$\left.\begin{array}{l} \wp_0 = 2, \\ \wp_{n'} = \mathfrak{u}(\wp_n), \end{array}\right\}$$

define the nth odd prime number $\wp_n$ as a function of n. Since the specifications of the functions $\mathfrak{q}(n)$ and $\mathfrak{u}(n)$, which we have here given in ordinary language, can be expressed without difficulty in terms of the recursive functions that we have already introduced, it follows that the sequence of prime numbers

$$\{\wp_0, \wp_1, \wp_2, \ldots\}$$

admits of recursive definition.

4   Recursive arithmetic as a formal system

So far we have been treating recursive arithmetic in the ordinary mathematical manner, arguing intuitively and avoiding formalization of the theory except in so far as this is necessary for the sake of clarity. It is by no means difficult, however, to formalize this way of presenting arithmetic, merely by using formal derivation everywhere instead of intuitive deduction, while keeping the main sequence of steps unchanged. Such a formalization is discussed by Hilbert and Bernays (*Grundlagen*, I, §7), and various metamathematical conclusions are drawn by them concerning the resulting system. In particular, they are able to compare formalized recursive arithmetic with their own axiomatic system (Z), and to show that the system (Z) is at least as comprehensive as the recursive system (see p. 269 below).

Before turning to the details of this comparison, we need to look at formalized recursive arithmetic itself, in order to see what the motives were that prompted its construction, and what means were found necessary for the carrying out of the project. The system was developed, as we have already indicated, with a quite specific purpose in view, and to think of it merely as a possible alternative to the axiomatic system (Z) as a formalization of intuitive arithmetic would be to miss a large part of its significance for the logic of mathematics. The recursive treatment of arithmetic was originally developed, and it has since become an object of intensive study, chiefly because many mathematicians have seen in it a reasonable hope of coming to terms, in this limited field of mathematics at least, with the intuitionist criticism of the non-constructive character of classical mathematics. In order to see how recursive arithmetic offers such a hope, we need to go back to the original formulation of the theory by Skolem. The order of development of recursive arithmetic that is adopted by Hilbert and Bernays, and that we have followed in the above informal presentation of the theory, is in fact taken with little change from Skolem's original paper (see p. 258 above).

Skolem's inspiration, as he himself has made quite clear, was essentially intuitionistic. The logic on which Russell and Whitehead based their mathematical system in *Principia Mathematica* is non-constructive, since it makes free use of universal and existential quantifiers, and propositions of the form $(x)\phi x$ or $(\exists x)\phi x$ are not in general finitely decidable when the domain of individuals is infinite. Skolem felt that, if a branch of mathematics can be handled constructively at all, a constructive treatment is preferable to one that depends on the unnecessarily hypothetical logical calculus of *Principia Mathematica*; and his paper was offered as an attempt to provide such a treatment of arithmetic.

Many general arithmetical statements can be formulated without quantifiers, by use of free variables only; but then they are really propositional functions and not propositions. The commutative law of addition, for example, which we express in the form $a + b = b + a$, is such a propositional function, and Skolem looked upon the statement of the law as an assertion that the relation $a + b = b + a$ holds for an *unspecified* pair of numbers a, b. For him, therefore, assertion of this arithmetical theorem was an instance of what is referred to in the first edition of *Principia Mathematica* as 'assertion of a propositional function' (cf. p. 165). Having made this clear, he described his purpose in these words:

'What I wish to show in this paper is the following: If we understand the general theorems of arithmetic as functional assertions, and if we base our argument on the recursive mode of reasoning, then this science [i.e. arithmetic] can be rigorously built up without the use of Russell and Whitehead's concepts of "always" and "sometimes". The same thing can also be expressed by saying that arithmetic can be set up as a logical system without use of apparent logical variables. It is indeed often convenient to introduce apparent variables; but only a finite domain of variation for such variables is needed, and with the aid of recursive definitions their use can always be avoided altogether. This will all become clear in the sequel.'

In the body of the paper Skolem worked out the details of recursive arithmetic, covering the same ground as we have done in our summary of Hilbert and Bernays's version of the theory. The entire treatment satisfies Skolem's own demand that it should be 'consistently finitary, being founded on Kronecker's principle that a mathematical determination is a real determination if and only if it leads to its goal with the help of a *finite* number of steps'.

We see, then, that Skolem's primary object was to devise a system of arithmetic based on a logic that corresponds more closely than does

Russell's to the essentially constructive nature of the theory of the natural numbers. In their subsequent formalization of this theory Hilbert and Bernays remained faithful to Skolem's original intention, and instead of using the full resources of the restricted calculus of predicates, as in their various axiomatic systems of arithmetic, they worked here with the *elementary calculus with free variables* (cf. p. 105 above). This elementary calculus uses the symbolism of the restricted calculus of predicates, but without quantifiers or bound variables. Special mathematical symbols, such as '0' and ' ' ', are allowed, and the symbol '=' and the axioms (J_1) and (J_2) are required. The rules of procedure provide for substitution of terms for individual variables, and formulae (which may possibly contain free individual, propositional, or predicate variables) for propositional variables; and to the purely logical rules is added the schema for induction

$$\frac{\mathfrak{A}(0) \qquad \mathfrak{A}(a) \to \mathfrak{A}(a')}{\mathfrak{A}(a),}$$

a being a free individual variable.

No mathematical axioms except $0' \neq 0$ are required, since the place of such axioms is taken by recursive definitions. Thus, for instance, the function $\delta(a,b)$ is defined recursively as on p. 262, and the predicate $a < b$ is then introduced by the explicit definition

$$a < b \leftrightarrow \delta(b,a) \neq 0.$$

When this is done, the axioms $(<_1)$, $(<_2)$, $(<_3)$ that we adopted on p. 210 for the formal system (A_0) all reduce to derivable formulae. The two Peano axioms (P_1) and (P_2) are also derivable (*Grundlagen*, p. 302). The essential difference between the recursive system and the axiomatic systems that we discussed in Chapter 7 is thus the admission in the new system of recursive definitions and the exclusion of bound variables.

5   Representability of recursive arithmetic in the system (Z)

We come now to the relation, already mentioned on p. 265, between formalized recursive arithmetic and the axiomatic system (Z). It is shown in detail by Hilbert and Bernays that the whole of recursive arithmetic is representable in (Z), in the sense that we made precise on p. 222. The proof of this interesting and important result is far from easy, and here we can do no more than indicate the stages of the argument and give appropriate references.

In the system (B), as we have already seen on p. 220, and therefore *a fortiori* in the system (Z), we can derive the principle of the least number in the form

$$A(a) \to (Ex)\mathfrak{M}(x),$$

and we can then introduce a formal expression for 'the least number x such that $A(x)$' by putting

$$\mu_x A(x) = \iota_x[((z)\overline{A(z)} \to x = 0) \,\&\, ((Ez)A(z) \to \mathfrak{M}(x))].$$

With the aid of this μ-symbol it is now possible to reduce every recursive definition to an equivalent explicit definition (*Grundlagen*, p. 412). In other words, if $\varphi(a, \ldots, k, n)$ is a function that is introduced by equations of recursion

$$\left.\begin{aligned}\varphi(a, \ldots, k, 0) &= \mathfrak{a}(a, \ldots, k),\\\varphi(a, \ldots, k, n') &= \mathfrak{b}(a, \ldots, k, n, \varphi(a, \ldots, k, n)),\end{aligned}\right\}$$

we can introduce a term $\mathfrak{f}(a, \ldots, k, n)$, which may possibly involve the μ-symbol, in such a way that the formulae

$$\begin{aligned}\mathfrak{f}(a, \ldots, k, 0) &= \mathfrak{a}(a, \ldots, k,),\\\mathfrak{f}(a, \ldots, k, n') &= \mathfrak{b}(a, \ldots, k, n, \mathfrak{f}(a, \ldots, k, n))\end{aligned}$$

are derivable from the axioms (Z) by the restricted calculus of predicates and the ι-schema. In order to show that the function $\varphi(a, \ldots, k, n)$ is representable in the system (Z) itself, without use of μ- or ι-symbols, we now proceed in the following way.

We first replace all μ-terms by the equivalent ι-terms, in accordance with the definition of the μ-symbol. The term $\mathfrak{f}(a, \ldots, k, n)$ thus becomes a term $\mathfrak{g}(a, \ldots, k, n)$. To any derivable relation in recursive arithmetic that involves the function $\varphi(a, \ldots, k, n)$ there now corresponds a formula $\mathfrak{F}$, involving the term $\mathfrak{g}(a, \ldots, k, n)$, which is derivable from the axioms (Z) by use of the ι-schema. It follows that, if $\mathfrak{a}, \ldots, \mathfrak{k}, \mathfrak{n}, \mathfrak{l}$ are any given numbers, then the formula

$$\mathfrak{g}(\mathfrak{a}, \ldots, \mathfrak{k}, \mathfrak{n}) = \mathfrak{l}$$

or its negation

$$\mathfrak{g}(\mathfrak{a}, \ldots, \mathfrak{k}, \mathfrak{n}) \neq \mathfrak{l}$$

is derivable in (Z) according as $\mathfrak{l}$ is or is not the value of $\varphi(\mathfrak{a}, \ldots, \mathfrak{k}, \mathfrak{n})$.

Consider now the formula

$$\mathfrak{g}(a, \ldots, k, n) = l,$$

in which $a, \ldots, k, n, l$ are variables. Although ι-symbols may be involved in $\mathfrak{g}(a, \ldots, k, n)$, these can all be eliminated. For suppose the formula in question is of the form $\mathfrak{B}(\iota_x\mathfrak{A}(x))$, where $\iota_x\mathfrak{A}(x)$ is a maximal

ι-term in it.   For this ι-term to occur at all in $\mathfrak{g}(a, \ldots, k,n)$, the uniqueness formulae

$$(Ex)\mathfrak{A}(x)$$

and

$$(x)(y)[(\mathfrak{A}(x) \ \& \ \mathfrak{A}(y)) \to x = y]$$

must be derivable.   It follows, then, that the bi-implication

$$\mathfrak{B}(\iota_x\mathfrak{A}(x)) \leftrightarrow (x)(\mathfrak{A}(x) \to \mathfrak{B}(x))$$

is derivable.   We give here the main steps of the derivation:

(i) $(x)(\mathfrak{A}(x) \to \mathfrak{B}(x)) \to [\mathfrak{A}(\iota_x\mathfrak{A}(x)) \to \mathfrak{B}(\iota_x\mathfrak{A}(x))]$ [(e)]

   $\mathfrak{A}(\iota_x\mathfrak{A}(x)) \to [(x)(\mathfrak{A}(x) \to \mathfrak{B}(x)) \to \mathfrak{B}(\iota_x\mathfrak{A}(x))]$ [Rule VII]

   $(x)(\mathfrak{A}(x) \to \mathfrak{B}(x)) \to \mathfrak{B}(\iota_x\mathfrak{A}(x))$.

(ii) $\mathfrak{A}(\iota_x\mathfrak{A}(x))$

   $\mathfrak{A}(a) \to (\mathfrak{A}(\iota_x\mathfrak{A}(x)) \ \& \ \mathfrak{A}(a))$

   $(\mathfrak{A}(\iota_x\mathfrak{A}(x)) \ \& \ \mathfrak{A}(a)) \to \iota_x\mathfrak{A}(x) = a$

   $\iota_x\mathfrak{A}(x) = a \to (\mathfrak{B}(\iota_x\mathfrak{A}(x)) \to \mathfrak{B}(a))$

   $\mathfrak{A}(a) \to (\mathfrak{B}(\iota_x\mathfrak{A}(x)) \to \mathfrak{B}(a))$

   $\mathfrak{B}(\iota_x\mathfrak{A}(x)) \to (\mathfrak{A}(a) \to \mathfrak{B}(a))$

   $\mathfrak{B}(\iota_x\mathfrak{A}(x)) \to (x)(\mathfrak{A}(x) \to \mathfrak{B}(x))$.   [($\gamma$1)]

It now follows that we can eliminate from the formula $\mathfrak{g}(a, \ldots, k,n) = l$ the ι-term $\iota_x\mathfrak{A}(x)$, and similarly each other ι-term in turn; and thus the formula is convertible with a formula $\mathfrak{G}(a, \ldots, k,n,l)$ in which no ι-symbol occurs.   In other words, the bi-implication

$$\mathfrak{g}(a, \ldots, k,n) = l \ \leftrightarrow \ \mathfrak{G}(a, \ldots, k,n,l)$$

is a derivable formula.

Combining this result with our earlier result on the connexion between $\mathfrak{g}$ and φ, we now see that, for any choice of numbers $\mathfrak{a}, \ldots, \mathfrak{k}, \mathfrak{n}, \mathfrak{l}$, either the formula $\mathfrak{G}(\mathfrak{a}, \ldots, \mathfrak{k},\mathfrak{n},\mathfrak{l})$ or the formula $\overline{\mathfrak{G}(\mathfrak{a}, \ldots, \mathfrak{k},\mathfrak{n},\mathfrak{l})}$ is derivable, according as $\mathfrak{l}$ is or is not the value of $\varphi(\mathfrak{a}, \ldots, \mathfrak{k},\mathfrak{n})$.   The derivation may use the ι-schema; but $\mathfrak{G}(\mathfrak{a}, \ldots, \mathfrak{k},\mathfrak{n},\mathfrak{l})$ does not involve any ι-symbol, and hence, by the theorem on the eliminability of the ι-symbol (p. 95), either $\mathfrak{G}(\mathfrak{a}, \ldots, \mathfrak{k},\mathfrak{n},\mathfrak{l})$ or $\overline{\mathfrak{G}(\mathfrak{a}, \ldots, \mathfrak{k},\mathfrak{n},\mathfrak{l})}$ is derivable by the calculus of predicates alone.   We thus have the required result, which we can express in the following terms:

THEOREM 1.   *If $\varphi(a, \ldots, k,n)$ is a function that is defined recursively by a pair of equations*

$$\varphi(a, \ldots, k,0) = \mathfrak{a}(a, \ldots, k),$$
$$\varphi(a, \ldots, k,n') = \mathfrak{b}(a, \ldots,k,n,\varphi(a, \ldots, k,n)),$$

then there is a formula $\mathfrak{G}(a, \ldots, k,n,l)$ of the formal system (Z) *with the*

property that, for any particular numbers $a, \ldots, \mathfrak{k}, \mathfrak{n}, \mathfrak{l}$, (i) $\mathfrak{G}(a, \ldots, \mathfrak{k}, \mathfrak{n}, \mathfrak{l})$
is derivable from the axioms (Z) *by the restricted calculus of predicates if* $\mathfrak{l} = \varphi(a, \ldots, \mathfrak{k}, \mathfrak{n})$, *and* (ii) $\overline{\mathfrak{G}(a, \ldots, \mathfrak{k}, \mathfrak{n}, \mathfrak{l})}$ *is derivable if* $\mathfrak{l} \neq \varphi(a, \ldots, \mathfrak{k}, \mathfrak{n})$.

6 Primitive recursive and other recursive schemata

The schema of recursive definition that we have so far been considering, namely

$$\left. \begin{aligned} \mathfrak{f}(a, \ldots, k, 0) &= a(a, \ldots, k), \\ \mathfrak{f}(a, \ldots, k, n') &= \mathfrak{b}(a, \ldots, k, n, \mathfrak{f}(a, \ldots, k, n)), \end{aligned} \right\}$$

is by no means the only type of schema that yields a constructive process for evaluating a new function for any assigned values of its arguments, and there are many other schemata that can reasonably be classified as recursive also.   In discussing a few of the more important of these, we shall find it useful to adopt the customary term *primitive recursive* for any function that is defined in accordance with the schema already given.

A common type of recursion is the *course-of-values recursion* (*Wertverlaufsrekursion*):

$$\left. \begin{aligned} \mathfrak{f}(a, \ldots, k, 0) &= a(a, \ldots, k), \\ \mathfrak{f}(a, \ldots, k, n') &= \mathfrak{b}(a, \ldots, k, n, \mathfrak{f}(a, \ldots, k, \mathfrak{t}_1(n)), \ldots, \mathfrak{f}(a, \ldots, k, \mathfrak{t}_r(n))), \end{aligned} \right\}$$

where $\mathfrak{t}_1(n) \leqslant n, \ldots, \mathfrak{t}_r(n) \leqslant n$ are demonstrable inequalities.   Here the value of the function $\mathfrak{f}$ for the value n' of the argument is given, not in terms of the immediately preceding value, but in terms of a fixed number $\mathfrak{r}$ of earlier values.

The course-of-values recursion can be made to depend on a primitive recursion by the following simple device.   We consider for simplicity the definition of a function of one argument only, without parameters, but it will be seen that the method is generally applicable.   We need to make use of the function $\nu(n,k)$ of two variables that is defined as the exponent of $\wp_k$, the kth member of the sequence of prime numbers, in the resolution of the number n into prime factors.   This function, as is well known, can be defined by primitive recursion (cf. *Grundlagen*, p. 319).   If we now put

$$\mathfrak{h}(n) = \prod_{k \leqslant n} \wp_k^{\mathfrak{f}(k)},$$

the general course-of-values recursion

$$\left. \begin{aligned} \mathfrak{f}(0) &= a, \\ \mathfrak{f}(n') &= \mathfrak{b}(n, \mathfrak{f}(\mathfrak{t}_1(n)), \ldots, \mathfrak{f}(\mathfrak{t}_r(n))) \end{aligned} \right\}$$

for $\mathfrak{f}(n)$ can be replaced by the primitive recursion

$$\mathfrak{h}(0) = 2^{\mathfrak{a}},$$
$$\mathfrak{h}(n') = \mathfrak{h}(n) \cdot \wp_{n'}^{\mathfrak{b}(n, v(\mathfrak{h}(n), t_1(n)), \ldots, v(\mathfrak{h}(n), t_r(n)))}$$

for $\mathfrak{h}(n)$, together with the explicit definition

$$\mathfrak{f}(n) = v(\mathfrak{h}(n), n).$$

Another variant of the schema of recursion involves direct specification of the first $\mathfrak{m} + 1$ values of the function to be defined, together with definition of the general value in terms of the $\mathfrak{m} + 1$ immediately preceding values:

$$\mathfrak{f}(a, \ldots, k, 0) = \mathfrak{a}_0(a, \ldots, k),$$
$$\mathfrak{f}(a, \ldots, k, 0') = \mathfrak{a}_1(a, \ldots, k),$$
$$\cdots \cdots \cdots \cdots$$
$$\mathfrak{f}(a, \ldots, k, 0^{(\mathfrak{m})}) = \mathfrak{a}_{\mathfrak{m}}(a, \ldots, k),$$
$$\mathfrak{f}(a, \ldots, k, n^{(\mathfrak{m}+1)}) = \mathfrak{b}(a, \ldots, k, n, \mathfrak{f}(a, \ldots, k, n), \ldots, \mathfrak{f}(a, \ldots, k, n^{(\mathfrak{m})})).$$

Such a schema is readily reducible to one of primitive recursive form. A suitable reduction is given by Hilbert and Bernays (*Grundlagen*, p. 327), who adduce as an example of this type of recursion Euclid's algorithm for the determination of the highest common factor of two numbers $\mathfrak{a}$ and $\mathfrak{b}$:

$$\mathfrak{a} = \mathfrak{q}_1 \cdot \mathfrak{b} + \mathfrak{r}_1$$
$$\mathfrak{b} = \mathfrak{q}_2 \cdot \mathfrak{r}_1 + \mathfrak{r}_2$$
$$\mathfrak{r}_1 = \mathfrak{q}_3 \cdot \mathfrak{r}_2 + \mathfrak{r}_3$$
$$\cdots \cdots \cdots$$

The numbers $\mathfrak{a}, \mathfrak{b}, \mathfrak{r}_1, \mathfrak{r}_2, \ldots$ are the values $\varrho(\mathfrak{a},\mathfrak{b},0)$, $\varrho(\mathfrak{a},\mathfrak{b},0')$, $\varrho(\mathfrak{a},\mathfrak{b},0'')$, $\varrho(\mathfrak{a},\mathfrak{b},0''')$, $\ldots$ of a function $\varrho(a,b,n)$, defined by the recursion

$$\varrho(a,b,0) = a,$$
$$\varrho(a,b,0') = b,$$
$$\varrho(a,b,n'') = \varrho(\varrho(a,b,n), \varrho(a,b,n')),$$

where $\varrho(x,y)$, already defined by primitive recursion on p. 264, is the remainder when y is divided into x.

As well as recursive definitions for a single function, we can also have simultaneous recursions for a number of functions introduced together. The original schema of primitive recursion generalizes in this way to the schema:

$$\mathfrak{f}_i(a, \ldots, k, 0) = \mathfrak{a}_i(a, \ldots, k),$$
$$\mathfrak{f}_i(a, \ldots, k, n') = \mathfrak{b}_i(a, \ldots, k, \mathfrak{f}_0(a, \ldots, k, n), \ldots$$
$$\ldots, \mathfrak{f}_{\mathfrak{s}-1}(a, \ldots, k, n)), \qquad (i = 0, \ldots, \mathfrak{s} - 1).$$

This schema reduces to an ordinary primitive recursion if we define a new function $\mathfrak{g}(a, \ldots, k, n)$ by putting

$$\mathfrak{g}(a, \ldots, k, n) = \mathfrak{f}_{\rho(n,\mathfrak{s})}(a, \ldots, k, \pi(n,\mathfrak{s})),$$

where

$$n = \mathfrak{s} \cdot \pi(n,\mathfrak{s}) + \varrho(n,\mathfrak{s}) \quad \text{and} \quad 0 \leqslant \varrho(n,\mathfrak{s}) < \mathfrak{s}.$$

All the schemata that we have considered so far are 'recursive' in the sense that they set up an iterative process for the determination of the values of a function for all possible values of its argument. We evaluate the function for any assigned value n of the argument by working up from 0 to n in a finite number of repetitions of a specified process. It might now be thought likely that every schema with this property could be made to depend, by a sufficient exercise of ingenuity, on a schema of *primitive* recursion; but this is not in fact the case. In a paper published in 1928 (Bibliography, [1]) Wilhelm Ackermann constructed a recursion which he showed to be essentially different from primitive recursions by demonstrating that the function defined by it increases more rapidly, with increasing values of the argument, than is possible for any primitive recursive function. Ackermann's recursion took the following form:[1]

$$\left.\begin{array}{l}
\xi(a,b,0) = a + b, \\
\xi(a,0,n') = \beta(n,1) + a \cdot \alpha(\delta(n)), \\
\xi(a,b',n') = \xi(a,\xi(a,b,n'),n).
\end{array}\right\}$$

This is an instance of what is known as an interlocking (*verschränkt*) recursion, since b is not a mere parameter, but a second variable that is involved, together with n, in the recursive process itself. The first three values of Ackermann's function $\xi(a,b,n)$ are $\xi(a,b,0) = a + b$, $\xi(a,b,0') = a \cdot b$, $\xi(a,b,0'') = a^b$; and we have here already an indication of the rapidity of growth of the function $\xi(a,b,n)$ as n increases.

7   General recursive functions

The schemata that we have now passed in review are abstract representations of some of the more important procedures for defining—or rather generating—arithmetical functions constructively, in such a way that the value of the function for any chosen value of the variable can be determined in a finite number of steps; and the determination of this value, moreover, shows characteristically 'recursive' or iterative features. About a quarter of a century ago, however, it came to be realized that what chiefly matters in definitions of the recursive type is the existence of a finite process of evaluation which is based on equations, the iterative nature of the more familiar recursive procedures

[1] For the definitions of the auxiliary functions involved, see p. 262 above.

being in fact of secondary importance; and a broadened concept of *general recursive function* was accordingly introduced, in which the iterative element no longer appeared. This concept, often referred to as the Herbrand-Gödel-Kleene concept,[1] has been analysed in a very lucid fashion by Kleene in his now classical paper 'General recursive functions of natural numbers' in *Mathematische Annalen*, **112** (1936), 727–742. Cf. also §4 of Church's paper 'An unsolvable problem of elementary number theory', in the *American Journal of Mathematics*, **58** (1936), 345–363.

The definition of general recursive function may be summarized as follows. Let us suppose that

$$\sigma_j(x_1, \ldots, x_{s_j}) \quad (j = 1, \ldots, \mathfrak{n})$$

is a set of unknown arithmetical functions, and that (E) is a given set of equations

$$\mathfrak{a}_i = \mathfrak{b}_i \quad (i = 1, \ldots, \mathfrak{m})$$

with the following properties:

(i) For each value of i, $\mathfrak{a}_i$ and $\mathfrak{b}_i$ are terms that involve only the symbol 0, the successor function n', numerical variables, and the function symbols $\sigma_1, \ldots, \sigma_n$.

(ii) For each i, $\mathfrak{a}_i$ and $\mathfrak{b}_i$ between them involve at least one of the functions σ_j.

(iii) For each j in the range $1, \ldots, \mathfrak{n}$, and each set of $\mathfrak{s}_j$ numbers $\mathfrak{k}_1, \ldots, \mathfrak{k}_{s_j}$, there is one and only one number $\mathfrak{k}$ such that the equality

$$\sigma_j(\mathfrak{k}_1, \ldots, \mathfrak{k}_{s_j}) = \mathfrak{k}$$

is deducible from the equations (E) in a finite number of steps, each of which involves only the replacement of numerical variables by particular numbers or the substitution of equals for equals.

When this is so, the equations (E) are said to define the functions $\sigma_1, \ldots, \sigma_n$ recursively; and every function that can be defined by a system of equations in this way is said to be *general recursive*.

It is plain that all primitive recursive functions, as well as all functions that can be defined by the more elaborate recursive schemata that we have considered in §6, are recursive in the Herbrand-Gödel-Kleene sense. The concept of general recursiveness serves to make precise, in the most direct manner possible, the simple intuitive idea of unambiguous determination of the whole course of values of an arithmetical function by means of a set of equations. Thus we see how the simple idea of recursive definition of a function, as originally conceived by

---

[1] Gödel proposed such an interpretation of recursiveness in his lectures at Princeton in 1934, saying that it had been suggested to him by Jacques Herbrand (1908–1931), the brilliant French mathematician and logician who was killed at an early age in a mountaineering accident. Kleene developed the idea on the formal side.

Dedekind, Peano, and Skolem, has by degrees been generalized, until in the end a concept has been reached which may be looked upon as embodying the pure notion of effective definition, freed from all non-essential features. This conception of 'effectiveness' or 'constructivity' in arithmetic has been the object of a number of profound inquiries, and several different ways of approaching it have been tried, mainly during the period 1930–1940. In the remaining sections of this chapter we shall consider the deepened understanding of the significance of general recursiveness that has resulted from these investigations.

8   The mathematical ideal of constructivity

As we remarked earlier on, when discussing the intuitionist movement, an examination of the recent history of mathematics reveals a pronounced and persistent strain of constructivism. Many eminent mathematicians in fact, from Kronecker onwards, have held that a mathematical entity is not properly defined unless the definition that is offered permits construction of the entity (or at least controlled approximation to it) by a finite process. This requirement of constructivity has perhaps its clearest meaning in arithmetic, where we take a function $\mathfrak{f}(n)$ to be defined in this strict sense if, for any assigned natural number $\mathfrak{n}$, the value $\mathfrak{f}(\mathfrak{n})$ of the function can be determined in a finite number of steps, and where in a similar way we may regard a real number α between 0 and 1 as properly defined if the nth digit in its decimal expansion is a well-defined function of n.

Now although the idea of a constructively defined function of n is tolerably clear and distinct as an intuitive mathematical notion, it is nevertheless far from precise when judged by the more exacting standards of metamathematics, and much work has indeed been done with the aim of making it more definite. Since intuitive notions are, by their very nature, more or less vague, there can be no question of ever defining a formal concept that is strictly equivalent to such an informal notion; but all the same it is sometimes possible to produce a formal concept that is generally acceptable to mathematicians as the 'natural', 'proper', or 'appropriate' formalization of an intuitive notion. In this sense, Dedekind's real numbers formalize linear magnitudes, and the primary truth-functions of the propositional calculus formalize the logical relations which are the basis of mathematical deduction. And now, at the appropriate intuitive level, we ask for a satisfactory formalization of the notion of a constructive sequence of natural numbers.

An answer to this demand was given in 1936 by Alonzo Church, in his paper 'An unsolvable problem of elementary number theory'. In that paper Church declared that the notion of 'effectively calculable function', as he called it, ought to be identified with that of 'general recursive function' in the sense of Kleene (cf. p. 273 above); and he supported this contention—which has since come to be known as *Church's thesis*—by adducing a number of general considerations that go some way towards making it plausible. The kind of weight that he gave to these arguments may be gauged from the remark with which he introduced them: 'This definition is thought to be justified by the considerations which follow, so far as positive justification can ever be obtained for the selection of a formal definition to correspond to an intuitive notion'. It may be added that, although Church's thesis has found wide acceptance, it has recently been disavowed by Kalmár in a paper 'An argument against the plausibility of Church's thesis', published in *Constructivity in Mathematics: Proceedings of the Colloquium held at Amsterdam*, 1957. Kalmár backs his rejection of the thesis by a number of plausibility arguments which counter those advanced by Church.

8.1   Church's calculus of λ-conversion

The tentative identification of effective calculability with general recursiveness derives strong support from the fact that certain other suggested formalizations of the notion of calculability have proved to be demonstrably equivalent to general recursiveness. One of these alternative formalizations, devised by Church and Kleene, is λ-*definability*. This concept is explained by Church in his paper of 1936, to which we have just referred; and details of the calculus of λ-conversion, on which it depends, are to be found in a number of earlier papers.[1]

The calculus of λ-conversion is a syntactically-defined formal system which provides a wholly abstract treatment of the notion of function of an argument. The symbols used in it are: (i) the *variables* of the calculus, which are postulated as a denumerably infinite set, but which in practice are the small Latin letters $a, b, \ldots$; (ii) three kinds of brackets $\{, \}$; $(,)$; $[,]$; (iii) the letter λ. Extensive use is made of syntactic variables, both in the development of the system itself and in the subsequent discussion of its metamathematical properties. For these variables, Church and Kleene employ small and capital letters in a bold-face Latin fount, not German characters as we have done hitherto—and their example, as we have seen, has been followed more recently by Bourbaki in the part of his *Éléments de Mathématique* that is devoted to logic.

There are two basic processes of formation that can be used in the construction of well-formed formulae. (i) If **F** and **X** are well-formed

---

[1] A. Church: 'A set of postulates for the foundation of logic', *Ann. of Math.*, **33** (1932), 346–366, and **34** (1933), 839–864; S. C. Kleene: 'Proof by cases in formal logic', *Ann. of Math.*, **35** (1934), 529–544, and 'A theory of positive integers in formal logic, I, II', *Amer. J. Math.*, **57** (1935), 153–173 and 219–244.

formulae, then $\{\mathbf{F}\}(\mathbf{X})$ is also a well-formed formula.   (ii) If $\mathbf{M}$ is a well-formed formula and $\mathbf{x}$ is a variable that occurs free in it, then $\lambda\mathbf{x}[\mathbf{M}]$ is a well-formed formula, and $\mathbf{x}$ is a bound variable in $\lambda\mathbf{x}[\mathbf{M}]$.   All variables that are not bound in this way by a 'λ' are free.   The two processes of formation can be applied repeatedly; and a well-formed formula is any formula that can be built up, from variables standing alone, by a finite number of repetitions of these processes.   Interpreted intuitively, $\{\mathbf{F}\}(\mathbf{X})$ is 'the function $\mathbf{F}$ of the argument $\mathbf{X}$', and $\lambda\mathbf{x}[\mathbf{M}]$ is 'that function which $\mathbf{M}$ is of $\mathbf{x}$'.   Thus, using the λ-notation in an ordinary mathematical context, we could say that $\lambda x[\sin x]$ is the function 'the sine of'; and in symbolic logic, $\lambda x[\phi x]$ would be an alternative way of writing the propositional function that Russell denotes by $\phi\hat{x}$ (cf. p. 166).   In the ordinary handling of the λ-calculus, brackets are omitted wherever this can be done without risk of confusion.

If $\mathbf{M}$ and $\mathbf{N}$ are two expressions, and $\mathbf{x}$ is a variable, $S_{\mathbf{N}}^{\mathbf{x}}\,\mathbf{M}\,|$ denotes the expression that is obtained when $\mathbf{N}$ is substituted for $\mathbf{x}$ throughout $\mathbf{M}$.

There are no axioms in the λ-calculus, which is a formalized treatment of the construction of functional expressions, and not a formal deductive theory; but there are three 'rules of procedure', which take the form of permitted transformations of well-formed formulae. Church specifies these operations as follows:

I. To replace any part $\lambda\mathbf{x}[\mathbf{M}]$ of a formula by $\lambda\mathbf{y}[S_{\mathbf{y}}^{\mathbf{x}}\,\mathbf{M}\,|\,]$, where $\mathbf{y}$ is a variable which does not occur in $\mathbf{M}$.

II. To replace any part $\{\lambda\mathbf{x}[\mathbf{M}]\}(\mathbf{N})$ of a formula by $S_{\mathbf{N}}^{\mathbf{x}}\,\mathbf{M}\,|$, provided that the bound variables in $\mathbf{M}$ are distinct both from $\mathbf{x}$ and from the free variables in $\mathbf{N}$.

III. To replace any part $S_{\mathbf{N}}^{\mathbf{x}}\,\mathbf{M}\,|$ (not immediately following λ) of a formula by $\{\lambda\mathbf{x}[\mathbf{M}]\}(\mathbf{N})$, provided that the bound variables in $\mathbf{M}$ are distinct both from $\mathbf{x}$ and from the free variables in $\mathbf{N}$.

Any finite sequence of these operations is called a *conversion*, and if $\mathbf{B}$ is obtainable from $\mathbf{A}$ by conversion we say that $\mathbf{A}$ is *convertible* into $\mathbf{B}$,[1] or '$\mathbf{A}$ conv $\mathbf{B}$'.

The symbols $1, 2, 3, \ldots$ are introduced, by explicit definition, as abbreviations for the particular well-formed formulae $\lambda ab\,.\,a(b)$, $\lambda ab\,.\,a(a(b))$, $\lambda ab\,.\,a(a(a(b)))$, $\ldots$, that is to say the formulae which would be written in full as $\lambda a[\lambda b[\{a\}(b)]]$, $\lambda a[\lambda b[\{a\}(\{a\}(b))]]$, etc.   In this way the natural numbers are represented formally in the system as the abstract patterns of formation of a simple function of an argument and the composite functions which result from iteration of this process any number of times.

---

[1] This use of the word 'convertible' has no connexion with our earlier use of the same word as a translation of 'überführbar' in the sense of Hilbert and Bernays (cf. p. 73).

The crucial concept of λ-definability of an arithmetical function is now defined as follows: 'A function F of one positive integer is said to be *λ-definable* if a formula **F** can be found such that, if $F(m) = r$ and **m** and **r** are the formulae for which the positive integers m and r (written in Arabic notation) stand according to our abbreviations introduced above, then $\{\mathbf{F}\}(\mathbf{m})$ conv **r**. Similarly, a function F of two positive integers is said to be λ-definable if it is possible to find a formula **F** such that, whenever $F(m,n) = r$, the formula $\{\{\mathbf{F}\}(\mathbf{m})\}(\mathbf{n})$ is convertible into **r** (m, n, r being positive integers and **m**, **n**, **r** the corresponding formulae). And so on for functions of three or more positive integers.'

The above specification of the calculus of λ-conversion is condensed from Church's paper of 1936. In that paper, moreover, two theorems are stated which assert respectively that every general recursive function of positive integers is λ-definable and that every λ-definable function of positive integers is general recursive. Since it can be argued with considerable persuasive force that both general recursiveness and λ-definability are natural formalizations of the intuitive notion of effective calculability, the fact that these two initially quite distinct properties prove in the end to be equivalent lends strong support to Church's thesis (p. 275), which identifies effectively calculable functions with those which are general recursive.

8.2   Turing's conception of computability

Yet another possible way of giving precise meaning to the intuitive notion of effective calculability was proposed by A. M. Turing, in his paper 'On computable numbers, with an application to the Entscheidungsproblem' (*Proc. London Math. Soc.*, **42** (1937), 230–265). Turing's method was to identify the notion of effective calculability with that of computability by a machine. In his paper he devised a suitable idealization of the intuitive idea of a computing machine, gave an abstract definition of 'machine' in his theoretical sense,[1] and then proceeded to investigate the range of the resulting concept of computability, showing in particular that a decimal is computable in his sense if and only if the sequence of its digits is λ-definable. No better summary of Turing's conception of a computing machine can be given than that in the following extract from his original paper:

'We may compare a man in the process of computing a real number to a machine which is only capable of a finite number of conditions $q_1, q_2, \ldots, q_R$ which will be called "*m*-configurations". The machine is supplied with a "tape" (the analogue of paper) running through it, and divided into sections (called "squares") each capable of bearing a

---

[1] Turing's interest in mechanical computing, though initially theoretical, was afterwards put to good practical account when he was in charge of the development of the computer ACE, built at the National Physical Laboratory.

"symbol". At any moment there is just one square, say the rth, bearing the symbol $\mathfrak{S}(r)$ which is "in the machine". We may call this square the "scanned square". The symbol on the scanned square may be called the "scanned symbol". The "scanned symbol" is the only one of which the machine is, so to speak, "directly aware". However, by altering its m-configuration the machine can effectively remember some of the symbols which it has "seen" (scanned) previously. The possible behaviour of the machine at any moment is determined by the m-configuration q_n and the scanned symbol $\mathfrak{S}(r)$. This pair q_n, $\mathfrak{S}(r)$ will be called the "configuration": thus the configuration determines the possible behaviour of the machine. In some of the configurations in which the scanned square is blank (i.e. bears no symbol) the machine writes down a new symbol on the scanned square; in other configurations it erases the scanned symbol. The machine may also change the square which is being scanned, but only by shifting it one place to right or left. In addition to any of these operations the m-configuration may be changed. Some of the symbols written down will form the sequence of figures which is the decimal of the real number which is being computed. The others are just rough notes to "assist the memory". It will only be these rough notes which will be liable to erasure. It is my contention that these operations include all those which are used in the computation of a number.'

The fact that Turing chose to discuss computability of a decimal and not of a function $F(n)$ is plainly of little moment; and what is of particular interest is that, by analysing the operations that are performed in the actual procedure of computation, and devising a machine that could carry out exactly these operations, he came finally to a precise concept of computability that proved to be equivalent once again to λ-definability. His investigation thus powerfully reinforced Church's thesis.

8.3 The decision problem for formalized theories

In definability and computability (which, as we have said, are both equivalent to general recursiveness) we have two possible means of freeing the important metamathematical notion of constructivity from vagueness, and indeed of freeing it altogether from dependence on intuition. When this notion has been made formal in one of these ways, much of the metamathematics of arithmetic gains substantially in precision. We may wish to ask, for example, whether a particular arithmetical problem is constructively or effectively solvable; and if the problem in question can be exhibited as one of finding a number which satisfies certain given conditions, its constructive solvability will now be understood as meaning computability of such a number. Or again, if the question arises of whether some particular arithmetical predicate is 'effective', we shall interpret this question as asking whether the characteristic function of the predicate is a computable (i.e. general recursive) function.

Now although arithmetic is only a limited and very elementary part of mathematics, when once the problem of formalizing the notion of effectiveness has been solved for arithmetic it has in principle been solved generally. For, by using the artifice of Gödel numbering (cf. p. 234), we are able to restate in terms of the metamathematics of arithmetic the metamathematics of all formal systems of the usual type. One of the most interesting general results obtainable in this way is concerned with what Hilbert called the *Entscheidungsproblem*, or decision problem, for a given formal system F. This is the problem of devising a procedure which, when applied to an *arbitrary* formula $\mathfrak{A}$ of F, will decide in a finite number of steps whether or not $\mathfrak{A}$ is derivable in F. From the point of view of the metamathematician (though admittedly not from that of the working mathematician) the solution of the decision problem for a system F would render the actual construction of derivations in F wholly superfluous.

One system for which the decision problem has been solved is the propositional calculus. We already know two alternative decision procedures for this system, namely construction of a truth-table for any given formula $\mathfrak{A}$, and reduction of $\mathfrak{A}$ to conjunctive normal form (see Theorem 2, p. 37, and Theorem 4, p. 48). We have here, moreover, decision procedures of a particularly strong kind, for before the process is actually carried out for any particular formula $\mathfrak{A}$, a bound can be set to the number of steps that will be necessary if a decision is to be reached. But in other cases decidability in this strong sense cannot be hoped for, and a system is to be reckoned decidable as long as both the derivable and the underivable formulae are recursively enumerable (i.e. their Gödel numbers can be formed into recursive sequences). For when this condition is satisfied we can, in principle, locate the Gödel number of any given formula $\mathfrak{A}$ by working systematically through the two sequences; and when this number has been found we shall know whether the formula belongs to the decidable or the undecidable class. We are not, however, in a position to assign in advance any bound to the number of 'observations' that will be required.

It was proved by Church and Turing, in papers that we have already referred to, that for the restricted calculus of predicates there can be no decision procedure at all, not even one of the weaker kind. Church proved that 'there is no recursive function of two formulae **A** and **B**, whose value is 2 or 1 according as **A** conv **B** or not' (Theorem 19 of the 1936 paper). In other words, the characteristic function of the predicate 'the formulae with Gödel numbers m and n are convertible into each other' is not general recursive. From this Church inferred that 'the Entscheidungsproblem is unsolvable in the case of any system of symbolic logic which is ω-consistent and is strong enough to allow certain comparatively simple methods of definition and proof'.[1]   And Turing proved, using his concept of an idealized computing machine, that 'there can be no general process for determining whether a given formula $\mathfrak{A}$ of the functional calculus **K** is provable, i.e there can be no machine which, supplied with any one $\mathfrak{A}$ of these formulae, will eventually say whether $\mathfrak{A}$ is provable'.   The 'functional calculus **K**' referred to by Turing is Hilbert and Ackermann's restricted calculus of predicates.

8.4*   Post's canonical form for formal systems

A different way of reaching the same conclusion concerning unsolvability of the decision problem has been followed by Emil Post, in researches begun in about 1920.   The germ of Post's work is to be found in his early paper 'Introduction to a general theory of elementary propositions' (*Amer. J. Math.*, **43** (1921), 163–185), but for details of the mature theory we must turn to 'Formal reductions of the general combinatorial decision problem' (*Amer. J. Math.*, **65** (1943), 197–215). A valuable complement to this latter paper is an address that Post presented before a meeting of the American Mathematical Society in 1944, in which he outlined in an informal manner the implications of his results.   This address was published under the title 'Recursively enumerable sets of positive integers and their decision problems' (*Bull. Amer. Math. Soc.*, **50** (1944), 284–316).

Post's method is to show that a very wide class of formal systems can all be expressed in a certain standard form, called by him *canonical form*.   The system under consideration is supposed to be developed in a strictly syntactic manner, its formulae being nothing but finite sequences of individual symbols, or 'strings of marks'.   To define the system, we have to prescribe the set of available symbols (required here to be a finite set), the primitive assertions or axioms, and the rules of procedure.   The rules of procedure are here conceived as 'productions', of the following form:

$$g_{11}P_{i'_1}g_{12}P_{i'_2}\ldots g_{1m_1}P_{i'_{m_1}}g_{1,m_1+1}$$

$$g_{21}P_{i''_1}g_{22}P_{i''_2}\ldots g_{2m_2}P_{i''_{m_2}}g_{2,m_2+1}$$

$$\cdots \cdots \cdots \cdots \cdots \cdots$$

$$g_{k1}P_{i_1^{(k)}}g_{k2}P_{i_2^{(k)}}\ldots g_{km_k}P_{i_{m_k}^{(k)}}g_{k,m_k+1}$$

produce

$$g_1P_{i_1}g_2P_{i_2}\ldots g_mP_{i_m}g_{m+1}.$$

---

[1] As thus formulated, the theorem does not apply to the restricted calculus of predicates, but Church extended it to this calculus in 'A note on the Entscheidungsproblem', *J. Symb. Logic*, **1** (1936), 40–41 and 101–102.

The gs are certain strings of marks (possibly empty) that are fixed in any particular rule; the Ps are variable strings; and every P that occurs in the final line must occur in at least one of the earlier lines. It will be seen that a rule of procedure, expressed in canonical form in this way, is essentially a schema. The rule of *modus ponens*, for example, which we have expressed by the following schema (β):

$$\frac{\mathfrak{A}}{\mathfrak{A} \to \mathfrak{B}}$$
$$\mathfrak{B},$$

could be written in Post's canonical form as

$$g_1 P g_1$$
$$g_1 P g_2 Q g_1$$
$$\text{produce}$$
$$g_1 Q g_1,$$

with g_1 standing for the empty string, g_2 standing for the string that consists of the single symbol $\to$, and P and Q standing for any strings that count as well-formed formulae.

A formal system in canonical form is specified by a finite number of rules of production, which are said to constitute its *basis B*, and these rules may possibly be of considerable formal complexity. Post was able to show however, in his paper of 1943, that if a formal system can be put in canonical form at all then it is equivalent to a system in a very much more special form, which he called *normal form*. For a system to be in normal form, the rules of procedure must be exclusively of the simple type

$$gP$$
$$\text{produces}$$
$$Pg',$$

where g and g' are fixed strings, and P is a variable string. The replacement of an arbitrary system in canonical form by a system in normal form is only possible, in general, at the cost of a substantial increase in the number of primitive symbols employed and in the lengths of the strings that occur in the system; but in many metamathematical investigations such cost is far outweighed by the advantage that we gain from being able to restrict the discussion to formal systems of a single very simple type. This result of Post's, that every system in canonical form can be put in normal form, opens up a possibility of development of a very general theory of the syntax of formal systems (cf. P. C. Rosenbloom: *The Elements of Mathematical Logic*, Chapter IV).

Post applied his method to a variety of questions of effectiveness and decidability, obtaining results closely related to those which have been obtained in other ways by Gödel, Church, Kleene, and other investigators of this subject. He arrived at his particular definition of effectiveness in arithmetic by constructing a formal system in which the strings operated upon consist exclusively of finite sequences of symbols which can only be 1 or b, and the particular sequences 1, 11, 111, ..., formed of 1s only, serve to represent the intuitive numbers 1, 2, 3, ... A set of numbers may then be taken to be effectively defined if a basis B can be found which is such that all the 'numbers' of the given set, and only such numbers, are producible by means of this basis. The resulting characterization of effectiveness proves to be equivalent to λ-definability and to computability in Turing's sense.

In his address of 1944, Post reviewed in general terms the conclusions concerning the inherent limitations of formal methods which he felt to be inescapable in view of the outcome of his own work and the results of the investigations into general recursiveness that had been made by other mathematicians. The following result is typical of those which he considered: The bases that can be used to define sets of numbers in formalized arithmetic involve a finite number of symbols only, and they are therefore effectively enumerable in a sequence $B_1, B_2, \ldots$. Now let us consider the set of all pairs $(B_\mathfrak{m}, \mathfrak{n})$, consisting of a particular basis $B_\mathfrak{m}$ and a particular number $\mathfrak{n}$. It can be proved that no effective decision process can exist for the predicate $n \in B_m$, i.e. that the set of pairs of numbers $(\mathfrak{m}, \mathfrak{n})$ with the property $\mathfrak{n} \in B_\mathfrak{m}$ and the set of pairs with the complementary property $\mathfrak{n} \notin B_\mathfrak{m}$ cannot both be generated by means of suitable bases. In Post's words: 'The decision problem for the class of all recursively enumerable sets of positive integers is recursively unsolvable and hence, in all probability, unsolvable in the intuitive sense.' This particular result, and other results of a similar character concerning systems of formalized mathematics and logic, prompted Post to make the following observation:

'The conclusion is unescapable that even for such a fixed, well defined body of mathematical propositions, *mathematical thinking is, and must remain, essentially creative*. To the writer's mind, this conclusion must inevitably result in at least a partial reversal of the entire axiomatic trend of the later nineteenth and early twentieth centuries, with a return to meaning and truth as being of the essence of mathematics.'

It might indeed be maintained that the general tendency of metamathematics, ever since 1931 when Gödel proved the first comprehensive incompleteness theorem, has been to suggest some such view as that here put forward by Post. As metamathematics has been made more formal—first by Gödel's device of mapping any formal system whatever on arithmetic, and then by the perfecting of the conception of general recursiveness, which gives precision to the intuitive idea of effective calculability—so the indications have increased that no reasonably strong formal system can be either closed, in the sense that problems arising within the system can all be solved within the system, or complete as a formalization of more intuitive mathematics.

SUPPLEMENTARY NOTES ON CHAPTER 10

1. *Books on recursive arithmetic.* Standard works on recursive arithmetic are the four books already referred to on p. 261, namely the first volume of Hilbert & Bernays: *Grundlagen der Mathematik*, Rózsa Péter: *Rekursive Funktionen*, Goodstein: *Recursive Number Theory*, and Kleene: *Introduction to Metamathematics.*

Skolem's original paper [2] is not easily accessible, but it is worth reading for the impressive sureness with which Skolem handled what was then a new treatment of arithmetic.

Goodstein has diverged somewhat from Skolem and those other writers on recursive arithmetic who have taken over the details of Skolem's treatment. He prefers to dispense with a calculus of deductive logic, whether explicit or implicit, and to treat arithmetic directly as a 'free-variable equation calculus'. He carries out this plan in his book, mentioned above.

A very elegant axiomatic presentation of part of recursive arithmetic has been given by Church in his paper 'Binary recursive arithmetic' [11].

2. *Books on constructivity in general.* A textbook in English on matters connected with constructivity is M. Davis: *Computability and Unsolvability* (1958), described by its author as 'an introduction to the theory of computability and non-computability, usually referred to as the theory of recursive functions'. In German, there is also H. Hermes: *Aufzählbarkeit, Entscheidbarkeit, Berechenbarkeit* (1961).

P. C. Rosenbloom: *The Elements of Mathematical Logic* (1950) contains a concise treatment of various logical systems as pure calculi, and the book ends with a good account of Post's theory of canonical languages.

A number of different aspects of constructivity are touched upon in the collection of essays by a number of authors which we classify, under the name of its editor, as Heyting [4]. This volume constitutes the proceedings of a colloquium on constructivity that was held in 1957.

Chapter 11

THE AXIOMATIC THEORY OF SETS

1 Pure mathematics as an extension of the theory of sets

In spite of the widespread concern with questions of constructive existence that has been for many years so prominent a feature of research into the foundations of mathematics, the fact nevertheless remains that the typical outlook of mathematicians is still, as it has traditionally been, one that may be characterized as 'existential'. The ordinary way of presenting a theory in pure mathematics is to postulate a totality of entities (i.e. a domain of individuals) and to make the hypothesis that this totality has a particular structure, defined by a set of relations governed by stated axioms. The entities to be considered in the theory are not conceived as resulting from any procedure of construction or generation, but are merely taken for granted as an existent totality; and, in consequence of this basic attitude, mathematics is seen in terms of logical relations, not in terms of processes.

Mathematical orthodoxy of the kind just described finds its most complete embodiment in Nicolas Bourbaki's treatise *Éléments de Mathématique* (cf. Chapter 4, §7, above). Mathematics, according to Bourbaki, is the theory of abstract structure; and in it we should study, in an orderly sequence, the various structures that have come to be accepted as interesting objects of mathematical thought, beginning with the simplest and by degrees proceeding to those which are more elaborate. How this is to be done will be explained more fully in §5 of the next chapter.

Now any such systematic exposition of the various types of structure that are of interest to mathematicians must have a first stage; and Bourbaki takes for this first stage the pure theory of sets (*théorie des ensembles*), which is presupposed in all the subsequent theories. The theory of sets may be regarded as the most abstract part of mathematics, involving no specific structural features at all. It has only its own intrinsic *logical* structure, arising from purely logical relations between sets and subsets, which are all expressible in terms of the one basic relation of membership, $x \in X$. In adopting this foundation for his system, Bourbaki is simply conforming to current mathematical practice, for, in his words, 'as every one knows, all mathematical theories can be considered as extensions of the general theory of sets'.

This being so, the theory of sets may be looked upon as the logical substructure of pure mathematics. Though we may not now wish any longer actually to identify mathematics with logic, as was attempted in *Principia Mathematica*, we can hardly do other than support mathematics on a foundation of pure logic. It does indeed seem to be the case that, for the working mathematician, the provision of a clearly articulated and securely based theory of sets is the best answer to the doubts that have been raised by Russell's antinomy, Gödel's theorem, Brouwer's attack on traditional logic, and all the other disturbing elements in the modern philosophy of mathematics. Whether or not such a theory can be made fully acceptable to philosophers of mathematics, we may at least hope that it will secure for mathematics itself a higher standard of rigour than this study has ever achieved before.

2 The naive theory of sets

The pioneer in the theory of sets was, of course, Cantor, who introduced the main concepts and formed them into a logical system which has since become an integral part of the fabric of mathematics. This earliest treatment of sets was linked, however, with a naive attitude to logic, since Cantor was prepared to treat abstract sets as if they were objects of common-sense thinking; and later research into the theory of sets has had for its main objective the replacement of this naive logic by stricter reasoning, better able to stand up to philosophical criticism and yet still capable of yielding the mathematically indispensable parts of the original theory.

Cantor regarded the basic notion of set or aggregate (*Menge*) as too fundamental to allow of mathematical analysis, and he began the paper which contains his most systematic presentation of his results[1] with the following definition: 'By a "set" we are to understand any comprehension (*Zusammenfassung*) into a whole *M* of definite and separate objects *m* of our intuition or our thought'.

Now this definition of set involves an implicit reference to an individual mind—namely the mind which performs the act of comprehending—and it needs therefore to be suitably amended before it can be used in a formal theory. For this reason, Cantor's definition has not been retained in quite its original form by later authors, but was replaced at an early stage by a more abstractly conceived principle or axiom that has come to be known as the *principle of comprehension*. This principle, which asserts that every property (i.e. every predicate) gives rise to a set, namely the set of all those things which possess the

---

[1] G. Cantor: 'Beiträge zur Begründung der transfiniten Mengenlehre', *Math. Ann.*, **46** (1895), 481–512, and **49** (1897), 207–246. English translation by P. E. B. Jourdain: *Contributions to the Founding of the Theory of Transfinite Numbers* (1915).

property, was adopted as fundamental by Frege (cf. p. 179) and also, in a modified form, by Russell (cf. p. 169).

The most direct way in which we can attempt to construct a formal theory of sets which is based on the principle of comprehension is by beginning with a suitable system of symbolic logic, for instance the restricted calculus of predicates, and extending this system by introducing a new primitive relation of membership $x \in y$ and adopting additional axioms in which this relation occurs. We need, first of all, one or more axioms which give expression to the principle of extensionality (i.e. the principle that a set is uniquely determined by its elements). A possible choice is the pair of axioms

$$(z)(x \in z \leftrightarrow y \in z) \rightarrow (u \in x \leftrightarrow u \in y)$$

and

$$(u)(u \in x \leftrightarrow u \in y) \rightarrow (x \in z \leftrightarrow y \in z).$$

The principle of comprehension itself may be expressed in the form

$$(Ez)(x)(x \in z \leftrightarrow H(x)).$$

Further axioms beyond these basic ones are also needed, and these will include formal counterparts of various axioms that are discussed in later sections of the present chapter, as for instance the axiom of infinity and the axiom of choice.

The formal system that we obtain in this way has been named the 'ideal calculus' (*Idealkalkül*).[1] Such a calculus may indeed be regarded as a reasonable formalization of Cantor's naive theory of sets; but as a mathematical theory it is not yet satisfactory, since it is demonstrably inconsistent. Russell's antinomy, for instance, can at once be derived within it if the principle of comprehension is applied to the property $x \notin x$. Nevertheless, the ideal calculus may be thought of as underlying all the various axiomatic treatments of sets that have been proposed—and indeed these differ principally in the means that are adopted in them for re-establishing consistency. One way in which the known contradictions can be excluded from the system is by incorporation in it of a theory of types, as has been done in *Principia Mathematica*, but the way that is now more usually adopted in mathematics is a rather different one. In accordance with the procedure that is now generally favoured, we do not regard sets as produced by predicates, but instead we postulate them directly as primitive entities, which are merely required to satisfy certain stated axioms (cf. the postulation of points, etc. in Hilbert's system of geometry, described above in Chapter 7, §2). These axioms, which assert such things as that to every entity there corresponds a set with this entity as its sole element, that the subsets of

---

[1] See H. Hermes and H. Scholz: 'Mathematische Logik', *Enzyk. Math. Wiss.*, I 1, 1, 1 (1952), p. 58.

any given set are the elements of another set, that every set of sets has a union set, and so forth, have to be strong enough to guarantee the existence, in the abstract system, of all sets that are needed for mathematical purposes, but they are taken in the weakest form that satisfies this minimal requirement.

Sixty years ago, when Burali-Forti and Russell had just derived their famous antinomies within the existing theory of sets, the reaction of the more intuitionistically minded mathematicians and philosophers was to turn right away from Cantor's ideas and to try to do without his mathematical innovations altogether; but there were also other mathematicians who interpreted the antinomies rather as an intimation that the theory of sets in its existing form was too naive, and that it must be made more rigidly axiomatic if it was to be granted an established place within mathematics. The leader of the movement of rehabilitation was Ernst Zermelo (1871–1953), and time has shown that it was he and those who shared his views who were in the main stream of twentieth-century mathematics.

3 Zermelo's axiomatic theory of sets

Zermelo's axiomatization of the theory of sets is to be found in his paper 'Untersuchungen über die Grundlagen der Mengenlehre, I' (*Math. Ann.*, **65** (1908), 261–281), which begins as follows:

'The theory of sets is that branch of mathematics whose task is to investigate mathematically the fundamental concepts of number, order, and function, in their primitive simplicity, and thereby to develop the logical foundations of all arithmetic and analysis; and it accordingly constitutes an indispensable component of mathematical science. At the present time, however, the very existence of this discipline appears to be threatened by certain contradictions or "antinomies", which can be derived from what appear to be its essential principles and which have not up to now found any fully satisfactory solution. In the face of Russell's antinomy of the "set of all sets which do not contain themselves as element", in fact, it does not today seem permissible any more to assign to any arbitrary logically definable concept a "set" or "class" as its extension. Cantor's original definition of a "set" as a "comprehension of definite distinct objects of our intuition or our thought into a whole" therefore certainly requires some limitation, although no one has yet succeeded in replacing it by another definition, equally simple, that is not exposed to any such doubt. In these circumstances we now have no choice but to try the reverse way and, starting from the historically existing "theory of sets", to seek out the principles which are required as a basis for this mathematical discipline. This problem must be solved in such a way that the principles are made narrow enough to exclude all contradictions, and yet made sufficiently wide for all that is valuable in this theory to be preserved.'

In the body of the paper Zermelo carries out his plan of presenting the theory of sets as a wholly abstract axiomatic theory, in which the concept of 'set' shall remain undefined except in so far as it has the properties attributed to it in the axioms. He does not say, in fact, what sets *are*, but only how they are to be manipulated mathematically.

A certain domain $\mathfrak{B}$ of abstract objects is postulated; and the elements of this domain, which are referred to as 'things' (*Dinge*), are represented by letters $a, b, \ldots$. Any statement of equality, $a = b$, is understood as an assertion that the two symbols 'a' and 'b' designate the same thing.

There is a primitive relation $a \in b$ which is defined for the domain $\mathfrak{B}$. If this relation holds for two particular things a and b, we say that b is a *set* (*Menge*) and that a is an *element* of this set. Thus some, but not necessarily all, of the things in $\mathfrak{B}$ are sets. In addition it will be postulated in Axiom II that there is a set without any elements at all.

If M and N are two sets such that, for every x, $x \in M$ implies $x \in N$, we say that M is a *subset* of N. Zermelo expresses this relation between M and N in symbols by writing $M \nsubseteq N$, adopting the notation already used by Schröder in his *Algebra der Logik* (see p. 187, above).

A crucial element in the theory is the concept of *definiteness*, which Zermelo introduces in the following way: 'A question or assertion $\mathfrak{E}$, the validity or invalidity of which is decided without arbitrariness by the basic relations of the domain, by means of the axioms and the universal laws of logic, is said to be "definite" (*definit*). In the same way a predicate (*Klassenaussage*) $\mathfrak{E}(x)$, in which the variable x can run through all the individuals of a class $\mathfrak{K}$, is said to be "definite" if it is definite for *every separate* individual x of the class $\mathfrak{K}$. Thus the question of whether $a \in b$ or not is definite, and likewise the question of whether $M \nsubseteq N$ or not.'

The following seven axioms are taken:

I. Axiom of determination (*Bestimmtheit*). If every element of a set M is at the same time an element of N, and conversely, then $M = N$; in short, every set is determined by its elements.

II. Axiom of elementary sets (*Elementarmengen*). There is an (improper) set, the 'null set' 0, which contains no element at all. If a is any thing of the domain, then there exists a set $\{a\}$ which contains a and only a as an element; and if a and b are any two things of the domain, then there exists a set $\{a,b\}$ which contains both a and b as elements, but no thing x that is distinct from both a and b.

III. Axiom of separating out (*Aussonderung*). If the predicate $\mathfrak{E}(x)$ is definite for all the elements of a set M, then M has a subset $M_{\mathfrak{E}}$ which contains as its elements all those elements x of M for which $\mathfrak{E}(x)$ is true, and only such elements.

IV. Axiom of the power set (*Potenzmenge*). To every set T there corresponds a second set $\mathfrak{U}T$ (the 'power set' of T) which contains as elements all the subsets of T, and only these.

V. Axiom of the union (*Vereinigung*). To every set T there corresponds a set $\mathfrak{S}T$ (the 'union set' of T) which contains as elements all the elements of the elements of T, and only these.

VI. Axiom of choice (*Auswahl*). If T is a set, all of whose elements are sets that are distinct from 0 and no two of which have any element in common, then the union set $\mathfrak{S}T$ contains at least one subset S_1 which has one and only one element in common with each element of T.

VII. Axiom of infinity (*Axiom des Unendlichen*). The domain contains at least one set Z which contains the null set as element and which is so constituted that to each of its elements a there corresponds a further element $\{a\}$, or which, with each of its elements a, contains also the corresponding set $\{a\}$ as element.

Axiom III is very much weaker than Cantor's unacceptable principle that every property that can be conceived at all 'creates' in some way a corresponding set. Zermelo's axiom merely asserts that any suitably defined property separates out, *from a set M that must already be given*, a subset of that set; and it does not permit the construction of paradoxical sets with elements defined in terms of the sets themselves. Furthermore, since a definite property is one that is decidable by the basic relations of the domain $\mathfrak{B}$, no such property as that of being definable in a finite number of words can be used in the definition of a set, and the semantic paradoxes are thus also excluded.

Zermelo is able to prove that the domain $\mathfrak{B}$ is not itself a set. For suppose M is any given set. Then, since the property $x \notin x$ is definite, M has a subset M_0 that consists of all those of its elements that are not elements of themselves. But then M_0 is not an element of itself (for, if it were, then M_0 would have an element M_0 with the property $x \in x$); and *a fortiori* M_0 is not an element of M. But M_0 is certainly in $\mathfrak{B}$, and therefore $\mathfrak{B}$ is not the same as M. Thus $\mathfrak{B}$ cannot coincide with any set at all.

Zermelo's last axiom, the axiom of infinity, guarantees the existence in $\mathfrak{B}$ of a set Z_0 with elements 0, $\{0\}$, $\{\{0\}\}$, ... This set serves to represent the progression 0, 1, 2, . . . of the natural numbers, i.e. the standard denumerably infinite set, in Zermelo's formal system.

The formulation and preliminary discussion of the axioms takes up only a small part of Zermelo's paper, the rest of which is devoted to a detailed discussion of equivalence (i.e. equipotency) of sets. Cantor's theory of cardinal numbers is here shown to follow from the seven axioms that we have just quoted.

The system of Zermelo has provided the basis of all later work on the theory of sets (except for investigations with an intuitionist aim) and most of the changes subsequently made have been of the nature of improvements in the details of the theory. A feature of the original presentation that gave rise to misgiving almost from the outset was the notion of definiteness, which Zermelo had undoubtedly left somewhat vague. He said that an assertion is 'definite' if its truth or falsity is 'decided by the basic relations of the domain $\mathfrak{B}$ by means of the axioms and the universal laws of logic', and he gave as instances of definite assertions $a \in b$ and $M \notin N$. The inadequacy of this discussion of Zermelo's was commented upon by Skolem in a paper entitled 'Einige Bemerkungen zur axiomatischen Begründung der Mengenlehre', read at the Fifth Congress of Scandinavian Mathematicians in 1922. In this paper (to which we shall return below in §7) Skolem pointed out that the concept of definiteness could in fact be made precise in a very natural way, namely by identifying definite assertions with the combinations, formed by means of the logical operators of the propositional calculus and the quantifiers, of atomic constituents of the two forms $a \in b$ and $a = b$.

In a paper of 1925, with the same title as Zermelo's original paper, Abraham Fraenkel elaborated this suggestion of Skolem's with the aid of the notion of 'function', which he defined with reference to sets in the following way:

(a) The power set of x, the union set of x, a pair that depends on x, and also any constant set, are all to be called *functions of x*. A function of a function of x is again called a function of x.

(b) Let $\varphi(x)$ and $\psi(x)$ be given functions of x, and let $\circ$ be one of the primitive symbols $=$, $\neq$, $\in$, $\notin$. Then, if m and m' are sets such that the elements of m' are precisely the elements y of m for which the relation $\varphi(y) \circ \psi(y)$ holds, m' is said to be an *Aussonderungsmenge* of m that is determined by $\varphi \circ \psi$, in symbols: $m' = m_{\varphi(y) \circ \psi(y)}$.

(c) If $m' = m_{\varphi(y) \circ \psi(y)}$, and if m is a function of the indeterminate x or if the indeterminate x is involved in the functions φ and ψ (apart from the auxiliary variable y), then m' (as dependent in general on x) is said to be a function of x.

Fraenkel went on to formulate the *Aussonderungsaxiom* (Zermelo's Axiom III) in the following modified form: If m is any set, $\varphi(x)$ and $\psi(x)$ are any two functions, and $\circ$ denotes one of the primitive relations $=$, $\neq$, $\in$, $\notin$, then there exists the *Aussonderungsmenge* $m_{\varphi(y) \circ \psi(y)}$.

The Fraenkel-Skolem treatment of definiteness, which has now become part of the standard theory of sets, may reasonably be held to fulfil Zermelo's original intention; but Zermelo himself did not accept it, on the ground that, being essentially inductive, it made the theory of sets depend on properties of the natural numbers, which ought only to be introduced at a later stage.

Besides giving greater precision to the notion of definiteness, Fraenkel also made Zermelo's theory more formal in other ways. Thus whereas Zermelo had chosen to interpret the relation $a = b$ semantically, as meaning that a and b designate the same 'thing', Fraenkel preferred to treat '$=$' as a primitive constant, with a similar status in the system to '$\in$'. He also took the step of dispensing altogether with the notion of a domain $\mathfrak{B}$ of 'things', of which some but not necessarily all are sets. Instead he simply postulated one basic domain of sets, which was to function as a 'domain of individuals' for his axiomatic theory. Such a wholly abstract theory of sets and relations between sets is indeed sufficient for all mathematical purposes, and no provision need be made in the system for elements that are not themselves sets (*Urelemente*, in the terminology of Zermelo).

Now although Zermelo's original axiomatization of the theory of sets provides an adequate basis for a rigorous development of the various modes of argument used by Cantor in his transfinite arithmetic, the axioms are only able to guarantee the existence of cardinal numbers that are not too large; and so, in a paper[1] of 1922, Fraenkel proposed the introduction of a further axiom. As he pointed out, Zermelo's Axiom VII affirms the existence of the infinite set Z_0 with elements $0, \{0\}, \{\{0\}\}, \ldots$, and Axiom IV then yields in turn the sets $Z_1 = \mathfrak{U}Z_0$, $Z_2 = \mathfrak{U}Z_1, \ldots$, with greater and greater cardinal numbers; but there is nothing in the original axioms to guarantee the existence of a set which is the union of all the sets $Z_0, Z_1, Z_2, \ldots$. The new axiom that Fraenkel proposed was the following axiom of replacement (*Ersetzung*):

If M is a set, and if every element of M is replaced by a 'thing of the domain $\mathfrak{B}$', then M becomes again a set.

In this formulation of his new axiom (which he proposed before he reconsidered the theory of sets as a whole) Fraenkel was still thinking in terms of Zermelo's domain of 'things', but this was in no way essential to the main idea, and the axiom of replacement came in due course to be adopted as one of the standard axioms of the theory of sets. The original axioms of Zermelo, as amended by Fraenkel, are now usually referred to as the 'Zermelo-Fraenkel axioms' for the theory of sets.

A curious feature of Zermelo's system, which was pointed out in 1917 by Mirimanoff, is that the axioms permit the existence of 'extraordinary sets', or sets which give rise to an infinite descending chain of relations of membership. A set a is *extraordinary* if there is a sequence of sets $a_1, a_2, a_3, \ldots$ such that $a_1 \in a$, $a_2 \in a_1$, $a_3 \in a_2, \ldots$. Sets with this property are plainly anomalous, and it is desirable that the axioms should make their occurrence in the formal system impossible. The

[1] A. Fraenkel: 'Zu den Grundlagen der Cantor-Zermeloschen Mengenlehre', *Math. Ann.*, **86** (1922), 230–237.

standard way of excluding them is by means of the following 'axiom of foundation' (*Fundierung*), which was proposed for this purpose by von Neumann:

Every non-empty set *s* contains an element *t* such that *s* and *t* have no element in common.

Von Neumann's contribution to the theory of sets extends far beyond the introduction of this additional axiom, however, and we must now consider his innovations in detail.

4   Von Neumann's new approach to the theory of sets

Johann (afterwards John) von Neumann was born at Budapest in 1903, and he died at Washington in 1957.   His range of interests within mathematics was wide, and it included, in particular, the theory of sets, the mathematical foundations of quantum mechanics, the design of computers, and the theory of games (see Note 2, p. 354).   His first major mathematical undertaking was to reconsider the Zermelo-Fraenkel treatment of sets, which we have just been discussing in §3. He did this in his doctoral dissertation (Budapest, 1925) on the axiomatic construction of the general theory of sets.   The dissertation was written in Hungarian, but von Neumann published the substance of it in German, in two important papers: (i) 'Eine Axiomatisierung der Mengenlehre' (*J. reine angew. Math.*, **154** (1925), 219–240); (ii) 'Die Axiomatisirung der Mengenlehre' (*Math. Z.*, **27** (1928), 669–752). In the first paper he gave the system of axioms on which he based his treatment of sets, with a brief explanation of the reasons why he had taken the axioms in this particular form; and he also discussed in general terms the question of whether any axiomatic characterization of the theory of sets can be categorical (i.e. such that all its realizations are isomorphic).   In the second paper he showed in detail how the theory of sets can be deduced from his axioms.

Von Neumann's treatment of sets is a generalization of the Zermelo-Fraenkel treatment, in which this older theory is substantially retained, though in a modified form.   At first sight the new axioms look very different from the old ones, but this is mainly the result of a change in the language adopted.   When notions belonging to the theory of sets are used in mathematics there are two possible languages in which they may be expressed—the language of sets and their members, and the language of functions and their arguments; and the two are equivalent, since any function can be interpreted as a set of ordered pairs and any set can be specified with the aid of a characteristic function.   The language preferred by Zermelo was that of sets; but the idea of function was already implicit in Zermelo's notion of *Aussonderung*, and in Fraenkel's improved theory it became fully explicit.   Von Neumann's choice of language is the opposite one to Zermelo's, and he states his axioms from the outset in terms of arguments and functions.

The more fundamental difference between the Zermelo-Fraenkel and von Neumann systems, however, is not one of language, but rather of the means adopted to exclude the paradoxes that occur in the naive theory of sets. This was done in the Zermelo-Fraenkel system by limiting the available means of set-formation to those which are indispensable for mathematical purposes. But, in von Neumann's view, the limitations imposed in this way are unnecessarily severe, and they deprive mathematicians of modes of argument that are sometimes useful and that in any case seem free from vicious circularity. He therefore takes the step of making provision both for sets in the strict Zermelo-Fraenkel sense and also for totalities in a wider sense, rather nearer to that of the principle of comprehension, while at the same time eliminating all danger from vicious circles by allowing the wider totalities to have members but disqualifying certain of them from being themselves members of other totalities. The paradoxes, it seems, can only arise from 'over-large' totalities—or more precisely, from totalities which can be mapped on the entire universe of sets—and it is such totalities that von Neumann excludes from membership. Whereas Fraenkel's system is based on a single postulated domain of sets, therefore, von Neumann's presupposes two overlapping domains. Or rather, since the language is in fact that of functions, von Neumann postulates a domain of arguments and also a domain of functions, the two intersecting in a domain of argument-functions.

If x is a function and y is an argument, von Neumann denotes 'the value of the function x for the argument y' (i.e. the functional value $x(y)$ in ordinary mathematical notation) by $[x \; y]$. In order to be able to represent totalities in his system by means of characteristic functions, he postulates two constant arguments A and B, and he then calls a function a a 'domain' (*Bereich*) if it is such that, for any argument x whatever, either $[a \; x] = A$ or $[a \; x] = B$. Such a function is to correspond intuitively to the totality of all those arguments x for which $[a \; x] \neq A$, i.e. for which $[a \; x]$ has the value B. If a domain, in this special sense, is not merely a function with the property just specified, but an argument-function with this property, von Neumann calls it a set (*Menge*).

Drawing a distinction between functions and argument-functions, then, is von Neumann's way of securing his theory against paradoxes such as those of Russell and Burali-Forti. By working with an axiomatic theory of sets (or rather functions), instead of with a logistic system, like *Principia Mathematica*, in which all mathematical notions are defined in terms of a few primitive ideas that belong to logic, he avoids the necessity for a full theory of types and is able to manage with a much simpler stratification of his entities into two interpenetrating layers. The axiom by which he prevents functions that would define over-large totalities from being arguments states that a function a fails to be an argument-function if and only if there is a function b (in the domain of functions postulated by the theory) such that, for every argument x, there exists an argument y for which $[a \ y] \neq A$ and $[b \ y] = x$. This is a way of expressing formally the condition for b to yield a mapping, on to the whole universe of arguments, of those arguments such that $[a \ y] \neq A$, i.e. of the 'domain' a, if a is in fact a domain.

Von Neumann's axiom of exclusion IV, 2, which we have just quoted, is an extremely powerful principle, and from it Zermelo's axiom of *Aussonderung* and Fraenkel's axiom of replacement are both derivable. A further consequence of the axiom is the theorem that every set can be well-ordered, which can be proved in von Neumann's system without appeal to the axiom of choice.

In the formal presentation of his theory, von Neumann drops the use of the terms 'argument', 'function', and 'argument-function', using instead a neutral terminology of 'I. thing', 'II. thing', and 'I. II. thing' (*I. Ding*, etc.).

Since the theory is in the first instance a theory of functions and not of sets, a special symbol (x,y) has to be provided for the ordered pair of two I. things x and y, the convenient representation $\{\{x\},\{x,y\}\}$ of Kuratowski not being available in these circumstances. In this and other ways the treatment of sets by means of functions is slightly awkward, and at times artificial; and one of the aims of more recent research into the theory of sets has been to take advantage of the very substantial improvements made by von Neumann, while at the same time returning as closely as possible to the more natural point of view of Cantor. This intention has been very largely realized in the system of Bernays, to which we turn next.

5 Bernays's unification of symbolic logic and the theory of sets

In §1 of the present chapter we said that mathematics is conceived nowadays as a study of abstract structure, the natural basis of which is the theory of sets; and we then went on to show how Zermelo took a decisive initiative in attempting to rehabilitate the theory of sets as a strictly mathematical theory, after it had been seriously discredited in the realm of logic by the discovery of the vicious-circle paradoxes. We have now followed the movement inaugurated by Zermelo as far as von Neumann's construction of an abstract theory of sets that is indeed complete and powerful enough to serve as basis for a fully rigorous treatment of the whole of pure mathematics. Once this much had been achieved, the most pressing task that had to be undertaken was that of bringing the Zermelo-Fraenkel-von Neumann axioms for sets into closer relation with the formalization of mathematical logic that was already in existence. This crucial task has now been carried through by Bernays, first of all in a series of articles in the *Journal of Symbolic Logic*, extending over the years from 1937 to 1954, and then in his book *Axiomatic Set Theory* (Amsterdam, 1958), which embodies a revised version of the complete system. In this book is thus offered a system of logic (in rather a wide sense) that is expressly designed to meet the needs of the working mathematician, no less than those of the metamathematician.

By far the greater part of the work on foundations of mathematics that we have discussed in earlier chapters has been primarily philosophical in inspiration, being intended to answer theoretical questions about mathematics rather than actually to produce an improved system of mathematics itself. The original aim of Peano, of course, had been to make ordinary mathematics rigorous by presenting it in a strictly formal manner, and Hilbert's early examination of the foundations of geometry was prompted by a similar motive; but the limited initial objective in the study of the foundations of mathematics was quickly lost to sight when it became apparent that the specifically mathematical part of this study could not be isolated from much wider philosophical issues, on which a definite stand had first to be taken. The result was that Russell's *Principia Mathematica* and Hilbert's metamathematical investigations, and equally the various intuitionist and constructivist undertakings that we have been examining, were concerned less with helping the working mathematician to attain the rigour that he seeks in the actual presentation of mathematical theories than with answering fundamental questions that arise in the realm of philosophy of mathematics. In recent years, however, mathematical and metamathematical inquiries have been found to converge, and now at last the working mathematician and the metamathematician or logician are able to re-establish contact. On the one hand, mathematics has become so abstract and so highly formalized that the techniques of symbolic logic are often indispensable to it; and on the other hand, research in logic has been carried so far that logicians are now able to provide the very tools that are needed by mathematicians.

There are now available two distinct logical instruments which appear to be sufficiently powerful for the formal handling of mathematics—namely the extended calculus of predicates with the simple theory of types, and the restricted calculus of predicates taken in conjunction with an axiomatic theory of sets—and there is, moreover, a close formal connexion between these instruments.

The extended calculus of predicates, which we have already referred to briefly in Chapter 4, §6, is discussed by Hilbert and Ackermann in the concluding sections of their book; and a somewhat different though related logical system has been developed by Quine in his *Mathematical Logic* (1940; revised 1951). When symbolic logic is taken as the sole basis of mathematics, a logical instrument that is definitely more powerful than the restricted calculus of predicates is essential. Bound predicate variables (or some logical equivalent of them) cannot be entirely avoided; and some form of separation of types is accordingly forced upon us if vicious-circle fallacies are to be rendered impossible. The full hierarchy of types, however, is unquestionably an encumbrance in mathematics, and so the alternative kind of logical system, in which the restricted calculus of predicates is reinforced by an axiomatic treatment of sets, is more acceptable to mathematicians. In such a system no attention need be paid to the finer differences of type, since, as we have already seen in §4, a simple distinction between two kinds of entities is sufficient to exclude vicious circularity. The particular system of Bernays, which we are about to discuss, has been devised with the needs of mathematics all the time in view, and in it the restricted calculus of predicates and the axioms of the theory of sets supplement each other in a particularly satisfactory way.

Bernays, like Zermelo and Fraenkel, treats sets in a strictly mathematical manner, simply postulating them, together with their basic properties, as primitive, without making any attempt to derive them from still more basic ideas of logic. At the same time, however, he does not exclude altogether from his system the notion of the extension of a predicate. Adopting in a slightly modified form von Neumann's distinction between I. things and II. things, Bernays works with both 'sets' and 'classes'. Sets, which are denoted by small Latin letters, are the essential entities of the theory—the 'individuals', in the sense in which this word is used in the phrase 'domain of individuals' (cf. p. 63 above)—whereas classes, denoted by capital Latin letters, are ideal entities, which we might perhaps liken in this respect to points at infinity in the geometry of the extended euclidean plane. A set, interpreted intuitively, is an aggregate, while a class is the extension of a predicate. For any two sets a and b, either $a \in b$ or $a \notin b$; and for any set a and any class $\mathfrak{B}$, either $a \in \mathfrak{B}$ or $a \notin \mathfrak{B}$, according as a does or does not have the property expressed in the defining predicate of $\mathfrak{B}$. But no *class* can ever be considered as a possible member, either of a set or of a class, and combinations of symbols of the form $\mathfrak{A} \in b$ or $\mathfrak{A} \in \mathfrak{B}$ are inadmissible, i.e. they are not well-formed formulae of the system that Bernays sets up.

It will be seen from this informal explanation[1] that Bernays's sets

---

[1] Here, as at various other places in this book, we have given a very loose explanation of what is primarily a formal theory, with the aim of directing the reader's attention towards those salient features which may prove especially useful as landmarks while

and classes correspond more or less to von Neumann's I. things and II. things. There are, strictly speaking, no analogues of the I. II. things in Bernays's system, since sets and classes are entities of essentially different kinds; but a set a and a class $\mathfrak{A}$ may have exactly the same members, and when this is so the class is said to be *represented* by the set. A class and a set that represents it behave together very much like a I. II. thing.

Bernays opens the formal presentation of his system by specifying the logical calculus on which it is based. First of all he introduces syntactically the restricted calculus of predicates, doing this in the manner that we have already described in Chapter 3, except that he now prefers to dispense altogether with the rule of relabelling. He avoids this rule by formulating his axioms and rules of derivation in terms of syntactic variables (i.e. small and large German letters) instead of in terms of the variables of the system itself.

The ι-symbol is used in the system, but with a certain modification that allows an ι-term to be formed from any predicate whatever, whether the associated uniqueness formulae have been derived or not (cf. p. 93 and p. 100, footnote). This change has the important effect of making the definition of (well-formed) ι-term purely syntactic, since the eligibility of ι-expressions as terms is now no longer dependent on what formulae have previously been derived. The device which Bernays uses to achieve this end depends on the introduction of a constant symbol a. The earlier type of ι-term $\iota_\mathfrak{x}\mathfrak{A}(\mathfrak{x})$ is replaced by $\iota_\mathfrak{x}(\mathfrak{A}(\mathfrak{x}),a)$, this new expression being defined syntactically in such a way that it has the intuitive interpretation 'the set with the property $\mathfrak{A}$ if there is one and only one such set, and the constant set a otherwise'. If the uniqueness formulae for $\mathfrak{A}(\mathfrak{x})$ can be derived, then $\iota_\mathfrak{x}(\mathfrak{A}(\mathfrak{x}),a)$ behaves in exactly the same way as the former $\iota_\mathfrak{x}\mathfrak{A}(\mathfrak{x})$; and thus the earlier theory of the ι-symbol still continues to apply.

Of the well-formed symbolic expressions, some are terms and some are formulae, and these two categories can be defined syntactically by simultaneous recursion. The terms, furthermore, can be either set-terms or class-terms; and a term may only be substituted for a free variable of the appropriate kind. Any formula $\mathfrak{A}(\mathfrak{x})$ that contains a free variable $\mathfrak{x}$ gives rise to a class-term $\{\mathfrak{x} \,|\, \mathfrak{A}(\mathfrak{x})\}$.

The relation of *identity*, $a = b$, is taken as primitive (cf. Fraenkel's usage, referred to on p. 291), and it always connects two *set*-terms. For class-terms there is a corresponding equivalence relation $A \equiv B$, but since classes are treated simply as extensions of predicates, this

---

the theory is still unfamiliar to him. It will be observed that in the present instance we have even disregarded, for this purpose, the basic distinction between variables and particular entities.

relation can be defined explicitly in terms of the logical relation of bi-implication, thus:

$$A \equiv B \leftrightarrow (x)(x \in A \leftrightarrow x \in B).$$

The only primitive atomic formulae that occur in the system are those of the three forms $\mathfrak{a} = \mathfrak{b}$, $\mathfrak{a} \in \mathfrak{b}$, and $\mathfrak{a} \in \mathfrak{K}$, where $\mathfrak{a}$ and $\mathfrak{b}$ are set-terms and $\mathfrak{K}$ is a class-term.

For class-terms we have *Church's schema*:

$$c \in \{\mathfrak{x} \mid \mathfrak{A}(\mathfrak{x})\} \leftrightarrow \mathfrak{A}(c).$$

This schema formalizes directly the principle of comprehension (cf. p. 285), but only allows it to be applied to classes, not to sets.

The axioms are introduced by stages, with the object of bringing out as clearly as possible their specific import. First we have the axioms of equality and extensionality:

E 1 $a = b \rightarrow (a \in A \rightarrow b \in A),$

E 2 $(x)(x \in a \leftrightarrow x \in b) \rightarrow a = b.$

If $\mathfrak{A}(x)$ is any predicate, we can derive the formula

$$a = b \rightarrow (\mathfrak{A}(a) \rightarrow \mathfrak{A}(b))$$

from E 1 with the aid of Church's schema, and in this way the second axiom of identity (J_2) of Hilbert and Bernays is effectively contained in the present system. The axiom (J_1) is no longer needed as a separate axiom, for the formula $a = a$ is immediately derivable from E 2. Thus we see that the logic on which Bernays's system is based is the restricted calculus of predicates, extended by the standard treatment of identity and descriptions.

The main connective in the formula E 2 is a simple implication, not a bi-implication; but the stronger formula

$$a = b \leftrightarrow (x)(x \in a \leftrightarrow x \in b)$$

is derivable, and it gives formal expression to the principle of extensionality, that is to say the principle that a set is uniquely determined by its membership. This is the principle that was taken by Zermelo and Fraenkel as their axiom of determination (*Bestimmtheit*).

Although only sets behave as 'individuals', and classes are treated as ideal entities, we can nevertheless build up a full algebra of classes in the formal system. We have already defined the relation of equivalence $A \equiv B$; and if we now define the complement of A and the union and intersection of A and B by putting

I, Df 3.3 $\overline{A} \equiv \{x \mid x \notin A\},$

I, Df 3.4 $A \cup B \equiv \{x \mid x \in A \lor x \in B\},$

I, Df 3.5 $A \cap B \equiv \{x \mid x \in A \ \& \ x \in B\},$

and the universal class and the empty class by putting

I, Df 3.6 $V \equiv \{x \mid x = x\}$

and

I, Df 3.7 $\Lambda \equiv \{x \mid x \neq x\}$,

we can at once develop formally the familiar boolean algebra of classes.

The very important concept of representability of a class by a set (see p. 297 above) is expressed in the formal system by the following definitions:

I, Df 4.5 $\mathrm{Rp}(A,a) \leftrightarrow (x)(x \in A \leftrightarrow x \in a)$,

I, Df 4.6 $\mathrm{Rp}(A) \leftrightarrow (Ex)(\mathrm{Rp}(A,x))$.

Passing now from these logical preliminaries to the theory of sets proper, we begin with the following three axioms:

A 1 $a \notin 0$,

A 2 $a \in b\,;c \leftrightarrow (a \in b \vee a = c)$,

A 3 $a \in \sum_{\mathfrak{x}} (\mathfrak{m},\mathfrak{t}(\mathfrak{x})) \leftrightarrow (E\mathfrak{x})(\mathfrak{x} \in \mathfrak{m}\ \&\ a \in \mathfrak{t}(\mathfrak{x}))$.

These axioms involve certain constant symbols (primitive symbols of the system) whose use can best be followed if we bear in mind their intuitive interpretation. 0 corresponds to the null set, $\mathfrak{b}\,;\mathfrak{c}$ to the union $\mathfrak{b} \cup \{\mathfrak{c}\}$ of the two sets $\mathfrak{b}$ and $\{\mathfrak{c}\}$, i.e. the set obtained by adding the further element $\mathfrak{c}$ to the existing elements of $\mathfrak{b}$, and $\sum_{\mathfrak{x}} (\mathfrak{m},\mathfrak{t}(\mathfrak{x}))$ to the union $\bigcup_{\mathfrak{x} \in \mathfrak{m}} \mathfrak{t}(\mathfrak{x})$, where $\mathfrak{t}(\mathfrak{x})$ is a set which depends on $\mathfrak{x}$.

It will be observed that Bernays does not state his axioms in the existential form $(Ex)(a \notin x)$, etc., which might be thought more natural, but instead he takes each time a new primitive symbol. In this way he secures directly axioms which are free from bound variables, without having to resort to the process of symbolic resolution, as would otherwise be necessary (cf. Chapter 4, §4.1, above).

The unit set $[a]$, the unordered pair $[a,b]$, and the ordered pair $\langle a,b \rangle$ are defined as follows:

II, Df 1.1 $[a] = 0\,;a$,

II, Df 1.2 $[a,b] = [a]\,;b$,

II, Df 1.3 $\langle a,b \rangle = [[a], [a,b]]$.

No *Aussonderungsaxiom* is needed in this system, since there is a derivable schema (II, 2.5) which formalizes the assertion that, for any set b and any predicate $\mathfrak{A}(x)$, there is a set that consists of all the elements a of b that satisfy $\mathfrak{A}(a)$. Since $\mathfrak{A}(x)$ can only be a predicate that is built up out of the basic constituents of the formal system, this schema effectively implements Skolem's proposal for making precise the notion of a 'definite' predicate (cf. p. 290, above).

An unusual feature of Bernays's treatment of the theory of sets is the early introduction of ordinal numbers, which precedes even the completion of the axiomatic foundation of the system. Bernays defines 'ordinals' without first developing a detailed theory of order, and he does so simply by considering a certain totality of sets which has the same structure as the system of ordinal numbers treated by Cantor, and identifying these sets with the ordinals. He is here adapting to his system one of the standard ways of constructing a theory of ordinals, which is to identify the finite ordinals 0, 1, 2, 3, . . . with the sets 0, {0}, {0,{0}}, {0,{0},{0,{0}}}, . . . , the ordinal ω with the union of all these sets, and so on, as described by Fraenkel in his *Abstract Set Theory* (p. 278). For any pair of distinct ordinals, as so defined, just one of the two is a member of the other, and so we have a natural ordering of the ordinals. Furthermore, every ordinal is the union of all the ordinals that precede it in the natural order.

It is this treatment of ordinals that is formalized by Bernays. 0 is, as usual, the null set. Every ordinal c has a *successor* c', defined as $c ; c$, and every set m of ordinals has a *sequent*, the ordinal $\sum m = \sum_{\mathfrak{x}} (m, \mathfrak{x})$. It will be seen that the three essential constituents of this treatment of the theory of ordinals—that is to say the initial ordinal 0, the successor of any particular ordinal, and the sequent of any set of ordinals—are provided for in the axioms A 1, A 2, and A 3 respectively. The resulting formal theory, moreover, may be seen as a natural extension into the transfinite of Peano's theory of the natural numbers.

Every ordinal is either a *successor number*, like $1 = 0'$ and $\omega + 1 = \omega'$, or else a *limit number*, like ω. Formally we have the definitions

III,   Df 2.2 $\mathrm{Suc}(c) \leftrightarrow (Ex)(\mathrm{Od}(x) \ \& \ x' = c)$

and

III,   Df 2.3 $\mathrm{Lim}(c) \leftrightarrow \mathrm{Od}(c) \ \& \ c \neq 0 \ \& \ (x)(x \in c \to x' \in c)$,

where '$\mathrm{Od}(c)$' means 'c is an ordinal'.

It can be proved by formal derivation that every non-empty class of ordinals has a lowest element (III, 1.12), that is to say that the natural ordering of the ordinals is a well-ordering. That being so, we have a *principle of transfinite induction* for the ordinals which provides a generalization of the ordinary principle of mathematical induction for the natural numbers. This new principle is embodied in the following derivable schema (III, 1.17):

$$(\mathfrak{x})((\mathrm{Od}(\mathfrak{x}) \ \& \ (\mathfrak{z})(\mathfrak{z} \in \mathfrak{x} \to \mathfrak{A}(\mathfrak{z}))) \to \mathfrak{A}(\mathfrak{x})) \to (\mathrm{Od}(c) \to \mathfrak{A}(c)).$$

A corresponding constructive procedure of *transfinite recursion* is also available, which extends to all ordinals the arithmetical procedure of recursive definition (see Bernays, Chapter IV).

A separate treatment of finite arithmetic, say on the lines laid down by Hilbert and Bernays in *Grundlagen der Mathematik*, is now no longer required, since the natural numbers may be identified with the finite ordinals. When this is done, proof by mathematical induction (or 'numeral induction', as Bernays now felicitously calls it) and definition by primitive recursion become merely special cases of the corresponding transfinite procedures.

The whole development of the theory of sets that we have outlined so far is based exclusively on the logical calculus and the five axioms E 1, E 2 (p. 298), and A 1, A 2, A 3 (p. 299). For the completion of the theory—which we shall not go into here—three more axioms are required. These further axioms, which deviate from the corresponding axioms in Zermelo's original system only in the manner of their formulation, are the axiom of potency (i.e. the axiom of the power set) A 4, the axiom of choice A 5, and the axiom of infinity A 6. In addition the *Fundierungsaxiom* may be added as a further axiom A 7, although it is not involved in the main development of the theory.

6 The theory of sets in Bourbaki's 'Éléments de Mathématique'

In Bernays's logico-mathematical treatment of the theory of sets we have the culmination of the efforts of mathematical logicians to devise a logical instrument capable of handling the full complexity of modern mathematics with rigour and clarity. From the early beginnings of symbolic logic in Frege's *Begriffsschrift* and Peano's *Formulaire* to the elaborate edifice of *Principia Mathematica*, and then by way of the strictly syntactic treatment of the restricted calculus of predicates and its extensions in Hilbert and Ackermann's *Grundzüge der theoretischen Logik* and Hilbert and Bernays's *Grundlagen der Mathematik* to the final fusion of the logical calculus with Zermelo's axiomatic theory of sets, the evolution of mathematical logic has passed through several distinct phases, and logic has been progressively enriched by ideas and techniques drawn from a wide variety of sources. And now we are left in the end with a surprisingly simple system, whose simplicity matches that of the mathematical disciplines in which it finds its most natural application.

In recent decades, indeed, mathematics as well as logic has undergone reform, and it is no accident that in Bourbaki's *Éléments de Mathématique*, which is as characteristic of mathematics in its present state as were the earlier *Cours d'Analyse*[1] of mathematics at the time when

---

[1] The tradition of publishing these *Cours d'Analyse* remained alive for a long time and produced a succession of influential works, e.g. C. Jordan: *Cours d'Analyse de l'École Polytechnique* (Paris, 1882), and Ch. J. de la Vallée Poussin: *Cours d'Analyse Infinitésimale* (Louvain, 1906).

it was still dominated by analysis, modern logic and modern mathematics are entirely complementary. The *Éléments* opens, as we indicated at the beginning of the present chapter, with a volume devoted to the *théorie des ensembles*; and the early sections of this volume contain a unified system of logic and theory of sets which is in many ways similar, in outlook no less than in content, to the system devised by Bernays. We have already described Bourbaki's logical calculus in Chapter 4, §7, and so all that now remains is for us to indicate very briefly the nature of his approach to the theory of sets.

Unlike Bernays, Bourbaki does not introduce any formalism for classes, and in his system all terms are set-terms. This is not a fundamental difference between the two treatments, however, since, by virtue of Church's schema, classes serve only to provide an alternative way of making statements that involve predicates. Where Bernays says that a class A is 'represented' by a set a, Bourbaki says that a predicate $R(x)$—or in his terminology a *relation*—is *collectivisante*. We can express the definition of *relation collectivisante* in our symbolism by writing

$$\text{Coll}_x R(x) \leftrightarrow (Ey)(x)(x \in y \leftrightarrow R(x)).$$

Bourbaki takes five axioms for sets, which we may write as follows:

A 1 $(x)(y)((x \subset y \ \& \ y \subset x) \to x = y)$,

A 2 $(x)(y)\text{Coll}_z(z = x \lor z = y)$,

A 3 $(x)(u)(y)(v)[(x,y) = (u,v) \to (x = u \ \& \ y = v)]$,

A 4 $(x)\text{Coll}_y(y \subset x)$,

A 5   There exists an infinite set.

A 1 is the axiom of determination or extension, A 2 the axiom of elementary sets, A 4 the axiom of the power set, and A 5 the axiom of infinity. A 3 serves to introduce axiomatically the ordered pair (x,y).

In addition to the axioms there is the powerful schema S 8, called by Bourbaki the *schéma de sélection et réunion*, which we may translate into our symbolism as follows:

$$(\mathfrak{y})(E\mathfrak{v})(\mathfrak{x})(\mathfrak{R}(\mathfrak{x},\mathfrak{y}) \to \mathfrak{x} \in \mathfrak{v}) \to (\mathfrak{w})(E\mathfrak{z})(\mathfrak{x})[(E\mathfrak{y})(\mathfrak{y} \in \mathfrak{w} \ \& \ \mathfrak{R}(\mathfrak{x},\mathfrak{y})) \leftrightarrow \mathfrak{x} \in \mathfrak{z}].$$

If we use the notation of *Principia Mathematica* for relations (see p. 172) we can write this schema more succinctly in the form

$$(\mathfrak{y})(E\mathfrak{v})(\overrightarrow{\mathfrak{R}}`\mathfrak{y} \subset \mathfrak{v}) \to (\mathfrak{w})(E\mathfrak{z})(\mathfrak{R}``\mathfrak{w} = \mathfrak{z}).$$

As we now show, Bourbaki's schema effectively absorbs Zermelo's *Aussonderungsaxiom* and his axiom of the union (see p. 288), as well as Fraenkel's axiom of replacement (see p. 291).

(i) Let $R(x,y)$ be independent of y, so that it can be written as $R(x)$. Then the schema justifies the assertion

$$(Ev)(x)(R(x) \rightarrow x \in v) \rightarrow (w)(Ez)(x)[((Ey)(y \in w) \text{ \& } R(x)) \leftrightarrow x \in z].$$

From this we can infer

$$(Ev)(x)(R(x) \rightarrow x \in v) \rightarrow (Ez)(x)[((Ey)(y \in \alpha) \text{ \& } R(x)) \leftrightarrow x \in z],$$

where α is any constant set. If, now, we take some particular non-empty set for α, we get

$$(Ev)(x)(R(x) \rightarrow x \in v) \rightarrow (Ez)(x)(R(x) \leftrightarrow x \in z).$$

This at once yields the *Aussonderungsaxiom* if we apply it with M as v and $(\mathfrak{E}(x) \text{ \& } x \in M)$ as $R(x)$, in Zermelo's notation.

(ii) To obtain the axiom of the union we need only apply the original schema with $x \in y$ as $\mathfrak{R}(\mathfrak{x},\mathfrak{y})$.

(iii) Finally, let $R(x,y)$ be a relation such that there is one and only one x that corresponds to any y. The left-hand side of the implication yielded by Bourbaki's schema is then true, since $(y)(\vec{R}^{\iota}y = \iota^{\iota}R^{\iota}y)$. The right-hand side is therefore true also; and thus we obtain the axiom of replacement.

Bourbaki does not need to take the axiom of choice as a separate axiom, since its functions are taken over by the τ-operator, i.e. Hilbert's ε-symbol (cf. p. 101, above).

It is plain, even from this brief survey, that Bourbaki fully endorses the view of Bernays, that the appropriate foundation for pure mathematics is a combination of symbolic logic and the axiomatic theory of sets. And so we see that the joint logic of predicates and sets is now very much more than an instrument of theoretical research that working mathematicians often find it convenient to use. It is indeed the very fundament of the greatest mathematical enterprise of the mid-twentieth century.

7 Limitations of the axiomatic treatment of sets

From a strictly mathematical point of view, the axiomatic theory of sets that we have been considering in the last two sections provides an acceptable answer to the demand for a secure foundation for the whole of pure mathematics. Mathematics can, in fact, be erected on this foundation; and although no actual proof has been given of the consistency of the theory of sets, contradictions appear to be ruled out by the logical safeguards incorporated in the system. When the theory of sets is approached from the side of philosophy, however, the axiomatic treatment is seen to leave many questions open.

A number of difficulties in Zermelo's original treatment of the theory were pointed out by Skolem in 1922, in a paper that we have already mentioned (see p. 290). Some of Skolem's objections have now been met—as for instance the one relating to the vagueness of the concept of definiteness—but others still point to unsolved problems. We shall mention two of these. The first concerns an apparent circularity in Zermelo's system. The axioms are intended to give precise meaning to the intuitive notion of set; but they refer to a certain postulated 'domain' $\mathfrak{B}$—and what is a domain if not a set? The theory has to be based on an appropriate 'domain of individuals'; but whereas this standard procedure is innocuous in other mathematical situations, where the logical basis of mathematics is in any case taken for granted, it is less obviously so here, where the theory that is being presented axiomatically includes part of this logical basis itself. Indeed, by pointing out this particular difficulty Skolem has drawn attention in a striking way to the importance in formalized theories of the postulated domain of individuals, which is no less a part of the primitive specification than the axioms.

Skolem's other point is one to which he has attached especial importance. He was led to it by a certain metalogical (or metamathematical) antinomy, now known as the *Skolem paradox*. There is a theorem of Löwenheim (cf. p. 78) according to which any well-formed formula of the restricted calculus of predicates that is identically true for some denumerably infinite domain of individuals is identically true for all domains of individuals; and by applying this theorem to the negation $\mathfrak{A}$ of a formula $\mathfrak{A}$, we can at once infer that, if $\mathfrak{A}$ is satisfiable at all, then it is satisfiable with a denumerably infinite domain of individuals. Skolem has generalized this last result and has shown that, subject to appropriate conditions, any formal theory that is realizable at all has a realization with a denumerably infinite domain of individuals. Now this theorem applies, in particular, to Zermelo's theory of sets, and hence if Zermelo's axioms are realizable they can be satisfied for a denumerably infinite domain $\mathfrak{B}$. But, within the Zermelo theory, we can demonstrate the existence of non-denumerable infinite sets, e.g. the set $\mathfrak{U}Z_0$. Thus, in the case of the model just referred to, (i) the domain $\mathfrak{B}$ is denumerable, and yet (ii) $\mathfrak{B}$ has a subset $\mathfrak{U}Z_0$ which is more than denumerable. This is the paradox. The solution which Skolem proposed ran as follows:

'The explanation of this is not hard to find. According to the axiomatic theory, a "set" does not signify an arbitrarily defined comprehension (*Zusammenfassung*); sets are simply things which are linked together by the relations that are expressed in the axioms. And so there is no contradiction if a set M of the domain $\mathfrak{B}$ is non-denumerable in the sense of the axioms; for this means only that, *within* $\mathfrak{B}$, there does not occur any one-one mapping Φ of M on Z_0. In spite of this the possibility remains open of an enumeration of all the things in $\mathfrak{B}$, and hence also the elements of M, by the positive integers; such an enumeration is naturally also a collection of certain pairs; but this collection is not a "set", i.e. it does not occur in the domain $\mathfrak{B}$. It is clear, further, that the set $\mathfrak{U}Z_0$ cannot have arbitrarily definable parts of the set Z_0 as elements. For, since the elements of $\mathfrak{U}Z_0$ are only some of the things of the domain $\mathfrak{B}$, they can be enumerated by the positive integers in the same way as the elements of Zermelo's number series and then a new part of Z_0 can be *defined* in a familiar way; but this is not a set, i.e. it does not belong to $\mathfrak{B}$.'

Skolem thus came to the conclusion that the concept of cardinal number can only be defined, by means of Zermelo's axioms, *relatively to the domain* $\mathfrak{B}$. If there are several realizations of Zermelo's axiomatic theory, with essentially different totalities taking the role of $\mathfrak{B}$, then the defined concept of cardinal number will have different content in the various cases.

This matter of the relativity of cardinal numbers was discussed by von Neumann in the second part of his paper of 1925, to which we have referred on p. 292. Von Neumann examined the possibility that a system Σ' of I. and II. things satisfying his axioms might be a sub-system of another such system Σ, both systems being contained in a more comprehensive system P in which the formal relations between them could be expressed. In such circumstances, Cantor's system of cardinal numbers would be obtainable in Σ and also in Σ'; but two sets with the same cardinal number in Σ could very well have different cardinal numbers in Σ', where less mappings were available—and so von Neumann found himself driven to the conclusion that the concept of cardinal number is in a sense illusory. He interpreted the relativity of cardinal numbers (powers) as a warning that there is a gulf which separates the axiomatic theory of sets from any ideas of a more intuitive kind. Admittedly we are now able to set up axiomatic theories which reproduce in exact detail the formal relations between sets, and 'in them all the known powers occur in their infinite magnitude, greater than any power whatever. But as soon as more delicate instruments of research are used ("higher" systems P) everything dissolves away. Nothing is left of all the powers but those which are finite and denumerable. Only these have real significance; all else is formalist fiction'.

More recently, the same question of whether an axiomatic treatment of the theory of sets can embody non-formal truth has been touched upon by Gödel, in a non-technical commentary on the continuum hypothesis and its wider significance.[1] Gödel makes the point first of all that he looks upon the axiomatic theory of sets as 'a satisfactory foundation of Cantor's set theory in its whole original extent'.

[1] K. Gödel: 'What is Cantor's Continuum Problem?', *Amer. Math. Monthly*, **54** (1947), 515–525.

'It might at first seem that the set theoretical paradoxes would stand in the way . . . but closer examination shows that they cause no trouble at all.   They are a very serious problem, but not for Cantor's set theory. As far as sets occur and are necessary in mathematics (at least in the mathematics of today, including all of Cantor's set theory) they are sets of integers, or of rational numbers (*i.e.* of pairs of integers), or of real numbers (*i.e.* of sets of rational numbers), or of functions of real numbers (*i.e.* of sets of pairs of real numbers), *etc.*; when theorems about all sets (or the existence of sets) in general are asserted, they can always be interpreted without any difficulty to mean that they hold for sets of integers as well as for sets of real numbers, *etc.* (respectively, that there exist either sets of integers, or sets of real numbers, or . . . *etc.*, which have the asserted property).   This concept of set, however, according to which a set is anything obtainable from the integers (or some other well defined objects) by iterated application [i.e. transfinite iteration] of the operation "set of", and not something obtained by dividing the totality of all existing things into two categories, has never led to any antinomy whatsoever; that is, the perfectly "naïve" and uncritical working with this concept of set has so far proved completely self-consistent.'

Having said this, Gödel goes on to discuss the continuum problem and its implications.   This famous problem—that of proving or disproving Cantor's conjecture that $2^{\aleph_0} = \aleph_1$—is extremely difficult, and very little progress has so far been made towards solving it.   One of the few results as yet obtained is Gödel's own theorem to the effect that the hypothesis $2^{\aleph_0} = \aleph_1$ is consistent with the axioms for the theory of sets, provided that these are themselves consistent.   It is quite possible that a proof will also eventually be found for the compatibility of the negation of Cantor's hypothesis with the axioms; and, if this should be the case, the theory of sets will then divide at this point, as geometry divides into euclidean and non-euclidean branches at the axiom of parallels.   This will mean that the existing axioms are not by themselves sufficient to characterize the theory of sets beyond a certain stage.   On this, Gödel makes the following comment:

'Only someone who (like the intuitionist) denies that the concepts and axioms of classical set theory have any meaning (or any well-defined meaning) could be satisfied with such a solution, not someone who believes them to describe some well-determined reality.   For in this reality Cantor's conjecture must be either true or false, and its undecidability from the axioms as known today can only mean that these axioms do not contain a complete description of this reality; and such a belief is by no means chimerical, since it is possible to point out ways in which a decision of the question, even if it is undecidable from the axioms in their present form, might nevertheless be obtained.'

The choice of the axioms for sets, for instance, has repercussions in remote parts of mathematics, 'even in the field of diophantine equations'; and so it would be possible for mathematical grounds to be found for a decision as to the truth of Cantor's hypothesis. There is indeed already a small amount of mathematical evidence which Gödel takes as an indication that the hypothesis is more likely to be false than true.

Gödel believes, then, that there is in some sense an objective reality which mathematicians are seeking to express in the axioms for sets, and that the present axioms only represent that reality in an incomplete way. He thinks it likely that further axioms, at present not even imaginable, will eventually be introduced, thus allowing rather more of the intuitive content of the notion of set to be represented in the formal theory; and he suggests that, if a more completely understood mathematical concept of set is ultimately evolved, this may lead to a solution of certain outstanding mathematical problems, and of the continuum problem in particular.

It appears, then, that the present theory of sets, as formulated by Bernays and Bourbaki, is sufficient for almost all strictly mathematical purposes. There is, however, a disturbing element of arbitrariness in the non-categorical character of its axiomatic basis, and the consequent relativity of the concepts defined with reference to it. Although the insufficiency of this basis is at present philosophical rather than mathematical, it may still have a bearing on mathematical issues, especially this very difficult problem of the continuum. And the very fact that there are such objections which can be raised against the existing theory is an indication that study of the foundations of mathematics still remains an open subject.

SUPPLEMENTARY NOTES ON CHAPTER 11

1. *Historically important papers on the theory of sets*. The successive stages in the evolution of the axiomatic theory of sets are marked by the following papers: Cantor [1], Zermelo [1], Fraenkel [1, 2], von Neumann [1, 2], Bernays [1]. Further important primary sources are Skolem [1], Gödel [4], and Bernays & Fraenkel [1].

See also Ackermann's paper [8] of 1956, and the review of it by Dana Scott in the *Journal of Symbolic Logic*, **23** (1958), 215–216.

2. *Additional reading*. (a) *Textbooks*. The most important single book is Bernays & Fraenkel [1]. Important also is the first volume of Bourbaki [1].

A more elementary textbook on the theory of sets is Suppes [2]; and a chapter on the boolean algebra of classes is included in Birkhoff & MacLane [1]. An excellent book on sets, written in 1914, when the subject was still a branch of mathematics that had not yet attained to independent existence, is Hausdorff [1].

A convenient survey of the main axiomatic treatments that have been proposed for the theory of sets is contained in Wang & McNaughton [1]. Wang's expository article [1] may also be consulted.

(b) *Works with a more general approach.*   Much has been contributed to the theory of sets, and also to the study of its history, by Fraenkel; and both Fraenkel: *Abstract Set Theory* (1953) and Fraenkel & Bar-Hillel: *Foundations of Set Theory* (1958) are of immense value.   Fraenkel's concise account of the Zermelo-Fraenkel axioms for sets which forms the introductory part of Bernays & Fracnkel [1] should also be noted.

Sierpiński [1] is a relatively non-formal account of the theory of sets and transfinite numbers, written by a mathematician who has done much work in this field.

Littlewood [1], a printed version of notes of lectures originally delivered at Cambridge in 1925 to students of mathematics, may be read as a brief introduction to a large subject.

PART III

Philosophy of Mathematics

'Dagegen muß behauptet werden, daß die Wahrheit nicht eine ausgeprägte Münze ist, die fertig gegeben und so angestrichen werden kann.'

G. W. F. Hegel: *Phänomenologie des Geistes*

'Logic considers . . . *quae non debentur rebus secundum se, sed secundum esse quod habent in anima.* That is, logic belongs to psychology, not to metaphysics.'

A. De Morgan: *On the Syllogism, No. III*

Chapter 12

THE EPISTEMOLOGICAL STATUS OF
MATHEMATICS

1 Retrospect

We have now pursued the more formal argument of this book as far as is appropriate in what is essentially an introductory survey of the whole field of mathematical logic and foundations of mathematics, and we turn finally to a consideration of the wider relevance of the ideas and points of view that have already been discussed in detail in earlier chapters.

We began by giving, in the four chapters of Part I, a general account of deductive logic, first in its traditional aristotelian form, and then as it is treated by more modern methods which make extensive use of mathematical symbolism. After that, we devoted the whole of Part II to the study of the foundations of mathematics, and we showed in particular how the techniques of symbolic logic have been applied in a variety of ways to the analysis of mathematical theories, and more especially of arithmetic. Our outlook up to now has been restricted by the necessity for keeping in close touch with the very specialized activity of mathematicians; but in the present concluding Part we shall need to view the whole terrain of mathematics from a vantage point that offers a prospect which is altogether more distant, and corresponding-ly more inclusive. Our final task must be, in fact, to consider mathematics in its relation to knowledge in general, and for this reason we give to Part III the title 'Philosophy of Mathematics'.

Mathematics originates in the mind of any individual, as it doubtless originated historically in the collective life of mankind, with the recog-nition of certain recurrent abstract features in common experience, and the development of processes of counting, measuring, and calculating, by which order can be brought into the manipulation of these features. It *originates* in this manner, indeed; but already at a very early stage it begins to transcend the practical sphere, and its character undergoes a corresponding change. Intellectual curiosity progressively takes charge, despite the fact that practical applications may for long con-tinue to be the main source of interest and may indeed never cease to stimulate the creation of new concepts and new methods. As mathe-matics breaks free from its early dependence on practical utility, its immediate 'significance' is at the same time lost; and the investigations that we have been concerned with in Part II have all been directed towards the goal of discovering what it is that makes 'emancipated' mathematics valid.

From what we have said in that Part, it appears that there are two possible ways of conceiving mathematics: (i) as a totality of deductive 'theories', all of which are grounded in pure logic, and (ii) as an autonomous rational activity, the ultimate source of which is a primordial faculty of 'intuition' (*Anschauung*).

The first way is exemplified in the logistic tradition, which found its most complete fulfilment in Russell's logistic theory of pure mathematics, but which can be traced, as we have seen, much further back— certainly to Dedekind, and perhaps even to Leibniz. An early but fully explicit manifesto of the logistic movement was Dedekind's essay *Was sind und was sollen die Zahlen?* (1888), which we have discussed in Chapter 6, §2; and this was soon followed by the three great systematic attempts to rewrite mathematics, in logical symbolism, as an edifice of entirely abstract assertions, namely Frege's *Grundgesetze der Arithmetik* (1893–1903), Peano's *Formulaire de Mathématique* (1894–1908), and lastly Whitehead and Russell's *Principia Mathematica* (1910–1913), which finally vindicated the logistic claim that pure mathematics can be based on logic alone.

The alternative interpretation of mathematics as an autonomous activity, which is by its nature much more an attitude than a definite thesis, has assumed a variety of different forms. We have met it in Hilbert's attempt to justify mathematics, as this is already known to mathematicians, by formalizing it and then establishing the consistency of the resulting formal system by finitary argument. And we have met it also in Brouwer's rejection of classical logic and his proposed reconstruction of mathematics in accordance with intuitionist principles. Besides Brouwer himself, moreover, there have been a number of other mathematicians whose attitudes towards mathematics, though differing considerably among themselves, may all be described in a general way as intuitionist.

2   The logistic conception of mathematics

The two general conceptions of mathematics that we have just distinguished correspond to basically different philosophical attitudes, and we shall now consider them separately in order to see what the nature of the underlying philosophy is in each case. We begin, in the present section, with the logistic conception. What is chiefly characteristic of the logistic attitude is its uncompromising insistence that mathematics must be based on logic alone, and that all appeal to intuition must be rigorously excluded from it. We have already seen this demand taking shape in the mind of Dedekind.   In his essay of 1872, *Stetigkeit und irrationale Zahlen*, Dedekind set out to show, as we have seen in Chapter 5, §4, that the infinitesimal calculus can be made purely arithmetical and freed entirely from dependence on geometrical evidence.   And then afterwards, in *Was sind und was sollen die Zahlen?* (1888), he took the further step of attempting a 'purely logical construction of the science of numbers' (cf. p. 158).   Here, then, was the first foreshadowing of what was ultimately to take definite shape in the mature logistic theory of *Principia Mathematica*.   As yet, however, only the first sketch had been drawn ; and when, five years later, Frege published the first volume of his *Grundgesetze der Arithmetik*—a work in which he undertook the immense task of carrying out in full the project that Dedekind had already attempted in his more summary fashion—he made the following observation :

'My purpose necessitates many deviations from customary mathematical usage.   The rigour that is demanded in argumentation leads unavoidably to an increase in length.   Anyone who does not keep this in mind will be surprised at the minuteness with which proofs are often given of theorems which he thinks he can apprehend immediately in a single cognitive act.   This is particularly striking if we compare Herr Dedekind's essay *Was sind und was sollen die Zahlen?*—the most profound work on the foundation of arithmetic that has come to my notice in recent times.   In a much smaller compass, that essay follows out the laws of arithmetic considerably further than is done here.   Such brevity is only attained, to be sure, because there is much that is not proved in the full sense.   Herr Dedekind often says merely that the proof follows from such and such theorems ; he uses dots as in "$\mathfrak{M}(A,B,C, \ldots)$" ; nowhere is there to be found a catalogue of the logical or other laws on which he takes his stand, and if there were such a catalogue we would have no means of testing whether other laws might not have been applied ; for this would only be possible if the proofs were not merely indicated but carried out in full detail.   Also Herr Dedekind is of the opinion that the theory of numbers is a part of logic ; but his essay does little to confirm this opinion, since the expressions "system" and "a thing belongs to a thing" that he employs are not customary in logic and cannot be reduced to what is generally acknowledged as logical.   I do not say this by way of reproach ; for his manner of proceeding may have been the most appropriate for his purpose ; I say it simply in order to put my own intention in a clearer light by contrast.'   (Preface, p. VII.)

Dedekind had shown, arguing much as a very careful mathematician might be expected to argue, that arithmetic is reducible to logic ; and now Frege proposed to cover similar ground in a more thorough fashion, formulating every definition and every proof in the precise symbolism of his concept-script (cf. Chapter 6, §4.1), with the intention not merely of convincing the reader of the truth of each theorem but also of making everywhere fully explicit all general principles to which appeal was made. This he began doing in the first volume of the *Grundgesetze*, and he completed his task in the second volume, which followed after an interval of ten years. In the meantime, however, Russell had communicated to him the discovery of the antinomy of the class of all classes that are not members of themselves, a discovery that showed that not even Frege's very carefully constructed logical foundation was sufficient to bear the weight of arithmetic. Frege's comment on this revelation, contained in a postscript to the second volume of the *Grundgesetze*, runs as follows:

'Scarcely can anything less welcome happen to a scientific author than that, when he has finished a work, one of the corner-stones of the edifice is shaken. I was placed in this situation by a letter from Herr Bertrand Russell as the printing of this volume was nearing completion. The letter was concerned with my basic principle (V).[1] I have never concealed from myself that this principle is not as evident as the others, or as evident as we ought to require a logical law to be. In the preface to the first volume, on p. VII, I accordingly drew attention to this weakness. I would have been happy to dispense with this support if I had known of any substitute for it. And yet even now I cannot see how arithmetic can be set up on a firm basis, and how numbers can be conceived as logical entities and made objects of thought, if we are not allowed—conditionally at least—to pass from a concept to its extension. Am I always permitted to speak of the extension of a concept, of a class? And if not, how are the exceptional cases to be recognized? Is it always legitimate to infer, from the fact that the extension of one concept coincides with the extension of another, that every entity that falls under the first concept falls also under the second? These questions are raised by the communication of Herr Russell.' (*Grundgesetze*, II, p. 253.)

Thus, although Frege had seen more clearly than anyone before him what was involved in reducing the whole of arithmetic without residue to logic, and although he had devised an admirable symbolism for this purpose, his attempt at a logistic justification of arithmetic was not in the end successful. And so the attempt was renewed almost at once by Russell and Whitehead, who made the logic of classes secure against paradox by their theory of types. Although their system also is open to criticism on certain grounds, we may on the whole accept it as a valid realization of the logistic intention—the more so as the extended calculus of predicates (with the theory of types that we have described in Chapter 4, §6.1) is now known to provide a demonstrably consistent

---

[1] Frege's principle (V), which we have quoted on p. 180, is a logical axiom, expressed in concept-script, which can be translated approximately as follows:

$$(\{x\,|\,F(x)\} = \{x\,|\,G(x)\}) \leftrightarrow (x)(F(x) \leftrightarrow G(x)).$$

system of logic, which we have every reason to suppose strong enough to support the entire edifice of the *Principia*.[1]

We see then that it is possible, though admittedly only with great difficulty, to analyse arithmetic in purely logical terms, and so to exhibit it as a product of abstract thought that is wholly independent of intuition; and it seems likely that, when once arithmetic has been thus analysed, most other branches of pure mathematics can be treated in the same way, since they have in fact already been reduced to arithmetic for purely mathematical purposes. The system of *Principia Mathematica* is accordingly the definitive embodiment of the logistic conception of mathematics—not, of course, a system of mathematics for the common use of mathematicians, but an ideal system of rigorous mathematics which supplies established general principles from which ordinary mathematical investigations can take their departure, and which is now available as a touchstone of meaningfulness of mathematical statements and validity of mathematical inferences.

Even though we may be able to accept *Principia Mathematica*, however, as a satisfactory analysis of mathematics in logical terms, the main problem with which the logistic movement began, that of making mathematics into a secure body of knowledge, has not been finally solved but has only been pushed further back. We still have to ask what justification is possible for logic itself, and whether the conception of logic that is presupposed in *Principia Mathematica* is philosophically acceptable. When we try to answer these questions we find that only the *formal* development of the logical calculus is treated fully in the *Principia*, and the philosophical aspect of logic is left surprisingly vague.

2.1   Mathematics as an edifice of propositions

One presupposition of *Principia Mathematica* which is made absolutely plain is that logic deals with propositions, not with mental acts; and it follows that, on the logistic view, mathematics likewise is essentially propositional. Indeed this is perhaps the most characteristic difference between the two conceptions of mathematics that we are contrasting in the present chapter. If mathematics is conceived logistically, then its ultimate nature is to be sought in the perfected theories which it produces; but if it is to be taken rather as an activity, then the *process* of mathematical reasoning itself is no less important than the products that it yields.

In a system such as that of *Principia Mathematica*, the whole of mathematics is required to be derived from a small number of primitive

---

[1] The system of logic to which we refer is Hilbert and Ackermann's *Stufenkalkül*, discussed above in Chapter 4, §6.2. A reference to the proof of consistency for this system, due to Gentzen, was given on p. 168.

ideas and primitive propositions; and once these primitive elements have been enumerated, the entire system is fixed. From that point on, mathematics is, theoretically speaking, purely combinatorial; and all that the mathematician has to do is to deduce consequences of the primitive propositions and to organize these consequences in theories which display the logical connexions between them. In practice he will have to sift those of the established truths which are mathematically 'significant' from those which are trivial, and he may also wish to isolate particular complex concepts by explicit definition in order to throw into relief those combinations of the primitive logical concepts that are mathematically interesting—but this part of his work is motivated more by aesthetic than by strictly logical considerations, and it has little to do with the *validity* of mathematics.

Such, then, is the broad implication of the logistic thesis, taken as a philosophical analysis of mathematical truth: Mathematics exists as an ideal totality of propositions, and the purpose of the mathematician's work is to discover these propositions and to form them into 'theories' which, when duly printed in books, *are* mathematics. All else that the mathematician may have occasion to do in the course of his work is made necessary simply by the limitations of finite minds.

2.2   Logic and objective reality

Interpreted logistically, then, mathematics is an edifice of propositions, arranged as a deductive system and based on a small number of axioms which express simple truths of logic. It is a formal system, in the sense that it is constructed syntactically by the use of a small number of rules of procedure, such as *modus ponens*; but at the same time it differs essentially from formal systems of the kind that we described in Chapter 4, §3. The difference is that primitive ideas and primitive propositions such as those of the *Principia* are not postulated arbitrarily, but are chosen because they are believed to correspond to objective logical principles.

One consequence of the allegedly necessary truth of the axioms is that mathematics, as interpreted in this way, is conceived as a *closed* totality of propositions—by no means all of them known, of course, and indeed not all knowable by any single individual, but all determined in advance by the axioms from which everything has to follow. Errors may perhaps have been made, and it is possible also that there are further logical axioms that have not yet been discovered; but no radical change in the basis of logic is to be expected. This means that a system such as *Principia Mathematica* can only be put forward in the belief that it is in principle irrevocable. New mathematical theories can subsequently be added to the system by the framing of suitable explicit definitions, but the essential logical framework, if once correctly set up, cannot afterwards be modified. And so we see that Russell at the beginning of the twentieth century (or at any rate Frege at the end of the nineteenth) was in effect committed, no less than had been Kant in his very different situation at the end of the eighteenth century, to the view that logic no longer left any room for discoveries which might necessitate a revision of its basic principles.

It is plain that in a logistically conceived system of formalized mathematics there can be nothing that is arbitrary, for the whole purpose of basing mathematics on a foundation of pure logic is to exhibit it, in Dedekind's phrase, as an immediate product of the laws of thought. Mathematics, as thus understood, is a collection of necessary truths, which are known in advance to hold for any contingent data that intuition or perception may subsequently supply. The logical principles that are taken as primitive must be absolute in this sense, and they must accordingly form part of the fabric of the knowable world. *Principia Mathematica* is in this way very much more than an arbitrary formal system of the kind familiar to mathematicians. It is *the* formal system which displays, in symbolic form, the logical structure of the actual world; and by implication, therefore, it presents an *a priori* theory of the world. A philosopher who clearly appreciated this aspect of the *Principia* was Ludwig Wittgenstein (1889–1951), who declared his position in the incisive aphorisms with which he opened his *Tractatus Logico-Philosophicus* (1921):[1]

'The world is everything that is the case. The world is the totality of facts, not of things. The world is determined by the facts, and by these being *all* the facts. For the totality of facts determines both what is the case and also all that is not the case. The facts in logical space are the world. The world divides into facts. Any one can either be the case or not be the case, and everything else remain the same.

'What is the case, the fact, is the existence of atomic facts. An atomic fact is a combination of objects (entities, things). It is essential to a thing that it can be a constituent part of an atomic fact.'

The view of the world and of logic that Wittgenstein presents in the *Tractatus*, which is far from conventional in substance and often exasperatingly enigmatic in the manner of its formulation, is much less fitted than the sober logical analysis that makes up *Principia Mathematica* to compel the assent of mathematicians. And yet the *Principia*

---

[1] This work was originally published in German in Ostwald's *Annalen der Natur-philosophie* (1921), with the title 'Logisch-Philosophische Abhandlung'. In 1922 it was issued in its present form, accompanied by an English translation that faithfully conveys the evocative power of Wittgenstein's own language. This translation (from which the above extract is taken) was replaced in 1961 by a new one, since Wittgenstein's train of thought can often be better understood now than it could in 1922, when most of his philosophical work was still to be done.

remains unsupported until answers are given to some of the questions that Wittgenstein had in mind when he wrote his brilliant and profound essay; and some such view as this early one of Wittgenstein's seems forced upon us if we demand a complete justification of the *Principia* as a system of objective knowledge.

That this is so is at once apparent if we ask the simple question 'What are the "individuals" in *Principia Mathematica*?'. Every formal system, of the type that we discussed in Chapter 4, has to be introduced by the postulation of (i) suitable axioms, namely the axioms of the logical calculus that is used, and possibly also special axioms for the particular theory that is being studied, (ii) the rules of procedure that are available for use in the derivation of new formulae, and (iii) a domain of individuals. In the *Principia* the logical axioms are clearly stated, and there are no special axioms since all mathematical entities are expressed in terms of logical entities by explicit definition. The rules of derivation are not fully explicit, but this omission can be made good without difficulty. It is thus only the domain of individuals that is left completely unspecified. The domain of individuals for a formal theory, as we have so far thought of it, is a non-logical primitive notion, determinable anew for each theory that is set up, as for example the class N_0 of natural numbers in Peano's system of arithmetic and the class of points in Hilbert's system of euclidean geometry. Russell, however, could not work with an *arbitrary* domain of individuals, or his logic would lack the objectivity that it was meant to possess; and he accordingly referred in formal statements always to one and the same universal domain, over which all bound individual variables were to range. Thus, in Russell's system, if ϕx is any propositional function with individuals for its arguments, $(x)\phi x$ can only mean 'every individual whatever has the property ϕ', and $(\exists x)\phi x$ can only mean 'there is some individual in the universal domain that has the property ϕ'.

Now although *Principia Mathematica* is a system of logic expressed in a symbolic language, and not merely an uninterpreted formal system, no clear indication is to be found of what makes up the totality of individuals. In the informal discussions that introduce the separate chapters, Russell often gives examples in which 'individuals' are taken to be men, mythical beings, and the like; but in doing this he is clearly only illustrating his logical symbolism by applying it to a simplified 'world', not too far removed from the world of common discourse; and in the main body of the formal development no such application would be possible. In that development the individuals can only be the ultimate entities into which the actually existing world is resolved by philosophical analysis; and in this way we are driven back upon some such analysis of the 'world' as that which was envisaged by Wittgenstein when he spoke of a world of atomic facts, which were in turn combinations of 'entities'. What the 'individuals' of logic are to be identified with must depend on the conception of the nature of the world that is presupposed. Russell, being a strict empiricist, may have thought of them as sense-data, the minimal particulars that are distinguishable from one another in perception.

It was in any case possible for the precise identification of the domain of individuals to remain in abeyance, for, since the system of logic was only to be used as a foundation for pure mathematics, particular individuals never needed to be named. Provided, in fact, that we have a hierarchy of individuals, etc., the different levels being kept separate by the theory of types, and that we pay strict attention to *relative* types, we need never ask whether the lowest level that we reach is in fact that of individuals which are not classes of any simpler entities (cf. the remarks made on p. 168, and also the remark on *Urelemente* on p. 291). All that we require of the individuals, therefore, is that they provide a basis for the hierarchy, and this they can do as long as certain essential requirements are met. In particular, the axiom of infinity requires that the domain of individuals shall not be finite. This is necessary because cardinal numbers are defined in the *Principia* as classes of equipotent classes; for if there were no class with more than a certain finite number N of members, all cardinal numbers greater than N would be equal.

The individuals, then, are conceived as existent entities which at the same time satisfy certain theoretical conditions. It thus appears that, when logic is interpreted as the formal structure of the world, to reduce arithmetic to logic is, paradoxically, to make it dependent ultimately on certain matters of fact.

3 The relativism of Brouwer's intuitionist outlook

According to the logistic view, as we have now seen, mathematics is both objective and absolute. Being grounded in pure logic, its statements (in so far as they are not infected by error) express ultimate truths, and they must therefore be understood as timeless. It is this claim, especially, that is rejected by those mathematicians and philosophers who prefer to look upon mathematics as a form of activity. It has been attacked with particular vehemence by Brouwer, whose intuitionist philosophy of mathematics is indeed an extreme form of anti-logistic philosophy. Brouwer holds, as he declared in the passage that we have quoted on p. 246, that all logic is historically conditioned, and no particular system of logic is binding on all men in all times; and his greatest merit may well be that of having drawn attention to the relativity of logic and having revealed the large element of arbitrariness in the supposedly objective mathematics that had finally resulted from the freeing of mathematical analysis from its long-standing dependence on geometrical intuition.

Intuitionism is something much more comprehensive than a philo-sophical clarification of mathematical theories, and Brouwer gave a sketch of the general background of his thought in an important address, 'Mathematik, Wissenschaft und Sprache' [Mathematics, Science, and Language], which he delivered in Vienna in 1928.[1] In this address he put forward a pragmatic interpretation of mathematics and its wider significance, based on the threefold subdivision of rational activity indicated in the title.

'Mathematics, science, and language constitute the principal func-tions in the activity of man, by means of which he rules over nature and maintains order in its midst. The origin of these functions is to be found in the three modes in which the will to live of the individual man shows itself: 1. the mathematical attitude of mind (*die mathematische Betrachtung*), 2. mathematical abstraction, and 3. the imposition of the will by means of sounds.'

Brouwer thus sets out from the notion of man as a being, in the world of nature and of human society, whose whole activity may be seen as a manifestation of the basic will to live; and he interprets mathematics in terms of this conception. Mathematics, in his view, plays an essen-tial part in enabling man to establish his privileged position in the world. It does so, not only in the more obvious ways, by enabling man to build bridges and to navigate the seas, but also at a very much more fundamental level, by making his surroundings rationally intelligible to him and thus enabling him to mould them to his wishes.

The mode of apprehension of the world that has been evolved by mankind can be resolved into two phases, the one temporal and the other causal (cf. Kant's discussion, in the *Critique of Pure Reason*, of the form of intuition and the categories, summarized below in Chapter 13, §4). The mind is able to apprehend as a temporal sequence that of which it is immediately aware; and then it is able further to distinguish enduring features in apprehended experience, relating these, by refer-ence to causal chains, to permanent objects. Time and causality thus make up the basic mathematical frame of the world as apprehended by the human mind. Unlike Kant, however, Brouwer maintains that this frame is a product of the human will.

'As has been said, the two stages of mathematical contemplation (*Betrachtung*) are in no way passive capacities but acts of will. Every-one can satisfy himself that it is possible at will either to sink into a reverie, taking no stand in time and making no separation between self and the external world, or else to effect such a separation by one's own

---

[1] *Monatsh. Math. Phys.*, **36** (1929), 153–164.

effort and to evoke the condensation of individual objects in the apprehended world.'

Even the most primitive human beings think mathematically in the
sense that we have just indicated; but the further step of mathematical
abstraction is only possible at a comparatively high level of cultural
development.   When this step is taken, the mind advances beyond the
mere ability to distinguish between different things to the abstract
notion of 'twoness'—the primordial intuition of mathematics—on
which can then be built the system of all the natural numbers, the system
of real numbers, and finally the whole of pure mathematics.   This
systematic construction of mathematical ideas makes possible the
development of theoretical science—which is yet another manifestation
of the universal will to live, since its primary function is to allow means
that are not in themselves desired to be pursued for the sake of desirable
ends which it is known that they will lead to.

Since man is a social being, he can only achieve his aims by securing
the cooperation of other men, and for this he must be able to impose
his will on them.   At the crudest stage of development, inarticulate
shouts may possibly suffice for this; but later on, more precise means
of communication are essential, and so there must be a developed
language.   Brouwer is most insistent, however, that language is nothing
but a means to a certain social end, and that neither language, nor the
logic which it reflects, can have any absolute significance.   The platonic
view of 'concepts' as entities which are in some sense more real or more
fundamental than directly apprehended features of the world, and also
the view of the principles of classical logic as the most certain of all
truths, are both without rational foundation, deeply rooted though
they may be in the history of thought.   For Brouwer, therefore, there
is nothing at all that can serve as a basis for a philosophical analysis of
mathematics on the logistic model.   Mathematics is a product of the
free activity of human beings, impelled simply by the will to live; and
we can only go back to this original source of activity, in order to build
anew if necessary, and with clearer awareness of what we are doing,
on the sole foundation that is available, namely primary intuition.

It is plain from the address on which the remarks just made are based
that Brouwer's general philosophy is no less extreme than his treatment
of mathematics, which we discussed in Chapter 9.   The complete lack
of sympathy that Brouwer shows with the main tradition of western
philosophy may possibly obscure the essential seriousness of his outlook; but his conception of mathematics as a form of activity has in
fact been shared by very many thinkers whose general position is not
in the least unorthodox.   To make this clear, we shall now turn from
philosophy of mathematics to mathematics itself, and see how mathematicians interpret the work that they are doing.

4 Hilbert's twenty-three mathematical problems

One mathematician whose testimony is especially valuable, in view of his leading role in many different fields of mathematics, is Hilbert, who in the year 1900 gave an account of his conception of mathematical research in his famous lecture on mathematical problems.[1] In the summer of 1900 the Second International Congress of Mathematicians met at Paris, and Hilbert seized the convenient opportunity which the occasion offered for marking the beginning of a new century by venturing, in an address to his fellow mathematicians, to 'lift the veil under which the future lies concealed, in order to cast a glance at the advances that await our discipline and into the secrets of its development in the centuries that lie ahead'. Characteristically, Hilbert chose as his way of indicating probable future developments within mathematics the drawing up of a catalogue of what he judged to be the most important unsolved problems already facing mathematicians. The problems that he selected were the ones that seemed to him most likely to stimulate important new advances. There were twenty-three of them in all, varying in character from the posing of quite specific mathematical questions to the indication of general topics that urgently demanded further research. Hilbert's schedule of problems can be summarized as follows:

1. Cantor's problem of the cardinal number of the continuum (i.e. the 'continuum hypothesis' $2^{\aleph_0} = \aleph_1$).
2. The consistency of the axioms of arithmetic.
3. Demonstration of the impossibility of proving, without appeal to considerations of continuity, that triangular pyramids with bases of equal area and with the same height have the same volume.
4. Systematic examination of geometries for which it is an axiom that the sum of two sides of a triangle is greater than the third side.
5. Treatment of continuous groups without postulation of differentiability of the functions involved.
6. Mathematical treatment of the axioms of physics.
7. Irrationality and transcendentality of particular numbers and classes of numbers.
8. Problems concerning prime numbers.
9. Proof of the most general law of reciprocity for an arbitrary number field.
10. A decision procedure for the solvability of diophantine equations.
11. Quadratic forms with arbitrary algebraic numbers as coefficients.
12. Extension of Kronecker's theorem on abelian fields to an arbitrary algebraic field.

[1] D. Hilbert: 'Mathematische Probleme', *Göttinger Nachrichten* (1900), 253–297. A French translation of the address appears in *Compte Rendu du Deuxième Congrès Internationale des Mathématiciens, tenu à Paris du 6 au 12 août* 1900.

13. Impossibility of solving the general equation of the seventh degree by means of functions of only two arguments.

14. Proof of the finiteness of certain complete systems of functions.

15. Rigorous foundation of Schubert's calculus in enumerative geometry.

16. The topological constitution of algebraic curves and surfaces.

17. Representation of any definite form as a quotient of sums of squares of forms.

18. Filling of space by congruent polyhedra.

19. The question of whether the solutions of regular variational problems are necessarily analytic.

20. Existence of solutions of partial differential equations with prescribed boundary conditions.

21. Proof of the existence of linear differential equations with a prescribed monodromy group.

22. Uniformization of analytical relationships by means of automorphic functions.

23. Extension of the methods of the calculus of variations.

The history of mathematics during the sixty years of the twentieth century that have so far elapsed is a sufficient vindication of Hilbert's judgement of what was of primary importance in the mathematics of his day; and we are now able to see, not only that his problems were well chosen, but also that by focusing attention on them he did much to guide mathematical inquiry in directions that led to important objectives. The address to the mathematical congress, however, was considerably more than just a scheme for research, for in presenting his programme Hilbert also gave reasons for ascribing the importance that he did to the particular problems selected, and indeed to mathematical problems at all. What he said can thus be taken as his personal affirmation of faith as a mathematician, and as an implicit answer to the question 'What is mathematics?'.

Beginning with the specific issue of the role of problems in mathematical research, Hilbert summed up his view in the following terms:

'The great significance of definite problems for the progress of mathematics in general and the important part that they play in the work of the individual mathematician are undeniable. As long as a branch of knowledge offers an abundance of problems, it is in a flourishing condition; but scarcity of problems is a sign of approaching death or of the cessation of independent development. As all human undertakings are directed towards goals, so mathematical research needs problems. By the solution of problems the mathematician develops his powers; he finds new methods and prospects, and he gains a wider and freer horizon.'

The problems that are necessary for the health and vigour of mathematics are produced by mathematics itself.   Again in Hilbert's words :

'Having surveyed the general significance of problems in mathematics, we now turn to the source from which mathematics draws its problems.   Assuredly the first and oldest problems in any branch of mathematics arise out of experience, and are suggested by the world of external phenomena. . . .   In the further development of a mathematical discipline, however, the human mind, encouraged by success in the solution of earlier problems, becomes conscious of its own independence ; and it then creates very successfully from within itself new and fruitful problems, often without apparent external stimulus and solely by logical combination, by generalization and specialization, by separation and assembling of concepts.   The mind thus comes to the fore as itself the propounder of questions. . . .   But even while this creative activity of pure thought is going on, the external world once again reasserts its validity, and by thrusting new questions upon us through the phenomena that occur, it opens up new domains of mathematical knowledge ; and as we strive to bring these new domains under the dominion of pure thought we often find answers to outstanding unsolved problems, and thus at the same time we advance in the most effective way the earlier theories.   On this ever-repeated interplay of thought and experience depend, as it seems to me, the numerous and astonishing analogies and the apparently pre-established harmony that the mathematician so often perceives in the problems, methods, and concepts of diverse realms of knowledge.'

Hilbert firmly rejected the opinion, evidently widely held at the time of his address, that mathematical rigour in the full sense can only be hoped for in analysis, and perhaps only in arithmetic.   He maintained that there is no inherent difference with regard to possible rigour between one branch of mathematics and another, and that arithmetic, geometry, and all other subjects that mathematicians may succeed in bringing within the scope of their general method are valid and indispensable constituents of mathematics.

'I hold that, whenever mathematical concepts arise, whether from the side of epistemology, or in geometry, or out of the theories of natural science, mathematics is faced with the problem of probing into the principles behind the concepts and isolating these principles by means of a simple and complete system of axioms in such a way that the precision of the new concepts and their applicability in deductive argument shall be in no respect inferior to what obtains in arithmetic.'

In Hilbert's view, then, mathematics deals always with the deductive structure of conceptual systems.   It begins with some body of concepts, possibly vague and intuitive and possibly sharply defined, perhaps forced upon us by experience and perhaps created deliberately by an act of postulation ; and it proceeds by isolating a small number of general principles to serve as axioms, and then developing the consequences of these axioms deductively. We know, as a matter of historical fact, that from extremely simple sets of axioms may be derived theories of great profundity, almost inexhaustible in their mathematical interest.

The choice of mathematical axioms is in one sense arbitrary (since no consistent set of axioms is ever 'incorrect' or 'invalid') but in practice it is conditioned by considerations of relevance—either relevance to experience of natural phenomena, or relevance to the world of mathematical knowledge that already exists. And when a branch of mathematics has become sufficiently well established for there to be a common consensus of opinion as to the fundamental principles on which it is based, its growth is promoted by the continued efforts of mathematicians to solve whatever problems may present themselves, either by proving conjectures or by disposing of them with a proof of their impossibility.

'The conviction of the solvability of every mathematical problem is a powerful spur to us in our work. We hear within us the steady call: There is the problem, seek the solution. You can find it by pure thought; for in mathematics there is no *Ignorabimus*!'

It is quite sufficient for mathematics that its concepts have been postulated, and nothing further need be done to ensure that the concepts have content. Hilbert considered internal consistency to be a sufficient criterion of meaningfulness in the realm of mathematical thought; and in his later work, as we have already seen in Chapter 7, he attempted a systematic justification of mathematical knowledge by a metamathematical proof of consistency.

We see, then, that the characteristic features of Hilbert's mathematical outlook at the time of his address can be summed up as follows:
(i) Mathematics is conceived as a pure, intellectual theory of deductively handled conceptual systems, which may with equal right be abstracted from experience or freely postulated; and there is a continual interplay between abstract mathematics and concrete experience.
(ii) Mathematics is an autonomous study, free to choose concepts and axioms and to evolve procedures, and limited only by the one overriding condition of consistency.
(iii) Mathematics is forward-looking, being more concerned with solving outstanding problems and creating powerful new concepts and methods than with merely contemplating knowledge that has already been won.

5 Bourbaki's interpretation of mathematics

At the time when Hilbert drew up his catalogue of problems, his whole interest was concentrated on the consolidation and extension of mathematical knowledge; and when he considered philosophical questions at all, as he did in the *Grundlagen der Geometrie* (1899), this was only because he had to do so in order to gain additional insight into the significance of particular mathematical theories. Hilbert's outlook was accordingly that of a working mathematician, and the opinions that he expressed at the Paris congress may thus be taken as direct testimony from a mathematician as to the nature of his activity. A comparision at once suggests itself with certain utterances of Nicolas Bourbaki, who has a clear right to speak for the mathematicians of a more recent generation, and we find indeed that Bourbaki confirms much of what Hilbert has said or implied. Bourbaki has remained very much a working mathematician, and he has not made any systematic study of the foundations of mathematics such as that which Hilbert undertook in his later work; but he has indicated his general philosophical outlook on a number of occasions, and we shall consider in particular the address which he delivered to the Association for Symbolic Logic in 1948 (cf. p. 118, above) and an article 'L'Architecture des Mathématiques' which he contributed to a collective volume of essays on modern mathematical thought.[1]

Before discussing Bourbaki's more philosophical utterances, however, we must first explain the nature of his interpretation of mathematics, as presented in the *Éléments de Mathématique*. We have already dealt both with the logical calculus on which this system is based and with the associated treatment of the theory of sets (see Chapter 4, §7, and Chapter 11, §6), and we now need to complete what we have already said by explaining the manner in which Bourbaki presents the whole of pure mathematics as an extension of the theory of sets.

Mathematics is understood by Bourbaki as a study of *structures*, or systematic patterns of relations, each particular structure being characterized by a suitable set of axioms. In mathematics, as it exists at the present time, there are three great families of structures, the 'mother-structures', which dominate the whole of mathematics: namely algebraic structures, topological structures, and ordinal structures. Any particular structure is to be thought of as inhering in a certain set E, which functions as a domain of individuals for the corresponding theory. An *algebraic structure* arises from one or more rules of composition. Such a rule may be an *internal rule of composition*, i.e. a three-term relation $x \top y = z$ which associates with any ordered pair (x,y) of elements of E a uniquely determined element z of E, or it may be an *external rule of composition*, which associates with any element x of E and any element α of a second fixed set Ω (called a *domain of*

---

[1] 'Foundations of Mathematics for the Working Mathematician', *J. Symb. Logic*, **14** (1949), 1–8; 'L'Architecture des Mathématiques', in *Les Grands Courants de la Pensée Mathématique* (Paris, 1948), edited by F. Le Lionnais, pp. 35–47.

operators) a definite element $\alpha \perp x$ of E.   In either case, the rule is to be
defined implicitly by appropriate axioms.   A *topological structure* is
defined for E when every element of E has assigned to it a set of subsets
of E as its family of *neighbourhoods*, the relation between element and
neighbourhood again being such that appropriate axioms are satisfied.
A set E with a topological structure is referred to as a *topological space*.
And lastly, an *ordinal structure* is defined by a relation xRy which is
transitive and reflexive.[1]

One of the simplest and most familiar of algebraic structures is that
of the *group*.   For this structure we need the basic set E, an internal
rule of composition $x \tau y = z$, and a fixed element e of E, these being
such that (i) for all x, y, z in E, $(x \tau y) \tau z = x \tau (y \tau z)$, (ii) for every x
in E, $e \tau x = x \tau e = x$, and (iii) for every x in E there is a y in E such
that $y \tau x = x \tau y = e$.   With two internal rules of composition we
can have the more elaborate structures of the *ring* and the *field*, and
with one internal rule (addition) and one external rule (multiplication
by a scalar) we can have that of the *vector space*.   Very many different
types of algebraic structure are possible, and the greater part of abstract algebra can be formulated as a theory of such structures.

Topological structures make possible an abstract treatment of ideas
of continuity.   Such structures may be present together with algebraic
structures in the same set E, as in the case of *topological groups*, where
the algebra and the topology are bound together by the postulated
continuity of the operation of composition in the group.   In the more
elaborate systems that are treated in mathematics, many structures
may all be present in a set at the same time.   The real continuum, for
instance, can be treated at pleasure as an additive group, a ring, a field,
a topological group, an ordered set, and so forth.

Unified treatment of the whole of pure mathematics in terms of an
interlocking system of typical structures has been made possible by the
perfecting of the axiomatic method; and in his paper on the architecture of mathematics Bourbaki has accordingly sought to dispel certain
widespread misconceptions concerning the use of this method.   The
axiomatic method is a universal one, equally applicable in all mathematical situations, and we may therefore be inclined to liken it, he says,
to the treatment of functions in classical analysis by means of their
Taylor expansions; but to regard it as a mechanical device that simply
increases the deductive powers of the unaided mind, rather as a
machine tool augments a manual worker's physical strength and
dexterity, would be to overlook its deeper significance.   Bourbaki then
makes the following comment:

---

[1] Bourbaki's usage is different in this particular from that of Russell and many other
logicians, who take ordering relations to be non-reflexive.   Bourbaki's ordinal relations
correspond to the arithmetical relation $x \leqslant y$, and Russell's to $x < y$.

'But here we have an inadequate analogy. The mathematician does not work mechanically, like a factory operative at the assembly-line. We cannot stress too emphatically the fundamental part that is played in his research by a special intuition, not the common intuition of sense but rather a kind of direct divination (in advance of all reasoning) of the normal behaviour that he seems justified in expecting from mathematical beings which long acquaintance has rendered as familiar to him as the beings of the real world. Now each structure carries with it its own proper language, full of particular intuitive resonances, derived from the theories from which axiomatic analysis has disengaged it; and for the research worker who suddenly discovers this structure in the phenomena that he is studying, it is like a sudden modulation that gives all at once to the intuitive flow of his thought a new and unexpected direction, and brings the light of a new day to the mathematical landscape in which he is moving about. Let us think—to take an old example—of the progress brought about at the beginning of the nineteenth century by the geometrical representation of imaginaries. From our point of view this amounted to the discovery in the set of complex numbers of a well-known topological structure, that of the euclidean plane, with all the possibilities of application that this involved. . . .

Such examples have multiplied in the last fifty years: Hilbert space, and more generally function spaces, introducing topological structures in sets of elements which were no longer *points* but *functions*; Hensel's p-adic numbers where, by a still more astonishing development, topology invaded what was up to then the domain of the discrete, the discontinuous *par excellence*, the set of whole numbers; Haar measure, enlarging beyond all expectation the field of application of the notion of integral, and making possible a very profound analysis of the properties of continuous groups—so many decisive moments in the progress of mathematics, turning points where a flash of genius has given a new orientation to a theory by revealing in it a structure that would not have appeared *a priori* to play any part there.

All this means that now mathematics is reduced less than ever to a purely mechanical manipulation of isolated formulae. More than ever before, intuition reigns over the genesis of discoveries; but from now on it is in a position to make use of the powerful levers that are provided by the theory of the great types of structure, and it sweeps in at a single glance immense domains now unified by the axiomatic method, where once the wildest chaos seemed to prevail.'

Mathematics, then, like most human activity, is a continual thrusting out into the unknown. The mathematician is not bound by any pre-existing limitation on what is to count as mathematics, but is free to create entirely new concepts and procedures, as was done, for instance, by Cantor. Bourbaki declares, indeed, that the three great families of mother-structures are only those which we can recognize in mathematics as it exists at the present time, and that quite new kinds of structure, as yet unimagined, may become equally significant in the future.

What ultimately counts is whether or not the domain of mathematics is permanently enlarged by the gaining of new territory, peopled by 'mathematical beings', as Bourbaki would say, that are no less 'real' than those with which we have for long been familiar.   On this view, what is chiefly to be expected from the study of foundations of mathematics is a classification of the structures and the controlling principles that logical analysis reveals in mathematics as it at present exists. The logician is only competent to say 'This is the structural organization of the mathematics of the present time'—or perhaps 'This is what the structural organization of the mathematics of the present time would be if it were wholly true to its own implicit principles'—not 'Here are principles that are eternally valid for mathematics as such'.

Logic itself might be described as 'mathematical criticism', for it cannot exist at all until the reasoning in which logical principles are exemplified is already there.   This point, which is very much in the spirit of Brouwer, was made by Bourbaki when he addressed the Association for Symbolic Logic :

'Proofs, however, had to exist before the structure of a proof could be logically analysed ; and this analysis, carried out by Aristotle, and again and more deeply by the modern logicians, must have rested then, as it does now, on a large body of mathematical writings.   In other words, logic, so far as we mathematicians are concerned, is no more and no less than the grammar of the language which we use, a language which had to exist before the grammar could be constructed.'

Mathematics is simply what is produced by the research of mathematicians, who work within a tradition that has evolved and become consolidated during a span of some twenty-five centuries, and who subject their results and theories always to the critical scrutiny of the entire mathematical world.   Mathematics is what it is, and it needs no certificate of legitimacy from logicians or philosophers.   Logicians, indeed, are obliged to take mathematics as a datum.   They can then analyse its structure, and thus make mathematicians more clearly aware of the formal side of their essentially intuitive work, and by doing this they make a now indispensable contribution to the development of mathematics itself.

But what, then, of Frege and Russell's vision of a mathematics securely based once and for all on an unchanging foundation of pure logic ?   What of Hilbert's attempt to guarantee the stability of mathematics by a metamathematical proof of its consistency ?   Bourbaki renounces altogether such grandiose projects, adopting instead what he calls a 'realist' attitude to the foundations of mathematics.   Contradictions may indeed occur in the future, as they have occurred many times in the past ; and mathematicians will continue to deal with them by making such modifications in their concepts and methods as may be necessary for the re-establishment of consistency. Systematic adoption of the axiomatic method, as in the *Éléments de Mathématique*, will greatly assist this process by allowing the sources of such contradictions to be traced.

Bourbaki is thus reverting, in a sense, to the practice of Dedekind and Peano, who did so much to improve the standard of clarity and rigour in mathematics, though without thinking in terms of a specific justification of mathematics as a whole. He does so because he is first and foremost a mathematician, determined to pursue mathematical research, and confident that this can be done significantly, whatever may be the philosophical difficulties that are as yet unresolved. He has summed up his 'philosophy of the working mathematician' in the following words, which form the conclusion of the introduction to the *Éléments*:

'In short we believe that mathematics is destined to survive, and that the essential parts of the majestic edifice will never collapse as a result of the sudden appearance of a contradiction; but we do not maintain that this opinion rests on anything but experience. That is not much, it may be said. But for twenty-five centuries mathematicians have been correcting their errors, and seeing their science enriched and not impoverished in consequence; and this gives them the right to contemplate the future with equanimity.'

Chapter 13

THE APPLICATION OF MATHEMATICS TO THE NATURAL WORLD

1 Pure mathematics and applied mathematics

In considering the various aspects of mathematical philosophy, we have so far limited the discussion almost exclusively to pure mathematics, which can be treated as a self-sufficient discipline, in no way dependent on more concrete knowledge. From our examination of the principal ways in which pure mathematics has been analysed, it appears that in recent years philosophical theories of the nature of mathematics have receded somewhat into the background, leaving as the main foci of research axiomatic systematizations of mathematics itself, as practised by working mathematicians. At the same time, the now traditional symbolic logic that we discussed in Part I has been superseded, as a foundation for mathematics, by a rather different kind of logical system in which the restricted calculus of predicates is combined with the axiomatic theory of sets. Such a system appears to be capable, in principle, of supporting the entire edifice of pure mathematics. As a practical counterpart to this theoretical foundation, moreover, there now exists Nicolas Bourbaki's *Éléments de Mathématique*, in which the whole of pure mathematics will eventually be derived from the basic properties of sets—not any longer, it is true, with that extreme degree of formal rigour and completeness that was deemed essential by Frege and Russell, but still strictly and fully enough to satisfy all reasonable demands of mathematicians.

From now on we shall accept the view, so powerfully urged by both Hilbert and Bourbaki, that mathematics is in the last resort an affair of mathematicians, who are not answerable in their work to any higher authority. Mathematics, in other words, is an independent mode of rational activity; and over the centuries it has produced its own subject-matter, its own methods, and its own criteria of correctness, all of which have subsequently been analysed by logicians.

Pure mathematics, in its modern form, is conceived as a theory of abstract structure. The types of structure with which it deals are many and varied, but they all go to make up a single mathematical organism, and all are studied by the same universal axiomatic method. Each individual type of structure, in fact, is defined implicitly by an appropriate set of axioms, and the deductive consequences of these axioms then furnish a detailed analysis of its properties. Pure mathematics offers in this way a wealth of structural patterns that have been systematically investigated, with the result that a great deal is known about them; and the mathematical knowledge that is thus available can now be applied in other spheres. By an *application* of a mathematical theory we understand the recognition that the structure with which the theory deals is present in a certain body of experience, and the consequential transfer to that experience of the knowledge about the structure that is contained in abstract form in the theorems of which the theory is composed.

As we have already observed, the theories that comprise pure mathematics are arrived at in a variety of ways.[1] Sometimes a mathematical theory is directly suggested by concrete experience, from which it is detached by a process of abstraction; sometimes pure mathematics and its applications evolve side by side, each fostering the growth of the other; and sometimes again a mathematical theory is worked out in the first instance as a purely intellectual exercise, and only afterwards does it prove to have a significant application. The first of these three possibilities is exemplified by euclidean geometry, the second by the theory of differential equations, and the third by the tensor calculus. The precise temporal relation between formation of a mathematical theory and application of the theory is in any event unimportant, except as a matter of historical interest; for when once a theory has been devised it exists in its own right as pure mathematics, and its formal relation to experience may then be studied *ab initio* as a philosophical problem.

The distinction between pure and applied mathematics is one that we first alluded to in Chapter 1, where we adduced as an example of applied mathematics the science of formal logic (see p. 5). To call logic applied mathematics may well have struck the reader as perverse at that early stage; but we can now see that to use the propositional calculus, say, in order to elucidate the logical structure of some such demonstrative procedure as proof by *reductio ad absurdum* is an entirely typical application of a mathematical theory, being in fact an application to deductive reasoning of boolean algebra. There are indeed no *a priori* restrictions whatever on the kind of 'experience' to which mathematics may properly be applied, and any domain in which entities are sufficiently well defined and relations sufficiently stable for a clear structural pattern to be discernible is a legitimate field of application for mathematics. It is the world of natural phenomena, however, that supplies the overwhelming majority of significant applications;

---

[1] A particularly instructive example of the creation of a mathematical theory is provided by the theory of games, devised by von Neumann. See Note 2, p. 354.

and in the discussion which now follows we shall accordingly confine our attention to the more familiar scientific applications of mathematical theories.

2   The spatial structure of the world

Since to apply mathematics means to identify an abstractly conceived structure with the structure that actually inheres in some particular body of experience, it might well be imagined that applied mathematics would present no philosophical problems of its own, beyond the problems that we have already discussed in relation to pure mathematics.   This is by no means the case, however, for the 'experience' to which mathematics is to be applied is itself a source of philosophical perplexities, and is indeed no less beset by problems than is mathematics.   Pure mathematics becomes a riddle as soon as we are aware of the essential inadequacy of 'naive logic'; and a similar development takes place in the field of possible applications of mathematics when 'naive epistemology' is brought under scrutiny.

One of the oldest and most familiar of mathematical theories that count as applied mathematics in the sense in which we are here using that term is euclidean geometry, understood as a mathematical theory of the spatial structure of the world of common experience; and this particular example, as we shall now see, offers a very clear illustration of the philosophical problems that are characteristic of applied mathematics.   We are not thinking here of euclidean geometry as an *abstract* theory, based say on Hilbert's axioms, but are treating it as a scientific analysis of space as in actual fact constituted.   This, of course, was the only interpretation given to geometry until the nineteenth century.

The naive conception of the natural world is of a world of objects that exist and events that occur in space and time.   At any particular time, every object is located at a definite 'place', and the totality of all possible places is what we call *space*.   Space endures while time passes; and continuous variation of position in space with time is known as *motion*.   Space, being the unchanging substratum of all observable phenomena, has a structure that can be elucidated once and for all. This structure is apprehended directly, in a rough and ready fashion, by common sense; and it can be studied with scientific precision, to whatever degree of accuracy may be considered worth while, with the aid of such instruments as graduated scales, protractors, and theodolites.   For purposes of theoretical investigation and discovery we confine our attention to the simplest possible shapes—triangles, parallelograms, circles, etc.—and to achieve a higher degree of precision we use carefully drawn diagrams in preference to pieces of gross matter. It is then a natural further step to substitute in imagination, for lines actually drawn with pencil upon paper, 'perfect' lines, having position but no thickness, which are conceived as the mathematical ideal to which the finest possible ruled lines approximate. At the same time it is assumed that the geometrical properties of 'perfect' figures are governed by a small number of simple first principles, which we can verify approximately by making suitable measurements. In this way we are led to accept euclidean geometry as an account of the spatial structure of the actual world, and to think of both material objects and geometrical diagrams as in some way immersed in a space that is made up of dimensionless points.

The view that euclidean geometry has an immediate application to the familiar world was taken for granted until recent times; but the rise of modern physics has now not merely thrown doubt on the supposed fact that space is euclidean, but has even upset the traditional presupposition that there *is* an objective space with a well-defined geometrical structure. As long as we remain at the level of crude common sense, where quantitative statements can at best be translated extremely roughly into facts of direct experience, no inadequacy becomes apparent in the assumption that the world possesses a euclidean structure; but this is no longer the case when more refined techniques of scientific measurement are developed. As long ago as 1854, Riemann declared in his famous *Habilitationsschrift* on the hypotheses of geometry[1] that we have no warrant for assuming that the structural properties of finite regions of space will continue to hold for indefinitely small regions:

'But now the empirical concepts on which spatial measurements are based, the concept of a rigid body and that of a ray of light, appear to lose their validity in the infinitely small. It is therefore indeed conceivable that the metrical relations of space in the infinitely small are not in accordance with the assumptions of geometry; and this would in fact have to be acknowledged to be the case as soon as phenomena could be explained more simply in that way.' (*Werke*, p. 267.)

Riemann's doubt was purely speculative, but the discovery of quantum mechanics and the development of nuclear physics have now shown that the situation is indeed as he conjectured, and that the physical world does not even behave as a continuous manifold, much less as a euclidean space.

Not only quantum mechanics, but also the theory of relativity has cast doubt on the finality of the application of euclidean geometry to the actual world. When Einstein had once questioned the longstanding presuppositions of absolute space and absolute time it soon came to be generally seen that space and time, as hitherto conceived,

---

[1] B. Riemann: 'Über die Hypothesen, welche der Geometrie zu Grunde liegen', *Werke* (1876), pp. 254–269.

were 'metaphysical' entities, inaccessible to observation and measurement, and therefore scientifically valueless.   That Einstein's new philosophical insight into the nature of space and time was more than a mere speculative idea, and that it must be taken seriously by practical scientists, was strongly suggested by the unsolved problem posed by the negative result of the celebrated experiment of Michelson and Morley (1887) for the determination of the earth's velocity through the ether, a result very difficult to explain as long as space was treated as absolute ; and the new theory was strikingly vindicated by observations made during the total eclipse of the sun in 1919, which yielded empirical confirmation of its predictions.

But in order to see that the traditional view of euclidean geometry is too simple, we do not even need to go as far as quantum mechanics and relativity.   It is quite sufficient to ask how, in fact, we find out about the structure of space.   We do so, of course, by measurement.   Using ruler, compasses, and protractor, we satisfy ourselves that the properties of material triangles, circles, etc., are in agreement with the theorems of Euclid ; and when we supplement these simple instruments with theodolites and astronomical telescopes we are able to extend our field of observation over the entire surface of the earth and far out into space.   The only weakness in this procedure is its indirectness.   We never measure distances between points in space by immediate comparison of the distance to be measured with a standard distance, but always by intervention of some physical system.   We may perhaps use a rigid scale, which we transfer from one position to another, or alternatively we may employ some optical means ; but in every case we have to interpret our results on the basis of appropriate physical assumptions—that a steel bar remains of invariable length when its temperature is kept constant, for instance, or that light travels in straight lines.   What we verify by our measurements is therefore not euclidean geometry as a theory of the geometry of the physical world, but euclidean geometry taken in conjunction with a substantial part of classical physics.

3   Naive realism and its inadequacy

As we now see, even the application of euclidean geometry to ordinary space, which we might imagine to be one of the least problematic of all applications of mathematics, raises perplexing questions, and appears even to demand a comprehensive philosophy of our knowledge of the physical world.   The essential difficulty is that, whereas a mathematical theory is ordinarily a highly developed deductive system, the experience to which we wish to apply it is almost always of a less tractable kind.   This is indeed to be expected, for 'experience' is concrete and largely empirical, with the result that it can never have the conceptual tidiness and simplicity of a theory based on freely postulated axioms.   The most that we can hope for is that experience may be clarified by philosophical analysis in such a way that its empirical content is freed as far as possible from unwarranted 'metaphysical' accretions (cf. p. 335), and its essential structure is laid bare.   Any serious discussion of an application of mathematics must accordingly be supported by a philosophical inquiry into the nature of the relevant kind of experience; and in the case of applications to physical reality this means a philosophical analysis of knowledge of the physical world. Such an undertaking is plainly too vast to be treated here, even in the most summary fashion, and we can only refer the reader to the standard books mentioned in Note 4 at the end of the chapter for a discussion of what it involves.   There are certain specific issues, however, that are of such direct relevance to our theme of the application of mathematics to the natural world that we must at least attempt an introductory discussion of them.

We have already seen, from the example of applied geometry discussed in §2, that experience of the physical world cannot be taken at face value.   The common-sense notion of a unique cosmic frame of space and time cannot be justified philosophically, comprehensible though its universal adoption may be when seen from the point of view of the history of thought; and what is true of the spatio-temporal frame of experience is true equally of the entire common-sense conception of physical reality.   This conception, which is often referred to as *naive realism*, is at best a very rough first approximation, and even the most elementary philosophical discussion of applied mathematics demands a considerably more mature notion of the physical world.

According to naive realism, the world is very much as it appears to be, when due allowance is made for obvious sources of error.   It consists of objects, located in space, which retain their identity through the passage of time.   Objects are capable of influencing one another in various ways, and the changes that take place in the world are all governed by intelligible relations of cause and effect.   Human beings have a twofold relation to the world, since they are both observers of what exists and what takes place, and also agents, capable of initiating changes by their own activity.   Knowledge of the natural world is all derived ultimately from information supplied by the senses—although the unaided senses may well be reinforced in practice by scientific instruments and by elaborate techniques of scientific investigation. In short, therefore, what exists corresponds closely to what we perceive. We must be on our guard against illusions, but we find no great difficulty in making due allowance for the apparent change in the size of an object as it moves away from us or for the apparent bending of a stick when it is immersed in water.   We are thus able to pass confidently in thought from the appearances of things seen and heard to what we take to be the reality behind such appearances.

Such are the principal features of naive realism, the normal outlook of the unphilosophical mind, and indeed also of the philosophical mind in most of the situations of everyday life. It should be added, however, that this conception of reality is encountered less frequently as an overtly held theory of the world than as an 'absolute presupposition', that is to say a conditioning factor in thought, which need not even be consciously present to the mind as something actively believed in, but which is nevertheless revealed by philosophical analysis of the thoughts and beliefs that are acknowledged.

The weakness in the outlook of naive realism is that the 'world' which it yields is everywhere subject to correction, as new ways are detected in which the senses can be misled. One supposedly objective feature after another is eroded away by criticism, until in the end we are left either with the merest shadow of the common-sense world or else with a reality so much 'corrected' that naive realism has ceased altogether to be realist and has turned into theoretical science. An early attempt to improve upon naive realism was made by John Locke in his *Essay Concerning Human Understanding* (1690), where he elaborated the distinction, made by Robert Boyle, between primary and secondary qualities (Book II, Chapter 8). Recognizing that much of what our senses tell us is subjective—since the response of an organ of sense to an external stimulus is conditioned by the responsive capacity of the organ as well as by the activating stimulus—Locke attempted to separate the secondary qualities of things, which are subjective, from the primary or objective qualities.

'Qualities considered in bodies are, first, such as are utterly inseparable from the body, in what state soever it be; such as in all the alterations and changes it suffers, all the force can be used upon it, it constantly keeps; and such as sense constantly finds in every particle of matter which has bulk enough to be perceived and the mind finds inseparable from every particle of matter, though less than to make itself singly be perceived by our senses. . . . These I call original or primary qualities of body, which I think we may observe to produce simple ideas in us, viz., solidity, extension, figure, motion or rest, and number. Secondly, such qualities which in truth are nothing in the objects themselves, but powers to produce various sensations in us by their primary qualities, i.e. by the bulk, figure, texture, and motion of their insensible parts, as colours, sounds, tastes, &c, these I call secondary qualities.'

Locke's distinction was an eminently reasonable one to make in the seventeenth century, when scientific observation was still mainly a matter of direct employment of the senses, and when physical science was as yet in its infancy; but today we are forced into a more radical attitude. What is now known of the ultimate constitution of matter makes it quite impossible for solidity to be retained as a primary quality; and as for extension, figure, and motion and rest, these all presuppose a conception of space and time that, on analysis, is found to lose its validity. Number alone remains as something that may still be thought to be objective. Naive realism, modified in the way that Locke indicated, is still adequate, of course, as a working conception of reality, sufficient for common sense and for the needs of everyday life; but it no longer corresponds to the scientific outlook, and in consequence it has little relevance to the philosophy of applied mathematics. Indeed, the data of science are now no longer the perceived qualities of things, but what have been referred to by Sir Arthur Eddington, in a characteristically apt phrase, as *pointer readings*.

An 'observation' in physical science now ordinarily means the reading of some instrument, and the result of the observation is a number or set of numbers. Numbers obtained in this way furnish the sole link between theoretical science and the observed world. Physical theories have become almost entirely structural, and they are therefore expressible without residue in strictly mathematical form. Testing such a theory experimentally means obtaining suitable pointer readings and seeing whether they are compatible with the structure prescribed by the theory. Individual pointer readings are now no longer immediately identifiable with objective properties of things—a reading on a measuring scale with the distance between points, the numbers read on the graduated circles of an astronomical telescope with the direction in which the instrument is pointing, the weights in the pan of a balance with the mass of the object being weighed, and so forth. It more often happens that observations can only be interpreted in physical terms when a considerable amount of physical theory is presupposed—as when the radial velocity of a celestial object is inferred from the amount of the shift in the lines of its spectrum, or when the behaviour of fundamental particles is studied by measurement of tracks in photographic emulsions. And now that we have so many instances of 'observations' that plainly involve a substantial amount of inference, we see that all scientific observations are in fact of this kind, though the inferences may possibly be so elementary that we overlook their presence altogether. We are never in direct contact with the 'real world'; and even to think in terms of such a world, existing independently of human minds, is philosophically unjustifiable.

4 The a priori form of the physical world

The aim of physical science is to produce a complete theory of the world of inanimate nature, in which all systematic relations between phenomena are exhibited as consequences of certain fundamental natural laws, in such a way that experimental results can be predicted in advance of actual observation.   The laws of physics, as well as the concepts that occur in them, are arrived at inductively, by use of what has come to be known as the scientific method, and they are therefore always liable to revision, or in extreme cases to rejection, if it should turn out that the further progress of science shows that conclusions which were once adequately supported by empirical evidence are no longer tenable.   But although the conclusions of physics are never certain, they are nevertheless more secure than almost any other part of human knowledge; and even when physics passes through one of its infrequent revolutions, the greater part of the earlier theory retains its validity when appropriately reinterpreted.   This extreme stability of natural knowledge has led some philosophers to ask whether the enduring core of physical theory may not after all have been supplied by the inquiring mind itself, as an *a priori* nucleus of knowledge, for in that case physical laws would certainly be exempt from empirical refutation.

One constituent of natural knowledge that indubitably is *a priori* is arithmetic.   Thus whenever we can be sure that we are dealing with discrete entities that retain their identity, we know without necessity of counting that seven things taken together with five things yield twelve things in all.   Or again, to take a less trivial example of the mathematical *a priori* in nature, the symmetrical external form of chemical crystals must depend on the finer structure of the material of which the crystals are composed.   Views may change as to what this material is or how it is constituted, but we can show mathematically that, whatever it may be that is distributed in space, the number of types of symmetry that the distribution can exhibit is finite; and the possible types can all be analysed by means of the algebraic theory of groups.   In this way we are able to derive *a priori* knowledge of the possible range of crystalline forms (cf. Note 3, p. 355).

The case for believing that a substantial part of natural knowledge is in fact *a priori* was powerfully argued by Kant (cf. Chapter 9, §2), in answer to Hume's sceptical argument that empirical evidence cannot justify general scientific laws, since it never shows more than that experience has exhibited certain regularities in the past.   Kant developed his thesis in detail in the *Critique of Pure Reason* (1781), and he also gave the gist of the argument, in a less closely reasoned form, in the *Prolegomena*[1] (1783), §§14–38.

As we have indicated in Chapter 9, §2, Kant draws a fundamental distinction between the world of *noumena*, or things in themselves, and the world of *phenomena*, or things as objects of knowledge for us.   The

---

[1] *Prolegomena zu einer jeden künftigen Metaphysik, die als Wissenschaft wird auftreten können.*

noumenal world, by its very nature, is for ever out of reach as an object of theoretical knowledge, and we can therefore know nothing but phenomena. Knowledge comes partly from sensory intuition (*Anschauung*) and partly from the understanding (*Verstand*), the business of the senses being to supply the intuitive content of awareness, and that of the understanding being to think. Sensory intuition has an *a priori* form, the matrix of space and time, which is an objective constituent of the phenomenal world; and the pure theory of the form of intuition is mathematics. But the phenomenal world is more than a mere array of perceptions in space and time; it is a coherent world, as known to a particular consciousness, and it acquires its coherence (unity of apperception) through an unconscious activity of synthesis which is the work of the understanding. This synthesis results from certain fundamental concepts or *categories*, which Kant believed to be twelve in number on the ground that, being anterior to all empirical content, they must correspond to the 'logical functions of the understanding in judgement', traditionally classified under the four headings of quantity, quality, relation, and modality, each of which gives rise to three subdivisions. Kant's table of the categories takes the following form:

1. Quantity — unity
   — multiplicity
   — totality
2. Quality — reality
   — negation
   — limitation
3. Relation — inherence and subsistence
   — causality and dependence
   — reciprocal action
4. Modality — possibility – impossibility
   — existence – non-existence
   — necessity – contingency.

These categories yield a conceptual unity which welds the perceptions of each individual into a coherent whole; and since the categories are the same for all minds, every individual is able to relate his perceptions to the same objectively existing phenomenal world. This world, moreover, has an *a priori* form, namely the form supplied by the categories. There is thus a twofold *a priori* element in scientific knowledge—first of all the mathematical form of sensory intuition, and then the conceptual unity of apperception, which includes, in particular, the causal structure of the totality of phenomena.

Although the conception of an unknowable world of things in themselves, which reveals its presence though not its nature through the phenomena that we are able to observe, is not one that has proved generally acceptable to philosophers, and although the entire Kantian philosophy has in a sense passed into history, the modern philosophical tradition has nevertheless been profoundly influenced by Kant's ideas. The best known among recent writers on the philosophy of natural science who have argued that physical knowledge is largely *a priori* is Eddington, who took up an extreme position on this issue. Eddington developed his ideas on the subject in a relatively non-technical way in his Tarner lectures of 1938, published under the title *The Philosophy of Physical Science* (Cambridge, 1939). It was in these lectures that he used his graphic illustration of the fishing-net to bring home his basic contention to his audience:

'Let us suppose that an ichthyologist is exploring the life of the ocean. He casts his net into the water and brings up a fishy assortment. Surveying his catch, he proceeds in the usual manner of a scientist to systematise what it reveals. He arrives at two generalisations:
   (1) No sea-creature is less than two inches long.
   (2) All sea-creatures have gills.
These are both true of his catch, and he assumes tentatively that they will remain true however often he repeats it.' (Page 16.)

From here Eddington went on to point out that the conclusion (2) is an empirical generalization, and as such it may at any time be disproved by the fishing up of a sea-creature without gills, but the same is not necessarily true of (1). If it so happens that the ichthyologist's net has a two-inch mesh, then this generalization *must* hold for every catch that he makes; and in such circumstances a philosopher could assert, as soon as he had inspected the ichthyologist's equipment, that (1) would be for him an irrefutable law. And if the ichthyologist were philosophically minded, he would himself be able to arrive at this *a priori* 'law of nature' from epistemological considerations alone.

Eddington believed that physical science is predominantly *a priori* in this sense, and that the laws of nature are inferable in detail from knowledge of the concepts that physicists presuppose and the methods of investigation that they recognize. Indeed, in his difficult and controversial book *Fundamental Theory*, published posthumously in 1946, he sought to derive physics from basic epistemological principles.

5   Whitehead's theory of natural knowledge

Now that we have given some general indication of the complexity of the philosophical problems raised by the application of mathematics to natural phenomena, we shall devote the second half of this chapter to one particular constructive attempt that has been made to devise an adequate theory of natural knowledge, namely that of A. N. Whitehead. We choose Whitehead's philosophy because, whatever may be the eventual judgement of history upon its acceptability as a philosophical basis for natural science, it is, beyond all doubt, a serious attempt to answer the right questions in the right kind of way.

Whitehead developed his ideas in three short books, published in quick succession: *An Enquiry concerning the Principles of Natural Knowledge* (1919), *The Concept of Nature* (1920), and *The Principle of Relativity* (1922). The philosophy of nature sketched in these three books led in the end to the more comprehensive philosophical system of *Process and Reality* (1929), and Whitehead himself came eventually to be widely acknowledged as the greatest of living philosophers[1]—a development that is not surprising in view of the depth of philosophical insight that is revealed by the earlier works. In those works, moreover, Whitehead was greatly helped, on the mathematical side, by his mastery of the axiomatic handling of geometry.[2] The account of his ideas that we shall now give will be based, in the main, on *The Concept of Nature*. This book is the published version of the inaugural course of Tarner lectures, which Whitehead delivered at Cambridge in 1919.

Whitehead worked out his theory of natural knowledge specifically as a reply to the challenge to philosophy that was contained in the newly developed theory of relativity. This challenge had already been foreshadowed towards the end of the nineteenth century in the critical writings of Ernst Mach (1838–1916), who, as a strict positivist, insisted that no statement is admissible in science unless it is empirically verifiable. But it was when Einstein put forward his theory of relativity that the idea rapidly gained acceptance that, notwithstanding the unbroken pragmatic justification enjoyed by the traditional conceptions of space and time ever since the age of Galileo and Newton, a thorough overhaul of these conceptions had now become imperative. And then, as frequently happens in such circumstances, when once the current conceptions had been questioned they were seen to involve wholly unjustifiable assumptions; and philosophy was accordingly faced with the task of giving a new analysis of space and time that would take account of all available knowledge. This was exactly what Whitehead sought to do in the theory now to be summarized.

Before reconstruction there has to come demolition, and Whitehead did not hesitate to make a thorough clearance of the ground. With a boldness equal to that of Brouwer (cf. p. 246), he refused to be overawed by any mere weight of tradition.

[1] For details of Whitehead's life and work see E. T. Whittaker: 'Alfred North Whitehead, 1861–1947', *Obituary Notices of Fellows of the Royal Society*, 6 (1948–1949), 281–296.
[2] Cf. Whitehead's two Cambridge Tracts, *The Axioms of Projective Geometry* (1906) and *The Axioms of Descriptive Geometry* (1907).

'The eighteenth and nineteenth centuries accepted as their natural philosophy a certain circle of concepts which were as rigid and definite as those of the philosophy of the middle ages, and were accepted with as little critical research. I will call this natural philosophy "materialism". Not only were men of science materialists, but also adherents of all schools of philosophy. The idealists only differed from the philosophic materialists on question of the alignment of nature in reference to mind. But no one had any doubt that the philosophy of nature considered in itself was of the type which I have called materialism. . . . It can be summarized as the belief that nature is an aggregate of material and that this material exists in some sense *at* each successive member of a one-dimensional series of extensionless instants of time. Furthermore the mutual relations of the material entities at each instant formed these entities into a spatial configuration in an unbounded space. It would seem that space—on this theory—would be as instantaneous as the instants, and that some explanation is required of the relations between the successive instantaneous spaces. The materialistic theory is however silent on this point; and the succession of instantaneous spaces is tacitly combined into one persistent space. This theory is a purely intellectual rendering which has had the luck to get itself formulated at the dawn of scientific thought. It has dominated the language and the imagination of science since science flourished in Alexandria, with the result that it is now hardly possible to speak without appearing to assume its immediate obviousness.

But when it is distinctly formulated in the abstract terms in which I have just stated it, the theory is very far from obvious. The passing complex of factors which compose the fact which is the terminus of sense-awareness places before us nothing corresponding to the trinity of this natural materialism. This trinity is composed (i) of the temporal series of extensionless instants, (ii) of the aggregate of material entities, and (iii) of space which is the outcome of relations of matter.

There is a wide gap between these presuppositions of the intellectual theory of materialism and the immediate deliverances of sense-awareness. I do not question that this materialistic trinity embodies important characters of nature. But it is necessary to express these characters in terms of the facts of experience.' (*The Concept of Nature*, page 70.)

The constructive task to be underaken, then, is to devise a better philosophy of the natural world, more firmly rooted than the traditional 'materialism' in direct awareness; and Whitehead accordingly begins with an examination of the immediate awareness of natural phenomena that is the only thing that gives science its empirical content.

The ultimate and indubitable fact is what Whitehead calls the 'passage of nature'. This passage is more fundamental than time, and temporal transition is derivative from it. Whitehead identifies it with *durée* as described by Bergson in [1], and more briefly in [2].

'It is in virtue of its passage that nature is always moving on. It is involved in the meaning of this property of "moving on" that not only is any act of sense-awareness just that act and no other, but the terminus of each act is also unique and is the terminus of no other act. Sense-awareness seizes its only chance and presents for knowledge something which is for it alone.'   (Page 54.)

What we apprehend in sense-awareness is 'something going on'. Within this something two kinds of constituent can be distinguished— the *discerned*, which is registered as actually present to the senses, and the *discernible*, which is inferred, consciously or unconsciously, from what is present.

'This general fact [of something going on] at once yields for our apprehension two factors, which I will name, the "discerned" and the "discernible". The discerned is composed of those elements of the general fact which are discriminated with their own individual peculiarities. It is the field directly perceived. But the entities of this field have relations to other entities which are not particularly discriminated in this individual way. These other entities are known merely as the *relata* in relation to the entities of the discerned field.'   (Page 49.)

It will be seen from this extract that Whitehead certainly does not conceive the mind as a *tabula rasa*, on which sense-impressions are passively received. The mind is already prepared by its own earlier experience, as well as by schooling, to interpret the 'something going on' as the world as it appears from a certain point of view at a certain epoch. What is thus apprehended might be described as the present state of the world for the epoch in question, but we must be careful not to be misled by the adjective 'present'. The present as perceived in sense-awareness is not a mathematical instant but a thin temporal slab. This *specious present*, as it is called, not only registers an epoch but also comprehends the passage of nature as it is taking place at that epoch. We are thus able to perceive passage directly, and the perceived passage of nature has, moreover, a definite sense from earlier to later that is an element in our awareness. The temporal boundaries of the specious present are vague and continually shifting and, in Whitehead's phrase, 'what we perceive as present is the vivid fringe of memory tinged with anticipation'.

Such then is the primitive 'deliverance of sense-awareness'—on the one hand immediate, concrete, and unique, while on the other hand it appears to be hopelessly elusive and imprecise. Sense-awareness is ultimately our only means of access to the natural world, and yet it seems altogether too vague to provide a secure foundation for exact science. Whitehead's main task is to show how such a foundation is possible. Briefly his argument is that, for all their imprecision, specious presents are able to function as 'neighbourhoods' in a topological sense, in terms of which moments of zero temporal thickness can be defined; and then, by making in thought the limiting transition from nature as passage to instantaneous states of nature, we are able to derive an idealized world of physical phenomena to which the precise methods of scientific inquiry are applicable.

The specious present of an individual at a particular epoch is an instance of what Whitehead refers to more generally as a *duration*, using this term to mean not an abstract temporal interval between two instants but the concrete slab of the whole of nature in its discerned and discernible passage through the interval.   A specious present is thus a very short duration, so short that it can be comprehended in a single act of awareness.   Durations can be very much longer than this; and indeed, since the world as posited for sense-awareness is made up of the intellectually discernible as well as the immediately discerned, they can be arbitrarily long or arbitrarily short.   By a *moment* we shall mean the ideal limit to which a duration approximates as it is made shorter and shorter.   A moment is thus an instantaneous state of the whole world.

For natural science to be possible at all, we must have both moments and durations.   Moments of time (and likewise points of space) are necessary in order that the world may be simplified sufficiently to allow of precise mathematical description and mathematical handling. Whitehead has formulated the following general principle, which he calls the *law of convergence to simplicity by diminution of extent*: 'If A and B are two events, and A' is part of A and B' is part of B, then in many respects the relations between the parts A' and B' will be simpler than the relations between A and B'.   This law, as he says, is the principle which presides over all attempts at exact observation.

But although science is directly based on moments, we cannot define moments at all, and hence we cannot link scientific theories effectively with data of direct observation, unless we go back to durations.   Among the famous paradoxes of Zeno of Elea (fifth century B.C.) there is one that effectively illustrates this necessity, namely the paradox of the flying arrow: At every instant of its flight the arrow is in some definite place, and therefore at rest.   How, then, can it move at all?   If the ultimate analysis of time is into discrete moments, then motion is incomprehensible; but if what is given is an overlapping system of durations, and moments are merely logical constructions out of durations, then there is no longer any mystery about motion.   And more generally, by going back to the durations out of which moments are formed we can hope to discover a basis for the many important differential properties of nature.

The fundamental philosophical problem thus reveals itself to be the reduction by logical analysis of the scientific world of phenomena in time and space to the world as presented in sense-awareness.   White-head's proposed solution to this problem is based on an essentially topological method, called by him the *method of extensive abstraction*, which makes possible the definition of a space-time frame for the physical description of nature.   When applied to durations this method yields moments, and when applied to events it can also yield points. But we have not yet explained what Whitehead understands by an event, and this omission must be made good before we turn to the more formal details of the theory of extensive abstraction.

An *event* is 'the specific character of a place throughout a period of time'.   Every duration is an event, but an event may also be only some spatially limited part of a duration, as for instance 'the natural fact which is the Great Pyramid throughout a day, meaning thereby all nature within it'.   One event can extend over another in time, in space, or in both respects, and the method of extensive abstraction is thus able to give a variety of limiting entities such as moments, points, and one-dimensional tracks.

5.1   The method of extensive abstraction

The domain within which the method of extensive abstraction is applied is the domain of events.   Since events are entities which possess extension, they behave in many ways like classes; but since they are here taken as primitive and unanalysed, no direct application to them of the algebra of classes is possible.   Instead we work with a primitive relation aKb (to be read as 'a extends over b'), this relation being interpreted as meaning that b is a *proper* part of a.   Thus the relation aKb for events is analogous to the relation $(b \subset a \,\&\, b \neq a)$ for classes.   Whenever the relation aKb holds, we say that the event b is a *part* of the event a.   Among the basic formal properties of the relation K are the following (*Enquiry*, p. 101):

(i) $aKb \rightarrow a \neq b$;

(ii) $(x)[(Ey)xKy \,\&\, (Ez)zKx]$;

(iii) $(x)(bKx \rightarrow aKx) \rightarrow (a = b \,\vee\, aKb)$;

(iv) $(aKb \,\&\, bKc) \rightarrow aKc$;

(v) $aKc \rightarrow (Ex)(aKx \,\&\, xKc)$;

(vi) $(x)(y)(Ez)(zKx \,\&\, zKy)$.

An *abstractive set* is a set of events which is such that (i) of any two of its members one extends over the other, and (ii) there is no event that is extended over by every event of the set.

An abstractive set α is said to *cover* an abstractive set β if every member of α extends over some member of β.   Two abstractive sets are said to be *K-equal* if each covers the other.

In less formal terms, an abstractive set is a nest of events which converges to an ideal limit (but not to a limiting *event*, since its intersection is empty), and K-equal abstractive sets define alternative modes of convergence to the same ideal limit. With the aid of this idea of convergence of sets of events we can now make more precise the law of convergence to simplicity by diminution of extent, which we quoted in a vague form on p. 345. In view of the fundamental importance of the law, we give in full the passage in *The Concept of Nature* in which Whitehead explains it.

'So far as the abstractive sets of events are concerned, an abstractive set converges to nothing. There is the set with its members growing indefinitely smaller and smaller as we proceed in thought towards the smaller end of the series; but there is no absolute minimum of any sort which is finally reached. In fact the set is just itself and indicates nothing else in the way of events, except itself. But each event has an intrinsic character in the way of being a situation of objects and of having parts which are situations of objects and—to state the matter more generally—in the way of being a field of the life of nature. This character can be defined by quantitative expressions expressing relations between various quantities intrinsic to the event or between such quantities and other quantities intrinsic to other events. In the case of events of considerable spatio-temporal extension this set of quantitative expressions is of bewildering complexity. If e be an event, let us denote by $q(e)$ the set of quantitative expressions defining its character including its connexions with the rest of nature. Let e_1, e_2, e_3, etc. be an abstractive set, the members being so arranged that each member such as e_n extends over all the succeeding members such as e_{n+1}, e_{n+2}, and so on. Then corresponding to the series

$$e_1, e_2, e_3, \ldots, e_n, e_{n+1}, \ldots,$$

there is the series

$$q(e_1), q(e_2), q(e_3), \ldots, q(e_n), q(e_{n+1}), \ldots.$$

Call the series of events s and the series of quantitative expressions $q(s)$. The series s has no last term and no events which are contained in every member of the series. Accordingly the series of events converges to nothing. It is just itself. Also the series $q(s)$ has no last term. But the sets of homologous quantities running through the various terms of the series do converge to definite limits. For example if Q_1 be a quantitative measurement found in $q(e_1)$, and Q_2 the homologue to Q_1 to be found in $q(e_2)$, and Q_3 the homologue to Q_1 and Q_2 to be found in $q(e_3)$, and so on, then the series

$$Q_1, Q_2, Q_3, \ldots, Q_n, Q_{n+1}, \ldots,$$

though it has no last term, does in general converge to a definite limit. Accordingly there is a class of limits $l(s)$ which is the class of the limits of those members of $q(e_n)$ which have homologues throughout the series

$q(s)$ as n indefinitely increases. We can represent this statement diagrammatically by using an arrow($\rightarrow$) to mean "converges to". Then

$$e_1, e_2, e_3, \ldots, e_n, e_{n+1}, \ldots \rightarrow \text{nothing},$$

and

$$q(e_1), q(e_2), q(e_3), \ldots, q(e_n), q(e_{n+1}), \ldots \rightarrow l(s).$$

The mutual relations between the limits in the set $l(s)$, and also between these limits and the limits in other sets $l(s')$, $l(s'')$, ..., which arise from other abstractive sets s', s'', etc., have a peculiar simplicity.

Thus the set s does indicate an ideal simplicity of natural relations, though this simplicity is not the character of any actual event in s. We can make an approximation to such a simplicity which, as estimated numerically, is as close as we like by considering an event which is far enough down the series towards the small end.' (Page 80.)

The relation of K-equality among abstractive sets is clearly an equivalence relation, and it accordingly divides up the totality of abstractive sets into classes of K-equal abstractive sets. Any such class of all the abstractive sets K-equal to a given abstractive set is said to be an *abstractive element*. Abstractive elements thus provide a representation, in the strict theory, of the 'ideal limits' to which we have already referred in a more informal way.

5.2   Definition of time and space by extensive abstraction

Whitehead applies his method of extensive abstraction first of all to durations. A duration, as we have said (p. 345), is the concrete slab of the whole of nature in its apprehended passage from one epoch to another. For any given person, all durations belong to a single family, which has the following characteristics: there are no maximal or minimal durations in the family; two durations are either disjoint or else they intersect in a duration; and any two durations are contained in a single duration which extends over them both. If we now take any abstractive set of durations of the family, this set can be thought of as converging to a *moment* or instantaneous ideal limit. We can, of course, avoid postulating moments as entities of a new and mysterious kind by the familiar mathematical device of identifying the moment defined by an abstractive set of durations with the abstractive element to which this abstractive set belongs. In this way we arrive at a totality of moments. It is easily shown that, if two moments are distinct, then any two abstractive sets that respectively define them will have members that are disjoint; and we accordingly say that the moments themselves are non-intersecting or *parallel*. Furthermore, a natural serial order of the parallel moments is determined by the unique sense of passage within all durations of the initial family.

Now it is an empirical fact that the world of sense-awareness is four-dimensional; and every moment therefore determines a three-dimensional section of this world, namely the instantaneous world as it exists at the corresponding epoch. If temporal sections of the four-dimensional world can only be taken in one way (at right-angles, so to speak, to the unique time-axis) then the instantaneous sections cannot be further differentiated by this means; but if genuinely different families of temporal sections were available, we could analyse the world ultimately into points, defined as common intersections of tetrads of non-parallel moments. Whitehead believes this to be possible, since the theory of relativity in fact demands a multiplicity of time-systems, associated with observers in relative motion.

Whitehead's method, then, is to begin by postulating different families of durations. He asserts that two durations belong to the same family if and only if either (i) there are durations which are common parts of both, or (ii) the two durations are entirely separate. In other words, two durations belong to the same family unless they intersect in common parts which are not durations. Then every family of durations gives rise to an associated family of parallel moments.

With a multiplicity of families of moments at his disposal, Whitehead is able to define various loci in the four-dimensional world by forming suitable intersections. Two non-parallel moments intersect in a *level*, three moments intersect in general in a *rect*, and four moments intersect in general in a *punct*. The artificial words 'rect' and 'punct' are used provisionally at this stage of the argument in order that the words 'line' and 'point' may be left free for more specific use later on. The strict definition of a punct is as 'the assemblage of abstractive elements which lie in each of four moments whose families have no special relation to each other'. Levels, rects, and puncts are 'mere logical notions without any route of approximation along entities posited in sense-awareness'. But although these ideal entities cannot be approached by direct approximation, they have nevertheless an indirect connexion with events, and this is what makes them scientifically useful.

Suppose we take some particular punct π, and we form a totality of abstractive sets as follows: An abstractive set p is to belong to the totality if and only if (i) it covers every abstractive element which is a member of π, and (ii) all the abstractive sets q which cover every abstractive element which is a member of π and are covered by p also cover p. The totality of abstractive sets so defined is in fact an abstractive element, and Whitehead calls it the *event-particle* associated with the punct π. A punct is thus a mere abstract position in the four-dimensional world, but an event-particle is a place in the concrete world of sense-awareness, conceived as the limit of its nest of neighbourhoods.

So far we have been dealing all the time with moments or instantaneous spaces, but what is needed by physics is a single timeless space that retains its identity while time passes (cf. p. 343). The importance of event-particles derives from the fact that, by virtue of their close relation to events, they are able to connect one instantaneous space with another, thus making possible an identification of the 'same' point at different times. The required identification is achieved by means of the 'stations' corresponding to the various event-particles, a station being a new kind of abstractive element that is defined in the following way.

By *cogredience* of an event with a duration we are to understand extension of the event throughout the duration. More precisely, an event is cogredient with a duration if and only if it is a part of the duration, and every part of the duration has among its own parts a part of the event. Suppose, now, that P is a given event-particle in a given duration d. If we consider abstractive sets of events such that (i) all the events are cogredient with d, and (ii) the event-particle P lies in each event, then we can derive an abstractive element which is called the *station* of P in d. If d' is a duration that forms a part of d, then the stations in d' are those parts of the stations in d that are contained in d'; and by means of overlapping durations we can prolong the finite stations in d to infinite *point-tracks* which extend throughout all durations of the same family α as d. Every moment of α is then met by every point-track in one and only one event-particle, and thus the point-tracks determine the required correlation between the instantaneous spaces of the different moments of α.

We have now succeeded in constructing physical time and space, by purely logical means, out of the primitive materials provided by sense-awareness. Time and space have as yet no metrical properties, however, but only relations of order. The metrical properties all follow from the theory of congruence that is developed by Whitehead on the basis of the construction that we have outlined. But even when this has been done, one further development is still required before we can claim to possess an adequate philosophy of natural knowledge. We still need a theory of objects.

5.3   Objects

The world of common sense is no heraclitean flux, but a world of persistent objects; and change is conceived as change in the properties of objects or in relations between objects. How, then, does it come about that we are able to find such objects amid the universal passage of nature? Whitehead's answer is that we do this by the activity of 'recognition', which must be taken as a primitive power of the discerning mind.

'Objects are elements in nature which do not pass. The awareness of an object as some factor not sharing in the passage of nature is what

I call "recognition". It is impossible to recognize an event, because an event is essentially distinct from every other event. Recognition is an awareness of sameness. But to call recognition an awareness of sameness implies an intellectual act of comparison accompanied with judgment. I use recognition for the non-intellectual relation of sense-awareness which connects the mind with a factor of nature without passage. On the intellectual side of the mind's experience there are comparisons of things recognized and consequent judgments of sameness or diversity. Probably "sense-recognition" would be a better term for what I mean by "recognition". I have chosen the simpler term because I think that I shall be able to avoid the use of "recognition" in any other meaning than that of "sense-recognition". I am quite willing to believe that recognition, in my sense of the term, is merely an ideal limit, and that there is in fact no recognition without intellectual accompaniments of comparison and judgment. But recognition is that relation of the mind to nature which provides the material for the intellectual activity.' (*The Concept of Nature*, page 143.)

Whitehead's theory of objects is much less formal than his theory of space and time, since we cannot deal even in the most general way with objects without going in detail into much of the complexity of the concrete world. For this reason Whitehead does not attempt to give an exhaustive theory of objects, but contents himself in the main with a clarification of the difference between three kinds of object that must be kept distinct if confusion is to be avoided in the philosophy of natural science, namely sense-objects, perceptual objects, and physical objects.

'These three types form an ascending hierarchy, of which each member presupposes the type below. The base of the hierarchy is formed by the sense-objects. These objects do not presuppose any other type of objects. A sense-object is a factor of nature posited by sense-awareness which (i), in that it is an object, does not share in the passage of nature and (ii) is not a relation between other factors of nature. It will of course be a relatum in relations which also implicate other factors of nature. But it is always a relatum and never the relation itself. Examples of sense-objects are a particular sort of colour, say Cambridge blue, or a particular sort of sound, or a particular sort of smell, or a particular sort of feeling. I am not talking of a particular patch of blue as seen during a particular second of time at a definite date. Such a patch is an event where Cambridge blue is situated.' (Page 149.)

To illustrate what he means by a perceptual object, Whitehead takes the example of an athlete's coat of Cambridge blue flannel:

'When we look at the coat, we do not in general say, There is a patch of Cambridge blue; what naturally occurs to us is, There is a coat. Also the judgment that what we have seen is a garment of man's attire is a detail. What we perceive is an object other than a mere sense-object. It is not a mere patch of colour, but something more; and it is that something more which we judge to be a coat. I will use the word "coat" as the name for that crude object which is more than a patch of colour, and without any allusion to the judgments as to its usefulness as an article of attire either in the past or the future. The coat which is perceived—in this sense of the word "coat"—is what I call a perceptual object.' (Page 153.)

Perceptual objects are thus the objects distinguished by unreflective common sense, 'the outcome of the habit of experience'. But then, as perception becomes more permeated by reflection, many perceptual objects are found to be delusive. By this we mean that they do not fit into a systematic pattern of causality, that they cannot also be perceived by other observers, and so forth. A distinction is thus arrived at between *perceptual* objects simply as appearances (e.g. a visual image, which may equally be of a thing directly seen or of a thing which appears delusively to be behind a mirror in which it is reflected) and *physical* objects as things objectively existing in space and time and perceptible by all observers.

'Physical objects are the ordinary objects which we perceive when our senses are not cheated, such as chairs, tables and trees.' (Page 156.)

Whitehead carries his analysis one stage beyond physical objects to what he calls 'scientific objects'. These are the objects which we postulate intellectually in order to account for perceived phenomena by means of scientific theories. Electrons, for example, are scientific objects. It is plain that the distinction between physical objects and scientific objects is only one of degree, and indeed that no precise classification of objects into distinct kinds can be made at all.

This last part of Whitehead's philosophy of natural knowledge, which treats of objects, is inclined to be somewhat vague and less satisfactory than the earlier part, because the distinctions dealt with in it are qualitative and therefore not amenable to abstract mathematical treatment. Where a mathematical approach is possible, as in the discussion of space and time, the system is very much more successful. In any case we shall not here go further into the details of the theory, since these are best studied from Whitehead's own writings.

6   Mathematics and the logical analysis of the natural world

The examination of Whitehead's philosophy of natural knowledge that we have just completed arose out of our general discussion of the application of theories belonging to pure mathematics. In order to justify philosophically an application of such a mathematical theory it is necessary to show that the structure which the theory analyses inheres in some particular body of experience; and so we found ourselves led to a consideration of the structural features of experience of natural phenomena. But on looking back we now see that, as often happens in philosophy, the attempt to solve a philosophical problem has shown the problem itself, in its original formulation, to be illusory.

We began with the idea of a mathematical theory (e.g. riemannian geometry) on the one hand and the observable world of physical phenomena on the other, the problem being to determine whether the theory fits the phenomena. But such a problem cannot be solved until the physical world is described in precise enough terms for its structure to admit of comparison with the ideal mathematical structure, and it was in this way that Whitehead's ideas became relevant. Whitehead has in fact provided a general description of the natural world that makes its structure fully explicit, and he has done so by logical analysis of the kinds of statement that we make about natural phenomena. His method, as we have seen, is to build up the descriptive 'language' of common sense and the 'language' of experimental science out of the most primitive 'language' of all, that of immediate impressions of sense. But in doing this he is obliged to use essentially mathematical methods, especially the method of extensive abstraction; and so we cannot any longer treat the world of described phenomena as something directly given, and available for confrontation with abstract mathematics. In this sense, then, the original problem of justifying the application of mathematics has been destroyed by the preparations that have been made for solving it.

Whitehead's attempt to say more precisely what constitutes the natural world has in fact lent support to Brouwer's conception of mathematics, which we considered in Chapter 12, §3. In his paper 'Mathematik, Wissenschaft und Sprache', on which our account of his ideas was based, Brouwer interpreted the mathematical approach to the world (which he separated into *mathematische Betrachtung* and *mathematische Abstraktion*) as the means that man has developed for moulding his world to his will by science and technology. Mathematics is not something applied to phenomena from without, but rather an element in our way of conceiving phenomena themselves. Thus both Brouwer and Whitehead suggest that it is a mistake to think of the natural world as something objectively given, in just the way in which it appears to us with our particular 'language' and cultural tradition. Here, indeed, we have a glimpse of an idea that has been central in post-Kantian philosophy—the idea of the active role of the mind in the production of knowledge. In the concluding chapter of this book we shall now turn to a more deliberate, though still introductory, consideration of the relevance of this idea to the philosophy of mathematics and mathematical science.

SUPPLEMENTARY NOTES ON CHAPTER 13

1. *Zeno's paradoxes of motion.* Zeno of Elea (c. 490–430 B.C.) devised four paradoxes concerning motion, which are quoted by Aristotle in the *Physics*, 239[b]. The following summary of them is taken from J. Burnet: *Greek Philosophy* (London, 1914):

'The celebrated arguments of Zeno concerning motion introduce the element of time, and are directed to showing that it is just as little a sum of moments as a line is a sum of points. (1) If a thing move from one point to another, it must first traverse half the distance. Before it can do that, it must first traverse half of the half, and so on *ad infinitum*. It must, therefore, pass through an infinite number of points, and that is impossible in a finite time. (2) Achilles can never overtake the tortoise. Before he comes up to the point at which the tortoise started, the tortoise will have got a little way on. The same thing repeats itself with respect to this little way, and so on *ad infinitum*. (3) The flying arrow is at rest. At any given moment it is in a space equal to its own length, and therefore at rest. The sum of an infinite number of positions of rest is not motion. (4) If we suppose three lines, one (A) at rest, and the other two (B, C) moving in opposite directions, B will pass in the same time twice the number of points in C than it passes in A.'

2. *The theory of games.* In their book *Theory of Games and Economic Behavior* (1947), von Neumann and Morgenstern explore heuristically the possibility of making economics into a mathematical science. Earlier attempts to do this by simply transferring to the new field the existing techniques of algebra and the infinitesimal calculus, already used to such good effect in physical science, have proved fruitless, since little has been achieved beyond the reformulation of existing statements in mathematical symbols instead of in words. There are two fundamental difficulties to be overcome: (i) the conceptual imprecision of descriptive economics, and (ii) the probable inappropriateness of mathematical methods that have been developed for quite other purposes. The subject-matter of economics needs first of all to be clarified by much patient research of a predominantly descriptive character, leading eventually to a stage where the concrete axiomatic method becomes applicable (cf. p. 201, above). And there must also be research on the mathematical side, in order that mathematical techniques may be developed that are capable of dealing with whatever formal problems are found to arise. The demands of physical science in the seventeenth century led to the creation of the calculus; and so 'it is to be expected that mathematical discoveries of a stature comparable to that of the calculus will be needed in order to produce decisive success in the field of economics'.

There are few short cuts in science, and it is absurd to try to by-pass an essential phase of development that may require many generations, or even centuries, to run its course. The time has not yet come for setting up comprehensive axiomatic theories, or even for trying to produce practical results by treating economic problems mathematically. We should rather concentrate on making ourselves thoroughly familiar with very simple situations that share in some of the essential features of economic activity, seeking to devise mathematical ways of investigating the structural properties of such economic microcosms. Then we can gradually enlarge the scope of the inquiry as we develop the means to do so. The theory of games is put forward as the initial phase of such an investigation:

'The field covered in this book is very limited, and we approach it in this sense of modesty. We do not worry at all if the results of our study conform with views gained recently or held for a long time, for what is important is the gradual development of a theory, based on a careful analysis of the ordinary everyday interpretation of economic facts. This preliminary stage is necessarily *heuristic*, i.e. the phase of transition from unmathematical plausibility considerations to the formal procedure of mathematics. The theory finally obtained must be mathematically rigorous and conceptually general. Its first applications are necessarily to elementary problems where the result has never been in doubt and no theory is actually required. At this early stage the application serves to corroborate the theory. The next stage develops when the theory is applied to somewhat more complicated situations in which it may already lead to a certain extent beyond the obvious and the familiar. Here theory and application corroborate each other mutually. Beyond this lies the field of real success: genuine prediction by theory. It is well known that all mathematical sciences have gone through these successive phases of evolution.'

3. *The mathematical theory of crystalline structure.* A fundamental work on the mathematics of crystalline symmetry (cf. p. 339) is A. Schönflies: *Krystallsysteme und Krystallstruktur* (1891). In this book, Schönflies traces the mathematical study of crystal structure as far back as to a publication of Hauy (1781), and he gives specific references to major contributions by a number of authors (see pp. 17–19 and 313–314 of his book). He begins his own account by first defining a crystal as 'a homogeneous rigid body, whose physical properties are in general different in different directions, and vary with direction in accordance with fixed laws of symmetry', and he goes on to adduce two basic experimental facts: (1) If, through an arbitrarily chosen fixed point O of a given crystal, a directed line g_1 is taken, there is a finite set of further directed lines $g_2, \ldots, g_N$ such that the physical properties of the crystal in all N directions $g_1, \ldots, g_N$ are identical; and the set of N lines has properties of symmetry that are independent of the choice of g_1. (2) For any axis of rotational symmetry in a crystal, the defining angle of rotation always has one of the four values $\pi, 2\pi/3, \pi/2, \pi/3$. Interpreting symmetry as invariance with respect to a group of transformations (rotations, reflections, etc.), Schönflies then shows in detail that there exist precisely 32 groups which are consistent with his two facts, and that the types of symmetry so defined are the ones already given, wholly or in part, in the classifications worked out by Möbius, Bravais, and other authors. Having done this, he then begins afresh with an examination of the mathematical consequences of the hypothesis that a crystal consists of molecules situated at the points of a three-dimensional lattice. He is able to show that the types of symmetry that are possible for such a lattice correspond exactly to his 32 groups of transformations, and furthermore that the restriction of angles of rotation

to multiples of π, $2\pi/3$, $\pi/2$, and $\pi/3$ is deducible from the hypothesis of the molecular lattice.

On the scientific value of such *a priori* investigations Schönflies makes the following comment (p. 248):

'To the mathematician thus falls, as is often the case in science, the role of an indispensable assistant but nothing more. He must mark out precisely the freedom that is left, in any theory, for further hypotheses about the nature of the bricks of which crystals are constructed, so that the crystallographer shall be in no doubt as to what latitude he has in each case for making permissible assumptions concerning the chemical or physical characteristics of molecules.'

In other words, there are certain *a priori* limitations on the physical constitution of crystals, and these can be worked out mathematically; but, when this has been done, all further details must be inferred from empirical data, and it is for the experimental scientist to complete the picture.

Books that may be consulted on the mathematics of crystal structure are A. Speiser: *Die Theorie der Gruppen von endlicher Ordnung, mit Anwendungen auf algebraischen Zahlen und Gleichungen sowie auf die Krystallographie* (Berlin, 1923) and H. Weyl: *Symmetry* (Princeton, 1952).

4. *Books on the philosophy of science.*   The following works may be taken as representative:

1. E. Mach: *Die Mechanik in ihrer Entwickelung, historisch-kritisch dargestellt* (Leipzig, 1883); English translation *The Science of Mechanics* (Chicago, 1893).
2. K. R. Popper: *Logik der Forschung* (Vienna, 1935); English translation *The Logic of Scientific Discovery* (London, 1959).
3. B. Russell: *The Analysis of Matter* (London, 1927).
4. B. Russell: *Human Knowledge: Its Scope and Limits* (London, 1948).
5. E. Nagel: *The Structure of Science. Problems in the Logic of Scientific Explanation* (London, 1961).

Chapter 14

LOGIC AND THE ACTIVITY OF THINKING

1   The limitations of formal logic

We have now considered, from many different points of view, the philosophical problems to which mathematical knowledge gives rise; and a recurrent theme throughout the discussion has inevitably been the connexion between mathematics and formal logic. In this final chapter we shall attempt an assessment of the extent to which logic is in fact able to provide a sufficient basis for mathematical truth, and we shall at the same time consider what new understanding of logic itself has resulted from the various investigations that have been made into the logic of mathematics.

We began our discussion, in Part I, by tracing the growth of modern mathematical logic from traditional aristotelian logic. The original system of logic, as devised by Aristotle, was intended as a theory of deductive argument, and subsequent developments have served in the main to extend the scope of this theory from demonstration of the classical geometrical type to the much more intricate deductive pattern of modern mathematical analysis. As we have seen, symbolic logic in its present form is powerful enough to deal with all currently used types of deductive reasoning, and it is therefore fully satisfactory for working needs. But the further claim has been made that this same logic is sufficient also as a theoretical foundation for the whole of mathematical knowledge, and this contention is altogether more doubtful.

The attempt to base mathematics on nothing but logic began in the nineteenth century, with the critical movement which we have described in Chapter 5. It came to be realized at that time that geometrical intuition is a source of uncertainty and weakness in mathematics, and that for greater rigour mathematics ought to be based on pure thought, that is to say on logic alone. The earlier critical movement led eventually to the attempts of Frege and Russell to reduce mathematics without residue to pure logic; but in the more recent history of the study of foundations of mathematics logic has been found insufficient by itself, and appeal has had to be made once again to some kind of intuition. In this way the attempted logistic reduction of mathematics to logic has resulted, not in the disappearance of further need for study of the foundations of mathematics, but in the realization that logic itself is much less simple than was at one time believed.

That logic is more than a formal calculus is not at all a new discovery, and indeed a much wider conception of logic was already an integral element in the imposing philosophical system of Kant's great successor, Georg Wilhelm Friedrich Hegel (1770–1831)—a system that strongly influenced European thought in the course of the nineteenth century.   But argument for or against a particular philosophical outlook is by its nature inconclusive; and the view that logic cannot be represented adequately by a formalism remained speculative until the fact was clearly established that such a treatment of logic is not sufficient even in the wholly abstract sphere of pure mathematics.   The essential insufficiency of formal logic was made apparent in a particularly striking way by the metamathematical theorem of Gödel on the occurrence of undecidable propositions in formalized mathematical theories (p. 238), a theorem which implies that formal logic is incapable of ever containing the whole of intuitive mathematics.   Exclusive reliance on formal logic would in fact necessitate complete formalization of the axioms on which mathematics is based; and Gödel has proved that, whatever system of axioms may be adopted, there will always be propositions which can be stated in the language of the system and even decided by intuitive means, but which are nevertheless logically inaccessible from the chosen starting-point.   Thus, indispensable though formal logic is to mathematics, it cannot provide an ultimate criterion of validity of mathematical assertions.

Although the difference between intuitively based knowledge and abstract theories can only be discerned with some difficulty in mathematics, it is clearly apparent in natural science; for scientific reasoning very often tends to be more of an interplay of concepts that are not fully articulated than an application of a formal scheme.   As has been explained in some detail in Chapter 13, our experience of natural phenomena is what it is by reason of the concepts that pervade it.   No experience, except possibly the most rudimentary deliverance of the senses, is passively received; and there has to be 'interpretation' before anything can be presented to the mind as fit material for reflection.   In the view of Whitehead, for instance, apprehended nature includes both the discerned and the discernible (p. 344), and the discernible is something that can only be grasped intellectually.   The discerned, too, is partly conceptual, as we see from Whitehead's account of physical objects.   And even if this particular theory of natural knowledge is rejected altogether, the conclusion remains inescapable that the natural world which we observe and think about is largely a product of the concepts which we use in apprehending it intellectually.

Now when, as most of the time, we treat the world as if it were simply given—a world consisting of entities of such and such kinds, related in such and such ways—we are able to argue about its constitution and its behaviour in a manner that can be analysed in terms of deductive logic. We may perhaps conclude that something or other cannot be the case because this would contradict something else that is already certain, or we may infer some particular fact from accepted general principles. In these and many other ways our thinking falls squarely within the scope of formal logic. But it has to be remembered that we can only presuppose a 'given' world at all because such a world has already been fashioned by earlier thinking. The barely differentiated 'primitive deliverance' of the senses has gradually been worked up in the course of history, as appropriate concepts have been developed, into the perception of natural phenomena that we now take for granted.

Now although formal logic may be adequate for assessing the validity of reasoning about the world as at present understood, it has nothing whatever to say on the subject of creation of new concepts or revision of old ones; and if we take logic always in this restricted formal sense, then the essential process of conceptual evolution will remain strictly outside its province. This will mean that, although logic is able to elucidate and criticize the deductive structure of scientific theories, it leaves out of account the more intuitive process by which the concepts used in such theories are produced; and logic must therefore fail just at the point where fundamental philosophical questions have to be asked. We are thus driven to the conclusion that formal logic constitutes only the initial phase in the philosophical examination of valid reasoning, being limited to the application of a simple mathematical formalism to the web of deductive relations. In this final chapter we shall accordingly consider what other features of thought must be given a place in a fully comprehensive system of logic.

2   The logic of concrete thought

Logic, taken in its widest sense, is that part of philosophy which treats of the cogency of reasoning; and its task is the dual one of analysing the structure of reflective thinking, as this exists in the world, and formulating general principles against which the validity of actual thinking can be judged. The theory of deductive argument is thus a very limited part of logic, for reflective thinking also includes not only the whole of inductive reasoning but also a great deal of discourse of a less formal character that is nevertheless intended to lend rational support to its conclusions.

We shall use the term 'reflective thinking', without much pretension to philosophical precision, to cover all kinds of mental activity that are carried on deliberately for the attainment of knowledge, or at least for reaching a considered judgement as to what may reasonably be accepted as true.   Reflective thinking is accordingly distinguished from other types of mental activity by the fact of its being both deliberate and cognitive.   The following types of activity, for instance, do not satisfy this requirement, although they all involve the operation of the mind: (a) guessing, idle musing, and habitual jumping to conclusions, all of which are subjects for psychology, not for philosophy; (b) writing poetry or romances; (c) carrying out intelligent courses of action simply by 'knowing how', without formulation of any conscious plan.[1]

Since reflective thinking is by its nature a deliberate process, it must always have a systematic form.   In some cases, as we have already seen, the form shows itself in a certain structural pattern, which can be represented mathematically by means of symbolic logic; but very often the form of reflective thinking is not structural in this special sense.   When reflective thinking is of such a kind that its validity can be assessed by the criteria of formal logic we shall say that it is *manipulative*, and in the contrary case we shall described it as *dialectical*.   Reasoning which is described as manipulative in accordance with this usage need not be presented formally—either in terms of syllogisms or by the use of a symbolic calculus—but it must be such that formalization would theoretically be capable of exhibiting the logical element which it involves.   What we now have to do is to elucidate the precise relationship between manipulative and dialectical thinking; and to do this we must first of all examine the nature and use of concepts.[2]

By a *concept* we understand some definite idea that can be recognized as a recurrent feature in thinking.   Concepts, in the realm of thought, are thus analogous in this respect to Whitehead's objects in the realm of sense-awareness (cf. p. 350).   In deductive reasoning, concepts behave rather like things, since they are treated as fixed and unchanging, and susceptible of precise delimitation by means of suitable definitions.   To them we can attach names (which may be names of entities, of properties of entities, of relations between entities, and so forth) and deductive argument is then a process of manipulation of the names involved.   This is what is achieved when an argument is formalized with the aid of symbolic logic.

In reasoning which is not wholly manipulative, concepts function in quite another way, since they are then no longer *objects* to be handled combinatorially but *foci of organization* in the flux of thought.   In

---

[1] Cf. G. Ryle: 'Knowing how and knowing that', *Proceedings of the Aristotelian Society*, **46** (1946), 1–16.

[2] Cf. G. T. Kneebone: 'Abstract logic and concrete thought', *Proceedings of the Aristotelian Society*, **56** (1956), 25–44.

order that we may be able to discuss this aspect of the work of concepts we need to have a name for the general object to which reflective thinking relates, and for this purpose we choose the word 'experience' —here to be used as a neutral term, with no specific reference to any particular content. For a given person, at a given moment in his life, his 'experience' is his entire world at that stage. It includes all that he knows and believes, his tacit presuppositions, his stock responses to words and situations—in brief everything, except external stimuli, capable of influencing what comes into his mind.

It will be seen that the totality of reflective thinking which we envisage in the present discussion extends far beyond the mere consideration of natural phenomena that was the main subject of the part of Whitehead's philosophy which we examined in Chapter 13. In developing his theory of natural knowledge, Whitehead related his argument all the time to the world of sense-awareness, which he analysed, as we have seen, into the discerned and the discernible. In the present context, where we are contemplating the whole of reflective thinking, we cannot restrict the object of awareness in this way, and we must think in terms of a world of 'total awareness'. This, the content of our experience, is the totality of all that can come before the mind, either as directly discerned or as merely discernible; and it includes the entire world of sense-awareness and much more besides. The world of total awareness is not a system of discrete entities, but rather a continuous field of sensation, emotion, and intellectual activity, sharply defined in some parts and nebulous and elusive in others, in which we are able to 'recognize' permanent features.

The experience of a person at a particular time may well be full of unresolved inconsistencies, but in spite of this it has an over-all coherence; and, for the person concerned, the form of his experience is in effect an *a priori* form, since it determines the possible ways in which new impressions can be fitted into the existing picture of the world. The form is supplied partly by the explicit concepts at the person's disposal and partly by his tacit presuppositions, that is to say the general notions and principles which he takes for granted, without necessarily articulating them. If Kant is right in asserting that the entire phenomenal world has an inescapable *a priori* form that is the same for all rational men, then this form constitutes a fixed nucleus of the *a priori* form of each individual's experience; and the objective nucleus is immersed in the totality of concepts and presuppositions peculiar to each separate individual. This totality is *a priori* for the individual to whom it belongs, since he cannot envisage the world in other terms, but it is not necessarily shared by any other individual. In practice, of course, people who live in the same age and the same society tend to have experiences of similar form[1]—and it is precisely for this reason that they are able to communicate with one another with tolerable freedom. And discussion between people, whether forming part of everyday conversation or conducted more systematically through the medium of print, is in its turn the principal means whereby separate experiences are enabled to interact, and thus to extend the common background.

By the operation of language, the concepts that a person has at his command are isolated and made stable. When a permanent feature of experience has been recognized, it can only be kept steadily before the mind and considered with intellectual detachment if a name is given to it; and in this way our experience is strongly conditioned by the language which we possess. It is easy to imagine that any word which refers to something in the world must have a clear, objective meaning; but reflection shows that this is far from being the case. Indeed, the normal thing is for such a word to be a condensation of a whole *theory* of the entity to which it refers—or perhaps of many theories, which are not even necessarily consistent with one another— a theory that has evolved, possibly over a very long period of time, and has eventually yielded the current concept of the entity, now enshrined in the word as at present used.

A word may thus sum up the history of an idea, and by its overtones, which a person is able to sense to the extent to which he is at home in the language used, it is able to keep part of this history alive in the present. This aspect of language can be illustrated by many of the most familiar words in the vocabulary of natural science and mathematics, and we may take as typical the three words 'force', 'point', and 'variable'. 'Force' is one of the key-words of newtonian mechanics, and whenever it is used we immediately place what is said in a setting of classical physics, with the result that the questions that naturally spring to mind are questions which likewise presuppose a newtonian background. The word 'point' has many associations—that which has neither parts nor magnitude, abstract position in space, an entity fixed by a set of coordinates, and so forth; and when it is used in modern mathematics any or all of these associations may become active, suggesting appropriate relations and analogies. And finally, the word 'variable' is now used (cf. p. 28) in such a way that, strictly speaking, all idea of variation is excluded, its place being taken by the more precise idea of substitution of a specific entity for an indeterminate; but what makes the word 'variable' almost indispensable is

---

[1] This is doubtless due in part to what Brouwer has called *Vernunftdressur*, the measures taken by human societies to condition the ideas and attitudes of their citizens in such a way that the community acknowledges a single loyalty and is responsive to a common will. See Brouwer's paper [2], quoted on p. 320 above.

precisely the fact of its associations, derived from its earlier application to quantities thought of as varying, which call to mind just the sort of formal behaviour that 'variables' exhibit.

Since the referential function of words accounts only for part of their significance, and the attachment which they have to particular sets of ideas or to specific theories may well be of even greater importance, it is evident that the language which we use plays an active part in our picturing of the world, whether this be the actual world or some ideal world of thought. Sometimes language impresses a particular form on the world as we understand it. This was the case, for instance, as we are now able to see, with the language used by physics in the nineteenth century. And again, language may also determine the kind of entities into which we analyse our world, for we can only think in terms of what we have words for. That the mere use of particular words can beg many questions is obvious enough if words are thought of which refer to things which are controversial, whether in politics, in religion, or in science ; but the same thing is no less true in wholly non-controversial contexts. For the most part it does not much matter that questions are continually begged,[1] for every one does this in the same way, in accordance with the common presuppositions of the age and society to which the language that is being used belongs. What does matter is the consequence that the *a priori* form impressed on experience by language is historically conditioned. The point was made vividly by William Whewell, in his account of scientific induction (1840):

'Although in every inductive inference an act of invention is requisite, the act soon slips out of notice. Although we bind together facts by superinducing upon them a new conception, this conception, once introduced and applied, is looked upon as inseparably connected with the facts, and necessarily implied in them. Having once had the phenomena bound together in their minds in virtue of the conception, men can no longer easily restore them back to the detached and incoherent condition in which they were before they were thus combined. The pearls once strung, they seem to form a chain by their nature. Induction has given them a unity which it is so far from costing us an effort to preserve, that it requires an effort to imagine it dissolved. For instance, we usually represent to ourselves the earth as round, the earth and the planets as revolving about the sun, and as drawn to the sun by a central force ; we can hardly understand how it could cost the Greeks, and Copernicus, and Newton so much pains and trouble to arrive at a view which is to us so familiar. These are no longer to us conceptions caught hold of and kept hold of by a severe struggle ; they are the

---

[1] Occasionally though, it matters very much. It was the question-begging use of words like 'space', 'time', and 'simultaneous' that concealed the inadequacy of the presuppositions of newtonian dynamics until Einstein drew attention to it.

simplest modes of conceiving the facts; they are really facts. We are willing to *own* our obligation to those discoverers, but we hardly *feel* it: for in what other manner (we ask in our thoughts,) could we represent the facts to ourselves?'[1]

It is important to observe, indeed, that the active context of a man's thought extends far beyond the limits of the society or nation in which he has grown up. He is in the first instance a member of a community of people who speak the same 'language' as himself. But his particular community is in turn only one among many related communities, all of which share in a common history; and consequently he is in touch, as an individual, with an extensive 'cultural tradition', consciously aware of a small part of it, and at the same time influenced in more subtle ways by more remote parts of which he may even be in complete ignorance.

The circumstances of reflective thinking may now be described in the following terms. The thinker possesses a certain experience, which includes both his existing knowledge and the means that he has of organizing the content of his mind, that is to say his concepts, presuppositions, logical principles, and so forth. He is also in touch with a cultural tradition, all of which is potentially available to him, although only small parts of it may be actually incorporated in his experience. His thinking is thus shaped both by his own experience and by the cultural tradition to which he belongs. In the limiting case of strictly manipulative thinking, the contribution that these two factors make to the form of an argument is summed up practically without residue in the principles of formal logic, and the pattern of reasoning may in consequence appear to be timeless and wholly objective. But, as Brouwer has declared with such insistence (cf. p. 246), philosophers have in fact no right to claim that any logical principles are eternal, no matter how long they may already have endured. Even in the deductive sphere, therefore, the historical character of the cultural tradition may need to be taken into account; and when reasoning is not manipulative the relevance of the specific background will be very much greater. In order to understand this we now need to look more closely at the way in which dialectical reasoning is carried out.

The fundamental difference between manipulative and dialectical thinking is that the former is essentially abstract and intellectual (even when carried out with a particular application to concrete experience in view) whereas the latter is inseparable from intuitive awareness; and this contrast shows itself in the very different functions exercised in the two modes of reasoning by concepts (cf. p. 360). When we are reasoning manipulatively, our ideal is to keep our concepts fixed and

---

[1] W. Whewell: *The Philosophy of the Inductive Sciences, founded upon their History* (London, 1840), Book XI, Chapter 5.

sharply delineated, so that language may be used with scientific precision. Concepts that are so employed might be called *definable* concepts, since their content, as required for the purpose in hand, can be specified finitely by a definition. But when concepts are transferred from a manipulative to a dialectical situation, they cease to be definable and become *intuitive*, for they are then foci of organization in total awareness. As so used, concepts do indeed pick out and register recognizable features in experience, but they do not circumscribe them. And while a formulated definition can only take account of certain predetermined facets of the concept which it defines, this same concept occurring as a focus or organization in experience can at any time be made specific in ways not previously envisaged.

Manipulative thinking serves to bring order into experience, and to make knowledge systematic, with the aid of those concepts which are already available. Dialectical thinking, on the contrary, produces new concepts, or at least gives new depth of meaning to existing ones. When we are faced, for instance, with experience of a radically new kind, our initial need is to find our bearings; and we accordingly apply a conceptual grid, consisting of the concepts which already offer themselves in a definable form. These concepts provide a language in which the experience under review can be described and discussed, but even as we use this language we are able to apprehend intuitively more than the existing meanings of our words take into account. Surrounding the central region of sharply defined meaning there is an intuitively apprehended penumbral zone of increasing indeterminacy. Although the intuitive penumbra is not part of the meaning as strictly understood, it is related to that meaning through the immediacy of direct awareness; and the meaning may be extended dialectically by incorporation of more of the intuitive content.

This, indeed, is the process by which concepts normally evolve. Existing concepts bring a measure of rational organization to the flux of total awareness, thus facilitating the recognition of further intuitively apprehended features; and the concepts act as centres of accretion, around which newly discerned characteristics are clustered. As time goes on, the concepts themselves are conceived in a more comprehensive way, and features that were at first only dimly discerned come at length to be accepted, by a process that we may refer to as *analytical absorption*, as forming part of the 'natural' definition of the concepts. In Whewell's phrase, the pearls seem to form a chain by their nature. Thus, in all kinds of reflective thinking, concepts evolve dialectically by absorption of what has first to be discerned intuitively; and by their evolution they both shape and transmit the collective 'experience' of society, i.e. its cultural tradition.

3   Inductive reasoning

A dominating constituent in the cultural tradition of the modern age is, of course, natural science and the scientific outlook on the world; and in the present section of this chapter we shall consider the logic of the inductive reasoning by which scientific knowledge is built up. Induction plays a considerable part in common life as well as in scientific research, but its most characteristic applications are those which are made in natural science when general laws are inferred from particular data. We shall here consider scientific induction only.

The distinction between deduction and induction is well established in the literature of philosophy, but there is a great difference in the degree of success with which these two types of reasoning are treated. Traditional logic—and still more symbolic logic—furnishes a theory of deductive inference that is generally accepted as sufficient, but the treatment of induction is often perfunctory and always controversial. The essential difference between deduction and induction is, very roughly, that in a deductive inference the conclusion asserts less than the premises, whereas in an inductive inference it asserts more.[1] For this reason, a valid deductive inference is always conclusive, but inductive inferences are inconclusive in all important cases.

Inductive inferences are not of a single uniform type, and for the sake of clarity we shall distinguish between two main kinds of induction, to be called *determinative induction* and *conceptual induction* respectively. Determinative induction is the mode of reasoning that is used when further details are added to a picture that has already been drawn, in outline at the very least. It comes into play, for instance, whenever the numerical value of a physical constant or a statistical parameter is estimated on the basis of empirical data, or when research is carried out in order to isolate the specific cause of some phenomenon that is already accounted for in a general way by a standard theory. Such induction is very much a matter of common sense and experience, often aided in scientific work by statistical methods. The reasoning that is involved in determinative induction is essentially manipulative, since the concepts that are used in the interpretation of the observations remain unaffected. An altogether more fundamental use of induction in natural science, however, is to enable thought to escape from the closed circle of completely defined concepts—on rare occasions cataclysmically, as in the recent upheaval in physics, but more often so unobtrusively that only the cumulative change over a long period can

---

[1] In the textbooks there is often some discussion of 'perfect' inductions (considered originally by Aristotle) in which the conclusion does not in fact go beyond the premises, e.g. 'January, February,..., December each have less than 32 days; hence all months have less than 32 days'. Such inductions are trivial from our present point of view, and we shall leave them out of account.

be detected at all. Whenever induction reacts in this way upon concepts themselves, instead of merely using them manipulatively as counters, it is of the kind that we call conceptual. Such induction involves not only manipulation but also revision of concepts, a process which we describe as dialectical (p. 360).

The basis of all determinative induction is a statistical principle of optimum choice : we are faced with a certain range of possibilities, and we have to select the one that is the most appropriate in the light of all available evidence. The evidence to be taken into account is made up of the specific data for the induction in question and also the 'experience' (in the sense given to this term on p. 361) into which the conclusion has to fit. In cases of direct statistical estimation, the possibilities are the admissible values for the parameter in question, and standard methods are available for choosing between them. In other cases, not of this numerical kind, a less abstract type of conclusion has to be inferred from specific data—a disease has to be diagnosed, say, from observation of the patient's symptoms. Here the person making the inference must first of all decide what *prima facie* possibilities need to be considered, and then he must make his choice from among them. In some situations, as when the cause of an unexplained natural phenomenon is being investigated, an initial exercise of inventiveness may be required before there are any possibilities to be weighed; and the conclusion reached may conceivably be that none of the explanations offered is acceptable, so that further hypotheses must be sought.

Determinative induction, then, involves a choice, and this choice ought to be made as prudently as possible. The policies ordinarily adopted, which find expression in standard methods of statistical estimation no less than in the 'scientific method' that is handed down in laboratories from master to apprentice, are such that there is good reason to believe that in the long run they will yield a higher proportion of true conclusions than would be yielded by alternative policies. A conclusion that is inferred inductively may in fact be false, even though it is the proper one to choose in the light of available evidence; and the most that can be demanded of induction is that, on balance, evidence shall be used to the best advantage. If certain very general assumptions are made about the uniformity of the behaviour of the natural world and the finiteness of the number of factors that effectively influence any particular phenomenon, the policy of induction can be treated theoretically in terms of the calculus of probabilities; and such a mathematical analysis of determinative induction appears to be the nearest approach that is possible to a formal logic of induction. It does in fact account for the main structural features of inductive reasoning of the determinative kind. Departures from the theoretical pattern are sometimes necessary, it is true, as when special safeguards are demanded by the exceptional seriousness of the consequences that might follow upon errors in one particular direction; but these involve only minor adjustments to the general scheme.

Now unlike determinative induction, which is used for such specific purposes as those of establishing a particular causal connexion or evaluating a natural constant, conceptual induction operates most typically in the production of scientific 'theories'. Such theories not only add to the total body of knowledge, but they make possible a more adequate understanding of facts already recorded. The concepts of a theory, which are arrived at dialectically, allow both the theory itself and the earlier facts to be given an interpretation that would not previously have been possible. In this way conceptual induction (usually in conjunction with determinative induction as well) prepares the ground for a more adequate understanding of natural phenomena. A scientist's knowledge of the facts of nature is a part of what we have called his experience, and as such it has both factual content and conceptual form. Strictly determinative induction merely makes an addition to the content while leaving the form unchanged; but conceptual induction extends or otherwise modifies the form, and it may in consequence have repercussions throughout the whole of experience.

3.1 The element of judgement in induction

As we said on p. 366, the broad difference between deductive and inductive reasoning is that in deduction the conclusion asserts less than the premisses, whereas in induction it asserts more; and we might now add that the conclusions go beyond the premisses (or the evidence) in both kinds of induction, determinative as well as conceptual. It is an immediate consequence of the basic contrast between deduction and induction that the relation between reasoning and formal logic (or in other words the possibility of applying mathematics to the structure of thought) is quite different in the two types of reasoning. When a set of premisses is given, it is fully determinate whether or not any suggested conclusion follows deductively, since this depends only on whether the conclusion is 'contained in' the premisses; and the logic of deduction is thus an entirely typical mathematical theory of a certain formal structure. But when an inference for which the premisses are laid down is inductive, the conclusion is envisaged as going beyond these premisses; and a conclusion which is merely required to be compatible with the data has infinite latitude. A valid induction cannot be characterized as such mathematically, since the essential criterion is not an objective one of formal inclusion but a subjective one of 'reasonableness in the circumstances'.

In practice, inductive reasoning is a matter of judgement, in the sense in which this word is understood in the phrase 'using one's judgement'; and even when we wish to treat induction theoretically, as an object of philosophical inquiry, we cannot idealize it to the extent of eliminating all reference to the judging mind. All actual thinking involves judgement, but in different ways and to varying degrees. In deduction, judgement is reduced to the absolute minimum of bare recognition. We have to recognize the inference in question as an instance of the syllogism in Barbara, say, or of *modus ponens*, and that is all. In determinative induction, judgement is involved in the decision that the weight of evidence is sufficient to warrant acceptance of the conclusion. Here, as we have seen (p. 367), judgement can be eliminated in favour of the formal theory of mathematical statistics by idealization that is not at all violent. But in the dialectical process of conceptual induction there is no fixed pattern, and here everything depends on the soundness of judgement of the thinker.

In natural science there is an empirical control over private judgement, and almost complete objectivity is attained by the cross-checking of inductively acquired knowledge with the results of observation and experiment. When theories have been established inductively to the extent necessary for them to be generally accepted as giving a true picture of the world, they are used systematically in the course of further investigations; and if they do not after all agree with empirical fact, this will sooner or later become apparent. In this manner the coherence that is demanded of scientific theory, both internally with itself and externally with the whole range of empirical observation, exercises continual control over scientific induction. In other domains of reflective thinking also, there is a similar controlling factor of coherence of the whole body of knowledge; but restraint is proportionately weaker as direct confrontation of theoretical assertions with inescapable facts is rarer and more difficult. In some parts of history, for instance, control is very effective; but in philosophy, on the contrary, where the 'facts' of experience against which theories can be checked are, by their nature, determined much more by the concepts through which they are interpreted than by their strictly empirical content, control is at its weakest.

Even in science, however, empirical observation is not the only check; and public discussion and criticism of ideas and theories is no less essential. In mathematics, indeed, such discussion is the only control apart from formal consistency, and it is virtually the only one in philosophy. The effect of wide discussion is to test individual inferences and interpretations of experience against a common tradition, and thus to ensure at least the internal coherence of the tradition.

3.2   The calculus of probabilities

We have already referred (p. 367) to the interpretation of the calculus of probabilities as a 'formal logic of induction'. The view has often been put forward that this calculus has a much closer connexion with inductive reasoning than we have so far admitted, and indeed that a full theoretical justification of every type of induction can be given in terms of the mathematical theory of probability. This is a question that we must now consider. The conclusion to which we are led is that, although the calculus of probabilities provides a foundation for the theory of statistics, it is still not capable of justifying the inductive element in scientific inquiry, for it is itself dependent on induction in its applications.

What the mathematical theory of probability does offer is an analysis of the structure of much of determinative induction, as we have already acknowledged. All that it yields, however, is a *structural analysis*, and not a philosophical justification; for the treatment has to be based on assumptions of uniformity of nature, existence of probability distributions, etc., which, though they would be made freely in scientific inquiry, nevertheless cannot be taken as basic principles. In other words, the formal treatment is not self-contained, but is based on assumptions which have to be weighed up afresh for each particular application. Whether the assumptions hold in any given case (that is to say, whether the argument is amenable to statistical treatment) is a matter of judgement. Thus even determinative induction is not wholly formal; and when we turn to conceptual induction, which is a much more fundamental element in scientific inquiry, there is no formal structure at all that we can attempt to treat mathematically.

The calculus of probabilities itself can be treated either as pure or as applied mathematics. Taken as pure mathematics, it can be developed rigorously as a formal system; and suitable sets of axioms have been formulated, in different ways, by Reichenbach and Kolmogorov. Reichenbach's treatment, given in his paper 'Axiomatik der Wahrscheinlichkeitsrechnung' (1932) in *Mathematische Zeitschrift* and his book *Wahrscheinlichkeitslehre: eine Untersuchung über die logischen und mathematischen Grundlagen der Wahrscheinlichkeitsrechnung* (Leyden, 1935), is based on the primitive expression

$$(i)(x_i \in O \underset{p}{\supset} y_i \in P),$$

in which O, P are class variables and p is a numerical variable which can take values in the range $0 \leqslant p \leqslant 1$. This symbolic expression corresponds to the statement 'the probability that an event of the kind O has the property P is p'. Axioms are taken which correspond closely to the elementary rules for addition and multiplication of probabilities, etc.　In Kolmogorov's treatment, given in his book *Grundbegriffe der Wahrscheinlichkeitsrechnung* (Berlin, 1933), events are treated as sets of 'elementary events', and the mathematical ideas that are used are those of the theory of sets and the theory of measure.　This treatment of Kolmogorov has been widely adopted, in particular by Cramér (1937) and by van der Waerden (1957).　The theory to which it leads is a normal branch of pure mathematics, and nothing need be said here about its foundations.

Now although the calculus of probabilities is no longer in the least questionable as pure mathematics, the basis of its application remains very much a matter of controversy.　There are two main views of what corresponds in intuition to a mathematical probability.　The older view, which goes back in a systematic form at least to Laplace (1812), is that probabilities are degrees of rational belief.　This view was developed very fully by J. M. Keynes in *A Treatise on Probability* (London, 1921), still a standard work on what is often referred to as the *a priori* theory of probability.　The rival view is the one advanced by R. von Mises in a paper with the title 'Grundlagen der Wahrscheinlichkeitsrechnung', published in *Mathematische Zeitschrift* in 1919, and afterwards developed more fully in his book *Wahrscheinlichkeitsrechnung und ihre Anwendungen in der Statistik und theoretischen Physik* (Leipzig, 1931).　Von Mises set out from the idea of a 'collective', or infinite random sequence of observations, and he identified the probability that an observation has a certain property A with the limiting frequency of occurrence of terms with that property in some given collective.

Each of the two main conceptions of probability gives rise to difficulties—the *a priori* conception because rational degree of belief is hard to define logically and even harder to measure numerically, and the frequency conception on several counts: (a) the definition of collective, as given by von Mises, is inconsistent, (b) infinite sequences can never be actually given, and (c) what is wanted is often more general than a probability in one particular collective.　These various difficulties are still not fully resolved; but it seems reasonable to say that if a satisfactory form of frequency theory can be developed, this will best meet the needs of natural science.　The calculus of probabilities is important chiefly as a foundation for the mathematical theory of statistics, and since statistics is directly concerned with what happens on the average or in the long run, the central problem is to give an account of probabilities on this basis.

What kind of entity, then, can possess a probability that is definable by reference to frequency of occurrence?　Considerations of probability, in this sense, only arise when an observation of a definite kind can be made repeatedly—at different times, in different places, upon different subjects, or with some other variation of the circumstances that has no systematic influence on the outcome.　We may accordingly look upon the probability as a function of two predicates, one of which specifies as closely as may be necessary the nature of the observation that is made, while the other defines the outcome that is looked for. Let us use the symbolic expression $\Pr[O(x); P(x)]$, or more shortly $\Pr[O,P]$, to stand for the probability that an observation in accordance with O has an outcome in accordance with P.　Typical probabilities are then $\Pr[x$ is a card drawn at random from a given pack ; x is a spade] and $\Pr[x$ is an inhabitant of London, alive on 1 January 1960 and then aged between 20 and 25 ; x dies before reaching the age of 70].

Any probability $\Pr[O,P]$ is supposed to possess a numerical value p in the range $0 \leqslant p \leqslant 1$, and this number gives an estimate of the proportion of observations in accordance with O that may be expected to have the property expressed by P.　What we have to do in devising a theory of applied probability is to give more precise meaning to this notion of an estimate.　We cannot identify the probability with any actual proportion, since potential observations in the future are envisaged as well as observations already made ; and moreover, any set of observations that we make may, by chance, yield a proportion widely divergent from the probability.　All that we can say is that 'it is likely' that, if we make a series of observations, we shall get a proportion that approximates to the probability, and by increasing the number of observations we can increase the likelihood of a good approximation.　The assertion that this is so can only be an inductive conclusion, although there are many ways in which it may be arrived at—by simple extrapolation of available data, by identification of cases that have equal probability on grounds of symmetry, by appeal to general laws such as Gauss's law of errors, and so forth.　The inductive inference (inductive in the determinative sense) involves an act of judgement ; and a feature of judgement that we have not so far had occasion to mention is that, when we judge that a conclusion is adequately supported by the evidence offered, we can at the same time make an assessment of *how* adequate the support is.　Such an assessment is necessarily intuitive and non-numerical, but it is sufficiently definite for us to be able to say significantly that, when $\Pr[O,P] = p$, the likelihood that the relative frequency of observations of type O with outcomes of type P will fall in a given interval $(p - \varepsilon, p + \varepsilon)$ increases with increase of the total number of observations, and that the likelihood approaches practical certainty as the number of observations is made indefinitely large.[1]

What we have said in the last three sections on the subject of induction and probability is no more than a first step towards systematic

[1] See also G. T. Kneebone: 'Induction and probability', *Proceedings of the Aristotelian Society*, **50** (1950), 27–42.

philosophical mapping of what is after all a vast new continent, as yet mostly unexplored. We have already seen, in Part I and Part II of this book, something of the scope and the difficulty of the study of deductive logic and the foundations of pure mathematics; and there is every reason to expect that even greater difficulty will be encountered in the domain of inductive reasoning. By emphasizing the role of the active mind, exercising its power of judgement in each particular situation, we have tried to bring out the fundamental difference between inductive reasoning (and indeed dialectical reasoning in general) and the kind of reasoning that can be idealized in the operation of a formal calculus. It would be inappropriate here to pursue the inquiry beyond this heuristic stage, since it is properly not so much an appendix to the theory and application of deductive logic as a prologue to a major branch of philosophy which as yet scarcely exists.

4   The genetic method in philosophy

Philosophy, as we have chosen to interpret it, is critical analysis of rational activity (cf. p. 3). The philosopher accepts as given the particular kind of rational activity which it is his purpose to investigate —moral activity, deductive argument, or whatever it may be—and by studying this activity as it actually exists, he tries to see as clearly as possible the aims towards which it is directed and the means employed for attaining them. And then, when he has acquired enough factual knowledge, he can turn to his proper philosophical task of disentangling the implicit principles which control the activity that he is studying, and thus making more explicit the rational element in this activity.

Of such a nature, in particular, is the study of logic, which we accordingly interpret as critical analysis of reflective thinking. It appears from what we have said on the subject of reflective thinking, that logic, taken in this sense, needs to be interpreted more widely than is possible within the bounds of formal logic, and indeed that it is inseparable from epistemology. We cannot properly understand the logical form of reflective thinking unless we take into account the particular product, namely knowledge, that it is intended to yield; neither can we understand the nature of knowledge without seeing it as a product of this activity.

Knowledge, according to the view that we have developed, evolves out of reflection upon 'experience', i.e. the amalgam of intuitive awareness and conceptual interpretation, of acknowledged facts and unanalysed presuppositions, that makes up a man's world; and to avoid falsifying or distorting knowledge, as we examine it philosophically, we must accordingly discuss it from a genetic point of view, that is to say in relation to the process by which it originates. A genetic analysis of knowledge of the natural world, for example, has been attempted by Bertrand Russell, in his book *Human Knowledge: Its Scope and Limits* (London, 1948). In this book Russell traces the beginnings of natural science to what he calls 'animal inference', the confident expectation of continuing regularity that is engendered in animals and young children by habit, and that remains an important factor in the life of even the most reflective human adult. The products of animal inference are worked up by common-sense reflection, aided by scientific or philosophical inquiry, into experience in its more highly developed forms; and this metamorphosis is made possible by the dialectical operation of concepts, temporarily supported at every stage by an extensive manipulative scaffolding.

In the evolution of experience, we can detect a characteristic rhythm, an alternation of phases which are predominantly dialectical with phases which are predominantly manipulative. Concepts change dialectically, in a way that we have already described; and then for a while they seem to be fixed, and until the next dialectical revision they are used manipulatively. In describing the process in these terms we are, of course, looking at it in historical perspective, and the 'experience' referred to is the collective experience of an age or community rather than that of a single person. Individuals cannot often be said to 'reason in a dialectical manner'. They employ concepts manipulatively, though with the shade of meaning that is felt to be appropriate to the situation; and over a period of time the gradual shift through many contiguous shades brings about what the historian of thought must interpret as a dialectical revision. It is for this reason that there is so little direct evidence of the dialectical functioning of concepts in scientific and mathematical literature. An author usually writes and argues from within a particular 'moment' of thought; and it takes a string of moments to reveal the development of concepts.

At a given epoch a concept is regarded as definable, although in practice no complete definition is as a rule attempted; but in reality it would be impossible for any definition to exhaust the implicit content of a concept, and the fact that a concept is more fundamental than any definable idea is shown by the way in which concepts retain their identity through a long history of revision and redefinition. In different ages, for example, very different accounts have been offered of the nature of number; but it is nevertheless more appropriate to speak of many specifications of a single concept than of so many different concepts. And it would not be altogether correct, either, to say that at most one of the accounts can be right and all the others must be wrong. There is no sharp discrimination between a right and a wrong treatment in such a situation, and the most that we can say is that a particular treatment meets satisfactorily the needs of the time to which it belongs, and that other treatments have become obsolete.

5   The outcome of the philosophy of mathematics

The drift of the argument in Part III has been in the direction of showing that there is much in the process of thinking that cannot be brought within the scope of formal logic, and that it is precisely at the most fundamental level of thought, moreover, that the inadequacy of formal logic is most pronounced. Reflective thinking is a conceptual activity, and concepts capable of giving a rational articulation to experience can only be produced by a creative, evolutionary process. This process has an intelligible form, various aspects of which have been studied by philosophers, but no general 'logic of concrete reasoning' can at present be said to exist.

The argument of this Part may seem to have carried us right away from our goal in the study of foundations of mathematics. For the most promising line of advance so far attempted in that study, and one that seemed for a time to offer a prospect of complete success—namely the logistic movement—was only possible if an objective logic could be presupposed. The logistic movement lost impetus, as we have seen, when the conceptions of logic and mathematical truth on which it was based were challenged by other conceptions that accorded better with prevailing mathematical attitudes; and the conclusion to be drawn from later research appears to be that no timeless account of mathematical truth is possible at all. The most that we can ask for from philosophers of mathematics is an analysis of the philosophical presuppositions of mathematics as it exists in our own time, and a justification of the mathematics of today in relation to these presuppositions. It is to be expected, moreover, that the attempt to make explicit the presuppositions on which mathematics is based will alter the presuppositions themselves, and will thus react eventually upon mathematics.

The history of mathematics during the period that we have been chiefly concerned with, the nineteenth and twentieth centuries, shows very clearly the mutual influence of mathematics and philosophy of mathematics. The initial critical movement (discussed in Chapter 5), which was at first purely mathematical in intention, with mathematicians simply trying to achieve greater clarity and rigour in their ordinary work, became progressively more philosophical, until it issued at length in the logistic philosophy of mathematics. The study of metamathematics, on the other hand, began as a philosophical attempt to justify mathematics by investigation of its formal structure, but in the end was largely instrumental in enabling mathematicians to develop new and powerful methods of their own, by turning their attention from properties of individual mathematical entities to structural features of entire mathematical systems—a development that prepared the way for the formation of new branches of mathematics of wide generality, such as functional analysis and algebraic topology.

The modern conception of mathematics as a study of abstract structure has indeed grown out of mathematics and metamathematics together; and it supplies both the current form of presentation of mathematics and the currently valid answer to the philosophical question 'What is mathematics?'.

Are we to conclude, then, that the ambitious enterprise of dismantling traditional mathematics and re-erecting it on a new and unshakable foundation has ended in failure, and that the purpose which inspired it must now be renounced? We should rather say that the purpose, as so conceived, can now be recognized as illusory, and that what the critical research of the past century has achieved is something rather different from what was looked for. Substantial progress has indeed been made towards the desired security of mathematical knowledge; but we now see that the kind of security that is appropriate to mathematics must be sought in continual dialectical revision of the concepts that are used, not in the quiescence of a completed system.

We thus find that mathematics, after all, is not radically different from other domains of knowledge (cf. p. 133). Although mathematical research appears on the surface to be a highly specialized and possibly even unique mode of rational activity, we eventually discover in the philosophy of mathematics a microcosm of philosophy as a whole. Such characteristics as absence of finality and advance by dialectical development of concepts are common to all philosophy; and it is also entirely typical of philosophy that an inquiry should begin with the attempt to answer certain questions or to establish certain theses, only to find that, when all the necessary preparatory work has been carried out, the initial questions cannot any longer be asked or the theses propounded. Constructive advance in philosophy has resulted again and again from the work of philosophers whose positions have in the end been rendered untenable by the further development of the very ideas on which they were initially based. Thus, for example, philosophy as it exists at the present time owes a great debt to Kant, and more recently and in a lesser way it has drawn significant inspiration from the logical positivists of the Vienna Circle; but neither the questions asked by Kant nor those asked by the early logical positivists could still be asked with the same meaning today.

The general view of the nature of philosophy to which we have been led, then, excludes any demand for final answers in a philosophical inquiry. Such an inquiry can at most yield understanding of rational activity that goes beyond the fullest understanding that has previously been attained; but then the primary activity, as so understood, no longer remains what it was before, and the inquiry has to begin again from the new position. If, now, we think of mathematics as successively understood by Euler, by Gauss and Cauchy, by Dedekind and

Peano, by Russell, by Hilbert and Bourbaki, we shall certainly not look upon the history of mathematical philosophy as a melancholy succession of unsuccessful attempts to provide mathematics with an enduring foundation. On the contrary, we shall see it as a process of evolutionary advance, and we shall marvel that the progress made since this branch of philosophy reached maturity has been so rapid and so unfaltering.

Appendix

DEVELOPMENTS SINCE 1939 IN THE STUDY OF FOUNDATIONS OF MATHEMATICS

The discussion of mathematical logic and the foundations of mathematics in this book has been limited in the main to theories constructed and results obtained during the classical period in the study of the subject—a period that we may conveniently regard as spanning the sixty years from 1879 to 1939, that is to say from the publication of Frege's *Begriffsschrift* (which contained the first fully developed logical calculus) to the rounding off of Hilbert's metamathematical work with the appearance of the second volume of *Grundlagen der Mathematik*. It is the purpose of the present appendix to give a brief indication of those parts of mathematical philosophy in which significant advances have been made since 1939, so that the reader may be enabled to discern some general pattern in the more recent literature of the subject.

This appendix, which is offered simply as an initial aid to further study, must not be treated as a balanced assessment of what has been achieved since 1939 over the whole field of mathematical logic and its applications; and the particular works that are referred to in it have not been selected with the primary object of giving a representative sample of all that has been written on the topics mentioned. A number of major areas in which progress has been made are indicated, and under each heading a few typical books and papers are listed, so that the reader will have sufficient references to set out with; but the omission of any particular topic or publication does not necessarily mean that this is judged to be of no significance. Details of all the works referred to are given in the bibliography which follows the appendix.

Fuller information concerning many of the developments touched upon here may be found in the comprehensive survey of E. W. Beth, *The Foundations of Mathematics* (1959), where a systematic and detailed account of many aspects of modern research is given.

A concise progress report on the study of foundations of mathematics, with special emphasis on the current work of Polish logicians and mathematicians, was prepared by Mostowski and a group of collaborators for presentation to the Eighth Congress of Polish

Mathematicians at Warsaw in 1953, and this interesting and informative document was published in 1955 in the series of monographs *Rozprawy Matematyczne*, with the title 'The present state of investigations on the foundations of mathematics'. It will be of most use to those readers who already have some general acquaintance with the topics with which it deals.

The more recent literature of mathematical philosophy is markedly different from that of the classical period, but its most characteristic features may nevertheless all be traced back to innovations made during the years 1930–1939. Various ideas and technical devices that were introduced at that time for specific purposes have since revealed wider possibilities of application, becoming in many cases part of the normal equipment of investigators of the foundations of mathematics. Among such basic elements in present-day research, the following are especially important:

(1) Arithmetization of metamathematics by the introduction of a Gödel numbering for whatever formal system is being studied.

(2) Use of general recursiveness (or one of the equivalent properties of computability, λ-definability, etc.) as a criterion of effectiveness.

(3) Routine appeal to standard 'non-existence theorems', such as Gödel's theorem on the impossibility of an internal proof of consistency and Church's theorem on the unsolvability of the decision problem.

(4) Use of Hilbert's ε-symbol—sometimes in the actual working out of mathematics, as in Bourbaki's *Éléments de Mathématique*, and sometimes as a metamathematical instrument.

(5) Use of models of axiomatic theories for a variety of metamathematical purposes (see below).

A prominent feature of more recent work on mathematical logic is the influence of the ideas of Gentzen on the formulation of systems of symbolic logic. Ackermann, for example, has brought *Grundzüge der theoretischen Logik* up to date in the fourth edition (1959) by replacing the axiomatic foundation that was adopted for the propositional calculus in the first edition (1928) by a system of the Gentzen type. The *Sequenzenkalkül* that Gentzen used in 'Die Widerspruchsfreiheit der reinen Zahlentheorie' (1936), in preference to the more familiar type of axiomatic logical calculus, has been clarified and made more rigorous by Schröter in 'Theorie des logischen Schließens, I, II' (1955, 1958).

In most modern accounts of symbolic logic, a careful distinction is drawn between syntax and semantics. Semantic considerations have assumed greatly increased importance since Tarski showed that a rigorous treatment of semantics is possible.

A change has now taken place in logic which is similar to that brought about in geometry when the mathematical validity of non-euclidean systems came to be generally recognized. Whereas the principal object in books such as *Principia Mathematica*, Hilbert and Ackermann's *Grundzüge der theoretischen Logik*, and Quine's *Mathematical Logic* was the setting up of a definitive and generally acceptable logical calculus which would faithfully reflect the unique formal pattern of ratiocinative argument, and which could then be applied to the analysis of the deductive structure of mathematical theories and perhaps also to the logical definition of mathematical concepts, the task undertaken in discussions of logic at the present time is more usually one of considering a whole range of calculi that may be entertained as theoretical possibilities, with the intention of elucidating their structural properties.

A further development with far-reaching consequences is the growth of what might be called metamathematics (and metalogic) in the large. Metamathematics began as a study of particular formal systems, and it was initially concerned with questions of consistency and completeness of given sets of axioms. But it now embraces investigations of altogether wider scope, designed to yield fundamental information about entire classes of formal systems of some particular kind. Gödel's discussion of the limitations of formal systems is of this nature, and so is the treatment of the ε-symbol and the ε-theorems in the second volume of *Grundlagen der Mathematik*. A more recent instance of metamathematics in the large, referred to below, is the general theory of models. The generalized conception of metamathematics that is illustrated by these examples is a product of the final and transitional decade of the classical period, and its evolution was in fact fairly complete by 1939. This may be seen, in particular, from Schmidt's article 'Mathematische Grundlagenforschung' in the *Enzyklopädie der mathematischen Wissenschaften*, which was written in 1939 although not published until 1950.

We now consider in turn some of the main topics in mathematical philosophy in which substantial advances have been made since 1939, giving a small number of references in each case.

1. *Mathematical logic*

In a number of recently published works by German logicians, mathematical logic is treated very fully; and the different authors between them provide a comprehensive treatment of the greater part of modern logic.

(a) The logicians of the Münster school—led by Heinrich Scholz (1884–1956), the founder of the Institut für mathematische Logik und Grundlagenforschung at Münster—have chosen to treat logic 'ontologically', taking as unproblematic the notion of existence in a postulated universe, and making free use of the principle of excluded middle. Since these logicians think of logic as concerned primarily with relations of truth between propositions and with the properties of identical truth and satisfiability of propositional functions (*Aussagenformen*), they naturally give semantic notions priority over syntactic notions. This is clearly apparent in the article 'Mathematische Logik' (1952) of Hermes and Scholz in the *Enzyklopädie der mathematischen Wissenschaften*, and also in the expanded version of this article in Scholz & Hasenjaeger: *Grundzüge der mathematischen Logik* (1961). In both of these accounts of logic, semantic ideas are discussed first of all, and are then taken as the basis of the subsequent syntactic development.

(b) The subordination of formal syntax to considerations of meaning is even more fundamental to the work of Schmidt, who wishes mathematical logic to be understood as a study of 'codifications'. Schmidt develops this view in detail in his book *Mathematische Gesetze der Logik* (1960), and it is also presupposed in his *Enzyklopädie* article 'Mathematische Grundlagenforschung', to which we have referred on p. 381. A *codification* is an abstract idealization of some more intuitive body of knowledge that is already deductively organized. The idea of codification goes beyond that of axiomatization, in that it extends to the logical form of the deductive theory as well as to its assertorical content. Axiomatization, in the sense typified by Hilbert's *Grundlagen der Geometrie*, means axiomatization on the basis of a supposedly objective classical logic; but now that mathematicians ultimately disagree as much over the logical principles which can be accepted as valid as over mathematical concepts and postulates, what really requires to be axiomatized is a particular theory *as developed in accordance with a particular outlook* (naive, classical, constructivist, intuitionist, or of whatever kind it may be). Such a total axiomatization is what Schmidt calls a codification.

Every codification is based on a conceptual network (*Begriffsnetz*) and a deductive scaffolding (*Deduktionsgerüst*). The former is defined by a list of basic notions and an inductive specification of the 'pertinent expressions' (*einschlägige Ausdrücke*), i.e. well-formed terms and formulae, that may be built up out of them; and the latter is defined by a list of basic assertions, i.e. axioms, and an inductive specification of 'derivable theorem'. If the conceptual network involves ideas of pure logic only, then we have what may be called a logical codification; and it is such codifications that are studied by Schmidt in *Mathematische Gesetze der Logik*—codifications of the propositional calculus in the volume already published, and codifications of the calculus of predicates in the promised second volume. When a codification also involves extralogical concepts (*Eigenbegriffe*) and extralogical principles (*Eigenaxiome*) in addition to the logical ones, we can treat it as an extension of the logical kernel around which it is formed.

(c) The representation of semantic relations by equivalent syntactic relations constitutes the central topic of Schröter's series of papers

'Theorie des logischen Schließens'. Schröter first points out that the kind of derivability which is important in mathematics is rather different from that formalized in the usual systems of symbolic logic. Consider, for example, the theory of groups in algebra. This can be based on three axioms (respectively asserting associativity of the group operation, existence of an identity element for the group, and existence of an inverse for each separate element), all individual variables in the axioms being bound by quantifiers. The axioms involve a certain ternary predicate $R(x,y,z)$, ordinarily written as $xy = z$, and this predicate behaves partly as a variable and partly as a constant. Since the abstract theory is schematic, in that it can be made by specialization to apply to *any* particular group whatever, R may be classified as a free variable. But since, in any derivation from the axioms, R must be kept fixed, and substitution of some other formula $\mathfrak{A}(x,y,z)$ for $R(x,y,z)$ is clearly not permitted, R is not free as regards derivation. Schröter refers to mathematical derivation of this kind, in which free variables that occur in the axioms of a theory have to be exempted from liability to replacement, as 'restricted derivation' (*beschränktes Ableiten*).

In 'Theorie des logischen Schließens', Schröter analyses both the syntactic concept of restricted derivability and the semantic concept of consequence for various logical calculi, among which are included Gentzen's calculus of natural deduction and also his calculus of sequences. Schröter's aim is to show that in a number of basic logical systems (in particular, in the propositional calculus, the restricted calculus of predicates, and the restricted calculus of predicates with identity) a conclusion is restrictedly derivable from given premisses if and only if it is a consequence of them. He is able to show further that, in the propositional calculus and the restricted calculus of predicates without identity, Gentzen's method of natural deduction also yields an exact formalization of the semantic relation of consequence.

Schröter understands *consequence* in the sense of Bolzano, and the definition that he gives may be expressed as follows: A formula H is a consequence of a set of formulae X, or X *Fol* H, if and only if H is satisfied for every model of X, i.e. for every assignment of values to the variables in X which is such that all the formulae in X become true propositions.

A formal definition of *restricted derivability* is also required, and this takes the following form: Let X and Y be two given sets of formulae (in the language of some formal system F) and let H be a further formula. We then say that 'H is restrictedly derivable from the set of premisses X on the basis of the set of axioms Y', or X *Babl*$_Y$ H, if H is the end-formula of a derivation in which all the initial formulae belong to the set $X \cup Y$, and no substitution is anywhere made for a variable that occurs free in some formula belonging to the set Y.

A discussion of symbolic logic from the point of view of Schröter's Berlin school is at present being given by Günter Asser in his *Einführung in die mathematische Logik*, a work in three small volumes, of which the first has already been published (1959). The volumes are concerned respectively with the propositional calculus, the restricted calculus of predicates, and the extended calculus of predicates with separation of types. This particular account of mathematical logic, which is considerably shorter than the very complete accounts given by Scholz and Schmidt, is introductory in so far as Asser deals only with the central parts of his subject, avoiding altogether such peripheral topics as many-valued logic and modal logic. The treatment throughout is strictly formal, however, and little trace now remains of the descriptive manner of introducing formal logic that was more usual during the classical period, as in such books as those of Hilbert and Ackermann (1928) and Lewis and Langford (1932).

(d) Unlike Scholz and Hasenjaeger, whose approach to logic is avowedly ontological, both Schmidt and Schröter make provision in their discussions for a wide range of logical attitudes, confining their own argument to a comparative study of the structures of different systems. A logician who has taken up a more exclusive position—at the opposite extreme from the Münster logicians—is Lorenzen, who has given a detailed account of his system in *Einführung in die operative Logik und Mathematik* (1955). Lorenzen seeks to interpret mathematics as a theory of formal systems (cf. Curry [1]), i.e. abstract calculi in which combinations of symbols are formed systematically in accordance with postulated rules of construction. Two such calculi are necessary for the definition of a mathematical theory: a preliminary one to generate a totality of well-formed expressions, and then the main one to yield formal counterparts of derived theorems.

With each calculus goes a metatheory, in which general assertions are made about the expressions that the calculus produces. In the metatheory, an additional axiom (i.e. initial expression) or an additional rule of procedure is said to be 'admissible' (*zulässig*) if its adoption does not lead to any extension of the totality of obtainable expressions. The method of establishing admissibility is by showing that every occurrence of the new axiom, or every application of the new rule, can be 'eliminated', that is to say that an equivalent formal transition can be devised in which only the original axioms and rules are used. Lorenzen's method is here seen to be only partially formal, since he often establishes eliminability merely by means of an example. Indeed he remarks that many things cannot be taught, since the learner has to develop for himself the necessary mastery over the manipulation of the formal system, together with the intuitive insight that such mastery brings.

The metatheory of any particular calculus includes theorems concerning the admissibility of various rules for that calculus, and among such rules there will be some that are admissible for any calculus whatever. Such rules are the equivalents for Lorenzen of principles of logic. Although the theoretical basis of Lorenzen's operative mathematics is very different from that of mathematics as more usually understood, it turns out in the end that this new system agrees closely in its formal structure with the traditional one; and much of ordinary symbolic logic accordingly has an operative interpretation.

Influential philosophical views on the requirements that an acceptable system of symbolic logic must satisfy have been expressed by Quine (see below, p. 399). The standard treatment of symbolic logic which Quine himself has given in his *Mathematical Logic* (1940) is in many ways to be regarded as a modern revision of the logic of *Principia Mathematica*, and thus it belongs, in spite of its date, more to the classical period than to the period that is the subject of this appendix. It is indeed based on Quine's important earlier paper 'New foundations for mathematical logic' (1937). The *Journal of Symbolic Logic* contains papers on Quine's system by a number of authors—both the fundamental papers of Rosser and Quine himself, relating to the derivability of the Burali-Forti antinomy in the system as originally formulated and the measures needed for the elimination of this inconsistency, and also several others in which variants of the system are discussed.

Also in the *Journal of Symbolic Logic* is a series of papers by Fitch on his 'basic logic', a kind of universal logical calculus. The series begins with 'A basic logic' (1942); and in 1944 there is a paper 'Representations of calculi' in which Fitch proves that every finitary logic can be defined within his basic system.

2. *Consistency of analysis*

In 1936 Gentzen succeeded in proving the consistency of the arithmetic of the natural numbers (*reine Zahlentheorie*)—not, of course, in a strictly finitary manner, but by a method which only goes beyond the bounds of finitary argument in using transfinite induction over a segment of the second number class as a means of showing that a certain process of reduction must always terminate. After this, the most pressing need was for a proof, using some sufficiently trustworthy procedure, of the consistency of the arithmetic of the real continuum. The first major advance in this direction was made by Fitch, whose paper 'The consistency of the ramified *Principia*' (1938) contains a proof, though not a constructive one, of the consistency of Whitehead and Russell's formalization of analysis. A more constructive proof on similar lines was given in 1951 by Lorenzen in 'Algebraische und logistische Untersuchungen über freie Verbände'.

Gentzen's original idea of using transfinite induction to show that a process of reduction terminates has been followed up in a number of subsequent investigations of consistency. In 'Zur Widerspruchsfreiheit der Zahlentheorie' (1940), Ackermann gave an alternative proof of Gentzen's result, in which he used Hilbert's ε-symbol in conjunction with transfinite induction over the same segment of the second number class as that considered by Gentzen, namely the series of all ordinals below the first ε-number ε_0 (i.e. the first transfinite ordinal α such that $\omega^\alpha = \alpha$). After this, Ackermann turned his attention from the natural numbers to the real numbers, devising first of all a system of logic that is both adequate as a basis for the formalization of analysis and also amenable to metalogical investigation. Instead of the *Principia* logic, with its ramified type-structure, he preferred a type-free system; but in order to make such a logic secure against inconsistency he had to relinquish the principle of excluded middle. He gave a proof of the consistency of the resulting system, using transfinite induction for this purpose; but now the induction had to range over a more extended segment of the second number class than in the case of *reine Zahlentheorie*. The segment required consists of all ordinals less than the first *critical* ε-number, i.e. the first ε-number η such that $\varepsilon_\eta = \eta$.

This part of Ackermann's work is contained in the following papers, published in 1950 and 1952 respectively: 'Widerspruchsfreier Aufbau der Logik, I. Typenfreies System ohne tertium non datur' and 'Widerspruchsfreier Aufbau einer typenfreien Logik (Erweitertes System)'. A further paper 'Widerspruchsfreier Aufbau einer typenfreien Logik, II' (1953) contains a brief indication of a way in which the rational and real numbers can be handled within the system of type-free logic.

At the same time as Ackermann, Schütte was also carrying out metamathematical investigations of similar scope, and he arrived at comparable results. In 'Beweistheoretische Erfassung der unendlichen Induktion in der Zahlentheorie' (1951) Schütte considered the principle of 'infinite induction', a demonstrative principle that can be formalized by a rule which permits passage from the infinite set of premisses $\mathfrak{A}(0)$, $\mathfrak{A}(1),\ldots$ to the conclusion $(x)\mathfrak{A}(x)$. Since the set of premisses is not finite, this new rule of procedure is not of the kind usually considered; but Gentzen's method for proving consistency can nevertheless be extended to systems which include it. In a further paper 'Beweistheoretische Untersuchung der verzweigten Analysis' (1952) Schütte went on to adapt his methods more closely to ordinary analysis. Setting up a system of 'ramified analysis'—that is to say an essentially predicative treatment of analysis, based on the ramified theory of types without an axiom of reducibility—he proved this system consistent by means of transfinite induction up to the first critical ε-number. Since the predicative nature of the underlying logic is sufficient by itself to secure consistency, Schütte was not compelled like Ackermann to give up the principle of excluded middle. The system that he worked with is not the classical analysis that is known to mathematicians, since it involves an elaborate type-structure, but much of the content of ordinary analysis can be incorporated in it. This seems to be as much as can reasonably be demanded; and if a more direct formalization of classical analysis is required, the natural foundation for this is the axiomatic theory of sets.

In two later papers, 'Zur Widerspruchsfreiheit einer typenfreien Logik' (1953) and 'Ein widerspruchsloses System der Analysis auf typenfreier Grundlage' (1954), Schütte turned away from ramified logic to type-free logic, adapting his methods to the kind of treatment of analysis already considered by Ackermann. A comprehensive account of recent work in metamathematics, and especially on the formal handling of analysis, is given by Schütte in his book *Beweistheorie* (1960).

Yet another possible logical foundation for analysis is Fitch's basic logic. See, in particular, Fitch's two papers, 'A demonstrably consistent mathematics, I, II', published in 1950 and 1951 in the *Journal of Symbolic Logic*.

3. *Constructive treatment of ordinal numbers*

Since some of the more recent proofs of consistency of mathematical systems go beyond the limits of Hilbert's finitary argument by using transfinite induction, it is important that there should be available a constructive theory of those parts of the second number class over which the induction extends. The need is for a constructive definition of a totality of symbolic expressions with the same structure as the system of ordinal numbers that is more usually defined non-constructively in terms of the theory of sets. Such a definition, capable of reaching far into the second number class, was devised by Ackermann and used by him in his work on type-free logic, considered in the previous section. Ackermann developed the basic ideas in a paper 'Konstruktiver Aufbau eines Abschnitts der zweiten Cantorschen Zahlenklasse' (1951), the scope of which he summarized in the following terms:

'In view of possible metamathematical applications, I attach importance to the fact that the definition of the ordinal numbers in question is carried out constructively. Conditions for a constructive definition of a segment of the second number class have been laid down by A. Church and S. C. Kleene. The following conditions, regarded by them as fundamental, are satisfied here: Each ordinal number that occurs is represented by one and only one symbol.   Given two ordinal numbers, represented by different symbols, we can decide by a recursive arithmetical process which is the greater and which the smaller.   The symbol for the first ordinal number is known.   For every other number, we can decide whether it has an immediate predecessor or not.   In the first case this predecessor can be determined.   In the second case a sequence of ordinal numbers, having the given number as its limit, can be defined by arithmetical recursion.   Furthermore, it can be shown in a constructive manner, for each ordinal number, that transfinite induction is valid up to that point.'

The titles of the papers of Church and Kleene to which Ackermann refers are respectively 'The constructive second number class' and 'On notation for ordinal numbers'.   Both papers were published in 1938.

A further paper on the justification of the use of transfinite induction in metamathematics is 'On the restricted ordinal theorem' (1944), by Goodstein.

4. *Modern views on proof of consistency*

Hilbert's ideal of a decisive justification of mathematics by finitary demonstration of its consistency was very much a product of the classical period.   As we have seen in Section 2, even after the original objective had been shown by Gödel to be unattainable further proofs of consistency still continued to be devised, in which the argument used was not strictly finitary; but such proofs can no longer be held to have the unique epistemological importance of proofs of consistency of the type formerly envisaged, and in recent years there has been a lessening of interest in the study of formal consistency, together with a shift of emphasis in the interpretation of what can be achieved by such means.   Although Lorenzen, for instance, is himself the author of a major proof of consistency, he ascribes less value to such proofs than many mathematical philosophers have done in the past.   This is because his outlook is more in sympathy with Brouwer's intuitionism than with Hilbert's formalism.   And Kreisel has asserted, in 'Mathematical significance of consistency proofs' (1958), that 'the purpose of the so-called finitist or constructive consistency proofs of a system consists, for us, not in the allegedly greater "evidence" or "reliability" of constructive proofs compared with non-constructive ones, but in this: they help us to keep track of the constructive (recursive) content in the (non-constructive) proofs of the system considered.'

The modified attitude towards proof of consistency shows itself particularly in a change that has now taken place from investigation of absolute consistency to investigation of relative consistency.   Instead of a proof, from first principles, that some formal system F is free from contradiction, what is now more often given is a proof that, *if* a certain system F is free from contradiction, then so also is some extension F' of F. Historically, the decisive example of a theorem on relative consistency was Gödel's result on the continuum hypothesis. In lectures at Princeton in 1938, afterwards published as *The Consistency of the Axiom of Choice and of the Generalized Continuum-Hypothesis with the Axioms of Set Theory* (1940), Gödel showed that, if a certain axiomatic treatment of sets is consistent, then it remains consistent when the axiom of choice and the generalized continuum hypothesis $2^{\aleph_\alpha} = \aleph_{\alpha+1}$ are adjoined to its axioms. He did this by constructing, within the original system, a model of the extended system—a technique that has become so fundamental in metamathematical research that a separate section of this appendix will now be devoted to the idea on which it is based, that is to say the idea of construction of a model of a given set of formulae.

5. *Models*

By a *model* of a set X of formulae in a formalized language L we may understand a particular determination of a domain of individuals and a particular assignment of 'values' of the appropriate kinds to all the variables concerned, for which all the formulae in X become true propositions (cf. the definition of satisfiability on p. 71). Models are sometimes introduced in a relatively informal manner (like the arithmetical model of axiomatic euclidean geometry that was used by Hilbert in *Grundlagen der Geometrie*), but they may also be specified within the syntax of a formalized language—either L itself or some other language L'. In modern metamathematical applications, models are usually treated formally; and the concept of model has itself been rigorously defined for metamathematical purposes.

Some of the fundamental theorems of metalogic can be expressed conveniently in the language of models. One such result is Löwenheim's theorem (or the Löwenheim-Skolem theorem, as it is often called in its more general forms). As we stated it on p. 78, this theorem asserts that any formula of the restricted calculus of predicates which is identical for a denumerably infinite domain of individuals is identical for any domain whatever. An equivalent assertion is that any formula which is satisfiable at all is satisfiable for a denumerable domain; and since any finite set of formulae can be combined into a single conjunction, we may also express the theorem by saying that any finite set of formulae of the restricted calculus of predicates which has a model at all must have a denumerable model. In an expository paper entitled 'Interpretations of sets of conditions' (1954), Quine has discussed the actual production of such denumerable models, not merely for finite sets of formulae, but for infinite sets as well.

In the paper 'The completeness of the first-order functional calculus' (1949) which contains his new proof of Gödel's completeness theorem (see p. 76), Henkin has established a basic metalogical result which we may formulate roughly as follows: Any consistent set of formulae, without free individual variables, in a formal system F that is based on the restricted calculus of predicates, possesses a model for which the domain of individuals has the same cardinal number as the set of primitive symbols of F.   Gödel's completeness theorem and Löwenheim's theorem both follow as simple corollaries from this main result, which also has applications in abstract algebra (see Section 11 of this appendix, p. 397).

More recently, in 'Über ω-Unvollständigkeit in der Peano-Arithmetik' (1952), Hasenjaeger has used a certain type of model—the non-absolute model—as a means of proving independence.

Models thus have a wide range of significant application in metalogic and metamathematics; and it is natural that attempts should have been made to develop a unified theory of models as a branch of semantics.   Some of the earliest systematic work in this field was carried out by Tarski, in the course of his general investigations into the handling of semantic ideas, as for instance in his basic paper 'The concept of truth in formalized languages' (1931), and more particularly in the paper 'On the concept of logical consequence' (1935), in which he uses the notion of model in the definition of the semantic notion of consequence (cf. p. 383 above).   In 'Contributions to the theory of models, I–III' (1954–1955), Tarski discusses relations between the syntactic properties of sets of sentences and the set-theoretical properties of classes of models defined by them.

Further contributions to the general theory of models have been made by Mostowski, in 'On models of axiomatic systems' (1952), and by Kemeny, in 'Models of logical systems' (1948).   Kemeny begins his paper by giving a general definition of 'logical system', and he then tries to make precise, for an arbitrary logical system, the four metalogical concepts of consistency, completeness, model, and equivalence, concentrating particularly on the concept of model.

The principal applications of the method of models that have been made so far are concerned with the theory of sets, where fundamental theorems on relative consistency have been proved by such means. Thus it was by the construction of a model that Gödel demonstrated the compatibility of the continuum hypothesis with the usual axioms for sets (see p. 389); and models have also been used as a means of showing the consistency of formulations of the theory of sets of the von Neumann-Bernays type, in which provision is made for classes as well as for sets in the proper sense, relative to that of the Zermelo-Fraenkel theory.

The first proof of the relative consistency of a theory of sets with a class-formalism was given by Ilse Novak in her thesis of 1948, afterwards published as 'A construction of models of consistent systems' (1950). Miss Novak considered a formal system S of a specified general kind, and also an extended system S', formally related to S in the manner in which Bernays's theory of sets is related to the Zermelo-Fraenkel theory. Having formalized the syntax of S, she extended this to the syntax of S_ε, the system obtained when Hilbert's ε-symbol is adjoined to the logic of S; and she then constructed, in the syntax of S_ε, a model of S'. It follows from the possibility of this construction that if S is consistent—and consequently, by the theorem on the eliminability of the ε-symbol, S_ε is consistent also—then S' is consistent. The relative consistency of Bernays's theory of sets is contained as a corollary in this general result.

A different way of reaching a similar conclusion, devised by Mostowski, was used by Rosser and Wang in their paper 'Non-standard models for formal logics' (1950). This paper contains an important general discussion of non-standard models (i.e. models which are such that the relations between entities when they are considered as elements of the model do not correspond to the 'natural' relations between the same entities as elements of the system from which they are taken), and it concludes with an alternative proof of the relative consistency of Bernays's theory of sets. The proof sets out from some postulated model guaranteed, say, by Henkin [1], of the narrower system—i.e. the system that corresponds to Ilse Novak's system S—and proceeds by construction of an extended model of the wider system.

Yet another demonstration of the relative consistency of Bernays's theory of sets has been given by Shoenfield in 'A relative consistency proof' (1954). This proof does not involve a model at all, but depends on direct use of the ε-symbol in the manner discussed by Hilbert and Bernays in their second volume. Shoenfield considers a narrower formal system C and a wider system C', and he extends C to a system equivalent to C' with the aid of the ε-symbol. But then any formula of C that is derivable in C' is also derivable in C; and thus if a contradiction were derivable in C' a contradiction would also be derivable in C. The proof given by Shoenfield, moreover, is constructive, in that any derivation of a contradiction in C' can actually be converted into a derivation of a contradiction in C.

A general examination of the use of models in the theory of sets has been undertaken by Shepherdson in his series of papers 'Inner models for set theory, I–III' (1951–1953). By an *inner model* of a formal system F is meant a model of F whose domain of individuals is a part of the domain for F itself. Shepherdson concludes, in particular, that the method of proving relative consistency by inner models has now been exhausted, at least as far as 'a fairly large family' of models is concerned.

Among recent examples of the use of models in proofs of relative consistency in the theory of sets are a paper by Orey and one by Gandy, both published in 1956. In 'On the relative consistency of set theory' Orey uses a model in order to demonstrate the consistency of Gödel's theory of sets relative to a modified version of Quine's *Mathematical Logic*; and in 'On the axiom of extensionality' Gandy proves by a model that 'if the simple theory of types (with an axiom of infinity) is consistent, then so is the system obtained by adjoining axioms of extensionality'.

Finally, models have been used by Specker in an investigation into the independence of certain of Bernays's axioms, published in 'Zur Axiomatik der Mengenlehre (Fundierungs- und Auswahlaxiom)' (1957).

6. *Decision procedures*

The term 'decision problem' (*Entscheidungsproblem*), which is due to Hilbert, refers to the general problem of setting up, for a given formal system F, a systematic and constructive process whereby it can be determined whether or not any selected formula of F is valid. By 'validity' may possibly be understood the syntactic property of formal derivability in F; but more often it is the semantic property of identical truth that is meant. And instead of decidability with respect to identical truth we may equally well consider decidability with respect to satisfiability (cf. p. 71).

The decision problem is easily solvable for the propositional calculus, but for the restricted calculus of predicates no general solution of it is possible. Church has proved, in fact, that there can be no decision procedure for this calculus that is constructive in the accepted sense of general recursive (cf. p. 279). In spite of this very strong non-existence theorem, however, the question of whether decision processes are possible for particular formal systems or fragments of such systems may still arise, and there is in fact an extensive literature on decidability. This literature takes two forms: (i) further results related to Church's theorem, and (ii) results on the existence of particular decision procedures.

(i) We have already referred, on p. 280, to Turing's alternative proof of Church's theorem. Other contributions to this part of the literature are the book *Undecidable Theories* (1953) by Tarski, Mostowski, and Robinson, and also Putnam's paper 'Decidability and essential undecidability' (1957), in which the decidability of a theory is considered in relation to the decidability of its extensions.

(ii) Many results have been obtained concerning decidability, with respect to identical truth or satisfiability, for special classes of formulae of the restricted calculus of predicates. In 'Special cases of the decision problem' (1951) Church gave a survey of existing knowledge in this field; and the subject has since been discussed more fully by Ackermann, in *Solvable Cases of the Decision Problem* (1954). See also Klaua: 'Systematische Behandlung der lösbaren Fälle des Entscheidungsproblems für den Prädikatenkalkül der ersten Stufe' (1955).

It was shown by Löwenheim as long ago as 1915, in 'Über Möglichkeiten im Relativkalkül', that a decision procedure exists for formulae of the restricted calculus of predicates in which no predicate variable has more than one argument-place; and in a paper of 1945, with the title 'On the logic of quantification', Quine has presented 'a new decision procedure for monadic schemata which seems convenient enough for practical and pedagogical use'.

Besides work on the actual solution of the decision problem in particular cases, a great deal has also been done on methods of reduction of the decision problem for arbitrary formulae to the same problem for formulae of some more restricted kind. Kalmár, for instance, has published a series of three papers entitled 'On the reduction of the decision problem' (1939–1950)—the second and third of them in collaboration with his pupil Surányi—and a unified account of the subject has since been given by Surányi in *Reduktionstheorie des Entscheidungsproblems im Prädikatenkalkül der ersten Stufe* (1959). A paper of McKinsey, 'The decision problem for some classes of sentences without quantifiers' (1943), is also concerned with reduction, in this instance in relation to formalized algebraic theories.

A particular decision problem that has been much discussed is the 'word problem' for groups and other related mathematical systems. The system considered must be such that there is a relation of equivalence that is meaningful for pairs of 'words', i.e. well-formed expressions, of the system. This relation may possibly be one of designating the same entity, in the way in which any two products such as *ab* and *ba* designate the same element in an abelian group. The word problem is simply the decision problem for the equivalence of an arbitrary pair of words. In a paper of 1947, 'Recursive unsolvability of a problem of Thue', Post gave a proof that the word problem is unsolvable for a certain abstractly defined type of system that had been considered by Thue; and a result equivalent to Post's was arrived at almost at the same time by Markov, and announced by him in his paper 'Невозможность некоторых алгорифмов в теории ассоциативных систем' [On the impossibility of certain algorithms in the theory of associative systems] (1947). Markov has his own way of characterizing constructivity, in terms of existence of algorithms instead of by the various means that we have already discussed; see his 'Теория алгорифмов' [Theory of algorithms] (1954).

The unsolvability of the word problem was demonstrated for semigroups with two generators by Marshall Hall in 1949, and for semigroups with cancellation by Turing in 1950. Turing's proof was incorrect in its details (see the review by Boone in the *Journal of Symbolic Logic*, **17**, 74–76) and a different proof of a similar theorem has since been given by Novikov and Adian in 'Проблема тождества для полугрупп с одиосторонним сокращением' [The word problem for semigroups with one-sided cancellation] (1958).

The first proof that the word problem is unsolvable for groups was announced by Novikov in 'Об алгоритмической неразрешимости проблемы тождества' (1952), and Novikov has since published the proof in full in the pamphlet 'Об алгоритмической неразрешимости проблемы тождества слов в теории групп' [On the algorithmic unsolvability of the problem of identity of words in the theory of groups] (1955), of which an English translation has been made. A new proof of the unsolvability of the word problem for groups has been given by Britton in 'The word problem for groups' (1958).

M. O. Rabin made decision procedures in the theory of groups the subject of his doctoral dissertation at Princeton in 1956, and he afterwards published his conclusions in 'Recursive unsolvability of group theoretic problems' (1958). Rabin considered other decision problems besides the word problem, and he was able to show, by using Novikov's result on the unsolvability of the word problem, that there are many properties of groups that are not effectively decidable. He proved in his paper that 'for a very extensive class of group theoretic properties there does not exist a general and effective method of deciding, for every given presentation [of a group by specification of a finite set of generators and a finite number of relations between them], whether the group defined by it has the property in question'.

7. *Effectiveness and constructivity*

As we have already seen in the notes at the end of Chapter 10, consideration of questions of constructivity occupies a central place in modern research into the foundations of mathematics. Constructivism as an attitude or a point of view has found expression, not only in Brouwer's intuitionism and in the reliance on primitive recursion of such metamathematicians as Skolem and Goodstein, but also in the 'operative' approach to mathematics that is favoured by Lorenzen. Another metamathematician who has been much concerned with constructivism is Kreisel, as for instance in his papers 'On the interpretation of non-finitist proofs, I, II' (1951, 1952).

The intuitive notion of 'constructive' has been given precise meaning, for metamathematical purposes, by being identified with 'general recursive'. Ideas of general recursiveness, moreover, have been used by Kleene as the basis for a fundamental scale of logical complexity of predicates of natural numbers, known as the 'Kleene hierarchy'. See Kleene's paper 'Hierarchies of number-theoretic predicates' (1955), and also Kreisel's review of it in *Mathematical Reviews*, **17** (1956).

The detailed elaboration of recursive arithmetic still continues, especially in the work of Rózsa Péter, Skolem, and Goodstein. See, for example, Rózsa Péter's paper 'Zusammenhang der mehrfachen und transfiniten Rekursionen' (1950).

Goodstein has published a sequel *Recursive Analysis* (1962) to his *Recursive Number Theory* (1957), and in it he extends his treatment of the natural numbers by a free-variable equation calculus to a treatment of functions in a rational field, a treatment that 'aims at formulating in the rational field analogues of theorems of classical analysis, entirely without the use of properties of the real field'. Goodstein's interpretation of constructivity in relation to analysis thus takes an extreme form; but there have also been other attempts to isolate the constructive content of classical analysis in which the less exacting standard of general recursiveness has been adopted. Klaua, for instance, in his Berlin dissertation 'Berechenbare Analysis' (1956), has examined the extent to which such typical concepts of analysis as continuity, differentiability, and integrability can be given a recursive interpretation. An earlier investigation with a similar intention is contained in Specker's paper 'Nicht konstruktiv beweisbare Sätze der Analysis' (1949), where recursiveness is defined in various possible ways for real numbers and real functions, and the strengths of the different definitions are compared. Specker shows that, when a restriction of recursiveness is imposed on the numbers and functions that are considered, various standard theorems of analysis are no longer true. This line of inquiry has been pursued further by Shanin in 'Некоторые вопросы математического анализа в свете конструктивной логики' [Some questions of mathematical analysis in the light of constructive logic] (1956), a paper concerned with the recursive treatment of sets measurable in the sense of Lebesgue, and of summable functions.

8. *Intuitionism*

The influence of the intuitionist philosophy of mathematics still persists; and Lorenzen, in particular, has attempted to bridge the gulf between strict intuitionism and a more liberal constructivism that makes substantial concession to the requirements of classical analysis. Lorenzen describes his operative mathematics as a further development of the semi-intuitionist treatment of analysis that was proposed by Weyl in *Das Kontinuum* (1918), cf. p. 256 above.

Intuitionist logic continues to be of interest as a formal system. In 1957, for instance, Schröter thought it worth while to give the details, in 'Eine Umformung des Heytingschen Axiomensystems für den intuitionistischen Aussagenkalkül', of an investigation into an alternative axiomatic treatment of Heyting's logical calculus that he had carried out twenty years earlier but not published, although the results had been made known and had in fact been used in 1938 by Wajsberg.

Kreisel has written on intuitionism as well as on constructivity in general; and two recent papers of his are 'Elementary completeness properties of intuitionistic logic with a note on negations of prenex formulae' (1958) and 'A remark on free choice sequences and the topological completeness proofs' (1958).

The nominalist philosophy of Quine, referred to below in section 15 of this appendix, should also be mentioned here, as having a certain affinity with Brouwer's philosophical outlook on mathematics.

9. *The theory of sets*

The perfecting of an axiomatic treatment of sets is one of the most significant developments brought about in mathematics by the attempt to achieve a satisfactory standard of rigour. The main problems were solved in principle by Zermelo and Fraenkel, and the theory that was devised by them is in fact sufficient for ordinary use in mathematics, when the attitude adopted towards logic is an essentially naive one. The Zermelo-Fraenkel theory can be formalized in the modern manner if this is desired, as Ernst-Jochen Thiele has shown in his Berlin dissertation 'Ein axiomatisches System der Mengenlehre nach Zermelo und Fraenkel' (1955).

The chief modifications subsequently made in this first axiomatic theory of sets are (i) the inclusion of a class-formalism in the system, and (ii) the fusion of the axioms for sets with the axioms of a logical calculus; and these changes have produced the more elaborate theory that has been given a generally accepted form by Bernays and Gödel— by Bernays in his series of papers in the *Journal of Symbolic Logic*, and by Gödel in his lectures on the consistency of the continuum hypothesis. This Bernays-Gödel theory is the one presented by Bernays in Bernays & Fraenkel: *Axiomatic Set Theory* (1958).

As we have already seen, the Bernays-Gödel treatment of sets is at present being used by Bourbaki as the basis of his unified study of mathematical structures in *Éléments de Mathématique*; and it is quite as important for mathematics itself as for mathematical philosophy.

Much of the theoretical work to which the Bernays-Gödel system has given rise is concerned with the comparative strengths of related systems of axioms—for instance systems in which weaker or stronger forms of the axiom of choice are adopted. Investigations of relative consistency are especially important; and some of these have already been mentioned in Section 5 of this appendix, where the metamathematical use of models is discussed.

10. *Many-valued logics*

In addition to the book of Rosser and Turquette, already referred to in Note 7, p. 56, and the earlier papers of the same authors in the *Journal of Symbolic Logic* out of which this book developed, the Berlin dissertation of Helmut Thiele, published as 'Theorie der endlichwertigen Łukasiewiczschen Prädikatenkalküle der ersten Stufe' (1958), should also be mentioned. Many-valued logics are here considered from a point of view similar to that of Schröter in his discussion of two-valued logic in 'Theorie des logischen Schließens'; and, like Schröter, Thiele gives an important place to the semantic relation of consequence in the sense of Bolzano.

In 'Bemerkungen zum Komprehensionsaxiom' (1957), Skolem has investigated the possibility that the contradictions which are produced in the theory of sets by unrestricted use of the principle of comprehension might be avoided if a many-valued logic were used in place of the usual two-valued logic.

11. *Metamathematics and algebra*

Originally the sole purpose of metamathematics was to guarantee the security of mathematics by establishing its freedom from contradiction, but more recently metamathematical ideas have been used in the proof of actual mathematical theorems. Such a possibility was foreseen, quite early on, by Tarski; but systematic exploitation of it is largely the work of Robinson, who has applied metamathematical methods to algebraic problems. See, in particular, Robinson's book *On the Metamathematics of Algebra* (1951).

Henkin, also, has been interested in this borderland between logic and mathematics, and it formed the subject of his Princeton dissertation of 1947. He published his results in 1953 in 'Some interconnections between modern algebra and mathematical logic'. This paper contains various mathematical applications of what Henkin calls 'our basic result from logic', namely the theorem that guarantees the existence of a model, of a certain specifiable cardinality, for any consistent set of formulae of a very general kind (see p. 390 above).

Not only is metamathematics capable of supplying information about algebra, but algebra in its turn has applications to metamathematics that are far from trivial, for instance applications of the theory of lattices. For a general indication of the connexions between mathematics and metamathematics see Mostowski's report 'The present state of investigations on the foundations of mathematics' (1955).

12. *Modal logic*

The volumes of the *Journal of Symbolic Logic*, from its foundation in 1936 down to the present time, reveal a continuing interest in modal logic, and in the systems of Lewis in particular (cf. Note 6, p. 54). Earlier volumes contain many contributions by McKinsey; and the paper 'Some theories about the sentential calculi of Lewis and Heyting' (1948), by McKinsey and Tarski, may serve as typical of these.

Lewis's original treatment of strict implication was confined to the propositional calculus, but it has since been extended to the calculus of predicates by Ruth Barcan in her paper 'A functional calculus of first order based on strict implication' (1946).

More recently, Ackermann has considered a relation of 'strenge Implikation' that is rather stronger than strict implication in the sense of Lewis. Ackermann's relation holds between A and B when B is a *logical* consequence of A, i.e. when the content of B is a part of the content of A. A system of logic based on this relation is developed in Ackermann's paper 'Begründung einer strengen Implikation' (1956).

A much wider view of modal logic has been taken by von Wright, in his papers on the subject and in his book *An Essay in Modal Logic* (1951). Von Wright considers four distinct kinds of modality: *alethic* (necessary, possible, contingent, impossible), *epistemic* (verified, undecided, falsified), *deontic* (obligatory, permitted, indifferent, forbidden), and *existential* (universal, existing, empty).

13. *Formalization of semantics*

The two pioneers in the formalization of semantics, as we have already indicated in Note 2, p. 128, are Tarski and Carnap; and the concepts which they have introduced are fundamental to all work in this field.

In a paper of 1956, 'A new approach to semantics', Kemeny has tried to meet some of the objections that have been advanced against the formal treatment of semantics, and against Carnap's ideas in particular. The characteristic feature of Kemeny's approach to the subject is that he begins with the concept of a model of a formal language, which he attempts to define in precise terms. Then he uses this basic concept of model in the definitions of further semantic concepts.

14. *Probability and induction*

Much modern work on the foundations of probability and induction has been centred on the concept of *confirmation* of one proposition by another, and more particularly on the concept of *degree of confirmation*, i.e. a suitable measure of the degree of confidence which a perfectly rational being would have in the truth of a proposition B as a result of knowing a proposition A to be true. See, for instance, Hempel: 'A purely syntactical definition of confirmation' (1943), and also Helmer & Oppenheim: 'A syntactical definition of probability and of degree of confirmation' (1945).

Carnap has argued, in his fundamental work *Logical Foundations of Probability* (1950), that a numerical measure of degree of confirmation can be rigorously defined. Among subsequent discussions prompted by Carnap's book are two papers of 1955 with rather similar content— Lehman: 'On confirmation and rational betting' and Kemeny: 'Fair bets and inductive probabilities'—and also a paper by Martin: 'A formalization of inductive logic' (1958).

One of the best general works on probability and induction is von Wright's thesis 'The logical problem of induction', originally published in Finland in 1941, and reprinted in England in 1957. Broad's long commentary on this thesis, published in *Mind* in 1944, is also of importance.

A clear account of probability from the point of view of a philosopher has been given by Kneale in his book *Probability and Induction* (1949).

An English translation of Reichenbach's *Wahrscheinlichkeitslehre* (1935), incorporating certain revisions, was published in 1949, and this new version of the book was reviewed by Kemeny in the *Journal of Symbolic Logic*, **16**, 48–51.

On the mathematical side, the foundations of probability have recently been examined once again by Richter in a series of papers 'Zur Grundlegung der Wahrscheinlichkeitstheorie' (1953–1954), and also in his book *Wahrscheinlichkeitstheorie* (1956).

15. *Nominalism and platonism*

Apart from the many discussions that are connected with intuitionism and constructivism, there is relatively little argument of a philosophical nature in the more recent literature of mathematical logic, where formal considerations predominate. An exceptional instance of an issue with a well-established philosophical ancestry that has been taken up by mathematical logicians is the question of the existence of universals, or the conflict of outlook between 'nominalists' and 'platonists'. Nominalists hold that predicates can only be applied significantly to concrete individuals, and they only permit mention of abstract entities when this can be shown to be a form of words from which all reference to such entities can be eliminated by appropriate reformulation. Platonists, on the contrary, are committed to granting some sort of existence to abstractions.

In their paper 'Steps towards a constructive nominalism' (1947), Goodman and Quine firmly rejected platonism: 'We do not believe in abstract entities. No one supposes that abstract entities—classes, relations, properties, etc.—exist in space-time; but we mean more than this.   We renounce them altogether.' In the body of the paper Goodman and Quine made an attempt to give a nominalist analysis of various ostensibly platonist modes of expression, and they developed a nominalist syntax for use in describing, in a strictly nominalist manner, the formal behaviour of systems of platonist mathematics and logic (cf. Hilbert's finitary metamathematical treatment of non-finitary mathematics).

The same dispute concerning the existence of universals is one of the principal themes of Quine's collection of logico-philosophical essays *From a Logical Point of View* (1953), in which various philosophical matters are discussed with a minimum of logical technicality.

16. *Logic and computing machines*

There is a two-way relationship between mathematical logic and mechanical computing, since (i) the theory of Turing machines is one of the possible foundations for a theoretical analysis of constructivity in mathematics, and (ii) boolean algebra and many-valued propositional logic have applications to the design of digital computers, switching systems for electrical circuits, and railway signalling apparatus.   There are a number of papers on these aspects of logic in the *Zeitschrift für mathematische Logik und Grundlagen der Mathematik*, and papers of this kind are taken into account in the reviews published in the *Journal of Symbolic Logic*.

The theory of computing machines mostly falls within the province of information theory, which here overlaps that of logic.

BIBLIOGRAPHY

The following bibliography is confined to works mentioned elsewhere in this book. For more complete bibliographical information the bibliographies in Fraenkel [3], Fraenkel & Bar-Hillel [1], Kleene [5], and Mostowski [3] may be consulted, as well as Church's separate bibliographies [4] and [9]. For an extensive bibliography of Russian publications on mathematical logic and the foundations of mathematics, and some general observations concerning the scope and character of Russian work in this field, see Küng [1].

A search for publications on a particular topic may be carried out with the aid of the reviews that are published and systematically indexed in *Mathematical Reviews, Zentralblatt für Mathematik,* and the *Journal of Symbolic Logic* (in which an index by authors of works reviewed and also an index by reviewers appear at the end of every second volume, and an index by subjects appears at the end of every fifth volume).

The *Journal of Symbolic Logic* and the *Zeitschrift für mathematische Logik und Grundlagen der Mathematik* are devoted entirely to papers on mathematical logic and the foundations of mathematics; and both *Mathematische Annalen* and *Mathematische Zeitschrift* also include many papers on these subjects.

ACKERMANN, W.
1. 'Zum Hilbertschen Aufbau der reellen Zahlen', *Math. Ann.*, **99** (1928), 118–133.
2. 'Zur Widerspruchsfreiheit der Zahlentheorie', *Math. Ann.*, **117** (1940), 162–194.
3. 'Konstruktiver Aufbau eines Abschnitts der zweiten Cantorschen Zahlenklasse', *Math. Z.*, **53** (1950–1951), 403–413.
4. 'Widerspruchsfreier Aufbau der Logik, I. Typenfreies System ohne tertium non datur', *J. Symb. Logic*, **15** (1950), 33–57.
5. 'Widerspruchsfreier Aufbau einer typenfreien Logik. (Erweitertes System)', *Math. Z.*, **55** (1951–1952), 364–384.
6. Widerspruchsfreier Aufbau einer typenfreien Logik, II', *Math. Z.*, **57** (1952–1953), 155–166.
7. *Solvable Cases of the Decision Problem* (Amsterdam, 1954).
8. 'Zur Axiomatik der Mengenlehre', *Math. Ann.*, **131** (1956), 336–345.
9. 'Begründung einer strengen Implikation', *J. Symb. Logic*, **21** (1956), 113–128.

AMBROSE, A. & LAZEROWITZ, M.
1. *Fundamentals of Symbolic Logic* (New York, 1948).
2. *Logic: The Theory of Formal Inference* (New York, 1961).

APOLLONIUS OF PERGA
1. *Treatise on Conic Sections*, edited in modern notation with introductions including an essay on the earlier history of the subject by T. L. Heath (Cambridge, 1896).

ARISTOTLE
1. *The Works of Aristotle*, translated into English under the editorship of J. A. Smith and W. D. Ross (12 volumes: Oxford, 1908–1952).

ASSER, G.
1. 'Theorie der logischen Auswahlfunktionen', *Z. für math. Logik und Grundlagen der Math.*, **3** (1957), 30–68.
2. *Einführung in die mathematische Logik. Teil I, Aussagenkalkül* (Leipzig, 1959).

BAIN, A.
1. *Logic*. Part first, Deduction. Part second, Induction (London, 1870).

BAKER, H. F.
1. *Principles of Geometry* (6 volumes: Cambridge, 1922–1933).

BARCAN, RUTH C.
1. 'A functional calculus of first order based on strict implication', *J. Symb. Logic*, **11** (1946), 1–16.

BELL, CLIVE
1. *Art* (London, 1914).

BELL, E. T.
1. *Men of Mathematics* (London, 1937).
2. *The Development of Mathematics* (New York & London, 1940).

BERGSON, H.
1. *Essai sur les données immédiates de la conscience* (Thesis: Paris, 1889); English translation by F. L. Pogson: *Time and Free Will* (London & New York, 1910).
2. *L'Évolution Créatrice* (Paris, 1907); English translation by Arthur Mitchell: *Creative Evolution* (London, 1911).

BERNAYS, P.
1. 'A system of axiomatic set theory, I–VII', *J. Symb. Logic*, **2** (1937), 65–77; **6** (1941), 1–17; **7** (1942), 65–89; **7** (1942), 133–145; **8** (1943), 89–106; **13** (1948), 65–79; **19** (1954), 81–96.
2. Review of Carnap [2], *J. Symb. Logic*, **14** (1949), 237–241.

BERNAYS, P. & FRAENKEL, A. A.
1. *Axiomatic Set Theory* (Amsterdam, 1958).

BETH, E. W.
1. *The Foundations of Mathematics* (Amsterdam, 1959).

BIRKHOFF, G. & MACLANE, S.
1. *A Survey of Modern Algebra* (New York, 1941).

BLACK, M.
1. *The Nature of Mathematics. A Critical Survey* (London, 1933).

BOLYAI, J.
1. *Appendix, scientiam spatii absolute veram exhibens: a veritate aut falsitate Axiomatis XI Euclidei (a priori haud unquam decidenda) independentem: adjecta ad casum falsitatis, quadratura circuli geometrica*, appended to Wolfgang Bolyai: *Tentamen Juventutem studiosam in elementa Matheseos purae, elementaris ac sublimioris, methodo intuitiva, evidentiaque huic propria, introducendi* (2 volumes: Maros-Vásárhely, 1832 & 1833); English translation by G. B. Halsted: *The Science Absolute of Space* (Austin, Texas, 1892), included in the 1955 reprint of Bonola [2].

BONOLA, R.
1. 'Sulla teoria delle parallele e sulle geometrie non-euclidee', *Questioni riguardanti la geometria elementare, raccolte e coordinate da Federigo Enriques* (Bologna, 1900).
2. *La geometria non-euclidea: esposizione storico-critica del suo sviluppo* (Bologna, 1906); English translation by H. S. Carslaw: *Non-Euclidean Geometry* (Chicago, 1912; reprinted New York, 1955).

BOOLE, G.
1. 'On a general method in analysis', *Phil. Trans. Roy. Soc.*, **134** (1844), 225–282.
2. *The Mathematical Analysis of Logic, being an Essay towards a Calculus of Deductive Reasoning* (Cambridge, 1847; reprinted Oxford, 1948).
3. *An Investigation of the Laws of Thought, on which are founded the Mathematical Theories of Logic and Probabilities* (London, 1854: reprinted New York, 1951).
4. *Studies in Logic and Probability*, edited by R. Rhees (London, 1952).

BOURBAKI, N.
1. *Éléments de Mathématique* (Paris, in progress since 1939).
2. 'L'architecture des mathématiques', *Les Grands Courants de la Pensée Mathématique*, edited by F. Le Lionnais (Paris, 1948), 35–47; English translation, *Amer. Math. Monthly*, **57** (1950), 221–232.
3. 'Foundations of mathematics for the working mathematician', *J. Symb. Logic*, **14** (1949), 1–8.

BRITTON, J. L.
1. 'The word problem for groups', *Proc. London Math. Soc.*, **8** (1958), 493–506.

BROAD, C. D.
1. 'Hr. von Wright on the logic of induction, I–III', *Mind*, **53** (1944), 1–24, 97–119, 193–214.

BROUWER, L. E. J.
1. 'Zur Begründung der intuitionistischen Mathematik, I–III', *Math. Ann.*, **93** (1925), 244–257; **95** (1926), 453–472; **96** (1927), 451–488.

2. 'Mathematik, Wissenschaft und Sprache', *Monatsh. Math. Phys.*, **36** (1929), 153–164.

BURALI-FORTI, C.
1. 'Una questione sui numeri transfiniti', *Rendiconti del Circolo Matematico di Palermo*, **11** (1897), 154–164.

BURNET, J.
1. *Greek Philosophy: Part I, Thales to Plato* (London, 1914).

CANTOR, G.
1. 'Beiträge zur Begründung der transfiniten Mengenlehre', *Math. Ann.*, **46** (1895), 481–512 and **49** (1897), 207–246; English translation by P. E. B. Jourdain: *Contributions to the Founding of the Theory of Transfinite Numbers* (Chicago & London, 1915; reprinted New York, 1952).

CANTOR, M.
1. *Vorlesungen über Geschichte der Mathematik* (4 volumes: Leipzig, 1880–1908). I. Von den ältesten Zeiten bis zum Jahre 1200 n. Chr. (Second edition, 1894). II. Von 1200–1668 (Second edition, 1900). III. Von 1668–1758 (Second edition, 1901). IV. Von 1759 bis 1799 (With the collaboration of various authors; 1908).

CARNAP, R.
1. *Introduction to Semantics* (Cambridge, Mass., 1942).
2. *Meaning and Necessity. A Study in Semantics and Modal Logic* (Chicago, 1947).
3. *Logical Foundations of Probability* (Chicago, 1950).
4. Review of [1] by Church, *Philosophical Review*, **52** (1943), 298–304.
5. Review of [2] by Bernays, *J. Symb. Logic*, **14** (1949), 237–241.

CASSINA, U.
1. 'Vita et opera de Giuseppe Peano', *Schola et Vita, Organo de Academia pro Interlingua*, **7** (1932), 117–148. I. Elogio. II. Tabula chronologico de vita de G. Peano. III. Indice chronologico de publicationes scientifico de Giuseppe Peano.
2. 'L'opera scientifica di Giuseppe Peano', *Rendiconti del Seminario Matematico e Fisico di Milano*, **7** (1933), 323–389.
3. 'Su la Logica matematica di G. Peano', *Bollettino dell'Unione Matematica Italiana*, **12** (1933), 57–65.

CHURCH, A.
1. 'A set of postulates for the foundation of logic', *Ann. of Math.*, **33** (1932), 346–366 and **34** (1933), 839–864.
2. 'An unsolvable problem of elementary number theory', *Amer. J. Math.*, **58** (1936), 345–363.
3. 'A note on the Entscheidungsproblem', *J. Symb. Logic.* **1** (1936), 40–41 and 101–102.
4. 'A bibliography of symbolic logic', *J. Symb. Logic*, **1** (1936), 121–218 and **3** (1938), 178–212.

5. 'The constructive second number class', *Bull. Amer. Math. Soc.*, **44** (1938), 224–232.
6. Review of Carnap [1], *Philosophical Review*, **52** (1943), 298–304.
7. *Introduction to Mathematical Logic, Part I*. Notes by C. A. Truesdell. Annals of Mathematics Studies (Princeton, 1944).
8. 'Special cases of the decision problem', *Revue philosophique de Louvain*, **49** (1951), 203–221.
9. 'Brief bibliography of formal logic', *Proceedings of the American Academy of Arts and Sciences*, **80** (1951–1954), 155–172.
10. *Introduction to Mathematical Logic, Volume I* (Princeton, 1956). A revised and much enlarged version of [7].
11. 'Binary recursive arithmetic', *Journal de Mathématiques Pures et Appliquées*, **36** (1957), 39–55.
12. 'Logic', *Encyclopaedia Britannica*, edition of 1959.
13. 'Modern History of Logic', Part IV of the article 'Logic, History of', *Encyclopaedia Britannica*, edition of 1959.

COURANT, R. & HILBERT, D.
1. *Methoden der mathematischen Physik* (2 volumes: Berlin, 1924 & 1937).

COURANT, R. & ROBBINS, H.
1. *What is Mathematics? An Elementary Approach to Ideas and Methods* (New York, 1941).

COUTURAT, L.
1. *La Logique de Leibniz d'après des documents inédits* (Paris, 1901).
2. *Opuscules et fragments inédits de Leibniz. Extraits des manuscrits de la Bibliothèque royale de Hanovre* (Paris, 1903).

CRAMÉR, H.
1. 'Random variables and probability distributions', *Cambridge Tracts in Mathematics and Mathematical Physics*, **36** (1937), 121 pp.
2. *Mathematical Methods of Statistics* (Uppsala, 1945; reprinted Princeton, 1946).

CURRY, H. B.
1. *Outlines of a Formalist Philosophy of Mathematics* (Amsterdam, 1951).

DAVIS, M.
1. *Computability and Unsolvability* (New York, 1958).

DEDEKIND, R.
1. *Stetigkeit und irrationale Zahlen* (Brunswick, 1872).
2. *Was sind und was sollen die Zahlen?* (Brunswick, 1888).
3. *Essays on the Theory of Numbers*, translations of [1] and [2] by W. W. Beman (Chicago, 1901).
4. *Gesammelte mathematische Werke*, edited by R. Fricke, E. Noether, Ö. Ore (3 volumes: Brunswick, 1930–1933). The third volume contains [1] and [2].
5. Landau [1], for biographical details.

DE MORGAN, A.

1. *Formal Logic: or, The Calculus of Inference, Necessary and Probable* (London, 1847; reprinted London, 1926).
2. 'On the Structure of the Syllogism, and on the Application of the Theory of Probabilities to Questions of Argument and Authority', *Trans. Camb. Phil. Soc.*, **8** (1842–1847), 379–408.
3. 'On the Symbols of Logic, the Theory of the Syllogism, and in particular of the Copula, and the application of the Theory of Probabilities to some questions of evidence', *Trans. Camb. Phil. Soc.*, **9** (1849–1856), 79–127.
4. 'On the Syllogism, No. III, and on Logic in general', *Trans. Camb. Phil. Soc.*, **10** (1856–1864), 173–230.
5. 'On the Syllogism, No. IV, and on the Logic of Relations', *Trans. Camb. Phil. Soc.*, **10** (1856–1864), 331–358 and 355*–358*.
6. 'On the Syllogism, No. V, and on various points of the Onymatic System', *Trans. Camb. Phil. Soc.*, **10** (1856–1864), 428–487.

DESARGUES, G.

1. *Brouillon proiect d'une atteinte aux éuénemens des rencontres d'un cone auec un plan* (Paris, 1639); German translation: *Erster Entwurf eines Versuchs über die Ergebnisse des Zusammentreffens eines Kegels mit einer Ebene*, Ostwald's Klassiker der exakten Wissenschaften (Leipzig, 1922).

DESCARTES, R.

1. *Discours de la Méthode* (Leyden, 1637).

EDDINGTON, A. S.

1. *The Philosophy of Physical Science*, Tarner Lectures, 1938 (Cambridge, 1939).
2. *Fundamental Theory*, edited posthumously by E. T. Whittaker (Cambridge, 1946).

EUCLID

1. *The Thirteen Books of Euclid's Elements*, translated from the text of Heiberg, with introduction and commentary, by T. L. Heath (3 volumes: Cambridge, 1908).

EULER, L.

1. *Lettres à une Princesse d'Allemagne sur divers sujets de physique et de philosophie* (3 volumes: Mitau & Leipzig, St Petersburg, 1770–1772).

FANO, G.

1. 'Sui postulati fondamentali della geometria proiettiva in uno spazio lineare a un numero qualunque di dimensioni', *Giornale de Matematiche*, **30** (1891), 106–132.

FITCH, F. B.

1. 'The consistency of the ramified *Principia*', *J. Symb. Logic*, **3** (1938), 140–149.
2. 'A basic logic', *J. Symb. Logic*, **7** (1942), 105–114.
3. 'Representations of calculi', *J. Symb. Logic*, **9** (1944), 57–62.

4. 'A demonstrably consistent mathematics, I, II', *J. Symb. Logic*, **15** (1950), 17–24 and **16** (1951), 121–124.

FRAENKEL, A. A.
1. 'Zu den Grundlagen der Cantor-Zermeloschen Mengenlehre', *Math. Ann.*, **86** (1922), 230–237.
2. 'Untersuchungen über die Grundlagen der Mengenlehre', *Math. Z.*, **22** (1925), 250–273.
3. *Abstract Set Theory* (Amsterdam, 1953).

FRAENKEL, A. A. & BAR-HILLEL, Y.
1. *Foundations of Set Theory* (Amsterdam, 1958).

FREGE, G.
1. *Begriffsschrift, eine der arithmetischen nachgebildete Formelsprache des reinen Denkens* (Halle, 1879).
2. *Die Grundlagen der Arithmetik. Eine logisch mathematische Untersuchung über den Begriff der Zahl* (Breslau, 1884); English translation by J. L. Austin: *The Foundations of Arithmetic* (Oxford, 1950).
3. 'Über Sinn und Bedeutung', *Zeitschrift für Philosophie und philosophische Kritik*, **100** (1892), 25–50.
4. *Grundgesetze der Arithmetik, begriffsschriftlich abgeleitet* (2 volumes: Jena, 1893 & 1903).
5. *Translations from the Philosophical Writings of Gottlob Frege*, edited by Peter Geach and Max Black (Oxford, 1952).

GANDY, R. O.
1. 'On the axiom of extensionality, Part I', *J. Symb. Logic*, **21** (1956), 36–48.

GAUSS, C. F.
1. *Disquisitiones Arithmeticae* (Leipzig, 1801).
2. *Gedenkband anlässlich des 100. Todestages am 23. Februar 1955*, herausgegeben von Hans Reichardt, Berlin (Leipzig, 1957).

GENOCCHI, A.
1. *Calcolo differenziale e principii di calcolo integrale, pubblicato con aggiunte dal D.r Giuseppe Peano* (Turin, 1884).

GENTZEN, G.
1. 'Untersuchungen über das logische Schließen, I, II', *Math. Z.*, **39** (1935), 176–210 and 405–431.
2. 'Die Widerspruchsfreiheit der Stufenlogik', *Math. Z.*, **41** (1936), 357–366.
3. 'Die Widerspruchsfreiheit der reinen Zahlentheorie', *Math. Ann.*, **112** (1936), 493–565.

GÖDEL, K.
1. 'Die Vollständigkeit der Axiome des logischen Funktionenkalküls', *Monatsh. Math. Phys.*, **37** (1930), 349–360.
2. 'Über formal unentscheidbare Sätze der Principia Mathematica und verwandter Systeme I', *Monatsh. Math. Phys.*, **38** (1931), 173–198.
3. *On Undecidable Propositions of Formal Mathematical Systems.* Mimeo-

graphed notes, by S. C. Kleene and J. B. Rosser, of lectures given at the Institute for Advanced Study, Princeton, February–May 1934.

4. *The Consistency of the Axiom of Choice and of the Generalized Continuum-Hypothesis with the Axioms of Set Theory.* Notes by George W. Brown of lectures delivered at the Institute for Advanced Study, Princeton, during the autumn term, 1938–1939. Annals of Mathematics Studies (Princeton, 1940; revised edition 1951).

5. 'Russell's mathematical logic', *The Philosophy of Bertrand Russell*, edited by P. A. Schilpp (Evanston & Chicago, 1944), 125–153.

6. 'What is Cantor's Continuum Problem?', *Amer. Math. Monthly*, **54** (1947), 515–525.

GOODMAN, N. & QUINE, W. V.

1. 'Steps towards a constructive nominalism', *J. Symb. Logic.* **12** (1947), 105–122.

GOODSTEIN, R. L.

1. 'On the restricted ordinal theorem', *J. Symb. Logic*, **9** (1944), 33–41.
2. *Mathematical Logic* (Leicester, 1957).
3. *Recursive Number Theory* (Amsterdam, 1957).
4. *Recursive Analysis* (Amsterdam, 1962).

GRASSMANN, H.

1. *Die lineale Ausdehnungslehre, ein neuer Zweig der Mathematik* (Leipzig, 1844).
2. *Die Ausdehnungslehre, vollständig und in strenger Form bearbeitet* (Berlin, 1862).

GRELLING, K. & NELSON, L.

1. 'Bemerkungen zu den Paradoxien von Russell und Burali-Forti', *Abhandlungen der Fries'schen Schule*, **2** (1907–1908), 300–334.

HALL, MARSHALL, JR.

1. 'The word problem for semigroups with two generators', *J. Symb. Logic*, **14** (1949), 115–118.

HAMILTON, W.

1. *Lectures on Logic, I, II*, constituting volumes III and IV of *Lectures on Metaphysics and Logic*, by Sir William Hamilton, Bart., and edited by H. L. Mansel and J. Veitch (4 volumes: Edinburgh, 1859–1860).

HAMILTON, W. R.

1. *Elements of Quaternions* (London, 1866).

HANSON, N. R.

1. 'The Gödel theorem. An informal exposition', *Notre Dame Journal of Formal Logic*, **2** (1961), 94–110.
2. 'A note on the Gödel theorem', *Notre Dame Journal of Formal Logic*, **2** (1961), 228.

HASENJAEGER, G.

1. 'Über ω-Unvollständigkeit in der Peano-Arithmetik', *J. Symb. Logic*, **17** (1952), 81–97.

HAUSDORFF, F.

1. *Grundzüge der Mengenlehre* (Leipzig, 1914); second revised edition *Mengenlehre* (Berlin & Leipzig, 1927); English translation *Set Theory* (New York, 1957).

HEATH, T. L.

1. Apollonius of Perga [1], edited by T. L. Heath.
2. Euclid [1], edited by T. L. Heath.
3. *A History of Greek Mathematics* (2 volumes: Oxford, 1921).

HECKE, E.

1. *Vorlesungen über die Theorie der algebraischen Zahlen* (Leipzig, 1923).

HEGEL, G. F. W.

1. *Phänomenologie des Geistes* (Bamberg, 1807); English translation by J. B. Baillie: *The Phenomenology of Mind* (London, 1910).

HELMER, O. & OPPENHEIM, P.

1. 'A syntactical definition of probability and of degree of confirmation', *J. Symb. Logic*, **10** (1945), 25–60.

HEMPEL, C. G.

1. 'A purely syntactical definition of confirmation', *J. Symb. Logic*, **8** (1943), 122–143.

HENKIN, L.

1. 'The completeness of the first-order functional calculus', *J. Symb. Logic*, **14** (1949), 159–166.
2. 'Some interconnections between modern algebra and mathematical logic', *Trans. Amer. Math. Soc.*, **74** (1953), 410–427.

HERMES, H.

1. *Aufzählbarkeit, Entscheidbarkeit, Berechenbarkeit. Einführung in die Theorie der rekursiven Funktionen* (Berlin, Göttingen, Heidelberg, 1961).

HERMES, H. & SCHOLZ, H.

1. 'Mathematische Logik', *Enzyklopädie der mathematischen Wissenschaften*, I 1, 1, I (Leipzig, 1952), 82 pp.

HEYTING, A.

1. 'Die formalen Regeln der intuitionistischen Logik' and 'Die formalen Regeln der intuitionistischen Mathematik, II, III', *Sitzungsberichte der Preußischen Akademie der Wissenschaften, Physikalisch-Mathematische Klasse* (1930), 42–56, 57–71, 158–169.
2. 'Mathematische Grundlagenforschung: Intuitionismus, Beweistheorie', *Ergebnisse der Mathematik und ihrer Grenzgebiete*, III, 4 (Berlin, 1934).
3. *Intuitionism. An Introduction* (Amsterdam, 1956).
4. *Constructivity in Mathematics. Proceedings of the Colloquium held at Amsterdam, 1957.* Edited by A. Heyting (Amsterdam, 1959).

HILBERT, D.

1. 'Die Theorie der algebraischen Zahlkörper', *Jahresbericht der Deutschen Mathematiker-Vereinigung*, **4** (1894–1895), 175–546; published 1897.

2. *Grundlagen der Geometrie* (Leipzig, 1899); English translation by E. J. Townsend : *The Foundations of Geometry* (Chicago, 1902).
3. 'Mathematische Probleme', Vortrag, gehalten auf dem internationalen Mathematiker-Kongreß zu Paris 1900, *Nachrichten von der Königlichen Gesellschaft der Wissenschaften zu Göttingen, Mathematisch-physikalische Klasse* (1900), 253–297; French translation in *Compte Rendu du Deuxième Congrès Internationale des Mathématiciens, tenu à Paris du 6 au 12 août 1900*, 58–114.
4. *Grundzüge einer allgemeinen Theorie der linearen Integralgleichungen* (Leipzig & Berlin, 1912).
5. *Gesammelte Abhandlungen* (3 volumes: Berlin, 1932–1935). I. Zahlentheorie. II. Algebra. Invariantentheorie. Geometrie. III. Analysis. Grundlagen der Mathematik. Physik. Verschiedenes. Nebst einer Lebensgeschichte.
6. Weyl [5], [6], for biographical details.

HILBERT, D. & ACKERMANN, W.
1. *Grundzüge der theoretischen Logik* (Berlin, 1928; fourth edition, completely revised, 1959); English translation *Principles of Mathematical Logic* (New York, 1950).

HILBERT, D. & BERNAYS, P.
1. *Grundlagen der Mathematik* (2 volumes: Berlin, 1934 & 1939).

HILBERT, D. & COHN-VOSSEN, S.
1. *Anschauliche Geometrie* (Berlin, 1932); English translation *Geometry and the Imagination* (New York, 1956).

HOBBES, T.
1. *Elementorum philosophiae sectio prima: De Corpore* (London, 1655); English translation *Elements of Philosophy, the first Section, concerning Body* (London, 1656).

HUNTINGTON, E. V.
1. 'Sets of independent postulates for the algebra of logic', *Trans. Amer. Math. Soc.*, **5** (1904), 288–309.

JEVONS, W. S.
1. *Pure Logic or the Logic of Quality apart from Quantity: with remarks on Boole's system and on the relation of Logic and Mathematics* (London, 1864).
2. *Elementary Lessons in Logic* (London, 1870).

JORDAN, C.
1. *Cours d'Analyse de l'École Polytechnique* (3 volumes: Paris, 1882–1887).

KALMÁR, L.
1. 'On the reduction of the decision problem. First paper. Ackermann prefix, a single binary predicate', *J. Symb. Logic*, **4** (1939), 1–9.
2. 'An argument against the plausibility of Church's thesis', *Constructivity in Mathematics: Proceedings of the Colloquium held at Amsterdam, 1957* (Amsterdam, 1959), 72–80.

KALMÁR, L. & SURÁNYI, J.
1. 'On the reduction of the decision problem. Second paper. Gödel prefix, a single binary predicate', *J. Symb. Logic*, **12** (1947), 65–73.
2. 'On the reduction of the decision problem. Third paper. Pepis prefix, a single binary predicate', *J. Symb. Logic*, **15** (1950), 161–173.

KANT, I.
1. *Critik der reinen Vernunft* (Riga, 1781; second edition 1787); English translation by J. M. D. Meiklejohn: *Critique of Pure Reason* (London, 1852).
2. *Prolegomena zu einer jeden künftigen Metaphysik, die als Wissenschaft wird auftreten können* (Riga, 1783).

KEMENY, J. G.
1. 'Models of logical systems', *J. Symb. Logic*, **13** (1948), 16–30.
2. Review of *The Theory of Probability* by H. Reichenbach, *J. Symb. Logic*, **16** (1951), 48–51.
3. 'Fair bets and inductive probabilities', *J. Symb. Logic*, **20** (1955), 263–273.
4. 'A new approach to semantics, Parts I & II', *J. Symb. Logic*, **21** (1956), 1–27 and 149–161.
5. 'Semantics as a branch of logic', *Encyclopaedia Britannica*, edition of 1959.

KEYNES, J. M.
1. *A Treatise on Probability* (London, 1921).

KLAUA, D.
1. 'Systematische Behandlung der lösbaren Fälle des Entscheidungsproblems für den Prädikatenkalkül der ersten Stufe', *Z. für math. Logik und Grundlagen der Math.*, **1** (1955), 264–270.
2. 'Berechenbare Analysis', *Z. für math. Logik und Grundlagen der Math.*, **2** (1956), 265–303.

KLEENE, S. C.
1. 'Proof by cases in formal logic', *Ann. of Math.*, **35** (1934), 529–544.
2. 'A theory of positive integers in formal logic, I, II', *Amer. J. Math.*, **57** (1935), 153–173 and 219–244.
3. 'General recursive functions of natural numbers', *Math. Ann.*, **112** (1936), 727–742.
4. 'On notation for ordinal numbers', *J. Symb. Logic*, **3** (1938), 150–155.
5. *Introduction to Metamathematics* (Amsterdam, Groningen, New York, 1952).
6. 'Hierarchies of number-theoretic predicates', *Bull. Amer. Math. Soc.*, **61** (1955), 193–213.

KLEIN, F.
1. 'Über die sogenannte Nicht-Euklidische Geometrie', *Math. Ann.*, **4** (1871), 573–625.
2. *Vorlesungen über die Entwicklung der Mathematik im 19. Jahrhundert*, edited by R. Courant, O. Neugebauer, and St. Cohn-Vossen (2 volumes: Berlin, 1926 & 1927).

3. *Vorlesungen über Nicht-Euklidische Geometrie*, edited by W. Rosemann (Berlin, 1928).

KLINGENBERG, W.
1. 'Grundlagen der Geometrie', *C. F. Gauss: Gedenkband anlässlich des 100. Todestages am 22. Februar 1955* (Leipzig, 1957), 111–150.

KNEALE, W.
1. 'Boole and the revival of logic', *Mind*, **57** (1948), 149–175.
2. *Probability and Induction* (Oxford, 1949).
3. 'Gottlob Frege and mathematical logic', *The Revolution in Philosophy* (London, 1956), 26–40.

KNEALE, W. & KNEALE, M.
1. *The Development of Logic* (Oxford, 1962).

KNEEBONE, G. T.
1. 'Induction and probability', *Proceedings of the Aristotelian Society*, **50** (1950), 27–42.
2. 'Abstract logic and concrete thought', *Proceedings of the Aristotelian Society*, **56** (1956), 25–44.

KOLMOGOROV, A. N.
1. 'Zur Deutung der intuitionistischen Logik', *Math. Z.*, **35** (1932), 58–65.
2. 'Grundbegriffe der Wahrscheinlichkeitsrechnung', *Ergebnisse der Mathematik und ihrer Grenzgebiete*, II, 3 (Berlin, 1933); English translation by N. Morrison: *Foundations of the Theory of Probability* (New York, 1950).

KÖRNER, S.
1. *The Philosophy of Mathematics. An Introductory Essay* (London, 1960).

KREISEL, G.
1. 'On the interpretation of non-finitist proofs, Part I', *J. Symb. Logic*, **16** (1951), 241–267.
2. 'On the interpretation of non-finitist proofs, Part II. Interpretation of number theory. Applications', *J. Symb. Logic*, **17** (1952), 43–58.
3. 'Mathematical significance of consistency proofs', *J. Symb. Logic*, **23** (1958), 155–182.
4. 'Elementary completeness properties of intuitionistic logic with a note on negations of prenex formulae', *J. Symb. Logic*, **23** (1958), 317–330.
5. 'A remark on free choice sequences and the topological completeness proofs', *J. Symb. Logic*, **23** (1958), 369–388.

KUMMER, E. E.
1. 'Zur Theorie der complexen Zahlen', *J. reine angew. Math.*, **35** (1847), 319–326.

KÜNG, G.
1. 'Bibliography of Soviet work in the field of mathematical logic and the foundations of mathematics, from 1917–1957', with a preface by I. M. Bocheński, *Notre Dame Journal of Formal Logic*, **3** (1962), 1–40.

KURATOWSKI, K.
1. 'Sur la notion d'ordre dans la théorie des ensembles', *Fund. Math.*, **2** (1921), 161–171.

LAGRANGE, J.-L.
1. *Théorie des fonctions analytiques, contenant les principes du calcul différentiel, dégagés de toute considération d'infiniment petits et d'évanouissans de limites ou de fluxions, et réduits à l'analyse algébrique des quantités finies* (Paris, 1797).

LANDAU, E.
1. 'Richard Dedekind', Gedächtnisrede, gehalten in der öffentlichen Sitzung der Königlichen Gesellschaft der Wissenschaften zu Göttingen am 12. Mai 1917, *Nachrichten von der Königlichen Gesellschaft der Wissenschaften zu Göttingen, Geschäftliche Mitteilungen aus dem Jahre 1917*, 50–70.
2. *Grundlagen der Analysis.* (*Das Rechnen mit ganzen, rationalen, irrationalen, komplexen Zahlen.*) *Ergänzung zu den Lehrbüchern der Differential- und Integralrechnung* (Leipzig, 1930).

LAPLACE, P. S.
1. *Théorie analytique des Probabilités* (Paris, 1812).

LEGENDRE, A.-M.
1. *Éléments de Géométrie* (Paris, 1794).

LEHMAN, R. S.
1. 'On confirmation and rational betting', *J. Symb. Logic*, **20** (1955), 251–262.

LEVI, B.
1. 'L'opera matematica di G. Peano', *Bollettino dell'Unione Matematica Italiana*, **11** (1932), 253–262.

LEWIS, C. I. & LANGFORD, C. H.
1. *Symbolic Logic* (New York, 1932; reprinted New York, 1951).

LITTLEWOOD, J. E.
1. *The Elements of the Theory of Real Functions* (Cambridge, 1926; reprinted in a revised version, New York, 1954).

LOBACHEVSKY, N.
1. *Geometrische Untersuchungen zur Theorie der Parallellinien* (Berlin, 1840); English translation by G. B. Halsted: *Geometrical Researches on the Theory of Parallels* (Austin, Texas, 1891), included in the 1955 reprint of Bonola [2].

LOCKE, J.
1. *Essay Concerning Human Understanding* (London, 1690).

LORENZEN, P.
1. 'Konstruktive Begründung der Mathematik', *Math. Z.*, **53** (1950–1951), 162–202.

2. 'Algebraische und logistische Untersuchungen über freie Verbände', *J. Symb. Logic*, **16** (1951), 81–106.

3. 'Die Widerspruchsfreiheit der klassischen Analysis', *Math. Z.*, **54** (1951), 1–24.

4. *Einführung in die operative Logik und Mathematik* (Berlin, Göttingen, Heidelberg, 1955).

LÖWENHEIM, L.

1. 'Über Möglichkeiten im Relativkalkül', *Math. Ann.*, **76** (1915), 447–470.

2. 'Einkleidung der Mathematik in Schröderschen Relativkalkul', *J. Symb. Logic*, **5** (1940), 1–15.

ŁUKASIEWICZ, J.

1. 'O logice trójwartościowej' [On three-valued logic], *Ruch Filozoficzny* (Lwów), **5** (1920), 169–171.

2. 'Philosophische Bemerkungen zu mehrwertigen Systemen des Aussagenkalküls', *Comptes Rendus des Séances de la Société des Sciences et des Lettres de Varsovie, Classe III*, **23** (1930), 51–77.

3. *Aristotle's Syllogistic from the Standpoint of Modern Formal Logic* (Oxford, 1951).

ŁUKASIEWICZ, J. & TARSKI, A.

1. 'Untersuchungen über den Aussagenkalkül', *Comptes Rendus des Séances de la Société des Sciences et des Lettres de Varsovie, Classe III*, **23** (1930), 1–21.

McCOLL, H.

1. 'The calculus of equivalent statements and integration limits', *Proc. London Math. Soc.*, **9** (1877–1878), 9–20.

2. 'The calculus of equivalent statements (second paper)', *Proc. London Math. Soc.*, **9** (1877–1878), 177–186.

3. 'The calculus of equivalent statements (third paper)', *Proc. London Math. Soc.*, **10** (1878–1879), 16–28.

4. 'The calculus of equivalent statements (fourth paper)', *Proc. London Math. Soc.*, **11** (1879–1880), 113–121.

MACH, E.

1. *Die Mechanik in ihrer Entwickelung, historisch-kritisch dargestellt* (Leipzig, 1883); English translation by Thomas J. McCormack: *The Science of Mechanics* (Chicago, 1893).

McKINSEY, J. C. C.

1. 'The decision problem for some classes of sentences without quantifiers', *J. Symb. Logic*, **8** (1943), 61–76.

McKINSEY, J. C. C. & TARSKI, A.

1. 'Some theories about the sentential calculi of Lewis and Heyting', *J. Symb. Logic*, **13** (1948), 1–15.

MARKOV, A. A. (Марков, А. А.)

1. 'Невозможность некоторых алгорифмов в теории ассоциативных систем', *Доклады Акад. Наук СССР*, **55** (1947), 587–590.

2. 'Теория алгорифмов', *Труды Матем. Инст. им. В. А. Стеклова*, **42** (1954), 375 pp.

MARTIN, R. M.
1. 'A formalization of inductive logic', *J. Symb. Logic*, **23** (1958), 251–256.

MILL, J. S.
1. *A System of Logic, Ratiocinative and Inductive, being a connected View of the Principles of Evidence, and the Methods of Scientific Investigation* (2 volumes: London, 1843).

MIRIMANOFF, D.
1. 'Les antinomies de Russell et de Burali-Forti et le problème fondamental de la théorie des ensembles', *L'Enseignement Mathématique*, **19** (1917), 37–52.

VON MISES, R.
1. 'Grundlagen der Wahrscheinlichkeitsrechnung', *Math. Z.*, **5** (1919), 52–99.
2. *Wahrscheinlichkeitsrechnung und ihre Anwendungen in der Statistik und theoretischen Physik* (Leipzig, 1931).

MÖBIUS, A. F.
1. *Der barycentrische Calcul ein neues Hülfsmittel zur analytischen Behandlung der Geometrie dargestellt und insbesondere auf die Bildung neuer Classen von Aufgaben und die Entwickelung mehrerer Eigenschaften der Kegelschnitte angewendet* (Leipzig, 1827).

MOSTOWSKI, A.
1. *Sentences Undecidable in Formalized Arithmetic. An Exposition of the Theory of Kurt Gödel* (Amsterdam, 1952).
2. 'On models of axiomatic systems', *Fund. Math.*, **39** (1952), 133–158.
3. 'The present state of investigations on the foundations of mathematics', *Rozprawy Matematyczne*, **9** (1955), 48 pp. Compiled in collaboration with A. Grzegorczyk, S. Jaśkowski, J. Łoś, S. Mazur, H. Rasiowa, and R. Sikorski.

NAGEL, E.
1. *The Structure of Science. Problems in the Logic of Scientific Explanation* (London, 1961).

NAGEL, E. & NEWMAN, J. R.
1. *Gödel's Proof* (London, 1959).

VON NEUMANN, J.
1. 'Eine Axiomatisierung der Mengenlehre', *J. reine angew. Math.*, **154** (1925), 219–240.
2. 'Die Axiomatisierung der Mengenlehre', *Math. Z.*, **27** (1928), 669–752.

VON NEUMANN, J. & MORGENSTERN, O.
1. *Theory of Games and Economic Behavior* (Princeton, 1947).

NEWMAN, M. H. A.
1. 'Hermann Weyl', *J. London Math. Soc.*, **33** (1958), 500–511.

2. 'Hermann Weyl, 1885–1955', *Biographical Memoirs of Fellows of the Royal Society*, **3** (1957), 305–328.

NOVAK, ILSE L. (L. NOVAK GÁL)
1. 'A construction of models of consistent systems', *Fund. Math.*, **37** (1950), 87–110.

NOVIKOV, P. S. (Новиков, П. С.)
1. 'Об алгоритмической неразрешимости проблемы тождества', *Докла-ды Акад. Наук СССР*, **85** (1952), 709–712.
2. 'Об алгоритмической неразрешимости проблемы тождества слов в теории групп', *Труды Матем. Инст. им. В. А. Стеклова*, **44** (1955), 143 pp. English translation by K. A. Hirsch : 'On the algorithmic unsolvability of the word problem in group theory', *Amer. Math. Soc. Translations*, **9** (1958), 1–122.

NOVIKOV, P. S. & ADIAN, S. I. (Новиков, П. С. и Адян, С. И.)
1. 'Проблема тождества для полугрупп с односторонним сокращением' [The word problem for semigroups with one-sided cancellation], *Z. für math. Logik und Grundlagen der Math.*, **4** (1958), 66–88. German summary.

OREY, S.
1. 'On the relative consistency of set theory', *J. Symb. Logic*, **21** (1956), 280–290.

PASCH, M.
1. *Vorlesungen über neuere Geometrie* (Leipzig, 1882).

PEANO, G.
1. Genocchi [1], written by Peano.
2. *Calcolo Geometrico, secondo l'Ausdehnungslehre di H. Grassmann, preceduto dalle operazioni della logica deduttiva* (Turin, 1888).
3. *Arithmetices Principia nova methodo exposita* (Turin, 1889).
4. 'Sur une courbe, qui remplit toute une aire plaine', *Math. Ann.*, **36** (1890), 157–160.
5. *Rivista di Matematica*, **1–5**, continued as *Revue de Mathématique*, **6 & 7**, and *Revista de Mathematica*, **8** (Turin, 1891–1906) ; edited by Peano.
6. *Formulaire de Mathématique*, the final edition issued as *Formulario Mathematico* (5 successive versions : Turin, 1894–1908).
7. *Opere scelte* (3 volumes : Rome, 1957–1959).
8. Cassina [1], [2], [3] and Levi [1], for details of Peano's life and work.

PEDOE, D.
1. *Circles* (London, New York, Paris, 1957).

PEIRCE, C. S.
1. 'On the algebra of logic', *Amer. J. Math.*, **3** (1880), 15–57 ; reprinted in *Collected Papers of Charles Sanders Peirce*, edited by C. Hartshorne and P. Weiss (8 volumes : Cambridge, Mass., 1931–1958), **3**, 104–157.

Péter, Rózsa
1. 'Zusammenhang der mehrfachen und transfiniten Rekursionen', *J. Symb. Logic*, **15** (1950), 248–272.
2. *Rekursive Funktionen* (Budapest, 1951).

Pieri, M.
1. 'I principii della geometria di posizione composti in sistema logico deduttivo', *Memorie della Reale Accademia delle Scienze di Torino*, **48** (1899), 1–62.

Poincaré, H.
1. *La Science et l'Hypothèse* (Paris, 1902); English translation by W. J. G., 1905.

Poncelet, J.-V.
1. *Traité des propriétés projectives des figures, ouvrage utile à ceux qui s'occupent des applications de la géométrie descriptive et d'opérations géométriques sur le terrain* (Paris, 1822).

Popper, K. R.
1. *Logik der Forschung* (Vienna, 1935); English translation, with supplementary material, *The Logic of Scientific Discovery* (London, 1959).

Post, E. L.
1. 'Introduction to a general theory of elementary propositions', *Amer. J. Math.*, **43** (1921), 163–185.
2. 'Formal reductions of the general combinatorial decision problem', *Amer. J. Math.*, **65** (1943), 197–215.
3. 'Recursively enumerable sets of positive integers and their decision problems', *Bull. Amer. Math. Soc.*, **50** (1944), 284–316.
4. 'Recursive unsolvability of a problem of Thue', *J. Symb. Logic*, **12** (1947), 1–11.

Prior, A. N.
1. *Formal Logic* (Oxford, 1955).

Ptolemy (Claudius Ptolemaeus)
1. *Syntaxis Mathematica*, the Greek text of the *Almagest*, edited by J. L. Heiberg (2 volumes: Leipzig, 1898 & 1903); German translation by K. Mantius: *Handbuch der Astronomie* (2 volumes: Leipzig, 1912 & 1913).

Putnam, H.
1. 'Decidability and essential undecidability', *J. Symb. Logic*, **22** (1957), 39–54.

Quine, W. V.
1. 'New foundations for mathematical logic', *Amer. Math. Monthly*, **44** (1937), 70–80; reprinted in a revised form in [6].
2. *Mathematical Logic* (New York, 1940; revised version, 1951).
3. 'Element and number', *J. Symb. Logic*, **6** (1941), 135–149.
4. 'On the logic of quantification', *J. Symb. Logic*, **10** (1945), 1–12.

5. 'On natural deduction', *J. Symb. Logic*, **15** (1950), 93–102.
6. *From a Logical Point of View. 9 Logico-Philosophical Essays* (Cambridge, Mass., 1953).
7. 'Interpretations of sets of conditions', *J. Symb. Logic*, **19** (1954), 97–102.

RABIN, M. O.
1. 'Recursive unsolvability of group theoretic problems', *Ann. of Math.*, **67** (1958), 172–194.

RAMSEY, F. P.
1. *The Foundations of Mathematics and other Logical Essays*, edited by R. B. Braithwaite (London, 1931).

REICHENBACH, H.
1. 'Axiomatik der Wahrscheinlichkeitsrechnung', *Math. Z.*, **34** (1932), 568–619.
2. *Wahrscheinlichkeitslehre: eine Untersuchung über die logischen und mathematischen Grundlagen der Wahrscheinlichkeitsrechnung* (Leyden, 1935); English translation by E. H. Hutten and Maria Reichenbach: *The Theory of Probability. An Inquiry into the Logical and Mathematical Foundations of the Calculus of Probability* (Berkeley & Los Angeles, 1949).
3. *Philosophic Foundations of Quantum Mechanics* (Berkeley & Los Angeles, 1944).

RICHARD, J.
1. 'Les principes de mathématiques et le problème des ensembles', *Revue Générale des Sciences Pures et Appliquées*, **16** (1905), 541–543, and *Acta Math.*, **30** (1906), 295–296.

RICHTER, H.
1. 'Zur Grundlegung der Wahrscheinlichkeitstheorie, I–V', *Math. Ann.*, **125** (1952–1953), 129–139, 223–234, and 335–343; **126** (1953), 362–374; **128** (1954–1955), 305–339.
2. *Wahrscheinlichkeitstheorie* (Berlin, Göttingen, Heidelberg, 1956).

RIEMANN, B.
1. Über die Hypothesen, welche der Geometrie zu Grunde liegen', Habilitationsschrift, Göttingen, 1854. Originally published in *Abhandlungen der Königlichen Gesellschaft der Wissenschaften zu Göttingen*, **13** (1866–1867), 133–152, and reprinted in *Bernhard Riemann's Gesammelte mathematische Werke und wissenschaftlicher Nachlass* (Leipzig, 1876), 254–269.

ROBINSON, A.
1. *On the Metamathematics of Algebra* (Amsterdam, 1951).

ROSENBLOOM, P. C.
1. *The Elements of Mathematical Logic* (New York, 1950).

ROSS, W. D.
1. *Aristotle* (London, 1923).

Rosser, J. B.
1. 'Extensions of some theorems of Gödel and Church', *J. Symb. Logic*, **1** (1936), 87–91.
2. 'An informal exposition of proofs of Gödel's theorems and Church's theorem', *J. Symb. Logic*, **4** (1939), 53–60.
3. 'The Burali-Forti paradox', *J. Symb. Logic*, **7** (1942), 1–17.

Rosser, J. B. & Turquette, A. R.
1. *Many-Valued Logics* (Amsterdam, 1952).

Rosser, J. B. & Wang, Hao
1. 'Non-standard models for formal logics', *J. Symb. Logic*, **15** (1950), 113–129.

Russell, B.
1. *A Critical Exposition of the Philosophy of Leibniz* (London, 1900).
2. *The Principles of Mathematics* (Cambridge, 1903; second edition, with a new introduction, London, 1937).
3. *Introduction to Mathematical Philosophy* (London, 1919).
4. *The Analysis of Matter* (London, 1927).
5. *Human Knowledge: Its Scope and Limits* (London, 1948).
6. *The Philosophy of Bertrand Russell*, edited by P. A. Schilpp (Evanston & Chicago, 1944).

Ryle, G.
1. 'Knowing how and knowing that', *Proceedings of the Aristotelian Society*, **46** (1946), 1–16.

Saccheri, G. G.
1. *Euclides ab Omni Naevo Vindicatus* (Milan, 1733); reprinted with an English translation by G. B. Halsted (Chicago & London, 1920).

Schmidt, H. A.
1. 'Mathematische Grundlagenforschung', *Enzyklopädie der mathematischen Wissenschaften*, I 1, 1, II (Leipzig, 1950), 48 pp.
2. *Mathematische Gesetze der Logik. I, Vorlesungen über Aussagenlogik* (Berlin, Göttingen, Heidelberg, 1960).

Scholz, H. & Hasenjaeger, G.
1. *Grundzüge der mathematischen Logik* (Berlin, Göttingen, Heidelberg, 1961).

Schönflies, A.
1. *Krystallsysteme und Krystallstruktur* (Leipzig, 1891).

Schröder, E.
1. *Vorlesungen über die Algebra der Logik (Exakte Logik)* (3 volumes: Leipzig, 1890–1905). I, 1890; II(i), 1891; II(ii), edited after Schröder's death by E. Müller, 1905; III, *Algebra und Logik der Relative*, 1895.

28 + M.L.

SCHRÖTER, K.
1. 'Theorie des logischen Schließens, I, II', *Z. für math. Logik und Grundlagen der Math.*, **1** (1955), 37–86 and **4** (1958), 10–65.   A third part to follow.
2. 'Eine Umformung des Heytingschen Axiomensystems für den intuitionistischen Aussagenkalkül', *Z. für math. Logik und Grundlagen der Math.*, **3** (1957), 18–29.

SCHÜTTE, K.
1. 'Beweistheoretische Erfassung der unendlichen Induktion in der Zahlentheorie', *Math. Ann.*, **122** (1950–1951), 369–389.
2. 'Beweistheoretische Untersuchung der verzweigten Analysis', *Math. Ann.*, **124** (1951–1952), 123–147.
3. 'Zur Widerspruchsfreiheit einer typenfreien Logik', *Math. Ann.*, **125** (1952–1953), 394–400.
4. 'Ein widerspruchsloses System der Analysis auf typenfreier Grundlage', *Math. Z.*, **61** (1954–1955), 160–179.
5. *Beweistheorie* (Berlin, Göttingen, Heidelberg, 1960).

SHANIN, N. A. (Шанин, Н. А.)
1. 'Некоторые вопросы математического анализа в свете конструктивной логики' [Some questions of mathematical analysis in the light of constructive logic], *Z. für math. Logik und Grundlagen der Math.*, **2** (1956), 27–36.

SHEPHERDSON, J. C.
1. 'Inner models for set theory, Parts I–III', *J. Symb. Logic*, **16** (1951), 161–190; **17** (1952), 225–237; **18** (1953), 145–167.

SHOENFIELD, J. R.
1. 'A relative consistency proof', *J. Symb. Logic*, **19** (1954), 21–28.

SIERPIŃSKI, W.
1. *Cardinal and Ordinal Numbers* (Warsaw, 1958).

SKOLEM, TH.
1. 'Einige Bemerkungen zur axiomatischen Begründung der Mengenlehre' *Conférences faites au Cinquième Congrès des Mathématiciens Scandinaves, tenu à Helsingfors du 4 au 7 juillet* 1922 (Helsingfors, 1923), 217–232.
2. 'Begründung der elementaren Arithmetik durch die rekurrierende Denkweise ohne Anwendung scheinbarer Veränderlichen mit unendlichem Ausdehnungsbereich', *Skrifter utgit av Videnskapsselskapet i Kristiania, I. Matematisk-naturvidenskabelig Klasse*, 1923, no. 6, 38 pp.
3. 'Bemerkungen zum Komprehensionsaxiom', *Z. für math. Logik und Grundlagen der Math.*, **3** (1957), 1–17.

SOMMERVILLE, D. M. Y.
1. *The Elements of Non-Euclidean Geometry* (London, 1914).

SPECKER, E.
1. 'Nicht konstruktiv beweisbare Sätze der Analysis', *J. Symb. Logic*, **14** (1949), 145–158.

2. 'Zur Axiomatik der Mengenlehre (Fundierungs- und Auswahlaxiom)',
Z. für math. Logik und Grundlagen der Math., **3** (1957), 173–210.

SPEISER, A.
1. *Die Theorie der Gruppen von endlicher Ordnung, mit Anwendungen auf
algebraischen Zahlen und Gleichungen sowie auf die Krystallographie* (Berlin,
1923).

STABLER, E. R.
1. *An Introduction to Mathematical Thought* (Reading, Mass., 1953).

VON STAUDT, G. K. C.
1. *Geometrie der Lage* (Nuremberg, 1847).
2. *Beiträge zur Geometrie der Lage* (3 parts: Nuremberg, 1856, 1857, 1860).

SUPPES, P.
1. *Introduction to Logic* (Princeton, 1957).
2. *Axiomatic Set Theory* (Princeton, 1960).

SURÁNYI, J.
1. *Reduktionstheorie des Entscheidungsproblems im Prädikatenkalkül der
ersten Stufe* (Budapest, 1959).

TARSKI, A.
1. 'Einige Betrachtungen über die Begriffe der ω-Widerspruchsfreiheit und
der ω-Vollständigkeit', *Monatsh. Math. Phys.*, **40** (1933), 97–112.
2. 'Der Wahrheitsbegriff in den formalisierten Sprachen', *Studia Philosophica*, **1** (1936), 261–405; English translation 'The concept of truth in
formalized languages' in [7]. Originally presented to the Warsaw Scientific
Society in 1931.
3. 'Über den Begriff der logischen Folgerung', *Actes du Congrès Internationale de Philosophie Scientifique* (Paris, 1936), **7**, 1–11; English translation 'On
the concept of logical consequence' in [7]. The address was delivered in
1935.
4. 'The semantic conception of truth and the foundations of semantics',
Philosophy and Phenomenological Research, **4** (1944), 341–376.
5. *Undecidable Theories*, written in collaboration with Andrej Mostowski and
Raphael M. Robinson (Amsterdam, 1953).
6. 'Contributions to the theory of models, I–III', *Indagationes Mathe-
maticae* and *Proceedings, Koninklijke Nederlandse Akademie van Weten-
schappen, Series A*, **57** (1954), 572–581 and 582–588; **58** (1955), 56–64.
7. *Logic, Semantics, Metamathematics.   Papers from 1923 to 1938*, translated
by J. H. Woodger (Oxford, 1956).

THIELE, E.-J.
1. 'Ein axiomatisches System der Mengenlehre nach Zermelo und Fraenkel',
Z. für math. Logik und Grundlagen der Math., **1** (1955), 173–195.

THIELE, H.
1. 'Theorie der endlichwertigen Łukasiewiczschen Prädikatenkalküle der
ersten Stufe', *Z. für math. Logik und Grundlagen der Math.*, **4** (1958), 108–142.

TURING, A. M.
1. 'On computable numbers, with an application to the Entscheidungs-problem', *Proc. London Math. Soc.*, **42** (1937), 230–265.
2. 'The word problem in semi-groups with cancellation', *Ann. of Math.*, **52** (1950), 491–505.

DE LA VALLÉE POUSSIN, CH. J.
1. *Cours d'Analyse Infinitésimale* (2 volumes: Louvain, 1906).

VEBLEN, O. & BUSSEY, W. H.
1. 'Finite projective geometries', *Trans. Amer. Math. Soc.*, **7** (1906), 241–259.

VENN, J.
1. 'On the diagrammatic and mechanical representation of propositions and reasonings', *Philosophical Magazine*, **10** (1880), 1–18.
2. *Symbolic Logic* (London, 1881).

VAN DER WAERDEN, B. L.
1. *Moderne Algebra* (2 volumes: Berlin, 1930 & 1931).
2. *Mathematische Statistik* (Berlin, Göttingen, Heidelberg, 1957).

WAJSBERG, M.
1. 'Untersuchungen über den Aussagenkalkül von A. Heyting', *Wiadomści Matematyczne*, **46** (1938), 45–101.

WANG, HAO
1. 'The formalization of mathematics', *J. Symb. Logic*, **19** (1954), 241–266.
2. 'The axiomatization of arithmetic', *J. Symb. Logic*, **22** (1957), 145–158.

WANG, HAO & MCNAUGHTON, R.
1. *Les Systèmes Axiomatiques de la Théorie des Ensembles* (Paris, 1953).

WEYL, H.
1. *Das Kontinuum. Kritische Untersuchungen über die Grundlagen der Analysis* (Leipzig, 1918).
2. 'Über die neue Grundlagenkrise der Mathematik', *Math. Z.*, **10** (1921), 39–79; reprinted, with 'Nachtrag Juni 1955', in *Hermann Weyl: Selecta* (Basle & Stuttgart, 1956).
3. 'Philosophie der Mathematik und Naturwissenschaft', *Handbuch der Philosophie* (1927); revised and augmented English edition: *Philosophy of Mathematics and Natural Science* (Princeton, 1949).
4. *The Classical Groups. Their Invariants and Representations* (Princeton, 1939).
5. 'David Hilbert and his mathematical work', *Bull. Amer. Math. Soc.*, **50** (1944), 612–654.
6. 'David Hilbert, 1862–1943', *Obituary Notices of Fellows of the Royal Society*, **4** (1942–1944), 547–553.
7. *Symmetry* (Princeton, 1952).

WHATELY, R.
1. *Elements of Logic* (London, 1826).

WHEWELL, W.
1. *The Philosophy of the Inductive Sciences, founded upon their History* (2 volumes: London, 1840).

WHITEHEAD, A. N.
1. *A Treatise on Universal Algebra with Applications, I* (Cambridge, 1898).
2. 'The axioms of projective geometry', *Cambridge Tracts in Mathematics and Mathematical Physics*, **4** (1906), 64 pp.
3. 'The axioms of descriptive geometry', *Cambridge Tracts in Mathematics and Mathematical Physics*, **5** (1907), 74 pp.
4. *An Enquiry concerning the Principles of Natural Knowledge* (Cambridge, 1919).
5. *The Concept of Nature*, Tarner Lectures delivered in Trinity College, November 1919 (Cambridge, 1920).
6. *The Principle of Relativity with applications to Physical Science* (Cambridge, 1922).
7. *Process and Reality. An Essay in Cosmology*, Gifford Lectures delivered in the University of Edinburgh during the session 1927–28 (Cambridge, 1929).
8. Whittaker [1], for biographical details.

WHITEHEAD, A. N. & RUSSELL, B.
1. *Principia Mathematica* (3 volumes: Cambridge, 1910–1913; second edition, 1925–1927; reprinted up to *56, Cambridge, 1962).

WHITTAKER, E. T.
1. 'Alfred North Whitehead, 1861–1947', *Obituary Notices of Fellows of the Royal Society*, **6** (1948–1949), 281–296.

WILDER, R. L.
1. *Introduction to the Foundations of Mathematics* (New York, 1952).

WITTGENSTEIN, L.
1. 'Logisch-philosophische Abhandlung', *Annalen der Naturphilosophie*, **14** (1921), 185–262; published separately as *Tractatus Logico-Philosophicus*, accompanied by an English translation (London, 1922), and reissued in 1961 with a new translation.

WOLF, A.
1. 'Logic', *Encyclopaedia Britannica*, 14th edition (1929).

VON WRIGHT, G. H.
1. 'The logical problem of induction', *Acta Philosophica Fennica*, **3** (1941), 258 pp.; revised edition, Oxford, 1957.
2. 'Deontic logic', *Mind*, **60** (1951), 1–15.
3. *An Essay in Modal Logic* (Amsterdam, 1951).

ZERMELO, E.
1. 'Untersuchungen über die Grundlagen der Mengenlehre, I', *Math. Ann.*, **65** (1908), 261–281.

THE GREEK ALPHABET

A	α	alpha	I	ι	iota	P	ϱ	rho
B	β	beta	K	$\varkappa$	kappa	Σ	σ	sigma
Γ	γ	gamma	Λ	λ	lambda	T	τ	tau
Δ	δ	delta	M	μ	mu	Y	υ	upsilon
E	ε	epsilon	N	ν	nu	Φ	φ	phi
Z	ζ	zeta	Ξ	ξ	xi	X	χ	chi
H	η	eta	O	o	omicron	Ψ	ψ	psi
Θ	θ	theta	Π	π	pi	Ω	ω	omega

THE GERMAN ALPHABET

𝔄𝔅ℭ𝔇𝔈𝔉𝔊ℌ𝔍𝔎𝔏𝔐𝔑𝔒𝔓𝔔ℜ𝔖𝔗𝔘𝔙𝔚𝔛𝔜ℨ

𝔞𝔟𝔠𝔡𝔢𝔣𝔤𝔥𝔦𝔧𝔨𝔩𝔪𝔫𝔬𝔭𝔮𝔯𝔰𝔱𝔲𝔳𝔴𝔵𝔶𝔷

GENERAL INDEX

(*No references are given in this index to the Bibliography, which is itself arranged alphabetically by authors.*)

Truth-table, 30, 40
Truth-value, 29, 178
Turing, A. M. (1912–1954), 277 ff., 279, 394
Turquette, A. R. (1914–   ), 56, 397
Twoness, 321
Type-free logic, 386, 387
Types, 115, 165 ff., 253, 286, 296, 314
Typical ambiguity, 168, 169

Understanding (Kant), 340
Undistributed middle, 16
Uniform convergence, 62, 70
Union, 54, 108, 298
Uniqueness formulae, 93, 269
Unit class, 159, 170 ff.
Unit set, 299
Universal class, 109, 169, 299
Universal proposition, 11
Universal quantifier, 60
Universe of discourse, 63, 71
Unravelling of strands or threads, 84, 125, 215
Urelemente (Zermelo), 291, 319
Use and mention, 88

Vacca, G. (1872–   ), 151
de la Vallée Poussin, Ch.-J. (1866–1962), 301
Value of a variable, 58
Variable, 27, 58, 59, 362
Veblen, O. (1880–1960), 227
Vectors, 148
Venn, J. (1834–1923), 24, 187
Venn diagrams, 24
Verifiable formula, 214
Vernunftdressur (Brouwer), 362

Vicious-circle principle, 113, 166

van der Waerden, B. L. (1903–   ), 140, 371
Wajsberg, M. (–   ), 396
Walton, Izaak (1593–1683), 31
Wang, Hao (1921–   ), 190, 308, 391
Was sind und was sollen die Zahlen? (Dedekind), 131, 146, 158 ff., 190, 259
Weakened conclusion, 17
Weierstrass, K. (1815–1897), 140
Well-formed formula, 65, 68, 98, 275, 296
Well-formed term, 98
Weyl, H. (1885–1955), 192, 193, 228, 244, 246, 248, 256, 356, 395
Whately, R. (1787–1863), 21, 25
Whewell, W. (1794–1866), 363
Whitehead, A. N. (1861–1947), 27, 157, 226, 341 ff.
Whittaker, E. T. (1873–1956), 342
Wilder, R. L. (1896–   ), 189
Will to live (Brouwer), 320
Wittgenstein, L. (1889–1951), 58, 317
Wolf, A. (1876–1948), 5
Word problem, 393
Working mathematician, 118, 326, 330
von Wright, G. H. (1916–   ), 398, 399

Zeno of Elea (495?–435? B.C.), 345, 354
Zermelo, E. (1871–1953), 245, 287 ff., 307
Zermelo-Fraenkel axioms, 239, 288, 291, 308, 396